Connecticut

Connecticut

Barnett D. Laschever and Andi Marie Cantele

Principal Photography by Kim Grant

SEVENTH EDITION

The Countryman Press ✷ Woodstock, Vermont

Seventh Edition

No entries or reviews in this book have been solicited or paid for.

ISBN-13: 978-0-88150-824-6

Maps by Mapping Specialists Ltd., Madison, WI, © The Countryman Press
Text and cover design by Bodenweber Design
Composition by PerfecType, Nashville, TN
Front cover photograph of Mystic, CT © Paul Rezendes

Published by The Countryman Press, P.O. Box 748, Woodstock, Vermont 05091

Distributed by W. W. Norton & Company, Inc., 500 Fifth Avenue, New York, NY 10110

Printed in the United States of America

10 9 8 7 6 5 4 3 2 1

To Maggie and Truman.
—AMC

To: Dolores, steadfast lifetime companion, in gloomy days and when the sun shines.

Jonathan, son for all seasons, dedicated, resourceful, witty and wise.
—BL

EXPLORE WITH US!

Welcome to the sixth edition of *Connecticut: An Explorer's Guide.* Our state-by-state guides to New England are the most personable, conscientiously researched, and knowledgeable guides available. As with every book in this series, all attractions, inns, and restaurants are chosen on the basis of personal experience, not paid advertising. Recommendations are given by the authors, both lifelong residents of the state and experienced writers about Connecticut.

WHAT'S WHERE

In the beginning of the book you'll find an alphabetical listing of special highlights, with important information and advice on everything from agricultural fairs to youth hostels.

LODGING

When making reservations, especially at B&Bs, we suggest you inquire about policies regarding smoking, children, pets, the use of cell phones, and the use of credit cards for payment. If it is important that you have a private telephone, air-conditioning, Internet access, and/or television, by all means ask, as they are not standard in country inns and B&Bs.

Prices: Please don't hold us or the respective innkeepers responsible for the rates, which are listed as of press time in fall 2005. Some changes are inevitable. In popular vacation areas, rates are often adjusted to the season. The most popular lodgings often require a 2-day minimum stay on weekends and holidays. There is a 12 percent state room tax in Connecticut; prices given in this book do not include tax or gratuity.

RESTAURANTS

In each section, please note a distinction between *Dining Out* and *Eating Out.* In the *Dining Out* and *Eating Out* listings, prices of entrées (not the cost of a full meal) are given to indicate the general price range. Prix fixe is specified. Remember that prices are likely to change. By their nature, restaurants in the *Dining Out* group are generally pricier and more upscale. Restaurants in the *Eating Out* category are generally inexpensive, with a casual atmosphere that's often appropriate for families; but their prices too are rising.

KEY TO SYMBOLS

Special value. The special value symbol appears next to lodging and restaurants that combine quality and moderate prices.

Pet-friendly. The pet-friendly symbol appears next to lodgings and venues that accept pets.

Child-friendly. The child-friendly symbol appears next to lodging, restaurants, activities, and shops of special appeal to youngsters.

ꝏ **Wedding rings.** The wedding ring symbol appears next to lodgings and restaurants that specialize in wedding ceremonies and/or receptions.

▼ **Gay/Lesbian-friendly.** The gay/lesbian-friendly symbol appears next to lodging, restaurants, and attractions that are of special interest to gay and lesbian travelers. Connecticut, in the main, is a tolerant state. For a more complete listing of individual lodgings and other venues that are gay/lesbian-friendly, gay/lesbian organizations are a good resource.

♿ **Wheelchair.** The wheelchair symbol appears next to lodging, restaurants, and attractions that are handicapped accessible.

We appreciate your comments and corrections about the places you visit. Address your correspondence to Explorer's Guide Editor, The Countryman Press, P.O. Box 748, Woodstock, VT 05091; or e-mail us at countrymanpress@wwnorton.com. Andi Marie Cantele can be e-mailed at andicantele@yahoo.com; Barnett Laschever can be e-mailed at barnlasch@optonline.net.

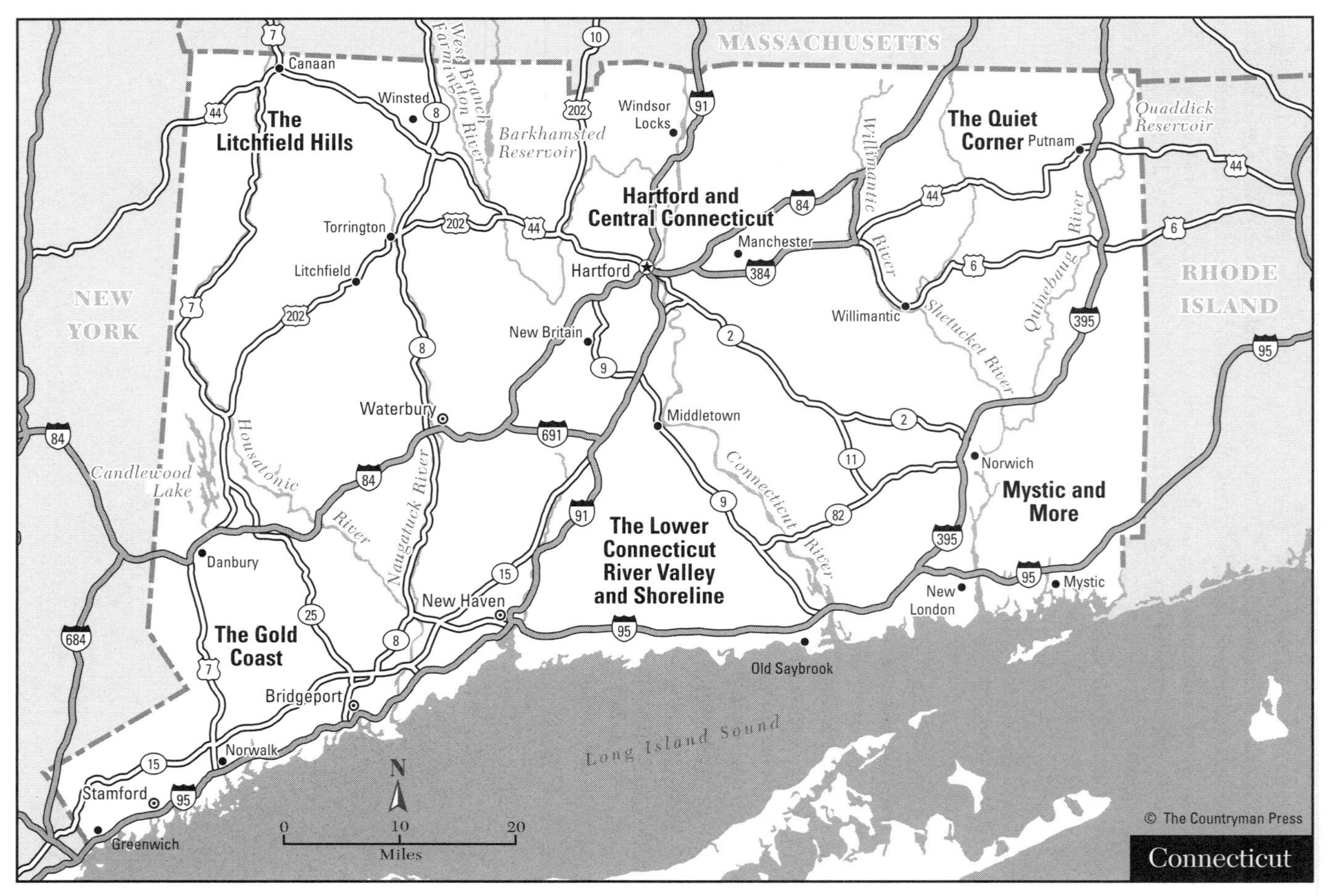
Connecticut
© The Countryman Press
MASSACHUSETTS
RHODE ISLAND
NEW YORK
The Litchfield Hills
Hartford and Central Connecticut
The Quiet Corner
Mystic and More
The Lower Connecticut River Valley and Shoreline
The Gold Coast
Canaan
Winsted
Torrington
Litchfield
Waterbury
Windsor Locks
Hartford
Manchester
New Britain
Middletown
Putnam
Willimantic
Norwich
New London
Mystic
Old Saybrook
New Haven
Danbury
Bridgeport
Norwalk
Stamford
Greenwich
West Branch Farmington River
Barkhamsted Reservoir
Quaddick Reservoir
Willimantic River
Quinebaug River
Shetucket River
Housatonic River
Naugatuck River
Connecticut River
Candlewood Lake
Long Island Sound
N
0
10
20
Miles

CONTENTS

INTRODUCTION

Welcome to Connecticut! This book is designed to bring you in and show you around our favorite state. We've selected hundreds of attractions, lodgings, restaurants, and shops to help you plan a visit that suits your own taste and budget. Beyond that, for the sake of background and entertainment, we've added a little spice to the mixture—nuggets of state history, both admirable and otherwise, and some of Connecticut's favorite legends and tall tales.

One example: Connecticut has an abundance of nicknames, principally the Nutmeg State and the Constitution State. But true Connecticut Yankees decry the sobriquet *Nutmeggers* as a base canard. It was written widely that wily Connecticut Yankee peddlers, whose annual shipload of nutmegs had not arrived on time, passed off wooden nutmegs as the real thing. More recently, historians have concluded that sailors, bored on the voyage home from Grenada, snitched real nutmegs from their bags and in their spare time carved wooden nutmegs to replace them! And then they sold them to unsuspecting tradesmen.

As you plan your trip, keep scale in mind. The nation's third-smallest state, Connecticut is less than 60 miles north to south and just 100 miles across. Diagonally it is 120 miles from Salisbury to Stonington. No point in the state is more than three hours from any other, making it easy to get around and opening up your options.

In such a small area, you might expect a similarity of landscape and lifestyle throughout, but you would be mistaken. Part of our task, in fact, has been to weave in the many aspects and images of Connecticut that exist side by side and sometimes seem to contradict one another. For instance, with three million people occupying an area of 5,000 square miles, we're unquestionably an urban state; yet nearly two-thirds of our land remains open—as forests, farms, gardens, and parks. Known as the Land of Steady Habits, Connecticut clings to tradition but was the first state to elect a woman governor—Ella Grasso—in her own right. As one of the original 13 colonies, Connecticut treasures its past, but no state has served as birthplace of more inventions and innovations—from the revolver to the hamburger, from interchangeable parts to the first telephone exchange. Some people think of Connecticut as the idyllic movie set for *Holiday Inn* and *Mr. Blandings Builds His Dreamhouse*; others see it as the home of the jet engine and the nuclear submarine. In fact, both these views are right.

To guide you into all this variety, we've divided our complex state into six regions: the Gold Coast area nearest New York City; the green and rolling Litchfield Hills; Hartford and surrounding towns; the northeast, known as the Quiet Corner; southeastern Connecticut—the Mystic–New London area; and the Lower Connecticut River Valley, with the adjacent shoreline. Each has its own distinct flavor, as you'll find.

The so-called Gold Coast is, among other things, commuter country, where dark-suited, briefcase-toting men and women wait on Metro-North platforms each morning and return each evening to their trim homes and well-clipped lawns. Along the shoreline are grand estates and marinas crowded with yachts and sailboats. Still, this is an area of cities—Bridgeport, Norwalk, Stamford, New Haven—each with its own background and special qualities. Stamford has attracted so many corporate headquarters that it's a commuter destination in its own right, with a striking skyline against Long Island Sound. New Haven, at the eastern edge of the region, is enriched by the presence of Yale University and many museums and theaters.

The northwestern corner of Connecticut, the Litchfield Hills, provides dramatic contrast to the Gold Coast, with wooded hills, clear streams, carefully preserved village greens, and white-steepled churches. The only signs of "progress" are antiques dealers, artisans' studios, and exquisite gift shops. Outdoor centers and state parks invite hikers and nature lovers to stretch their legs, while the picturesque villages offer colonial and Victorian homes and visible history, from a collection of handmade tools to the nation's first law school—a neat little building about the size of your grandfather's one-car garage.

The central portion of the state, Hartford and its neighbors, is split by the Connecticut River, a smooth-flowing example of the possibility of recovery. A polluted embarrassment 25 or so years ago, the river today is clean enough to swim in. The new facilities, among them a boathouse and a riverboat landing, have made the shore of Hartford, blocked for so many years by the necessary flood dike, "river-friendly"—all part of the Riverfront Recapture project. Hartford, once the nation's insurance capital, is crowned with a splendid state capitol—a wedding cake of grand proportions, with a golden dome, Gothic arches, brackets, crockets, niches,

FARMINGTON VALLEY IS A PLEASING MIX OF SMALL TOWNS AND RURAL COUNTRYSIDE.

© S. Wacht, GeminEye Images

and stained glass. It surely must have appealed to Mark Twain, who lived some 20 years in his own elaborate Hartford mansion, now open to visitors along with a Twain museum; the neighboring home of Harriet Beecher Stowe is also open to visitors. Hartford's XL Center presents concerts, trade shows of every description, and sports events—notably hockey and men's and women's college basketball. The excellent Hartford Stage Company, the Wadsworth Atheneum Museum of Art, and the original Old State House are among the downtown attractions.

A new convention center has been constructed along with a massive architectural makeover called Adriaen's Landing. The complex also includes a hotel and restaurants, all a continuation of Hartford's stunning riverfront revitalization project. For icing on the cake, a football stadium, on Rentschler Field across the river in East Hartford, is the home of the UConn football team.

Only a few miles away, in the historic district of Wethersfield, plain clapboard homes bear plaques declaring their 18th-century origins. George Washington, true to form, slept in at least one. The towns of Rocky Hill and Glastonbury are linked by the nation's oldest ferry service (started in 1655), which handles half a dozen autos at a time. To the west, the lively Farmington River Valley combines history, art, and scenery; and to the north and east, the small towns where shade-grown tobacco for cigar wrappers once ruled, the fertile alluvial land now sprouts condos, and museums devoted to trolleys, firefighting equipment, and aircraft.

The Quiet Corner is the northeastern section of the state. With no large cities, it has retained an unhurried atmosphere that suits its rural character. In early times, the combination of hills and streams fostered mills of all sorts, and in the 19th century this part of the state became a major textile manufacturing area. The mills are gone now, but as you drive the tree-lined roads, you'll occasionally see an old mill complex beside a river or a cluster of former workers' homes. You'll also discover colonial houses virtually untouched by time, and miles of stone walls that undulate over the hills and into the woods, marking boundaries of long-abandoned farmsteads. The area remains bucolic. It provides an ideal setting for the University of Connecticut in Storrs, which, fittingly, started as an agricultural land grant college and has blossomed into a full-fledged university whose men's and women's basketball teams have won national championships back-to-back. Like Boston, the state in many ways is a schoolmarm to the nation, with its plethora of prestigious prep schools and Ivy League colleges that can boast of many graduates who have occupied the Oval Office or sat on the bench of the U.S. Supreme Court.

Mystic Seaport, the re-created 19th-century maritime community on the Mystic River, is the state's best-known single attraction, dedicated to the traditions of shipbuilding and whaling. Southeastern Connecticut's maritime tradition is further enhanced by the Mystic Aquarium & Institute for Exploration, the U.S. Coast Guard Academy, and the U.S. Navy Submarine Base at Groton. (*Note:* The submarine base, the largest in the country, was in danger of being shut down in the 2005 wave of military base closures but was saved through a massive effort by state legislators, local officials, and submariners, and by the only U.S. president to have served on a submarine, Annapolis graduate Jimmy Carter. A physicist, Carter helped Admiral Rickover build the *Nautilus*.) They have been joined by myriad lodgings, restaurants, and shops, making the region the state's number one tourist area. The presence of two world-class Native American–operated gaming casinos nearby, Foxwoods Resort Casino and Mohegan Sun, has further increased the area's popularity.

Our final division, the lower valley of the Connecticut River and the central shoreline, offers another approach to serenity. Middletown, home of Wesleyan University, was once the state's largest city and busiest trading port. Barges and pleasure boats still ripple the waters here, and Harbor Park on the riverbank affords a vantage point for watching the traffic. If you like, you can board an excursion boat for a ride. South of Middletown, Haddam, Chester, Deep River, and Essex are a treasure trove of small gems strung along the river. Gillette Castle looms on a high bluff above the water, and directly below, an ancient ferry operation offers a three- to five-minute crossing between Chester and Hadlyme. The engine of the Essex Steam Train and Riverboat Ride huffs and puffs its way north along the river from Essex. As the river enters Long Island Sound, Old Saybrook and Old Lyme stand on opposite banks—one offering shoreline history, the other continuing its tradition as an artists' colony. The other shoreline towns of Westbrook, Clinton, Madison, Guilford, and Branford are best known as summer havens for the beach crowd, where concerts and crafts shows enliven greens laid out in the 17th century.

Although we've been speaking of summertime visits, bear in mind that Connecticut is definitely open year-round. Skiers have four choices for downhill skiing and virtually all the great outdoors for cross-country skiing, with trails open in most of the state's 100 state parks and 31 state forests. Those same trails are perfect avenues for hiking into the splendor of autumn foliage displays or the miracle of wildflowers in spring. State parks, in fact, are a largely undiscovered treasure in what's thought of as a highly industrial state. The parks are usually well marked and well maintained, with picnic spots, toilet facilities, and activities that may include saltwater and freshwater swimming, boating, and camping. Some have special or unexpected attractions, from the dramatic Kent Falls in Kent to the Harkness Mansion in Waterford, and from the implausible Gillette Castle in its own state park to a tower fit for Rapunzel on Talcott Mountain.

Along with abundant outdoor life, you find artistic stimuli as well. There are a dozen museums scattered around the state, featuring modern artists in Ridgefield, American artists in New Britain, Connecticut artists in Waterbury, British artists in New Haven, and an inclusive collection representing virtually all periods and all media in Hartford. Visiting performers and local talent present music year-round in big cities and small villages—classical, bluegrass, rock, experimental, and jazz—and dance programs of equal variety.

Connecticut theaters have earned so many drama awards in the past dozen

CONNECTICUT STATE SYMBOLS

Motto: *Qui Transtulit Sustinet.* (He who transplanted still sustains.)
Nickname: The Constitution State
Hero: Nathan Hale
Heroine: Prudence Crandall
Composer: Charles Edward Ives
Song: "Yankee Doodle"
Folk Dance: Square dance
Animal: Sperm whale
Bird: American robin
Insect: Praying mantis
Flower: Mountain laurel
Tree: White oak
Mineral: Garnet
Fish: American shad
Shellfish: Eastern oyster
Fossil: *Eubrontes giganteus*
Ship: USS *Nautilus*

Courtesy Coastal Fairfield County Convention & Visitors Bureau

HARBORS ON THE GOLD COAST ARE SAFE HAVENS FOR ALL MANNER OF PLEASURE BOATS.

years that critics speak of the state as a challenge to New York City and London in introducing successful new plays and landmark productions. Such recognition is based on the creativity of Yale Repertory and Long Wharf theaters in New Haven, the Hartford Stage Company, and the Goodspeed Opera House in East Haddam. New London was the boyhood home of Eugene O'Neill, America's only Nobel laureate in drama. In his memory, each summer in Waterford the Eugene O'Neill Playwrights Conference brings together promising new playwrights to try out and polish their creations, many of which subsequently appear on stages in the state and in New York City.

Connecticut's many craftspeople are known for innovation and quality. The state's major centers are in Guilford, Avon, Middletown, and Brookfield. Each has its own exhibit space. Outdoor summer crafts shows are numerous and enormously popular.

If you travel with children, you'll be glad to know that Connecticut has museums designed specifically for them in New Haven, New Britain, Manchester, Bridgeport, Stamford, West Hartford, Norwalk, Middletown, and Bristol. Other ideas for youngsters: Dinosaur State Park in Rocky Hill; Yale University's Peabody Museum of Natural History in New Haven (with the world's largest dinosaur skeleton); the Essex Steam Train and Riverboat Ride, with its working steam train in Essex, and the Naugatuck Railroad in Thomaston; trolley museums and rides at Warehouse Point in East Windsor and in East Haven; the *Nautilus*, the world's first nuclear submarine, in Groton; and the creaking planks and claustrophobic belowdecks of the *Charles W. Morgan*, the last of the wooden whaling ships, in Mystic. (*Note:* The *Morgan* will be in dry dock beginning in 2008 for a three-year, $2.5 million restoration.) Youngsters love to picnic and swim with their moms and dads. Many of the state's myriad state parks and forests offer swimming at safe saltwater or freshwater sandy beaches, and picnic tables with individual fire pits.

A word about the people of Connecticut: They're as varied as the landscape. You may run into a wry, laconic Yankee whose family has been here since 1636, but don't count on it. Connecticut's brand of Yankee ingenuity led to early industrialization, creating jobs that brought people from all over Western Europe, the Balkans, Russia, French Canada, and the American South. Connecticut's population today is made up of many ethnic and racial groups, drawn here by the prospect of work to be done. More recent settlers have been attracted by the state's advantageous location between Boston and New York City, by its natural beauty, and by that nebulous quality called lifestyle. Among those who have chosen to live in Connecticut is a long list of notables from the worlds of books, theater, art, broadcasting, music, politics, and sports—past and present. Examples range from Mark Twain to Henry Kissinger and include Paul Robeson, Jackie Robinson, Paul Newman, William Styron, Marian Anderson, Katharine Hepburn, Rosalind Russell, Tom Brokaw, Arthur Miller, Philip Roth, Maurice Sendak, Sam Waterston, and Oscar de la Renta. The list of historic figures born or raised in Connecticut could serve as a crib sheet on U.S. history: General Israel Putnam, Nathan Hale, Noah Webster, Benedict Arnold, Harriet Beecher Stowe, John Brown, Samuel Colt, P. T. Barnum, Eli Whitney, and J. P. Morgan, for example.

A quick look at New England's cuisine, past and present, may help first-time visitors understand why we eat what we do—and serve it to you. The frugal Pilgrims from England who landed at Plymouth in December survived the first winter on pumpkins; hence, pumpkin pie is a Yankee classic. As more English colonists arrived, they found that in the region's short growing season, they could successfully bring beans to harvest. Boston quickly earned its popular sobriquet, Beantown, through its ubiquitous baked beans. Bordered by the sea, New Englanders soon were eating in great quantities clam and fish chowders, and later corn chowders. Lobsters were in such abundance that some early diaries record settlers complaining of being "glutted with lobster." Shad swarmed up the Connecticut River, and to this day they still appear each year for a short interval when we gorge on planked shad and shad roe.

Native Americans taught us to marry corn and lima beans for another regional favorite, succotash. Because olive trees find New England inhospitable but pigs are easy to raise here, salt pork became the oil of choice in beans and chowders. So it was, too, that the New England boiled dinner was born. Legend has it that the Pilgrims served turkey and venison to their Native American guests at the first Thanksgiving. Today turkey dinners enhanced by cranberries from the bogs of Cape Cod and Nantucket are on restaurant menus year-round. Wild blueberries blanket sections of Maine, and blueberry festivals are annual events. Finally, you'll find no sugarcane fields in New England, but the Indians gave us yet another culinary gift: They showed us how to tap the myriad maple trees to create the maple syrup that drenches our pancakes and waffles on Sunday morning—and sweetens our baked beans. There was a time when a little cottage cheese relish and crackers were placed before you to nibble on in almost every Connecticut restaurant. Today the tradition lives on only in the Curtis House in Woodbury, the state's oldest inn.

That's New England and Connecticut cuisine in a nutshell, though it's not the whole story. As in the rest of America, the ethnic mix is shifting. Italians are 20 percent of the population, hence the plethora of pizza shops and Italian eateries.

Hispanics are a fast-growing ethnic group, and their cuisine is reflected in Cuban, Puerto Rican, Mexican, and Tex-Mex barbecue restaurants. Japanese, Thai, Vietnamese, Cambodian, and Indian chefs, along with the state's many Chinese cooks, have created an Asian food quilt. Sushi has joined baked beans and lobster on many of our menus. Many of the Chinese, of late, have shifted from sit-down restaurants to buffets, their version of fast food.

All this being said, restaurants in the Nutmeg State run the gamut, from sturdy old traditional diners—dozens of diners still ballyhoo steak, meat loaf, and mashed potatoes to a happy clientele—to some of the country's most acclaimed gourmet temples, with every degree of eatery in between. A note to visitors from the South: Most restaurants do not serve grits, and long-haul drivers will realize that creamed chipped beef on toast is hard to find in these parts.

A brief word about historical societies. Almost every city, town, and hamlet has one, and each tells its own story. Many are located in a historic house, staffed by volunteers, and are open irregularly and infrequently. We have not included a historical society unless it offers unique exhibits or, as Torrington's does, it's in an architecturally outstanding building and is more accessible to the public than the small town houses.

The authors of this book claim less fame than the celebrities singled out earlier but share equal enthusiasm for the state. Andi Marie is a true-blue Yankee, having been born in Litchfield County and spent every childhood summer on the Connecticut shore. A degree in journalism from Boston University began her career in writing for a variety of publications, from a community newspaper in Boston to an entertainment magazine in London. Andi Marie lives in the rural Litchfield Hills, where she enjoys biking, rowing, canoeing, gardening, and hiking in the woods with her husband, Brian, and dogs Maggie and Truman. She is the author of three bicycling guidebooks for The Countryman Press, as well as *New Jersey: An Explorer's Guide* and *52 Weekends in Connecticut*, also published by The Countryman Press.

Barney, another legitimate Yankee, was born and raised in Hartford and now lives in an 1810 garrison colonial in Goshen. He has left the state on occasion—to earn his degree at the University of Michigan; to write for *Stars and Stripes*, the U.S. Army's newspaper, in Germany during World War II; and to serve for 10 years as the travel editor of the *New York Herald Tribune*. Back in God's country, as his father instructed him to think of Connecticut, Barney resumed travel writing as an editor for Eugene Fodor, pioneer of the modern travel guidebook. He is author of five children's books, put in time as a reporter and Sunday editor at the *Hartford Times*, and was also a garden columnist for the *Hartford Times*, the *Hartford Courant*, the *Norwich Bulletin*, and the *Lakeville Journal*. He has written on travel for the *Providence Journal*, the *Boston Globe*, the *Torrington Register Citizen*, and the *Litchfield County Times*. For 17 years he served as director of tourism for the state of Connecticut. Since his retirement, like his father, Barney too has found his affection for the state unabated. Among his special interests is gardening, and he writes a weekly vinegary newspaper column, the "Ranting Retiree"; cohosts a radio show; and takes short hikes and long naps.

Both authors owe deep thanks to all those at The Countryman Press who have been simultaneously supportive and exacting: Kermit Hummel, Lisa Sacks, Jennifer Thompson, Laura Jorstad, Doug Yeager, Kelly Thompson, and Fred Lee.

And thanks to everyone in the Connecticut tourism industry who so graciously gave of their time, advice, knowledge, and wisdom.

WHAT'S WHERE IN CONNECTICUT

AGRICULTURAL FAIRS Though Connecticut holds no official state fair, some 57 local fairs between July and October celebrate the season's bounty: ox pulls, baking contests, livestock judging, ribbons for eggplants and string beans and for quilts and peach preserves. The largest is the **Durham Fair**, held in Durham in late September. The **Four Town Agricultural Fair** in Somers, one of the state's oldest, has been held in mid-September every year since 1838. Two of the largest fairs, in two of the smallest towns and in opposite corners of the state, attract thousands: the **Goshen Fair** in the Litchfield Hills and the **Woodstock Fair** in the Quiet Corner. A complete directory can be viewed on the **Association of Connecticut Fairs** Web site (www.ctfairs.org); for a printed copy, contact the association at info@ctfairs.org.

AIR SERVICE **Bradley International Airport** (860-292-2000; 888-624-1533; www.bradleyairport.com) at Windsor Locks (Exit 40 off I-91) is New England's second-largest airport, with national flights on a daily basis, as well as new international service to Amsterdam. Major airlines into Bradley are Air Canada Jazz, American, American Eagle, Continental, Continental Express, Delta, Frontier, Northwest, Skyway, Southwest, United, United Express, US Airways, and US Airways Express. **Groton–New London Airport** (860-445-8549; www.grotonnewlondonairport.com) in Groton, on the state's southeastern coast, serves only corporate and private planes. **Tweed–New Haven Regional Airport** (203-466-8833; info line 203-466-8888; www.flytweed.com) in New Haven is served by US Airways Express. **Westchester County Airport** (914-285-4860), just outside Greenwich in White Plains, New York, serves the Gold Coast area with daily flights by Air Canada, AirTran, American, Continental, Delta, Independence Air, JetBlue, Northwest, United, and US Airways. International arrivals also access the state through New York's **John F. Kennedy International**

Cory Mazon

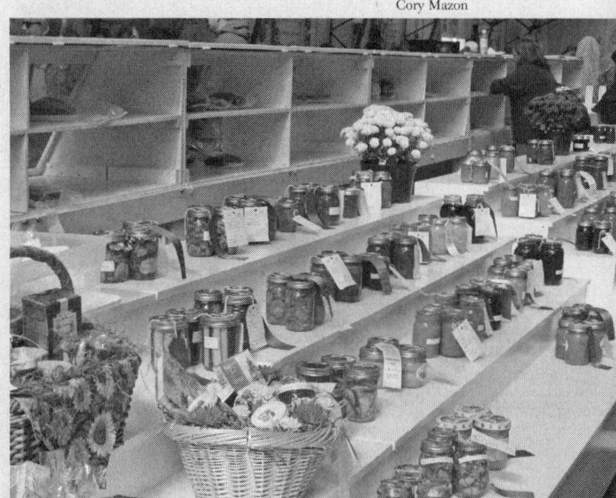

Airport (718-244-4444; www.kennedy airport.com).

AMUSEMENT PARKS In Middlebury, **Quassy Amusement Park** (203-758-2913; 800-367-7275; www.quassy.com) offers more than 24 rides (mostly for small visitors), a family entertainment center, and a water play area, plus swimming and boating on Lake Quassapaug. Bristol's **Lake Compounce Theme Park** (860-583-3300; www.lakecompounce.com), the oldest amusement park in the country, has Connecticut's biggest water park, live shows, and other thrills. In southeastern Connecticut, **Ocean Beach Park** (860-447-3031; 800-510-7263; www.ocean-beach-park.com) in New London has a saltwater beach and a swimming pool, a waterslide, an arcade, mini golf, and a boardwalk.

ANTIQUES Dealers are found virtually everywhere in the state, but certain sections—for example, the towns of **Woodbury**, **New Preston**, **Bantam**, **Ridgefield**, and **Putnam**, the city of **Stamford**, and the area around **Coventry** and **US 7 north of Norwalk**—have attracted many dealers in concentrated areas. In addition, there are more and more marketplaces—in **Mystic** and **Old Saybrook**, for instance—where dealers share spaces in a single building, offering shoppers variety and choice.

© S. Wacht, GeminEye Images

APPALACHIAN TRAIL Just 52 of the Appalachian Trail's total 2,174 miles from Maine to Georgia are in Connecticut, but local hikers claim it's the most diverse part of the entire trail! About one-quarter of the trail land in Connecticut is owned by the state; the rest is privately held. Hikers are reminded to observe the usual courtesies regarding these rights-of-way. White blazes mark the Appalachian Trail, which runs from **Sherman** north to **Cornwall** and through **Salisbury**, complete with challenging ascents to long vistas up Mount Riga and Lion's Head, and an easy amble along a quiet stretch of the Housatonic River. Many sections of the AT can be accessed by spur trails, making for good day hikes or weekend backpacking excursions. Popular day hikes on the AT go to **Bear Mountain** in Salisbury, **Pine Knob** in Sharon, and **St. John's Ledges** in Kent. For more information, contact the **Appalachian Trail Conservancy** (304-535-6331; www.appalachiantrail.org), the **Appalachian Mountain Club** (617-523-0655; www.outdoors.org), or the AMC's Connecticut chapter (www.ct-amc.org).

AQUARIUMS The state's largest is **Mystic Aquarium & Institute for Exploration** (860-572-5955; www.mysticaquarium.org) in Mystic. More than 6,000 sea-life specimens can be seen, from sea lions and harbor seals to penguins and the only beluga whales in New England. Connecticut's other aquarium is the **Maritime Aquarium at Norwalk** (203-852-0700; www.maritimeaquarium.org) in South Norwalk, with 259 species native to Long

Island Sound and one of the state's only IMAX movie theaters.

AREA CODES Connecticut has two area codes. Fairfield and New Haven counties (the shoreline area in the western part of the state) have the **203** prefix, while the area code for the rest of Connecticut is **860**.

ART MUSEUMS The **Connecticut Art Trail** (215-913-9706; www.arttrail.org) highlights 14 museums and historic sites with an emphasis on art. Most renowned is Hartford's **Wadsworth Atheneum Museum of Art** (860-278-2670; www.wadsworthatheneum.org), the nation's oldest public art museum, with more than 45,000 works representing all media and virtually all periods. The **New Britain Museum of American Art** (860-229-0257; www.nbmaa.org) in New Britain has some 5,000 American works of art. In Old Lyme, the **Florence Griswold Museum** (860-434-5542; www.florencegriswoldmuseum.org), a late-Georgian mansion, is the site of one of America's first art colonies. Its strength is works by American impressionists. In Ridgefield, the top-notch **Aldrich Contemporary Art Museum** (203-438-4519; www.aldrichart.org) showcases cutting-edge and provocative exhibitions. The **Mattatuck Museum Arts and History Center** (203-753-0381; www.mattatuckmuseum.org) in Waterbury showcases the industrial history of the Naugatuck Valley, but its largest gallery is devoted exclusively to Connecticut scenes. Three other museums showcasing American impressionists are the **Hill-Stead Museum** (860-677-4787; www.hillstead.org) in Farmington, the **Lyman Allyn Art Museum** (860-443-2545; www.lymanallyn.org) in New London, and the **Bush-Holley Historic Site** (203-869-6899; www.hstg.org) and **Bruce Museum of Arts and Science** (203-869-0376; www.brucemuseum.org) in Greenwich. The **William Benton Museum of Art** (860-486-4520; www.thebenton.org) on the campus of the University of Connecticut at Storrs, mounts changing exhibits of European and American works. Housatonic Community College in Bridgeport has on its campus the **Housatonic Museum of Art** (203-332-5053; www.hcc.commnet.edu), with many works by 19th- and 20th-century European and American artists. At Yale University in New Haven, the **Yale Center for British Art** (203-432-2800; www.ycba.yale.edu) is a prestigious showcase for British paintings, drawings, prints, sculptures, and rare books. Also on the Yale campus, the **Yale University Art Gallery** (203-432-0600; www.artgallery.yale.edu) has a collection of some 100,000 objects dating from ancient Egypt to the present. **Weir Farm National Historic Site** (203-834-1896; www.nps.gov/wefa) in Wilton is Connecticut's first property in the National Park System and the only national park in the country devoted to American painting.

In addition, many communities—Washington, Essex, Chester, and Ridgefield, for instance—have their own art guilds that showcase the work of local artists.

Kim Grant

BALLOONING Hot-air balloon flights are available throughout the state virtually year-round. Climb into a wicker basket and get the birds' perspective; in fall, a great way to see Connecticut's gold-and-crimson landscape is from the air. Check the index or specific chapters (under *To Do*) in this book for companies in a particular region; the **Connecticut Lighter Than Air Society** (www.lighterthanair.org) maintains a statewide list. Most companies require reservations; call ahead of your visit.

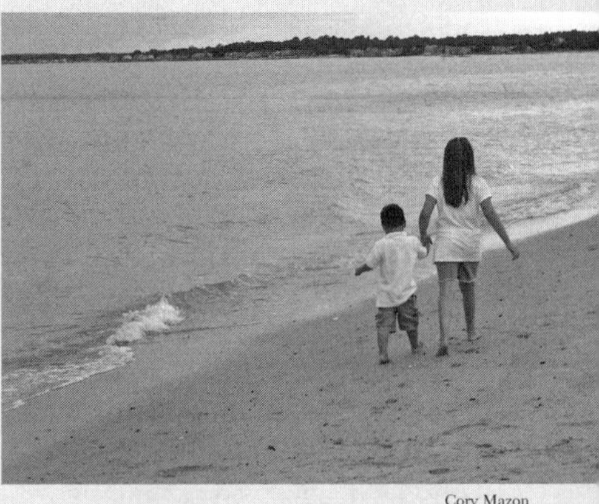
Cory Mazon

BEACHES Connecticut offers 20 state-run beaches open to the public—4 on Long Island Sound (easily accessible from I-95) and 16 on inland lakes, ponds, and rivers. **Hammonasset Beach State Park** (203-245-2785) in Madison is the largest, with 2 miles of water frontage and facilities for swimming, camping, picnicking, fishing, scuba diving, hiking, and boating for more than a million annual visitors. **Rocky Neck State Park** (860-739-5471) in East Lyme has a mile-long crescent beach, with swimming, camping, hiking, fishing, and picnicking. **Sherwood Island State Park** (203-226-6983) in Westport has two large picnic groves, swimming, fishing, scuba diving, field sports, and interpretive programs, as well as a 1.5-mile-long beach. In Milford, **Silver Sands State Park** (203-735-4311) offers fishing, swimming, and a boardwalk in a largely undeveloped setting. **Ocean Beach Park** (800-510-7263), New London, is a city-owned public beach and major recreation area, with saltwater and pool swimming, a waterslide, a boardwalk, and picnicking. New Haven's **Lighthouse Point Park** (203-946-8005) is an urban oasis with a beach, nature trails, a picnic grove, and 50-cent rides on an antique carousel. On hot summer weekends, parking lots at the four big state park saltwater beaches fill up quickly; plan accordingly. For additional information on state beaches, contact the **Connecticut Bureau of Outdoor Recreation, State Parks Division** (860-424-3200; www.ct.gov/dep). The online **Connecticut Coastal Access Guide** (www.lisrc.uconn.edu/coastalaccess) lists close to 300 sites where the public can access the shoreline.

BED & BREAKFASTS B&Bs throughout the state include elegant estates, gracious mansions, colonial and country homes, farmhouses, and centuries-old captains' houses. The following B&B reservation services list Connecticut properties either regionally or throughout the state: **Nutmeg Bed & Breakfast Agency** (860-236-6698; 800-727-7592; www.nutmegbb.com), P.O. Box 271117, West Hartford 06127; **Bed and Breakfasts of the Mystic Coast** (www.thebbmc.com), P.O. Box 555, Old Mystic 06372; **Litchfield Hills Bed and Breakfast Association** (www.litchfieldhillsbandb.com).

BICYCLING For a state map showing suggested on-road bicycle routes and other helpful information, contact the **Connecticut Department of Transportation** (860-594-2000; www.ct.gov/

dot). An online guide to the state's multiuse trails is available on the DOT Web site. We also recommend the guidebook *Backroad Bicycling in Connecticut* by coauthor Andi Marie Cantele.

For guided trips around the state, contact **Bicycle Tour Company** (860-927-1742; 888-711-5368; www.bicycletours.com), 9 Bridge St., Kent. If you're heading out on your own, contact a local bike shop for supplies, repairs, help in planning a route, or information on group rides and local cycling events.

BIRDING In the coastal area, birders flock to the following: **Earthplace: The Nature Discovery Center**, Westport; **Lighthouse Point Park**, New Haven; **Hammonasset Beach State Park** in Madison; and **Bluff Point Coastal Reserve State Park** in Groton. The **Connecticut Audubon Society** (www.ctaudubon.org) operates 19 wildlife sanctuaries and maintains centers in Greenwich, Fairfield, Pomfret, Southbury, Hampton, Glastonbury, and Sharon, as well as a **Connecticut Audubon Society Birdcraft Museum and Sanctuary** in Fairfield and the **Connecticut Audubon Coastal Center** in Milford. Other favorite spots are **Denison Pequotsepos Nature Center** in Mystic and the state's largest sanctuary, **White Memorial Foundation and Conservation Center**, in Litchfield. There's been talk in local birding circles of a **Connecticut Coastal Birding Trail**—a highway-based trail including more than 50 prime bird habitats along Long Island Sound—but no firm plans exist as of press time. (See also *Eagle Viewing*; *Nature Centers*; and *Nature Preserves, Coastal* and *Inland.*)

Andi Mari Cantele

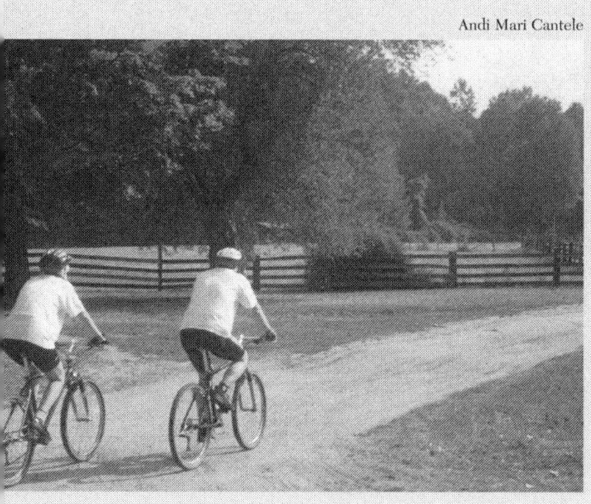

BOAT EXCURSIONS In Connecticut, the abundance of water makes boating a popular activity. You can choose boat rides on lakes, up and down the rivers, and along or across Long Island Sound to other Northeast ports of call. Excursions range from dinner cruises and bald eagle cruises to short hops around small islands where pirate legends still echo. (See also *Ferries* and *Windjammers.*)

BOATING Opportunities for boating and fishing abound on Connecticut's many lakes, ponds, and rivers, not to mention along its 253-mile shoreline on Long Island Sound. More than 100 state-operated public boat launches provide access to these areas. For a complete listing of boat-launching locations, as well as state boating laws and regulations, and registration information, contact the **State Department of Environmental Protection's Boating Division** (860-434-8638), P.O. Box 280, Old Lyme 06371-0280. You can also access the DEP's ***Connecticut Coastal Access Guide*** online (www.lisrc.uconn.edu/coastalaccess), or pick up a copy of the ***Connecticut Boater's Guide*** at any town clerk's office. Motorized boats and sailboats more than 19.5 feet must be registered with the state **Department of Motor Vehicles** (860-566-3781); applications and certificates are

Kim Grant

available at any DMV branch office. Anyone operating a boat must obtain a **Safe Boating Certificate** from the State Department of Environmental Protection.

BUS SERVICE **Greyhound Lines** (800-231-2222; www.greyhound.com) and **Peter Pan Bus Lines** (800-343-9999; www.peterpanbus.com) serve some two dozen communities in Connecticut, including Hartford, New Britain, Stamford, Bridgeport, New Haven, and New London. **CTTRANSIT** (860-522-8101; www.cttransit.com) provides local bus service for Hartford, New Haven, Stamford, and their surrounding towns.

CAMPING The state has a variety of campsites in more than 50 private campgrounds and 13 state parks and forests. Contact the **Connecticut Campground Owners Association (CCOA)** (860-521-4704; www.campconn.com), 14 Rumford St., West Hartford 06107, and ask for the current ***Connecticut Campground Directory***, which can also be viewed online. Basic services at CCOA campgrounds generally include hot showers, water and electric hookups, and dump stations; a few offer rustic camping cabins for those who don't want to pitch a tent. In general, family rates run from $26 to $60, depending on amenities provided. For those seeking quiet and solitude in a more rustic setting, 1,400 campsites are available in designated state parks and forests from mid-April through September; in some areas, off-season camping is available from October to December. Campgrounds in Natchaug and Pachaug state forests are designated exclusively for equestrian use. Pets can spend the night at state forest campgrounds, but not in state parks. For information and reservations for state park and forest sites, contact the **Connecticut Bureau of Outdoor Recreation, State Parks Division** (877-668-2267; www.reserveamerica.com).

CAMPS, FOR CHILDREN There are more than 200 youth camps licensed by the State Department of Health. These can be found in the annual publication ***Connecticut Summer Youth Camps***, which lists resident and day camps, some offering short-term stays and others an entire summer experience. For a copy, call 860-561-6000. The **Connecticut Camping Association** maintains an online directory at www.ctcamps.org.

CANOEING AND KAYAKING, TOURS AND RENTALS A number of outfitters offer rentals or guided canoe tours, some with instruction. **Clarke Outdoors** (860-672-6365) in

Kim Grant

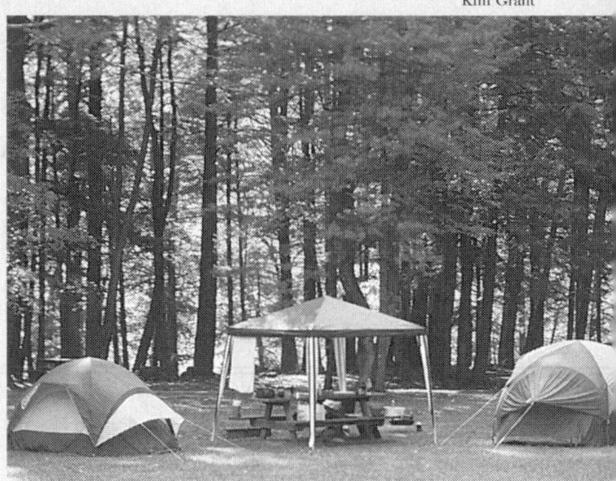

West Cornwall offers canoeing, kayaking, rafting, and tubing trips; they also rent canoes and kayaks at **Burr Pond State Park** in Torrington, and **Lake Waramaug State Park** in New Preston. **Huck Finn Adventures** (860-693-0385) and **Main Stream Canoes and Kayaks** (860-693-6791) in New Hartford offer trips on the Farmington River; **Collinsville Canoe and Kayak** (860-693-6977) in Collinsville leads trips on the Farmington and Connecticut rivers, and around the Norwalk Islands; Norwalk's **Small Boat Shop** (203-854-5223) offers day trips via kayak to the Norwalk Islands; and **Machias Adventures** (203-454-1243) in Westport leads kayak excursions on the Mystic River and in Branford Harbor. (See also *Whitewater Rafting*.)

CASINOS Two of the world's biggest casinos are tucked into the southeastern Connecticut's rural wooded countryside. **Foxwoods Resort Casino** (800-369-9663; www.foxwoods.com) is located on CT 2 in Mashantucket on the Mashantucket Pequot Indian Reservation. This is the second-largest gaming and entertainment complex in the world, with six casinos, more than 7,000 slot machines, 400 table games, high-stakes bingo, dozens of restaurants and eateries, championship golf, and more than 1,400 guest rooms in three hotels. Just down the road, **Mohegan Sun** (888-226-7711; www.mohegansun.com), off CT 2A in Uncasville, has more than 300 gaming tables, 6,000 slot machines, gourmet dining, boutique shopping, headline entertainment at the 10,000-seat Mohegan Sun Arena, the world's largest planetarium dome, and a 1,200-room luxury hotel and spa. Both casinos unveiled huge expansions in 2008: the 30-story **MGM Grand at Foxwoods** (866-646-0050; www.mgmatfoxwoods.com) added 825 guest rooms, a 4,000-seat theater, and 1,400 new slot machines to the tune of $700 million. Mohegan Sun opened its new Casino of the Wind, which added slots, tables games, and a 42-table poker room. A House of Blues–style hotel is slated to open in the near future. Together the two casinos draw about 25 million visitors annually.

CHILDREN, ESPECIALLY FOR Throughout this book, the ✐ symbol indicates child-friendly lodging, dining, and attractions. Bridgeport has several attractions that appeal to children: **The Barnum Museum** (203-331-1104; www.barnum-museum.org), **Connecticut's Beardsley Zoo** (203-394-6565; www.beardsleyzoo.org), and the **Discovery Museum** (203-372-3521; www.discoverymuseum.org), with its planetarium and *Challenger* Learning Center. **The Children's Museum** (860-231-2824; www.thechildrensmuseumct.org) in West Hartford has many exhibits specifically for youngsters, including a planetarium, a laser light show, and a small-animal collection. Two small museums—**Stepping Stones Museum for Children** (203-899-0606; www.steppingstonesmuseum.org) in Norwalk and **Kidcity Children's Museum** (860-347-0495; www.kidcitymuseum.com) in Middletown—

Kim Grant

are full of hands-on, interactive exhibits that inspire creative play and exploration. Other museums designed for children are located in Manchester, New Britain, New Haven, and Bristol. The brand-new **Connecticut Science Center** (www.ctsciencecenter.org) in Hartford, the **Essex Steam Train and Riverboat Ride** (860-767-0103; 800-377-3987; www.essexsteamstrain.com) in Essex, the **"Naugy" Railroad** (860-283-7245; www.rmne.org) in Thomaston, and the **New England Air Museum** (860-623-3305; www.neam.org) in Windsor Locks are other possibilities. Many of the state's nature centers offer walks, activities, and exhibits for children.

CLIMATE Connecticut's weather is relatively mild. In the Hartford area, on average there are just 19 days a year when the temperature goes above 90 degrees and only 6 days when it falls to zero or below. Some variations occur over the state, with temperatures in the northeastern and northwestern hills occasionally as much as 10 degrees lower than those in the central valley. Appreciable precipitation (.01 inch or more) is experienced about 127 days a year. Average highs and lows (in degrees Fahrenheit) in the Hartford area: **January** 35/18, **February** 36/19, **March** 46/28, **April** 59/38, **May** 70/48, **June** 79/57, **July** 84/63, **August** 81/61, **September** 74/53, **October** 64/42, **November** 51/22, **December** 38/23.

COTTAGE RENTALS Most cottage rentals in Connecticut are in the communities along Long Island Sound or on the shores of the state's many lakes and ponds. Contact the regional tourism district offices listed under *Guidance* in each chapter or real estate agents in the area where you want to stay.

COVERED BRIDGES Only three traditional covered bridges remain in Connecticut. **Bull's Bridge** in South Kent on US 7 continues to carry traffic, as does **West Cornwall Bridge** on CT 128, just off US 7. The latter has been in operation since 1837. The **Comstock Bridge** in East Hampton, built in 1873, crosses the Salmon River and is limited to pedestrian traffic, with picnicking and fishing nearby at Salmon River State Park.

CRAFTS CENTERS Four crafts centers, all with galleries and shops, are scattered around Connecticut. **Guilford Art Center** (203-453-5947; www.guilfordartcenter.org) offers classes and hosts several shows a year. In Middletown, **Wesleyan Potters** (860-344-0039; www.wesleyanpotters.com) is known for its pottery and weaving studios. The **Brookfield Craft Center** (203-775-4526; www.brookfieldcraftcenter.org) is a school for fine craftsmanship, with a gallery and book- and gift store in a colonial-era vintage restored mill. In Avon the **Farmington Valley Arts Center** (860-678-1867; www.fvac.net) has 20 artists' studios, an exhibition gallery, and shops.

DOG TRACK **Shoreline Star Greyhound Park** (203-576-1976; 888-463-

© S. Wacht, GeminEye Images

6446) in Bridgeport offers live dog racing as well as simulcast events.

EAGLE VIEWING The **Shepaug Eagle Observation Area** on the Housatonic River in Southbury features viewing from December to mid-March; call 800-368-8954 for reservations, which are required. **Connecticut River Expeditions** (800-996-8747; www.ctriverexpeditions.org) offers eagle-viewing trips along the lower Connecticut River aboard ***RiverQuest*** in winter and early spring.

EDUCATIONAL INSTITUTIONS Preparatory schools, like colleges and universities, for the most part welcome campus visitors, both those interested in attending and those who appreciate the landscape and architectural variety of these institutions. **Hotchkiss** in Lakeville and **Gunnery** in Washington, **Miss Porter's** in Farmington and **Ethel Walker** in Simsbury, **Taft** in Watertown, **Loomis-Chaffee** in Windsor, and **Kent School** in Kent are just a few of the names that ring bells among educators. Colleges and universities, both public and private, abound. Campuses offer architectural delights, museums, and musical and other programs by faculty, students, and visiting performers. **Yale University** in New Haven, **Wesleyan University** in Middletown, and **Trinity College** in Hartford are among Connecticut's—and America's—top private colleges. Public institutions include the **U.S. Coast Guard Academy** in New London and state schools (see also *U.S. Service Academy*). The **University of Connecticut at Storrs**, with branches in Groton, Stamford, Torrington, West Hartford, and Waterbury, as well as the four universities of the state system, in Danbury, Willimantic, New Britain, and New Haven, have their own particular specialties, from planetarium shows to natural science collections.

EVENTS This guidebook lists a variety of annual events at the end of each chapter. The **Connecticut Commission on Culture & Tourism** (888-288-4748; www.ctvisit.com), as well as the five regional tourism districts (see *Information*), produce comprehensive event calendars, and the major daily and weekly newspapers print weekly events listings. Look for the free ***Hartford Advocate***, ***New Haven Advocate***, and ***Fairfield County Weekly*** arts and entertainment newspapers for information on local arts and nightlife.

FALL FOLIAGE Peak season for autumn leaf-peeping getaways in Connecticut falls around **Columbus Day weekend**. Experts say that peak foliage has been pushed back about a week in recent years owing to climate change. All parts of the state offer excellent viewing, but the woods are especially colorful in the hilly northeast and northwest sections. The legendary brilliance of fall in New England comes from the presence of abundant and varied hardwoods. Scarlet and sugar maples, ash, birch, beech, dogwood, tulip tree, oak, sassafras, hickory—even the undistinguished sumac—all take part in the festival of color. Beginning in mid-September, you can contact the **Connecticut Commission on Culture & Tourism** (888-288-4748; www.ctvisit.com) for up-to-date reports on the status of fall foliage hues around the state. Want to get out of the car? Top picks for panoramic views of fall colors via hiking trail include **Cobble Mountain** in Kent's Macedonia Brook State Park, **Heublein Tower** at Talcott Mountain State Park in Simsbury, the **Stone Tower** in Hamden's Sleeping Giant State Park, the overlook atop **Mount**

Misery in Voluntown's sprawling Pachaug State Forest, and the lookout tower on **Mohawk Mountain** in Cornwall.

FARMER'S MARKETS There are 87 open-air farmer's markets scattered throughout Connecticut during the growing season; most of them are held on village greens, in parking lots, and in other central locations. For a statewide listing of market locations, log onto **www.ctfarmersmarkets.com**. The **Hartford Regional Market** (860-713-2503), 101 Reserve Rd., Hartford, is the biggest: a vast 32-acre outdoor market selling fruits, vegetables, perennials, trees, and other farm products. To obtain a copy of the **Connecticut Farm Map**, which lists more than 200 farmer's markets, sugarhouses, pick-your-own farms, and orchards, send a self-addressed, stamped business-sized envelope with $1.14 postage to Connecticut Farm Map, Connecticut Department of Agriculture, Marketing Department, 165 Capitol Ave., Room 129, Hartford 06106. You can also view the map online at **www.ctfarms.uconn.edu**.

Courtesy Coastal Fairfield County Convention & Visitors Bureau

FERRIES Two ferries across the Connecticut River are the oldest in the country still in operation: The **Glastonbury–Rocky Hill Ferry** departs from Meadow Road (CT 160) in Rocky Hill and carries six cars and passengers daily from May through October. About 20 miles downriver, the **Chester–Hadlyme Ferry** carries eight to nine cars from April to November, leaving daily from Ferry Road (CT 148) in Chester. For more information on both ferries, call 860-443-3856. To cross Long Island Sound to New York, there are four ferry services. The **Bridgeport and Port Jefferson Steamboat Co.** (203-335-2040; 888-443-3779; www.bpjferry.com) carries both cars and people and operates year-round, leaving from the Water Street Dock in Bridgeport and arriving in Port Jefferson, New York. **Cross Sound Ferry Services, Inc.** (860-443-5281; www.longislandferry.com), takes cars and passengers from New London to Orient Point, Long Island, New York, year-round; it also runs free shuttle buses to Foxwoods Resort Casino and Mohegan Sun. **Fishers Island Ferry District** (860-442-0165; www.fiferry.com) takes cars and passengers from New London to Fishers Island, New York, year-round. During the summer, the high-speed **Viking Ferry** (631-668-5700; www.vikingferry.com) shuttles foot passengers and bicycles from New London to Montauk, Long Island. **Block Island Ferry Express** (860-444-4624; www.goblockisland.com) carries passengers and bicycles via high-speed ferry from New London to Block Island, Rhode Island, late May through mid-October.

FISHING Freshwater fish—trout, pickerel, bass, and shad, among

Andi Mari Cantele

them—abound in Connecticut's lakes, ponds, streams, and its main rivers: the Connecticut, Thames, Housatonic, and Quinnipiac, all stocked by the State Department of Environmental Protection. Bluefish, striped bass, flounder, and other saltwater species are found in Long Island Sound and beyond. A fishing license, obtainable from designated tackle shops, any town hall, or by phone (860-424-3700), is required for anyone 16 or older fishing on inland waterways. Licenses are issued on a calendar-year basis, expiring on December 31. For nonresidents, the fee is $40 for the season; a three-day license is $16. Free licensing is available to handicapped individuals, as well as residents over 65 years of age. Many areas are open all year to fishing; in restricted waterways, the season opens at 6 AM on the third Saturday in April. Complete information on the above and on fishing sites, restrictions, season length, and species limitations is available from the DEP's **Fisheries Division** (860-424-3474; www.dep.state.ct.us), 79 Elm St., Hartford 06106. Ask for the ***Connecticut Angler's Guide***, which lists lakes and public boat ramps, as well as the species of fish available at each location. Other sources for additional information: **Marine Fisheries** (860-434-6043), **Conservation Law Enforcement** (860-424-3012), and **Parks and Recreation** (860-424-3200). Special fishing areas for children have been set aside and are so posted. These include both trout streams and ponds in various parts of the state. (See also *Fishing, Saltwater.*)

FISHING, SALTWATER Connecticut's recommended charter and party fishing boats are operated by U.S. Coast Guard–licensed captains. Charter fishing boats cater to private groups that book the vessels for their own use. Party fishing boats are open to the public on a first-come, first-served basis, sailing January through mid-November. For fishing- and charter-boat captains, see the *To Do* sections throughout this book. The **Connecticut Charter and Party Boat Association** (www.ctsportfishing.com) maintains an online directory of boats and captains.

FLOWER FESTIVALS You can get an early start on spring and follow the blooming flowers right through into summer. The preview comes in late February with the annual **Connecticut Flower and Garden Show** in Hartford. In April, watch for the **Daffodil Festival** in Meriden. In May, the **Dogwood Festival** takes over Greenfield Hill in Fairfield. June brings the **Laurel Festival** in Winsted, the **Rose Arts Festival** in Norwich, and **Rose Weekend** at Elizabeth Park, Hartford. (See also *Gardens.*)

FORTS Connecticut is rich in history, including the American Revolution and the Civil War. In Groton, **Fort Griswold Battlefield State Park**

Cory Mazon

(860-449-6877), overlooking the mouth of the Thames River, is the site of a famous 1781 battle between the Continentals and the British. In New Haven, **Black Rock Fort**, from the Revolutionary War era, and **Fort Nathan Hale** (203-466-1596), dating from the Civil War, have both been reconstructed; the site affords a spectacular view of New Haven Harbor. **Fort Saybrook Monument Park** (860-395-3123) in Old Saybrook is an 18-acre park with an exhibit on the history of the original settlement in the Connecticut colony (circa 1635) and a view of the mouth of the Connecticut River. **Putnam Memorial State Park** (203-938-2285) in Redding is the site of **Little Valley Forge**, where Connecticut's General Israel Putnam and his army of Continental soldiers spent the harsh winter of 1779. An on-site museum has exhibits and artifacts centering on the encampment, as well as reconstructed officers' quarters. **Fort Trumbull** (860-444-7591), guarding New London Harbor since the American Revolution, has been restored and is open to the public.

GARDENS In addition to its annual flower festivals (see *Flower Festivals*), the state offers many opportunities to enjoy flowers, herbs, and other growing things. Many museums and historic homes open to the public feature recreated period gardens. Eleven of these are part of **Connecticut Historic Gardens**: In the Litchfield Hills are **Bellamy-Ferriday House & Garden** (203-266-7596), Bethlehem; the **Glebe House Museum** and the **Gertrude Jekyll Garden** (203-263-2855) are in Woodbury. In the Greater Hartford region are **Butler-McCook House & Garden** (860-522-1806) and **Harriet Beecher Stowe Center** (860-522-9258), both in Hartford; **Hill-Stead Museum** (860-677-4787), Farmington; and **Webb-Deane-Stevens Museum** (860-529-0612), Wethersfield. In the Quiet Corner, look for **Roseland Cottage-Bowen House** (860-928-4074), Woodstock. **Osborne Homestead Museum and Kellogg Environmental Center** (203-734-2513) Derby, is in the Gold Coast region. **Florence Griswold Museum** (860-434-5542, Old Lyme, and **Harkness Memorial State Park** (860-443-5725), Waterford, are along the shoreline. The **Garden Conservancy** runs an **Open Days** program (845-265-5384; www.gardenconservancy.org) that allows visitors to tour many of the state's finest private gardens during the growing season.

Barnett D. Laschever

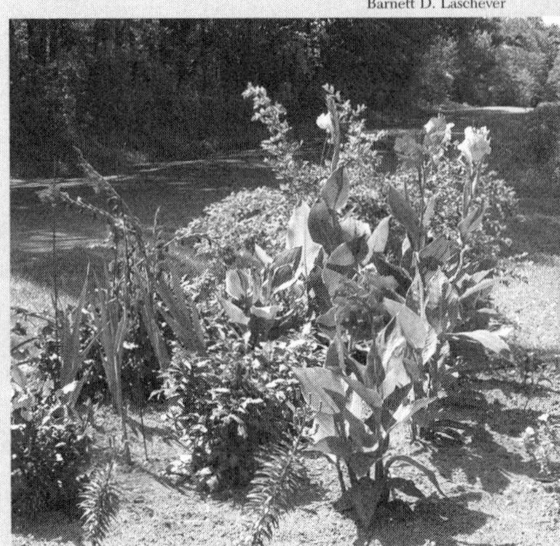

GENEALOGY As one of the nation's original 13 colonies, Connecticut is the ancestral home of many families across the country. It's no wonder that so many who are researching their family trees wind up here. Family, church, town, and other records of the **Connecticut State Library** (860-757-6500; www.cslib.org), 231 Capitol Ave., Hartford 06106, make an excellent place to start. Many museums and historic homes operated by local historical societies include research libraries that are open to the public; see the listings in each chapter.

GEOGRAPHY Although Connecticut is the third-smallest state, it has a surprising variety of terrain—rocky heights, wooded hills, fertile valleys, and plentiful streams, brooks, rivers, and lakes, as well as 253 miles of shoreline. Its highest point is at 2,380 feet on Mount Frissel in Salisbury. The state is divided into 169 towns, the capital being Hartford. There are 100 state parks and 31 state forests. Amazingly, two-thirds of Connecticut is green—open land, woods, and farms.

GOLF Connecticut's golf courses add many acres of green to the state total. The **Connecticut State Golf Association** (860-257-4171; www.csgalinks.org) maintains an online directory of its members; similarly, **www.ctgolfer.com** is an online guide to the state's public and private courses and driving ranges. In this guide, we describe only those courses that we know are open to the public. New England's premier golf tournament, the **Travelers Championship**, takes place every August in Cromwell.

HANDICAPPED ACCESS Throughout this book, the ♿ symbol indicates restaurants, lodgings, and attractions that are handicapped accessible.

HIKING Whether your preference is tough terrain or easygoing trails, Connecticut state parks have outstanding trails for hiking. For instance, **Talcott Mountain State Park** in Simsbury takes you on a rigorous, 1-mile hike to a spectacular overlook with views of four states on a clear day, and a picnic area and tower to enjoy while you're up there. **Macedonia Brook State Park** in Kent and **Sleeping Giant State Park** in Hamden are also known for particularly scenic trails. For information, contact the **Connecticut Bureau of Outdoor Recreation, State Parks Division** (860-424-3200; www.ct.gov/dep). There's the **Appalachian Trail** (see also *Appalachian Trail*), and the Connecticut **Blue Trails**, which total 700 miles throughout the state. The latter are maintained by the **Connecticut Forest and Park Association** (CFPA) (860-346-2372; www.ctwoodlands.org). Each year on **Connecticut Trails Day** in early June, the CFPA offers more than 70 hikes led by knowledgeable guides. You can, of course, hike the trails on your own any day.

HISTORIC HOMES AND SITES As one of the original colonies, Connecticut has a number of historic structures. In an effort to preserve the state's architectural past, there are more than 150 house museums in Connecticut—a remarkable number in a state with 169 cities and towns. Many of these houses have been carefully preserved and are open to the public. The towns of Wethersfield, Litchfield, Essex, and Norwich are especially known for their historic districts. The **Henry Whitfield State Museum** in Guilford is believed to be the oldest stone house in New England. There are also notable Victorian homes in Norwalk (the **Lockwood-Mathews Mansion**); Hartford (the **Mark Twain**

House & Museum and the **Harriet Beecher Stowe Center**); and Torrington (the **Hotchkiss-Fyler House**). **Connecticut Landmarks** (formerly the Antiquarian and Landmarks Society; 860-247-8996; www.ctlandmarks.org) provides excellent information on its eight historic properties that are open to the public. The **Connecticut Trust for Historic Preservation** (203-562-6312; www.cttrust.org) is another excellent resource. (See also *Museums.*)

HORSEBACK RIDING **Lee's Riding Stable, Inc.** (860-567-0785), Litchfield, has trail rides through open and wooded land. There's also **Diamond A Ranch** (860-779-3000) in Dayville.

HOTELS AND MOTELS In this guide, we have rarely listed chain hotels and motels since they're easy to locate and contact. You will find a few, though, either because lodging choices are scarce in that particular area or because of a desirable location (such as at the airport terminal). Clearly, the major cities—Hartford and New Haven—have a full complement of chain establishments. For the purposes of this book, we have concentrated on the resorts, inns, and B&Bs that are one-of-a-kind and especially identified with New England.

Barnett D. Laschever

HUNTING Connecticut offers opportunities for hunting deer, turkey, and waterfowl. A wide variety of small game is found in abundance throughout the state's fields and forests. Pheasant are stocked in state and private lands open to hunting. Waterfowl abound in freshwater ponds and marshes, along rivers, and in the coastal estuaries and bays of Long Island Sound. Hunting is not permitted in Connecticut on Sunday. For Connecticut residents a hunting license costs $14, and for nonresidents $67; both licenses must be renewed annually and are obtained through town clerks' offices or at the **State Department of Environmental Protection's Licensing and Revenue Office**, 79 Elm St., Hartford 06106-5127.

INFORMATION The **Connecticut Commission on Culture & Tourism** (860-256-2800; 888-288-4748; www.ctvisit.com), 1 Financial Plaza, Hartford 06103, publishes an annual ***Connecticut Vacation Guide*** and a variety of other publications geared to special interests. There are also five regional tourism districts throughout the state that produce guide/event brochures for their areas: **Coastal Fairfield County Convention & Visitor Bureau** (203-853-7770; 800-866-7925; www.visitfairfieldcountyct.com); **Greater New Haven Convention & Visitors Bureau** (203-777-8550; 800-332-7829; www.visitnewhaven.com); **Eastern Regional Tourism District** (860-444-2206; 800-863-6569; www.mysticcountry.com); **Central Regional Tourism District** (860-244-8181; 800-793-4480; www.enjoycentralct.com); and **Northwest Connecticut Convention & Visitors Bureau** (203-597-9527; www.litchfieldhills.com). Although the **Greater Hartford Convention and Visitors**

Bureau (860-728-6789; 800-446-7811; www.enjoyhartford.com) isn't an official state tourism bureau, it is a significant source of information for visitors to the state.

INFORMATION CENTERS Connecticut has six welcome centers located on its major roadways and at its largest airport, **Bradley International Airport, Terminal A**, in Windsor Locks. The others are located as follows: on I-95 in **North Stonington** (southbound), **Darien** (northbound), and **Westbrook** (northbound); on I-84 in **Danbury** (eastbound) and **Willington** (westbound); and on the Merritt Parkway in **Greenwich** (northbound). Some tourist brochures also are available at the **other McDonald's locations on I-95**. In **Litchfield** an information booth is operated seasonally on the green. Another assists tourists at the bus depot in **Southbury** off I-84. The **Old State House**, the **state capitol**, the **Legislative Office Building**, and the **Central Regional Tourism District** office on Pratt Street in Hartford also dispense tourist literature. A number of other towns—Glastonbury, Mystic, Stamford, Coventry, and Old Saybrook, among them—staff small visitor centers.

INNS Connecticut is dotted with more than 200 country inns and B&Bs, covering every style from colonial to Victorian to modern. The guest rooms of country inns—lodgings that serve dinner as well as breakfast—are typically furnished with antiques (and often four-poster beds), and many feature working fireplaces. (See also *Bed & Breakfasts.*)

INTERSTATES Connecticut is served by **I-95** along the shoreline. **I-91** from New Haven runs through the center of the state and intersects in Hartford with **I-84**, which crosses the state from Danbury to Union, where it joins the Massachusetts Turnpike. **I-91** then continues northward through New England to Canada. **I-395** runs north–south in the eastern part of the state, and the **Merritt Parkway (CT 15)**, an extension of the Hutchinson River Parkway in New York, roughly parallels the shoreline from Greenwich to Milford. From here to Meriden, it becomes the **Wilbur Cross Parkway**, which then merges with **I-91**. Major limited-access highway **CT 8**, in the western part of the state, links Bridgeport with Winsted.

ISLANDS **Sheffield Island** off Norwalk, with its now inactive lighthouse, is open to the public by ferry from Norwalk Harbor. On the island is a U.S. Fish and Wildlife Sanctuary. Also in Norwalk Harbor, **Chimon Island** is a natural wildlife preserve, accessible to the public only by boat. Near Guilford, **Faulkner's Island** is a wildlife preserve open to the public. Off Stony Creek in Branford, the **Thimble Islands** are privately owned and not accessible to the public, but three skippers offer short cruises around the harbor and the islands on launches that primarily serve island residents. The mini cruises are enlivened by legends—some of them true—of pirates and early settlers (see *To Do—Boat Excursions* in the relevant chapters).

LAKES There are more than 3,500 lakes and ponds in Connecticut. Many are in state parks and forests and are available for fishing, swimming, boating, ice skating, iceboating, and ice fishing. The state's largest is **Candlewood Lake**, a constructed waterway in New Milford, Sherman, and New Fairfield. Many lakes have boat-launching facilities, and some post restrictions regarding powerboats,

Kim Grant

speed limits, and times of operation. **Bantam Lake** is the state's largest natural lake. Contact the **Connecticut Bureau of Outdoor Recreation, State Parks Division** (860-424-3200; www.ct.gov/dep) for locations and regulations. Many towns have swimming lakes or ponds open to visitors of residents or to guests staying in a commercial lodging in the town.

LIGHTHOUSES Connecticut has 21 lighthouses, most of them off-limits to the public but close enough for photographers with long lenses. **Sheffield Island Lighthouse** was originally built in 1826 and is accessible by boat. **Penfield Reef Lighthouse** in Fairfield was built in 1874 and is not open to the public. In Stratford, the **Stratford Point Lighthouse** is the most powerful lighthouse along the Sound, originally built in 1821 and not open to the public. Two lighthouses are in Bridgeport—**Tongue Point Lighthouse** (built in 1891) and **Black Rock Harbor Lighthouse** (built in 1823)—but neither is open to visitors. Built in 1804, **New Haven Harbor Lighthouse** was retired in 1877 and replaced by **Southwest Ledge Lighthouse** at Lighthouse Point Park; this one is available to the public. A bird sanctuary is located near the active **Faulkner's Island Lighthouse**, south of Guilford Harbor. There are two lighthouses in Old Saybrook: **Lynde Point Lighthouse** was built in 1803 (not open), and **Saybrook Breakwater Lighthouse**, built in 1886, is presently active but not open. **Avery Point Lighthouse** in Groton was built in 1942 by the U.S. Coast Guard but never illuminated. It's now a research center. The town of New London has two lighthouses: **New London Harbor Lighthouse** (not open), built in 1706 and automated in 1978, and the **New London Ledge Lighthouse**, built in 1909 and automated in 1986. Tour boats put in at the **Ledge light**. **Stonington Harbor Lighthouse** was built in 1823 and discontinued in 1889. It's now the **Old Lighthouse Museum**, open to the public, and has an exciting story to tell.

LODGING This book lists select lodgings from among some 400 hotels, motels, inns, resorts, B&Bs, and camp-

Kim Grant

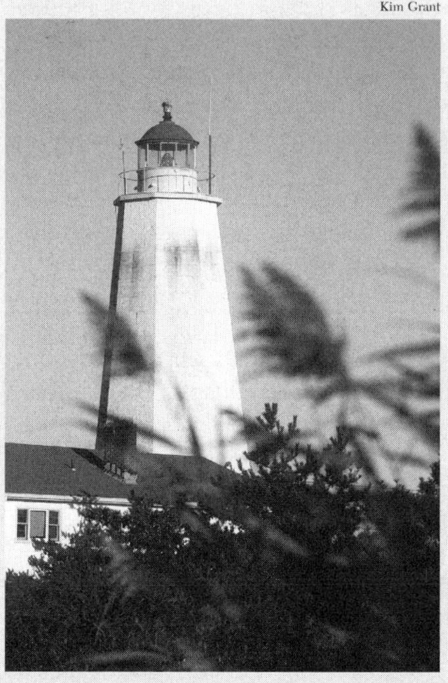

grounds throughout the state. A more complete list that includes chain properties is contained in the state's annual ***Connecticut Vacation Guide***. On the state's tourism Web site, **www.ctvisit.com**, each of the five tourism districts provides additional detailed information on lodging and dining out.

LYME DISEASE Because it was named for a town in Connecticut, travelers coming here often wonder about it. Lyme disease is traced to the bite of the deer tick, a creature about the size of a pinhead (or a poppy seed). Campers, hikers, and mountain bikers who spend time in grassy, wooded, or brushy areas should take the following precautions: Wear light-colored clothing; tuck pants legs into socks or boots, and shirt into pants; use insect repellent; wear a hat and a long-sleeved shirt; keep long hair tied back. After being outdoors, inspect your body, your children, and your pets, and remove any ticks. If a tick is found, save it in a jar for later testing in case a problem develops; record the date, the body location of the bite, and the place where the tick was acquired. Check the bite area for about a month for the appearance of a skin rash. For more information, contact the **Lyme Disease Foundation** (860-870-0070; www.lyme.org), Box 332, Tolland 06084.

MAPLE SUGARING Connecticut produces 12,000 gallons of syrup each year. The maple sugaring season is from early February until late March, depending on the weather. **Sharon Audubon Center** in Sharon and **Flanders Nature Center** in Woodbury conduct demonstrations on weekends; in **Hebron**, an annual festival celebrates the sugaring season and offers tours of several sugarhouses in town. The **Connecticut Department of Agriculture** (860-713-2503; 800-861-9939) offers a guide to Connecticut maple producers who welcome visitors during sugaring off. For a free copy, send a self-addressed, stamped envelope to the department's Marketing Division at 165 Capitol Ave., Hartford 06106.

MUSEUMS As you might expect, the state is liberally sprinkled with 200 or so museums of local history, many housed in centuries-old and well-preserved homes. But Yankee ingenuity does not rest with the home scene. Some of our favorites are the **New England Carousel Museum** (860-585-5411; www.thecarouselmuseum.com) in Bristol; the brand-new **Connecticut Science Center** (860-727-0457; www.ctsciencecenter.org) in Hartford; **Timexpo Museum** (203-755-8463; www.timexpo.com) in Waterbury; the **Submarine Force Museum** and **USS *Nautilus* Memorial** (860-694-3174; 800-343-0079; www.ussnautilus.org) in Groton; **Yale Collection of Musical Instruments** (203-432-0822) in New Haven; the **Institute for American Indian Studies** (860-868-0518; www.birdstone.org) in Washington; and the **Mark Twain House & Museum** (860-247-0998; www.marktwainhouse.org) in Hartford. (See also *Art Museums*; *Museums, Maritime*; and *Museums, Trolley and Rail.*)

MUSEUMS, MARITIME Connecticut has two outstanding maritime museums. **Mystic Seaport—The Museum of America and the Sea** (860-572-0711; www.mysticseaport.org) in Mystic is a re-creation of a 19th-century maritime village where visitors explore the local link to the sea. There are costumed docents, continuing crafts demonstrations, historic ships to board, period homes to visit, museum exhibits, and special events throughout the year. In South Norwalk, the **Maritime Aquarium at Norwalk** (203-852-0700; www.maritimeaquarium.org) explores the marine life and maritime culture of Long Island Sound with the help of an aquarium, an IMAX movie theater, and a history museum.

MUSEUMS, TROLLEY AND RAIL The **Shore Line Trolley Museum** (203-467-6927; www.bera.org) in East Haven is a National Historic Site. The collection consists of nearly 100 restored classic cars, and visitors are offered a ride on the old shoreline tracks. In East Windsor, the **Connecticut Trolley Museum** (860-627-6540; www.ceraonline.org) invites you to tour the car barns and hop aboard one of the restored beauties for a 3-mile jaunt. The **Danbury Railway Museum** (203-778-8337; www.danbury.org/drm) combines dioramas with a yard of vintage locomotives and coaches. The **Railroad Museum of New England/Naugatuck Railroad** (860-283-7245; www.rmne.org), Thomaston, takes you on a 20-mile ride on a restored rail through forests, along the Naugatuck River, and across the top of a dam. **Connecticut Eastern Railroad Company** (860-456-9999), Willimantic, is a railroad museum village with a station, freight house, section house, and roundhouse. The **Essex Steam Train and Riverboat Ride** (860-767-0103; 800-377-3987; www.essexsteamstrain.com) chugs along the banks of the Connecticut River to Deep River, where you board a boat that continues to the Goodspeed Opera House during its ride back into history. (See also *Train and Trolley Rides.*)

Kim Grant

MUSIC FESTIVALS, SUMMER In addition to weekly concerts on town greens and in bandshells around the state every summer, major festivals draw music lovers to Connecticut. They include the **Greater Hartford Festival of Jazz** (866-943-5299; www.hartfordjazz.com) in Hartford's Bushnell Park; the **New Haven Jazz Festival** (203-777-2800; www.newhavenjazz.com) on the New Haven green; the **Litchfield Jazz Festival** (860-567-4162; www.litchfieldjazzfest.com) in Kent; Roxbury's **Pickin' 'n' Fiddlin' Contest** (860-354-2912); the **Great Connecticut Traditional Jazz Festival** (800-468-3836; www.ctjazz.org) in Moodus; and the **Podunk Bluegrass Music Festival** (860-291-7350; www.podunkbluegrass.net) in East Hartford's Martin Park.

MUSIC SERIES, SUMMER **Music Mountain** (860-824-7126; www.musicmountain.org) in Falls Village, America's oldest continuing summer chamber music festival, provides enchantment on a 120-acre mountaintop from mid-June to early September. The **Norfolk Chamber Music Festival** (860-542-3000; www.yale.edu/norfolk) is presented by the Yale Music School from late June to mid-August on the Ellen Battell Stoeckel Estate in Norfolk. Summer concerts feature a diverse mix of world-class artists performing in a beautiful shed on 10 landscaped acres that accommodates an audience of 1,500 in the shed and on the lawn. **Levitt Pavilion for the Performing Arts** (203-221-2153; www.levittpavilion.com) in Westport schedules more than 50 free concerts every summer. **Charles Ives Concert Park** (203-837-9226; www.ivesconcert park.com), on the campus of Western Connecticut State University, honors Connecticut composer Ives as well as the late famed contralto Marian Anderson, a longtime Danbury resident, in a series of concerts. In Simsbury, the **Talcott Mountain Music Festival** (860-244-2999; www.hartford symphony.org) features the Hartford Symphony Orchestra. Performances by the **U.S. Coast Guard Band** (860-701-6826; www.uscg.mil/band) at the New London–based academy are free and open to the public.

NATIONAL HISTORIC SITES The **Weir Farm National Historic Site** (203-834-1896; www.nps.gov/wefa), 735 Nod Hill Rd., Wilton, was the state's first spot so designated, and one of only two such parks in the country recognizing American art. The former summer home and studio of noted American impressionist painter J. Alden Weir sits on a pastoral hilltop in the Housatonic Valley. Weir turned his 153-acre farm into a retreat that attracted famed impressionists—from John Singer Sargent to Childe Hassam—who came to paint the rural landscape of rambling stone walls, meadows, and woodlands. Weir Farm offers walking trails, galleries, and programs for visitors and artists, who can set up their easels right on the grounds. In 2007, the former home of the late architect Philip Johnson in New Canaan, known as **The Glass House** (203-594-9585; www.philip

Courtesy Glass House

johnsonglasshouse.org), opened as a National Trust Historic Site. It's a celebrated example of modernist architecture; tours are by reservation only and fill up quickly.

NATURE CENTERS **Ansonia Nature and Recreation Center** (203-736-1053; www.ansonianature center.org) in Ansonia is a 104-acre park with nature trails and award-winning gardens and offers hiking, cross-country skiing, a fishing pond, and picnic pavilions. **Connecticut Audubon Center at Fairfield** (203-259-6305; www.ctaudubon.org) in Fairfield is adjacent to **Larsen Sanctuary**, a 160-acre park with 6 miles of trails, ponds, and a walk for the blind, disabled, and elderly. In the Hartford suburbs, **Connecticut Audubon Society at Glastonbury** (860-633-8402) connects with **Earle Park** and its trail system. In Pomfret, the **Connecticut Audubon Center at Pomfret** (860-928-2939) offers 700 acres of forests and meadows laced with trails. **Denison Pequotsepos Nature Center** (860-536-1216; www.dpnc.org) in Mystic has self-guiding trails, including one for the blind, in a 125-acre sanctuary. In Woodbury, **Flanders Nature Center** (203-263-3711) has a trail system, geological sites, woodlands, wildlife, and a bog. **H. C. Barnes**

Memorial Nature Center (860-585-8886) in Bristol contains 70 acres with trails. In Westport, there's a 62-acre wildlife sanctuary at **Earthplace: The Nature Discovery Center** (203-227-7253). Along with 40 acres of diverse habitats with walking trails, **New Canaan Nature Center** (203-966-9577) has a Discovery Center with hands-on natural science exhibits and live animals. **Roaring Brook Nature Center** (860-693-0263) in Canton has self-guiding trails, a Native American longhouse, and live animals. In Stamford, the **Stamford Museum and Nature Center** (203-322-1646), on 118 acres, has a 19th-century working farm, a country store, woodland trails, a wildlife and picnic area, galleries, and planetarium shows on Sunday. The 146-acre **Woodcock Nature Center** (203-762-7280) in Wilton has 2 miles of hiking trails and a swamp boardwalk trail. (See also *Nature Preserves, Coastal* and *Inland.*)

NATURE PRESERVES, COASTAL

Hammonasset Beach State Park (203-245-2785) in Madison is the state's largest shoreline sanctuary, with 2 miles of sandy beaches, dunes, and salt marshes. The park's **Meigs Point Nature Center** offers exhibits and interpretive programs, including guided walks. **Bluff Point Coastal Reserve State Park** (860-444-7591) in Groton is a paradise for hikers and birders. Cars are not allowed in the 800-acre park; all exploring is done on foot. The 10-acre barrier beach at **Connecticut Audubon Center at Milford Point** (203-878-7440) is a feeding area for great blue herons and snowy egrets, which nest on nearby **Chimon Island**, a 70-acre nature reserve in Norwalk Harbor. **Sheffield Island**, also in Norwalk Harbor, is a 60-acre nature refuge.

NATURE PRESERVES, INLAND

The **Lucius Pond Ordway–Devil's Den Preserve** (203-226-4991) spans 62 acres in Weston, with self-guiding woodland trails and an arboretum. **McLean Game Refuge** (860-653-7869) in Granby off CT 10 offers 3,400 acres with hiking trails over varied terrain, and an abundance of small animals and birds. **White Memorial Foundation and Conservation Center** (860-567-0857) in Litchfield, the state's largest nature center, with 4,000 acres, offers bird-watching with observation platforms, hiking, boating, swimming, camping, horseback riding, and many self-guiding trails, including one for the blind. At **Connecticut College Arboretum** (860-439-5020) in New London, half of its 200 acres is preserved for nature itself and for hikers; the other half is maintained as an arboretum with a small stand of virgin pine, trees almost as high as California's famed redwoods. The **Laurel Sanctuary at Nipmuck State Forest** (860-684-3430) in Union is a cloud of

Kim Grant

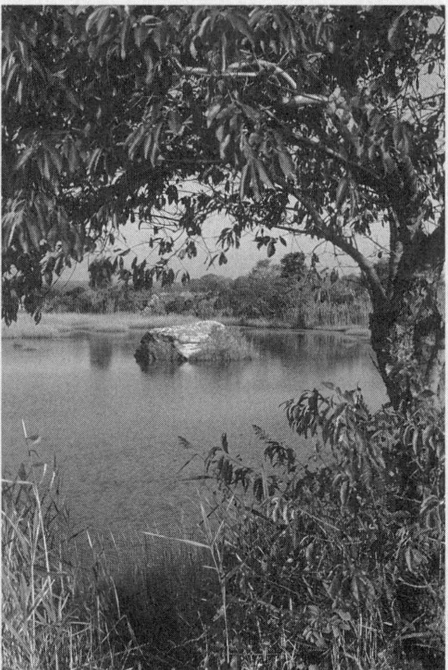

pink and white flowers in late June and early July, when the state flower, the mountain laurel, is in bloom.

PARKS AND FORESTS, STATE In all, Connecticut has 131 state parks and forests. Much of the traprock ridge that runs roughly down the center of the state has been judged unsuitable (or impossible) for development, and as a consequence some choice hiking areas remain pristine woodlands. The state has purchased a number of parcels for preservation, and in addition, generous citizens have donated lands to the system of parks and forests that so successfully interrupt the crush of megalopolis. Boating, fishing, camping, picnicking, swimming, cross-country skiing, snowmobiling, rock climbing, hunting, mountain biking, and, of course, hiking are among the activities available in various developed parks and forests. All state parks are open from 8 AM until sunset; some charge daily or weekend parking fees. For detailed information on developed and undeveloped but accessible parks and forests, contact the **Connecticut Bureau of Outdoor Recreation, State Parks Division** (860-424-3200; www.ct.gov/dep, click on "Outdoor Recreation").

PERFORMING ARTS CENTERS Centers around Connecticut offer a full roster of music, dance, theater, and film. In Hartford, the **Bushnell Center for the Performing Arts** (860-987-5900) is the state's premier performing arts center, presenting more than 300 events annually. Top repertory and the best of Broadway's plays are mounted in the **Stamford Center for the Arts** (203-325-4466). At the University of Fairfield in Fairfield, the **Regina A. Quick Center for the Arts** (203-254-4010) offers music, dance, theater, and lectures. The **Chevrolet Theatre** (203-265-1501) is in Wallingford. The **Warner Theatre** (860-489-7180), Torrington's elegant art deco facility, is listed on the National Register of Historic Places, as is Waterbury's historic art deco theater, **the Palace** (203-755-4700). The **Center for the Arts** (860-685-3355) at Wesleyan University in Middletown offers year-round dance and theater performances. The **Garde Arts Center** (860-444-7373) in New London is a historic vaudeville/movie theater that presents national and international touring companies. At the University of Connecticut at Storrs, the **Jorgensen Center for the Performing Arts** (860-486-4226) hosts dance, theater, live music, and other entertainment.

PETS, TRAVELING WITH Throughout this book, the 🐾 symbol indicates lodgings, parks, and other places that are pet-friendly.

PICK-YOUR-OWN Fall is harvest-time, when apple orchards and pumpkin patches open to visitors looking to pick their own seasonal produce. Connecticut farms invite you to help. You can pick strawberries, blueberries, apples, peaches, and pumpkins; later in the year, tag and cut your own Christmas trees. Signs along the roads point the way to pick-your-own farms; for a copy of the **Connecticut Farm Map**—which includes vineyards, greenhouses, and farmer's markets as well as pick-your-own farms—send a business-sized envelope with $1.14 postage to The Connecticut Farm Map, Connecticut Department of Agriculture, Marketing Department, 165 Capitol Ave., Room 129, Hartford 06106. To view the map online, go to www.ctfarms.uconn.edu. You can also download brochures at www.ctgrown.gov; click on "Publications."

Cory Mazon

POPULATION Connecticut's population, according to the 2006 U.S. Census, is 3,504,809.

RESORTS Connecticut has several resorts that offer swimming, either on ocean beaches or on lakeshores, and organized activities, as well as golf, tennis, fishing, boating, pools, health club facilities, and more. In Moodus, **Cave Hill Resort** (860-873-8347) and **Sunrise Resort** (860-873-8681; 800-225-9033) are casual, family-friendly choices. More upscale options include **Dolce Heritage** (203-264-8200; 800-932-3466; www.heritage.dolce.com) in Southbury; **Water's Edge Resort and Spa** (860-399-5901; 800-222-5901) in Westbrook; and **Interlaken Inn, Resort and Conference Center** (860-435-9878; 800-222-2909) in Lakeville. **Club Getaway** (860-927-3664) in South Kent is a sports resort for adults. Don't forget **Foxwoods Resort Casino** (800-369-9663) in Mashantucket and **Mohegan Sun** (888-226-7711) in Uncasville (see also *Casinos*).

SAFETY As is the case elsewhere, Connecticut cities call for common-sense precautions. Pay attention to your surroundings, and do your walking in the daytime; at night stick to the brightly lit areas where you find other tourists, diners, and theatergoers. Each chapter includes hospital and emergency numbers. Dial **911** in an emergency.

SCENIC ROUTES In 1940, the nation's second median-divided, limited-access parkway (passenger cars only) was opened to traffic: The **Merritt Parkway**, a 38-mile roadway across Fairfield County from Greenwich to Stratford, is a designated National Scenic Byway today. Described by one historian as "one of the most beautiful and best-engineered highways of the time," it is neatly landscaped and treats the driver to a succession of 35 ornamental bridges, each of them different. **CT 169**, Lisbon to Woodstock, 32.1 miles, is Connecticut's other National Scenic Byway. Other stretches of road selected by the Department of Transportation and designated scenic include **CT 234**, the **Pequot Trail**, from Stonington to Westerly, 3.16 miles; **CT 146**, Branford to Guilford for 12.2 miles and then **CT 77** north to Durham for 11.56 miles; **CT 4** in Sharon, 3.9 miles; **US 7** in Sharon at the Cornwall bridge and north for 4.29 miles, and also from New Milford north to Cornwall, 10.5 miles; **CT 41** in Sharon, 8.4 miles; **CT 160** in Glastonbury, 1.06 miles, ending at the Ferry Landing; **CT 202**, Canton

Kim Grant

to New Hartford, 5.1 miles; **CT 53** in Redding, 2.03 miles; **CT 49** in the Quiet Corner, 18.8 miles; and **US 44** in Salisbury, 3.1 miles.

SKIING, CROSS-COUNTRY The **White Memorial Foundation** in Litchfield offers 35 miles of trails. **Winding Trails Cross-Country Ski Center** in Farmington has 12 miles of trails. In Cornwall you'll find **Mohawk Mountain Ski Area** with 5 miles of cross-country trails. And in Woodbury, **Woodbury Ski Area** maintains 20 miles of cross-country trails with night skiing and snowmaking. Many state parks and forests permit cross-country skiing on hiking trails; contact the **Connecticut Bureau of Outdoor Recreation, State Parks Division** (860-424-3014; www.ct.gov/dep, click on "Outdoor Recreation"), for a complete listing.

SKIING, DOWNHILL Connecticut has five major ski areas, all with snowmaking capability, ski shops, night skiing, snowboarding, and food service. None of these offers lodging on the property. In Cornwall, **Mohawk Mountain Ski Area** is where snowmaking was invented. This area has 23 downhill trails and 5 miles of cross-country trails. **Mount Southington Ski Area** in Southington has 14 trails. **Powder Ridge Ski Area** in Middlefield was closed as of press time. **Ski Sundown** in New Hartford offers 15 trails. **Woodbury Ski Area** has 14 downhill trails and 20 miles of cross-country trails.

SNOWMOBILING In 11 designated areas in some Connecticut state forests, the use of snowmobiles is authorized on established trails and forest roads. There are more than 95 miles of trails on state lands, including seasonal hiking trails, unplowed logging roads, abandoned railroad rights-of-way, and fire access lanes. For locations of trails, policies, procedures, and regulations, contact the **Connecticut Bureau of Outdoor Recreation, State Parks Division** (860-424-3200; www.ct.gov/dep, click on "Outdoor Recreation").

SPAS The **Spa at Grand Lake** (860-642-4306; www.thespaatgrandlake.com) is a weight-loss health spa with daily activities ranging from massage to yoga. It's in Lebanon in a scenic and rural setting overlooking Lake Williams. In Norwich, the **Spa at Norwich Inn** (860-886-2401; 800-275-4772; www.thespaatnorwichinn.com) is a turn-of-the-20th-century luxury inn with modern resort atmosphere and a full-service health spa. **Saybrook Point Inn and Spa** (860-395-2000; 800-243-0212; www.saybrookk.com) in Old Saybrook, and Westbrook's **Water's Edge Resort and Spa** (860-399-5901; 800-222-5901; www.watersedgeresortandspa.com), offer upscale facilities on Long Island Sound. In recent years, day spas have sprung up in virtually every community in the state; check the Yellow Pages for local listings. In southeastern Connecticut, luxury spas are found at **Foxwoods Resort Casino** (800-369-9663;

www.foxwoods.com), **Mohegan Sun** (888-226-7711; www.mohegansun.com), and the **Mystic Marriott Hotel & Spa** (860-446-2600) in Groton.

THEATER, SUMMER First-rate summer theater is available in the state where it all really began. Before air-conditioning, New York thespians abandoned the city, but not their calling, during the summer months, traveling up to the cool "country"—Connecticut. Here they performed comedy, tragedy, high drama, and slapstick in makeshift theaters, often barns, and—voilà!—strawhat theater was born. Now the tradition continues nationwide. In Hartford, the **Centennial Theater Festival** schedules performances June through August at **Hartford Stage**. In Bridgeport, **Playhouse on the Green** holds performances June through October. The **Tri-Arts Sharon Playhouse** in Sharon has reopened with a schedule of musicals. The **Eugene O'Neill Theater Center** in Waterford was founded in 1964 in honor of Nobel Prize–winning playwright—and New London native—Eugene O'Neill. In New Haven, **Summer Cabaret at Yale** stages performances when Yalies are on summer break.

THEATER, YEAR-ROUND Connecticut's award-winning professional theaters are recognized worldwide. Among them: The **Hartford Stage Company** (860-525-5601) received a Tony Award for Outstanding Achievement in Resident Theater. New Haven's twin theater giants, the **Shubert Theater** (203-624-1825) and **Long Wharf Theatre** (203-787-4282), have between them garnered dozens of Obie, Golden Globe, and other awards. All three have initiated runs of innumerable new plays that went on to Broadway and national stages. Also in the Elm City are **Yale Cabaret** (203-432-1566) and **Yale Repertory Theatre** (203-432-1234). The **Goodspeed Opera House** (860-873-8668) in East Haddam has become famous as the birthplace and nurturer of American musical theater. Other professional-quality theater is found throughout the state. In Westport, the acclaimed **Westport Country Playhouse** (203-227-4177), originally a summer-stock professional theater, is now a year-round venue. In New Britain, the **Hole in the Wall Theater** (860-229-3049) plays throughout the year. The **Ivoryton Playhouse** (860-767-7318) is the country's oldest professional self-supporting theater. Middletown's **Oddfellows Playhouse Youth Theater** (860-347-6143) is the state's oldest and

Kim Grant

largest theater for children. Similarly, **Connecticut Repertory Theatre** (860-486-4226) at the University of Connecticut at Storrs offers theater with a combination of professional and student actors. The **Theatre of Northeast Connecticut at the Bradley Playhouse** (860-928-7887) is located in the rural Quiet Corner town of Putnam. A year-round venue, **Connecticut Cabaret Theatre** (860-829-1248) is in Berlin.

TIDES Click on **www.saltwatertides.com** to view tide tables for locations along the Connecticut shore, including New London Harbor, Saybrook Point, New Haven Harbor, Bridgeport, and the state's tidal rivers.

TRAILS, TOURISM Several special "trails" have been designed to guide visitors to collections or sites with common themes. See the index for individual listings of the properties, and see also *Art Museums*; *Crafts Centers*; and *Wineries*.

The **Connecticut Freedom Trail** (www.ctfreedomtrail.com) spotlights more than 100 sites associated with African American heritage in Connecticut. Homes, churches, and sites are included, many of them connected with the Underground Railroad and with the *Amistad* incident, which involved Mende tribesmen who seized control of the ship carrying them into slavery and came ashore in Connecticut. Sites along the trail, not all open to the public, include the homes, or their remains, of such notables as John Brown in Torrington, Marian Anderson in Danbury, Paul Robeson in Enfield, and other citizens, black and white, who have contributed to African American history. For a brochure, contact the Connecticut Commission on Culture & Tourism (860-256-2800; 888-288-4748; www.cultureandtourism.org), 1 Constitution Plaza, Hartford 06103.

The **Connecticut Women's Heritage Trail**, founded by the state's Women's Hall of Fame, features 13 sites that celebrate the accomplishments of women in Connecticut. The trail includes the Prudence Crandall House Museum in Canterbury, the Harriet Beecher Stowe Center in Hartford, the Florence Griswold Museum in Old Lyme, and the Connecticut Audubon Birdcraft Museum and Sanctuary in Fairfield. For more information, contact the Connecticut Women's Hall of Fame (860-768-5642; www.cwhf.org), 1265 Asylum Ave., Hartford 06105.

A national effort is under way to create a **Washington Rochambeau Revolutionary Route National Historic Trail** to recognize the French contribution to Washington's army during the American Revolutionary War. It will trace the 600-mile march route of the French troops under the command of the comte de Rochambeau from Newport, Rhode Island, to Yorktown, Virginia, where they joined the Continentals in forcing the surrender of General Cornwallis, the effective end of the war. In Connecticut, markers have been placed along the state's 120-mile portion of the route. For more information, contact the Connecticut Commission on Culture & Tourism (860-256-2800; 888-288-4748; www.cultureandtourism.org), 1 Constitution Plaza, Hartford 06103.

TRAIN SERVICES **Amtrak** (800-872-7245; www.amtrak.com) links New York City's Penn Station and Boston, with Connecticut stops at Stamford, Bridgeport, New Haven, Old Saybrook, New London, and Mystic. Service to Springfield, Massachusetts, connects with New Haven, with the following stops in Connecticut:

Wallingford, Meriden, Berlin, Hartford, Windsor, and Windsor Locks. The high-speed **Acela Express** stops in Stamford, New Haven, and New London on its route between Washington, DC, and Boston.

Metro-North (800-638-7646; www.mta.info/mnr) commuter line runs from New York City (Grand Central Terminal) to New Haven, scheduling stops at Greenwich, Cos Cob, Riverside, Old Greenwich, Stamford, Norton Heights, Darien, Rowayton, South and East Norwalk, Westport, Green's Farms, Southport, Fairfield, Bridgeport, Stratford, and Milford. A spur line to New Canaan serves Glenbrook, Springdale, and Talmadge Hill; one to Danbury stops at Merritt 7, Wilton, Cannondale, Branchville, Redding, and Bethel; the line to Waterbury also serves Derby–Shelton, Ansonia, Seymour, Beacon Falls, and Naugatuck. Metro-North and Amtrak connect at Union Station in New Haven.

Commuters in eastern Connecticut can get to Metro-North trains in New Haven via **Shore Line East** (203-777-7433; 800-255-7433; www.shorelineeast.com), a weekday commuter rail service that connects New Haven and New London, with stops in Branford, Guilford, Madison, Clinton, Westbrook, and Old Saybrook. **Shore Line Express** provides service between Bridgeport and Stamford.

TRAIN AND TROLLEY RIDES **Essex Steam Train and Riverboat Ride** (860-377-3987; www.essexsteamtrain.com) in Essex gives you an opportunity to ride in 1920s coaches behind an authentic, coal-fired steam locomotive along the Connecticut River, then continue upstream via riverboat. The **Naugatuck Railroad Company** (860-283-7245; www.rmne.org) follows the tracks that crisscross the Naugatuck River, from Thomaston south to Waterbury, once a major world center of brass manufacturing. Tours are run by the Railroad Museum of New England.

In Connecticut you get not one but two chances to ride the trolley into the past. At the **Shore Line Trolley Museum** (203-467-6927; www.bera.org) in East Haven, visitors are offered a ride on the old shoreline tracks. At Warehouse Point, East Windsor, the **Connecticut Trolley Museum** (860-627-6540; www.ceraonline.org) invites you to hop aboard one of the restored beauties for a 3-mile jaunt. (See also *Museums, Trolley and Rail.*)

U.S. SERVICE ACADEMY In New London, the **U.S. Coast Guard Academy** (860-444-8444; 800-883-8724; www.cga.edu) is open to the public daily May through October. Visitors can take a close-up look at a military academy at work and watch the cadets on parade on many Friday afternoons. The Visitors Pavilion and the museum provide an overview of the Coast Guard's history and mission. When the tall ship *Eagle*, a training vessel for the academy cadets, is in port, visitors are invited to go aboard. The Coast Guard is the first military service to give women officers command positions as captains of cutters.

WATERFALLS Some of Connecticut's highest falls are in state parks and forests. The most spectacular—and the state's tallest series of waterfalls—is **Kent Falls**, a series of three cascades that drop 250 feet over a quarter mile in Kent Falls State Park in the town of Kent on US 7. In East Haddam, Devil's Hopyard State Park on CT 156 has **Chapman Falls**, plunging some 60 feet down a rocky cliff. Wadsworth Falls State Park is on CT 157 in Middlefield. **Southford Falls**, located on

CT 188 in Southbury–Oxford, is a series of several easily accessible falls, with the added attraction of a covered bridge at the bottom. Spruce Brook Ravine in Naugatuck State Forest hides a pretty stream in a setting of evergreens and a steep-walled gorge. Pine Knob Trail, across from Housatonic Meadows State Park, is on US 7 in West Cornwall in a miniature canyon you can climb into.

WHITEWATER RAFTING **Clarke Outdoors** (860-672-6365; www.clarkeoutdoors.com) offers guided whitewater rafting on the Housatonic River in Bulls Bridge Gorge in South Kent during spring's high water. (See also *Canoeing and Kayaking, Tours and Rentals.*)

WINDJAMMERS In Mystic, Voyager Cruises (860-536-0416; www.voyagermystic.com) offers a variety of trips aboard ***Argia***, a replica of a 19th-century, gaff- rigged schooner with 20th-century appointments, and ***Mystic***, a new three-masted tall ship. The classic schooner ***Mystic Whaler*** (860-535-1556; 800-697-8420; www.mysticwhaler.com) has modern berths and sails for one-, two-, three-, and five-day getaways along the New England coast from New London. Long Island Sound yields its secrets on half-day, all-day, and summer cruises out of New Haven Harbor aboard the ***Quinnipiack*** (203-865-1737; www.schoonerinc.org). The 91-foot gaff-rigged wooden schooner is also available for charters, and sailing courses for students and adults. ***SoundWaters*** (203-323-1978; www.soundwaters.org), a replica of a 19th-century schooner, sails out of Stamford for two-hour ecology cruises or three-hour sunset cruises on Long Island Sound. Help haul in a net full of denizens of the deep, or climb the rigging and help set the sails.

Kim Grant

WINERIES The **Connecticut Wine Trail** invites swillers, snuffers, and tasters to tour 19 state vineyards that are open to the public on a regular basis. Some benefit from maritime microclimate near Long Island Sound; others sit high in the state's northern reaches. Wineries on the trail are **Bishop's Winery** (203-453-2338), Guilford; **Di Grazia Vineyard and Winery** (203-775-1616), Brookfield Center; **Jones' Winery** (203-929-8425), Shelton; **McLaughlin Vineyards** (203-426-1533), Sandy Hook; **Chamard Vineyard** (860-664-0299), Clinton; **Sharpe Hill Vineyard** (860-974-3549), Pomfret; **Taylor Brooke Winery** (860-974-1263), Woodstock; **Hopkins Vineyard** (860-868-7954), New Preston; **Land of Nod Winery** (860-824-8225), East Canaan; **Haight-Brown Vineyard and Winery** (860-567-4045), Litchfield; **Miranda Vineyard** (860-491-9906), Goshen;

Heritage Trail Vineyards (860-376-0659), Lisbon; **Priam Vineyards** (860-267-8520), Colchester; **Jonathan Edwards Winery** (860-535-0202), North Stonington; **Stonington Vineyards** (860-535-1222), Stonington; **Gouveia Vineyards** (203-265-5526), Wallingford; **Jerram Winery** (860-379-8749) and **Connecticut Valley Winery** (860-489-9463), both in New Hartford; and **White Silo Farm & Winery** (860-355-0271), Sherman. For a brochure, call 860-267-1399 or visit www.ctwine.com.

The Gold Coast

GREENWICH AND STAMFORD

WESTPORT AND NORWALK

BRIDGEPORT AND FAIRFIELD

THE NEW HAVEN AREA

THE HOUSATONIC VALLEY

Courtesy Coastal Fairfield County Convention & Visitors Bureau

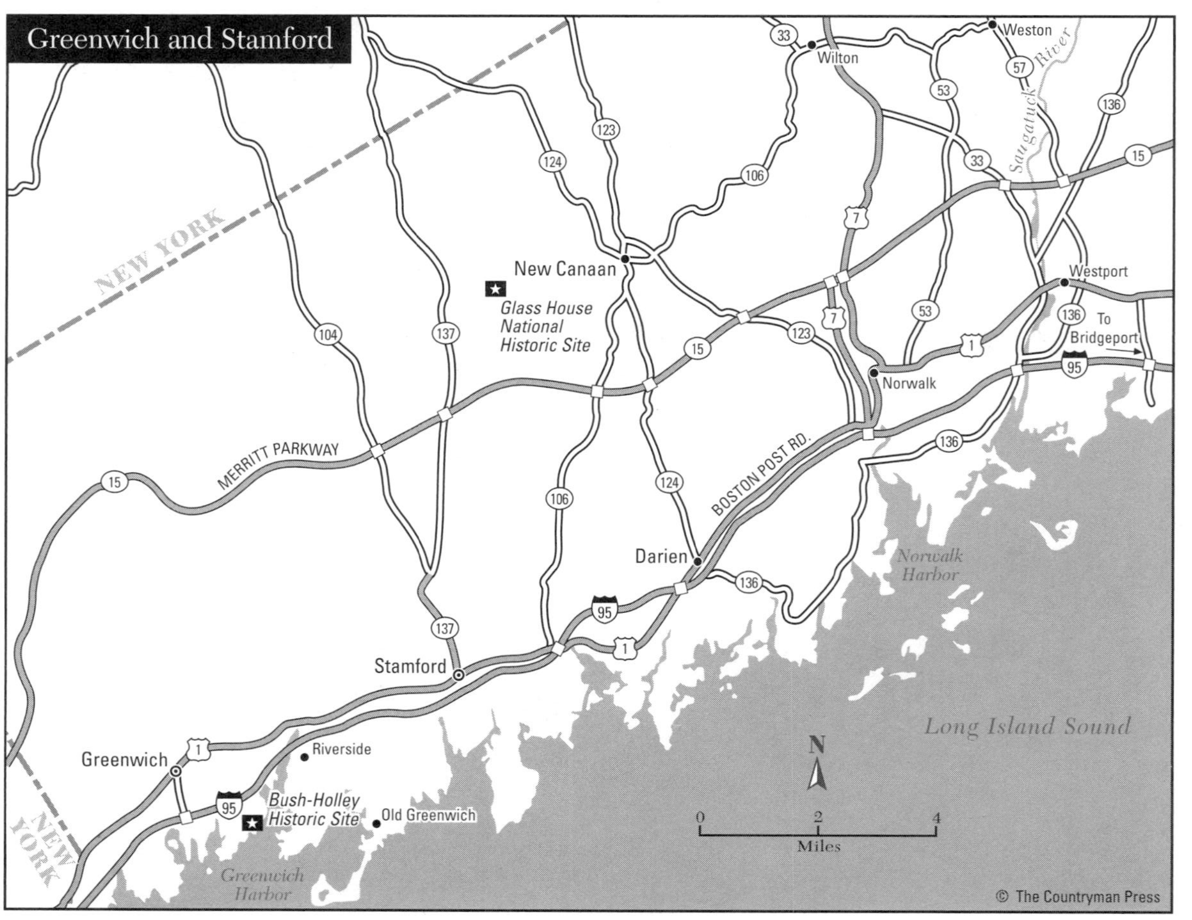
Greenwich and Stamford
NEW YORK
Weston
Wilton
Saugatuck River
New Canaan
Glass House National Historic Site
Westport
To Bridgeport
Norwalk
MERRITT PARKWAY
BOSTON POST RD.
Darien
Norwalk Harbor
Stamford
Long Island Sound
Greenwich
Riverside
Bush-Holley Historic Site
Old Greenwich
Greenwich Harbor
N
0
2
4
Miles
© The Countryman Press

GREENWICH AND STAMFORD

Travelers entering Connecticut's southwestern corner take their first steps into New England, although Yankee customs, architecture, and culture are not readily apparent. This is what has been dubbed the Gold Coast, where the cosmopolitan suburbs of New York City meet historic New England. Here in Fairfield County, bustling cities and gentrified towns are strung together along the coastline of Long Island Sound by two major arteries, I-95 and US 1, the colonial-era New York–Boston Post Road. It's a living image of exclusive, stylish, and moneyed Connecticut suburbia. It's also one of the wealthiest regions in America, the land of blue-chip companies and haute couture, Hummers and Jaguars parked in front of stately mansions. You must ply farther north to find New England's true flavor, its colonial greens and picturesque countryside. But by no means should you rush through the Gold Coast. It has its own charms, and much to offer the visitor. There's a thriving and well-respected arts scene, for one, not to mention dining and shopping, historic sites, even peaceful open spaces.

With the advent of the railroad and later the automobile, once-rural Fairfield County became a bedroom community for people working in New York City. In Greenwich's earliest days, it was home to farmers and fishermen; the commuters it sent to New York were potatoes and oysters, shipped daily on sailing packets. The 19th century brought passenger trains and the first of the rich and famous, looking for a retreat from the city. Today, Greenwich is the quintessential commuter's town, a string of exclusive gated shoreline neighborhoods where the good life is indeed more than good (the median house costs a million). It's a haven of wealth and good taste that offers its residents a prestigious address, quiet exclusivity, and proximity to Manhattan. Many people here have a lot of money and have had it for quite a while. It's called Wall Street by the Sea given the number of financial firms it hosts. Because the town is so attractive and so accessible to New York City (Times Square is a mere 30 miles away), it has attracted some of the world's greatest international corporations. Indeed, some of the wealthiest people in the world live on great estates in this moneyed enclave, ranked second among the top 10 places to live in America in a recent Robb Report. This is the land of country clubs, yacht clubs, manicured woodlands, and long driveways leading to grand old mansions, where some people sail and others play polo. Greenwich is the address of many of Connecticut's rich and famous, an interesting mélange of top professionals in law, science, literature, and even sports; movie stars; and those making their fortune in the business world. Even such a politico as New York's infamous Boss Tweed once had a Greenwich estate where he entertained his cronies.

As the region's name justly suggests, there is plenty of gold on this coast, but also plenty of places for the public to explore. Tour the restored Revolutionary War headquarters of General Washington's second in command, General Israel Putnam, or art and natural history exhibits at the Bruce Museum. See the house where 19th-century American impressionist painters lived and worked in the country's first artists' colony. Shoppers should head to chic Greenwich Avenue—or The Avenue, as it is known here—a critical mass of world-class galleries, sleek boutiques, haute bistros, and Fifth Avenue favorites like Gucci, Prada, Tiffany, Saks, and Hermès. Where a trolley once traveled up and down, gleaming SUVs now jockey for parking spaces. Visitors should also wander the rolling hills of Greenwich's exclusive Back Country, in the rural northern part of town, where quiet roads lead past horse paddocks, rambling stone walls, and opulent gated estates that run the architectural gamut from Mediterranean villa to English manor.

Few Connecticut towns are as closely associated with fine dining as Greenwich. Gourmets come from far and away for the seriously upscale scene that includes some of the best restaurants in the Northeast. It's not uncommon for Manhattan-based chefs to drift out to the suburbs to continue honing their talents, which run from haute French to the much-ballyhooed trend of small-plate noshing, edgy sushi bars to Old World patisseries, neighborhood haunts to elegant hotel dining rooms. Be advised, however, that entrée prices in Greenwich might induce sticker shock among the uninitiated. Another word of caution: Gold Coast restaurants open and close with head-spinning frequency; it's wise to phone ahead before setting out.

Stamford's big-city vibe belies its age. One of the Gold Coast's most metropolitan areas is also one of New England's oldest communities (founded in 1641). It was a stagecoach stop on the New York–to–Boston route and a rural farming town before evolving into a thriving industrial center. Today a bustling commercial hub sports a core center of high-rise hotels and steel-and-glass corporate towers, home to one of the nation's largest concentrations of Fortune 500 companies. It's 40 minutes on the Metro-North commuter rail from Manhattan, a method of travel favored by many suburbanites who avoid the perpetual traffic gridlock on I-95—the main truck route between Boston and New York—at all costs. For visitors, there is an abundance (more than 75, at last count) of lively downtown restaurants and bars, hipster havens, as well as first-rate performance venues and a burgeoning antiques scene that is boosting the city's reputation as a major antiquing center.

While Fairfield County is famous for its glitzy shoreline communities, there are reasons aplenty to explore the area's interior delights. New Canaan and Darien are enclaves of exclusivity, stylish without being flashy, dotted with antiques shops, boutiques, and restaurants ranging from eclectic to international. New Canaan is the only Gold Coast community without a shoreline, an upscale town whose quaint center mixes upscale chains like Talbots and Ann Taylor with one-of-a-kind shops (think books, antiques, high-end kitchenware) and cafés. Tucked among the magnificent New England clapboard farmhouses and grand Georgian mansions is one of the most famous modern houses in the world: Philip Johnson's Glass House, the boldly designed contemporary home of the iconic architect (he died in 2005) that, following his wishes, achieved museum status in 2007. For art and culture, head to the galleries and studios of the Silvermine Guild Arts Center and the Carriage

Barn Arts Center. As in New Canaan, wealthy "summer people" began retreating to Darien after the Civil War, taking the new railroad from New York and building large rambling houses perfect for entertaining fellow city folk and escaping the urban heat. Today the Post Road bustles with eclectic local shops as well as Lilly Pulitzer, Polo Ralph Lauren, Orvis, and other highbrow national chains. In both towns, local historical societies offer tours of their lovingly preserved centuries-old homes, chock-full of vintage furniture and period artifacts.

This is Connecticut's densely populated southern tier, but it's still woodsy if you know where to look. Despite huge development pressures, there's a pleasing amount of open space. Woodsy and exclusive well-heeled New Canaan and Darien

FAMOUS RESIDENTS, THEN AND NOW

An impressive number of icons in history, literature, sports, and entertainment have ties to Connecticut. In the early colonial days, there were Ethan Allen, Benedict Arnold, and Nathan Hale, who all gained fame during the American Revolution. Abolitionist John Brown, landscape designer Frederick Law Olmsted, lexicographer Noah Webster, educator and reformer Prudence Crandall, circus impresario Phineas (P. T.) Barnum, and a host of inventors from Eli Whitney (cotton gin) to Samuel Colt (.45 revolver) have roots in the Constitution State.

From the world of politics, there's President George W. Bush, who was born in New Haven, and his father, George H. W. Bush, whose boyhood home is now a private residence in Greenwich. Today former Secretary of State Henry Kissinger resides quietly in the rural Litchfield Hills.

An impressive number of film and television stars have roots in Connecticut. While actress Glenn Close was born in Greenwich, and actress Amy Brenneman was born in New London, Meryl Streep, Lynn Redgrave, Dustin Hoffman, Denis Leary, Sam Waterston, Mia Farrow, Kevin Bacon, and Kyra Sedgwick make their homes here today. So do late-night TV hosts David Letterman and Conan O'Brien, daytime favorite Regis Philbin, comedienne Joan Rivers, and writer-producer-director Barry Levinson.

In the music world, Connecticut claims icons like Diana Ross and Keith Richards, as well as Michael Bolton and guitarist José Feliciano, and natives Moby and John Mayer. There are literary luminaries past (Mark Twain, Harriet Beecher Stowe, Eugene O'Neill, Wallace Stevens) and present (Dominic Dunne, Maurice Sendak, Frank McCourt), as well as fashion designer Diane von Furstenberg and her business mogul husband, Barry Diller, and gold-medal figure skater Dorothy Hamill, who grew up in Fairfield County.

Sadly, Connecticut lost some of its most notable residents in recent years, including fashion designer Bill Blass, architect Philip Johnson, playwright Arthur Miller, composer Skitch Henderson, actress Katharine Hepburn, and actor Paul Newman.

lack the glam factor of their high-profile neighbors, instead offering unique shops, good restaurants, nature centers; Greenwich's Audubon Center is known for its hiking trails and new $5 million nature education facility; and Stamford's arboretum is a serene oasis and a gardener's delight. Corporate Stamford also has, of all things, a 19th-century working farm, where visitors can watch sheepshearing, crop harvesting, and other farm chores. And while much of the Gold Coast's shoreline is off-limits to the public, Greenwich, Stamford, and Darien (like towns throughout the state) allow out-of-towners access to their beaches.

Entries in this section are arranged in roughly geographic order.

AREA CODE 203.

GUIDANCE **Coastal Fairfield County Convention & Visitor Bureau** (203-853-7770; 800-866-7925; www.visitfairfieldcountyct.com), Gate Lodge, Mathews Park, 297 West Ave., Norwalk 06850. A self-service visitor information center is located in Stamford at the Stamford Town Center Mall, 100 Greyrock Place, Exit 7 off I-95.

Stamford Downtown Special Services District (203-348-5285; www.stamford-downtown.com) maintains an online directory of the city's restaurants, clubs, and shops, and sponsors performances, festivals, and other events in the downtown area.

A **Connecticut Welcome Center** is open year-round at the McDonald's on I-95 northbound in **Darien** between Exits 12 and 13; another center, open seasonally, is on the northbound side of the Merritt Parkway in **Greenwich** between Exits 27 and 28.

GETTING THERE *By car:* Three major east–west arteries link the Long Island Sound shoreline cities and towns of Connecticut with Boston and New York. Keep in mind that, while I-95 heads in a southerly direction from New York almost all the way down the Atlantic coast, the interstate runs east and west while in Connecticut. It is, however, still inscribed with north and south directions here.

I-95 hugs the coast and carries the most traffic; in other words, it is perpetually jammed and chronically overburdened. A few miles to the north, and proceeding to New Haven, where it veers off northward toward Hartford, the beautiful Merritt Parkway (CT 15) is a historic highway that prohibits big rigs. Then there's the venerable granddaddy of all American highways, historic US 1, named the Post Road in colonial days. Starting in Maine and ending in the Florida Keys, it snakes through all the metropolitan areas, a minefield of stoplights and shopping malls. At the same time, it's the most interesting of the southern arteries.

By air: **Westchester County Airport** (914-285-4860), near Greenwich in White Plains, New York, serves the area with daily flights by nine airlines: Air Canada, AirTran, American, Continental, Delta, JetBlue Airways, Northwest, United, and US Airways. It's also home base to one of the largest fleets of corporate aircraft in the country. **Tweed–New Haven Regional Airport** (203-466-8833; www.flytweed.com) is the airport of Greater New Haven and is served by US Airways Express. International arrivals access the Gold Coast through New York's **JFK Airport** (718-244-4444) or **Bradley International Airport** (860-292-2000; 888-624-1533; www.bradleyairport.com) in Windsor Locks, both about 1½ hours away.

By rail: There are two railroads: **Amtrak** (800-872-7245; www.amtrak.com), the main line along the entire Atlantic Coast, stops in Stamford. **Metro-North** (800-638-7646; www.mta.info/mnr), the busy New York commuter line, is a welcome alternative to navigating I-95 by car. Metro-North stops in Greenwich, Stamford, New Canaan, and Darien. Originating out of New York City's Grand Central Terminal, it runs express and local trains to its final terminal at New Haven. Check schedules for the towns and times you plan to visit.

By bus or limo: **Greyhound Lines** (800-231-2222; www.greyhound.com) and **Peter Pan Bus Lines** (800-343-9999; www.peterpanbus.com) stop at 30 Station Place (203-327-7622) in Stamford. **Connecticut Limousine Service** (800-472-5466; www.ctlimo.com) serves Bradley International, JFK, Newark, and LaGuardia airports.

GETTING AROUND *Taxi service:* In Stamford: **Stamford Taxi** (203-325-2611) and **Yellow Cab** (203-967-3633). In Greenwich: **Brand Taxi** (203-618-1100), and **Greenwich Taxi** (203-869-6000; 800-979-8295). In Darien: **Lloyd's Taxi of Darien** (203-655-2266; 866-628-8294). **Canaan Parrish Taxi** (203-966-6866) in New Canaan also serves the area.

Connecticut Transit (203-327-7433; www.cttransit.com) provides bus service to Stamford, Darien, and Greenwich.

MEDICAL EMERGENCY The statewide emergency number is **911**.

Greenwich Hospital (203-863-3000), 5 Perryridge Rd., Greenwich. The emergency number is 203-863-3637.

Stamford Hospital (203-276-1000), 30 Shelburne Rd., Stamford. The emergency number is 203-325-7777.

✷ To See

CHURCH **First Presbyterian Church** (203-324-9522; www.fishchurch.org), 1101 Bedford St., Stamford. Open year-round, Mon.–Fri. 9–5; July and Aug., weekdays 9–3. Donation suggested. You'll find here the largest mechanical-action pipe organ in Connecticut. The church, designed by Wallace K. Harrison, is a modern structure shaped like a fish—a nod to the symbol of early Christianity. The stained-glass windows, crafted with 20,000 pieces of faceted glass, are from France.

MUSEUMS ♿ **Bruce Museum of Arts and Science** (203-869-0376; www.brucemuseum.org), 1 Museum Dr., Greenwich. Open Tue.–Sat. 10–5, Sun. 1–5; closed Mon. and major holidays. Adults $7; students and seniors $6; children under 5 free; no charge on Tue. The home of wealthy textile magnate Robert Moffat Bruce was the nucleus for what is now a major museum with a variety of art galleries and educational workshops. The natural science collection includes fossils and minerals, mounted New England birds and mammals, a live-animal marine tank, and a Native American woodland wigwam. This town-owned museum mounts more than a dozen art exhibitions a year, as well as an annual outdoor crafts festival in mid-May and an outdoor arts festival on Columbus Day weekend. The museum's permanent collection of American paintings includes works by impressionists like

Courtesy Coastal Fairfield County Convention & Visitors Bureau

A MARINE TOUCH TANK AND ENVIRONMENTAL GALLERIES ARE HIGHLIGHTS OF GREENWICH'S BRUCE MUSEUM OF ARTS AND SCIENCE.

Childe Hassam and other key figures in Cos Cob's 19th-century art colony, and a full-sized bronze reproduction of Rodin's famous sculpture *The Kiss*, an anonymous gift. Call for schedules of other programs. The museum also operates a kid-friendly nature center at Greenwich Point Beach (see *Swimming*).

Putnam Cottage (203-869-9697; www.putnamcottage.org), 243 East Putnam Ave. (US 1), Greenwich. Open Apr.–Dec., Sun. 1–4; tours by appointment Jan.–Mar. Popular lore has it that Connecticut hero General Israel Putnam caught a glimpse of a British patrol here while looking in his shaving mirror in February 1779. Separated from his troops, Ol' Put rushed to his horse and escaped by riding down a set of steep steps in a cliff in the Horseneck section of Greenwich. The paunchy old warrior—he was in his mid-60s—did escape the British by riding down the cliff; however, the steps were not cut into the cliff until after the Revolution! The fish-scale-shingled house, built around 1700, is Greenwich's oldest and features antique furnishings, wide-board floors, hand-hewn beams, and seven fireplaces. The grounds contain an herb garden and a restored barn.

PUTNAM COTTAGE IS A REVOLUTIONARY WAR–ERA TAVERN NAMED FOR CONNECTICUT'S LEGENDARY WAR HERO GENERAL ISRAEL PUTNAM, WHO NARROWLY ESCAPED BRITISH CAPTURE HERE.

Jenny Larkin

History Center of Stamford (203-329-1183; www.stamfordhistory.org), 1508 High Ridge Rd., Stamford. Open Tue.–Sat. noon–4; closed major holidays. Adults $5; seniors and students $3. Permanent and changing exhibits, mostly featuring local history. Research library on the premises. Ask about the current schedule of Victorian teas and other special events. The society also operates **Hoyt-Barnum House**, a restored blacksmith's home built in 1699 and located at 713 Bedford St.

🖍 ♿ **Stamford Museum and Nature Center** (203-322-1646; www.stamfordmuseum.org), 39 Scofieldtown Rd. (off CT 137), Stamford. Open year-round, Mon.–Sat. 9–5, Sun. 11–5; closed Thanksgiving, Christmas, and New Year's. **Heckscher Farm** open daily 9–4; **Nature's Playground** open daily (weather permitting) 9–5. Adults $8; seniors and students $6; children 4–17 $4; children under 4 free. A pleasant relief in one of the state's most densely populated cities: 118 acres of forests, fields, and farmland that was once the estate of department store magnate Henri Bendel. The center holds one of the few planetariums in the state, with special shows on Sun. (separate admission charge). There is also considerable culture here; the center contains several galleries devoted to family-oriented topics. There's a country store, a picnic area, and woodland trails. Of special interest to children, however, is the 19th-century working farm, with demonstrations—goat milking, harvesting, sheepshearing—and an area for petting domestic animals.

Kim Grant

A NEW ENGLAND WORKING FARM ON 118 RURAL ACRES IS A BUCOLIC OASIS IN ONE OF CONNECTICUT'S MOST DENSELY POPULATED REGIONS.

New Canaan Historical Society (203-966-1776; www.nchistory.org), 13 Oenoke Ridge (CT 124), New Canaan. Hours vary for each building; call for schedules. Donation suggested. Five buildings housing seven museums and a library tell the story of this exclusive and historic Gold Coast town. Weaver and tavern keeper Stephen Hanford built this handsome center-chimney saltbox, now known as the **Hanford-Silliman House**, in 1764. Following his death in 1784, the Silliman family occupied the house for generations and made many architectural changes, including a Greek Revival facade added in the 1920s. Other historic buildings on the property run the gamut, including a **tool museum**, displaying the hand tools of a house builder, farmer, shoemaker, cooper, and farrier; a **sculptor's studio** (a registered National Historic Landmark) with a large collection of statuary; the **Cody Drug Store** with its mortars, pestles, and centuries-old potions and remedies; and the **Rock School**, a one-room schoolhouse built in 1799.

HISTORIC HOMES **Bush-Holley Historic Site** (203-869-6899; www.hstg.org), 39 Strickland Rd., in the Cos Cob section of Greenwich. Open year-round, Tue.–Sun. noon–4; closed Mon. and major holidays. In Jan. and Feb., house tours are conducted on Sat. and Sun. only. Admission includes the museum exhibition and guided house tour. Adults $6; students and seniors $4; children under 7 free; free admission on Tue. Built in 1732 by farmer David Bush, the Bush-Holley home was run as a boardinghouse from 1890 to 1925 by the Holley family and attracted a number of young American artists escaping the heat of New York City to spend the summer on Cos Cob harbor. Childe Hassam, John Henry Twachtman, J. Alden Weir, and others who summered at the house organized the famous 1913 Armory Show of impressionism in New York City. Journalist Lincoln Steffens, a visitor, records in his autobiography that the artists complained bitterly when the New Haven Railroad started building its main-line bridge over the Cos Cob River. When Steffens returned some months later, he found the members of what became known as the Cos Cob School of Artists busy painting pictures of the bridge girders that poked out over the river. Galleries display an outstanding collection of 18th-century Connecticut antiques and hands-on history exhibits, and the studio of artist Elmer Livingston MacRae has been re-created here. As the site of the first impressionist art colony in America, the classic saltbox house was designated a National Historic Landmark in 1991. The Greenwich Historical Society runs a visitor center in a restored 1805 village post office. The center includes a museum shop and changing exhibitions, as well as a mid-19th-century barn, where history and art workshops for adults and children take place.

The Philip Johnson Glass House (203-594-9884; 866-811-4111; www.philipjohnsonglasshouse.org), 199 Elm St., New Canaan. Open Apr.–Oct. for guided tours only; reservations are essential (plan well in advance, since tours sell out quickly). Tickets $25–40. Connecticut's newest National Trust Historic Site (it opened to the public in 2007) is one of the world's most famous modern houses, not to mention an icon of midcentury modernist architecture. It was also the home the late architect Philip Johnson and his longtime partner, the art collector David Whitney. And in case you aren't tipped off by the name, the simple glass-and-steel cube is virtually see-through, offering unobstructed views of the lovely New Eng-

PHILIP JOHNSON'S GLASS HOUSE IS AN ICON OF MODERN ARCHITECTURE.

Courtesy Glass House

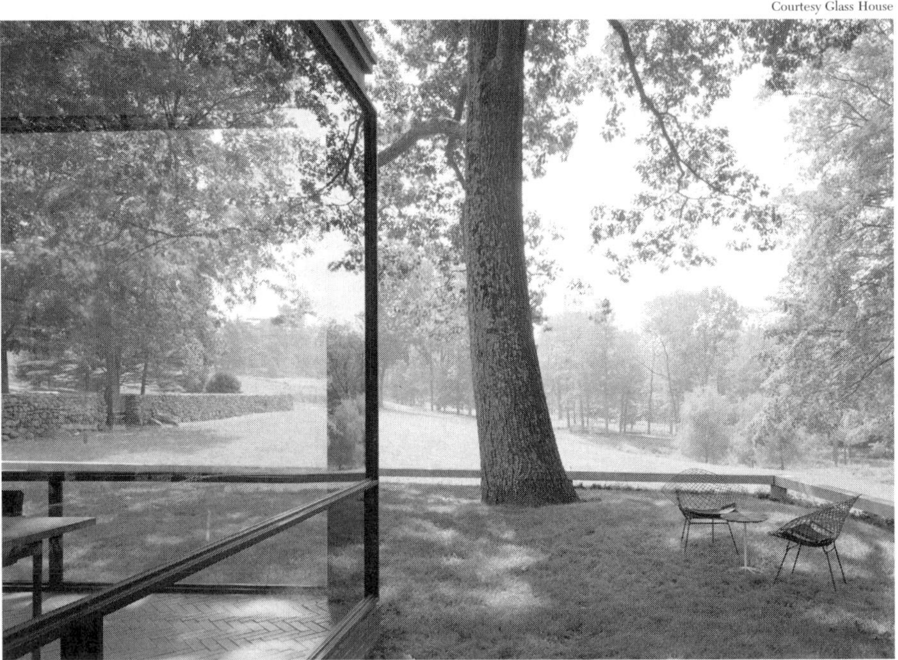

land countryside surrounding it. Johnson, who designed the AT&T Building in New York, the Bank of America building in Houston, and the garden at New York's Museum of Modern Art, among other high-profile projects, designed the Glass House as his private residence. He moved in when it was completed in 1949, and lived here until his death in 2005 at the age of 98. The 14 buildings and collection of contemporary art on the manicured 47-acre property reflect Johnson's famous anything-goes modernist design aesthetic. Visitors assemble at the Glass House Visitor Center, across the street from the train station in downtown New Canaan, where they are shuttled to the estate a short distance away. In addition to the Glass House, the walking tour includes two galleries on the property and Da Monsta, the estate's concrete-and-Styrofoam sculpture-like gatehouse.

Bates-Scofield House Museum (203-655-9233), 45 Old Kings Hwy. North, Darien. House tours Wed. and Thu. 2–4. Call for admission prices. There are period furnishings, embroidered curtains, and a huge center chimney in this classic circa-1736 New England saltbox. The herb garden is of special interest, with more than 30 varieties of culinary and medicinal herbs used in 18th-century Connecticut. Farmer John Bates built the house, raised nine children here, and held the first organized meetings in the community—then called Middlesex Parish. In addition to a beehive oven and spinning wheel, the house features interesting vintage Connecticut-made furnishings, including a blanket chest that dates from 1699.

✵ To Do

BOAT EXCURSIONS **Fjord Charters** (203-622-4020; 800-925-2622; www.fjordcatering.com), 143 River Rd., in the Cos Cob section of Greenwich. Open year-round; reservations are essential. Sunday brunch and Friday-night dinner cruises on Long Island Sound aboard the luxury yachts *Cayah Michele* and *Cayah Sarita* as well as the *Katinka*, a Mississippi-style paddle-wheel boat.

✐ *SoundWaters* Community Center for Environmental Education (203-323-1978; www.soundwaters.org), Cove Island Park, 1281 Cove Rd., Stamford. The center is open year-round, Tue.–Sat. 10–5; closed Sun. and Mon.; free admission. Boat trips Apr.–Nov. (call for a schedule): adults $30; children 12 and under $20. *SoundWaters* is a replica of a 19th-century, three-masted schooner and serves as a floating classroom in Long Island Sound. Help hoist the sails as the naturalists tell the eco-story of the Sound and how we must mobilize to clean and save the waters of what is probably the most heavily used recreational waterway in the world. More than 8,000 children and adults annually sail *SoundWaters* on its marine adventures. Public sails—2½-hour daytime ecology sails (adults and children) and evening sunset trips (adults only)—depart from

THOUSANDS OF VISITORS TAKE PART IN ENVIRONMENTAL EDUCATION PROGRAMS ANNUALLY ON LONG ISLAND SOUND ABOARD *SOUNDWATERS*, A REPLICA OF A 19TH-CENTURY THREE-MASTED SCHOONER.
Courtesy Coastal Fairfield County Convention & Visitors Bureau

Stamford's Brewer's Yacht Haven Marina. Exhibits at the center focus on the animals and habitats of Long Island Sound.

FISHING **Cove Island Park** (203-977-5217), at the junction of Cove Rd. and Weed Ave., Stamford. An 80-acre park on Long Island Sound with a marina and access to fishing and crabbing.

GOLF **E. Gaynor Brennan Public Golf Course** (203-324-4185), 451 Stillwater Rd., Stamford. A small municipal golf course close to downtown. Par 71, 18 holes, 5,931 yards. Restaurant and pro shop.

Sterling Farms Golf Course (203-461-9090; www.sterlingfarmsgc.com), 1349 Newfield Ave., Stamford. A historic farm turned municipal golf course. Par 72, 18 holes, 6,082 yards. Restaurant and pro shop.

MARINA **Brewer Yacht Haven Marina** (203-359-4500), Washington Blvd., Stamford. A full-service facility with visitors' services on Stamford Harbor.

SWIMMING **Byram Beach** (203-531-8938), Byram Shore Rd., Greenwich. Beach, swimming pool, tennis courts, picnicking, playground. On Byram Harbor. A $6 guest pass and $20 parking pass may be purchased at the Greenwich Town Hall and the Eastern Greenwich Civic Center.

Greenwich Point Beach (203-531-8938), Shore Rd., Old Greenwich. A 147-acre waterfront park on a peninsula that's known locally at Tod's Point. A day pass for nonresidents is $6 for the beach, $20 for parking; passes can be purchased at the Greenwich Town Hall and the Eastern Greenwich Civic Center. Sure there's a stretch of sand, and it's lovely, but be sure to check out the beachside nature museum (admission is free with your beach pass), where a touch tank and coloring area appeal to youngsters; parents like the guided walks and exhibits that highlight environmental issues facing Long Island Sound. The center is open July and Aug., Wed.–Sun. 10–4. Green thumbs will love the Secret Garden, a peaceful retreat under the care of a local garden club.

Cove Island Park (203-977-5214), at the junction of Cove Rd. and Weed Ave., Stamford. Admission $20; passes can be purchased in the Stamford Government Center or by mail. The park's 83 acres on Cove Harbor offer supervised swimming; there's also a snack bar, a bathhouse, fishing, and picnic areas.

Cummings Park and **Cummings Park West (West Beach)** (203-977-4140), Shippan Ave., Stamford. A one-day $20 permit can be purchased at the Stamford Government Center. Boardwalk, fishing pier, tennis courts, ball fields.

* Green Space

NATURE CENTERS **Audubon Greenwich** (203-869-5272; www.greenwich.audubon.org), 613 Riversville Rd., Greenwich. Open year-round, daily 9–5. Grounds open daily dawn to dusk. Adults $3; seniors and children $1.50 (fee is for the center, not the grounds). Don sturdy hiking boots, bring your binoculars, and stroll along 7 miles of trails through woods and meadows in a 285-acre nature sanctuary. A new $5 million nature education center features interactive exhibits, an indoor beehive, an art gallery, a nature store, and a weather station. Call for a schedule of demonstrations and educational programs. This was the first nature education facility established by the National Audubon Society more than 65 years ago, and you'd be hard-pressed to find more open space along the Gold Coast than here.

The Bartlett Arboretum & Gardens (203-322-6971; www.bartlettarboretum.org), 151 Brookdale Rd., Stamford. Grounds open year-round, daily 8:30–sunset. Visitor center open Mon.–Fri. 8:30–4:30. Admission $5. An oasis in an otherwise congested urban area, these 91 acres of natural woodlands are blanketed with significant collections of rhododendrons and dwarf conifers. Take your children for a hike on a boardwalk through the swamps and along marked ecology trails. The visitor center in the 19th-century Bartlett House has an extensive botanical research library, an art gallery with changing exhibits, a horticultural gift shop, a greenhouse full of exotic plants, and information on activities, nature walks, and classes and workshops on gardening.

Darien Nature Center (203-655-7459; www.dnc.darien.org), 120 Brookside Rd., in Cherry Lawn Park, Darien. Open Mon.–Fri. 9–4; Sat. 10–2; closed Sun. Free admission. A child-friendly spot with a children's zoo (including chinchillas and tarantulas), a theater, a nature science library, nature trails, summer garden tours, and other special events.

New Canaan Nature Center (203-966-9577; www.newcanaannature.org), 144 Oenoke Ridge (CT 124), New Canaan. Center open Mon.–Sat. 9–4; closed Sun. and Mon.; trails open year-round dawn to dusk. Donation suggested. On 40 acres, the center offers an interesting mix of walking trails, indoor exhibits, and active learning projects. Show your children how cider is made; peek into the maple sugar shed. Hands-on natural science exhibits are featured in the Discovery Center. The solar greenhouse is part of Project LEAF (Learning and Environmental Action for the Future). Gardeners in the family will enjoy browsing in the perennial, herb, and wildflower gardens. Nature art gallery and gift shop. There's a boardwalk through marshland and meadows, as well as an observation tower, where you might spy the ospreys, turtles, wild turkeys, and other creatures that call this beautiful oasis home.

A BOARDWALK TRAIL AT BARTLETT ARBORETUM & GARDENS IN STAMFORD

Kim Grant

✱ Lodging

INNS

In Greenwich 06830

Cos Cob Inn (203-661-5845; 877-549-4063; www.coscobinn.com), 50 River Rd., in the Cos Cob section of Greenwich. A large Federal manor home with a widow's walk, set in a spacious yard overlooking yachts bobbing on the Mianus River. Twelve pleasant rooms, bright and airy and nicely furnished, all with private bath, many with water views; suites are upgraded with sitting area, fireplace, whirlpool tub, and private porch. The reproduction American impressionist paintings are a nod to the 19th-century Cos Cob art colony, which brought Childe Hassam, John Twachtman, and other painters to Greenwich. Continental breakfast. $119–219.

Homestead Inn (203-869-7500; www.thomashenkelmann.com), 420 Field Point Rd. A stately white-clapboard Italianate Gothic home built in 1799 resides on a hill in the exclusive neighborhood of Belle Haven. Today it's furnished with Victorian antiques and offers a quiet night's rest in one of 18 impeccably decorated rooms and suites. The attentive service is reminiscent of a fine European hostelry, with a touch of old New England. Innkeepers Theresa and Thomas Henkelmann have decorated the guest rooms with a designer's eye, outfitting them in original artwork, rich fabrics, Frette linens, Bulgari personal amenities, and other luxurious accoutrements. Thomas Henkelmann serves elegant French cuisine in his eponymous restaurant (see *Dining Out*). The inn has earned the prestigious Relais & Châteaux designation. $250–495.

Stanton House Inn (203-869-2110; www.shinngreenwich.com), 76 Maple Ave. Overnight guests have been coming to this early-1900s mansion designed by Stanford White since the 1930s, when it first opened its doors as an inn. Common areas are formal yet inviting, and the 23 guest rooms and two suites are simply furnished with country-comfortable pieces; all have private bath, some come with upgraded amenities like a fireplace or balcony. Outside, guests can while away the day by the pool, on the patio, and in the "secret" garden. Continental breakfast and passes to local beaches are included. $159–239.

In Old Greenwich 06870

Harbor House Inn (203-637-0145; www.hhinn.com), 165 Shore Rd. A sprawling Victorian house with 23 rooms, all with private bath, coffeemaker, and refrigerator. Business travelers will appreciate the fax machines, copiers, and ample meeting space. Passes for the nearby beach are sold at the front desk; it's a 10-minute walk down the road, quicker if you take one of the inn's bikes. The lobby, filled with dark wood, rich fabrics, and Victorian-style furnishings, is a welcoming place to sit and relax; so is the living room and spacious wicker-filled porch. Continental breakfast, and evening tea and refreshments. $149–279.

In New Canaan 06840

Main Street Inn (203-972-2983), 190 Main St. A restored Victorian near the public library with three comfy guest rooms, all with private bath, one with a Jacuzzi tub and a balcony. The downtown shops on Elm Street are just a couple of blocks away. Continental breakfast. $90–150.

The Maples Inn (203-966-2927; www.maplesinnct.com), 179 Oenoke Ridge (CT 124). In the late 19th century, when New Yorkers escaped to the "country," this rambling mansion was the grand Hampton Inn. Today the full-service Victorian-style inn has 22 rooms—a mix of standard accommodations, suites, and corporate relocation apartments, outfitted with canopied four-poster beds and antiques. Fax, copy, high-speed WiFi. Wraparound porch. For dinner, the highly acclaimed Roger Sherman Inn (see

Dining Out) is right next door. Continental breakfast. $105–236.

🐾 **Roger Sherman Inn** (203-966-4541; www.rogershermaninn.com), 195 Oenoke Ridge (CT 124). A charming 18th-century colonial inn (parts of the building date from 1740) presided over by host Thomas Weilenmann, across the road from the New Canaan Nature Center and less than a mile from downtown. The 17 guest rooms, including a two-bedroom suite, all have charming country-style decor, private bath, TV, phone, and mini bar. Guests can stay in the elegant main house, above the restaurant (see *Dining Out*), or in a converted turn-of-the-20th-century carriage house. Continental breakfast. Rooms $115–205; suite $350.

HOTELS

In Greenwich 06830

🐾 ♿ **The Delamar Greenwich Harbor** (203-661-9800; 866-335-2627; www.thedelamar.com), 500 Steamboat Rd. The Gold Coast's priciest and most luxurious waterfront hotel is styled after a grand Tuscan villa, from the yellow stucco exterior to the lobby's 19th-century Italian landscape paintings and wood-paneled library. Polished, impeccable service and all the amenities and hospitality you'd expect from a fine European hotel. Most of the 83 rooms and suites have private balconies overlooking the harbor. L'Escale serves top-notch French-Mediterranean haute cuisine (see *Dining Out*), and the inviting bar/lounge is a good place to linger after dinner. Don't let the opulence fool you—this is a Fido-friendly establishment, with a handful of rooms outfitted with dog beds and bowls. A short walk from the Metro-North railroad station and the Greenwich Avenue shopping district. Rooms $399–549; suites $600–1,700.

In Old Greenwich 06870

♿ **Hyatt Regency Greenwich** (203-637-1234; 800-233-1234; www.greenwich.hyatt.com), 1800 East Putnam Ave. An unusually attractive hotel, more like an English manor house than a clone of a chain. Minutes to shopping and sightseeing in Greenwich and Stamford. The 374 luxurious rooms and suites are tastefully decorated. Have cocktails at the **Gazebo Bar & Grille**, in the lobby's dramatic conservatory-style, plant-filled atrium; there are also two restaurants, a business center, a European spa, an indoor pool, and close to 40 conference rooms. **Winfield's Restaurant** (203-409-4409) serves New American cuisine at three meals, and Sun. champagne brunch. $129–350.

In Stamford

♿ **Courtyard Stamford Downtown** (203-358-8822), 275 Summer St., Stamford 06901. This first-rate boutique hotel is popular among both business travelers and visitors, both who frequent the fantastic Napa & Co. (see *Dining Out*). There are 105 guest rooms and five suites, and amenities including a fitness center and indoor pool. $229–269.

♿ **Holiday Inn Stamford Downtown** (203-358-8400; www.histamford.com), 700 East Main St., Stamford 06901. Fresh off an $18 million renovation, a downtown hotel with 383 rooms and suites with flat-screen TVs; free high-speed Internet; a café, restaurant, and bar; a 24-hour fitness center; and an indoor heated pool. Leave the car in the indoor parking garage: Many restaurants, bars, and theaters are within walking distance; there's also a free shuttle to whisk you around. The hotel does a lot of weekday corporate business, which means good deals for weekend visitors. $125–225.

♿ **Marriott Stamford Hotel & Spa** (203-357-9555; reservations 800-732-9689; www.marriottstamford.com), 2 Stamford Forum, across from the Stamford Town Center shops, Stamford 06901. A downtown hotel that's also close to I-95, with 506 rooms (six suites), a restaurant, a health club, indoor and outdoor pools, racquetball courts, and a track. There's an indoor golf training center with a full-time PGA golf pro on hand for lessons. A full-service spa, **Agora**, offers body wraps, massages, facials, and Swiss showers. Take the elevator to **Restaurant Vuli**, the hotel's revolving rooftop dining room. $129–319; golf and spa packages available.

♿ **Stamford Suites Hotel** (203-359-7300; reservations:= 866-394-4365; www.stamfordsuites.com), 720 Bedford St., Stamford 06901. In the heart of Stamford's shopping and entertainment district. The 45 suites have newly refurbished kitchens, baths with whirlpool tubs, and free high-speed wireless Internet access. Amenities include a health club, a pool, tennis courts, and a business center. Continental breakfast. $129–299.

♿ **The Westin Stamford Hotel** (203-351-1865; 800-338-9115), 1 First Stamford Place, Stamford 06902. The 462 elegant rooms and suites in this downtown luxury hotel center on a stunning atrium lobby. There's a brand-new restaurant, recently refurbished rooms and meeting areas, and a pool, health club, and local shuttle-van service. $139–349.

🐾 ♿ **Sheraton Stamford Hotel** (203-359-1300), 2701 Summer St., Stamford 06905. A downtown hotel with 448 guest rooms nicely furnished with contemporary decor; business travelers appreciate the oversized work desks and high-speed Internet access. Upgraded accommodations include spacious suites with flat-screen TVs in roomy sitting areas. A health club, indoor pool, tennis court, and running track round out the amenities. $239–339.

✷ Where to Eat

DINING OUT

In Greenwich

♿ **Gaia** (203-661-3443; www.gaiarestaurant.com), 253 Greenwich Ave. Open for lunch Mon.–Fri.; dinner daily; brunch on Sat. and Sun. Fine dining, Greenwich-style, in surroundings at once opulent (soaring arches, grand mirrors) and rustic (hand-hewn tables, farmhouse antiques). In Greek mythology, Gaia is the goddess of Earth, an apt name for a restaurant whose menu emphasizes fresh ingredients and natural flavors. Chef Frederic Kieffer puts a sophisticated spin on familiar favorites, using high-quality ingredients to create elegant French country cuisine. The menu is extensive; starters like fresh oysters lead to entrées like quail, braised short ribs, and herb-crusted rack of lamb. Peanut, chocolate, and caramel ganache cake is just one of the decadent desserts. The wine list is 1,000 labels strong. $26–45.

♿ **L'Escale** (203-661-4600; www.lescalerestaurant.com), 500 Steamboat Rd., at the Delamar Greenwich Harbor hotel. Lunch Mon.–Sat.; dinner nightly; brunch on Sun. Reservations are recommended. Quite possibly the most elegant and upscale hotel dining in Connecticut. The dining room, with antique terra-cotta tiles, 18th-century French fireplace, and chandeliers, frames a stunning view of Greenwich Harbor. The name means "port of call," and with good reason: It has the only public boat dock on the harbor, so hungry yachters can stop by for the outstanding Provençal cuisine or champagne cocktails on the terrace.

(It's also a quick walk from the Metro-North commuter rail.) The menu emphasizes fresh seafood (Mediterranean sardines, Atlantic salmon) but has other creative offerings, like house-smoked duck with fingerling potatoes, or roasted rack of lamb with Niçoise olive jus. Desserts like black-and-white chocolate soufflé with pistachio sauce are delicious works of art. Service is French: knowledgeable, professional, efficient. The lounge serves sophisticated snacks and expertly crafted elixirs like the rum-and-champagne-based L'Escale Fizz in highly civilized surroundings. $24–45.

♿ **Nuage Restaurant & Bar** (203-869-2339; www.nuagerestaurant.com), 203 East Putnam Ave., in the Cos Cob section of Greenwich. Open for lunch Mon.–Fri.; dinner daily. *Nuage* is French for "cloud," perhaps an allusion to an ethereal dining experience that discriminating diners have been raving about since this small restaurant opened in a Cos Cob shopping center. Incredibly fresh fish, shellfish, and sashimi are skillfully prepared with a fusion of predominantly French and Japanese ingredients and techniques, notably artful presentation and attention to detail. Start with salmon tartare in mustard soy sauce, then try the sautéed lobster with champagne butter sauce over risotto. End with fried green tea ice cream. Eat in the chic dining room, at the copper-topped bar, or on the outdoor terrace overlooking a millpond. $22–38; seven-course tasting menus $45–90.

♿ **Palomino** (203-698-9033; www.palominorestaurants.com), 1392 East Putnam Ave., Old Greenwich. Open for lunch Mon.–Fri.; dinner daily; Sun. brunch. A newer star on Greenwich's dining scene, where "American market cuisine" means Montana rib-eye steak, Maine lobster, and other regional dishes with inventive pairings like roasted beet and arugula salad and saffron mashed potatoes. Save room for divine desserts like white chocolate bread pudding, and homemade blackberry Cabernet sorbet. Surroundings are chic and sophisticated, service is flawless. $16–42; five-course tasting menu $68.

Polpo (203-629-1999; www.polporestaurant.com), 554 Old Post Rd., Greenwich. Open for lunch and dinner daily. In Italian, *polpo* means "octopus"—here it comes grilled with garlic and rosemary and shouldn't be missed. If you're hit with the urge to splurge, order the Kobe steak ($125). The piano bar features live music every night. $26–44.

♿ **Rebeccas** (203-532-9270; www.rebeccasgreenwich.com), 265 Glenville Rd., in the Glenville section of Greenwich. Open for lunch Tue.–Fri.; dinner Tue.–Sat.; closed Sun. and Mon. Make reservations well in advance. Rebecca Kirhoffer and Reza Khorshidi were Manhattan chefs before taking their considerable culinary talents to a storefront eatery in the suburbs. Today the husband-and-wife team is at the helm of a local favorite among Greenwich gourmets, known for its fabulous and pricey contemporary New American cuisine with Asian and French touches. Rebecca works the sleek and modern dining room; Reza is at the helm in the open kitchen, which can be seen through a glass window. $36–65.

♿ **Restaurant Jean-Louis** (203-622-8450; www.restaurantjeanlouis.com), 61 Lewis St. Open for dinner Mon.–Sat.; lunch Mon.–Fri.; closed Sun. Reservations suggested. Just off Greenwich Avenue is a restaurant with a national reputation for its extraordinary contemporary French cuisine, and a longtime favorite (25 years strong) among celebrities and foodies. With his wife, Linda, alongside him at the helm, chef Jean-Louis Gerin runs this elegant establishment, considered one of Connecticut's best restaurants. It's decidedly romantic, with candlelight, linen, and fresh flowers, a 900-bottle wine cellar, and a staff that raises service to an art form. A loyal coterie of fans doesn't seem to mind the Manhattan prices: Starters like sautéed sweetbreads and oxtail consommé are in the $16–29 range. Expect big-ticket ingredients like caviar, foie gras, and truffles. The experience isn't cheap, but for a very special night out, this is worth the splurge. À la carte $38–41; prix fixe and tasting menus $59–79.

♿ **Tengda Asian Bistro** (203-625-5338; www.tengdaasianbistro.com), 21 Field Point Rd. Open daily for lunch and dinner. Reservations are recommended. This hip Fairfield County sushi bar and Asian-fusion hangout artfully blends the past and the present, with its restored Victorian facade and edgy modern interior and high-octane atmosphere. Chef Matthew Reddington brings diners a French-inspired taste of Indonesia, Malaysia, Thailand, and Vietnam. The result: lemongrass coconut-chicken soup, ginger-braised short ribs, roasted Chilean sea bass with sesame soba noodles, spicy tamarind-glazed duck breast, and spiced green-tea-rubbed salmon with lobster-wasabi mashed potatoes. For something more traditional, try shrimp teriyaki or stir-fried pad Thai. Desserts like *panna cotta* and gelato are decidedly more European than Asian. $22–36. There's a second location in Westport (203-255-6115) at 1330 Post Rd. East (US 1).

♿ **Thomas Henkelmann** (203-869-7500; www.thomashenkelmann.com), at Homestead Inn, 420 Field Point Rd. Serving lunch Tue.–Fri.; dinner Tue.–Sat.; closed Sun. and Mon. Reservations are suggested, as are ties; jackets are required. Looking for an extraordinary culinary experience that more than lives up to its formal setting? You won't go wrong if master chef Thomas Henkelmann, hands-down one of Connecticut's top chefs, is in the kitchen. Dine before the fireplace in winter or on the enclosed porch in summer in this rambling Italianate house turned inn. The setting is intimate and sophisticated, and the French cuisine is simply magnificent. Try the grilled salmon with braised asparagus and fingerling potato puree, or the poached Dover sole with saffron mousse, Maine lobster, and champagne sauce. Exquisite desserts include warm Valrhona chocolate soufflé, and marzipan-filled baked peaches with white chocolate ice cream. A favorite with locals and visitors, and recipient of the prestigious Relais Gourmands designation from Relais & Châteaux. $30–40.

In Stamford

♿ **Grand** (203-323-3232; www.stamfordgrand.com), 15 Bank St. Open for dinner Mon.–Sat.; closed Sun. and Mon. Reservations are recommended. A tiny, unobtrusive storefront space hides a stylish and Manhattan-chic dining room that puts a gourmet spin on the familiar. The menu of New American comfort food is divided into diminutive dishes perfect for snacking and sharing, and big plates for those who arrive hungry. Punched-up favorites include macaroni-and-cheese with truffles and Gruyère, or rack of lamb with olive-whipped potatoes; finish with apple-cherry crisp with vanilla ice cream, or silky chocolate fondue. The cuisine keeps pace with the dramatic decor, from the curving steel staircase to towering panels suffused with colorful lights. See-and-be-seen hipsters crowd the two bars and lounge, where martinis come in flavors ranging from watermelon to chocolate. If noise and crowds are not your bag, dine early to avoid the thriving bar scene. Later in the evening a DJ starts spinning house music, and the crowd gets livelier and louder. Sushi lounge every Wed. $16–36.

♿ **Il Falco** (203-327-0002; www.ilfalco.com), 59 Broad St. Lunch Mon.–Fri.; dinner Mon.–Sat.; closed Sun. Reservations suggested. Traditional Italian cuisine representing Italy's 21 regions, in elegant surroundings of painted wall murals and linen-clad tables. The kitchen re-creates the classics with fresh ingredients and solid techniques. Seasonal fresh seafood, veal, and homemade pasta are specialties; or try the signature *pollo falco:* chicken sautéed with wine, garlic, mushrooms, and sun-dried tomatoes; or the Dover sole with white wine, butter, and lemon. End with tiramisu or espresso. There's something for everyone on the 2,000-bottle wine list. $20–39.

♿ **Long Ridge Tavern** (203-329-7818; www.longridgetavern.com), 2635 Long Ridge Rd. Open for lunch Tue.–Sat.; dinner Tue.–Sun.; Sun. brunch; closed Mon. A quintessential 19th-century New England tavern with wide-board floors, a fieldstone fireplace, and hanging brass lanterns, serving innovative twists on American classics. You might start with watercress and endive salad with goat cheese and glazed walnuts, then continue to herb-crusted pork tenderloin with rhubarb and apple risotto, or pan-seared trout with lemon butter and corn bread stuffing. Top it off with wild berry shortcake or crème brûlée. There's live jazz and cabaret in the taproom, and a lighter menu of New England favorites, from ale-battered fish-and-chips to chicken potpie. $19–30.

♿ **Meera** (203-975-0479), 227 Summer St. Open daily for lunch and dinner. Reservations suggested. Paintings of Indian legends on the walls hint at the specialty here—authentic northern Indian cuisine based on centuries-old recipes and traditions. Watch the chefs at work through glass windows as they prepare breads, chicken, lamb, shrimp, and fish dishes in an almost authentic tandoori clay oven. (In India, tandoori ovens generally are in the ground.) If you fancy eggplant and lean toward vegetable dishes, try the *bhurtz baingan*, a medley of eggplant, tomatoes, and herbs. $13–25.

Napa & Co. (203-353-3319; www.napaandcompany.com), at the Courtyard by Marriott, 75 Broad St. Open for breakfast and dinner daily; lunch Mon.–Fri. Reservations are highly recommended. A cutting-edge 45-seat eatery with hot Connecticut chef Bill Taibe at the helm; his hallmark is homespun farm-fresh dishes with ingredients sourced from local producers. The motto, "From the farm to the plate without delay," is inspired by the light and healthy cuisine of California's Napa Valley. To wit: The ever-changing menu might feature sheep's-milk ricotta gnocchi, or duck breast braised in honey and thyme. $28–42.

♿ **Ocean 211** (203-973-0494; www.ocean211.com), 211 Summer St. Open for lunch Mon.–Fri.; dinner Mon.–Sat.; closed Sun. A stylish and sophisticated downtown favorite where it's all about seafood. The daily-changing menu features a bounty of fish and shellfish from around the globe. Sample bluepoints or littlenecks, or something from the raw bar (which usually features at least a dozen East and West coast choices on the half shell); but save room for super-fresh seafood meals such as pan-seared New Zealand snapper with lobster, corn, and fava bean hash; diver sea scallops with oxtail mushroom risotto and a porcini truffle emulsion; or coriander-crusted yellowfin tuna with marinated baby bok choy. There's an award-winning wine list, and live jazz on Fri. and Sat. $24–36.

♿ **Plateau** (203-961-9875; www.plateaurestaurant.com), 25 Bank St. Open for lunch and dinner daily. Reservations recommended. One of the best restaurants in town, a chic and elegant setting offering reborn Southeast Asian classics that have earned high marks from the *New York Times*, Zagat, and other heavy hitters for the kitchen's authentic, exotic dishes from Vietnam, Malaysia, and Thailand. Start with prawns glazed in Grand Marnier, or a Thai salad of grilled beef and green papaya, then move on to curry chicken with fresh cilantro; wok-seared steak with garlic, basil, and plum sauce; or crispy snapper with tamarind sauce. Desserts are equally exotic: fresh mango mousse, fried banana with green coconut paste, green tea ice cream, and mango sticky rice with coconut cream, served in a banana leaf. $13–25.

Saltwater Grille (203-391-6500; www.saltwatergrille.net), 183 Harbor Dr. Open for lunch Mon.–Sat.; dinner daily; Sun. brunch. A smack-on-the-water bistro serving New American cuisine. Cheddar popovers are a creative substitute for the traditional bread basket; on the menu, the lobster fritters with roasted corn rémoulade are a nice start, followed by pan-roasted Idaho trout, grilled tuna steak with Merlot butter, and other mostly seafood selections. $17–34.

♿ **Telluride** (203-357-7679; www.telluriderestaurant.com), 245 Bedford St. Open for lunch Mon.–Sat.; closed Sun. Reservations suggested. Dine on global cuisine in surroundings reminiscent of a rustic-yet-stylish mountain lodge, a scene that buzzes with energy but is as easygoing and casual as the American West. Generous portions of hearty made-from-scratch contemporary American cuisine are given a southwestern spin. Start with wild rice and chorizo chowder with basil pesto and roasted corn, raw oysters, or braised-lamb spring rolls, then Colorado trout, free-range meats, or exotic wild game. End with the artisanal cheese plate or homey desserts like English toffee bread pudding that are off-the-charts delicious. The award-winning 300-bottle wine list includes 30 wines by the glass. In all, everything you'd expect from a restaurant named for a hip Colorado ski town cum film festival. $23–48.

♿ **Republic Grill Asian Bistro** (203-353-8005), 235 Bedford St. Lunch Mon.–Sat.; dinner daily. An intimate storefront bistro serving sushi platters and Japanese lunch boxes by day, and upscale New Asian cuisine later on. Start with Thai crabcakes, then wok-grilled garlic shrimp with pineapple and baby bok choy. Chef-owner Jason Chen also helms Fairfield County's wildly popular Tengda Asian restaurants (see above). $16–22.

♿ **Duo** (203-252-2233; www.duoeurojapanese.com), 25 Bank St. Open for lunch Mon.–Sat.; dinner daily; Sun. brunch. Eclectic Euro-Japanese fusion cuisine in a high-ceilinged sleek space that manages to be both trendy and comfortable. Eat off the better-than-usual sushi menu or sample the main courses, which imaginatively pair Asian staples with flavors from around the world. $23–34.

♿ **Market** (203-348-8000; www.marketstamford.com), 249 Main St. Open for lunch Mon.–Fri.; dinner daily. As the name implies, inventive seasonal New American cuisine using the bounty of local farmers is the trademark of this stylish and modern newcomer with an open kitchen. You might try fried baby artichokes with garlic aioli for a starter, move on to wild halibut with roasted corn succotash, then wrap things up with the warm raspberry and nectarine cobbler. $23–42.

Dragonfly Restaurant & Lounge (203-357-9800; www.dragonflyloungect.com), 488 Summer St. Open for lunch Mon.–Fri., dinner Mon.–Sat.; closed Sun. Dragonfly is part Gothic-inspired restaurant, part sleek New York–style cocktail lounge. You can order a bunch of little plates and nibble on adventurous New American dishes such as grilled elk, Mediterranean snapper, smoked Gouda ravioli, and chocolate-dipped peanut butter cheesecake. Many come simply for the live jazz and creative cocktails. $18–42.

In New Canaan

♿ **Bistro Bonne Nuit** (203-966-5303), 12–14 Forest St. Open for dinner daily. Reservations recommended. Romantic and unhurried dining in the spirit of the classic French bistro. Step past the cascading window boxes into a collection of small linen-covered tables amid vibrant decor reminiscent of Provence. Diners feast on French-Mediterranean bistro-inspired fare that's elegant yet robust and simple: escargots, onion soup gratiné, rosemary lamb brochette, duck confit. A decent wine list includes many by-the-glass choices. $25–40.

♿ **Cava Wine Bar & Restaurant** (203-966-6946; www.cavawinebar.com), 2 Forest St. Open for lunch Tue.–Fri.; dinner daily. A storefront space transformed by an ambience reminiscent of a rustic Tuscan wine cellar: candlelight, dramatic arched ceilings, and a wood-fired oven. The walls are lined with racks of wine, a treat for both oenophiles and entry-level wine enthusiasts. Authentic rustic Italian dishes like grilled calamari, osso buco, and roasted fish and poultry. Wines—more than 120 varieties—are from California and Italy, with some two dozen by-the-glass choices. $17–37.

🏵 **Ching's Table** (203-972-8550; www.chingstablecafe.com), 64 Main St., across from town hall. Open daily for lunch and dinner. Regarded as one of Fairfield County's best pan-Asian restaurants, this stylish storefront eatery features primarily Chinese and Thai cuisine with accents of Vietnam, Indonesia, and Malaysia. Standouts include the crispy red snapper and Vietnamese summer rolls. The exotic flavors of ginger, lemongrass, and curry predominate, while the exquisite sauces carry hints of lime, mango, and coconut. The extensive menu, including more than a dozen varieties of noodle bowls, is a remarkable feat for Ching's little kitchen. $10–24.

Harvest Supper (203-966-5595), 15 Elm St. Open Tue.–Sat. for lunch and dinner; closed Sun. and Mon. A pair of Manhattan restaurateurs turned a tiny pizzeria into a bistro with rustic farmhouse decor and a sophisticated menu. Small plates of "New England market cuisine" means bluepoint oysters, mustard-glazed Kobe skirt steak, and shrimp coquettes with horseradish aioli. You can get a coffee crème brûlée, but no coffee or tea. $7–17; five-course tasting menu $50.

♿ **Roger Sherman Inn** (203-966-4541; www.rogershermaninn.com), 195 Oenoke Ridge (CT 124). Dinner served daily; lunch Tue.–Sat.; Sun. brunch. This elegant house was built in 1740 as the home of the niece of Roger Sherman, the colonial jurist whose "Connecticut Compromise" broke the deadlock in Philadelphia and made it possible for the delegates to the Constitutional Convention to agree on the final draft of the U.S. Constitution. Five downstairs rooms serve as intimate dining areas where you can enjoy well-prepared contemporary Continental cuisine with Swiss specialties. Start with smoked salmon, housemade country pâté, or cold vichyssoise. Move on to roasted rainbow trout with pine nut sage butter, or roasted rack of lamb with mustard cream sauce and rosemary fingerling potatoes. $24–54.

♿ **Sole** (203-972-8887; www.soleofnewcanaan.com), 105 Elm St. Open for lunch Mon.–Sat.; dinner daily. A chic establishment with pastel walls, columns, an intricately tiled floor, and a sophisticated menu that matches its clientele. Northern Italian dishes such as Tuscan bread salad with fresh mozzarella and prosciutto, grilled chicken and fennel on focaccia, and housemade potato gnocchi with sausage, mushrooms, and basil. Among the exquisite desserts is *torta di formaggio*, a white chocolate cheesecake with almond brittle and fruit compote. $25–38.

In Darien

♿ **The Black Goose Grille** (203-655-7107; www.theblackgoosegrille.com), 972 Post Rd. (US 1). Open daily for lunch and dinner; Sun. brunch. Reservations suggested. This lovely old brick house with gleaming black shutters offers some of the best fine dining in town. Well-prepared, classic American dishes, from Black Angus sirloin to old-fashioned beef stew and roast pork chops, can be enjoyed in the rustic bar with its massive fireplace, on the terrace, or in the elegant dining room. The menu also offers combinations, such as grilled chicken and filet mignon, or crabcakes and grilled swordfish. $18–30.

♿ **Coromandel Cuisine of India** (203-662-1213; www.coromandelcuisine.com), in the Good Wives Shopping Center, 25-11 Old Kings Hwy. North. Open daily for lunch and dinner. Menu of traditional regional Indian favorites and dishes of India's Coromandel coastal region, with an emphasis on healthy ingredients and low-fat dishes. Coromandel's fare wins high marks for authenticity and tops readers' polls on a regular basis. A gustatory trip to India, with traditional dishes ranging from mildly seasoned to fiery-hot. Try tandoor-cooked New Zealand lamb chops flavored with yogurt and nutmeg; a stew of tiger prawns, coconut milk, ginger, and curry; or favorites like chicken tikka masala, a Punjabi classic. $12–25.

♿ **Giovanni's** (203-325-9979; www.giovannis.com), 2748 Post Rd. (US 1). Open for lunch Mon.–Fri.; dinner daily. An inviting family-owned steak house in an 18th-century carriage house, Giovanni's serves traditional Italian-inspired fare with an emphasis on seafood and steak. $21–48; prix fixe $41–51.

EATING OUT

In Greenwich

♿ **Abis** (203-862-9100; www.abisjapanese.com), 381 Greenwich Ave. Open daily for lunch and dinner. Traditional Japanese cuisine in an airy space full of blond wood, mirrors, and greenery. Watch chefs in the open kitchen prepare tempura, *donburi*, and teriyaki dishes, as well as sushi and sashimi. For dessert, try cream *mitsumame*, an unusual combination of vanilla ice cream atop beans, peaches, mandarin oranges, and Jell-O. $14–27.

♿ **Centro** (203-531-5514; www.centroristorante.com), 328 Pemberwick Rd. Open for lunch Mon.–Sat.; dinner daily. Reservations suggested.

An appealing restaurant in a former felt mill overlooking a 30-foot waterfall on the Byram River. Serves homemade pasta, thin-crusted European pizza, panini sandwiches, and grilled fish and meat. In-season there's seating inside and out. $12–28. Other locations in Darien (203-655-4772) and Fairfield (203-255-1210).

The Ginger Man (203-861-6400; www.gingermangreenwich.com), 64 Greenwich Ave. A beer pub on The Avenue? People who love neighborhood joints will feel at home in this casual and fun place. The bar offers more than 80 varieties of beer—mostly microbrews—including two dozen Belgian ales, as well as single-malt scotches and a decent list of wines. The dining room features snacks a few notches above the usual pub fare and a menu of pasta, beef, and seafood. The first Ginger Man opened in Houston in the 1980s; there's another in Manhattan. It's named not for the holiday cookie, but for the infamous J. P. Donleavy novel *The Ginger Man*, about the misadventures of a young American living in Ireland after World War II. $10–33.

Meli-Melo (203-629-6153; www.melimelogreenwich.com), 362 Greenwich Ave. Don't let the cramped quarters deter you from indulging in one of the standout buckwheat crêpes. Regulars squeeze into the tiny storefront restaurant, whose name, which translates from the French as "hodgepodge," is a direct hint at the eclectic little-of-everything menu. Among the freshly made paper-thin buckwheat crêpes, fillings range from sweet (chocolate-hazelnut) to savory (smoked salmon and chives). There are also a dozen or so soups, an even longer list of fresh juices, and creative salads and sandwiches. Finish with homemade ice cream in a freshly made waffle cone. There's seating for only 20 people at a time, so expect to wait; this is a popular stop among Greenwich Avenue shoppers who come to refuel and recharge. $7–16.

Terra Ristorante Italiano (203-629-5222; www.terraofgreenwich.com), 156 Greenwich Ave. Open for lunch Mon.–Sat.; dinner daily. The cozy dining room's arched ceiling painted with frescoes of cherubs, clouds, and blue skies is dreamy; so is the northern Italian fare. The wood-fired oven busily churns out chicken, fish, light pasta dishes, and pizzas. $14–40.

In Stamford

Black Bear Saloon (203-324-4448; www.blackbearstamford.com), 261 Main St. Open daily for lunch and dinner. Live music and pro sports on a plethora of TVs (some booths have their own) are the draws at this lively downtown watering hole. The appetizer menu offers up familiar favorites like potato skins and nachos, and hearty entrées, from pasta and burgers to steak and seafood. $10–20. A second location in South Norwalk (203-299-0711).

♿ **City Limits Diner** (203-348-7000; www.citylimitsdiner.com), 135 Harvard Ave. Open daily for breakfast, lunch, and dinner; open until midnight on Fri. and Sat. A fun, energetic, 1950s-style art-deco-inspired diner where new creations feel like familiar favorites. Of course you can get burgers, milk shakes, and eggs Benedict around the clock, but this place offers so much more than retro comfort food. Asian steamed dumplings, Maryland crab-lobster cakes, and wild mushroom leek ravioli are among the dressed-up choices. Artisan breads are prepared in-house, as are the smoked fish and meat. There's a full bar with an impressive selection (70 in all) of beers and microbrews. Desserts like the white chocolate espresso truffle tart, and the pineapple-coconut bar paired with house-made toasted coconut sorbet, will make you swoon. $13–25.

Kotobuki (203-359-4747), 457 Summer St. Open Tue.–Fri. for lunch; Tue.–Sun. for dinner; closed Mon. Reservations suggested. For the sashimi and sushi lover in you; other Japanese specialties, too, including teriyaki-glazed salmon, shrimp tempura with udon noodles, and sliced pork sautéed in ginger sauce. $12–22.

SBC Downtown Restaurant & Brewery (203-327-2337; www.southportbrewing.com), 131 Summer St. Open daily for lunch and dinner. A lively brewpub next door to the Palace Theater in the heart of Stamford with house-brewed ales, stouts, porters, and pilsners, including some (Stamford Red, Palace Pilsener, Summer Street IPA) that pay tribute to the city. Appetizers are the usual suspects (wings, calamari, quesadillas) and lead to light brick-oven pizzas, salads, and sandwiches, as well as heartier steaks and seafood. Standouts among the house specialties are Maryland crabcakes, fish-and-chips in beer batter, and baby back ribs basted in tangy beer-infused barbecue sauce. Outdoor patio dining in-season. $14–27. Five locations along the Connecticut coast, including Southport.

In New Canaan

Cherry Street East (203-966-2100), 45 East Ave. This neighborhood bar and grill, an on-the-go lunch spot and equally popular destination later on, recently reopened after a devastating fire. Once again, regulars are happily rubbing shoulders with Manhattanites spending the weekend in the country. $8–20.

JP's Country Cupboard (203-966-6163; www.jpscountrycupboard.com), 17 Elm St. Open daily for breakfast and lunch; dinner Tue.–Sun. The walls are hung with Norman Rockwell prints, classic oldies are piped in on the sound system, and comfort food is on the menu. Together they lend a homey vibe to this local spot tucked behind Harvest Supper that's frequented by old-timers, moms with toddlers, and high school kids, who know that the best seats in the house are at the counter. Breakfast means fluffy banana walnut pancakes and hearty omelets; sandwiches, snacks, and specials like meat loaf and prime rib later on. $8–18.

♿ **Plum Tree Japanese Restaurant** (203-966-8050; www.plumtreejapanese.com), 70 Main St. Open for lunch Mon.–Sat.; dinner daily. The indoor fishpond and lovely hand-painted murals set a soothing tone for sushi and other authentic Japanese dishes. For a fun way to try a little of everything at lunchtime, order a bento box—a traditional black lacquer box filled with an artfully presented sampling that changes daily and might include tempura, sushi, rolls, or soup. Later on, tasting plates (edamame, skewered teriyaki beef) sport diminutive dimensions; main-dish favorites (coconut lobster, hibachi filet mignon) satisfy hearty appetites. $14–26.

♿ **Tequila Mockingbird** (203-966-2222), 6 Forest St. Open for dinner daily; reservations suggested on weekends. Specializing in the regional dishes of Mexico. Sip on a colossal margarita while the chef prepares chiles rellenos that melt in your mouth. A heartier dish: grilled steak, Mexican-style (it's listed as *Arrachera al Carbon* on the menu). The bright pink-and-green exterior hints at the lively fun inside, where colorful decorative tiles recall the rosy glow of a New Mexico sunset. $11–28.

Thali (203-972-8332), 87 Main St.

Open daily for lunch and dinner. Reservations recommended. Take a trip to India without leaving Connecticut. A high-ceilinged, early-20th-century bank building decorated with rich velvet drapes, colorful saris, and a cascading waterfall makes an exotic backdrop for regional Indian haute cuisine. The lamb curry and chicken tikka masala are done well, but many diners opt for a *thali*—a sampling platter of soup, bread, rice, and Indian dishes. For a lighter meal, the Bread Bar offers appetizers and a variety of Indian breads—*poori*, naan, *paratha*, and the like. Lots of vegetarian options. According to Zagat, this is Connecticut's best Indian restaurant. The Sunday-evening dinner buffet lets you try a little of everything. $15–28. Other locations in Ridgefield (203-894-1080) and New Haven (203-777-1177).

In Darien

♿ **The Cookhouse** (203-655-6663; www.thecookhouse.com), 154 Post Rd. (US 1). Open daily for lunch and dinner. Full-flavored, slow-cooked southern barbecue arrived in the Gold Coast when a satellite of Litchfield County's famous barbecue joint opened in 2005. They call it "American country food," which means tangy short ribs, buttery corn bread, and smoky-sweet pulled pork. The ribs—lean baby back or meaty St. Louis–style—are perennial award winners. $14–29.

The Melting Pot (203-202-3958), 14 Grove St., in the Grove Street Plaza. Open for dinner daily. Reservations recommended. An aptly named fondue restaurant with locations around the country; this, however, was the first in New England. For a fun dining experience that's both whimsical and time-honored, fondue is the ultimate share-friendly way to nosh. For dinner, dip fruit, veggies, and hunks of bread into your choice of cheese (aged cheddar, Swiss, Gruyère, or Fontina gets a flavor boost with white wine, sherry, or lager beer); for dessert, chocolate fondue is paired with fruit, marshmallows, and cake. The Flaming Turtle (milk chocolate, caramel, pecans) and the Amaretto Meltdown (white chocolate and amaretto liqueur) are flambéed tableside. There's also an à la carte menu of chicken, steaks, and seafood. On the list of specialty martinis, Godiva white chocolate liqueur keeps company with ice cream for an unexpected twist. $16–26.

♿ **Post Corner Pizza** (203-655-7722), 847 Post Rd. (US 1). Open daily for lunch and dinner. Clean and friendly, often filled with families. The Sofronas family have been serving Greek specialties and satisfying pizzeria fare here since 1971. The souvlaki and moussaka are authentic and delicious. Locally liked, moderately priced. $7–20.

The Sugar Bowl (203-655-1259), 1033 Post Rd. (US 1). Open for breakfast and lunch. A cozy and homey eatery with a nostalgic diner-inspired menu and atmosphere to boot. Lots of regulars come here just for the old-fashioned doughnuts, which are made fresh daily and come plain or sugared. Within walking distance of the Metro-North commuter rail station. $6–12.

SNACKS ♿ **Aux Delices** (203-698-1066; www.auxdelicesfoods.com), 1075 East Putnam Ave. (US 1), Greenwich. Open daily from 7:30 AM, to eat in or take out. Debra Ponzek's innovative hand has won her many accolades; samplings from her gourmet and specialty foods shop prove that the praise is highly deserved. In the morning, order fresh-baked scones and coffee, and seat yourself at a shiny copper café table. Lunch and dinner offer a changing selection of outstanding dishes, such as crabcakes with cilantro-mint sauce, butternut squash and goat cheese lasagna, and green olive and almond tapenade tea sandwiches. Exquisite desserts include chocolate pear espresso tarts and petits fours. Sandwiches around $8; entrées $10–20. Another location in Greenwich at 3 West Elm St. (203-622-6644), and in Darien at 25 Old King's Hwy. North (203-662-1136).

Black Forest Pastry Shop (203-629-9330), 52 Lewis St., Greenwich. Open daily. Authentic German cakes, tortes, pies, and pastries in a locally beloved European-style pastry shop. Stop in for coffee and a made-from-scratch Danish pastry, scone, or muffin. Of the seasonal specialties, the whimsical gingerbread houses crafted during the Christmas holidays are the most magical. The handmade truffles and chocolates are sublime.

Plum Pure Foods (203-869-plum; www.plumpurefoods.com), 236 East Putnam Ave., Cos Cob. Open Mon.–Fri. 7:30–6; closed Sat. and Sun. Look for the plum-hued awning shading a shoe-box storefront eatery with just four tables (most come for take-out). The kitchen works magic with made-from-scratch soups, salads, and sandwiches; standouts include the grilled chicken and hummus with goat cheese, roasted peppers, and olive tapenade on pumpernickel baguette. $4–8.

Arcadia Coffee Co. (203-637-8766; www.arcadiacoffee.com), 20 Arcadia Rd., Old Greenwich. Open daily. A cozy and friendly spot to get a caffeine kick, featuring local artwork, local bands, and a menu of soups, salads, sandwiches, baked goods, and sweets.

Crab Shack (203-967-7229; www.crabshell.com), 46 Southfield Ave., at Stamford Landing Marina, Stamford. *The* place to hang out in summer is this lively waterfront outdoor bar on the dock in front of the Crab Shell Restaurant. There's live music and a shoreline menu of steamers, lobster rolls, and clam chowder. $8–21.

♿ **Ole Mole** (203-461-9962), 1030 High Ridge Rd. (CT 137), Stamford. Open Tue.–Sun. for lunch and dinner; closed Mon. A tiny, bustling take-out spot, with four self-seating tables in a Mexican-tiled store. Generous portions of tasty Mexican food with rice, beans, and guacamole and chips on the side. Delicious moles and salsas made on the premises; the *mole negro* is a rich, earthy blend of Mexican chocolate, tomatoes, and dried chiles. Of the burritos, one is stuffed with eggs, chorizo sausage, beans, and chipotle sauce; the quesadilla Sedona is filled with smoked mozzarella, cilantro, grilled onions, and poblanos. $5–15.

Connecticut Muffin (203-972-7557), 108 Main St., New Canaan. Crack open your eyelids with coffee and generously proportioned muffins at this charming little coffee shop in New Canaan's equally charming downtown. Favorite flavors—as many as 20 varieties are available daily—include lemon poppy seed, morning glory, and blueberry; the cherry-walnut and chocolate scones are equally good. Go early before yours is gone. Soups and sandwiches are served later in the day. Local artwork, old wooden floorboards, and hand-painted furniture lend a pleasingly homey aesthetic.

T-Party Antiques and Tea Room (203-662-9689; www.tpartyantiques.com), 2 Squab Lane, off US 1, Darien. Afternoon tea (reservations recommended) Wed.–Sat. at 1:30 and 3 PM; shop open Tue.–Sat. 11–5; closed Sun. and Mon. A cozy 19th-century restored farmhouse-cum-tearoom just off busy Post Road is crammed with vintage finds, from furniture and pottery to kitchenware and collectibles. Browse at your leisure, but don't miss the traditional ritual of lingering over afternoon tea. Choose from 14 varieties of loose tea, accompanied by delicate finger sandwiches, home-baked scones with jam and clotted cream, and a variety of sweets that might include fruit tartlets or chocolate-dipped strawberries. $12–17.

♿ **Uncle's Deli** (203-655-9701; www.unclesdeli.com), 1041 Post Rd. (US 1), Darien. Breakfast and lunch daily. A snug deli in a tiny green-and-white shack dressed up with checked curtains. Primarily take-out, except in summer, when you can bring your picnic fixings to a table outside. Locals love the roll-ups; the Thanksgiving version (crammed with turkey, stuffing, and cranberry sauce) is a tasty reminder of the holiday dinner table. $4–8.

Versailles Patisserie (203-661-6634), 315 Greenwich Ave. Open for lunch Mon.–Fri.; breakfast and dinner daily. This is the place to embrace your inner Francophile. Many come to this cute French bistro and pastry shop, a longtime Greenwich Avenue institution, for a quick bite. In the morning, you can't go wrong with the flaky, buttery croissants; in the afternoon, enjoy an espresso and dessert from the patisserie, whose glass showcases are filled with exquisite works of edible art.

✷ Entertainment

MUSIC AND THEATER

In Stamford

Avon Theatre Film Center (203-967-3660; www.avontheatre.org), 272 Bedford St. Watching the latest flicks in an old-fashioned movie house is a refreshing change of pace from the neighborhood homogenized multiplex. Here, a historic theater that first showed films in 1939 reopened its doors in 2004, beautifully refurbished, from the neo-colonial-style exterior to the dramatic art-deco-style vertical marquee. Today it's a nonprofit film center that mixes current features with classics, foreign and independent films, and documentaries.

Sterling Farms Theatre Complex (203-329-8207; www.curtaincallinc.com), 1349 Newfield Ave. **Curtain Call** is a local theater group that performs comedies, murder mysteries, dramas, and Broadway musicals. Some performances are staged in a cabaret-style setting where you can bring your own dinner and drinks.

Stamford Center for the Arts (203-325-4466; www.stamfordcenterforthearts.org), or SCA, operates two first-rate performance venues: The **Palace Theatre** (61 Atlantic St.), designed by noted theater architect Thomas Lamb, which was a vaudeville house when it was built in 1927 and is now home to **Connecticut Grand Opera & Orchestra** and **Stamford Symphony Orchestra**; and the nearby state-of-the-art **Rich Forum** (307 Atlantic St.). Together they offer varied fare: Broadway musicals, comedies, plays, dance, and music.

Stamford TheatreWorks/Purple Cow Children's Theatre (203-359-4414; www.stamfordtheatreworks.org), 200 Strawberry Hill Ave. Year-round professional theater presenting new and experimental plays for adults and children in an intimate 150-seat barn theater; call for a schedule. Family productions are presented by the Purple Cow Children's Theatre during summer and the Christmas and Hanukkah holiday seasons. School for the performing arts also on-site.

✱ Selective Shopping

ANTIQUES

In Stamford

The Antique and Artisan Center (203-327-6022; www.stamfordantiques.com), 69 Jefferson St. Open Mon.–Sat. 10:30–5:30; Sun. noon–5. This 150-dealer antiques showplace was the city's first major antiques center. Garden antiques, lighting, period furniture and paintings, home furnishings.

Braswell Galleries (203-357-0753), 24 Harborview Ave. Open Mon.–Sat. 10:30–5:30; Sun. 11–5. More than 40,000 square feet of one-of-a-kind finds, perfect for treasure hunting or if you have a house to redecorate. Antiques, lighting, furniture, garden furniture, paintings, and other home decor items fill a huge gallery shop; there's also an auction house on the premises.

Connecticut Antiques Center (203-355-9335; www.connecticutstyle.com), 850 Canal St. Ninety dealers offering antique jewelry and lighting, fine art and silver, midcentury modern furniture.

Harbor View Center for Antiques (203-325-8070), 101 Jefferson St. Open Mon.–Fri. 10:30– 5:30; Sun. noon–5. More than 70 American and international dealers in 18th-, 19th-, and 20th-century antiques.

Hiden Galleries (203-363-0003; www.hidengalleries.com), 47 John St. Open daily 10–6. A consortium of 350 dealers in American and European furniture, paintings, lamps, silver, and textiles.

Elsewhere

Church Street Antiques (203-661-6309), 77 Church St., Greenwich. Fine antiques and decorative pieces.

Guild Antiques (203-869-0828), 384 Greenwich Ave., Greenwich. Specialties include 18th- and 19th-century English furniture and Chinese and English porcelain.

Antiques of Darien (203-655-5133), 1101 Post Rd. (US 1), Darien. Eight dealers, each with a specialty—fine art, Oriental carpets, country furniture, lamps, mirrors. Many unique finds.

Knock on Wood Antiques (203-655-9031), 355 Post Rd. (US 1), Darien. European antiques and home furnishings and reproductions on display in a spacious gallery.

ART GALLERIES **Cavalier Galleries** (203-869-3664; www.cavaliergalleries.com), 405 Greenwich Ave., Greenwich. A Greenwich Avenue gallery with a focus on photography, paintings, and sculpture.

Greenwich Arts Center–Bendheim Gallery (203-622-3998; www.greenwicharts.org), 299 Greenwich Ave., Greenwich. Changing exhibits of paintings, sculpture, prints, and other works, run by the Greenwich Arts Council.

583 Art Factory (203-324-9750; www.583artfactory.com), 583 Pacific St., Stamford. Open Tue.–Sat. 10–6. A SoHo-inspired gallery in a turn-of-the-20th-century brick factory building in Stamford's downtown antiques district. Visitors can tour a working art studio and view exhibits by local artists in the gallery.

Stamford Art Association (203-325-1139), 39 Franklin St., Stamford. Gallery open Thu. and Fri. 11–3, Sat. and Sun. noon–3. A community fine arts guild offering changing exhibits and juried shows featuring local painters, sculptors, photographers, and printmakers.

Geary Gallery (203-655-6633; www.gearygallery.com), 576 Boston Post Rd. (US 1), Darien. A full schedule of exhibitions from fall to spring featuring

Connecticut and East Coast artists.

The Carriage Barn Arts Center (203-972-1895; www.carriagebarn.org), Waveny Park, 681 South Ave. (CT 124), New Canaan. Gallery open Tue.–Fri. 11–4, Sat. and Sun. 1–5; closed Mon. Free admission. A community arts center run by the New Canaan Society for the Arts, a group that dates from the 19th century. A restored 1895 stone carriage barn houses a rustic and contemporary spacious gallery, a charming setting for art exhibitions, concerts, lectures, and other special programs.

Silvermine Guild Arts Center (203-966-5617; www.silvermineart.org), 1037 Silvermine Rd., New Canaan. Open Tue.–Sat. 11–5; Sun. 1–5; closed Mon. and major holidays. Admission $2. The arts center campus includes a school and five galleries featuring changing exhibitions of contemporary art. Silvermine is among the most beautiful and prestigious galleries in New England, with rotating exhibits of works by top professionals for sale and for viewing. The Guild of Artists was formally established in 1922 and founded by local sculptor Solon Borglum, whose barn was the setting for regular gatherings of a group known as the Knockers Club, local artists who were drawn here by the bucolic landscape that inspired their work.

BOOKSTORES ✐ **Diane's Books** (203-869-1515; www.dianesbooks.com), 8A Grigg St., Greenwich. Open Mon.–Sat. 9–5. A quaint Tudor-style shop with books and guest authors for readers of all ages, especially children. They stock an impressively large selection of family books, many more than most national retailers stock.

Just Books Inc. (203-869-5023; 800-874-4568; www.justbooks.org), 11 East Putnam Ave., Greenwich. Open Tue.–Fri. 9–9; Mon. and Sat. 9–5; closed Sun. The name says it all. A cozy neighborhood independent bookshop that invites browsing and sponsors a variety of book clubs, book signings, a children's story hour, and other events. A second location, **Just Books Too** (203-637-0707), is in Old Greenwich at 28 Arcadia Rd.

Barrett Bookstore (203-655-2712; www.barrettbookstore.com), Noroton Heights Shopping Center, 314 Heights Rd., Darien. A longtime independent neighborhood bookstore with author events and thoughtful staff picks.

Elm Street Books (203-966-4545; www.elmstreetbooks.com), 35 Elm St., New Canaan. Open Mon.–Sat. 9:30–5:30; Sun. noon–5. This beloved New Canaan bookshop reopened its doors in 2006, just up the road from their old location. Everything that made it great is still here: a knowledgeable staff, opinionated book selections, and a full schedule of author talks and other events in comfy surroundings. Bonus: **Rosie's**, an adjoining café, serves drinks, snacks, and light meals to hungry bibliophiles.

SPECIAL SHOPS **Greenwich Avenue** in the center of Greenwich is a mecca for upscale shopping, lined with chic boutiques, art galleries, antiques shops, and stellar restaurants. A great place for window-shopping and crowd-watching. Among the shops are: ✐ **Best & Co.** (203-629-1743), 289 Greenwich Ave. Fashion designer Susie Hilfiger's shop carries high-end European and American children's clothing in handsome surroundings. **Kate's Paperie** (203-861-0025), 125 Greenwich Ave., a branch of the New York–based stationery giant known for its ornate exquisite papers, fine journals, pens, and accessories. **Seacloth** (203-422-6150), 107 Greenwich Ave., is the place for chic furnishings and decorative accessories for stylish digs. **Giggles** (203-622-6775), 102 Greenwich Ave., is a new shop offering eco-friendly goods for babies and kids. **Knitting Niche** (203-869-6205), 115 Mason St. Knitting has become a popular pastime, and not just among grandmothers. Knitting classes teach adults how to purl; the shop, just a block away from Greenwich Avenue, carries hand-dyed yarns and others made of silk, cashmere, and other luxurious fibers.

Home Boutique of Greenwich (203-866-2550; www.homeboutique.com), 14 Lewis St., Greenwich. French hand-embroidered table linens are the raison d'être at this downtown boutique.

The Drawing Room (203-661-3406; www.thedrawingroom.cc), 5 Suburban Ave., off US 1, Cos Cob. Open Tue.–Sat.; closed Sun. and Mon. A stylish home furnishings and accessories store that's as elegant and chic as the goods: art, handbags, body products, furniture, and gifts. A tea and espresso bar serves sweets, snacks, and high tea during store hours.

Agabhumi: The Best of Bali (203-325-2274; www.agabhumi.com), 22 Magee Ave., Stamford. Regina and Michael Kirshbaum take regular jaunts to Bali for the handiwork of local artisans. There's a whimsical selection of housewares and clothing, plus lots of must-have accessories such as exquisite jewelry, leather goods, and one-of-a-kind pottery.

Schakolad (203-359-1886; www.schakolad.com), 172 Bedford St., Stamford. Open Mon.–Sat.; closed Sun. Here's where to shop for the chocoholic in your life: The bonbons and truffles are exquisite, but the sculpted creations are over the top. Using hundreds of molds, they can craft just about anything from chocolate, from picture frames and champagne glasses to credit cards.

Shanti Bithi Nursery (203-329-0768; www.shantibithi.com), 3047 High Ridge Rd., Stamford. Open Mon.–Sat. 9–5; closed Sun. *Shanti bithi* means "path of peace," an apt name for such a magical and serene Japanese-style setting. The specialty of this unique nursery is bonsai—one of the country's most extensive collections—and bonsai-related garden accessories. Ask about workshop classes held in spring and fall, as well as lectures by guest bonsai specialists at the nursery's annual fall open house.

Stamford Town Center (203-324-0935; www.shopstamfordtowncenter.com), 100 Greyrock Place, across from the Stamford Marriott. Clustered in a huge covered mall in the center of downtown are the cream of New York City's stores and boutiques, such as Macy's and Saks Fifth Avenue. New Yorkers make the short train trip to Stamford because they argue that in New York they may be able to visit one or two stores on a good shopping day, but in Stamford, more than 100 are all together and easily accessible under one roof.

United House Wrecking (203-348-5371; www.unitedhousewrecking.com), 535 Hope St., Stamford. Open Mon.–Sat. 9:30–5:30 and Sun. noon–5. Connecticut's largest antiques emporium and home furnishings showroom evolved from a vast family-owned architectural salvage yard, beloved by home owners and decorators for half a century. Wander through rooms filled with stained and beveled glass, old mantels, butcher blocks, fireplace accessories, unusual furniture, Victorian gingerbread, weather vanes, English statuary, or cast-iron urns for the garden. The list is endless and ever-changing, and the sheer volume is staggering. An exclusive line of hand-crafted vintage furniture appeals to those searching for new treasures.

Smith and Hawken (203-972-0820), 30 East Ave., New Canaan. Open Mon.–Sat. 10–6; Sun. 11–5. Like the legendary gardening catalog, this shop has every conceivable gadget to make your garden grow, while making it (and the gardener) look snazzy. Decorative spigots, galvanized plant markers, imported hand tools, rubber rain shoes, and the like. This was the first East Coast outpost for the California-based garden decor giant.

The Summer House (203-594-9550; www.thesummerhouseonline.com), 3 Forest St., New Canaan. The specialty is 18th- and 19th-century Swedish antiques, from hand-painted furniture to elegant home accents.

Darien Cheese & Fine Foods (203-655-4344; www.dariencheese.com), 25-10 Old Kings Hwy. North, in the Goodwives Shopping Center, Darien. Open Tue.–Sat.; closed Sun. and Mon. Supplies for gourmet picnics and elegant suppers.

Orvis (203-662-0844), 432 Post Rd. (US 1), Darien. Open Mon.–Sat. 10–6 (Thu. until 8); Sun. noon–5. The Orvis name is synonymous with the sport (and art) of fly-fishing. Fly-fishing and fly-tying equipment, clothing, and everything else to satisfy your inner fly-fisherman. Call for a schedule of workshops and seminars.

✷ Special Events

March: **Darien Antiques Show** (www.darienantiquesshow.org), 14 Brookside Rd., Darien. Dozens of dealers have been selling rugs, paintings, furniture, silver, maps, European china, and jewelry here for more than 40 years.

May: **Outdoor Crafts Festival of the Bruce Museum** (203-869-0376), Bruce Museum of Arts and Science, 1 Museum Dr., Greenwich. A popular show with more than 80 crafts exhibitors, live music, and educational crafts activities for children and families.

June: **Ox Ridge Charity Horse Show** (203-655-2559), Ox Ridge Hunt Club, Darien. Jumper- and hunter events in a show running more than 75 years. **Greenwich Concourse D'Elegance** (203-618-0460), Roger Sherman Baldwin Park, Greenwich. World-class exhibition of vintage European cars and antique boats.

Summer: **French Market** (203-348-5285; www.stamford-downtown.com), Bedford St., Stamford. Farmer's market offering fresh produce, baked goods, and flowers. Sat., June–Nov. **Greenwich Polo Club** (203-661-5420), 80 Field Point Rd., Greenwich. On Sundays from June to September, the public is welcome to watch polo matches featuring players from around the world. **Greenwich Arts Council Summer Concerts** (203-862-6750; www.greenwicharts.org), Roger Sherman Baldwin Park, Greenwich. free. **Stamford Downtown Outdoor Summer Concert Series** (203-348-5285; www.stamford-downtown.com), Columbus Park, Stamford. Free.

September: **Hawk Watch Festival** (203-869-5272), Audubon Center of Greenwich, Greenwich. Help volunteers spot and identify hundreds of hawks passing through on their annual southern migration.

October: **Outdoor Arts Festival** (203-869-0376), Bruce Museum, 1 Museum Dr., Greenwich. Juried show attracting artists from around the country.

November: **Stamford Balloon Parade Spectacular** (203-348-5285), Stamford. This downtown celebration is the country's largest parade of giant helium character balloons—24 in all—accompanied by more than 60 marching bands, floats, and special groups.

December: **Rappelling Santa and Colossal Tree Lighting** (203-348-5285), Landmark Square and Latham Park, Stamford. Santa and elves rappel from Stamford's tallest building, then light the holiday tree in Latham Park. **Winterfest** (203-869-6899), Bush-Holley Historic Site, in the Cos Cob section of Greenwich. **Old Greenwich First Light Festival** (203-637-0217), downtown Old Greenwich. Retailers and merchants open their doors on the first Saturday in December, when holiday carols, horse-drawn carriage rides, hot chocolate, wine tasting, and Santa Claus bring locals and visitors together.

WESTPORT AND NORWALK

Though sitting cheek by jowl on the western shores of Long Island Sound, Westport and Norwalk couldn't be more different in geography, topography, character, purpose, and population. Norwalk started life as a bustling industrial town—its 1800s storefronts and redbrick factory buildings once produced derbies and corsets—that also drew its sustenance from the water with a once-thriving oyster fishing industry. Although the bulk of the factories have skipped town, commercial oystering is still in business here. South Norwalk (south of US 1 and the main-line railroad tracks) was particularly hard hit, but enterprising city officials and civic leaders launched a remarkable restoration project in the early 1980s. They targeted the urban blight plaguing the shabby waterfront area where the Norwalk River empties into the harbor, transforming abandoned Beaux-Arts factories and warehouses into what is now a thriving enclave of edgy galleries, funky boutiques, and cool, trendsetting nightspots packed with dressed-to-impress hipsters. This cosmopolitan world-within-a-world, known simply as SoNo, resides mostly on and around Washington Street. Naturally, the bohemian vibe attracts a lively crowd and a vibrant artistic community and offers unparalleled people-watching opportunities and buzz-worthy festivals. It's home to some of the area's hottest cuisine, which runs the culinary gamut from cutting-edge Nuevo Latino and down-home southern barbecue to African-Caribbean fusion and, as you'd expect in a waterfront town, just-off-the-boat seafood, in surroundings as stylish and energetic as the neighborhood the restaurants reside in.

The high trend factor aside, SoNo is an artsy community that hasn't forgotten its nautical roots. Its centerpiece is the Maritime Aquarium, a decidedly un-chic destination but one that brings families and others in touch with exhibits devoted to the region's maritime history and ecological life, plus more than 1,000 native marine animals and one of the state's only IMAX theaters. Excursions aboard the aquarium's research vessel *Oceanic* bring visitors up close to the creatures that inhabit Norwalk Harbor and Long Island Sound. The Norwalk Seaport Association hosts the must-see Norwalk Oyster Festival, a summertime celebration of the area's seafaring heritage. Ferry cruises to Sheffield Island offer tangy Long Island Sound breezes and tours of a historic 19th-century lighthouse. The rest of the rocky, windswept Norwalk Islands are havens for birding and sea kayaking. A bit inland, Norwalk's Mathews Park offers two different attractions: one a shrine to golden age grandeur, another with hands-on fun just for youngsters. The Lockwood-Mathews Mansion Museum was the Civil War–era retreat of a railroad

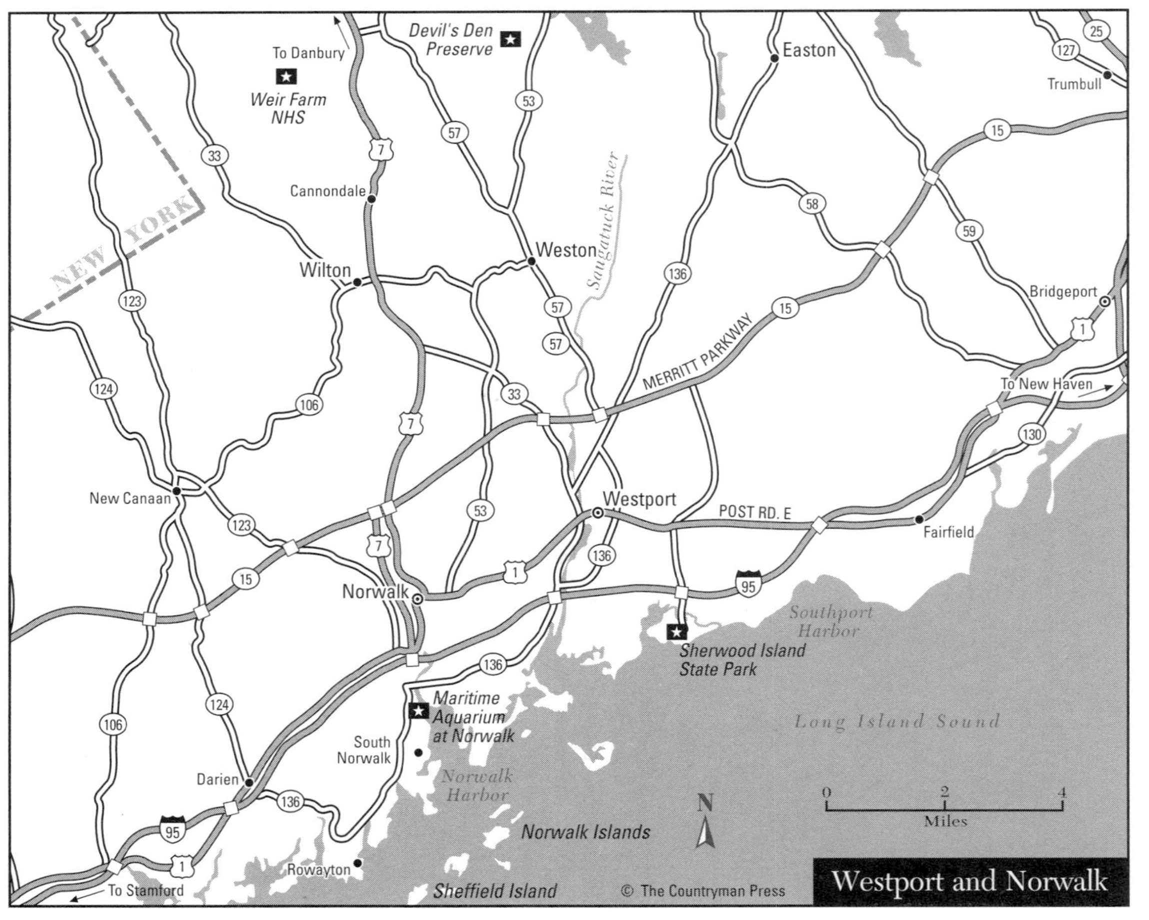
Westport and Norwalk
To Danbury
Weir Farm NHS
Devil's Den Preserve
Easton
Trumbull
Cannondale
Wilton
Weston
Saugatuck River
NEW YORK
MERRITT PARKWAY
Bridgeport
To New Haven
New Canaan
Westport
POST RD. E
Fairfield
Norwalk
Southport Harbor
Sherwood Island State Park
Maritime Aquarium at Norwalk
South Norwalk
Long Island Sound
Norwalk Harbor
Darien
Norwalk Islands
Rowayton
To Stamford
Sheffield Island
© The Countryman Press
N
0
2
4
Miles

magnate; more recently it was the opulent setting for the "boys' club" in Frank Oz's remake of *The Stepford Wives* (based on Ira Levin's satirical novel about 1950s housewives), the dark comedy starring Nicole Kidman in the "perfect" Connecticut suburbs. Just down the road, Stepping Stones Museum for Children is one of the top kid-friendly museums in America. Silvermine Tavern is a mecca for live jazz, gourmet cuisine, romantic overnight lodging, and nostalgic surroundings straight out of 18th-century New England. The quiet Rowayton section of town, on the banks of Five Mile River, offers a top-notch seafood restaurant, kayaks for hire, and a market that has catered to locals since 1753.

The chic-yet-genteel bedroom community of Westport has been called Beverly Hills East; it has also been called a "snooty commuter town" (in *New York* magazine's October 2005 issue). Just 40 miles from Manhattan, it became home to the affluent New York commuter almost from the day it was connected to Manhattan by rail. In the mid–19th century, onions put Westport on the map; in the 1920s, it was the infamous Gatsby-esque summer playground of F. Scott and Zelda Fitzgerald. Around that time, artists and writers from the city began retreating to what was quickly becoming a bustling artists' colony. Today numerous celebrities and corporate CEOs enjoy their privacy, and one another's company, at lavish parties on their palatial estates. One of the customs in "the Land of Steady Habits" is to respect your neighbors' privacy no matter what their fame. So follow the lead of the locals and don't bother longtime Westporter Joanne Woodward if you bump into her in the aisle of a supermarket.

The Westport Country Playhouse is one of the oldest in the nation, founded in 1931. Its board of directors sounds like a roster of Oscar winners and brings luminaries to the stage in local productions. When Woodward and her late husband, Paul Newman, came onto the scene in the 1960s, they became deeply involved in the playhouse—Woodward is co–artistic director. Martha Stewart made her name as a domestic diva from her home in Westport, where she began the small catering business that evolved into the Martha Stewart Living Omnimedia empire.

Though Westport can't point to many conventional tourist attractions, its haute cuisine, stylish galleries, and fancy-schmancy boutiques in the core of town—radiating off bustling Main Street—annually draw thousands of visitors. High-end national retailers like Anthropologie, Restoration Hardware, and Pottery Barn are mixed with one-of-a-kind local favorites to create a vibrant shoppers' paradise. Nearby, the oh-so-refined Inn at National Hall, an 1873 Italianate gem on the banks of the Saugatuck River, is *the* place to stay in town, the centerpiece of the restoration of Westport's 19th-century waterfront, which is now a National Historic District. Nature lovers head to the beach at Sherwood Island State Park on Long Island Sound, or to the hiking trails and perennial gardens at Earthplace: The Nature Discovery Center, whose 63 woodsy acres serve as a refuge for both birds of prey and solitude seekers.

The sleepy towns of Wilton, Weston, Monroe, and Easton are for the most part affluent residential areas, as is the polished seaside village of Southport. Of interest to visitors are their inns and restaurants, open spaces, and historical societies. America's Giverny, the Wilton studio-farm of J. Alden Weir—the 19th-century painter in the vanguard of American impressionism—is Connecticut's only National Historic Site.

Entries in this section are arranged in roughly geographic order.

GUIDANCE **Coastal Fairfield County Convention & Visitor Bureau** (203-853-7770; 800-866-7925; www.visitfairfieldcountyct.com), Gate Lodge, Mathews Park, 297 West Ave., Norwalk 06850. Stop by to pick up brochures and maps, or get travel advice on what to see and do in Fairfield County from the friendly, knowledgeable staff.

WPA Murals (203-854-7900), Norwalk City Hall, 125 East Ave., Norwalk. Open Mon.–Fri. 9–5. During the Great Depression of the 1930s, President Franklin Roosevelt's Works Project Administration (WPA) created federal jobs in every endeavor, from constructing schools and municipal buildings to promoting arts and culture—not to mention putting local artists back to work. Hundreds of impoverished artists throughout the country were employed to paint murals in the new public buildings. Most murals have been destroyed, but Connecticut, recognizing their historic value, has restored and now displays 33 murals of life in the Norwalk area, the largest collection in the country of this unique art form. Several depict the city's historic oyster industry, remembered to this day at the annual summertime Norwalk Oyster Festival. Other examples of the huge murals can be seen in other city buildings: Two in the Maritime Museum depict oystering; two children's scenes are in the public library (203-899-2780) on Belden Ave.; and another pair are hung in Norwalk Community College (203-857-7000) on Richards Ave.

MURALS IN SOUTH NORWALK DEPICT LIFE IN EARLIER CENTURIES.

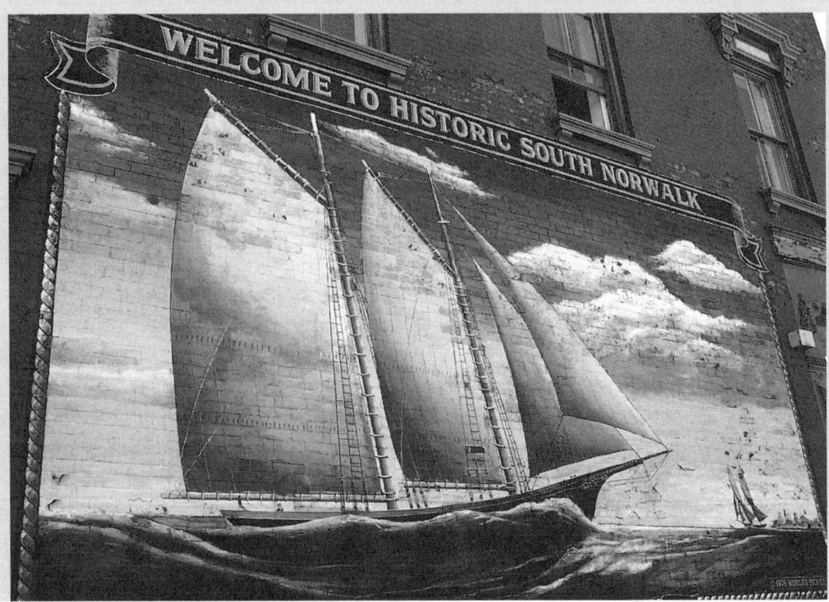

Kim Grant

GETTING THERE *By air:* **Westchester County Airport** (914-285-4860), just outside Greenwich in White Plains, New York, serves the area with daily flights by Air Canada, AirTran, American, Continental, Delta, JetBlue, Northwest, United, and US Airways. **Tweed–New Haven Regional Airport** (203-466-8833; www.flytweed.com) is the airport of Greater New Haven and is served by US Airways Express. International arrivals access the Gold Coast through New York's **JFK Airport** (718-244-4444) or **Bradley International Airport** (860-292-2000; 888-624-1533; www.bradleyairport.com) in Windsor Locks, both about 1½ hours away.

By car: Westport and Norwalk, and adjoining towns and villages, are accessible by car from I-95, the Merritt Parkway (CT 15), and US 1 (the Post Road).

By rail: **Metro-North** (800-638-7646; www.mta.info) commuter trains from Grand Central Station in New York City stop in Westport, Norwalk, and Wilton.

By bus or limo: **Greyhound Lines** (800-231-2222; www.greyhound.com) and **Peter Pan Bus Lines** (800-343-9999; www.peterpanbus.com) stop in Stamford and Bridgeport. **Connecticut Limousine Service** (800-472-5466; www.ctlimo.com) serves Bradley International Airport and the major metro New York airports.

GETTING AROUND **Westport Star Taxi** (203-227-5157), **Wilton Taxi Service** (203-227-3063), **Saugatuck Taxi Service** (203-571-1111), **Norwalk Taxi** (203-855-1764), and **Yellow Cab** (203-853-1267) serve the area.

MEDICAL EMERGENCY The statewide emergency number is **911**.

Norwalk Hospital (203-852-2000), 34 Maple St., Norwalk. The emergency number is 203-852-2160.

Greenwich Hospital (203-863-3000), 5 Perryridge Rd., Greenwich. The emergency number is 203-863-3637.

Stamford Hospital (203-276-1000), 30 Shelburne Rd., Stamford. The emergency number is 203-276-7777.

✷ To See

MUSEUMS ♿ **Norwalk Museum** (203-866-0202; www.norwalkmuseum.lbu.com), 41 North Main St., Norwalk. Open year-round, Wed.–Sun. 1–5; closed Mon. and Tue. Free admission. Housed in the imposing former city hall, displays of local manufacturing, retail, and artistic history showcase period furnishings, paintings, and decorative art. A merchants' courtyard depicts shops selling Dobbs hats and 19th-century Norwalk pottery. The gift shop carries Norwalk pottery reproductions along with Raggedy Ann and Andy dolls, whose creator, Johnny Gruelle, lived in Norwalk.

✐ **Stepping Stones Museum for Children** (203-899-0606; www.steppingstonesmuseum.org), Mathews Park, 303 West Ave., Norwalk. Open Memorial Day–Labor Day, daily 10–5; Labor Day–Memorial Day, Tue. 1–5, Wed.–Sun., 10–5; closed Mon. Adults and children $9; seniors $7; under age 1 free. *Child* magazine designated this happy place as one of America's top 50 children's museums. It's an interactive discovery museum for children ages 1–10, based on the belief that little ones learn best through hands-on interaction in a fun and nurturing multidimensional environment. The weather station, musical instruments, and simulated helicopter are favorites among more than 80 hands-on activities that entertain as well as educate. Programs in arts, science, technology, culture, and heritage appeal to children's natural curiosity and provide a fun way for families to spend time together. Special programs and events take place throughout the year, from holiday-themed activities and toddler workshops to storytelling performances.

The Maritime Aquarium at Norwalk (203-852-0700; www.maritimeaquarium.org), 10 North Water St., South Norwalk. Open daily 10–5; July and Aug. daily 10–6; closed Thanksgiving and Christmas. Additional IMAX hours Fri. and Sat. evening. Adults $11; seniors $10; children $9; IMAX and simulated adventure ride extra. Unlike Mystic Seaport, which is spread over 17 acres, this maritime museum is contained in a former 19th-century iron factory. It attracts half a million visitors a year with exhibits devoted to the maritime history and ecological life of Long Island Sound, plus more than 1,000 marine animals native to the area, from loggerhead turtles and jellyfish to sharks, harbor seals, and river otters (be sure to catch them at feeding time)—more than 259 species in all. A 110,000-gallon Open Ocean tank is home to bluefish, stingrays, sand tiger sharks. One of the few IMAX theaters in the country, and one of only two in the state; images on the six-story screen make you feel like you're in every scene, whether flying over the Grand Canyon or scaling Mount Everest. There are hands-on exhibits (including two touch pools) for children, and a working wooden-boat shop. To see seals and waterfowl in their natural environment, hop aboard the 40-foot research vessel *Oceanic* on one of the aquarium's wildly popular **Winter Creature Cruises** and help survey the harbor seal population; or from spring to fall, take one of the **Marine Life Study Cruises**, which give visitors a chance to study and test the waters of Norwalk Harbor like a real marine biologist (see *Boat Excursions*).

SoNo Switch Tower Museum (203-246-6958; www.westctnrhs.org), 77 Washington St., South Norwalk. Open May–Oct., Sat. and Sun. noon–5. Admission by

STEPPING STONES MUSEUM FOR CHILDREN ENTERTAINS AND EDUCATES YOUNG VISITORS WITH INTERACTIVE EXHIBITS.

Courtesy Coastal Fairfield County Convention & Visitors Bureau

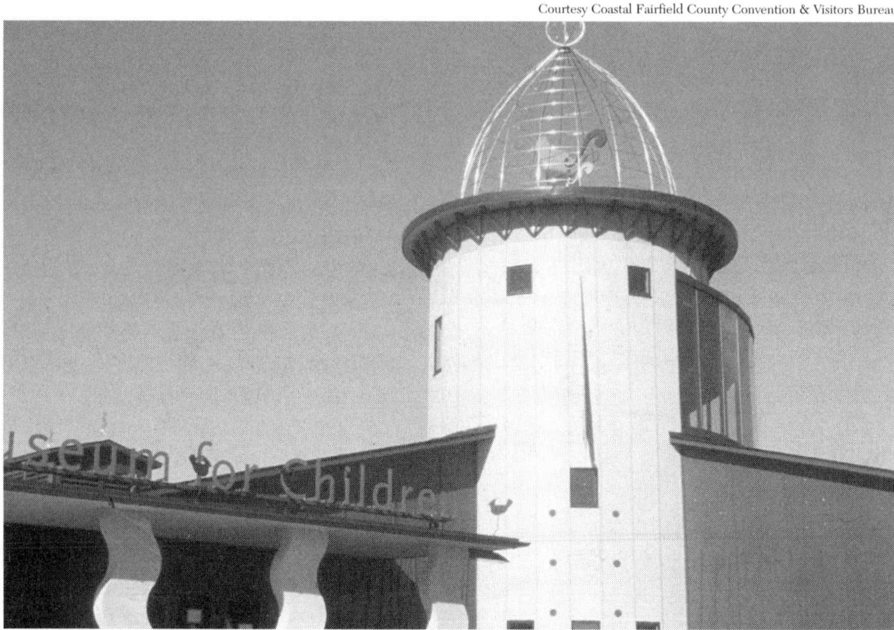

Weir Farm National Historic Site (203-834-1896; www.nps.gov/wefa), 735 Nod Hill Rd., Wilton. Burlingham House Visitor Center open Nov.–Apr., Thu.–Sun. 9:30–4; May–Oct., Wed.–Sun. 8:30–5; grounds open year-round daily from dawn to dusk. Free admission. Julian Alden Weir, one of the founders of the American school of impressionism, traded a still-life painting worth $650 in 1882 for some 153 acres of pristine land in Wilton and the Branchville section of Ridgefield, where he farmed and set up his studio. Not far from New York City, the humble farm, with its subtle, simple beauty and rolling countryside, attracted other landscape artists—Childe Hassam, John Twachtman, and John Singer Sargent among them—and Weir soon founded the famous School of Ten group of American impressionist painters. The public began enjoying Weir's sanctuary in 1967 when one of his daughters, Cora Weir Burlingham, donated 37 acres to The Nature Conservancy. Today the property and antique buildings are Connecticut's first site in the National Park System (established by an act of Congress in 1990) and one of only two in the country dedicated to art. At a mere 60 acres, it's no Yellowstone (which is roughly the size of Connecticut), but in the thickly settled Fairfield County suburbs, it's a bucolic, albeit diminutive, soul-soothing oasis. It embodies all that is wonderful about Connecticut's quintessential—and rapidly disappearing—rural landscape: sloping pastures laced with stone walls, and peaceful woodlands studded with dense stands of mountain laurel and rock outcroppings. Park rangers lead free tours of the grounds and studio; you can also pick up a brochure and hike the self-guided **Painting Sites Trail**, which leads to the fields, pond, and orchard where some of the greatest artists of Weir's time were inspired; you can compare prints of paintings with the actual views that they depict. See the studio built by Weir's artist daughter Dorothy and her sculptor-husband, Mahroni Young, in the 1930s. In a nod to its roots, the park still fosters creativity: Artists at work behind easels are a common sight around the grounds; a visiting-artist program allows artists to live and work here, and summertime art classes are offered for children.

donation. A unique railroad museum, housed at signal station 44, a restored 1896 switch tower. Visitors can operate the levers that controlled the signals and switches on the tracks for more than 100 years. Passenger and freight trains often rumble by on the main line connecting New York, New Haven, and Hartford. Railroad memorabilia and artifacts are on display; a gift shop sells souvenirs.

HISTORIC DISTRICT **National Hall Historic District**, on the west bank of the Saugatuck River, Westport. Wharves, factories, and warehouses have been restored on 3 scenic acres, once a bustling seaport where Captain Kidd put in with his treasure-laden ships. Local lore has it that the dashing pirate buried his ill-gotten gains on nearby Sherwood Island, now a state park. Take a walk along the shoreline boardwalk. Photograph a replica of the original 1894 horse-watering trough. The cornerstone of the restoration is The Inn at National Hall (see *Lodging*).

HISTORIC HOMES **Wheeler House** (203-222-1424; www.westporthistory.org), 25 Avery Place, Westport. Open year-round, Sat. and Sun. 11–3. Admission by donation. This Victorian Italianate villa (which actually started life in 1795 as an austere saltbox) is the home of the Westport Historical Society and features a 19th-century parlor, kitchen, and bedroom as they appeared in the elegant Victorian era. The striking cobblestone barn—the only barn in the state with an octagonal roof—is the keeper of Westport's heritage, from the days of the Native Americans to the present.

Lockwood-Mathews Mansion Museum (203-838-9799; www.lockwoodmathews mansion.org), Mathews Park, 295 West Ave., Norwalk. Open Apr.–Dec., Wed.–Sun. noon–4; closed Mon. and Tue. Guided tours on the hour, noon–3. Adults $8; seniors and students $5; children under 12 free. Group tours $4, by appointment. In 1864, long before the coal barons and railroad tycoons built their "summer cottages" in Newport, railroad investor and banker LeGrand Lockwood built a magnificent 50-room Second Empire–style mansion on the banks of the Norwalk River that for years was a showcase of American wealth and opulence. Under meticulous restoration for the past 20 years, the Victorian mansion, now a National Historic Landmark, is a wondrous display of the art of interior decoration, from parquet floors to frescoed walls, with ornate trim, a 42-foot-high octagonal rotunda, and a lovely plant-filled conservatory. When Paramount Pictures filmed the 2004 remake of *The Stepford Wives*, the dark comedy starring Nicole Kidman, the mansion served as the Stepford Men's Association, the secretive "boys' club" whose members included Stepford husbands played by Matthew Broderick, Christopher Walken, and Jon Lovitz. The studio assisted with renovations and added a group of massive reproduction Hudson River school landscape paintings that hang in the rotunda. Changing exhibits and special events; gift shop.

Wilton Historical Society and Heritage Museum (203-762-7257; www.wiltonhistorical.org), 224 Danbury Rd. (US 7), Wilton. Open Mon.–Thu. 9:30–4:30; call for special Sun. hours, and tour and event schedule. Adults $4; seniors $3; children free. Two classic 18th-century houses—the **Betts-Sturges-Blackmar House** and the **Sloan-Raymond-Fitch House**—feature 14 newly restored period rooms, including a Queen Anne–style parlor and colonial kitchen with massive fireplace, that show changes in family life, the economy, and style from 1740 to 1910. Details like period paint colors, handmade wallpapers, and reproduction fabrics and floor coverings lend striking authenticity and beautifully showcase a sampling of the museum's major collections: Norwalk-made stoneware, toys, dolls, dollhouses, costumes, and textiles. A 19th-century barn contains a working blacksmith shop and major tool exhibit. Special programs and events include significant antiques and crafts shows.

✷ To Do

BOAT EXCURSIONS ***G. W. Tyler*** **Lighthouse Ferry** (203-838-9444; www.seaport.org), Seaport Dock, between the Maritime Aquarium at Norwalk and the

Norwalk River Bridge, South Norwalk. Weekends Memorial Day–mid-June; daily mid-June–Labor Day; weekends in Sept. Adults $20; children 4–12, $12; 3 and under, $5. Reservations are a must on weekends. A 30-minute narrated trip aboard this 49-passenger, covered-deck ferryboat heads through Norwalk Harbor to **Sheffield Island**, one of the 11 barrier islands protecting the Connecticut shoreline along the Gold Coast. The 1868 stone lighthouse at the western tip of the rocky and windswept island was in service until 1902; today it's cared for by Norwalk Seaport Association volunteers, who maintain the lighthouse and grounds. Climb the steep stairs to the 60-foot-high tower, where views of the New York City skyline are visible on a clear day. Visitors can see rooms furnished in keeping with the 19th century, when light keepers and their families lived here. Afterward, wander the nature trail through the federal bird sanctuary or enjoy a picnic on the rocky shore.

Marine Life Study Cruises (203-852-0700; www.maritimeaquarium.org), Maritime Aquarium at Norwalk (see *Museums*), 10 North Water St., South Norwalk. Cruises on the research vessel *Oceanic* depart from the dock near the Aquarium's IMAX entrance Apr.–Oct.; contact the aquarium for a schedule and reservations, which are recommended. Collect marine life from the water's surface down to the bottom and get a firsthand look at some of Long Island Sound's vibrant animal communities. Aquarium educators demonstrate how to use real sampling techniques to collect fish, crabs, lobsters, and sea stars—along with occasional surprises. Dec.–Mar., the *Oceanic* embarks on **Winter Creature Cruises** to look for seals and waterfowl that migrate here from points north, and aquarium staff talk about the changes that take place on the Sound during the winter months. Dress warmly and bring binoculars.

BOATING **Norwalk Cove Marina** (203-838-2326), 48 Calf Pasture Beach Rd., Norwalk. Open year-round. Dry dock, repair shop, and supplies; 400 slips. Mini golf, arcade, and restaurant. The marina hosts an annual boat show in fall.

All Seasons Marine Works (203-838-9038), 167 Rowayton Ave., in the Rowayton section of Norwalk. Open year-round; full services.

Rex Marine Center (203-831-5234), 144 Water St., South Norwalk. Open year-round. Dry dock, full services, 676 slips. Within walking distance of historic South Norwalk.

Total Marine (203-838-3210), 160 Water St., is also within walking distance of SoNo. Open Apr.–Oct.

Short-term docking is available in Norwalk at **Veteran's Memorial Park** (203-854-7806) on Seaview Ave., and at

A SEASONAL FERRY TAKES VISITORS TO SHEFFIELD ISLAND, KNOWN FOR ITS A 19TH-CENTURY STONE LIGHTHOUSE THAT STANDS SENTINEL OVER NORWALK HARBOR.
Courtesy Coastal Fairfield County Convention & Visitors Bureau

the **Norwalk Visitor Docks** (203-849-8823) on Donohue Dr. A state boat launch is located on the east side of the Saugatuck River, off Compo Rd. in Westport. Call the **Norwalk Recreation and Parks Department** (203-854-7806) for locations of 18 offshore islands where you can fish, swim, picnic, or bird-watch.

FISHING ***My Bonnie* Charters** (203-866-6313; www.mybonniecharters.com), Village Creek, South Norwalk. Captain Sal Tardella takes up to six passengers on charter trips into Long Island Sound aboard a 25-foot fishing boat.

Westport Outfitters (203-831-8036; www.saltwater-flyfishing.com), Norwalk Cove Marina, 44 Calf Pasture Beach Rd., Norwalk. Arrange for a fishing trip around the Norwalk Islands, or stop by to pick up bait, tackle, charts, and other fishing necessities.

GOLF **Oak Hills Park Golf Course** (203-838-0303; www.oakhillsgc.com), 165 Fillow St., Norwalk. Open mid-Mar.–Nov. Par 71, 18 holes, 6,307 yards. Restaurant and pro shop.

HIKING **Lucius Pond Ordway–Devil's Den Preserve** (203-226-4991), 33 Pent Rd., Weston. Open daily sunrise to sunset. Free admission. Owned and maintained by The Nature Conservancy, this wooded oasis in the suburbs is named for local conservationist Katherine Ordway but is known locally simply as The Den. At 1,756 acres, it's the largest contiguous nature preserve in southwestern Connecticut, so naturally it attracts a lot of visitors; in fact, this is the most-visited Nature Conservancy property in Connecticut. A 21-mile network of well-marked trails and old woods roads lace through rugged terrain for hiking, birding, and cross-country skiing. Pick up a trail map at the parking lot kiosk. Hike by **Godfrey Pond**, an 18th-century millpond, to **Ambler Gorge**, a rocky ravine, and up to the **Great Ledge** for views of the Saugatuck Reservoir. Call for a schedule of guided hikes.

See also *Green Space.*

SAILING **Longshore Sailing School** (203-226-4646; www.longshoresailingschool.com), 260 South Compo Rd., Westport. Open

SOUTH NORWALK'S 19TH-CENTURY STOREFRONTS AND FACTORY BUILDINGS ARE NOW A HIP NEIGHBORHOOD OF BOUTIQUES AND BISTROS ON NORWALK HARBOR.

Courtesy Coastal Fairfield County Convention & Visitors Bureau

May–Sept. Sailing lessons for all skill levels; reservations required. Kayak and small-sailboat rentals available.

Norwalk Sailing School (203-852-1857; www.norwalksailingschool.org), Calf Pasture Beach Rd., East Norwalk. Private and group lessons for all skill levels; sailboat, Windsurfer, and sea kayak rentals are available, as are guided tours to the Norwalk Islands, an archipelago stretching from Stamford to Westport along the coastline. Call for reservations.

Sound Sailing Center (203-838-1110; www.soundsailingcenter.com), Norwalk Cove Marina, 54 Beach Rd., East Norwalk. Next to Calf Pasture Beach. Instruction for novices and rentals for experienced sailors, on 23- to 44-foot sailboats.

See also *Boat Excursions.*

SEA KAYAKING **Below Deck** (203-852-0011; www.coastalprovisions.com), 157 Rowayton Ave., in the Rowayton section of Norwalk. Kayak rentals, gear, and equipment for paddling and other water sports. Stop at the Rowayton Market for provisions before you venture out.

Kayak Adventure (203-852-7294; 888-454-0300; www.kayak-adventure.net), Norwalk. Open daily year-round. Guided tours and lessons, plus rentals for experienced paddlers and a full schedule of clinics, events, and trips.

The Small Boat Shop (203-854-5223; www.thesmallboatshop.com), 144 Water St., South Norwalk. May–Oct., weekends only. Day trips around the Norwalk Islands for beginning kayakers and experienced paddlers June–Sept. Instruction and equipment provided; bring lunch and water. Call for information and reservations. The shop also sells canoes, kayaks, rowing shells, and sailboats.

See also *Sailing.*

SWIMMING **Compo Beach** (203-341-5090), Compo Beach Rd., Westport. Open daily, sunrise to sunset. Parking fee $30 weekends, $15 weekdays, May–Sept. A pricey-yet-popular summertime spot, within an hour's drive of Manhattan. The 29-acre park has a long white sand beach, a playground, a boardwalk, a picnic area, playing fields, and a skate park.

Sherwood Island State Park (203-226-6983), Westport, Exit 18 off I-95. Open year-round, daily 8 AM–sunset. Seasonal parking fee on weekdays: residents $7, nonresidents $10; on weekends: $10 and $15. This is Connecticut's first state park, and of the state's three major beach parks along Long Island Sound it's closest to New York City. The gentle surf along the 1.5-mile-long strand is ideal for children. Indulge in their food service or bring a picnic basket. Tables and grills are set in groves of beachside trees. Visitors can also enjoy fishing, shellfishing, and hiking here. Staff members lead a variety of interpretive programs. On sizzling summer weekends, come early to make sure you can get in.

✷ Green Space

NATURE CENTERS ♿ **Earthplace: The Nature Discovery Center** (203-227-7253; www.earthplace.org), 10 Woodside Lane, Westport. Grounds open daily 7 AM–dusk. Nature center open Mon.–Sat. 9–5, Sun. 1–4; closed major holidays. Adults and children 12–17 $7; seniors and children 12 and under $5; free admission to grounds. Call or check the Web site for a schedule of nature programs. A

63-acre wooded retreat in the suburbs with nature trails, including one that is handicapped accessible. Outside are bird and butterfly gardens, and exhibits featuring owls, falcons, hawks, and other birds of prey. The center's brand-new exhibit hall features hands-on nature displays, wildlife dioramas, and a collection of resident snakes, owls, turtles, and other critters.

Woodcock Nature Center (203-762-7280; www.woodcocknaturecenter.org), 56 Deer Run Rd., Wilton. Grounds open daily, dawn to dusk; nature center open Mon.–Sat. 9:30–4; closed Sun. and holidays; closed weekends in summer. Free admission. A 149-acre nature preserve spread across Wilton and Ridgefield invites visitors to hike along four trails and on a swamp boardwalk across rich wetlands forested with maple, oak, and hickory. An Interpretive Center, with exhibits and a small store overlooking scenic Woodcock Pond, offers birding, lectures, and year-round natural-history and outdoor recreation programs, such as cross-country skiing clinics and geology lectures.

NATURE PRESERVE **Lucius Pond Ordway–Devil's Den Preserve** (203-226-4991), 33 Pent Rd., Weston. Open daily, sunrise to sunset. Regulars come to this Nature Conservancy–run 1,756-acre oasis for hiking, birding, and cross-country skiing. Conscientious birders can spot 145 species, especially around the preserve's streams and swamps; there are 23 species of mammals, too, including the red fox, the bobcat, and the now ubiquitous coyote, not to mention reptiles and salamanders. Gardeners delight in identifying myriad trees and wildflowers. Archaeologists have uncovered the site of prehistoric Native American encampments.

PARKS **Cranbury Park** (203-854-7806), Grumman Ave., Norwalk. Open year-round, daily 8–8. The parks department maintains 190 acres of parkland with walking and hiking trails, picnic groves, and even cross-country skiing when nature cooperates. The park was once the grounds of a private estate; picnicking is popular in the open fields surrounding the mansion.

Sherwood Island State Park (203-226-6983), Exit 18 off I-95, Westport. Open year-round, daily 8 AM–sunset. Seasonal parking fee on weekdays: residents $7, nonresidents $10; on weekends: $10 and $15. Not actually an island, but rather a spit of land stretching into Long Island Sound. It had been farmed since the 1600s (lastly by the Sherwood family) before it was acquired in 1917 by the state, which intended to establish a military base. At more than a mile long, it's the most spacious beach in Fairfield County. In all, 234 acres of beach, wetlands, woods, fields, and salt marsh offer swimming, fishing, biking, hiking, and birding. A brand-new nature center has display areas and classrooms; stop by for a park map or birding guide before exploring the adjacent nature trail. A 9/11 memorial—a lone cherry tree—sits at Sherwood Point in view of the New York City skyline on a clear day. The park's proximity to Westchester County, as well as the Bronx and Queens, means weekend crowds swell in summer; but winter is wonderfully serene.

✷ Lodging

INNS **The Inn at Longshore** (203-226-3316; www.innatlongshore.com), 260 Compo Rd. South, Westport 06880. A charming clapboard Victorian on expansive parklike grounds fronting Long Island Sound. It was a summer estate at the turn of the 20th century, then for a time an exclusive country club that entertained the likes of F. Scott Fitzgerald. Today it offers nine guest rooms and three suites; all have private bath. Anticipate warm New England–inspired decor and graciously comfortable surroundings that will entice you to take off your shoes and put your feet up. Guests have privileges at the town beach; there's also an outdoor pool, tennis, and golf. Splash has cutting-edge cuisine and choice water views (see *Eating Out*). $185 and up.

The Inn at National Hall (203-221-1351; 800-628-4255; www.innatnationalhall.com), 2 Post Rd. West, Westport 06880. In the National Hall historic district. You'd be hard-pressed to find grander surroundings in which to spend the night on the Gold Coast. Go for the history, and treat yourself to a night of opulence and elegance. The stately brick Italianate building dating from 1873 was, in succession, a bank, plumbing business, newspaper office, high school, and state police headquarters. It was rescued from the wrecking ball and converted with the utmost taste into what is hailed as a European manor house on the banks of the Saugatuck River. The 16 lavishly designed and furnished rooms and loft suites boast 18-foot-high ceilings, gold-leaf-stenciled walls, carved oak chandeliers, and Flemish oil paintings. Expect luxe linens, utter privacy, and gracious service. Continental breakfast. $355–900.

🐾 ✐ ♿ **The Westport Inn** (203-259-5236; reservations 800-446-8997; www.westportinn.com), 1595 Post Rd. East (US 1), Westport 06880. Close to everything, The Westport Inn appeals to a wide audience—families, couples, business travelers—looking for clean and comfy rooms and a friendly atmosphere. The 115 rooms and two suites have all the standard features: A fitness center, a sauna, an indoor pool, and a business center highlight the amenities. Coffee and cookies in the lobby, and evening wine receptions, are nice touches. **Spyglass Restaurant** is the inn's eclectic bistro. Continental breakfast. $169–199.

Silvermine Tavern (203-847-4558; 888-693-9967; www.silverminetavern.com), 194 Perry Ave., Norwalk 06850; Exit 40-A off the Merritt Parkway or Exit 15 off I-95. Easily the most welcoming inn in town, this 1785 hostel at the edge of a rushing waterfall is what you probably had in mind when you conjured up an image of a romantic country getaway. The old-fashioned sense of hospitality appeals to urbanites looking to leave the stresses of city life behind, just for a while, without traveling too far. Antiques in each of the 11 cozy rooms (one suite); all have private bath. Two of the rooms have porches overlooking the river, and there are working fireplaces in the parlor and dining room. Continental breakfast. Highly acclaimed restaurant (see *Dining Out*) and live jazz that draws musicians from far and wide. $95–210.

HOTELS 🐾 ✐ **Doubletree Hotel Norwalk** (203-853-3477; 800-222-8733), 789 Connecticut Ave., Norwalk 06854. Close to historic South Norwalk and the Maritime Aquarium. A major renovation in 2005 spiffed up the hotel's common areas and its 265 guest rooms. Amenities include a fitness center, an indoor pool, a business center, and **Sapphire's**, a restaurant serving American cuisine. $140 and up.

♿ **Norwalk Inn and Conference Center** (203-838-5531; www.norwalkinn.com), 99 East Ave., Norwalk 06851. The inn offers 72 rooms, including one suite with a Jacuzzi tub. Outside, there's a pool and barbecue pits; indoors, a restaurant and coffee shop, lounge, sauna, fitness center, and free WiFi. Continental breakfast. $139–169.

Main Avenue in Norwalk offers a variety of chain-hotel accommodations, including **Courtyard by Marriott Norwalk** (203-849-9111; 800-321-2211), 474 Main Ave.; **Four Points Hotel by Sheraton** (203-849-9828; 800-325-3535), 426 Main Ave.; **Homestead Studio Suites** (203-847-6888; 800-782-9473), 400 Main Ave.; and **Hilton Garden Inn** (203-523-4000; 800-445-8667), 560 Main Ave.

✷ Where to Eat

DINING OUT

In Westport

♿ **Acqua Ristorante** (203-222-8899; www.acquaofwestport.com), 43 Main St. Open Mon.–Sat. for lunch and dinner; closed Sun. A chic downtown restaurant with surroundings reminiscent of a Tuscan villa, from the hand-painted wall murals and graceful arches to the cherub-clad frescoed ceiling and elegant white-linen decor. The view of the Saugatuck River from the upstairs dining room makes it clear how the restaurant got its name. The Mediterranean menu features French and Italian dishes like whole roasted fish, veal Milanese, and dressed-up pizzas, as well as American classics like Black Angus steak and Maryland crabcakes. Berry crisp with lavender-mint sauce, and a variety of soufflés for dessert. Chef Christian Bertrand, who comes to Westport by way of New York's Lutece, used to cook for French president Charles de Gaulle. $16–38.

Blue Lemon (203-226-2647; www.bluelemonrestaurant.com), Sconset Square, 15 Myrtle Ave. Open for lunch Mon.–Sat.; dinner daily. Reservations recommended. In summer, the flower-clad porch hints at the romantic atmosphere inside, where plush banquettes fill a dining room whose lemony color scheme is a nod to the restaurant's name. The modern American menu has Mediterranean touches, especially from Italy and Spain, in dishes that are artfully presented and expertly prepared. Starters like grilled baby squid with a ginger-lime vinaigrette, and foie gras with butternut squash chutney, lead to equally inventive entrées. Seared Atlantic salmon comes atop braised lentils and watercress; diver scallops are paired with polenta, and ginger spinach with pomegranate vinaigrette; and roast duck is accompanied by wild rice and a black cherry sauce. $20–26.

♿ **Via Sforza** (203-454-4444; www.cantinasforza.com), 243 Post Rd. West (US 1). Open for lunch Mon.–Sat.; dinner daily. Italian-born Dino Sforza and his family are at the helm of this charming dining room that's reminiscent of an elegant Tuscan farmhouse. Here, fine dining has a warm and friendly feel. Traditional Italian dishes (seafood, chicken, veal) followed by equally classic desserts (tiramisu, biscotti, gelato). A massive wood-burning pizza oven turns out thin-crust pies. $21–32.

♿ **Conte's Market & Grill** (203-226-3474; www.contesmarketandgrill.com), 540 Riverside Ave. Open for lunch Tue.–Fri.; dinner Tue.–Sun.; closed Mon. The menu at this popular seafood restaurant depends on what's available, fresh, and best. One day it may feature snapper and skate, the next, lobster, salmon, and scallops. The adjacent fish market sells fillets and shellfish. On weekends, there's live music in the bar, which is a popular see-and-be-seen spot on Friday and Saturday nights. Oysters are the stars of the raw bar. $21–34.

♿ **DaPietro's** (203-454-1213; www.dapietros.com), 36 Riverside Ave. Dinner Mon.–Sat.; closed Sun. Reservations required. For truly authentic cuisine from northern Italy and southern France, step through the door of this tiny storefront into a romantic, elegant space with bistro-like charm. Chef-owner Pietro Scotti's award-winning menu includes a variety of veal dishes, game in-season, duck, and roast rack of lamb that ranks with the best on the Gold Coast. The meatballs—his grandmother's recipe—are made with beef, pork, raisins, and pine nuts. $19–32.

The Dressing Room (203-226-1114; www.dressingroomhomegrown.com), 27 Powers Court, behind the Westport Country Playhouse. Open for lunch Wed.–Sun.; dinner Tue.–Sun.; closed Mon. Reservations are recommended. Before his death in 2008, longtime Westport resident and playhouse benefactor Paul Newman teamed up with star chef Michel Nischan to debut what they called their "homegrown restaurant." The seasonal menu spotlights high quality, mostly organic ingredients from local and regional farms, which might mean heirloom squash, fresh Connecticut oysters, pasture-raised lamb, or just-picked apples. The dining room is a rustic timber-and-fieldstone space, oft packed with theatergoers and health-conscious locals. $25–34.

♿ **Positano's** (203-454-4922; www.positanoswestport.com), 233 Hills Point Rd. Open for lunch daily; dinner Mon.–Sat. Take a flight to the coast of Italy without leaving Fairfield County. A romantic Italian restaurant on Long Island Sound combines lovely water views with hand-painted murals depicting romantic coastal scenes. Dishes are familiar, delicious, and generously portioned: calamari, seafood, game, veal. End with homemade classic desserts like tiramisu, cheesecake, and crème brûlée, or a supercharged double espresso. $21–32.

The Red Barn (203-222-9549; www.redbarnrestaurant.com), 292 Wilton Rd. (CT 33). Open daily for lunch and dinner; brunch on Sat. and Sun. A longtime favorite just off the Merritt Parkway (Exit 41), and one of the top spots in Connecticut for traditional American cuisine for more than half a century. The rustic interior and pretty grounds make this a popular special-occasion destination. $10–33.

♿ **Seminara's Ristorante Italiano** (203-222-8955; www.seminarasrestaurant.com), 256 Post Rd. East. Open for lunch Tue.–Fri.; dinner Tue.–Sun.; closed Mon. Reservations suggested. Enjoy upscale Italian regional cuisine with flavors of the Middle East in elegant surroundings. The *zuppa di pesce*, an enticing mélange of fresh fish in red or white sauce, is a must. The location, within walking distance of the Westport Country Playhouse, makes this perfect for pretheater dining. $19–32.

Tavern on Main (203-221-7222; www.tavernonmain.com), 146 Main St. Open daily for lunch and dinner. Reservations suggested. Innovative takes on traditional Yankee fare in an elegant 1810 sea captain's home with low-beamed ceilings, dark wood floors, and a double-sided fireplace. Start with the tavern's award-winning New England clam chowder or wild mushroom ravioli with white truffle butter, then try the Wellfleet oysters, or the Parmesan and herb crusted lamb chops with vegetable ratatouille. Leave room for desserts like cappuccino bread pudding and maple sugar crème brûlée. *Bon Appétit* magazine dubbed this place one of "America's Great Neighborhood Restaurants." $22–33.

♿ **Three Bears Restaurant** (203-227-7219; www.threebearsrestaurant.com), 333 Wilton Rd. (CT 33), just north of the Merritt Parkway. Open for lunch Tue.–Sat.; dinner Tue.–Sun.; Sun. brunch; closed Mon. Named for the classic children's tale, this former stagecoach stop now has six dining rooms filled with Tiffany lamps and a priceless collection of antique glass, a charming setting for award-winning contemporary American cuisine that garners rave reviews from locals and critics. Chef Steve Vazzano's seasonal menu includes many seafood, pasta, and game choices. You might start with pan-fried zucchini blossoms and continue to lemon sole stuffed with three-onion whipped potatoes and seared spinach, or roast veal chops accompanied by a caramelized onion beggar's purse with a celery-root puree. Desserts come highly recommended. $18–30.

♿ **Zest** (203-226-9378; www.zestcafeandrestaurant.com), 8 Church Lane. Open daily for breakfast, lunch, and dinner. This lively and often noisy epicurean hot spot, tucked away in a basement, couldn't have been branded with a better name. Chef Pietro Scotti, who also owns DaPietro's (see above), turns out authentic Italian cuisine that's "presented with artistic panache." The decor is stylish, too, but gourmands come for the food, which is prepared with fresh produce and imported Italian ingredients. The risotto is a must-try on the ambitious menu of nearly two dozen entrées. $15–30.

In Norwalk and South Norwalk

♿ **Barcelona Restaurant & Wine Bar** (203-899-0088; www.barcelonawinebar.com), 63 North Main St., South Norwalk. Additional locations in Greenwich (203-983-6400); Fairfield (203-255-0800); New Haven (203-848-3000); and West Hartford (860-218-2100). Open daily for dinner. Diners in this chic SoNo enclave come for the adventurous Spanish-inspired tapas, from a simple medley of house-cured olives, to risotto cakes stuffed with fresh mozzarella, or crispy calamari with roasted tomato aioli. Full entrées run the gamut from steaks to game to fish, all with a Mediterranean touch—ample garlic and olive oil. A young, lively crowd packs the inviting courtyard patio and the wine bar. Tapas $4–14; dinner entrées $20–27.

Bacchus (203-855-9469; www.bacchussono.com), 120 Washington St., South Norwalk. Open Tue.–Sat. for lunch and dinner; closed Sun. and Mon. A gem of a hideaway named for the mythological Roman god of wine, thus making it a favorite for romantic dining. The changing menu of Tuscan-inspired cuisine is par excellence. Ostrich or buffalo might appear alongside the signature beet salad or fried artichoke hearts. Servers will help you pair each dish with the ideal glass of wine. Live jazz. $22–45.

♿ **Brasserie Molliere** (203-855-7660), 15 North Main St., South Norwalk. Open for lunch Mon.–Fri.; Sun. brunch; dinner daily. This new hot spot is tucked away from the frenetic pace of ultrachic Washington Street. A long zinc bar and Parisian posters on the walls lend an authentic French bistro feel, as does the menu of contemporary and classic French dishes (think pâté, onion soup, foie gras, cassoulet, soufflés). Seafood is a specialty; mussels alone are prepared eight ways. $23–33.

Habana (203-852-9790; www.habanasono.com), 70 North Main St., South Norwalk. Open daily for dinner. SoNo meets South Beach in this energetic spot, where the menu is your passport to Brazil, Mexico, Peru, and, of course, Cuba. You can expect a trendy crowd filling the tropical and sensual space (ceiling fans, banana trees, island music) and noshing on cutting-edge dishes like empanadas stuffed with chorizo or minced duck. $18–30.

♿ **Match** (203-852-1088; www.matchsono.com), 98 Washington St., South Norwalk. Open daily for dinner. Reservations suggested. The aptly named Match is as hot a restaurant as they come in SoNo. The cavernous wood-burning oven turns out pizza with such imaginative toppings as roasted potato and garlic with rosemary and caramelized onion; or black truffles, goat cheese, and truffle oil. If pizza doesn't suit you, start with seared wasabi-rubbed tuna, a house specialty; then try the pan-roasted salmon with caramelized bananas and a mango-papaya relish, or the juicy wood-oven-roasted organic chicken. After dinner, flit across the street to **The Loft**, their upscale lounge whose silky chocolate martini (Godiva Liqueur, vodka, white crème de cacao) is a Food Network award winner. $22–39.

Meigas (203-866-8800; www.meigasrestaurant.com), 10 Wall St., Norwalk. Open for lunch Tue.–Fri.; dinner Tue.–Sun.; closed Mon. *Meigas* means "sorceresses" in Galician, and loyal patrons of Spanish haute cuisine will tell you there's magic going on in the kitchen. This is the sister restaurant to New Haven's wildly popular Ibiza, handsomely outfitted in wood, exposed brick, and vibrant Spanish artwork. The ever-changing contemporary menu reinterprets traditional Spanish recipes with gusto. Start with gazpacho or one of the creative tapas, artfully served on ceramic spoons. Most entrées emphasize fish; others might include grilled duck breast, or short ribs braised in ginger and red wine. Sunday features paella in half a dozen delicious renditions, studded with seafood or chorizo, rabbit or snails. *Wine Spectator*, the *New York Times*, and *Esquire* magazine have all given rave reviews. $24–36.

Ocean Drive (203-855-1665; www.oceandrivesono.com), 128 Washington St., South Norwalk. Open daily for dinner. Reservations recommended. The perfect name for what's arguably the best and freshest seafood on Washington Street, if not in Fairfield County. The menu offers "rambunctious seafood"—that is, ambitiously crafted and stunningly presented. For an American-fusion twist, look no farther than the Thai bouillabaisse, the oyster bar's fresh-from-the-ocean shellfish, or the sushi, sashimi, and specialty rolls.

COMMERCIAL FISHING BOATS, PLEASURE CRAFT, AND SEA KAYAKS PASS THROUGH NORWALK HARBOR ON THEIR WAY TO LONG ISLAND SOUND AND BEYOND.

Courtesy Coastal Fairfield County Convention & Visitors Bureau

The dining room is sleek and inviting: Check out the magnificent 7-foot-long glass sculpture resplendent in pink and blue ocean hues. For the ultimate in privacy, request one of the curtained booths. $20–35.

♿ **Pasta Nostra Restaurant** (203-854-9700; www.pastanostra.com), 116 Washington St., South Norwalk. Open for dinner only, Wed.–Sat. Reservations essential. In a neighborhood where restaurants come and go with alarming frequency, it's no small feat that this SoNo trattoria has reigned supreme for 20 years. A made-from-scratch menu emphasizes traditional food—*bàccala al forno, pasta con sarde*—and changes weekly. $21–35.

♿ **The Restaurant at Rowayton Seafood** (203-866-4488; www.rowayton seafood.com), 89 Rowayton Ave., in the Rowayton section of Norwalk. Open for lunch and dinner daily; Sun. brunch. A hidden gem in a quiet village of Norwalk, popular with well-dressed suburbanites and yachters who can dock and dine here. From the enclosed waterfront dining room, you can watch boats ply to and from Long Island Sound on the Five Mile River as you feast on some of the best seafood on the shoreline. Fresh fish is prepared with an expert hand yet kept simple. Depending on your inclinations, lunch can go from nice to fancy—from chopped Cobb salad to steamed Maine lobster. Dinner gets even more swank; think pecan-crusted brook trout with roasted squash and balsamic glaze, or grilled Atlantic king salmon with sweet potato and pear cream. $25–45.

Silvermine Tavern (203-847-4558; www.silverminetavern.com), 194 Perry Ave., Norwalk. Open for lunch Wed.–Sat.; dinner Wed.–Sun.; Sun. brunch; closed Mon. and Tue. Reservations are a must. In a town chock-full of super-chic bistros, it's reassuring to find this classic New England tavern with creaky wide floorboards, slanted beamed ceilings, antiques, and fireplaces. A long-running favorite for chicken potpie, herb-crusted salmon, roast duckling, crab-stuffed fillet of sole, or osso buco. Dine on the tree-shaded terrace overlooking the waterfall and duck pond in warm weather. Take care—don't fill up on the inn's secret-recipe signature honey buns. Live jazz on the weekends; call for a schedule. The tavern runs a country store across the street, selling New England foods and gifts; a collection of antique tools and Currier and Ives prints are on display. Spend the night in one of 11 guest rooms (see *Lodging*). $22–34.

Elsewhere

The Schoolhouse at Cannondale (203-834-9816; www.schoolhouseat cannondale.com) 34 Cannon Rd., Wilton. Open for lunch and dinner Wed.–Sat.; Sun. brunch; closed Mon. and Tue. Reservations are recommended. This cozy and sophisticated jewel box of an eatery, housed in an 1872 schoolhouse on the Norwalk River, is winning raves for its inventive farm-fresh cuisine. Chef-owner Tim LaBant turns out dishes as good as any in a fancy dining room. His menu offers a short selection of season-based starters, entrées, and desserts, but what a selection! You might start with seared Hudson Valley foie gras with pomegranate-truffle honey; then pork loin stuffed with sage, dried cherries, and candied pecans; ending with strawberry napoleon with rhubarb sorbet. $28–40.

Cobb's Mill Inn (203-227-7221; www.cobbsmillinn.com), 12 Old Mill Rd. (CT 57), Weston. Lunch and dinner daily; brunch on Sun. Delightfully off the beaten path—but not too far off—this rambling 200-year-old colonial gristmill and lumber mill overlooks a dramatic Saugatuck River waterfall. Its nine dining rooms are decidedly romantic. A revitalized American Continental menu has such classics as French onion soup gratiné, Long Island duckling, and escargots. Award-winning wine list. $27–42.

Carl Anthony Trattoria (203-268-8486; www.carlanthonytrattoria.com), 477 Main St., in Clocktower Square, Monroe. Open for lunch Tue.–Sat.; dinner daily. This local pizza joint turned contemporary trattoria serving upscale Italian cuisine enjoys best-kept-secret status, and it's worth the trip to find it. Splendid renderings of upscale Italian cuisine, from the wood-roasted wild salmon with an olive raisin rub atop whipped parsnips to the stalwart chicken parmigiana. Desserts are traditional: tiramisu, crème brûlée, and bread pudding. $21–36.

EATING OUT

In Westport

Bobby Q's Barbeque & Grill (203-454-7800; www.bobbyqsrestaurant.com), 42 Main St. Open daily for lunch and dinner. The big draw here is barbecue, of course, and lots of it. Beef brisket, pulled pork, and spice-rubbed pork ribs, slow cooked in a hickory-wood-fired pit-oven smoker. Accompaniments are straight out of the South: grits, jicama slaw, and roasted sweet potato salad. Seafood choices include spicy Creole-style shrimp; wraps, burgers, and salads accommodate small appetites. Their most famous dessert is the fried Twinkie, battered, fried, and drizzled with raspberry sauce. Live music on weekends. $14–27.

Mario's Place (203-226-0308), 36 Railroad Place, in the Saugatuck section of Westport. Open for lunch and dinner. In a town filled with pricey restaurants, this convivial and reasonably priced spot is a refreshing change of pace. Commuters coming off Metro-North and Amtrak trains pack this casual, unpretentious eatery for traditional Italian cuisine as well as steaks, seafood, and chops, especially the prime rib. $14–25.

Sakura (203-222-0802; www.sakurarestaurant.com), 680 Post Rd. (US 1). Lunch Mon.–Fri.; dinner daily. Reservations suggested. Watch the chef deftly cook your dinner on the hibachi, or relax on tatami while nibbling on sushi. More than 20 kinds of sushi and sashimi, and 11 different delicately prepared rolls; try the outstanding snow crab and asparagus roll. Other standards include tempura, teriyaki, and *nabe* (Japanese pot-cooked dinners). Wall screens and painted murals lend a peaceful aesthetic to a restaurant whose name translates from the Japanese as "flowering cherry tree." $15–25.

Splash Restaurant & Bar (203-454-7798), at the Inn at Longshore, 260 South Compo Rd. Open for lunch and dinner. Location, location, location. This vibrant and contemporary restaurant and bar tucked into a corner of the historic inn is one of the top alfresco dining spots around. Even the Food Network gave a nod to the choice Long Island Sound locale. An up-to-the-minute modern menu includes many seafood options. Come early to drink in the water view; stay late for the lively bar scene. Asian-influenced Amerian cuisine. $15–25.

Viva Zapata (203-227-8226; www.vivazapata.com), 530 Riverside Ave. Open for lunch Mon.–Sat.; dinner daily. Since 1969, Viva Zapata has been the go-to place for authentic Mexican fare and killer frozen drinks. Nearly a dozen varieties of nachos come with homemade refried beans; margaritas are blended with fresh-squeezed lime juice. The bar and outdoor patio are quite lively. $8–16.

In Norwalk and South Norwalk

The Brewhouse Restaurant (203-853-9110; www.sonobrewhouse.com), 13 Marshall St., South Norwalk. Open for lunch and dinner daily; Sun. brunch. Reservations suggested. This 1920s factory was once home to SoNo's own microbrewery, the New England Brewing Company. The brewery moved to bigger digs, but the menu of microbrewed bottles and drafts—including New England Brewing Company's own Atlantic Amber—is impressive. There's seating inside and out, and a casual pub-like atmosphere with decor collected from breweries around New England. It's just half a block up from the Maritime Aquarium, making this a popular stop for hungry families. The kitchen churns out beer-steamed mussels, fish-and-chips, baby back ribs, fresh seafood, and German specialties. $14–24.

Dry Dock Café (203-847-1333), 215 Main St., Norwalk. A convivial local spot for more than 35 years, with bar fare encompassing nachos and chili, pizza and burgers. The bar and dining room are perpetually full of regulars.

Kazu (203-866-7492; www.kazusono.com), 64 North Main St., South Norwalk. Open for lunch Mon.–Fri.; dinner daily. This stylish yet casual Asian eatery next to the SoNo Cinema attracts a young, hip clientele as well as lavish accolades. Sushi, sashimi, and bento boxes are among the favorites. $15–24.

The Lime (203-846-9240; www.limerestaurant.com), 168 Main Ave. (CT 123), Norwalk. Open daily. Enthusiasts of vegetarian cooking should run, not walk, to this modest storefront café. The menu of made-from-scratch dishes, which includes meat options, has had a loyal following for 30 years. Where else can you can get a New York strip *and* soy-carrot loaf? $14–22.

Burger Bar & Bistro (203-853-2037; www.burgerbarsono.com), 58 North Main St., South Norwalk. The cow theme may be a tad cutesy for some tastes, but it's a fun and casual spot for hand-cut fries and organic beef burgers with creative toppings such as goat cheese, pancetta, fried egg, and chorizo. $7–17.

SoNo Seaport Seafood (203-854-9483; www.sonoseaportseafood.com), 100 Water St., South Norwalk. Open daily for lunch and dinner; fish market open daily. For super-fresh seafood, it doesn't get any better than a restaurant that has its own fishing fleet. This fish market turned seafood restaurant boasts a prime location right on Norwalk Harbor. In warm weather, the outdoor tables are SoNo's best place for a relaxing, alfresco harborfront lunch of bay scallops, swordfish, shrimp, and other fresh catches. $12–20.

Elsewhere

Georgetown Saloon (203-544-8003; www.georgetownsaloon.com), 8 Main St., at the junction of CT 57 and CT 107, in the Georgetown section of Wilton. Open daily for lunch and dinner; Sun. brunch. A casual western-style bar and restaurant, complete with knotty-pine walls hung with rifles and powder horns. Regulars come here for the steaks, barbecue, and Mexican specialties, as well as the live blues, country, and acoustic music. New: bluegrass open-mike nights on Wednesday. $10–28.

The Lunch Box (203-227-4808), 190 Weston Rd., in the Weston Shopping Center, Weston. A pair of former grade school teachers serve homey diner fare (pizza, fried chicken, ice cream) out of this popular eatery. They recently expanded, adding freshly made doughnuts and crullers to the menu.

SNACKS

In Westport

♿ **Balducci's** (203-254-5200; www.balduccis.com), 1385 Post Rd. East (US 1). An upscale specialty-food store (formerly Hay Day) with satellites in Greenwich (203-637-7600) and Ridgefield (203-431-4400). Open Mon.–Sat. 8–8; Sun. 8–7. Full meals, soups, salads, and baked goods to take home or eat here. While the big sellers are European-style artisan breads and desserts like triple chocolate mousse cake, the grilled-lamb burgers and organic horseradish-encrusted salmon are perfect for dinner.

Chef's Table (203-226-3663), 44 Church Lane, and 1035 Post Rd. East (US 1) (203-454-2433). Open Mon.–Sat.; closed Sun. The motto of this humming take-out spot is "Fine food fast," and its menu emphasizes healthy eating. An ever-changing menu features creative soups (balsamic lentil), gourmet salads (tomato and roasted eggplant), and hearty sandwiches (barbecue pulled pork and cheddar on brioche).

Gold's Delicatessen (203-227-0101), 421 Post Rd. East (US 1). Open daily 8–6. This authentic Jewish-style deli has been a neighborhood icon since 1959. Gold's delivers knishes, chicken soup with matzo balls, pastrami, corned beef, and unbeatable New York cheesecake. Seat yourself at the back of the store—you're likely to rub elbows with some very loyal patrons.

In Norwalk and South Norwalk

Jeff's Cuisine (203-852-0041; www.jeffscuisine.com), 54 North Main St., Norwalk. Open for lunch and dinner Tue.–Sun.; closed Mon. Chef-owner Jeff Esaw cooks up generously portioned down-home southern-style favorites in a homey storefront space. Dishes are straight out of his South Carolina childhood: fried chicken, slow-cooked barbecued pulled pork, jambalaya, corn bread, ribs (Kansas City– or Memphis-style) with tangy barbecue sauce or rubbed with earthy spices. Peach cobbler for dessert.

Rowayton Market (203-852-0011), 157 Rowayton Ave., in the Rowayton section of Norwalk. Open daily 7–7. An old-fashioned neighborhood market since 1753, with a back porch overlooking the Five Mile River; there's even a dock in case you arrive by boat. Groceries and gourmet delicacies include artisan cheeses, an olive bar, freshly prepared specialty foods, and creative sandwiches. Pick up lunch to take on a kayak excursion.

♿ **Swanky Frank's** (203-838-8969), 182 Connecticut Ave., Norwalk. Open daily 11–6. Famous since the 1940s for its grilled dogs, cheese steak, and hand-cut fries. Popular among devotees of Formica countertops, vinyl stools, and other staples of the traditional American roadside diner.

SoNo Baking Co. (203-847-7666; www.sonobaking.com), 101 South Water St., South Norwalk. Open Mon.–Sat. 7–6 for breakfast and lunch; Sun. 7–5 for brunch. Food-savvy locals flock to this culinary rave for all-natural hearth-baked breads, European-style pastries, and cakes that put Grandma's to shame. Fans of domestic doyenne Martha Stewart take note: This bakery and café was opened in 2005 by John Barricelli, senior food editor of *Martha Stewart Living*, and Margot Olshan, chef at Martha Stewart Living Omnimedia's Westport studios. The duo also appear on the Stewart-produced PBS television show *Everyday Food.* In addition to seasonal favorites like bite-sized petits fours, panettone, and stollen around the December holidays (they go fast), there are a dozen different artisanal breads available every day, including the house sourdough and potato rosemary. Be sure to get here early for the handmade chocolate bread, made only on Sunday.

SoNo Caffeine: Coffee & Chocolate Lounge (203-857-4224), 133 Washington St., South Norwalk. Open daily for breakfast, lunch, and dinner. A trendy, be-all-things coffee shop, with breakfast pastries, sandwiches, and soups; an espresso bar; live jazz, folk, cabaret, and blues; and evening snacks. The menu is as eclectic as the decor: a comfy array of mix-and-match chairs, tables, and sofas; a 1970s-era disco ball; and chandeliers. Most of the funky assortment of antiques and collectibles is for sale. Chocolate caramel turtles and decadent truffles are handmade on the premises.

In Wilton

Café Cogolulu (866-421-1366), 991 Danbury Rd. (US 7). Creamy Italian gelato is richer and smoother than American ice cream because it contains less air, but it has half the butterfat! Chocolate, hazelnut, plum, kiwi, and rum-raisin are among the dozen or so flavors available every day. Also on the menu: pastries and espresso in the morning, panini for lunch, to-go Italian dishes for dinner.

Dexter's Dog House (203-788-6831), 713 Danbury Rd. (US 7). A drive-in hot dog joint where the dogs come topped with Kuhn's chili sauce. Hamburgers, too.

✷ Entertainment

MUSIC AND THEATER **Levitt Pavilion for the Performing Arts** (203-221-2153; www.levittpavilion.com), South Compo Rd. (behind the Westport Public Library), Westport. A free summer festival staged in a landscaped open-air amphitheater by the Saugatuck River. Jazz, classical, cabaret, big band, blues, and rock—more than 50 events in all—draw big crowds; bring a picnic blanket or lawn chair. Check the schedule for special ticketed events.

Westport Country Playhouse (203-227-4177; www.westportplayhouse.org), 25 Powers Court, next to Winslow Park, Westport. If you take in one show in Connecticut, let it be here. Since the playhouse was founded in 1931 as a venue for summer stock, more than 700 productions have attracted a who's who of Broadway and the big screen to its stage. Originally a 19th-century tannery, the playhouse has also served as a cow barn. Joanne Woodward and the late Paul Newman, who moved to Westport in the 1960s, had been very active in the playhouse, of which she was co–artistic director until early 2009. Newman starred in *Our Town* in 2003. Westport's landmark cultural center received an $18 million face-lift for its 75th season in 2005, becoming sleeker and more state-of-the-art but still loaded with country charm. Dressing Room, the playhouse's new gourmet restaurant helmed by star chef Michel Nischan, is one of the state's hottest tables (see *Dining Out*).

The **Fairfield Orchestra** and the **Norwalk Symphony Orchestra** (203-866-4100; www.norwalksymphony.org) are two outstanding orchestras that perform in the acoustically renowned auditorium attached to the **Norwalk Concert Hall** (203-854-7746), 125 East Ave. (in City Hall), Norwalk. In addition to their own performances, they host visiting musical groups and guest soloists.

Shakespeare on the Sound (203-299-1300), Pinkney Park, 177 Rowayton Ave., Rowayton. In a park on the banks of the Five Mile River. Spread a picnic blanket on the ground and enjoy free open-air professional productions of Shakespeare's plays on summer nights.

The Wilton Playshop (203-762-7629; www.wiltonplayshop.org), 15 Lovers Lane (CT 33 and 106), Wilton. Since 1937, this community theater group has staged musicals, dramas, mysteries, and comedies. Performances Nov.–May; call for a schedule.

✷ Selective Shopping

In Westport

Balducci's (203-254-5200), 1385 Post Rd. East (US 1). Every specialty-food item imaginable, plus an impressive selection of fresh produce and herbs. A popular spot for gourmet take-out lunch and dinner. Other locations along the shoreline.

Dovecote (203-222-7500; 866-999-2241; www.dovecote-westport.com), 56 Post Rd. East (US 1). Open daily. Sleek and stylish home furnishings, Parisian antiques, 19th- and 20th-century accessories and furniture.

Downtown Westport. Main Street is lined with hip stores, from Gap to J.Crew and other high-end national chains (think Brooks Brothers and Tiffany & Co. Also look for chic boutiques, antiques shops, and eateries.

Wish List (203-221-7700; www.shopwishlist.com), 606 Post Rd. East, Westport. Trendy teen fashions attract hordes of teenage girls to the likes of Juicy Couture, Michael Stars, 7 For All Mankind. Quirky accessories, even candy. Other locations in Greenwich, Darien, and New Haven.

In Wilton

Cannondale Village (203-762-2233), 30 Cannon Rd., in the Cannondale section of Wilton, off US 7. Open Tue.–Sun. 11–5; closed Mon. A small collection of restored pre–Civil War buildings offering antiques, collectibles, crafts, and gourmet food in an old New England schoolhouse.

The New England Historical Connection (203-761-8646; 800-647-5719), 300 Danbury Rd., at the junction of US 7 and CT 33. Open daily. A shop known for its handcrafted reproductions of 18th-century American country furniture and home accessories made by a variety of artisans and craftspeople. The changing inventory might feature dining tables, sets of chairs, chests of drawers, beds, and highboys. Home accessories include prints, quilts, pottery, and reproduction sconces and chandeliers.

Open Book Shop (203-834-2028; www.wiltonopenbook.com), 5 River Rd. Open daily. This popular local bookstore has been in town since the 1930s. There are more than 12,000 titles, including many children's books, as well as a fun selection of gifts and toys.

In Norwalk and South Norwalk

Stew Leonard's Dairy Store (203-

SONO'S WASHINGTON STREET IS PACKED CHEEK BY JOWL WITH TRENDY SHOPS, HIP EATERIES, AND LIVELY BARS.

Courtesy Coastal Fairfield County Convention & Visitors Bureau

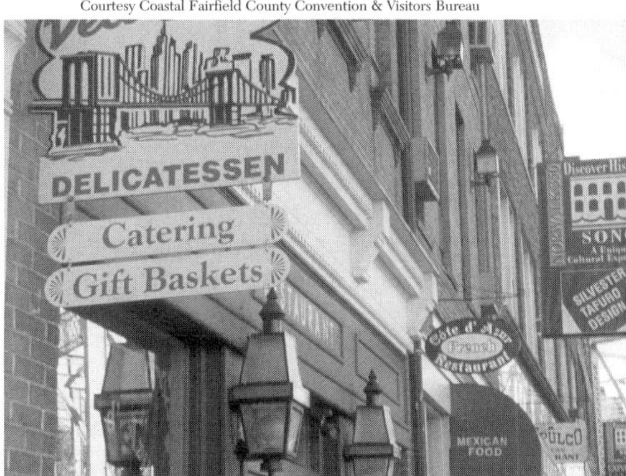

847-7214; www.stewleonards.com), 100 Westport Ave. (US 1), Norwalk. A dairy store in a guidebook? A fair question. What started out as a small dairy operation in the 1920s has evolved into a grocery amusement park. Fresh foods are made right in front of the customer, and the world's only in-store dairy plant comes complete with animated cows, singing farm animals, and costumed characters. The 3-ton granite rock perched at each store's entrance proclaims that the customer is king. Sister stores in Danbury and Newington are just as mobbed: each store attracts about 100,000 customers a week!

A Touch of New England (203-840-1911), 99 New Canaan Ave. (CT 123), Norwalk. Open daily. A store full of Connecticut souvenirs and products and crafts made in New England, from handblown glass to pewter. Toys and quilts are sold in the shop, which also carries candles, regional specialty foods, and homemade gelato.

Pymander (203-854-5596; www.pymanderbooks.com), 37 Wall St. The Egyptian name of this New Age bookshop translates as "messenger of the gods." Books include self-help, metaphysical, and recovery titles; gifts run the gamut from CDs and jewelry to gemstones and singing bowls. Ask about author signings and book discussions.

Chocopologie (203-838-3131; www.chocopologie.com), 125 South Main St., South Norwalk. A chocolate shop and café where you can watch chocolates being made through the kitchen's glass walls. These are treats for sophisticated tastes, with gourmet flavors such as hot chili, peppercorn, and rosewater.

✐ **Sweet Rexie's** (203-853-2513; www.sweetrexies.com), 136 Washington St., South Norwalk. In addition to more than 200 kinds of bulk candy (including nostalgic favorites like gummi alligators, Good & Plenty, Bit-O-Honey, and Bazooka bubble gum), owner Nanci Lewis stocks art, books, toys, jewelry, and other quirky and curious gifts.

ANTIQUES **L'Antiquaire** (203-454-2750; www.lantiquaireweb.com), 18 Post Rd. West (US 1), Westport. The specialties here are 18th- and 19th-century French and Continental furniture, art, and home accessories.

Cannondale Antiques (203-762-0244; www.cannondaleantiques.com), 26 Cannon Rd., in Cannondale Village, off US 7 in the Cannondale section of Wilton. Open Wed.–Sat. 11–5; Sun. noon–5; closed Mon. and Tue. Antique and vintage ceramics, with a particular emphasis on Asian ceramics and Arts and Crafts–era pottery, tastefully displayed throughout two floors of gallery space.

ART GALLERIES

In Westport

ARTredSPOT Gallery (203-254-2698; www.artredspot.com), 1869 Post Rd. East (US 1). Open Wed.–Sat. 10–5; Sun. noon–5; closed Mon. and Tue. A contemporary art gallery housed in the Old Sasco Mill on the Westport-Fairfield town line. Look for glass art, paintings, handcrafted furniture, and fine ceramics.

Gallerie Je Reviens (203-227-7716; www.galleriejereviens.com), 991 Post Rd. East (US 1). Open Wed.–Sat. 11–5; Sun. noon–5; closed Mon. and Tue. Post-impressionism, American folk art, and French masters.

Kismet Gallery (203-222-8880; www.kismetspace.com), 9 Sconset Square, 15 Myrtle Ave. Open Mon.–Sat. 10–6; Sun. by appointment. More than 100 artists from around the world are represented at this art gallery and gift store, with an emphasis on contemporary Asian-inspired art, antiques, and wearable art.

Vintage Poster Gallery (203-222-1525; 866-897-1525; www.postergroup.com), 563 Riverside Dr. Open Tue.–Sat. 10–6; closed Sun. and Mon. A vast collection of original vintage posters from the past. Some 40,000 in stock, from late-18th-century belle epoque to 20th-century art deco.

Westport Arts Center (203-222-7070; www.westportartscenter.org), Seabury Center, 51 Riverside Ave. A gallery on the Saugatuck River with a busy schedule of changing exhibits, literary discussions, workshops, films, and dramatic performances.

In Norwalk and South Norwalk

Center for Contemporary Printmaking (203-899-7999; www.contemprints.org), Mathews Park, 299 West Ave., Norwalk. Open Mon.–Sat. 9–5; closed Sun. Studio and gallery displaying photography, artists' books, works on paper, and original prints.

Rowayton Arts Center (203-866-2744; www.rowaytonartscenter.org), 145 Rowayton Ave., Rowayton. Open Tue.–Sat. noon–5, Sun. 1–4. A trio of galleries in a 1905 former firehouse on the banks of Five Mile River. Changing exhibits feature the work of local artists; a retail shop sells small works of art, crafts, and gifts.

Quester Gallery (203-523-0250; www.questergallery.com), 119 Rowayton Ave., Rowayton. Open Mon.–Sat. 10–6; closed Sun. Marine art from the 18th, 19th, and 20th centuries, including paintings, ship models, carvings, and marine antiques.

FARMS AND GARDENS **Gilbertie's Herb Gardens** (203-227-4175; www.gilbertiesherbs.com), 7 Sylvan Lane, Westport. Open daily. More than 400 varieties of herbs (19 kinds of thyme, 15 basils, and 18 sages, to name a few!) makes Gilbertie's the country's largest herb grower. In addition to the greenhouses, you'll find a retail shop and 15 formal gardens to explore. The public is invited to a full schedule of demonstrations, workshops, and lectures.

✐ **Silverman's Farm** (203-261-3306; www.silvermansfarm.com), 451 Sport Hill Rd., Easton. Open daily 9–5; closed major holidays. Pick your own apples, plums, nectarines, and peaches, or cut your own sunflowers. Kids will love the buffalo, llamas, longhorn cattle, and other resident wildlife at the animal farm and petting zoo. Tour the vintage cider mill or take a hayride in fall. You can get fresh-baked cookies and 17 varieties of pie, as well as native honey, maple syrup, and New England jams at the farm market.

Twombly Nursery (203-261-2133), 163 Barn Hill Rd., off CT 111, Monroe. Featured in the display gardens at this 11-acre facility is a design scheme not found at many Connecticut nurseries: a winter garden filled with ornamental plants that look their best during New England's harshest cold months. More than 50,000 varieties of flowers, trees, and shrubs are on display and for sale, including lots of hard-to-find plants.

✳ Special Events

June: ✐ **Round Hill Highland Scottish Games** (203-324-1094), Cranbury Park, Norwalk. Tossing the caber, bagpipe competitions, Scottish food, and a parade of the clans in their distinctive tartans. ✐ **Norwalk Harbor Splash! Festival** (203-853-7770; www.norwalkharborsplash.com), South Norwalk. Dragon boat races, clam chowder cook-off, live music. **Strawberry Festival** (203-452-1339), on the Monroe town green. An old-fashioned church festival, a tradition born in the 1800s, features the sweet, crimson berries topping shortcake, dipped in chocolate, and baked into pies. Around 2 tons of berries used each year.

July: **Victorian Ice Cream Social** (203-838-9799), Lockwood-Mathews Mansion Museum, Norwalk. Annual celebration on the lawn, petting zoo, pony rides, kids' games, and, of course, lots of ice cream. **Westport Fine Art Festival** (203-836-2041), Main St., Westport. More than 130 artists from the United States, Canada, and Europe working in glass, metal, and wood; works of fine art in photography, sculpture, painting, and mixed media. The downtown festival draws tens of thousands of visitors every year.

August: **SoNo Arts Celebration** (203-840-0770; www.sonoarts.org), South Norwalk. A festival of visual and performing arts on the historic streets of South Norwalk. More than 150 juried artists and craftspeople, live music, a kinetic sculpture race, and, for children, an art playground and a puppet parade. The festivities wind up with an exuberant block party.

September: Enjoy crafts, entertainment, live music, and, of course, great food at the **Norwalk Oyster Festival** (203-838-9444; www.seaport.org), in Veterans Memorial Park, Norwalk. See tall ships and vintage boats in port or take a harbor tour during this popular festival celebrating Long Island Sound's seafaring history. **Norwalk International In-Water Boat Show** (212-984-7000), Norwalk Cove Marina, East Norwalk. **Fairfield County Concours d'Elegance** (203-227-7988; www.fairfieldcountyconcours.com), Fairfield County Hunt Club, Westport. Something for every car aficionado: classic automobiles, rare motorcycles, muscle cars, hot rods, and the like.

December: The halls, rooms, and rotunda of Norwalk's Lockwood-Mathews Mansion Museum are decorated for its **Victorian Holiday Celebration** (203-838-9799). **First Night Westport/Weston** (203-454-6699; www.firstnightww.com) is a family-friendly end-of-the-year fete complete with live music, carriage rides, films, and fireworks.

Cory Mazon

BRIDGEPORT AND FAIRFIELD

Connecticut's largest city is not as cosmopolitan as, say, Stamford, or as stylish as Fairfield, its affluent neighbor. In fact, working-class Bridgeport sits smack in the state's richest county, yet it has struggled for years with a seemingly unshakable image of a downtrodden city with a checkered past. From I-95 you see an industrial landscape pockmarked with hulking smokestacks and empty factory buildings, grim reminders that the city's heyday, when it was a manufacturing giant and major port city, has long since gone. Its bustling factories had fed America's war machines since the Civil War; but even before the Cold War ended, big corporations left town and factories slipped away to the South and to Asia. Much of the city sadly fell into a state of neglect, beleaguered by crime, political scandals, and unemployment.

All along, the city has quietly boasted a respectable number of attractions beneath its gritty exterior, but 21st-century Bridgeport is experiencing a turnaround the likes of which it has never seen. An earnest effort is under way to polish up the city's image and reclaim the grandeur it enjoyed in the 19th century, when Phineas Taylor (P. T.) Barnum, the legendary circus impresario and creator of the Greatest Show on Earth, made Bridgeport his home and served as its mayor. He later contributed most of his estates to the city as parks, hence the nickname Park City. Developers and city leaders are banking on an economic revival in a city that many thought was past its prime. Myriad revitalization projects are taking place—notably, an extreme makeover of the historic downtown into a retail-office and entertainment district and artsy residential neighborhood. Real estate developers are converting long-abandoned 1800s commercial buildings into apartments and upscale loft-style condominiums, catering to those who can't afford to live in higher-priced Gold Coast communities like Norwalk and Stamford. A historic department store, for example, is today's Sterling Market Lofts, a space for painters, sculptors, and other artists to live and create.

There's more in the works: A $50 million transportation center on Bridgeport Harbor, with ferry service, buses, taxis, and trains in one location. A billion-dollar waterfront development with hotels, restaurants, and a high-end outlet mall. An arts and entertainment complex whose centerpiece is the 1908 Bijou Theater, the oldest movie house in America. While the restored Bijou will cater to independent-film fans, a nightclub will host nationally touring acts, and a café will stage poetry readings, book signings, and live acoustic shows.

So what's been the appeal all along? Plenty of culture, for starters. Black Rock is

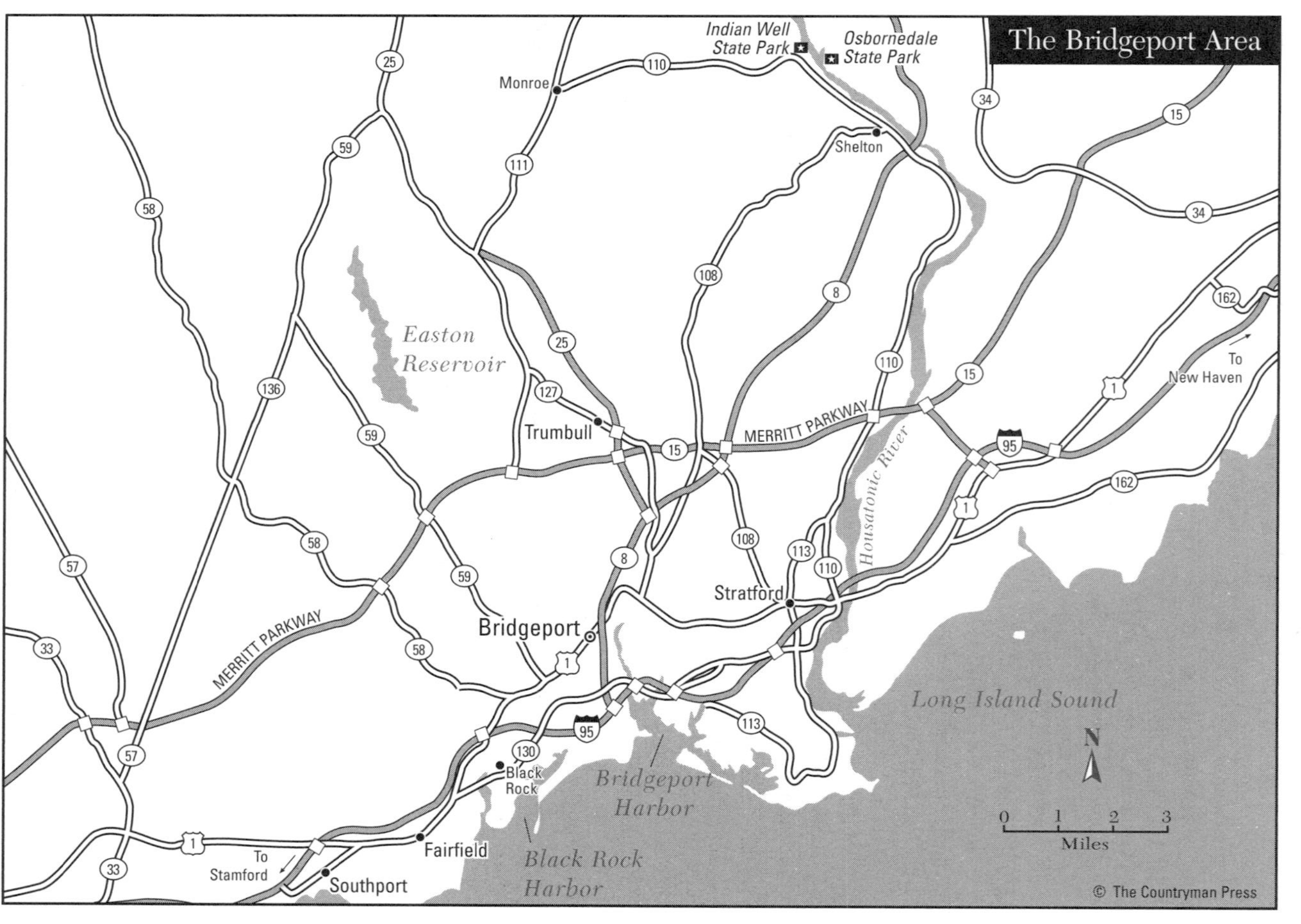
The Bridgeport Area
Indian Well State Park
Osbornedale State Park
Monroe
Shelton
Easton Reservoir
Trumbull
MERRITT PARKWAY
Housatonic River
To New Haven
Stratford
Bridgeport
Long Island Sound
Bridgeport Harbor
Black Rock
Black Rock Harbor
Fairfield
Southport
To Stamford
N
0 1 2 3
Miles
© The Countryman Press

the city's unpretentious arts district, loaded with galleries, unique shops, and ethnic eateries. Picassos, Warhols, and Renoirs reside at the Housatonic Museum of Art. There's a resident symphony orchestra, and an active thespian community supporting a Shakespeare festival and two professional theaters. Families favor Bridgeport's kid-friendly attractions—professional baseball and hockey, Siberian tigers and timber wolves at the state's largest zoo, the "please touch" Discovery Museum and Planetarium, and Victorian-style boardwalk shops at Captain's Cove Seaport, a popular destination that overflows with visitors on summer weekends. Foodies take note: Italian cooking is taken seriously in Bridgeport; here "prosciutto" becomes *prsut*, "pizza" becomes *apeetz*, and "risotto" becomes *rizot*. Voices chattering in Italian can still be heard in restaurant kitchens. You can also dine in an Old World steak house, a feminist vegetarian restaurant, and a new bistro reminiscent of a Parisian sidewalk cafe.

All told, Bridgeport is becoming, leaders believe, a city rife with potential. With buildings going up and people and businesses moving in, the city seems to be making up for lost time; and developers are hoping it won't take outsiders long to see that the Park City is an up-and-coming city. It's a show grand enough to impress Barnum himself.

Just west of Black Rock Harbor, the shoreline community of Fairfield is as well heeled as its neighbor is urban. Founded in 1639 as a farming and coastal shipping center, it was one of the earliest settlements along the old Post Road linking Boston and Philadelphia. Today the presence of Fairfield University has fostered its own respectable arts community. The town green, with requisite white church steeples and elegant town hall, offers a glimpse of colonial history amid the Gold Coast's suburban sprawl. In late spring, Fairfield's annual Dogwood Festival draws thousands of visitors who come to view the profusion of pink and white blossoms on more than 30,000 dogwood trees in the historic Greenfield Hill district. The home of the late Leonard Bernstein is among the handsome dwellings in this austere old neighborhood. US 1, the 21st-century name for the Post Road, bustles with mom-and-pop shops, national chains, and upscale boutiques selling everything from antiques to evening gowns and organic produce, and restaurants serving dishes from New England, the Côte d'Azur, the Pacific Rim, and beyond. You can explore the residential towns of Stratford, Trumbull, Southport, and Shelton by visiting their parks, small museums, restaurants, shops, and carefully preserved historic homes.

Entries in this section are arranged in roughly geographic order.

AREA CODE 203.

GUIDANCE **Coastal Fairfield County Convention & Visitor Bureau** (203-853-7770; 800-866-7925; www.visitfairfieldcountyct.com), Gate Lodge at Mathews Park, 297 West Ave., Norwalk 06850. A friendly and well-informed staff will answer questions and offer suggestions on how to explore the area; the office is loaded with travel literature. A self-service visitor information center is located at the Barnum Museum, 820 Main St., Bridgeport.

GETTING THERE *By car:* The Bridgeport and Fairfield area is accessible by car from I-95; the Merritt Parkway (CT 15); US 1, the heavily trafficked historic Post Road that passes through the centers of towns and cities; and CT 8 (a highway) from the north.

By air: **Bradley International Airport** (860-292-2000; 888-624-1533; www.bradleyairport.com) in Windsor Locks serves the entire state. **Tweed–New Haven Regional Airport** (203-466-8833; www.flytweed.com), Exit 50 off I-95 in New Haven, is served by US Airways Express.

By rail: **Amtrak**'s (800-872-7245; www.amtrak.com) main-line trains running from Boston to New York and Washington make scheduled stops at Bridgeport's main station (525 Water St.). There is frequent commuter service to New York City by **Metro-North** (800-638-7646; www.mta.info/mnr); from Bridgeport, daily connecting trains make local stops up the Naugatuck Valley to Waterbury. **Shore Line Express** (800-255-7433) provides weekday commuter service between Bridgeport and Stamford.

By bus: **Greyhound Lines** (800-231-2222; www.greyhound.com) and **Peter Pan Bus Lines** (1-800-343-9999; www.peterpanbus.com) offer frequent service to the **Bridgeport Bus Terminal** on Water St.

By ferry: **Bridgeport and Port Jefferson Steamboat Company** (203-335-2040; reservations 888-443-3779; www.bpjferry.com), 330 Water St., Bridgeport. The "Port Jeff" ferry, in operation since 1883, runs daily year-round; in summer, leaving on the hour 6 AM–9 PM; in winter, every 90 minutes 6 AM–9 PM. Reservations are suggested for vehicles. Car (90–100) and passenger (1,000 in summer, 500 in winter) ferries cross the Sound between Bridgeport and Port Jefferson on the North Shore of Long Island.

GETTING AROUND *Taxi service:* In Bridgeport: **Ace Cab Co.** (203-334-6161); **Town Taxi** (203-366-8534); **Metro Taxi** (203-333-3333); and **Yellow Cab** (203-334-2121). In Fairfield: **Fairfield Cab Co.** (203-255-5797).

MEDICAL EMERGENCY The statewide emergency number is **911**.

Bridgeport Hospital (203-384-3000), 267 Grant St., Bridgeport. The emergency number is 203-384-3566.

St. Vincent's Medical Center (203-576-6000), 2800 Main St., Bridgeport. The emergency number is 203-576-5171.

✻ To See

SPECIAL ATTRACTION ✐ **Captain's Cove Seaport and Marina** (203-335-1433; www.captainscoveseaport.com), 1 Bostwick Ave., Bridgeport, on Old Black Rock Harbor. Open daily Apr.–Oct. Free admission. A favorite summertime spot for families just west of Bridgeport Harbor. Among the attractions on this historic harbor is the **Dundon House**, a restored Queen Anne Victorian displaying exhibits on local maritime history. Among the photos and artifacts are 18th-century navigational instruments, boat models, and sailmaker's tools. The boardwalk is lined with colonial- and Victorian-style shops selling candy, crafts, toys, gifts, and ice cream. A restaurant (see *Eating Out*), charter fishing trips, and weekend boat excursions in Black Rock Harbor (see *Boat Excursion*) are also available here, as are free outdoor concerts, car shows, and other events on weekends. (See also *Boating*, *Fishing*, and *Selective Shopping*.)

MUSEUMS ✐ **Discovery Museum and Planetarium** (203-372-3521; www.discoverymuseum.org), 4450 Park Ave., Bridgeport. Open Sept.–June: Tue.–Sat.

10–5; Sun. noon–5. July–Aug.: Mon.–Sat. 10–5; Sun. noon–5. Closed major holidays. Adults $8.50; seniors, children, and students $7; under 5 free. Easily one of the most child-friendly museums in the country, with its 100 hands-on science exhibits on electricity, sound, magnetism, computers, and energy. Youngsters can learn all about the stars in one of the state's few planetariums. The ***Challenger* Learning Center**, the only such facility in Connecticut, is devoted to space travel and honors the memory of the *Challenger* crew. Make reservations for computer-simulated space missions in a rocket ship. Gift shop and food court.

Housatonic Museum of Art (203-332-5052; www.hcc.commnet.edu), Housatonic Community College, 900 Lafayette Blvd., Bridgeport. Open Sept.–May, Mon.–Fri. 8:30–5:30 (Thu. until 7); Sat. 9–3; Sun. noon–4; closed during academic holidays. Free admission. The permanent collection boasts more than 4,500 pieces and includes an interesting mix of modern Connecticut art, contemporary Latin American art, European and American art of the 19th and 20th centuries, and Asian and African collections. Names in the collection that will ring a bell—Picasso, Rodin, Warhol, Renoir, Miró, Matisse—are on display alongside works by local artists in a series of galleries. There's a full schedule of changing exhibitions, lectures, and special programs; call or check the Web site for details.

Connecticut Audubon Society Birdcraft Museum at Fairfield (203-259-0416; www.ctaudubon.org), 314 Unquowa Rd., Fairfield. Open Tue.–Fri. 10–5; Sat. and Sun. noon–4; closed Mon. Adults $2; children $1. This small natural history museum in the historic Greenfield Hill section of town is a National Historic Landmark, and the adjacent private songbird sanctuary is the oldest in the country (see *Birding*). Mabel Osgood Wright not only established the sanctuary in 1914, she also founded the Connecticut Audubon Society here in 1898 and cofounded the National Audubon Society. In the museum, wildlife exhibits, antique wildlife

KIDS LOVE THE HANDS-ON DISPLAYS, PLANETARIUM SHOWS, AND *CHALLENGER* LEARNING CENTER IN BRIDGEPORT'S INTERACTIVE SCIENCE MUSEUM.

Courtesy Coastal Fairfield County Convention & Visitors Bureau

✐ ♿ **The Barnum Museum** (203-331-1104; www.barnum-museum.org), 820 Main St., Bridgeport. Open year-round, Tue.–Sat. 10–4:30; Sun. noon–4:30; Mon. during July and Aug., 10–4:30; guided tours at 2 PM on weekends; closed major holidays. Adults $5; seniors and students $4; children $3. The Byzantine–Romanesque Revival building was a gift of Bridgeport's most famous citizen, the great circus impresario Phineas Taylor (P. T.) Barnum. The museum features a complete scale model of Barnum's world-famous Three-Ring Circus. Other exhibits and memorabilia tell the story of General Tom Thumb and Jenny Lind, the opera singer Barnum brought to America and sent on wildly successful tours as the Swedish Nightingale. Changing exhibits are devoted to art, as well as the city's industrial history.

Barnum (1810–1891) is best known as the legendary mastermind behind the Greatest Show on Earth, but he was also a journalist, entrepreneur, and politician, serving as both a state legislator and Bridgeport's mayor. Barnum's three mansions were all destroyed, but donations of his estates earned Bridgeport the nickname Park City. A statue of the famous showman resides in Seaside Park; he's honored every summer in the city's Barnum Festivalwith music, parades, car shows, and fireworks over Bridgeport Harbor.

CIRCUS IMPRESARIO PHINEAS (P. T.) BARNUM WAS MAYOR OF BRIDGEPORT AS WELL AS THE MASTERMIND BEHIND THE GREATEST SHOW ON EARTH.

Courtesy Coastal Fairfield County Convention & Visitors Bureau

dioramas, hands-on children's activities, nature paintings, and changing exhibits highlight the natural history of Connecticut.

Fairfield Museum and History Center (203-259-1598; www.fairfieldhs.org), 370 Beach Rd., Fairfield. Open Mon.–Fri. 10–4; Sat. and Sun. noon–4; open until 6 on Thu. Adults $5; students $3; children 5 and under free. A new museum and history center on the town green with changing exhibits, a theater, library, and museum shop.

Catharine B. Mitchell Museum (203-378-0630; www.stratfordhistoricalsociety.com), 967 Academy Hill, Stratford. Open June–Oct., Wed. and Sun. noon–3.

Adults $3; seniors $2; students $1. A modern museum with permanent and changing exhibits on local Stratford history, from local Native Americans and early African American history to the town's soldiers who fought with the British in the French and Indian War. The museum is maintained by the Stratford Historical Society, which is headquartered next door in the **Captain David Judson House**. Captain Judson built this stately red circa-1750 Georgian home on the site of his great-grandfather's 1639 stone house. Displays feature farming and oystering tools, antiques, a collection of Chinese porcelain, and locally crafted period furnishings.

Garbage Museum (203-381-9571; www.crra.org), 1410 Honeyspot Rd. Extension, Stratford. Open Sept.–June: Wed.–Fri. noon–4. July–Aug.: Tue.–Fri. 10–4. Free admission. An innovative environmental education center for children. This regional recycling plant can be observed from a glass-walled observatory, where visitors watch plastic, aluminum, glass, and paper being crushed or baled. Children love the Trash-O-Saurus, a 24-foot-long dinosaur constructed from a full ton of rubbish. Interactive exhibits (the Worm Tunnel replicates a compost pile) and sculptures use found materials in an imaginative way and elevate household garbage to an art form.

♿ **National Helicopter Museum** (203-375-8857; www.nationalhelicoptermuseum.org), 2480 Main St., at the eastbound railroad station, Stratford. Open Memorial Day–mid-Oct., Wed.–Sun. 1–4; closed Mon. and Tue. Free admission. A small but fascinating museum with hundreds of photos, models, and documents tracing the history of the helicopter in Connecticut (including Stratford's Sikorsky Aircraft, long associated with helicopter technology) and around the world, from the early 1900s to the present.

HISTORIC HOMES AND SITES **P. T. Barnum Statue** in Seaside Park, Bridgeport, depicts "the Greatest Showman on Earth," a Connecticut native, sitting atop a high block of marble and looking out to Long Island Sound in one of the parks he gave to the citizens of Bridgeport. He served as mayor of the city and as a state legislator. Close by is a statue of Elias Howe, the inventor of the sewing machine. Three great Bridgeport showplace homes of Barnum, including Iranistan—a model of a Persian mosque—sadly were all destroyed.

Ogden House & Gardens (203-259-1598), 1520 Bronson Rd., Fairfield. Open June–Sept., Sun. 1–4. Adults $2; children $1. Visitors can tour the austere house and the well-tended colonial-style kitchen and herb gardens at this preserved and restored 18th-century saltbox farmhouse run by the Fairfield Historical Society. The house was built around 1750 by David Ogden, whose family would live and farm here for 125 years. (See also *Special Events*.)

Boothe Memorial Park and Museum (203-381-2046), 5774 Main St., Putney, Stratford. Park open year-round, daily 9–5; museum open Tue.–Fri. 11–1; Sat. and Sun. 1–4; house tours led June–Oct. Free admission. Two wealthy, eccentric brothers left a 32-acre estate with a collection of 20 buildings and exhibits that can only be described as, well, eccentric. There's nothing quite like it in all of New England, where eccentricity is commonplace. The **Boothe Homestead**, in the Boothe family since 1725, is full of furniture, clothing, Civil War artifacts, and other items that belonged to several generations of the family. The **Blacksmith Shop** has 44 corners and 44 sides and houses 2,000 ancient implements. The brothers loved lighthouses, so they built a model lighthouse. The outdoor basilica and organ house have attracted thousands of people to Easter sunrise services. The **Technocratic Cathedral** defies description. The **Clock Tower Museum** houses hundreds of artifacts collected by the brothers during their world travels.

WINERY **Jones Winery** (203-929-8425; www.jonesfamilyfarms.com), 266 Israel Hill Rd., Shelton. Open daily for tastings May–Dec. Tasting fee $5. A vineyard and dairy barn turned winery is the latest venture of a family that's been farming the white hills for six generations. Winemaker Jamie Jones produces traditional reds and whites, and fruit wines crafted with the farm's homegrown strawberries, as well as raspberries and black currants grown on local farms. Huntington Red, Harvest Time (apple and pear), and the dry and flavorful Stonewall White are some of the varieties available in the gift shop, which also sells specialty foods and other unique items. See also *Selective Shopping*.

ZOO **Connecticut's Beardsley Zoo** (203-394-6565; www.beardsleyzoo.org), 1875 Noble Ave., Beardsley Park, Bridgeport. Open year-round, daily 9–4; rain forest and carousel buildings open 10:30–4; closed Thanksgiving, Christmas, New Year's. Adults $9; seniors and children $7; children under 3 free. A 36-acre nature preserve just off CT 8, Connecticut's only accredited zoo is popular with families, for it's relatively small compared with the big zoos in New York, and many New Yorkers find a day here less tiring for the children. The zoo has a rustic New England farmyard especially for youngsters with goats to feed and pet, friendly cows, and a children's stage. Wildlife includes the timber wolf, mountain lion, and bison; boa constrictors, monkeys, parrots, and other exotic animals in the Tropical Rainforest exhibit; plus 120 other species of animals, including the endangered Siberian tiger. Kids love the restored Victorian carousel and carousel-horse exhibit. Snack bar, gift shops, and special events.

CONNECTICUT'S BEARDSLEY ZOO IN BRIDGEPORT IS HOME TO MORE THAN 300 ANIMALS REPRESENTING 125 SPECIES, INCLUDING THE LYNX SHOWN HERE.

Connecticut's Beardsley Zoo

✷ To Do

AMUSEMENTS **Sports Center of Connecticut/The Rinks at Shelton** (203-929-6500; www.sportscenterct.com), 784 River Rd. (CT 110), Shelton. Open daily year-round. A little something for everyone in the family. The weather-protected golf center has a driving range, miniature golf, and batting cages. Inside, a double-decker ice-skating arena (they claim it's the only one in the world) offers public skate times, figure skating, and hockey. There's also a Lazer Tag arena, kiddie water rides, a health club, a sports rehabilitation center, and a sports training program for elite athletes.

BALLOONING **A Yankee Balloon** (203-255-1929; www.ayankeeballoon.com), 120 Flax Rd., Fairfield. Year-round balloon flights over central and western Connecticut; tether rides are available for the timid.

BIRDING **Connecticut Audubon Society Birdcraft Museum at Fairfield** (203-259-0416; www.ctaudubon.org), 314 Unquowa Rd., Fairfield. Open Tue.–Fri. 10–5; Sat. and Sun. noon–4. Adults $2; children $1. This 6-acre songbird sanctuary, established by Connecticut Audubon Society founder Mabel Osgood Wright in 1914, was the first private birding sanctuary in the country to welcome visitors. An observation deck off a stone cottage is a good spot for spying resident and migratory birds; more than 120 species have been documented here. The museum features antique dioramas of birds and other Connecticut wildlife, changing art exhibits, and hands-on children's activities. Outside, take a guided walk to the meadows, woods, and ponds, or attend a bird-banding demonstration (by appointment) on weekdays in spring or fall.

♿ **Connecticut Audubon Society Center at Fairfield** (203-259-6305; www.ctaudubon.org), 2325 Burr St., Fairfield. Grounds open daily, dawn to dusk; nature center, Tue.–Sat. 9–4:30; Sun. noon–4; closed Mon. and major holidays. Adults $2; children $1; free admission to sanctuary grounds. The 152-acre **Larsen Wildlife Sanctuary** has ponds, meadows, marshes, woodlands, and wetlands, and 7 miles of raised boardwalks and trails, including one that's handicapped accessible (see *Green Space*). In the nature center, check out the natural history exhibits, library, nature store, solar greenhouse, and the enclosed compound for nonreleasable owls and hawks.

BOAT EXCURSION **Captain's Cove Seaport and Marina** (203-335-1433), 1 Bostwick Ave., Bridgeport. Weekends May–Sept.; call for rates. Hour-long narrated tours of historic Black Rock Harbor aboard *Chief*, a 40-foot navy launch that once brought sailors ashore on leave during World War II. Sights along the way include the restored 1823 Black Rock Harbor Lighthouse on Fayerweather Island, and the Penfield Reef Lighthouse, which, your guide may tell you, is haunted by the ghost of a former keeper.

BOATING **Captain's Cove Seaport and Marina** (203-335-1433), 1 Bostwick Ave., Black Rock Harbor, Bridgeport. Open year-round; reservations requested. A full-service marina with 400 slips; restaurant and shops along a lively waterfront boardwalk.

Cedar Marina (203-335-6262), 86 Bostwick Ave., Black Rock Harbor, Bridgeport. Open May–Oct. Full services, snack bar.

Brewers Stratford Marina (203-377-4477), at the foot of Broad St., Stratford. Open year-round; full services; restaurant. Reservations recommended.

Marina at the Dock (203-378-9300), 955 Ferry Blvd., Stratford. Open Apr.–Oct. Full services.

FISHING Charter boats are available for hire for various fishing excursions; reservations are required. From **Captain's Cove Seaport and Marina** in Bridgeport, you can fish for striped bass, flounder, and bluefish aboard ***Daystar*** (203-615-0070); the ***Carol Marie*** (203-264-2891) heads offshore for tuna, shark, and

Courtesy Coastal Fairfield County Convention & Visitors Bureau

A VICTORIAN-STYLE BOARDWALK ON BRIDGEPORT'S HISTORIC BLACK ROCK HARBOR IS A POPULAR SUMMERTIME DESTINATION FOR FAMILIES.

marlin; the ***Catherine E*** (203-335-1433) is a traditional lobster boat available for fishing. ***Middlebank II*** (203-655-5918; www.middlebank.com) is the only party fishing boat in southwestern Connecticut.

GOLF **D. Fairchild Wheeler Golf Course** (203-373-5911), 2390 Easton Turnpike (CT 59), Fairfield. Par 71, 36 holes, 6,559 yards. Bridgeport's municipal golf complex has two 18-hole courses.

H. Smith Richardson Golf Course (203-255-7300), 2425 Morehouse Hwy., Fairfield. Par 72, 18 holes, 6,676 yards. Distant views of Long Island Sound can be glimpsed from the back nine.

South Pine Creek Golf Course (203-256-3173), Old Dam Rd., Fairfield. Par 27, 9 holes, 1,240 yards.

Short Beach Golf Course (203-381-2070), 1 Dorne Dr., Stratford. Par 27, 9 holes, 1,369 yards. Views of Long Island Sound from every hole on the course.

Tashua Knolls Golf Club (203-452-5186), 40 Tashua Knolls Lane, Trumbull. Par 72, 18 holes, 6,540 yards.

SPECTATOR SPORTS 🏵 ✐ **Bridgeport Bluefish** (203-345-4800; www.bridgeportbluefish.com), Ballpark at Harbor Yard, 500 Main St., Bridgeport. Games Apr.–Sept.; call or check online for a schedule of home games. Fairfield County's only minor-league baseball team plays home games in the city's new $19 million, 5,300-seat stadium that resembles an old-time neighborhood ballpark. The Bluefish play in the Independent Atlantic League, which includes professional teams from throughout the Northeast. Here it's all about family-friendly fun: Kids love the dog tricks and other sidelines attractions, the between-innings entertainment, and the Friday-night fireworks.

✐ **Bridgeport Sound Tigers** (203-334-4625; www.soundtigers.com), Arena at Harbor Yard, 600 Main St., Bridgeport. Games are played Oct.–Apr.; call or check the Web site for the current schedule. The Sound Tigers, a professional affiliate of the New York Islanders, play in the American Hockey League.

Shoreline Star Greyhound Park and Entertainment Complex (203-576-1976; 888-463-6446; www.shorelinestar.com), 255 Kossuth St., Bridgeport. Open year-round for matinee and evening events; closed on Christmas Day. This dog track was built next to the city's former jai alai fronton. Greyhounds race on the outdoor track from mid-May to mid-October; simulcast thoroughbred, harness, and greyhound races, as well as jai alai and other sporting events, are viewed inside on giant screens all year long.

✷ Green Space

✐ ♿ **Connecticut Audubon Society Center at Fairfield** (203-259-6305; www.ctaudubon.org), 2325 Burr St., Fairfield. Sanctuary open daily, dawn to dusk; nature center, Tue.–Sat. 9–4:30; closed major holidays. Adults $2; children $1. Free admission to sanctuary grounds. In the nature center: natural history exhibits, a library, nature store, solar greenhouse, and rehabilitation area for birds of prey. Outside, trails lace through the 152-acre **Larsen Wildlife Sanctuary**, where woods, ponds, meadows, and marshes feature interpretive signs, an observation platform, and a replica of an Algonquin wigwam. Classes, lectures, and workshops on environmental topics are offered, including wildlife photography sessions for adults. See also *Museums*.

✐ **Short Beach Park** (203-385-4052), 1 Dorne Dr., Stratford. Admission $5. A 30-acre waterfront park and beach fronts Long Island Sound and the Housatonic River. Lots of amenities, including picnic areas, ball fields, tennis, volleyball, mini golf, and a skateboard park.

Indian Well State Park (203-735-4311), Howe Ave. (CT 110), Shelton. Open year-round, daily 8 AM–sunset. Parking fee on weekdays: $5 residents, $7 nonresidents; on weekends and holidays: $7 residents, $10 nonresidents. The unusual name of this park comes from the pools at the base of its scenic waterfalls. The wide sandy beach on a calm stretch of the Housatonic River is a perfect spot to spend a hot summer day. Most people come for the fishing, hiking, boating, and picnicking in a tree-shaded waterfront grove. The Head of the Housatonic regatta (see *Special Events*) is held here in October.

✷ Lodging

HOTELS AND MOTELS 🐾 ♿ **Black Rock Inn** (203-659-2200; 866-922-7625; www.blackrockinn.com), 100 Kings Hwy. Cutoff, Fairfield 06824. A new property in the Best Western chain with 60 clean and comfortable rooms and suites. Guest rooms have refrigerators, satellite TV, and free high-speed Internet; there's also a fitness room and a business center. Continental breakfast. $130–160.

🐾 ♿ **The Inn at Fairfield Beach** (203-255-6808; www.innatfairfieldbeach.com), 1160 Reef Rd., Fairfield 06430. A friendly inn in a residential neighborhood close to Fairfield Beach with 14 roomy and uniquely themed studio suites. Accommodations are clean and nicely furnished; each suite has a kitchenette and cable TV; many come with cathedral ceilings, balconies, and views of Long Island Sound; some have a fireplace. Balcony flower boxes add a cheerful, homey touch. Fairfield Beach is a five-minute walk down the road. $140–250.

Bridgeport Holiday Inn Hotel & Conference Center (203-334-1234; reservations 877-863-4780; www.holidayinn.com), 1070 Main St., Exit 27A off I-95, Bridgeport 06604. A major hotel in the heart of the city, within walking distance of train and bus stations and the Barnum Museum. The 234 rooms (six suites) have all the usual amenities, including free WiFi. There's a health club and an indoor pool; **Parc 1070** is known for its bountiful Sun. brunch; and there's a carnival ambience in the **PT** (as in P. T. Barnum) **Lounge**. $140 and up.

Marnick's Motel (203-377-6288), 10 Washington Parkway, in the Lordship section of Stratford 06497. Open year-round. A no-frills, family-owned motel right on the beach with clean, comfortable rooms, many with private balconies overlooking Long Island Sound. Restaurants are close by, including Marnick's own, which serves breakfast, lunch, and dinner every day. $70–100.

Homewood Suites by Hilton (203-377-3322; reservations: 800-238-8000; www.stratford.homewoodsuites.com), 6905 Main St., Exit 53 off the Merritt Parkway (CT 15), Stratford 06615. This all-suite hotel overlooking the Housatonic River has a warm, fireplaced lobby and New England–style decor. The 135 suites—studios and one- and two-bedroom units—are designed for extended stays and come with fully equipped kitchens and separate living and sleeping areas. The fitness center and business center are both open around the clock; there's also a library, convenience store, laundry facility, indoor pool, and whirlpool. Evening social gatherings (Mon.–Thu.) and daily continental breakfast are included. $109–229.

Trumbull Marriott (203-378-1400; reservations: 800-228-9290), 180 Hawley Lane, Trumbull 06611. Often the alternative hotel when the downtown Bridgeport Holiday Inn is full. Quiet country setting but close to the Merritt Parkway; 324 rooms and suites, health club, sauna, indoor and outdoor pools. $104–169.

Courtyard by Marriott (203-929-1500; reservations 866-296-2296; www.sheltoncourtyard.com), 780 Bridgeport Ave., Exit 12 off CT 8, Shelton 06484. The 160 newly renovated units include 16 roomy suites, all with free high-speed Internet and upgraded work spaces. A restaurant and lounge, a fitness room, an indoor pool, a sauna, and a new business center round out the amenities. $99–199.

✷ Where to Eat

DINING OUT

In Bridgeport

Joseph's Steakhouse (203-337-9944; www.josephssteakhouse.com), 360 Fairfield Ave. Open for lunch Mon.–Fri.; dinner daily. Reservations recommended on weekends. Classic steak house fare is served at this handsome downtown restaurant. The dark-hued dining room is decked with brick walls and lots of gleaming wood, from the mahogany bar to the oak floors. The menu keeps things simple, with an emphasis on top-quality cuts of aged prime beef and a handful of alternatives, such as twin lobster tails, lamb chops, and broiled salmon. Dishes are decidedly old school—when's the last time you saw herring with sour cream among appetizer offerings? The specialty, of course, is meat, and they do it well. You can get filet mignon with mushrooms or order steak for up to four people. Traditional sides like sautéed onions and creamed spinach are extra. Desserts feature the usual players: pecan pie, apple strudel, key lime pie, carrot cake. Owner Josef Kustra is a gracious and attentive dining room host. $23–53.

King & I (203-374-2081; www.kingandict.com), 545 Broadbridge Rd. Open for lunch Mon.–Sat.; dinner daily. Another location in Fairfield (203-256-1664) at 260 Post Rd. (US 1). When you want satay, curry, or pad Thai, this is where you should go—locals say King & I has some of the best anywhere. The dining room is intimate, peaceful, and oft filled with regulars, who come for the attentive service and top-quality authentic Thai cuisine at moderate prices. $12–20.

La Scogliera (203-333-0673; www.lascoglierarestaurant.com), 697 Madison Ave. Open Tue.–Sun. for lunch and dinner; closed Mon. Reservations recommended. The north end of Bridgeport is the city's Italian section, a residential neighborhood where you'd expect to find authentic Italian home cooking. Carmelo and Carmelina Maione opened their warm and friendly eatery in 1978 (*scogliera* is Italian for "cliff," a nod to the rugged coastline of their native southern Italy), and it has been a favorite ever since. Loyal patrons come for Italian favorites like veal chops with porcini mushrooms, homemade gnocchi, and the house specialty: chicken breast sautéed with tomatoes, peppers, prosciutto, and artichoke hearts. Ordering off the menu is welcome here; just ask. Live entertainment by Italian artists. $15–34.

♿ **Ralph 'n Rich's** (203-366-3597), 815 Main St. Open Mon.–Sat. for lunch and dinner; closed Sun. Traditional Italian cuisine and white-linen dining in a tasteful, high-ceilinged dining room where you might rub elbows with the city's movers and shakers. Start your meal with an excellent hot antipasto, then choose from a variety of pasta, steak, and seafood dishes—even a few vegetarian choices, like polenta primavera. Live piano on Friday and Saturday nights. $12–26.

State Street Bistro (203-540-5705; www.statestreetbistro.com), 211 State St. Open for lunch Mon.–Fri.; dinner Mon.–Sat.; closed Sun. A new face on Bridgeport's culinary scene, with elegant surroundings reminiscent of a Parisian sidewalk café and a vibe that's casual and relaxed. Arched ceilings, tall windows, European tapestries, candlelit tables, and crimson walls combine into a warm and inviting backdrop for classic French bistro cuisine. The kitchen shows its mettle with house-cured salmon, bouillabaisse, duck a l'orange, and mussels steamed with garlic, white wine, and shallots. White chocolate crème brûlée is the dessert menu's pièce de résistance. Close to the **Playhouse on the Green** and the **Arena at Harbor Yard**. $23–32.

♿ **Tuscany Ristorante** (203-331-9884), 1084 Madison Ave. Michele Rotondi, owner of this cozy and upscale eatery, is a native of Tuscany, which naturally influences the menu. A long list of daily additions accompanies the steak, seafood, and house-made pasta offerings. When you arrive, the day's special appetizers are on display, as if to beckon you in. In warm months, the French doors facing the sidewalk are flung wide open, to the delight of diners. $15–32.

In Fairfield

Barcelona Restaurant & Wine Bar (203-255-0800; www.barcelonawinebar.com), 4180 Black Rock Turnpike. Open daily for lunch and dinner, Sun.–Thu. until 1 AM; Fri. and Sat. until 2 AM. A chic tapas joint and wine bar catering to the dining desires of well-dressed suburbanites and hip young patrons. Spanish and Mediterranean cuisine can be ordered in tapas-style portions or as full entrées. The small plates are fun to pass around and share—little tastes of lobster risotto, empanadas, chorizo and figs, or a sampling of house-cured olives or roasted garlic bulbs with olive oil. One entrée pairs pepper-rubbed filet mignon with garlic mashed potatoes and a brandy reduction; in another, grilled swordfish is accompanied by heirloom tomatoes, fresh basil, and toasted peasant bread. The flavorful cooked-to-order paella blends saffron rice, chicken, chorizo, and seafood. There's a daily selection of cured meats, sausages, and artisan cheeses.Small plates $4–11; entrées $19–27. Other locations in South Norwalk, Greenwich, New Haven, and West Hartford.

♿ **Centro** (203-255-1210; www.centroristorante.com), 1435 Post Rd. (US 1). Lunch Mon.–Sat.; dinner daily. High ceilings, white columns, and walls sponged in yellow, pink, and peach create a sophisticated yet relaxing atmosphere that attracts a stylish crowd. An imaginative repertoire of Italian dishes, such as portobello mushrooms stuffed with spinach, goat cheese, sun-dried tomatoes, and garlic—or penne tossed with shrimp, beans, arugula, and onions and sauced with roasted garlic and olive oil—complements the list of hearty thin-crust pizzas. Diners flock to the umbrella tables on the patio as soon as the weather allows. $14–25. Other locations in Darien and Greenwich.

♿ **Cinzano's** (203-367-1199), 1920 Black Rock Turnpike. Open daily for lunch and dinner. Reservations suggested. The pink-hued walls set the style as Victorian; the large mural of peasants at harvest bent over in the fields north of Rome flags the cuisine as northern Italian. Sole is layered with eggplant, mushrooms, and mozzarella; veal is sautéed in a wine sauce with peas and sun-dried tomatoes and topped with fresh mozzarella; and Chicken Portuguese is a tasty commingling of tomatoes, shrimp, and black olives. $14–32.

Piatto D'Oro (203-615-0100; 866-651-9993; www.piattodororestaurant.net), 770 Commerce Dr. Open daily for lunch and dinner. Reservations are recommended. The menu of authentic northern Italian cuisine revolves around classic dishes like veal osso buco, handmade pasta, and Dover sole served tableside. $15–30.

♿ **Sarabande** (203-259-1493; 12 Unquowa Place. Open for lunch Tue.–Fri.; dinner Mon.–Sat.; closed Sun. Chef-owner Phillis Bodek offers exceptional fusion cuisine at her sophisticated yet casual (the decor is described as "California post-modern") downtown bistro just off the Post Road. The diminutive open kitchen turns out made-from-scratch breads, soups, and desserts, as well as creative riffs on seafood, chicken, steak, and gourmet thin-crust pizza. $17–30.

♿ **St. Tropez** (203-254-8094; www.saint-tropez-bistro.com), 52 Sanford St. Open for lunch Mon.–Sat.; dinner daily. Reservations recommended. A lively French bistro whose tasteful decor and lovely mural of the Côte d'Azur hint at the authentic goings-on in the kitchen. The menu of French and Mediterranean classics has a strong emphasis on the sea. You might start with avocado and crab salad with orange vinaigrette, or escargots sautéed in white wine, garlic, and tomatoes. Next, bouillabaisse, filet mignon in black peppercorn sauce, braised monkfish with fresh fennel sauce, or oven-roasted lobster plucked out of the shell and served with champagne sauce. For dessert, profiteroles *au chocolat* is a decadent puff pastry filled with vanilla ice cream and topped with chocolate sauce; if you call the day before, the kitchen will make you a lighter-than-air soufflé. The **"O" Bar** martini lounge offers libations, a light menu, and a DJ on weekends. $20–33.

Elsewhere

♿ **Shell Station** (203-377-1648; www.shellstationrest.com), at the railroad station, 2520 Main St., Stratford. Open for lunch Mon.–Fri.; dinner daily. A sushi bar is the latest venture of this local favorite known for its seafood—lobster, shrimp, and scallops—and fresh pasta made daily. The name refers to the scalloped seashell, not the gas station. $11–21.

♿ **Il Palio Ristorante** (203-944-0770; www.ilpalioct.com), 5 Corporate Dr. (Enterprise Corporate Park), Shelton. Open for lunch Mon.–Fri.; dinner Mon.–Sat.; closed Sun. Elegant northern Italian cuisine in an equally elegant dining room, set in perhaps the most unlikely of locations: a suburban office park. It's fitting, then, that this is a popular spot for business lunches. Everything about this place is refined, however, from the gracious service to the taffeta drapes, contemporary Tuscan artwork, and warm lighting. And then there's the food. You might start with house-smoked salmon or beef carpaccio with shaved Parmesan and truffle oil, then move on to lobster ravioli or creative renditions of the more traditional osso buco and filet mignon. Extensive wine list. $18–24.

Paci Restaurant (203-259-9600; www.pacirestaurant.com), 96 Station St., Southport. Open for dinner Tue.–Sat.; closed Sun. and Mon. A popular Italian restaurant in Southport's train station, and winner of a James Beard award for its design. There's an open kitchen, and the dramatic high-ceilinged dining room features a clock projected against one of its soaring walls; the other walls are exposed brick. The aforementioned kitchen works magic with top-notch imported Italian ingredients, from olive oil and balsamic vinegar to fresh mozzarella, handmade cured meats, and aged cheeses. The menu of regional cuisine changes daily, based on what's available and fresh. For a traditional starter, go for the lightly breaded squash blossoms stuffed with ricotta and Parmesan, or grilled hot peppers with cured black olives, caramelized garlic, and aged provolone. Among the entrées, veal Milanese is a house favorite, along with pan-seared grouper, prime dry-aged sirloin, and fresh ricotta ravioli. Homemade desserts like coconut cake drizzled with bittersweet chocolate espresso sauce are well worth saving room for. The carefully chosen wine list features mostly Italian bottles. $23–55.

EATING OUT

In Bridgeport

Café Roma (203-333-0055), 269 Fairfield Ave. Open daily for lunch and dinner. This new café, formerly J. R. Bijou Café, is a good place to get a bite before a game or performance at the nearby **Arena at Harbor Yard**. There's a northern Italian menu of seafood, chicken, veal, homemade pasta, and other familiar favorites, and paninis at lunch. $8–15.

▼ ♿ **Bloodroot** (203-576-9168; www.bloodroot.com), 85 Ferris St. Open for lunch Tue., and Thu.–Sat.; dinner Tue.–Sat.; Sun. brunch; closed Mon. Quietly tucked away in a residential neighborhood on Black Rock Harbor, Bloodroot might be easily overlooked. Yet for 30 years, this feminist collective has been a beloved institution, filled with devoted fans eager to taste Selma Miriam and Noel Furie's homespun vegetarian and vegan fare. There's no cash register and no wait staff. When you arrive, order from the blackboard menu at the open kitchen, collect your food, then bus your table when you're done. Made-from-scratch dishes change with the seasons, feature mostly organic ingredients, and take inspiration from virtually every corner of the globe. Summer means baby eggplant stuffed with bulgur, sun-dried tomatoes, and garlic; fall is time for lima bean squash soup and three-grain pilaf with fried kale and parsnip puree; in winter, try the *llapingachos*, Ecuadoran potato cakes with spicy peanut sauce. Save room for desserts like tofu mousse in blueberry, strawberry, pumpkin, and other seasonal flavors. Save time to browse the feminist titles, photography, and artwork in the bookshop. Ask about classes in weaving, spinning, vegan cooking, and other topics. Dinner entrées $14.50.

The Field (203-333-0043; www.thefieldrestaurant.net), 3001 Fairfield Ave. Open for lunch Mon.–Sat.; dinner daily; Sun. brunch. A restaurant and bar in the Black Rock section of town, with burgers, pizza, and pasta for light meals; steaks, chicken, and seafood for dinner. Extensive wine list and more than 40 bottled beers. Live bands on weekends. $17–22.

Home on the Range (203-336-3514), 2992 Fairfield Ave., Bridgeport. Open Tue.–Sat. for breakfast and lunch; breakfast on Sun.; closed Mon. A popular Black Rock breakfast spot; whole wheat pancakes with homemade yogurt and fresh fruit, and the omelet with mushrooms, Gorgonzola cheese, and flank steak are standouts on the creative morning menu. $6–12.

Restaurant at Captain's Cove (203-335-7104; take-out 203-368-3710; www.captainscoveseaport.com), 1 Bostwick Ave. Open daily May–Oct. Two-level spacious dining rooms serve vast quantities of fish and seafood from the restaurant's own tanks, all accompanied by hearty fries and a bowl of coleslaw. A scale model of the RMS *Titanic* dominates the center of the second-floor bar. A great place to bring the kids after a day spent at the seaport. $6–20.

Taco Loco (203-335-8228; www.tacoloco.com), 3170 Fairfield Ave. Open Tue.–Sun. for lunch and dinner; closed Mon. A popular, casual Mexican café in the Black Rock section of the city. Well-prepared classics made with fresh ingredients. Try the quesadillas with shrimp, avocado, and pimiento, or the swordfish with mango salsa. The paella is delicious: Spanish saffron rice with a mélange of lobster, mussels, clams, chicken, and chorizo. A good selection of vegetarian options. $11–21.

Vazzy's (203-371-8046; www.vazzysrest.com), 513 Broadbridge Ave., on the Trumbull town line. The calzones at this bustling and noisy family restaurant are especially popular, stuffed with fresh lobster, pesto, meatballs, or simple and delicious mozzarella and ricotta. Among the house specialties: grilled sirloin steak topped with Gorgonzola butter; chicken sautéed with artichokes in a mustard cream sauce; eggplant rolled around ricotta and prosciutto, topped with homemade marinara. Generous portions, reasonable prices. $11–19. This is the original, with other locations, including Monroe (203-459-9800), Milford (203-877-7475), and Stratford (203-375-2776).

In Fairfield

Andros Diner (203-384-8176; www.androsdinerfairfield.com), 651 Villa Ave. Of all the diners in Fairfield

County, this open-around-the-clock locale is consistently at the top of readers' polls, especially for its hearty breakfasts and global menu. The Andros family have been at the helm for more than 30 years. $8–16.

♿ **Archie Moore's** (203-256-9295), 48 Sanford St., just off the Post Road (US 1). A popular tavern within walking distance of the Metro-North train station; the original location in New Haven (203-773-9870; 188 Willow St.) opened in 1898 and is still in business, along with a handful of others across the state. The reasonably priced pub menu features burgers, nachos, and other hearty American dishes, but the signature Buffalo chicken wings take center stage. $7–18.

♿ **The Reef at Ash Creek** (203-256-2737; www.thereefct.com), 93 Post Rd. (US 1). Open daily for lunch and dinner; reservations are necessary for weekends. The longtime Ash Creek Saloon has been reinvented as a seafood restaurant. The menu has shifted from country-western to coastal. Clams casino is a good way to start; then again, so is the fried calamari with homemade garlic butter. Both dishes are made on the premises. If you pass on the seafood, tasty alternatives include steaks, chicken, and pasta. $17–30.

Frank Pepe Pizzeria Napoletana (203-333-7373), 238 Commerce Dr., on the Bridgeport city line. Open daily. This is the first outpost of the legendary New Haven pizzeria that opened in the city's Wooster Square in 1925. Watch them make their famous white clam pizza in the open kitchen's huge tiled oven. As in New Haven, the line here often stretches out the door.

Elsewhere

♿ **SBC Restaurant & Brewery** (203-256-2337; www.southportbrewing.com), 2600 Post Rd. (US 1), Southport. Open for lunch daily; dinner Mon.–Sat.; brunch Sun. This is an honest-to-goodness brewery, so it should come as no surprise that many dishes feature beer in the list of ingredients. House specialties include, for instance, fish-and-chips battered with their own Big Head Blonde beer, or baby back ribs basted with ale-infused barbecue sauce. Thin-crust pizza, fresh pasta, Maryland crabcake salad, and warm goat cheese salad with balsamic-honey vinaigrette are among the more popular menu choices. On tap, 16 varieties of home-brewed ales, IPAs, stouts, and pilsners, including Pequot IPA, Connecticut Pale Ale, and Black Rock Stout. $12–27. Other locations in Stamford, Branford, Hamden, and Milford.

Knapp's Landing (203-378-5999; www.knappslanding.com), 520 Sniffens Lane, Stratford. Reservations are recommended on weekends. An off-the-beaten-path favorite spot for lobster rolls and a lovely view of the Housatonic River. The something-for-everyone menu encompasses burgers, pastas, bar bites, and seafood. $15–27.

♿ **Outriggers** (203-377-8815; www.outriggersrestaurant.com), Brewer's Stratford Marina, at the foot of Broad St., Stratford. Open for lunch Mon.–Sat.; dinner daily. In warm weather, the expansive open-air deck overlooking the Housatonic River fills with patrons who come for the views of the river, salt marsh, and marina. The menu items are what you'd expect from a place on the water: New England clam chowder, fried clam strips, grilled fish, and lobster ravioli, plus a lighter selection of sandwiches, salads, and stone-baked pizzas. Slips are available for pleasure boaters to dock and dine. $18–26.

♿ **Old Towne Restaurant** (203-261-9436; www.oldtownerestaurant

.net), 60 Quality St., Town Hall Shopping Plaza, Trumbull. Open daily for three meals. Typically we avoid steering visitors to restaurants in shopping plazas, but in this part of crowded Fairfield County, the mall eateries are convenient, and they serve quality food. This popular family restaurant starts breakfast at 7 AM and is still satisfying diners until 11 PM with generous portions of steak, seafood, veal, chicken, and a variety of pasta dishes. $8–23.

Huntington Street Café (203-925-9064; www.hs-café.com), 90 Huntington St., Shelton. Open daily. The eclectic menu boasts more than 25 gourmet salads, wraps, and sandwiches inspired by song titles, like Steely Dan's "Hey Nineteen" (steak, cheese, caramelized onions) and Bob Dylan's "Maggie's Farm" (fresh mozzarella, pesto, and roasted red peppers with a tomato and balsamic vinaigrette). Desserts like chocolate cake with airy whipped cream are big and homey. The drink menu features specialty coffees, whole-leaf organic teas, and wines crafted at a local vineyard. Local poets and musicians take the stage almost every night. $5–10.

SNACKS

In Bridgeport

Helados Vazquez (203-333-9393), 2871 Fairfield Ave. Open daily until 10:30 PM. A new Euro-style gelateria in the city's artsy Black Rock neighborhood with a twist: homey Mexican dishes at lunch. For dessert, icy cool sorbettos and creamy gelatos; go truly Italian with chocolate and vanilla (*stracciatella*) or hazelnut (*nocchia*).

Luigi's Italian Pastry Inc. (203-374-4225; www.luigisbakery.com), 4090 Main St. *The* place to get your cannoli, since 1968. This Italian shop crafts numerous renditions of the classic Italian pastry; they start with freshly baked shells (plain or chocolate), then stuff them with creamy ricotta cheese and other decadent fillings. Cannoli fly out of this shop faster than anything, but Luigi's is also famous for its éclairs, ricotta pie, and spectacular wedding cakes.

Micalizzi's (203-366-2353; www.micalizzis.com), 712 Madison Ave. Open daily; extended summer hours. Folks hankering to beat the heat with a cup of soft Italian ice happily line up Micalizzi's walk-up window. Favorites on the list of 21 homemade flavors include root beer, watermelon, chocolate, cherry, honeydew, and cotton candy.

Port Coffeehouse (203-345-8885; www.portcoffeehouse.com), 2889 Fairfield Ave. Open daily. Black Rock hipsters and creative types gather here for organic and fair-trade coffee and tea, as well as made-right-here baked goods, including gluten-free options.

Soul of the World Tea Room (203-362-2306), 670 Brewster St. A sign by the door of this little tea shop in the city's Black Rock section promises GOOD KARMA IN EVERY CUP. Infused teas—black, green, white, and other varieties—are organic and fair-trade certified, which means they're grown by farmers who receive fair profits and don't use chemical pesticides. The whimsical pastel decor is inviting, and the handwritten menu board describes the teas in depth, from how they taste to where the leaves are grown.

Timothy's Ice Cream (203-366-7496), 2974 Fairfield Ave., in the Black Rock section of Bridgeport. Timothy's house-made ice cream is, loyal patrons insist, the best there is. Hot waffles are made in an iron behind the counter—some are rolled into cones, others are left bowl-shaped, big enough to cradle a generously sized sundae. Of the 80 or so kid pleasers and familiar favorites in their repertoire, a dozen or so are available every day. There are all kinds of wonderful flavors, including Black Rock (vanilla flecked with chocolate-covered almonds), peach, caramel crunch, and others that will make your taste buds sing. If you desire, they'll spread your choice of ice cream onto the counter and mash in all sorts of mix-ins.

In Fairfield

Chef's Table (203-255-1779; www.chefstable.com), 1561 Post Rd. (US 1), Fairfield. "Fine food fast" is the mantra of this bustling eatery, whose blackboard menu is packed with creative riffs on soups, sandwiches, and salads. It's also a gallery of rock-and-roll art. Other locations in Westport.

♿ **Firehouse Deli** (203-255-5527), 22 Reef Rd. Open daily. Don't despair at the long line—a cadre of workers busily assembles gargantuan Dagwood-style sandwiches and grinders with amazing speed. Check the blackboard for daily soup, sandwich, and quiche specials, then grab a sidewalk table for prime people-watching. Sandwiches around $7.

Las Vetas Lounge (203-255-1958), 1462 Post Rd. (US 1). Open daily. Comfy couches and a baby grand piano are among the mismatched retro-styled furnishings (think monkeys hanging from a vintage pressed-tin ceiling) at this kitschy hangout in Fairfield's historic town center that's popular with Fairfield University students. It's a laid-back coffee joint by day, a bohemian alternative to Starbucks, and a venue for open-mike nights and live local bands later on. Specialty coffee drinks, light meals, and desserts constitute the menu.

Layla's Falafel (203-384-0100; www.laylasfalafel.com), 2088 Black Rock Turnpike. Open daily. This popular Middle Eastern and vegetarian eatery does a brisk take-out business, but there are a dozen or so tables if you feel like enjoying your baba ghanoush, tabbouleh, hummus, stuffed grape leaves, or (naturally) falafel right here. This is authentic Middle Eastern home cooking, so everything is fresh. Sandwiches and platters are paired with traditional sides like lentil rice and salad. Although the menu is mostly vegetarian, they offer healthy meat dishes like grilled chicken or lamb kebabs. There's a satellite location in Stamford (203-468004) at 926 High Ridge Rd.

Rawley's Drive In (203-259-9023), 1886 Post Rd. (US 1). Open Mon.–Sat.; closed Sun. This inconspicuous hot dog stand on the Post Road has been a Fairfield County icon since 1946. They make hot dogs the old-fashioned way: deep-fried (not split), then grilled and topped with raw onions, sauerkraut, and bacon. Domestic doyenne (and former Westport resident) Martha Stewart once proclaimed Rawley's as her favorite spot to eat.

Super Duper Weenie (203-334-3647; www.superduperweenie.com), 306 Black Rock Turnpike. Open daily. How can the name not make you smile? Grilled dogs generously smothered with homemade condiments like chili, sauerkraut, bacon, hot or sweet relish, and other classics. Fresh-cut fries and onion rings are signature sides. The New Englander (sauerkraut, bacon, onions, mustard, relish) is an all-time favorite.

Billy's Bakery (203-337-5349; www.billysbakery.com), 1885 Black Rock Turnpike. Open daily. A busy bakery specializing in European-style pastries, hearth-baked artisan breads, and decadent desserts. If you come, as many do, for the chocolate cake, phone ahead to avoid disappointment—they go fast.

Elsewhere

Danny's Drive-In (203-378-6728), 940 Ferry Blvd., Stratford. An all-American drive-in (since 1935) with an old-time menu of favorites. This is where to go for burgers and foot-long dogs topped with fiery chili. French fries come crisp and plain, or smothered in chili, melted cheese, onions, and jalapeño peppers. Hungry? Order up the Triple Piggie, a three-burger creation topped with three slices of cheese and three strips of bacon.

The White Lilac Tea Room (203-378-7160), 2410 Main St., Stratford. Open Tue.–Thu. 11:30–4; Fri. and Sat. 11:30–5; closed Sun. and Mon. Reservations suggested. This quaint tearoom may remind you of visiting a dear, old aunt. Afternoon tea—a daily changing selection of English and Russian teas—is served by the pot with scones and tea sandwiches, as well as Cornish pasties and other British classics. The family photos on the walls lend to the warm and welcoming atmosphere.

Liquid Lunch (203-924-0200; www.liquidlunchrestaurant.com), 434 Howe Ave., Shelton. Open Mon.–Sat.; closed Sun. It's all about the soup at this popular downtown spot that bustles at lunchtime, when locals pack in for freshly made soups. More than 10 varieties are on the daily rotation, from standbys like French onion to creative specials ranging from chicken-spinach-Gorgonzola to Louisiana crab Florentine. On weekends, it morphs into a hip café with live music. You can also get egg sandwiches at breakfast, and homemade ice cream from nearby Rich Farm in Oxford. Another location in Milford (203-877-7687).

Pasta Fina (203-922-0041), 609 Howe Ave., Shelton. Handmade pasta is the raison d'être at this little pasta factory. In autumn, the savory pumpkin ravioli stuffed with ricotta and sage in a butternut squash cream sauce is a must-have. Most come to take out; phone ahead if you want to eat here.

Stockbridge's Gourmet Cheesecakes & Delectables (203-924-7853; www.sbcheesecakes.com), 509A Howe Ave., Shelton. Open Tue.–Sun.; closed Mon. Cheesecake aficionados take note: A dozen varieties of the sweet and creamy treat (they make 42 flavors in all) are available each day. You can stick with the traditional (lemon, chocolate chip) or opt for the unusual (sweet potato, green tea, gingerbread); there are also some sugar-free and organic varieties. They've opened a new café on the premises with indoor and outdoor seating.

✷ Entertainment

ARTS CENTERS ♿ **Black Rock Art Center** (203-367-7917; www.blackrockartcenter.org), 2838 Fairfield Ave., Bridgeport. Open mid-Feb.–mid-May, and mid-Sept.–mid-Dec. An old bank building turned arts center with a variety of cultural offerings: performances in a black-box theater, galleries with changing art exhibits, and live music. A summertime world music series takes place at venues around the city.

Edgerton Center for the Performing Arts (203-374-2777; www.edgertoncenter.org), on the campus of Sacred Heart University, 5151 Park Ave., Fairfield. Performances Sept.–June, Fri.–Sun. Symphony performances, cabaret-style shows, concerts, comedy, and professionally produced plays and musicals featuring a mix of established actors and students.

Quick Center for the Arts (203-254-4010; 877-278-7396; www.quickcenter.com), on the campus of Fairfield University, 1073 North Benson Rd., Fairfield. Music, dance, theater, and lectures at the 742-seat **Kelley**

Theatre and in the more intimate **Wien Experimental Theatre** during the school year; family programs in July and Aug.

MUSIC The city's **Black Rock** section, which also encompasses part of Fairfield, is becoming increasingly known as a lively arts district. There are a variety of venues for live music, from national acts to up-and-coming local talent, including **The Acoustic Café** (203-335-3655; www.acousticafe.com), 2926 Fairfield Ave., where live shows feature jazz, folk, blues, hip-hop, and other music styles in a casual atmosphere. **Two Boots** (203-331-1377; www.twoboots.com), 281 Fairfield Ave., is a bar and pizzeria in Bijou Square with live music and open-mike nights. Big-name acts play at the **Arena at Harbor Yard** (203-345-2400; www.arenaatharboryard), 600 Main St.

Klein Memorial Auditorium (203-576-8115; www.theklein.org), 910 Fairfield Ave., Bridgeport. The city's major—and newly renovated—1,478-seat auditorium is home to the **Greater Bridgeport Symphony** (203-576-0263; www.bridgeportsymphony.org).

Summer Concert Series (203-256-3000), at the Sherman Green Gazebo, Post Rd. at Reef Rd., Fairfield. Free performances Memorial Day–Aug., Wed., Thu., and Sun. at 7 PM. Orchestras, country-western, big band, jazz, polkas, and oldies under the stars. Call for a schedule.

THEATER **Bijou Theater**, Fairfield Ave., Bridgeport. Restoration of the city's historic 300-seat theater—the oldest movie house in America—is the centerpiece of the downtown revitalization plan for the Bijou Square arts district. Outside, the mosaic brick facade of the 1908 building has been newly restored; inside is a state-of-the-art cinema with three screens showing independent and foreign films. The theater will also be home to the newly created **Bridgeport Film Society**.

Downtown Cabaret Theatre (203-576-1636; www.downtowncabaret.org), 263 Golden Hill St., Bridgeport. Performances year-round, Fri.–Sun. A popular, award-winning cabaret-style venue for Broadway favorites, comedies, musical revues, and original works starring professional actors. Year-round schedule; children's shows, running Oct.–May, include cutting-edge musical adaptations of children's literary classics and fairy tales, as well as original works. Bring your own dinner and bottle of wine.

Playhouse on the Green (203-333-3666; www.playhouseonthegreen.org), 177 State St., Bridgeport. A year-round schedule of weekend performances, from comedies and musicals to dramas and children's theater. This state-of-the-art downtown theater is the former **Polka Dot Playhouse**, the area's oldest continually running professional theater.

Fairfield Community Theatre (203-255-6255), 1424 Post Rd., Fairfield. This historic landmark movie theater, complete with old-time marquee, first opened its doors as a silent-movie house in 1920. Today it's a volunteer-run facility showing independent films, classics, and second-run mainstream pictures.

Fairfield Theatre Company (203-259-1036; www.fairfieldtheatre.org), 70 Sanford St., Fairfield. A professional theater staging Off-Broadway productions all year long. A children's theater workshop is held in summer.

Square One Theatre Company (203-377-8778; www.squareonetheatre.com), 2422 Main St., Stratford. Performances Oct.–June. Stratford's only resident theater company stages dramas and comedies in the **Stratford Theater**, a revitalized art-deco-style former movie house.

✷ Selective Shopping

ANTIQUES SHOPS **Pickets** (203-254-0012), 1894 Bronson Rd., Fairfield. Open Mon.–Sat. 10–5; closed Sun. An English garden shop specializing in antiques, ornaments, sconces, mirrors, cast-iron urns, stone planters, vintage jewelry, architectural pieces, and unique gifts.

Stratford Antique Center (203-378-7754; www.stratfordantique.com), 400 Honeyspot Rd., Stratford. Open daily 10–5; open until 9 on Thu. in Dec. Look for the massive 16,000-square-foot blue warehouse, where more than 200 dealers offer a huge selection of antiques and collectibles.

ART GALLERIES **City Lights Gallery** (203-334-7748), 37 Markle Court, Bridgeport. Open Mon.–Fri. 10–5:30; Sat. 10–4. Changing exhibits feature the work of emerging and established local and regional artists; there's a full schedule of opening receptions, lunchtime art demonstrations, concerts, and movies.

Greenwich Workshop Gallery (203-255-4613), 1657 Post Rd. (US 1), Fairfield. Open Mon.–Sat.; closed Sun. Original works and limited editions of more than 50 artists; high-quality and affordable fine art prints, sculpture, art books.

J. Russell Jinishian Gallery (203-259-8753; www.jrusselljinishiangallery.com), 1657 Post Rd. (US 1), Fairfield. Open Tue.–Sat. 10–5 and by appointment. One of the best-known U.S. galleries specializing in contemporary and antique marine art—paintings, ship models, scrimshaw, and sculpture.

Walsh Art Gallery (203-254-4000), Quick Center for the Arts, on the campus of Fairfield University, 1073 North Benson Rd., Fairfield. Open Tue.–Sat. 11–5; Sun. noon–5. Six changing exhibitions—contemporary art and grand masters' works—are presented every year, including traveling exhibits and works by local artists.

BOOKSTORES ▼ **Bloodroot** (203-576-9168; www.bloodroot.com), 85 Ferris St., Bridgeport. Open Tue.–Sun. during restaurant hours. A cozy shop tucked into a corner of Black Rock's venerable vegetarian restaurant (see *Eating Out*) is well stocked with cookbooks (including the restaurant collective's own series of published cookbooks) and books on feminism, holistic healing, poetry, politics, environmental issues, gardening, and craftwork. Owners Selma Miriam and Noel Furie have read most of the titles and can offer suggestions.

The Dinosaur Paw (203-256-0797), 1300 Boston Post Rd. (US 1), Fairfield. A sunny, cheerful bookstore devoted exclusively to young readers. An impressive stock of quality children's books. Masks of Clifford, Arthur, Max (of *Where the Wild Things Are* fame), and other heroes of children's literature line the walls. The shop is named for a children's book by Patricia Reilly Giff, whose family owns the shop.

The Whistle Stop Bookshop (203-375-4146), 2505 Main St., Stratford. Comprehensive selection of new and used books in a browser-friendly shop. Many children's programs; call for a schedule.

Written Words Bookstore (203-944-0400; www.writtenwordsbookstore.com), 194 Leavenworth Rd., in the White Hills Shopping Center, Shelton. Open daily. A friendly independent shop with children's story time, knitting classes, and complimentary coffee and tea.

FARMS AND GARDENS **Beardsley's Cider Mill & Orchard** (203-926-1098; www.beardsleyscidermill.com), 89 Pearmain Rd., Shelton. Open mid-Sept.–Dec., Mon.–Fri. noon–6; Sat. and Sun. 10–6. The Beardsley family have been farming here since 1849; today visitors who come to pick apples in fall (weekends and holidays in Sept. and Oct.) can also stop by the cider mill, where they can watch as apples are pressed into cider, then enjoy free hot or cold samples. Home-baked pies, jams and jellies, local honey, fruit butters, and New England–made products are available at the farm market.

Jones Family Farms (203-929-8425; www.jonesfamilyfarms.com), 266 Israel Hill Rd., Shelton. Six generations of the Jones family have worked this 400-acre farm since 1848. In summer and fall, visitors can pick their own strawberries, blueberries, and pumpkins (via hayride); around the holidays, there are 200 acres of Christmas trees for customers to cut themselves. A winery and vineyard is their latest venture (see *To See*). The **Holiday Gatherings** gift shop sells holiday home decor, crafts, and baked goods in Nov. and Dec.

SPECIAL SHOPS **Captain's Cove Seaport and Marina** (203-335-1433), 1 Bostwick Ave., Bridgeport, on Old Black Rock Harbor. Open daily Apr.–Oct. A favorite summertime spot for families just west of Bridgeport Harbor. The boardwalk is lined with colonial- and Victorian-style shops selling candy, crafts, collectibles, toys, nautical gifts, and ice cream.

Westfield Shoppingtown (203-372-4500), 5065 Main St., Exit 48 off the Merritt Parkway (CT 15), Trumbull. More than 200 national and regional retailers, including Macy's and other anchor stores.

Special Events

March: **The Garden Expo** (203-259-1847), Fairfield High School, Fairfield. More than 70 exhibitors bring their wares to this popular annual kick-off to the spring gardening season.

Early May: **Dogwood Festival** (203-259-5596), in the Greenfield Hill section of Fairfield, Exit 20 off I-95 and just south of the Merritt Parkway (CT 15). Some 30,000 dogwood trees burst into pink and white bloom on the village green and on the streets radiating from the center. Garden lovers have made an annual pilgrimage to this breathtaking floral display for more than 70 years. Lunch is served at the Greenfield Hill Congregational Church during the multiday festival, which also features guided garden tours, historical walks, children's activities, a juried art show, and free concerts.

May: **Garlicfest** (203-374-4053), Notre Dame Catholic High School, Fairfield. Area restaurants offer a variety of garlicky foods and desserts (really!) featuring the pungent bulb. **Market & Craft Fair** (203-334-5245), Fairfield. The Fairfield Women's Club puts on this annual show on the historic town hall green.

Summer: **Barnum Festival** (203-367-8495; 866-867-8495; www.barnumfestival.com), Bridgeport. A series of events from May through July honors P. T. Barnum, the city's former mayor and the "Greatest Showman on Earth." Car shows, parades, concerts, and fireworks in Bridgeport Harbor.

June: **Fairfield County Irish Festival** (203-333-4736; www.irishfestival

.org), Indian Ledge Park, Trumbull. A family celebration with Irish music, pipe-band marches, art, and sporting events. Children's tent with activities and rides.

Summer: **Connecticut Free Shakespeare** (203-393-3213), Connecticut's Beardsley Zoo, Bridgeport. Outdoor productions of classic Shakespeare works by professional actors and local students.

August: **Bluefish Tournament** (203-366-2583), Captain's Cove Seaport, Bridgeport. Billed as the "Greatest Bluefish Tournament on Earth"; hundreds of anglers cast into Long Island Sound and vie for thousands in prize money. **St. Vincent's Swim Across the Sound** (203-576-5451), Captain's Cove Seaport, Bridgeport. A 15-mile swim across Long Island Sound—from Port Jefferson, Long Island, to Captain's Cove Seaport in Bridgeport—to raise money for cancer research.

September: **Early American Festival** (203-378-0630), David Judson House, Stratford. Demonstrations of 18th-century crafts, period music, military reenactments, and children's colonial games, hosted by the Stratford Historical Society. **Trumbull Arts Festival** (203-452-5065), town hall green, Trumbull. A juried show of artists and crafters, presented by the Trumbull Arts Commission.

October: **Head of the Housatonic** (203-734-0125), Indian Well State Park, Shelton. The New Haven Rowing Club hosts this annual 2.5-mile-long head race up the Housatonic River that brings thousands of high school, collegiate, and masters rowers to town. Crews launch their boats from the beach and row upstream to the finish. **Fall Festival at Ogden House** (203-259-1598), Ogden House Museum and Gardens, 1520 Bronson Rd., Fairfield. Early American crafts and games for children, carriage rides, food, music, and crafts demonstrations.

THE NEW HAVEN AREA

If visitors tend to think of Connecticut as suburban and staid, then New Haven exists to shatter that common misperception. This city about midway between Boston and New York City blends a spirit of collegiate energy and urbane sophistication with a thriving arts community. It's peppered with theaters, museums, and restaurants of every stripe and is shaped as much by the presence of one of the world's most prestigious universities as by its colonial history. White-steepled churches and Yale University's neo-Gothic arches and turrets frame a stage-set town green laid out by Puritan settlers in the 1600s.

New Haven, it seems, has always been destined to stand out. For a time after the Revolutionary War, as the seat of state government alternated between New Haven and Hartford, New Haven came close to becoming Connecticut's capital. Instead, the Elm City became the state's arts and culture capital, in the form of top-flight museums, galleries, and concert halls, not to mention stellar global cuisine and a dance-till-you-drop club scene. While Yale may have put New Haven on the map, there's much to savor beyond its storied campus. New Haven is a city that walks a comfortable line between historic and hip, with a cosmopolitan air that is unique within Connecticut. What's more, it's decidedly walking scale, a plus for out-of-towners looking to leave the car behind and explore.

When it comes to world-class academia, New Haven is synonymous with Yale. The 300-year-old ivied campus offers plenty to keep visitors busy, from art, music, and drama to truly amazing neo-Gothic architecture, as well as a few modernist gems, including the Yale Center for British Art and the newly revamped Yale University Art Gallery, both designed by renowned architect Louis Kahn. Its no-admission-fee museums hold a collective treasure trove: rare British paintings, a 15th-century Gutenberg Bible, the world's largest mural depicting the age of the dinosaurs, and the oldest college art gallery in the country. There's a noteworthy roster of intellectually gifted alums, from dictionary publisher Noah Webster and submarine inventor David Bushnell to presidents (George W. Bush, Bill Clinton) and celebrities (Meryl Streep, Clare Danes, Paul Newman). Yale students even started the game of Frisbee, throwing around pie tins from the Frisbee Pie Company. If you happen to be here in November, nothing beats "The Game," the annual Yale–Harvard contest that's also college football's oldest rivalry, celebrated with lavish tailgate parties and students painted up in crimson and blue.

While the campus lends the feel of a different century, the swanky shops and eateries along Chapel Street cater to 21st-century tastes, with a mishmash of

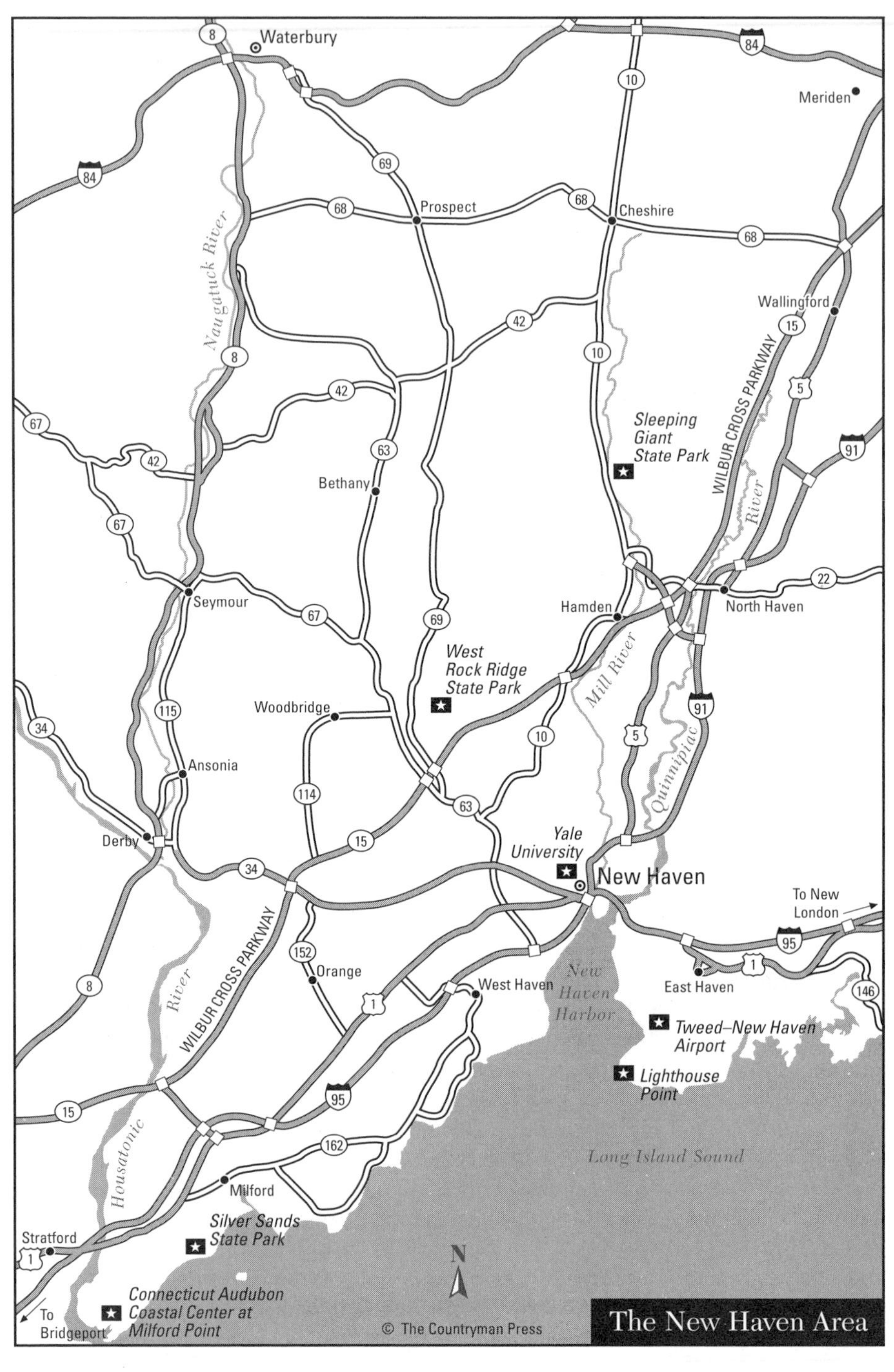

Waterbury
Meriden
Prospect
Cheshire
Naugatuck River
Wallingford
WILBUR CROSS PARKWAY
Sleeping Giant State Park
Bethany
River
Seymour
Hamden
North Haven
West Rock Ridge State Park
Mill River
Woodbridge
Ansonia
Quinnipiac
Derby
Yale University
New Haven
To New London
Orange
West Haven
New Haven Harbor
East Haven
River
Tweed–New Haven Airport
Lighthouse Point
Housatonic
Long Island Sound
Milford
Silver Sands State Park
Stratford
N
Connecticut Audubon Coastal Center at Milford Point
To Bridgeport
© The Countryman Press
The New Haven Area

unique boutiques and bookshop cafés, ethnic eateries, and eclectic galleries. The shopping district around Broadway is jam-packed with youthful retailers like Urban Outfitters and J.Crew, as well as Cutler's Record Shop, a New Haven icon. Bistros and bars line State Street; the Audubon Arts District along Whitney Avenue is known for art spaces and upscale gift shops. And then there's IKEA. In 2004, the Scandinavian home furnishings behemoth chose New Haven for its first New England store and has achieved nothing short of cult status ever since.

Shopping works up an appetite, and fortunately New Haven packs a culinary punch, with more dining options than some cities far greater in size. Ever since the lollipop was invented in a local candy factory in 1892, and Louis' Lunch served the nation's first hamburger three years later, the city has been in the vanguard when it comes to food. It's hands-down one of Connecticut's top dining destinations, and foodies are more than willing to drive here from all around the state to eat at restaurants of every ethnic persuasion, from Thai to Turkish, Ethiopian to Italian, Malaysian to Middle Eastern. Don't be surprised if you stumble upon soul food just a stone's throw away from a cozy wine bar. And while there's nothing cozy about Zinc, it dishes out among the most modern and jazzed-up cuisine the city has seen. Institutions like Claire's Corner Copia and the Union League Café rub shoulders with Nuevo Latino hot spots like Roomba and Pacifico. Did someone say something about pizza? It has been a local staple since the 1920s, and the famed brick ovens on Wooster Street—New Haven's Little Italy—offer some of the best. Get in line with the locals and ponder the age-old question of who makes America's best thin-crust pie. Pepe's? Sally's? Modern? Who knows? Maybe you'll settle the great New Haven pizza debate once and for all. These days, the Ninth Square District, one of the city's newly chic neighborhhods, seems to be where the hot new restaurants are setting up shop.

THE YALE UNIVERSITY CAMPUS IS KNOWN FOR ITS NEO-GOTHIC ARCHITECTURE.

Kim Grant

New Haven, in the finest college-town tradition, has cornered the market on cultural diversity and, well, culture. Lots of creative types—artists, writers, musicians—call it home. This is a city that supports six symphony orchestras, five dance companies, and 16 musical ensembles, not to mention galleries (at last count there were 22). Artists and artisans open their studio doors several times a year, giving visitors a peek at the creative process. New Haven's theaters also draw

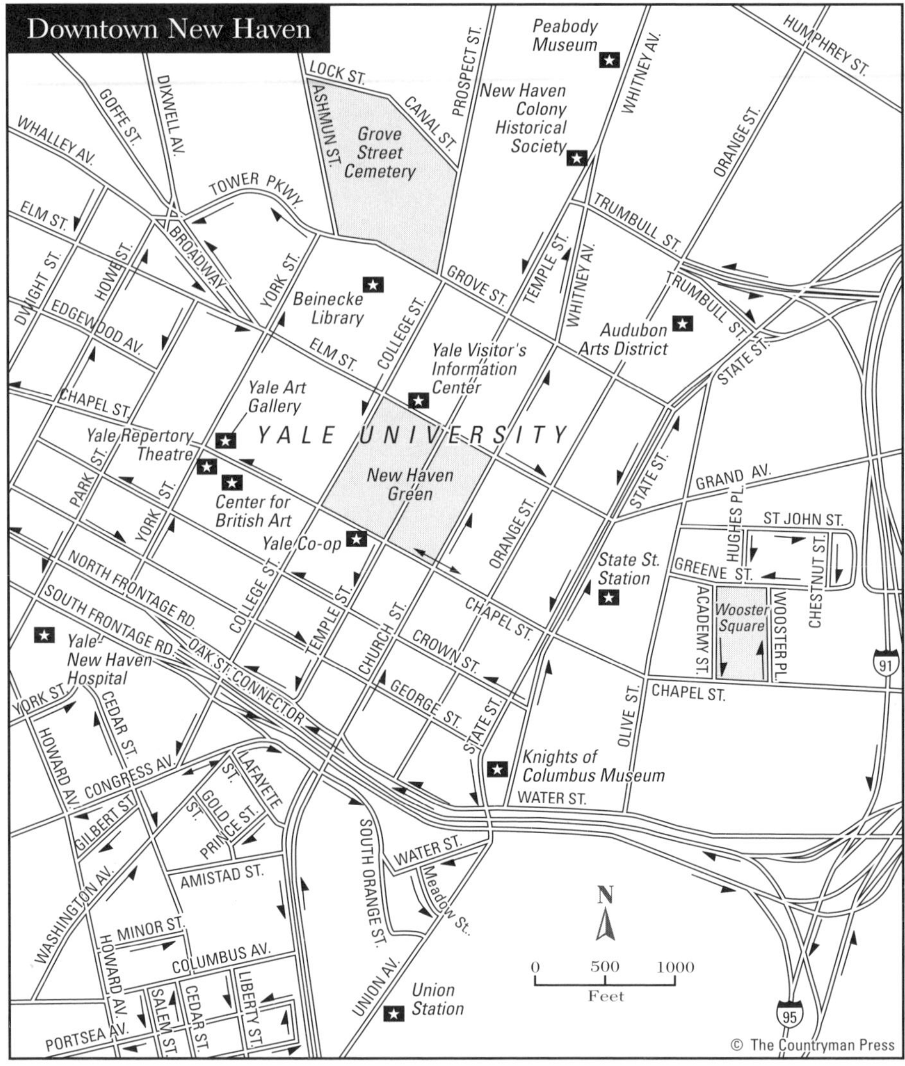

crowds. The historic Shubert, known as the "birthplace of the nation's greatest hits," was the storied venue for new shows (*My Fair Lady*, *A Streetcar Named Desire*, *The Sound of Music*) with Broadway on their minds. Al Pacino, Mia Farrow, and Christopher Walken all played the Long Wharf; and Jodie Foster, David Duchovny, and Henry Winkler performed in Yale Repertory Theatre dramas and Yale Cabaret musicals before they were stars. New Haven has always nurtured a burgeoning nightlife scene; these days, outlets for late-night partying run the gamut, and downtown hums into the wee hours. You can quaff a Guinness at Anna Liffey's, get the groove to move at Alchemy, join martini-sipping hipsters at The Blue Pearl, or catch a band at Toad's Place, the iconic rock club where the Rolling Stones once launched a world tour.

All these enticements are reason enough to visit, but first-timers shouldn't miss the myriad events that seem to increase exponentially when warm weather kicks in. The Pilot Pen Tennis Tournament draws some of the top pros—think Lindsay Davenport and Venus Williams. The pleasures of summer can be as intellectually stimulating at the International Festival of Arts and Ideas, a two-week-long cultural smorgasbord that mixes discussion and debate with the arts, or as simple as free films and live jazz on the New Haven green, itself a National Historic Landmark.

The leafy public space smack in the center of downtown was once a burying ground as well as a colonial meeting place. When the first Pilgrims from Massachusetts settled here in 1638, their village plan (the first of its kind in the nation) called for a grid of nine squares, one being the 16-acre green. Here, a bronze sculpture in front of city hall pays tribute to Connecticut's abolitionist heritage, specifically the *Amistad* revolt. Following their illegal capture by Spanish slave traders, 53 Mende African captives led by Joseph Cinque seized their schooner, *La Amistad*, and sailed into New Haven Harbor in 1839. The memorial sits in the exact location of the prison that held the surviving slaves as they awaited the historic court battle—which started in New Haven and ended in the U.S. Supreme Court—that won their freedom.

Besides enjoying New Haven's urban energy, take time to head toward the water—in this case, New Haven Harbor. For outdoor fun, stop by Long Wharf Pier, just shy of downtown, where you can tour the Freedom Schooner *Amistad*, which is berthed in New Haven when it's not visiting ports around the world. Young children in tow? You can't miss at Lighthouse Point Park, with its public beach, historic lighthouse, and 50-cent rides on a vintage carousel. To admire it all from above, hike to the summit of West Rock and savor the views of the Yale campus and Long Island Sound. A historical footnote: During New Haven's early days, three judges presided over the trial of King Charles I in England, and they sentenced him to death. When his supporters seized power again, the judges were accused of regicide and were, in turn, sentenced to the chopping block. They escaped to the New World and for a while hid out in a cave near the summit, now known as the Three Judges Cave. Their memory lives on in the names of three major city streets: Whalley, Goffe, and Dixwell.

Outside the city is a string of shoreline towns that beckons summer visitors. West Haven has Connecticut's longest stretch of public beach on the Sound—some 7.5 miles—and folks flock here to stroll the seaside boardwalk and eat some of the state's best lobster rolls and fried clams. Milford's vibrant downtown district offers bistros, antiques, galleries, and a historic village green a short walk from the town's picturesque harbor, where you can watch fishing boats ply to and fro. Nearby, the Connecticut Audubon Coastal Center protects an 840-acre refuge teeming with migrating and nesting shorebirds and songbirds. Youngsters love East Haven's Shore Line Trolley Museum, where restored antique trolleys still chug along the tracks, keeping nostalgic time with a long-ago era. Hamden boasts a museum devoted to cotton gin inventor Eli Whitney, and leafy towns like Bethany, Woodbridge, Derby, and Ansonia offer historic houses for touring and nature centers for solitude. And Wallingford, a town that once enjoyed a worldwide reputation for the manufacture of pewter and silverware, has hung on to some of its orchards and farms; today there's even a vineyard and a pair of bed & breakfasts.

Entries in this section are arranged in roughly geographic order.

GUIDANCE **Greater New Haven Convention & Visitors Bureau** (203-777-8550; 800-332-7829; www.visitnewhaven.com), 169 Orange St., New Haven 06510.

INFO New Haven (203-773-9494; www.infonewhaven.com), 1000 Chapel St., New Haven 06510. Open Mon.–Thu. 10–9; Fri. and Sat. 10–10; Sun. noon–5. A fully staffed downtown visitor information center stocked with brochures, maps, and events calendars. They will make restaurant and theater reservations, answer questions, and offer advice. Ask about one-hour guided walking tours around the New Haven green, by appointment Apr.–Oct. A satellite location at 351 Long Wharf Drive is open June–Oct. Ask about self-guided walking tours of Yale, the green, Audubon Street, and the theater district.

Yale Visitor Center (203-432-2300; www.yale.edu/visitor), 149 Elm St., between College and Temple streets, New Haven 06510. This is where you hook up with the highly popular student-led campus tours, or pick up a self-guided tour pamphlet to explore the ivied campus on your own (see *To See*).

GETTING THERE *By car:* New Haven is accessible by car from I-95, north- or southbound. From Hartford and other points north, I-91 joins I-95 at New Haven. CT 34 links New Haven to US 8 in Derby.

By air: **Tweed–New Haven Regional Airport** (203-466-8833; info line 203-466-8888; www.flytweed.com), Exit 50 off I-95, 10 minutes from downtown New Haven, is served by US Airways Express. **Bradley International Airport** (860-292-2000; 888-624-1533; www.bradleyairport.com) in Windsor Locks is about 45 minutes north of New Haven on I-91.

By rail: **Amtrak** (800-872-7245; www.amtrak.com) links Boston and New York with stops at historic Union Station in New Haven. The city is also served by **Acela Express**, Amtrak's high-speed train. **Metro-North's New Haven Line** (800-638-7646; www.mta.info) is the busy New Haven–New York commuter line that runs in and out of Union Station; it also drops off passengers at State Street Station during the week. **Shore Line East** (203-777-7433; 800-255-7433; www.shorelineeast.com) is a weekday commuter service that stops at New Haven's Union Station and State Street Station, and it connects the city to towns along the shoreline, as well as to New London. **Shuttle buses** (203-624-0151) connect Union Station to downtown New Haven and the Sargent Drive–Long Wharf area.

By bus: **Greyhound Lines** (800-231-2222; www.greyhound.com) and **Peter Pan Bus Lines** (800-343-9999; www.peterpanbus.com) offer frequent service from Union Station. **CTTRANSIT** (203-624-0151; www.cttransit.com) provides bus service to the Greater New Haven area.

GETTING AROUND *By taxi:* **Metro Taxi** (203-777-7777), **New Haven Taxi Company** (203-877-0000), **Checker Cab** (203-468-2678), and **Yellow Cab** (203-777-5555) serve Greater New Haven. **Connecticut Limousine** (203-878-2222; 800-472-5466), **Red Dot Airport Shuttle** (800-673-3368), and **Prime Time Shuttle Service** (203-891-1280; 800-377-8745) provide airport transportation and stops at area hotels.

By trolley: The **New Haven Trolley Line** (203-288-6282), a free downtown electric trolley, runs every 15 minutes, Mon.–Sat. 11–6.

MEDICAL EMERGENCY The statewide emergency number is **911**.

Yale–New Haven Hospital (203-688-4242), 20 York St., New Haven. The emergency number is 203-688-2222.

Hospital of St. Raphael (203-789-3000), 1450 Chapel St., New Haven. The emergency number is 203-789-3464.

Milford Hospital (203-876-4000), 300 Seaside Ave., Milford. The emergency number is 203-876-4100.

Griffin Hospital (203-735-7421), 130 Division St., Derby. The emergency number is 203-732-7222.

✷ To See

UNIVERSITY **Yale University** (203-432-2300; www.yale.edu/visitor), New Haven. **Visitor Information Center**, 149 Elm St., between College and Temple, New Haven. The campus of one of the world's greatest universities is home to several unique attractions, so many, indeed, that the campus tour office hosts thousands every year on free daily tours conducted by student guides. They cover Yale's campus life, magnificent gargoyle-clad Gothic architecture, and 300-year-old history. Rather venture out on your own? Pick up a self-guided pamphlet at the information center; it will guide you along the same sites. Be sure to stroll Hillhouse Avenue, the leafy campus avenue that Charles Dickens once called "the most beautiful street in America"; and High Street, home to the headquarters of the all-male secret society Skull and Bones, which counts former student President George W. Bush among its members. See the building, now a dormitory, where Connecticut hero Nathan Hale lived and studied before joining Washington's army. Behind these ivy-covered walls, former presidents William Howard Taft, Gerald Ford, George Bush Sr., and Bill Clinton also studied, not to mention Noah Webster, Eli Whitney, Samuel Morse, Sinclair Lewis, James Fenimore Cooper, and a host of other American luminaries (more recently, Paul Newman, Meryl Streep, Jodie Foster, Clare Danes, and Natalie Portman). Plan to spend time at the other Yale attractions, including the largest collection of British art outside the United Kingdom. (See also *Museums* and *Entertainment.*)

MUSEUMS ♿ **Beinecke Rare Book & Manuscript Library** (203-432-2972; events info 203-432-7325; www.library.yale.edu/beinecke), 121 Wall St., New Haven. Open year-round, Mon.–Thu. 8:30–8; Fri. 8:30–5; Sat. 10–5; closed Sun. and major holidays. Free admission. Unique architecture with translucent marble wall panels protecting the rare and fragile manuscripts from light. Among the treasured gifts from an affluent Yale alumnus is one of the world's few remaining Gutenberg Bibles, the first books printed with movable metal type in the 15th century. There's also a large collection of original manuscripts (several million!) of such authors as Dickens. The 600,000-volume library overlooks a sunken sculpture garden.

Yale University Collection of Musical Instruments (203-432-0822; www.yale.edu/musicalinstruments), 15 Hillhouse Ave., New Haven. Open Sept.–June, Tue.–Fri., Sun. 1–5; closed Sat. and Mon.; closed July and Aug. Admission $2. This collection of magnificent and unusual instruments—started in 1900 by piano manufacturer M. Steinert & Sons—boasts more than 850 European and American instruments from the 16th to the 20th centuries, including a Stradivarius and two pianos from the 1840s. Concerts featuring classic and antique instruments are held often on Sunday afternoons.

Yale University Peabody Museum of Natural History (information tape 203-432-5050; www.peabody.yale.edu), 170 Whitney Ave., New Haven. Open Mon.–Sat. 10–5; Sun. noon–5; closed major holidays. Adults $7; seniors $6; college students and children 3–18 $5; free admission on Thu. 2–5. Marvel at the huge skeleton of the brontosaurus and of other dinosaurs in the Great Hall, which houses *The Age of Reptiles*, the world's largest mural depicting the age of the dinosaurs. Expeditions to the far corners of the world by Yale archaeologists fill other exhibit rooms with minerals, fossils, and rare birds in one of the top natural history museums in the country. Ongoing lecture series and special events. Books, dinosaur models, paintings, and prints in a well-stocked gift shop.

Yale University Art Gallery (203-432-0600; www.artgallery.yale.edu), 1111 Chapel St., New Haven. Open Tue.–Sat. 10–5, Sun. 1–6; open until 8 PM on Thu., Sept.–June; closed Mon. and major holidays. Free admission. This is the oldest university art museum in America, founded in 1832 with Colonel John Trumbull's collection of his paintings of the American Revolution. Innovative, changing exhibits complement the gallery's more than 185,000 objects—paintings, sculpture, and artistic artifacts ranging from ancient Egypt, the Middle East, and Europe through French and American impressionists to the present. Works from the massive collection—the largest in Connecticut, and considered one of the finest in the world—appear in exhibitions around the country. A recent $44 million renovation of the Louis Kahn–designed building added more gallery space for viewing the Reniors, Monets, and Pissarros.

Yale Center for British Art (203-432-2800; www.ycba.yale.edu), 1080 Chapel St., New Haven, across the street from the Yale University Art Gallery (see above). Open Tue.–Sat. 10–5; Sun. noon–5; closed Mon. and holidays. Free admission. A modern steel-and-glass building, the last work of iconic American architect Louis Kahn, is a Chapel Street landmark, and it sets a dramatic stage for the largest and most comprehensive collection of British art outside the United Kingdom. It began with a gift from philanthropist and Yale grad Paul Mellon; today the treasure trove—30,000 prints, 20,000 drawings and watercolors, 2,000 paintings, and several hundred sculptures—reflects British art, life, and culture since the Elizabethan period. A fine museum shop features reproduction prints, books, handcrafted jewelry, educational toys, and games.

New Haven Colony Historical Society Museum and Library (203-562-4183; www.nhchs.org), 114 Whitney Ave., New Haven. Open Tue.–Fri. 10–5; Sat. noon–5; closed Sun. and Mon. Adults $4; seniors $3; students $2; children 5 and under free. Special exhibits tell the story of New Haven from colonial times to the present in pictures, artifacts, industrial exhibits. The **Whitney Library** is open for local history research.

Knights of Columbus Museum (203-865-0400; www.kofc.org), 1 State St., New Haven. Open Labor Day–Apr., Wed.–Sat. 10–5; Sun. 11–5; closed Mon. and Tue. May–Labor Day, open daily 10–5. Free admission. This worldwide Catholic fraternal order was founded in 1882 by Waterbury native Michael J. McGivney at New Haven's St. Mary's Church and maintains its world headquarters here. Today it's a state-of-the-art downtown museum that's not just for Catholics. Changing and permanent exhibits chronicle the history of this 1.6-million-member organization—the largest such group in the world—founded on the four principles of fraternity, charity, unity, and patriotism. The permanent collection offers a sweeping look at world history, from religious art and artifacts that trace the history of Catholicism in the New World and the founding of the Knights, to papal memorabilia, and a 400-year-old copper cross that once graced the most famous basilica in the world—St. Peter's in Rome.

Connecticut Children's Museum (203-562-5437; www.connecticutchildrens museum.org), 22 Wall St., New Haven. Open Fri. and Sat. noon–5. Admission $5. Creative programs for parents and young children. Eight rooms are filled with hands-on exhibits appealing to children's multiple intelligences—logical-mathematical, linguistic, spatial, kinesthetic, musical, and more. Little ones love the pint-sized post office, the observation beehive, and the exact replica of a scene from the classic bedtime story *Goodnight Moon.*

♿ **Eli Whitney Museum** (203-777-1833; www.eliwhitney.org), 915 Whitney Ave., Hamden. Open year-round, Wed., Thu., Fri., and Sun. noon–5, Sat. 11–4; daily 11–4 in summer. Explore the site where one of Connecticut's, and America's, first inventive geniuses worked. While living in the South, Whitney invented the cotton gin; little did he know that his invention would shape the cotton economy in the South, though with unintended consequences. The invention led to the agricultural slave economy that eventually tore the country apart. Back in Connecticut, he devised a system for dividing the labor of producing muskets through jigs and fixtures. Whitney's innovations sparked the Industrial Revolution in the North. His greatest contribution: America's confidence in the power of invention. Clearly, here was a man whose impact on the lives of millions of people after him was incalculable. The museum is a workshop in the Whitney tradition: It offers projects for children ages 5–15 to invent. Kids love the **Water Learning Lab** on the Mill River, where they can test their experiments from June to August.

Shore Line Trolley Museum (203-467-6927; www.bera.org), 17 River St., East Haven. Open Memorial Day–Labor Day daily 10:30–4:30; check ahead for off-season weekend hours. Adults $8; seniors $6; children 2–15 $4; under 2 free. Visit 100 vintage electric cars in various stages of restoration, collected from municipal transit systems all over the country. The museum is a registered National Historic Site, and the trolley line has starred in several Hollywood movies. A 3-mile round-trip ride along the country's oldest continuously operating suburban trolley line offers a unique perspective on Connecticut's shoreline region (see *To Do*).

HISTORIC HOMES **Ward-Heitmann House Museum** (203-932-9823; www .wardheitmann.org), 277 Elm St., West Haven. Open Tue.–Fri. 10–2; closed Sat.–Mon. This restored circa-1700 home is the oldest pre-Revolutionary building in town; while the year it was built is unclear, it could be as early as 1684. It stands proudly behind a picket fence; inside is a 19th-century schoolroom and five fireplaces used for hearth cooking, candle making, and other colonial demonstrations. Docents in period dress tell the story of the families that lived here over the centuries. Events like wine tastings, teas, and holiday displays take place throughout the year.

Jonathan Dickerman House (203-248-6030), 105 Mount Carmel Ave., Hamden. Open July and Aug., Sat. and Sun. 1–4; Sept.–June by appointment. Free admission.

A meticulously restored 1792 farmhouse. Also on the site: an early-19th-century barn, one-room schoolhouse, and historic herb garden featuring plants used in folk medicines.

General David Humphreys House (203-735-1908; www.derbyhistorical.org), 37 Elm St., Ansonia. Open Mon.–Fri. 1–4; group tours by appointment. Adults $5; seniors and children $2. The restored 1698 red-clapboard home of General Washington's aide-de-camp. After the war, the general (and Yale graduate, author, and poet) imported the first merino sheep from Spain and opened a woolen mill. Antique spinning wheels are among the artifacts on display in the house's meticulously restored rooms.

Osborne Homestead Museum (203-734-2513), 500 Hawthorne Ave., Derby. Open May–Oct., Thu. and Fri. 10–3; Sat. 10–4; Sun. noon–4. Holiday house tours, late Nov.–mid-Dec., Thu.–Sun. 10–4. Donation suggested. Guided tours highlight the outstanding collection of antiques and fine art in the elegant Colonial Revival–style estate of pioneering conservationist Frances Osborne Kellogg, local business leader and dairy farmer. Her estate, with formal rose and flower gardens, borders the 415-acre Osbornedale State Park and Kellogg Environmental Center (see *Green Space*).

Stone-Otis House (203-795-6465; www.orangehistory.org), 615 Orange Center Rd. (CT 152), Orange. Open June–Oct., Sun. 1–4, or by appointment. Tours of a restored circa-1830 home with herb garden, original general store, and blacksmith shop. The house and adjacent 1878 Academy Building, with its schoolroom and small local history museum, are managed by the Orange Historical Society. Ask about their schedule of traditional Victorian teas.

Thomas Darling House (203-387-2823), 1907 Litchfield Turnpike (CT 69), Woodbridge. Open by appointment. The headquarters of the Amity and Woodbridge Historical Society are in this 18th-century home, which is on the National Register of Historic Places and contains period furnishings and vintage quilts. It was built in 1772 by Yale alum and wealthy merchant Thomas Darling, who counted Benedict Arnold and Benjamin Franklin among his illustrious friends. The restored horse barn features a collection of farm implements. Outside, walking trails lead to West Rock Ridge State Park.

HISTORIC SITES

All entries are in New Haven

***Amistad* Memorial**, 165 Church St. A majestic 14-foot, three-sided bronze relief sculpture at the entrance to city hall—the site of the former New Haven jail—recalls a stirring story of an early fight against slavery. In 1839, 53 Africans were kidnapped for the slave market in Cuba. Under the leadership of Sengbe Pieh (known as Joseph Cinque), they seized their prison ship, *La Amistad*, and wound up in New Haven Harbor. Former president John Quincy Adams came out of retirement to plead before the U.S. Supreme Court and won their freedom. A replica of the *Amistad* was built at Mystic Seaport and is now berthed in New Haven when it's not visiting ports around the world.

Fort Nathan Hale and **Black Rock Fort** (203-466-1596; www.fort-nathan-hale.org), 36 Woodward Ave. Grounds open year-round, daily 10–4; visitor center open Memorial Day weekend through Labor Day, daily 10–4. Free admission. A

20-acre park with two important relics from American military history. Black Rock Fort is a reconstructed Revolutionary War–era structure built in the spring of 1776 on a ledge overlooking the harbor to repel British attackers. Fort Nathan Hale was constructed on the east shore of New Haven Harbor to protect the city from British invaders during the War of 1812; today it's a backdrop for reenactments of barracks life and maneuvers.

Grove Street Cemetery/New Haven Burying Ground (203-787-1443; 203-230-9858; www.grovestreetcemetery.org), 227 Grove St. Free guided tours May–Nov., Sat. at 11 AM, first and third Sun. at noon; for self-guided tours, pick up a map at the cemetery office. Enter through an imposing 1845 Egyptian Revival gate and visit the well-manicured final resting places of some of Connecticut's most inventive and creative minds: lexicographer Noah Webster, author of America's first dictionary; Charles Goodyear, inventor of vulcanized rubber; cotton gin inventor Eli Whitney; Samuel F. B. Morse; an original member of the Plymouth colony; many Yale presidents; and early leaders of the New Haven colony. This is one of America's oldest cemeteries, incorporated in 1796. Many of the graves here were moved from their original site—beneath the New Haven green.

Harkness Memorial Tower, High St. This soaring Gothic tower climbing 201 feet above the Yale campus was built from 1917 to 1921 and modeled after St. Botolph's Tower in England. The turrets and ornately carved figures are typical of the university's neo-Gothic architecture.

New Haven Crypt (203-787-0121; www.newhavencenterchurch.org/crypt), Center Church, 311 Temple St. Free tours Apr.–Oct., Thu. and Sat. 11–1. Beneath the upper portion of the city's historic green, settlers were laid to rest in the 17th and 18th centuries. This early colonial burial ground, now in a crypt in the church basement, allows visitors to see tombstones dating as far back as 1687; in all, there are 137 gravestones dating to 1812.

WINERY

Gouveia Vineyards (203-265-5526; www.gouveiavineyards.com), 1339 Whirlwind Hill Rd., Wallingford. Open Fri.–Sun. Bring a picnic to fully enjoy this hilltop vineyard's 360-degree panorama. You can lunch by the pond or by the winery's double-sided stone fireplace in the rustic tasting room. Gouveia, pronounced *go-veya*, grows many varieties of grapes, among them Chardonnay, Cabernet Franc, Pinot Noir, and Zinfandel.

✱ To Do

AMUSEMENTS 🍼 **The Only Game in Town** (203-234-7166; www.theonlygameintown.com), 275 Valley Service Rd., North Haven. Open daily, Apr.–Oct. A large entertainment complex that will keep every member of the family busy, with attractions ranging from a go-cart track—with banked curves, a bridge, and a tunnel—to eight batting cages for baseball and softball. There's also a lighted driving range, 18 holes of miniature golf, and an arcade.

🍼 **Smiles Entertainment Center** (203-877-3229; www.smilesentertainment.com), 1607 Boston Post Rd. (US 1), Milford. Open year-round, Sun.–Thu. 10 AM–midnight; Fri. and Sat. 10 AM–2 AM. An indoor/outdoor family entertainment facility, with batting cages, an arcade with more than 300 pinball machines and video games, miniature golf, bumper boats, 26 pool tables, kiddie rides, and many other activities.

BALLOONING ♿ **Gentle Breezes and Soft Landings** (203-397-0521), 170 Ohman Ave., Orange. Year-round daily flights over central Connecticut, departing at sunrise. Specializing in single-person rides and instruction. Call for reservations.

BIRDING The shoreline in the Greater New Haven area is a refuge for shoreline birds and migrating waterfowl and is becoming increasingly popular as one of Connecticut's top birding destinations. The region is a stop on the Atlantic Flyway, the major route for songbirds, waterfowl, birds of prey, and butterflies that head south for the winter. New Haven's **Lighthouse Point Park** and **East Rock Park** draw birders to Morris Creek, where migrating songbirds and birds of prey travel through on their spring and fall migrations. In Milford, the **Connecticut Audubon Coastal Center at Milford Point** (203-878-7440; www.ctaudubon.org) protects a barrier beach, and an 840-acre salt marsh where the Housatonic River flows into Long Island Sound. Shorebirds feed in the marsh at low tide and roost on the sandbars at high tide. Important birding areas in West Haven include **Sandy Point**, known for its American oystercatchers and threatened species like piping plovers, while the mouth of the **Oyster River** is a prime vantage point for viewing many kinds of gulls.

BOAT EXCURSIONS **Freedom Schooner *Amistad*** (203-495-1839; 866-264-7823; www.amistadamerica.org), Long Wharf Pier, 389 Long Wharf Dr., New Haven. The Freedom Schooner *Amistad* is a replica of the cargo ship on which Africans bound for slavery revolted before arriving in New Haven, where they were put on trial and later freed. Connecticut's Tall Ship Ambassador and Flagship visits ports around the world and serves as a floating classroom when it's home on New Haven Harbor. Check ahead to see when the *Amistad* will be in New Haven; don't miss the guided tours and public sails on Long Island Sound.

Schooner Sound Learning (203-865-1737; www.schoonerinc.org), Long Wharf Pier, New Haven (office: 60 South Water St.). Public sails Memorial Day weekend–Labor Day weekend; reservations are required. Three-hour trips aboard New Haven's flagship the *Quinnipiack*, a gaff-rigged, 91-foot wooden schooner. On some trips, sailor-guides explain the ecology, culture, and history of the Sound; other excursions range from sunset trips to historical reenactments.

BOATING The state operates boat launches at **Lighthouse Point Park** in New Haven, on the east side of the **Housatonic River** in Milford, and **off Naugatuck Avenue** in the Devon section of town. Another public launch in Milford is at the head of **Milford Harbor**. Visiting yachters may rent slips at area marinas or put in for a short visit to take on supplies and fuel. Most of the New Haven–area marinas are in the waters off Milford. Call ahead for reservations and information.

In New Haven and West Haven

New Haven Yacht Club (203-469-9608), 156 Cove St., in the Morris Cove section of New Haven. Reciprocal hospitality for members of other clubs.

Oyster Point Marina (203-624-5895), 98 South Water St., New Haven.

West Haven Cove Marina (203-933-3000), 13 Kimberly Ave., West Haven. Open May–Nov. A marina on the West River with full services, 120 slips, and winter storage.

In Milford

Flagship Marina (203-874-1783), 40 Bridgeport Ave. Open year-round, full services, 80 slips.

Milford Harbor Marina (203-878-2900), 2 High St. Open year-round, 250 slips, dry dock, full services.

Milford Landing Marina (203-874-1610), 37 Helwig St. Open daily mid-May–Columbus Day. A municipal marina at the head of Milford Harbor and close to restaurants and shops in Milford's historic downtown. The landscaped waterfront promenade includes a rose garden and a picnic area.

Milford Yacht Club (203-783-0065), 131 Trumbull Ave. Transient slips are available for visiting boaters; full services, restaurant, and bar.

Port Milford (203-877-7802), 164 Rogers Ave. Full services, dry dock, open year-round, 100 slips.

Spencer's Marina, Inc. (203-874-4173), 44 Rose St. Open spring through fall, full services, dry dock.

CANOEING **Canoe New Haven** (203-946-6768; www.cityofnewhaven.com/parks), various locations. Canoe guides lead trips on rivers, lakes, and New Haven Harbor mid-May–Oct. Beginners and novice boaters are welcome; instruction in basic paddling techniques is included, as is use of canoes, paddles, and other equipment. Trips offer wildlife viewing. Ask about special excursions (a fee is charged) like the popular full-moon paddle trips and sea kayaking.

See also the Connecticut Audubon Coastal Center under *Green Space.*

FISHING Stocked-trout fishing is available at **Sleeping Giant State Park** (203-789-7498), 200 Mount Carmel Ave., Hamden, and **Wharton Brook State Park** (203-269-5308), CT 5, New Haven. Lake Wintergreen in **West Rock Ridge State Park**, Hamden (203-789-7498), is another prime fishing spot. In Milford, **Gulf Beach** (203-783-3280), Exit 39 off I-95, has a fishing pier on Gulf Pond; and **Silver Sands State Park** (203-735-4311), Exit 35 off I-95, is a popular fishing spot, both on the beach and along the sandbar that stretches to Charles Island at low tide. At low tide, the exposed tidal pools and sandbars are a beachcomber's delight.

In New Haven, **Reel Crazy Sportfishing** (203-619-4753) offers charter fishing trips out of Oyster Point Marina.

GOLF **Alling Memorial Golf Course** (203-946-8014), 35 Eastern St., New Haven. Par 72, 18 holes, 6,283 yards.

Laurel View Country Club (203-281-0670; www.laurelviewcc.com), 310 West Shepard Ave., Hamden. Par 72, 18 holes, 6,924 yards.

Sleeping Giant Golf Course (203-281-9456), 3931 Whitney Ave., Hamden. Par 35, nine holes, 2,671 yards. A busy course near Sleeping Giant State Park.

Grassy Hill Country Club (203-795-1422; www.grassyhillcountryclub.com), 441 Clark Lane, Orange. Par 70, 18 holes, 6,208 yards.

Orange Hills Country Club (203-795-4161; www.orangehillscountryclub.com), 389 Racebrook Rd., Orange. Par 71, 18 holes, 6,499 yards.

Great River Golf Club (203-876-8051; www.greatrivergolfclub.com), 130 Coram Lane, Milford. Par 72, 18 holes, 7,209 yards. A scenic course along the banks of the Housatonic River.

Woodhaven Country Club (203-393-3230), 275 Miller Rd., Bethany. Par 36, nine holes, 3,387 yards.

HAYRIDES AND SLEIGH RIDES

Maple View Farm (203-799-6495), 603 Orange Center Rd., Orange. Available year-round daily by appointment only. Pony rides plus horse-drawn wagon rides, depending on the season. A party barn with petting zoo is available for groups, with prior arrangement.

HIKING **West Rock Ridge State Park** (203-789-7498), Wintergreen Ave., Hamden. Open daily 8 AM–sunset. Free admission. New Haven is flanked by two huge outcroppings—East Rock and West Rock. Scenic views of New Haven and the Sound can be found along the hiking trails on the park's 40 acres: Try the challenging 6.3-mile **Regicides Trail**, which follows the ridge crest north to Hamden. From the top at 627 feet, the panorama takes in the Yale campus, New Haven Harbor, and Long Island Sound. The **West Rock Nature Center** has a small zoo with reptiles, mammals, and native birds.

Sleeping Giant State Park (203-789-7498; www.sgpa.org), 200 Mount Carmel Ave., off CT 10, Hamden. Open daily 8 AM–sunset. Fee on weekends and holidays: $7 residents, $10 nonresidents. The name of the 1,533-acre park comes from its distinguishing crest, which resembles the head of a sleeping giant arising from its center. Picnicking, hiking, and more than 30 miles of trails—some popular, others solitary—featuring cliffs, views, and spectacular rhododendron displays in spring. This rugged, suburban oasis attracts hikers year-round. The 1.6-mile **Tower Trail** leads to sweeping views from the park's Depression-era stone lookout tower. Check the Web site for a calendar of more than 15 guided hikes scheduled each year.

See also *Mountain Biking* and *Green Space.*

MOUNTAIN BIKING **Sleeping Giant State Park** (203-789-7498; www.sgpa.org), 200 Mount Carmel Ave. (CT 10), Hamden. Open daily 8 AM–dusk. Explore a network of 11 trails in this 1,533-acre park. A popular route is the 1.6-mile path to the stone tower at the summit.

In New Haven, **College Street Cycles** (203-865-2724; www.collegestreetcycles.com), 252 College St., and **The Devil's Gear Bike Shop** (203-773-9288; www.thedevilsgear.com), 433 Chapel St., are good sources for repairs, equipment, and advice on other local places to ride, as is **Baybrook Bicycles** (203-933-4576; www.baybrookbicycles.com), 243 Captain Thomas Blvd., West Haven.

SPECTATOR SPORTS **Sports Haven** (203-946-3201), 600 Long Wharf Dr., New Haven. Open daily. There are no thoroughbred racing tracks in Connecticut, but this is the world's first simulcast racing theater. Four movie-sized screens—

along with hundreds of monitors—broadcasting live jai alai, as well as thoroughbred, harness, and greyhound racing, are a nice substitute. A game room, a 17-foot-tall aquarium with exotic sharks, and restaurants round out this unique entertainment complex.

SWIMMING In addition to freshwater swimming at inland state and municipal parks and nature centers, visitors are welcome at the Long Island Sound saltwater beaches of New Haven, West Haven, East Haven, and Milford. Be advised that these beaches do not boast the pure white sands and crystal-clear waters of the Caribbean; but on a hot day when the kids are cranky, as we say, any port in a sweaty storm. Special fees for nonresidents.

🖍 **Lighthouse Point Park** (203-946-8019), 2 Lighthouse Point Rd., Exit 50 off I-95, New Haven. Open year-round, daily 7 AM–sunset. Summer parking fee $10; carousel 50 cents. Swim, hike, and picnic on 82 acres on Long Island Sound. The antique carousel, replete with 72 vibrant, ornately carved horses, operates Memorial Day weekend–Labor Day, daily 11–5. Nature trails, bird sanctuary, picnic grove.

The West Haven Recreation Department operates a string of beaches, all accessible from Exit 42 off I-95: **Bradley Point**, **Morse**, **Oak Street**, and **Sandy Point beaches** (203-937-3651). Sandy Point is a birding hot spot, while Bradley Point is known for its 3.5-mile boardwalk, popular with walkers and bikers. Beaches open 9 AM–dusk; lifeguards are on duty Memorial Day–Labor Day. Daily fee $10; $5 after 4 PM.

In Milford, swimmers can head to three lifeguard-staffed beaches that have public parking: **Gulf Beach** (203-783-3280), Gulf St., Exit 39 off I-95, has a fishing pier at the mouth of Milford Harbor, as well as a concession stand, and a pond for birding and paddling. **Walnut Beach** (203-783-3280), on Viscount Dr., Exit 34 off I-95, has picnic tables and the best sand—it hosts a popular sand-castle contest in August. The daily fee at both beaches is $5. Also in town, **Silver Sands State Park** (203-735-4311), Exit 35 off I-95, is largely undeveloped, so it's your best bet for a quiet summertime day at the beach. At low tide, you can walk out on a sandbar to Charles Island, where—like many spots along the coast of Long Island Sound—treasure was reputedly buried by Captain Kidd in 1699. Today the 14-acre island is a nature preserve. The wooden seaside boardwalks at this 310-acre state park—Connecticut's newest state beach—are popular with strollers. Admission is free.

TROLLEY RIDE 🖍 **Shore Line Trolley Museum** (203-467-6927; www.bera.org), 17 River St., East Haven. Open Memorial Day–Labor Day, daily 10:30–4:30; check ahead for off-season weekend hours. Adults $8; seniors $6; children 2–15 $4; under 2 free. Take the children or the trolley buff in your family on a 3-mile round-trip ride along the country's oldest continuously operating suburban trolley line, bumping along tracks and trestles through tidal estuaries and salt marshes from Sprague Station in East Haven to Short Beach in Branford. Afterward, check out the collection of vintage electric cars (see *To See*).

✳ Winter Sports

ICE SKATING State and local parks, some already listed, offer skating on outdoor ponds when the mercury dips below freezing and stays there long enough to create safe ice. Indoor rinks make their own ice. Rentals, a food concession, and a fireplace are available at the **Ralph Walker Skating Pavilion** (203-946-8007), 1080 State St., New Haven. Rentals also are available at the **Edward L. Bennett Skating Rink** (203-931-6890), West Haven High School, 1 Circle St., West Haven; the **Louis Astorino Ice Arena** (203-287-2610), Hamden High School, 595 Mix Ave., Hamden; the **Milford Ice Skating Pavilion** (203-878-6516), 291 Bic Dr., Milford; and the **Veterans Memorial Ice Rink** (203-468-3367), 71 Hudson St., East Haven.

✷ Green Space

NATURE CENTERS **Ansonia Nature and Recreation Center** (203-736-1053; www.ansonianaturecenter.org), 10 Deerfield Rd., Ansonia. Trails open daily sunrise to sunset; interpretive center open daily 9–5. Two miles of wooded nature trails meander past a pond, meadows, and upland swamp spread across 146 acres near the Woodbridge town line. Families like the picnic areas, playground, and playing fields. Check out the butterfly, hummingbird, native fern, and wildflower gardens; then head inside to browse the shop and library in the nature center. Special programs, including guided hikes, take place on Sundays.

Connecticut Audubon Coastal Center at Milford Point (203-878-7440; www.ctaudubon.org), 1 Milford Point Rd., Milford. Grounds open daily, dawn to dusk. Nature center open Tue.–Sat. 10–4; Sun. noon–4; closed Mon. Free admission. Excuse the pun, but birders have a field day on the **Smith-Hubbell Wildlife Refuge**, an 8.4-acre barrier beach, and the adjoining 840-acre spit of land known as the **Charles E. Wheeler Salt Marsh**, which curls into the Housatonic River, splitting it off from Long Island Sound. In pleasant weather, plan on spending an hour or two watching shoreline birds and migrating waterfowl. Bring binoculars, the bird books of Connecticut naturalist Roger Tory Peterson, and your own notepads. Call for a schedule of nature programs, including guided canoe trips, lectures, and family activities.

THE CHARLES E. WHEELER SALT MARSH AT THE CONNECTICUT COASTAL AUDUBON COASTAL CENTER IN MILFORD IS A BIRDER'S PARADISE.

✐ ♿ **Kellogg Environmental Center** (203-734-2513), 500 Hawthorne Ave., Derby. Open Tue.–Sat. 9–4:30; closed Sun. and Mon. Free admission. Environmental and hands-on science programs, lectures, exhibits, guided field walks, and many activities for children. Located on the grounds of the Kellogg estate and surrounded by lovely gardens. A research library, solar greenhouse, and nature store are also on the premises.

PARKS Unless otherwise noted, the parks are open all year from sunrise to sunset. Call for program schedules.

In New Haven

🐾 ✐ **East Rock Park** (203-946-6086; www.newhavenparks.org), at Orange and Cold Springs streets, on the New Haven–Hamden town line. Access to the summit, Apr.–Nov., daily 8 AM–sunset; closed Nov.–Apr. 1, except on Fri., Sat., and Sun. when the roads are open, weather permitting. From atop the huge promontory, you get a panorama of New Haven, West Haven, and more, almost to Bridgeport—a spectacular view of the harbor (marred only by an oil tank firm) and Long Island Sound beyond. The **Pardee Rose Garden** (203-946-8142), 180 Park Rd., is open daily Apr.–Oct. In June and July, more than 50 varieties of roses bloom in a riot of vibrant hues; herb, annual, and perennial gardens provide color throughout the growing season. The **Trowbridge Environmental Center** offers nature programs, guided hikes, and bird walks on Thu. and Fri. from 10 to 5. Hiking trails, a playground, and picnic facilities round out the park's amenities.

♿ **East Shore Park** (203-946-8790; www.newhavenparks.org), Woodward Ave. This 82-acre park on the shore of New Haven Harbor includes a shoreline walking trail, lighted playing fields, and tennis and basketball courts. Hanna's Dream is a handicapped-accessible playground.

✐ **Edgerton Park** (203-777-8009; www.edgertonpark.org), 75 Cliff St. Open daily sunrise to sunset. Turn-of-the-20th-century greenhouses with a variety of perennials set amid an 18th-century landscaped garden. This 22-acre former estate of 18th-century inventor Eli Whitney is popular with picnickers; concerts and theater productions are staged during summer months.

🐾 ✐ **Edgewood Park** (203-946-8028; www.newhavenparks.org), 720 Edgewood Ave. Nature trails, a children's fishing pond, and wildlife displays in a 140-acre park. Tennis and basketball courts, and special family programs round out the amenities.

The New Haven green is the city's Central Park. Bordered on one side by buildings of Yale University, it is a grassy retreat in the heart of downtown. Three churches of Gothic, Federalist, and Georgian design dominate the center of the green. Concerts and other community events are held here in warm weather. Legend has it that hundreds, perhaps thousands, of Continental soldiers are buried under the green. Although generally regarded as the property of the city, the green is actually owned by five proprietors—an arrangement dating from colonial days—who have the final say on its uses.

New Haven Sea Walk (203-946-8019), at the end of Howard Ave. Open daily dawn to dusk. A pleasant path along the shore of New Haven Harbor, looking out toward Long Island Sound.

Wooster Square, bordered by Wooster Place and Chapel St., is a picture-perfect copy of a typical square in London—an oasis of grass and trees flanked by gracious

Kim Grant

WOOSTER SQUARE, IN DOWNTOWN NEW HAVEN, IS REMINISCENT OF LONDON'S PUBLIC PARKS.

homes. In Wooster Square, the Victorian homes, slated for demolition, were saved and from 1958 to 1963 were restored by community action and the government. They are now the town houses of fortunate New Haven residents who have but a short commute to work in the city. Behind the homes is a row of some of the best Italian eateries—and most famous pizza restaurants—in New England (see *Eating Out*).

Elsewhere

Bradley Point Park and Promenade (203-937-3651), Beach St., West Haven. Open daily 9 AM–dusk. Daily fee $10; $5 after 4 PM. Fly kites over Long Island Sound. Bicycle trails and a long and sandy stretch of beach popular with picnickers at the site where British troops landed on shore in July 1779.

🐾 ✐ **Brooksvale Park** (203-287-2669), 524 Brooksvale Ave., Hamden. Domestic-animal zoo, picnicking, maple sugaring demonstrations, ice skating, and 195 acres covered with ball fields and hiking trails that connect to the adjacent Naugatuck State Forest.

🐾 **Sleeping Giant State Park** (203-789-7498; www.sgpa.org), 200 Mount Carmel Ave., off CT 10, Hamden. Open daily 8 AM–sunset; fee charged weekends and holidays, Apr.–Nov. Most come here for the more than 30 miles of hiking trails, especially the trail to the park's historic stone tower, but there's more on offer: trout fishing, picnicking, and group camping. The unusual name of the 1,533-acre park refers to the 2-mile-long ridgeline, which resembles the head of a sleeping giant, arising from its center.

♿ 🐾 **West Rock Ridge State Park** (203-789-7498), Wintergreen Ave., Hamden. Open daily 8 AM–sunset; park road to summit open to vehicles Memorial Day–Oct., Thu.–Sun. Scenic views from the summit take in downtown and Long

Island Sound. A pile of glacial boulders near the summit marks the site of the Three Judges Cave (see the chapter introduction).

Osbornedale State Park (203-735-4311), 555 Roosevelt Dr., Derby. Open 8 AM–sunset; free admission. Tour the restored 19th-century Osborne Homestead Museum and the Kellogg Environmental Center, or just explore the hiking trails lacing the park's 415 wooded acres. There's also picnicking and fishing on Pickett's Pond.

✷ Lodging

BED & BREAKFASTS

In New Haven

In addition to the listings below, a number of B&B reservation services offer access to rooms available in establishments throughout the state. For a list, see *Bed & Breakfasts* in "What's Where in Connecticut."

Farnam Guest House Bed and Breakfast (203-562-7121; 888-562-7121; www.farnamguesthouse.com), 616 Prospect St., New Haven 06511. When vacationing couples and parents of Yale students want a home away from home, this friendly B&B does the trick. It's housed in a handsome brick Georgian colonial mansion just a mile from the green and the Yale campus in the city's Prospect Hill neighborhood. The seven guest rooms—some with private bath, others with shared—are cozy, and free WiFi, as well as kitchen and laundry facilities, is available to guests. Full breakfast. $79–149.

Historic Mansion Inn (203-865-8324; 888-512-6278; www.thehistoricmansioninn.com), 600 Chapel St., New Haven 06511. A butter-yellow 1842 Greek Revival mansion elegantly furnished with Queen Anne reproductions. While surroundings are grand—polished mahogany, lofty ceilings—the atmosphere is decidedly relaxing and informal. Seven guest rooms with private bath. First-floor rooms—and two upstairs—have 12-foot ceilings, four-poster queen beds, marble fireplaces, and armoires. Three smaller rooms on the second floor have shared baths and are ideal for single travelers. In a bustling neighborhood of eateries, shops, theaters; close to Yale University. Full breakfast. $139–189; higher during Yale events.

The Inn at Oyster Point (203-773-3334; 866-697-8377; www.oysterpointinn.com), 104 Howard Ave., New Haven 06519. A century-old former oysterman's residence with uniquely themed guest rooms evoking the style of Tuscany, Paris, the French Riviera, New England, and the tropics. The whirlpool baths, cozy window seats, stained glass, and fireplaces make a stay at this inn a luxurious treat. Six guest rooms and suites have queen beds; most have private bath. Yale University and the New Haven green are close by. Continental breakfast. $99–289.

Swan Cove B&B (203-776-3240; www.swancove.com), 115 Sea St., New Haven 06519. A lovely white-pillared 1890s Queen Anne–style home turned inn in Oyster Point, a quiet neighborhood of historic 19th-century residences with views of Long Island Sound. Innkeeper Raquel Seacord offers two rooms and two uniquely themed suites with a kitchenette, a private entrance, and lots of room. Next door, "The Barn" offers total privacy and the ambience of a rustic farmhouse in Provence. Yale parents, weekend travelers, and corporate execs love the comfy home-away-from-home feel and proximity to downtown. Full breakfast. Rooms $139–224; suites $195–425; more during Yale events.

Touch of Ireland Guest House (203-787-7997; 866-787-7990; www.touchofirelandguesthouse.com), 670 Whitney Ave., New Haven 06511. A warm and friendly bed & breakfast in the city's East Rock section, where Irish hospitality means genuine warmth and a kettle always on for tea. Innkeepers Jeannine and Michael McCann opened their 1920s-era center-hall colonial to visitors in 1999, inspired by their travels around the Emerald Isle. The names of the four cozy and period-furnished guest rooms, each with private bath, honor the hosts' Irish roots. Complimentary snacks and beverages always available. It's just a short walk to the Yale University Peabody Museum of Natural History and a quick drive to downtown. The gourmet candlelit breakfast is a treat. $135–150; more during Yale events.

Elsewhere

The Lily Pad (203-876-9996), 44 Prospect St., Milford 06460. A charming bed & breakfast in a classic 1820 French colonial on the Wepawaug River. Innkeeper Lily Flannigan offers six Victorian-style guest rooms that share three baths. Cozy common rooms as well as a gazebo and lawn swing to relax in. Continental breakfast. $125–135.

High Meadow Bed and Breakfast (203-269-2351; www.high-meadow.com), 1290 Whirlwind Hill Rd., Wallingford 06492. Those who love old New England will like this smartly restored 18th-century post-and-beam colonial. It was a tavern when it was built in 1742; today it's a small B&B in well-preserved historic surroundings. Innkeepers Bob and Nancy Charles offer a guest room, two suites, and a cottage. Full breakfast. $110–250.

Wallingford Victorian Bed & Breakfast (203-269-4492; www.bedandbreakfastwallingford.com), 245 North Main St., Wallingford 06492. Innkeepers Becky and Dave Barrett's Queen Anne Victorian has three rooms, two suites, and an apartment for extended stays. There's free WiFi and a stocked kitchenette for guests to use. Full breakfast. $129–169; lower rates for a room without breakfast are available.

HOTELS AND MOTELS For a complete list of lodgings, call the Greater New Haven Convention & Visitors Bureau (203-777-8550; 800-332-7829; www.newhavencvb.org). Milford, just west of New Haven, and Hamden, to the north of the city, have a plethora of budget accommodations on main thoroughfares, most of them medium-sized motels.

All entries are in New Haven

♿ **The Study at Yale** (866-930-1157; www.studyhotels.com), 1157 Chapel St., New Haven 06511-4892. For years, this was The Colony, a European-style hotel overlooking busy Chapel Street and next to the Yale campus. In late 2008 it was preparing to reopen as The Study, a luxury boutique hotel with 124 rooms and suites, all with high-speed wireless Internet access and the usual amenities. Restaurant and lounge, health club privileges. Room rates were not available as of press time; inquire when planning your stay.

♿ **Courtyard New Haven at Yale** (203-777-6221; reservations 800-321-2211; www.courtyardmarriottyale.com), 30 Whalley Ave., New Haven 06511. In historic York Square, New Haven's Courtyard has all the amenities you'd expect, and 160 newly renovated rooms and suites. Bathrooms are done in granite and marble, and high-speed Internet is free. There's a restaurant, lounge, fitness center, business center, and outdoor pool. Continental breakfast. $119–199.

Hotel Duncan (203-787-1273), 1151 Chapel St., New Haven 06511. Stay cheap at the oldest hotel in New Haven, which rubs shoulders with the Yale campus and is within walking distance of the Shubert and Yale Repertory theaters. You can't beat the price, but don't expect a lot frills here—there aren't any. Just 90 simply furnished rooms (eight suites), all with private bath, in an unbeatable location. $60–90.

♿ **New Haven Hotel** (203-498-3100; reservations 800-644-6835; www.newhavenhotel.com), 229 George St., New Haven 06510. They call this the "quiet hotel in the heart of the city," and indeed it is. A gracious small hotel with the amenities of a much larger one, with 92 Queen Anne–style rooms (four suites). Amenities include a health club and two pools. $99–239.

♿ **Omni New Haven Hotel at Yale** (203-772-6664; 800-843-6664; www.omninewhaven.com), 155 Temple St., New Haven 06510. Housed in the former Park Plaza, an elegant four-star hotel with 306 rooms (seven suites), all with private bath. An acclaimed American restaurant, **John Davenport's at the Top of the Park**, offers a bird's-eye view of the New Haven green and Yale campus from the 19th floor; on the ground floor, Barcelona is a chic restaurant and wine bar (see *Dining Out*). Health club. $199–360.

🐾 ♿ **Premiere Hotel & Suites** (203-777-5337; 866-458-0232; www.newhavensuites.com), 3 Long Wharf Dr., New Haven 06511. This former Marriott underwent a $4 million renovation in 2008; today each of the 112 suites—designed for extended stays—has a full kitchen, and some have fireplaces. Outdoor pool, Jacuzzi tub, free WiFi, and continental breakfast. $159–229.

✷ Where to Eat

DINING OUT The city has been enjoying a restaurant renaissance for several years and shows no sign of stopping; hot new places continue to pop up all over. The choice eating places in downtown New Haven, if you're visiting the major museums of the university or attending performances at Yale Repertory Theatre, are clustered along Chapel Street and its immediate side streets. Some of the finest Italian restaurants in the state have been serving satisfied gourmets—and gourmands—in the area for years. With the cosmopolitan mix of folks who eat out, in good part from the Yale student body, the New Haven area has an unusually varied mix of ethnic restaurants, from Mexican, Indian, and Turkish to African, Thai, Vietnamese, and Japanese. In the towns strung along the shoreline, locally popular beachfront seafood shacks serve up lobster rolls, fish-and-chips, fried oysters, and clam chowder. **INFO New Haven** (see *Guidance*) can help with reservations.

In New Haven

Barcelona (203-848-3000; www.barcelonawinebar.com), 155 Temple St., in the Omni New Haven Hotel. Open daily for dinner. The latest in a wildly popular statewide chain of chic Spanish tapas restaurants/wine bars (also in Greenwich, South Norwalk, Fairfield, and West Hartford), this sleek steel-and-glass space is in a heart-of-downtown location that's close to Yale. Small plates $7–14; entrées $19–24.

Basta Trattoria (203-772-1715; www.bastatrattoria.com), 1006 Chapel St.

Open for lunch Mon.–Fri.; dinner daily. Food-savvy locals cheered the opening of this lively spot by Claire and Frank Criscuolo, owners of the city's legendary Claire's Corner Copia (right next door). It has all the charm of a warm and friendly Italian trattoria, complete with ethereal mural scenes on the ceiling. Ingredients are fresh and organic, many are imported from Italy, others are locally grown, and the menu reflects that. The tiny kitchen, dominated by a wood-burning oven, shows off its smarts in dishes like Pizza Basta (topped with Gorgonzola, pears, onions, almonds, and honey), wild sea bass, and *zuppa di pesce* studded with calamari, mussels, clams, scallops, and tiger shrimp. $14–30.

Bentara (203-562-2511; www.bentara.com), 76 Orange St. Open daily for lunch and dinner; dinner only on summer weekends. Malaysian-inspired cuisine in the city's historic Ninth Square district. The kitchen takes inspiration and ingredients from traditional Malaysian cooking (the chef's mother still runs the original Bentara in Malaysia), which means many dishes are spicy and hot. There are so many enticing dishes, it's hard to know which to choose. One entrée pairs curry-rubbed filet mignon with lemon-garlic pan-fried baby potatoes; in another, grilled chicken is basted with the house lime and coconut sauce and comes with steamed baby bok choy and grilled tomatoes. Traditional satay—skewered and grilled beef or chicken—are served with the requisite peanut sauce. An interesting selection of noodle bowls and vegetarian dishes rounds out the offerings. $15–27.

♿ **bespoke** (203-562-4644; www.bespokenewhaven.com), 266 College St. Open for dinner Tue.–Sun.; closed Mon. This three-level restaurant, lounge, and rooftop café is New Haven's newest hip spot. The decor is smart and stylish ("industrial-chic" is how some have described it), the contemporary American cuisine impeccable. Chef Arturo Camacho, already the city's culinary darling, confounds expectations with sophisticated dishes in the vein of goat cheese and roasted beet salad, or ginger-seared Scottish salmon in a burgundy sauce. Entrées $26–32; prix fixe dinner $29.

♿ **Caffe Adulis** (203-777-5081; www.cafeadulis.com), 228 College St. Open daily for dinner. Reservations suggested. In a city with a year-round international community, an Eritrean/Ethiopian restaurant should come as no surprise. Traditional specialties include *tibsie*, a medley of chicken, tomatoes, sun-dried peppers, and garlic; *alitcha*, a vegetable stew with a curry base; and *gored gored*, filet mignon sautéed with curried vegetables. $9–25.

Central Steakhouse (203-787-7885; www.centralsteakhouse.com), 99 Orange St. Open for dinner Mon.–Sat.; closed Sun. This all-American establishment stands out in a city teeming with ethnic restaurants. Classic, hearty steak house fare is given a creative spin and served in hip surroundings. The pan-roasted scallops with seaweed salad and pineapple-Riesling reduction is a nice way to start off, and the grilled-veal porterhouse and New Zealand rack of lamb are as hearty as you'd expect steak house fare to be. $19–47.

♿ **Hot Tomato's** (203-624-6331; www.hottomatos.net), 261 College St. Open for lunch Mon.–Fri.; dinner daily. The monumental building next to the Shubert Theater is the former 1912 Taft Hotel; today it houses a beautifully designed and inviting restaurant and bar, filled with elegant Old World touches like ornate pillars, a grandly embellished ceiling, soaring windows, and a dramatically curving staircase. The surroundings are the perfect backdrop for the contemporary menu. As expected, the namesake tomato is well represented—it is oven roasted in the house salad, sautéed with the calamari, and studded in the shrimp Piccata. House specialties show the kitchen's expert hand—pan-seared diver scallops with butternut squash and shiitake mushroom risotto, for one, or roast chicken with fried polenta, braised escarole, and a native-honey vinaigrette. Whatever you order, be sure to include their not-to-be-missed garlic bread stuffed with melted cheese, piping hot and delightfully garlicky. A spin-off of the popular Hartford original. $18–34.

♿ **Ibiza** (203-865-1933; www.ibizanewhaven.com), 39 High St. Lunch Wed.–Sat.; dinner Tue.–Sun.; closed Mon. The rich and vibrant flavors of traditional Spanish cuisine dominate the menu at this restaurant, named for the island off the coast of Spain. Foodies rave about and flock to this place for dishes like tomatoes stuffed with sautéed duck, squid, and sweetbreads, doused with mussel broth; or braised veal in a sauce of ginger and red wine. Dessert, including *bunuelos*—delicately fried puffs of pastry filled with passion fruit and vanilla cream—are a must, but then everything is. *Esquire* dubbed Luis Bollo its Chef of the Year, and *Wine Spectator* has also sat up and taken notice. $23–30.

♿ **Istanbul Café** (203-787-3881; www.istanbulcafect.com), 245 Crown St. Open daily for lunch and dinner. A lively Turkish restaurant with vibrant decor and catering to a diverse crowd. Exotic spices and flavors enhance the hummus, kebabs, and other familiar and exotic dishes. Try the *ispanak ezme*, spinach pureed with garlic and paprika; or *lavrek izgara*, a kebab of sea bass accented with *raki*, an anise-flavored marinade. End your meal with aromatic Turkish coffee or *sultac*, rice pudding with walnuts and cinnamon. $14–19.

Kudeta (203-562-8844; www.kudetanewhaven.com), 27 Temple St. Open for lunch and dinner Tue.–Sun.; closed Mon. This ultra-hip Asian fusion spot—a relative newcomer to the city's dining scene—is winning raves for its gorgeous decor and eclectic dishes with haute-cuisine twists. Try the wok-fried calamari with tamarind garlic sauce; follow it with Malaysian-style curried seafood served in a clay pot, or the sliced pork with lemongrass in a spicy coconut and peanut sauce. Just like New Haven itself, this Ninth Square hot spot draws an eclectic crowd. $13–35.

L'Orcio (203-777-6670; www.lorcio.com), 806 State St. Open for lunch Tue.–Fri.; dinner Tue.–Sun.; closed Mon. Reservations are recommended. A romantic little place that turns out stellar Italian cuisine and wine in pretty surroundings. The sleek and stylish interior is bright, airy, and uncluttered. The menu is reminiscent of central and southern Italy; service is friendly and smart. Start with paper-thin beef carpaccio with shaved Parmesan, or *insalate di pesce* studded with clams, calamari, and mussels in a lemon-wine dressing. Follow with grilled pork tenderloin, filet mignon with porcini mushrooms, herb-rubbed lamb chops, or handmade pasta with meat sauce studded with pork, veal, and beef. Specials usually feature fresh fish, sometimes served whole. If willpower doesn't crumble in the face of homemade desserts like chocolate-rum mousse, end the night with grappa or espresso. $22–33.

Pacifico (203-772-4002; www.pacificorestaurants.com), 220 George St. Open for lunch Mon.–Fri.; dinner Mon.–Sat.; closed Sun. This is the kind of place where you'll decide on what you'll have "next time" before you leave. Nuevo Latino cuisine is typically fun and lively; presentation is bold and flavors are exotic. Here it's no exception. Belly up to the blue-tile bar for cool cocktails, then head upstairs to the dining room awash in Caribbean colors—cheery pinks, cobalt blues, bold yellows, and tropical greens. Chef-owner Rafael Palomino has penned a couple of cookbooks on South American cooking, so he knows his stuff—as if the cuisine isn't proof enough. He presents you with the world on a plate, by way of flavors like saffron, cumin, and chipotle, and ingredients like plantains and chorizo. Most of the menu items come from the sea, including roast Mediterranean sea bass and robust seafood paella served in a copper pan. $18–25.

♿ **Scoozzi Trattoria and Wine Bar** (203-776-8268; www.scoozzi.com), 1104 Chapel St. Lunch Mon.–Sat.; dinner daily; Sun. jazz brunch. Reservations suggested. Chef Jeff Caputo turns out exemplary trattoria fare with a creative twist. Adventurous palates opt for black peppercorn ravioli stuffed with goat cheese, with chicken sausage, escarole, and garlic in a toasted fennel seed glaze; or grilled tilapia sautéed with mango asparagus and leeks and served over Indian basmati rice. Never mind next time—the dessert menu shines on cannoli, biscotti, tiramisu, and other Italian favorites. Dining spills onto the wisteria-clad courtyard when the weather permits. $22–28.

Tre Scalini Ristorante (203-777-3373; www.trescalinirestaurant.com), 100 Wooster St. Open for lunch Mon.–Fri.; dinner daily. Many insist this is the best Italian food in the city; Zagat apparently agrees, bestowing upon it the coveted "excellent" rating. For white linen and candlelight, head to this high-toned Wooster Street trattoria, where diners come from throughout the region, looking for the perfect place to feast on authentic Italian cuisine, delicious and beautifully served. Dinner starts with broccoli rabe and Italian sausage with garlic and olive oil, or homemade *pasta e fagioli.* For dinner, classics like shrimp and scallop scampi are excellent. Another winner is a variation of veal scaloppini with grilled eggplant, baby peas, mozzarella, and roasted-garlic *pomodoro* sauce. Desserts include all the expected players—cheesecake, crème brûlée, and a selection of sorbets. $19–29.

♿ **Union League Café** (203-562-4299; www.unionleaguecafe.com), 1032 Chapel St. Lunch Mon.–Fri.; dinner Mon.–Sat.; closed Sun. Reservations suggested. An elegant building, the former home of the Union League, has been converted into a French bistro. Crêpes with smoked salmon, duck leg confit, and steamed mussels top the list of appetizers. Alaskan halibut, braised veal cheeks, and poached Maine lobster highlight the entrées. For dessert, don't pass up the *crêpes cerise-pistache.* $20–34.

Zinc (203-624-0507; www.zincfood.com), 964 Chapel St. Open for lunch and dinner Mon.–Fri.; dinner Sat.; closed Sun. "Market inspired and globally infused" is the mantra of this urbane bistro with decor as cool and modern as its name suggests. Dishes are cutting edge and imaginative, peppered with ingredients like Italian couscous, Peruvian lima beans, Thai rice, and Singaporean peanut sauce, as well as artisan cheeses from Connecticut. From the menu divided into small plates (appetizers) and main plates (entrées), you can start with Saigon beef in lettuce wraps with chile-garlic sauce, or smoked-duck nachos with fried wonton skins and chipotle aioli. Then try specialties like pan-seared Scottish salmon with shaved fennel and rocket salad, or charred Vietnamese chicken breast with black Thai rice, sautéed Asian vegetables, and lemon-pepper dipping sauce. For a sweet finale, try the ginger crème brûlée or lemon mascarpone cheesecake with blueberry compote. Service is polished and friendly. $20–30.

In Milford

Beach House (203-877-9300; www.beachhousemilford.com), 141 Merwin Ave., in the Woodmont section of Milford. Open for lunch Mon.–Sat.; dinner daily. A Hollywood mogul once owned this Mediterranean villa, now a stylish restaurant with emphasis on steak and seafood that attracts gourmands from all over. The changing menu might feature organic roast chicken stuffed with aged prosciutto and baby spinach, or pan-seared sea scallops with roasted corn salsa. $24–36.

Citrus (203-877-1138; www.citrus-ct.com), 56 South Broad St. Open for dinner daily. Reservations recommended. Chef Ole Knudsen's eclectic American-Caribbean fusion menu is your passport to the tropics—coconut-crusted shrimp with pineapple dipping sauce is an island vacation on a plate. Pair the dish with grilled marinated skirt steak over tabbouleh salad and cilantro-garlic pesto, and you'll have no room for dessert. But if you must, chocolate peanut butter pie or any of the decadent specialty coffee drinks are stand-outs. $16–32.

♿ **Stonebridge Restaurant** (203-874-7947; www.stonebridgerestaurant.com), 50 Daniel St. Open daily for lunch and dinner. A venerable establishment on the banks of the Wepawaug River. Regulars love the veal porterhouse with roasted-tomato vodka sauce, seafood potpie, and pan-blackened chicken with portobello mushrooms and Gorgonzola. The bar offers lighter bites like wings, quesadillas, and half-pound Angus burgers. In warmer months, the crowd spills out onto the patio, where there are lobster bakes, a raw bar, and DJs on Friday and Saturday nights. $16–35.

In Hamden

Mickey's Restaurant & Bar (203-288-4700; www.mickeysgroup.com), 2323 Whitney Ave. Open for lunch Mon.–Fri.; dinner Mon.–Sat.; closed Sun. Israeli chef-owner Mickey Josephs's cooking is on par with that of New Haven's top chefs. Enjoy contemporary Mediterranean dishes like Greek paella and risotto studded with asparagus and wild mushrooms, and Grand Marnier molten chocolate cake for dessert. $17–26.

Restaurant Luce (203-407-8000; www.ristoranteluce.net), 2987 Whitney Ave. Open for lunch Mon.–Fri.; dinner daily. Reservations are recommended. Luce is serious about its wine; the list is award winning and spans the globe, with some 15,000 bottles filling the wine cellar. The well-executed regional Italian cuisine keeps pace. $21–28.

EATING OUT

In New Haven

♿ **Bangkok Gardens Restaurant** (203-789-8684), 172 York St. Lunch and dinner daily. New combinations of spiced, diced, and sliced chunky vegetables added to classic Thai fried rice make for a satisfying main course. Ask for a seat in the greenhouse atrium and watch the passing parade of Yale students with their ubiquitous book bags. $6–17.

Bella Rosa Café (203-387-7107), 896 Whalley Ave. Open Mon.–Sat. for breakfast and lunch; Sun. brunch. Grab breakfast—say, blueberry pancakes or stuffed French toast—at this cozy enclave in New Haven's historic and artsy Westville neighborhood. Regulars happily wait on the sidewalk for Saturday's all-day breakfast. For lunch, think homemade comfort food with a gourmet twist. $6–13.

Caseus Fromagerie Bistro (203-624-3373; www.caseusnewhaven.com), 93 Whitney Ave., on the corner of Trumbull St. Open for lunch Mon.–Sat.; dinner Wed.–Sat.; closed Sun. *Caseus*, Latin for "cheese," is perhaps as appropriate a name as there is for a bistro and cheese shop. The French-inspired menu includes cheese soufflés, and hanger steak with *pommes frites*. The selection of more than 100 artisan cheeses comes from farms around the world as well as Connecticut. $11–22.

Chow (203-772-3002; www.chownewhaven.com), 962 Chapel St., in the Temple Plaza Courtyard (just behind Zinc). Open Tue.–Thu. noon–10, Fri. and Sat. noon–midnight; closed Sun. and Mon. A former fur vault is one of New Haven's more adventurous culinary destinations, but most notably the city's first dim sum wine bar. As *dim sum* is Cantonese for "heart's delight," here an Asian-inspired menu of excellent small plates is easy to mix and match. Red curry shrimp with jasmine rice; pork and ginger dumplings with soy-lime sauce; warm duck confit salad with asparagus, walnuts, and mango vinaigrette; and honey- and hoisin-glazed pork ribs are followed by desserts like steamed chocolate buns with passion fruit coulis, and a crispy banana roll with tamarind dipping sauce. Sample artisan wines and beers from Vietnam, Thailand, and Japan at the wine bar, where you can hear piano music, jazz, and cabaret. In warm weather, the hip and lively crowd takes the food and fun outdoors, onto the patio overlooking Temple Plaza. $8–11.

♿ **Claire's Corner Copia** (203-562-3888; www.clairescornercopia.com), 1000 Chapel St. Open daily. Claire Criscuolo's gourmet vegetarian restaurant is a neighborhood landmark, offering home cooking to students and others with healthy appetites for close to 35 years. The Mexican specialties should not be missed; neither should the quiche. Many come just for the Lithuanian coffee cake and other incredible desserts. $6–12.

Frank Pepe Pizzeria Napoletana (203-865-5762; www.pepespizzeria.com), 157 Wooster St. Open daily. Nothing as synonymous with the city as this humble pizzeria in town since Frank Pepe hung his shingle on Wooster Street in 1925. Local lore has it that folks all the way from Vermont make a pilgrimage to New Haven for Pepe's white clam pizzas. Prepare to stand in line, no matter when you arrive. If it's too crowded, go down the alley to **The Spot**, 163 Wooster St. (203-865-7602), which is owned by Pepe's. New outposts are open in Fairfield and, more recently, in Manchester.

♿ **Louis' Lunch** (203-562-5507; www.louislunch.com), 261–263 Crown St. Open Tue.–Wed. 11–4; Thu.–Sat. noon–2 AM; closed Sun., Mon., and the month of August. Louis declared that he cooked the first hamburger sandwich in the United States in 1900. Who is to deny him? In this unprepossessing building, now crowded at noon with business types, Yalies, and knowing tourists, fourth-generation owner Jeff Lassen keeps the legacy of Connecticut's undisputed burger king alive. The beef, ground fresh daily, is cooked in upright broilers built in 1898. You can get cheese, tomato, or onions, no ketchup, mustard, or relish. Burgers around $5.

Modern Apizza (203-776-5306; www.modernapizza.com), 874 State St. Open Tue.–Sun.; closed Mon. An Elm City favorite since 1934 that's attracted a coterie of devoted fans ever since. There's nothing like the heady aroma of simmering sauce and melting cheese atop a blackened crust, the telltale result of a 700-degree brick oven. You can't miss with the simple Pizza Margarita, but hearty appetites might go for the Italian Bomb, loaded with half a dozen meats and veggies. The repertoire isn't limited to pizza, however. Calzones, pasta dishes, and chicken Parmesan are among the Italian staples on the menu.

♿ **Sally's Apizza** (203-624-5271), 237 Wooster St. Open Tue.–Sun. from 5; closed Mon. Guess who else serves clam pizza? Sally, that's who. Like Pepe, the menu brims with standard Italian American pizzas, a staple of Yale law students Bill Clinton and Dick Blumenthal, Connecticut's attorney general, when they were studying together in a drab Olive Street rooming house.

Elsewhere

Eli's Brick Oven Pizza and Market (203-288-1686; www.elisbrickoven

NEW HAVEN PIZZA

Foodies from around the country know about New Haven's Wooster Street, where coal-fired brick pizza ovens have been churning out thin-crust "tomato pies" since the 1920s, when Frank Pepe arrived in America from Naples and crafted the perfect crispy-yet-chewy crust. Lots of people started waiting in long lines, and the legend of New Haven pizza was born. In 1938, Pepe's nephew Sal broke ranks and opened Sally's Apizza, just down the street. Today each pizzeria draws legions of hungry fans, many of whom proclaim a steadfast devotion to Pepe's or Sally's, Modern or Abate's. Pepe's signature clam pizza is worth the hour-plus wait on weekends, locals will explain, but so is the spicier sauce on Sally's pies. People drive long distances and wait as long as it takes to feast on either one, so pick a line and discover what it takes for food to become legendary. And remember: On Wooster Street, it's not "mozzarella," it's *mutz*, and pizza is pronounced *a-peets.*

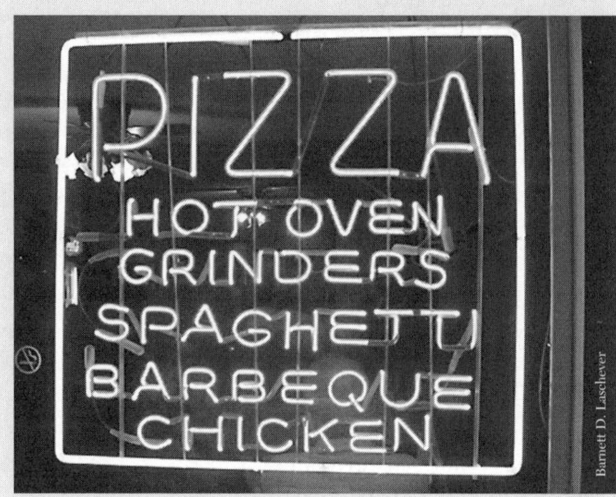

Barnett D. Laschever

pizza.com), 2402 Whitney Ave., Hamden. Open daily. Seriously authentic brick-oven pies are in the spotlight at this local favorite. Other traditional Italian dishes, pastas and the like, round out the menu.

♿ **Sono Bana** (203-281-4542; www.sonobana.com), 1206 Dixwell Ave., Hamden. Open daily for lunch and dinner. For years this was Hama, but while the owners changed the name they kept the attentive and gracious service and well-prepared sushi. The entire menu of authentic cuisine makes it one of the shoreline's best and most popular Asian restaurants. $12–23.

Seven Seas Restaurant and Pub (203-877-7327), 16 New Haven Ave., Milford. Open daily 10 AM–1 AM. A friendly, casual, neighborhood pub (downtown's oldest) near Milford harbor that serves some of the best fish-and-chips on the shore. Generous portions of clam strips, fried shrimp, and scallops accompany typical pub fare—burgers, sandwiches, and chili—as well as hearty entrées like steak and pasta. $6–17.

Daiko Japanese (203-392-3626; www.daikojapaneserestaurant.com), 400 Derby Ave. (CT 34), West Haven. Open for lunch Mon.–Sat.; dinner daily. The sushi bar here, they say, is the largest in Connecticut. They also say that this is the best Japanese cuisine in New Haven County. It's indeed impressive, with a wide selection of sushi, sashimi, and specialty rolls. $12–16.

Jimmie's (203-935-3212), 5 Rock St., West Haven. Open daily for lunch and dinner. A shoreline institution in the Savin Rock neighborhood, catering to generations of locals. Sure, you can get burgers and dogs, but most make the trip for huge portions of seafood in all its incarnations. $10–20.

Zuppardi's Apizza (203-934-1949; www.zuppardisapizza.com), 179 Union Ave., West Haven. Open daily for lunch and dinner. If you can't make it to Wooster Street for a pizza fix, Zuppardi's will fit the bill. It might not look like much from the outside, but inside is a homey local joint with killer pies. $8–16.

SNACKS

In New Haven

Atticus Bookstore Café (203-776-4040), 1082 Chapel St., just opposite the Yale University Art Gallery. Open daily, 7 AM–midnight. A fully stocked bookstore best known as a gathering place for students and professors, who sit and kibitz over coffee, hot chocolate, and pastry at its coffee bar. Sandwiches, soups, breads, and desserts all made in-house.

Keys to the City @ Caffé Bottega (203-624-6200; www.bottegane whaven.com), 910 Chapel St. Open Mon.–Sat. for breakfast, lunch, and dinner; closed Sun. Is it a nightclub/café, or is it a luncheonette/bistro? All of that and more, actually. You can grab latte in the morning, come back for a grilled panini sandwich at lunch, then return for cocktails at the end of the day. The menu covers soups, made-to-order salads and pizzas, and 24 flavors of gelato made fresh daily. Nightly entertainment ranges from live music and DJs to movie nights. $4–12.

Chabaso Bakery (203-562-9007; www.chabaso.com), 360 James St. Freshly baked, all-natural cranberry-pecan and seven-grain bread, as well as golden loaves of *ciabatta* and seeded baguettes, fly off the shelves of this family-run bakery. *Ciabatta* is flavored with roasted garlic or olive oil; the cranberry-nut multigrain loaf is another winner.

Gastronomique (203-776-7007; www.thegastro.com), 25 High St. Open Mon.–Sat. 10–9; closed Sun. Eating on the go has never been this haute. The first thing you'll wonder when you squeeze your way into this tiny sliver of a take-out spot is: How do they do it? Their motto is "The art of good eating," and it's taken seriously. Creative and expertly prepared French-inspired dishes range from beer-battered fish-and-chips with rémoulade sauce to tuna tartare with fried salmon skin and seaweed salad. On the simple-yet-satisfying side: pancakes and waffles, soups and sandwiches. The organic juice bar will have you feeling healthy in short order. Energy shakes come with protein powder, sea moss, and linseed; build your own concoction with fresh fruit, bee pollen, aloe, and other high-test healthy additions. On a college budget? Ask about their student meal plans. $5–18.

Gourmet Heaven (203-787-4533), 15 Broadway. Open daily, 24 hours. A second location at 44 Whitney Ave. (203-776-0400). Gourmet groceries and hot and cold prepared foods are available around the clock at these two upscale downtown grocery stores.

Libby's Italian Pastry Shop (203-772-0380), 139 Wooster St. A Wooster Square institution (since 1922) for cannoli made from an old family recipe. Deep-fried pastry shells are stuffed with fresh ricotta and flavors like vanilla, chocolate chip, and many others.

Sweet Relief Café (203-789-9800; www.sweetreliefcafe.com), 99 Audubon St. Open Mon.–Fri. 8–5; Sat. 11–4; closed Sun. Everything's house-made at this local meeting place in the city's arts district that serves up, according to a note at the door, "Food your Mom wants you to eat!" Indeed, the soups are homemade (Cajun chicken corn chowder), the wraps are stuffed with inventive combinations (grilled chicken, white cheddar, and strawberries), and the desserts are baked in-house. Fruity smoothies and more than 60 varieties of tea round out the menu. Everything is wonderfully fresh, familiar, and appealing, and the prices are gentle. $3–8.

Elsewhere

Chick's Drive-In (203-934-4510), 183 Beach St., West Haven. Life's a lot tastier, it seems, when it's summer and you're eating outdoors. Chick's has it all: piles of crispy fried clams, lobster rolls, hot dogs, onion rings, chowder, and a bevy of similar road-food staples. The kind of old-fashioned drive-in where you eat in the rough, with an ocean view to boot.

Stowe's Seafood (203-934-1991), Beach St., West Haven. Open Tue.–Sun.; closed Mon. One of the shoreline's best seafood shacks, run by the same family since 1923. Join the locals, who line up for quintessential summer eats like lobster rolls, shellfish, fried clams, fish-and-chips, and chowder and bisque. Eat at the picnic tables across from the beach, or at the handful of tables inside.

Bobette's Take Out (203-874-9414; www.bobettes.com), 93 Boston Post Rd. (US 1), Milford. Open Mon.–Sat.; closed Sun. Here, satisfying homestyle cooking means salads, sandwiches, and—locals rave about these—soups. In autumn, don't miss the butternut squash bisque, piping hot and topped with chopped walnuts and brown sugar.

Café Ra (203-269-2960; www.cafera.com), 1163 South Broad St., off CT 5, Wallingford. Open Mon.–Sat. for breakfast and lunch; closed Sun. Inside a large barn full of country decor, there's a menu of soups, salads, and more than two dozen sandwiches. After eating, browse the interesting selection of gourmet foods, teas, and gifts.

COFFEE AND TEA

In New Haven

Celtica Tea Room (203-785-8034), 260 College St. Tearoom open daily noon–4:30; reservations are accepted. For tea aficionados, this quaint tearoom is a welcome respite from the city's bustling java scene. High tea and a menu of light Celtic fare (scones, finger sandwiches, smoked salmon on Irish brown bread) are served in a snug room in the back of a shop full of Irish imports (see *Selective Shopping*).

Cosi Coffee and Bar (203-495-9869), 338 Elm St. Open daily until late. You can stop in for a latte in the morning, then return for a cocktail or specialty coffee drink when the day is done. The menu ranges from breakfast fare to pizza, sandwiches, and salads.

Koffee on Audubon (203-562-5454), 104 Audubon St. Open daily. A popular hangout in the trendy Audubon Arts District where the coffee is organic and fair trade. There's a second location, **Koffee on Orange** (203-752-0052), 141 Orange St., in the city's Ninth Square neighborhood.

The Publick Cup (203-787-9929; www.thepublickcup.com), 276 York St. Open late. As you'd expect in a college town, another coffee shop that bustles with students who bring their laptops and tap into the fee WiFi. Wraps, panini sandwiches, and salads are on the health-conscious menu.

Willoughby's Coffee and Tea, 258 Church St. (203-777-7400). Open daily. A good spot to slug down coffee made with beans harvested around the globe—Honduras, Papua New Guinea, Kenya, and Costa Rica, to name a few—and roasted here. They even sell mini roasters that fit perfectly in a home kitchen.

In Milford

Café Atlantique (203-882-1602; www.cafeatlantique.us), 33 River St. Open daily for breakfast, lunch, dinner, and late-night snacks. A Parisian-style downtown coffeehouse/bistro/wine bar, housed in a former record shop near the Milford green, is where an artsy crowd gathers to sip espresso, latte, and French-style lemonade. Breakfast items; creative salads, sandwiches, and soups; and rich crêpes made with Nutella, caramel, and other decadent fillings. If something you want isn't on the menu, just ask. Everything is made fresh, and the staff aim to please. In the evening, the café hosts poetry readings; open-mike nights; live folk, blues, and jazz; foreign films; beginner French lessons; and art shows. Outdoor seating in warm weather on the patio and lawn.

M-Bellish Café and Tea Room (203-283-5472; www.mbellishtearoom.com), 116 Bridgeport Ave., Milford. A charming enclave in the center of the Devon neighborhood. The formal afternoon tea with warm scones and tea sandwiches is a relaxing respite; the gift shop is stocked with antiques and other unique finds.

ICE CREAM **Ashley's Ice Cream Café** (203-288-7497), 2100 Dixwell Ave., Hamden; and 280 York St. (203-776-7744), New Haven. The original Ashley was a champion Frisbee dog, hence the colossal ice cream sundae served atop a Frisbee. More than 150 flavors of the ultimate hot-weather treat are on the roster, with 25 available on any given day. A New Haven–area institution since 1973.

Kelly's Kone Konnection (203-287-0872), 2538 Whitney Ave. (CT 10), Hamden. It's not summer without a delectable dollop of Kelly's homemade ginger ice cream. Three dozen daily flavors might include vanilla (a national award winner), the supercharged espresso chip, or eggnog and pumpkin around the winter holidays. The perfect dessert stop after noshing on burgers and dogs at the adjacent Glenwood Drive-In.

Wentworth's Old-Fashioned Ice Cream (203-281-7429), 3697 Whitney Ave. (CT 10), Hamden. Wentworth's is a local institution thanks to its rich, creamy homemade ice cream. Loyal patrons sing the praises of many flavors, such as pumpkin in fall, and peppermint stick and eggnog during the holidays. Canine Crunch is a favorite with the four-legged set (at least that's what my basset hound, Cecil, tells me). A good stop after hiking at Sleeping Giant State Park. A second location in downtown Wallingford (203-265-2814).

Walnut Beach Creamery (203-878-7738), 17 Broadway, Milford. Open daily. One side of this Laurel Beach spot is an ice cream parlor with homemade flavors; the other, a sculptor's studio and gallery. They make some of the best from-scratch ice cream around; an excellent case in point is the best seller, Nutty Yankee, packed with almonds, dried cranberries, and coconut. Other creative flavors include lavender, honey, fig, and banana bread.

Entertainment

With the Yale drama and music schools as a catalyst, New Haven has become one of the most important entertainment cultural centers in the country. At one time, nearly all major Broadway shows staged their pre-Broadway "tryouts" at the old Shubert Theater in New Haven. If it didn't make it in New Haven, it rarely made it to the Great White Way. Although the Shubert no longer is Broadway's principal tryout theater, it has been renovated and, as a performing arts center, mounts roadshow performances of the best in American dramatic arts. But New Haven is now much more than just the Shubert. In addition to the theaters and performing groups listed below, every town in this culture-crazed area has an active arts council. Check for schedules of performances and exhibits. Pick up a free copy of the *New Haven Advocate*, the venerable weekly entertainment guide, to see what's going on around the city.

All entries are in New Haven

MUSIC **New Haven Symphony Orchestra** (information: 203-865-0831; box office: 203-562-5666; 800-292-6476; www.newhavensymphony.org), 70 Audubon St. Regular season Sept.–May; summer events. Now entering its second century, the New Haven is the fourth-oldest continuously operating symphony in the United States: It first performed in 1895. Its regular concert series is held in Yale's beautiful, spacious Woolsey Hall on College and Grove streets. The New Haven also brings international symphonies and guest soloists to Woolsey. Summertime performances are held on the city's historic green.

Orchestra New England (203-777-4690; tickets: 888-736-2663; www.orchestranewengland.org), P.O. Box 200123, New Haven 06520-0123. A traveling orchestra that performs regularly at Yale's Battell Chapel, College and Elm streets. A family concert series is held in various locations.

Yale Institute of Sacred Music (203-432-5062; www.yale.edu/ism), 409 Prospect St. Performances by Yale faculty, students, and guest artists in a variety of locations; they also offer a series of films, art exhibits, dramas, lectures, and literary readings.

Yale School of Music (203-432-4158; info line: 203-432-4157; www.yale.edu/music). Performance venues vary; call ahead. Season runs Sept.–May; most events are free. The Graduate School of Music presents more than 300 performances throughout the school year, featuring **New Music New Haven**, the **Yale Symphony Orchestra**, **Yale Opera**, **Faculty Artists Series**, **Great Organ Music**, and others.

THEATER **Criterion Cinemas** (203-498-2500), 86 Temple St. The soaring mural in the lobby of this restored neo-Classical building is a clue that this isn't your average multiplex. In addition to new releases, you can catch late-night cult classics on Friday and Saturday, or movies and mimosas on Sunday morning.

♿ **Long Wharf Theatre** (203-787-4282; 800-782-8497; www.longwharf.org), 222 Sargent Dr., Exit 46 off I-95. Performances Sept.–May, Tue.–Sun. Tony Award–winning Long Wharf has attracted top stars, top dramatic works, and appreciative New England, New York, and international audiences to prizewinning plays—from classic revivals to world premieres—for more than 40 years. In excess of 30 Long Wharf Theatre productions were later staged on Broadway and Off-Broadway. A long-talked-about new downtown venue, on the site of the old New Haven Coliseum, will be the theater's first new location since it was founded in 1965. The $50 million complex, slated for a 2012 opening, will be part of the city's newly redeveloped Ninth Square retail, dining, and entertainment district.

✐ ♿ **Shubert Theater** (203-624-1825; box office: 888-736-2663; www.shubert.com), 247 College St. Evening performances Tue.–Sat.; matinees Wed.–Sun. An intimate 1,600-seat theater best known for Broadway plays, the Shubert also offers dance, opera, music, cabaret, and family productions. The Shubert brothers opened their first namesake theater in New York in 1912, two years before launching this location, a longtime venue for pre-Broadway hopefuls. More than 300 shows that debuted here (think *South Pacific*, *Sound of Music*, *The King and I*) would go on to open on the Great White Way.

Summer Cabaret at Yale (203-432-1567; www.summercabaret.org), 217 Park St. Performances June–Aug., Wed.–Sat. at 8 PM; preshow dinner at 6:30. Reservations recommended. Professional summertime theater—comedies, one-act plays, original works, and the like—since 1974.

Yale Cabaret (203-432-1566; www.yale.edu/cabaret), 217 Park St. Performances Oct.–Apr., Thu. at 8 PM; Fri. and Sat. at 8 and 10:30 PM. Dinner served before the weekend shows (at 6:30 PM and 9:30 PM); light meals and drinks before the later performance. Reservations strongly encouraged. Most works in this intimate 95-seat basement theater are written, directed, produced, and performed by Yale School of Drama students—20 cutting-edge productions each season.

♿ **Yale Repertory Theatre** (203-432-1234; www.yalerep.org), 1120 Chapel St.; **New Theater**, 1156 Chapel St.; and **University Theatre**, 222 York St. Sept.–May. In this Tony Award–winning professional theater, located in an old church, students of the Yale School of Drama and other new playwrights have an opportunity to present new works and bold interpretations of the classics.

NIGHTLIFE **Alchemy Night Club** (203-777-9400; www.alchemynightclub.com), 223 College St. Open Thu.–Sat. The trend factor is high at this downtown nightspot that's actually three different clubs under one roof, with a lively view in all directions and energy that amps up as the night goes on. The soundtrack—DJs spin hip-hop every night—complements the slick aesthetic. The café serves dinner and late-night snacks.

Anna Liffey's (203-773-1776; www.annaliffeys.com), 17 Whitney Ave. Lunch and dinner daily; brunch on Sun. A downstairs watering hole that's just what you'd expect an Irish pub to be—dark wood, Guinness on tap, musicians playing tunes from the motherland. A favorite spot among Yalies and dressed-down locals.

Bar/The Bru Room (203-495-8924; www.barnightclub.com), 254 Crown St. Open every day of the year. Something for everyone—a bar jammed with students and suits; pool tables; a dark, intimate space with overstuffed couches; a brick-oven pizzeria; and a dance club where DJs spin salsa, house, R&B, and tribal music most nights.

The Blue Pearl (203-789-6370; www.thebluepearlnewhaven.com), 130 Court St. Open for lunch Wed.–Fri.; dinner Tue.–Sat.; bar open late. This sexy cocktail lounge is a see-and-be-seen hot spot that also serves inventive small plates of upscale bar food. On weekends, it's mobbed with 20- and 30-something hipsters sipping trendy cocktails and sharing fondue.

Bottega Lounge (203-562-5566), 956 Chapel St., in the Temple Plaza Courtyard. A young, hip crowd caps off the night with specialty martinis at the marble bar of this chic nook behind the Shubert Theater. Late-night bites of regional Italian cuisine from the Adriatic coast—risottos, pasta dishes, fresh seafood, and imported desserts. Weekend DJs spin hip-hop, reggae, rock, jazz, and funk.

116 Crown (203-777-3116; www.116crown.com), 116 Crown St. There's no shortage of coolness at this Ninth Square newcomer. The tapas-style bar food, exotic cocktails, and well-chosen by-the-glass wines keep pace with the crush to see and be seen.

The Playwright (203-752-0450), 144 Temple St. Lunch and dinner daily. Part lively Irish pub, part lively nightclub, this is a downtown institution. Locals and students come during the week for the traditional Irish fare (think shepherd's pie), Guinness and other imported drafts, and on weekends for live music, fresh-spun house music, and dancing.

Richter's (203-777-0400), 990 Chapel St. Renowned for the large selection of small-batch bourbons and single-malt scotches, as well as beer, stout, and ale by the pint and in half-yard glasses. The **Taft Tap Room** in back dates from 1858, but the best spot is a seat at the gleaming dark-wood bar.

Toad's Place (203-624-8623; www.toadsplace.com), 300 York St. This is the place! For 35 years, reggae, blues, jazz, and alternative rock fans have crowded in to hear rock legends from the Rolling Stones and Bob Dylan to U2 and Bruce Springsteen, as well as the newest bands on the music scene. Call or check online for schedules.

✷ Selective Shopping

New Haven has several shopping districts, each with its own flavor. **Chapel Street**, primarily between Temple and Howe streets, is lined with chic boutiques, galleries, upscale clothing stores, museum shops, and bookstores. The **Broadway** shopping district is popular with students and young trendsetters, who haunt places like J.Crew and Urban Outfitters. For antiques, head to State Street or Whalley Avenue in the city, or go to the town green in Milford. The **Audubon Arts District** is full of galleries selling artwork, handcrafted jewelry, and contemporary crafts. In the city's old

Chapel Square Mall along the green, shops face the street instead of inside, and the city's historic **Ninth Square** district is being revitalized into a retail district.

ART GALLERIES

In New Haven

A Leaf Photography Studio & Gallery (203-562-5323), 91 Orange St. Open Tue.–Fri. 1–6; Sat. and Sun. by appointment; closed Mon. One of the latest galleries to open in the city's Ninth Square district.

Artspace (203-772-2709; www.artspacenh.org), 50 Orange St., at the corner of Crown St. Open Tue. noon–5; Wed.–Sat. noon–8; closed Sun. and Mon. Artist- and volunteer-run exhibition galleries and performance center for visual, literary, and performing arts. Call for a schedule of performances and events. This is the force behind the annual City-Wide Open Studios event every October (see *Special Events*).

♿ **Creative Arts Workshop** (203-562-4927; www.creativeartsworkshop.org), 80 Audubon St. Open Mon.–Fri. 9:30–5:30 (until 8 on Thu.); Sat. 9–noon; closed Sun. Gallery exhibitions, workshops for professional and amateur artists, and studios for painting, weaving, and jewelry making. In the crafts gallery and shop, fine craftswork in wood, glass, and metal is displayed and on sale. The annual **Celebration of American Crafts** is a popular venue for unique holiday shopping, offering fine contemporary crafts by more than 400 artists.

Elm City Artists Gallery (203-444-3100), 13 Broadway. Open Mon.–Wed. 10–6; Thu.–Sat. 10–9; Sun. noon–5. Traditional and contemporary art by New Haven artists.

John Slade Ely House (203-624-8055; www.elyhouse.org), 51 Trumbull St. Open Sept.–July, Wed.–Fri. 11–4; Sat. and Sun. 2–5. An Elizabethan-style house in the Audubon Arts District that has been a contemporary-art

BOOKSTORES, ANTIQUES SHOPS, BOUTIQUES, AND A PLETHORA OF ETHNIC EATERIES FRONT THE CAMPUS OF YALE UNIVERSITY.

Kim Grant

center for more than 40 years; it was the city's first arts center when it opened in 1961. Today it mounts several exhibitions every year.

Small Space Gallery (203-772-2788), 70 Audubon St. Open Mon.–Fri. 9–5; closed Sat. and Sun. A second-floor space, home to the Arts Council of Greater New Haven, with a dozen rotating exhibits every year featuring the work of local artists.

White Space Gallery (203-495-1200; www.whitespacegallery.com), 1020 Chapel St. Open Mon.–Sat. 10–6; closed Sun. A fine art gallery featuring classic and contemporary works, including hand-signed limited-edition lithographs by Dalí, Miró, Picasso, and other surrealist artists.

Elsewhere

Gilded Lily Gallery (203-878-7007; 877-684-5576; www.gildedlilygallery.com), 101 River St., Milford. Open Tue.–Sun.; closed Mon. This gallery in Milford's historic district specializes in sculpture, paintings, jewelry, art glass, and pottery by local and nationally known artists.

MFAC Firehouse Art Gallery (203-306-0016), 81 Naugatuck Ave., Milford. Open Thu.–Sun. noon–5; closed Mon.–Wed. The Milford Fine Arts Council runs this firehouse turned art gallery as a community arts center, with a gallery, gift shop, and studio space, and a full schedule of classes and workshops. Changing exhibits take place throughout the year.

BOOKSTORES

In New Haven

Atticus Bookstore Café (203-776-4040), 1082 Chapel St. Open daily 8 AM–midnight. This full-service independent bookstore with a bustling café is a Chapel Street fixture, where a lively mix of professors, students, and bibliophiles gather to read and snack on pastries and light meals, day and night. (see *Where to Eat*).

Book Trader Café (203-787-6147), 1140 Chapel St. Open Mon.–Fri. 7:30 AM–9 PM; Sat. and Sun. 9–9. Used titles, from general books to textbooks, and a gourmet café with outdoor seating during the warm-weather months. A popular hangout with the Yale crowd.

Bryn Mawr Book Shop (203-562-4217), 56½ Whitney Ave. Two floors' worth of out-of-print and used books makes for delightful browsing.

Labyrinth Books (203-787-2848), 290 York St. Independent shop, new and used titles, specializing in academic and serious general interest: social sciences, humanities, literature, architecture, and the like.

The Yale Bookstore (203-777-8440), 77 Broadway at York Square. Open daily. The official bookstore of Yale, described by locals as the Yale Department Store. Though it caters primarily to the needs of the students, it is open to the public (it's run by Barnes & Noble). There's a wider variety of esoteric and intellectual books than you'll find at the average bookstore, and a full complement of Yale accessories and souvenirs. A café serves coffee, pastries, and snacks.

Elsewhere

Whitlock's Book Barn (203-393-1240), 20 Sperry Rd. (off CT 69), Bethany. Open Tue.–Sun. 9–5; closed Mon. Down a pasture-lined country lane, a pair of red wooden 19th-century barns, known as the Book Barns, is chock-full of treasures: tens of thousands of old, out-of-the-ordinary books; rare first editions; and maps (20,000), prints, records, and ephemera. A Connecticut institution, and a browser's, bibliophile's, and bargain hunter's delight.

✐ **Barnett Books Warehouse** (203-265-2013; www.barnettbookswarehouse.com), 20 North Plains Industrial Rd., Wallingford. Open Fri.–Sun. The huge inventory of bargain books, many of them children's titles, includes over-stock, damaged, and remainders.

FARMS AND GARDENS

✐ **Hindinger Farm** (203-288-0700), 835 Dunbar Hill Rd., Hamden. Farm stand open May–Dec., Tue.–Sun. 9–5; closed Mon. Pick up fresh fruits and vegetables—sweet corn, tomatoes, pears, peaches—at the farm stand, pick strawberries in June, and come back in summer and fall for festivals devoted to peaches and pumpkins. Say hello to the resident goats while you're here.

SPECIALTY SHOPS

In New Haven

archetype (203-562-6772; www.archetypeclothing.com), 265 College St. If you want to know what's in—and, more important, what's next—look no farther than this chic shop. It attracts women looking to dress themselves in must-have pieces (think Theory, Diane von Furstenberg, Trina Turk, Plenty). If your style falls under funky, there's plenty of fun garb for you, too.

Celtica (203-785-8034), 260 College St. Open Mon.–Sat. 10–7; Sun. noon–5. This is where to go for authentic Celtic and Irish goods, from jewelry and pottery to clothing and gifts, straight from Ireland. Look for hard-to-find Irish china and crystal imported from the Emerald Isle, and traditional hand-knit wool sweaters from the Aran Islands. A tearoom in back serves high tea and a menu of light Celtic fare (see *Where to Eat*), and is open daily noon–4:30.

Cutler's (203-777-6271; www.cutlers.com), 25–27 Broadway. Open daily. Audiophiles beware: step into this independent record shop and you'll never want to leave. Ever. It's an area treasure, where passion for music is evident everywhere, from the CDs and DVDs to LPs and 45s (remember those?). Rare live recordings, indie labels, and hard-to-find music are all here, too.

Fair Haven Furniture (203-776-3099; ww.fairhaven-furniture.com), 72 Blatchley Ave. Open Thu.–Mon. A haven for furniture fanatics, it also stocks clothing, jewelry, and whimsical gifts (we love the jewelry trees) spread across three floors in a converted factory building. The first-floor River Street Gallery has changing art exhibits.

Group W Bench Gallery (203-624-0683), 1171 Chapel St. They call themselves a gallery, but this place is more of a throwback to the 1960s, crammed with all things funky—from toys and jewelry to offbeat home accessories.

✐ **IKEA** (203-865-4532; 800-434-4532), 450 Sargent Dr., Exit 46 off I-95. Open Mon.–Fri. 10–9; Sat. 9–9; Sun. 10–8. New England's first IKEA lures thousands of shoppers with affordably priced, unfussy Scandinavian-designed furniture and accessories. Ingvar Kamprad founded the home furnishings behemoth in 1943, selling functional furniture with a clean, simple look. In all, 50 showrooms display kitchens, dining and living rooms, bedrooms and bathrooms, offices, and children's playrooms. They know how to make shopping easy—there's a supervised play area for the kids, a café serving traditional Swedish and American fare, and a food market with smoked salmon, lingonberries, pickled herring, and other imported treats to take home.

Sogno Boutique of Dreams (203-777-3226; www.sognoboutique.com),

83B Audubon St. A good place to score chic fashion staples and accoutrements for the home.

Ten Thousand Villages (203-776-0854; www.newhaven.tenthousandvillages.com), 1054 Chapel St. Open daily. One-of-a-kind fair-trade handicrafts from around the world, meaning a fair income is paid to artisans and crafters working in third-world countries. You might find jewelry from Haiti, sculpture from Peru, or ceramic planters made in Vietnam. The other Connecticut location is in West Hartford.

Elsewhere

H. Mangels Confectioner (203-783-9770; www.hmangels.com), 58 River St., Milford. The Mangels family have been purveyors of high-quality chocolates since Henry Mangels opened a chocolate shop in New York City in 1898. Their chocolate truffles, handmade in small batches with all-natural ingredients (chocolate, heavy cream, butter, liqueur), are beyond decadent. Flavors like espresso, champagne, banana schnapps, and double Dutch chocolate fly off the shelves.

The Villa Gourmet (203-878-8646; www.thevillagourmet.com), 11 River St., Milford. Open daily. Gourmands will think they've died and gone to heaven: Here the shelves are stocked with the likes of caviar, artisan cheeses, tapenades, and aged balsamic vinegars. The homemade ravioli—stuffed with smoked chicken, crabmeat artichokes, and other inventive fillings—make a quick and easy gourmet dinner, as does the fresh fish, available on Saturdays.

L.L. Bean (203-795-3500), 560 Boston Post Rd. (US 1), in the Orange Meadows Shopping Center, Orange. Open daily. A new outlet store of the venerable Maine outfitter; returns, overstock, and discontinued items are up to 60 percent off retail.

✷ Special Events

March: **St. Patrick's Day Parade** (203-248-4826; www.stpatricksdayparade.org), downtown New Haven. A city tradition since the 1950s.

April: **Communiversity Day** (203-432-0591), on Yale's Old Campus, New Haven. A celebration with city and university. **Wooster Square Cherry Blossom Festival** (203-865-8961), Wooster Square, New Haven. This festival in one of the city's historic neighborhoods heralds the arrival of spring.

✐ *May:* **Meet the Artists and Artisans** (203-874-5672), Milford green, Broad St., Milford. Juried arts-and-crafts show with more than 200 hand-selected exhibitors from around the nation. Photographers, painters, sculptors, and other artisans display and discuss their work. A popular exhibition for nearly 50 years. (See also *September.*)

June: **International Festival of Arts and Ideas** (203-562-5666; 888-736-2663; www.artidea.org), New Haven. A cultural festival offering more than two weeks of theater, music, dance, and poetry, as well as discussions, debates, and family programs featuring "artists and thinkers from around the globe." Most events are free. **St. Andrew Society Annual Festa** (203-776-0693), 515 Chapel St., New Haven. An Italian festival held in Wooster Square for more than 100 years; live music, parade, all kinds of Italian food.

July: ✐ **Celebrate New Haven Fourth** (203-946-7821), Long Wharf Park, Long Wharf Dr., New Haven. Festivities include one of the state's largest fireworks displays, strolling musicians, waterfront picnicking, live music. Other Independence Day fireworks celebrations on Long Island Sound at the town beach in East Haven, and at Bradley Point in West Haven.

Summer: **Pilot Pen Tennis Tournament** (203-776-7331; 800-997-4568; www.pilotpentennis.com), Connecticut Tennis Center, 45 Yale Ave., New Haven. Main court and adjoining side courts attract the top professional tennis players in the world for this weeklong tournament on the Yale campus. **Free Friday Flicks on the Green** (203-776-6789; www.filmfest.org), on the green, New Haven. Film series showing classic movies beginning just after dark. Bring a lawn chair or picnic blanket. **Summer Concert Series**, on the green, New Haven. **Shakespeare in the Park** (203-393-1436; www.elmshakespeare.org), Edgerton Park, New Haven. The Elm Shakespeare Company performs the works of Shakespeare with a cast that includes professional actors and students. Do like the locals and come early with a picnic.

August: **New Haven Jazz Festival** (203-393-3002; www.newhavenjazz.com), on the green, New Haven. Free live jazz concerts on the city's historic green. ✐ **Milford Oyster Festival** (203-878-5363; www.milfordoysterfestival.org), at and around Milford Harbor, Milford. A 35-year community tradition—arts and crafts, children's activities, musical entertainment, a classic car show, farmer's market, fresh oysters.

Labor Day weekend: **New Haven Road Race** (203-481-5933; www.newhavenroadrace.org), New Haven green, New Haven. Three races—20K, 5K, and a half-mile children's run—attract more than 5,000 participants, including nationally ranked elite runners.

September: ✐ **Connecticut Folk Festival** (877-928-3655); www.ctfolk.org), various locations, New Haven. ✐ **North Haven Fair** (203-239-3700; www.northhaven-fair.com), North Haven Fairgrounds, Washington Ave. (CT 5), North Haven. A traditional fair featuring livestock and agricultural exhibits, pony rides, a petting zoo, entertainment, vendors, rides, and food; since 1942. ✐ **Engine 260 Antique Fire Apparatus Show and Muster** (203-874-2605), Eisenhower Park, CT 121, Milford. A great family event for nearly 40 years. The largest such show on the East Coast, with a parade of 100 fire engines, muster competitions, and fire-safety demonstrations. **Meet the Artists and Artisans** (203-874-5672), Milford green, Broad St., Milford. Juried crafts show with more than 200 exhibitors, held in spring (see *May*) and fall. ✐ **Orange Country Fair**, CT 152, Orange. A small-town fair with old-fashioned fun, in the form of tractor pulls, pie-eating contests, pigeon races, and a women's skillet-toss competition.

October: **City-Wide Open Studios** (203-772-2709; www.cwos.org), New Haven. More than 400 artists around the city open their studios so visitors can see work representing every medium, from painting to pottery. Three weekends; call for a schedule.

November: **Yale v. Harvard Football** (203-432-1400), New Haven. Yale hosts Ivy League gridiron contests in the Yale Bowl; but nothing beats "The Game," when the Crimson boys come to town. Join the alumni in blue at the world's most lavish tailgate luncheons celebrating college football's oldest rivalry.

December: ✐ **Fantasy of Lights** (203-777-2000), Lighthouse Point Park, New Haven. Drive through an enchanting land of more than 200,000 twinkling lights and 38 spectacular displays, many animated. **Celebration of American Crafts** (203-562-4972), Creative Arts Workshop, 80 Audubon St., New Haven. More than 400 craftspeople from around the country come to this holiday-season juried show.

THE HOUSATONIC VALLEY

Visitors to the Housatonic Valley—known as the western gateway to Connecticut—often notice the scenery unfold as the Gold Coast's air of exclusivity makes way for the quaint colonial villages synonymous with quintessential New England. The valley is a link between the sophistication of the Gold Coast and the history and charm of the Litchfield Hills, and the result is a pleasing blend of both. The area is anchored by the city of Danbury, where the "hat that won the West"—the 10-gallon Stetson—was first fashioned. But in colonial days Danbury was known (take notice, Bostonians) as Beantown, because its major crop was beans, which were exported to Norwalk. Then came men's hats in 1780, and some 40 factories in America's Hat City that produced fedoras, derbies, top hats, and stovepipe hats. Then in the 1960s, when President Kennedy went bareheaded in all his public appearances, hats trickled out of style in America, and Danbury went into a decline.

Today Danbury is a city of 76,000 with historical and cultural attractions as well as ethnic eateries—Peruvian, Brazilian, and Italian, to name a few—that reflect the city's diverse immigrant population. The local historical society museum explores Danbury's glory days as America's hatmaker, as well as its colonial history and Revolutionary War ties. Nationally known musicians grace the stage at Ives Concert Park, a beautiful open-air venue named for native son Charles Ives, Pulitzer Prize–winning composer and "Father of American Music." There are museums for rail buffs (Danbury Railway Museum) and military aficionados (Military Museum of Southern New England), and for gourmets, one of the finest French restaurants in Connecticut (Bernard's).

By contrast, the Housatonic Valley is dotted with well-heeled rural suburbs and charming colonial centers that could each serve as a model for a Norman Rockwell painting. Of these, Ridgefield is best at mixing classic old Yankee with cultural sophistication. It's a Hollywood set designer's dream, particularly the lovely tree-lined Main Street, where most buildings date from the 18th and 19th centuries. Stately mansions reside side by side with a Revolutionary War tavern turned house museum, gracious inns and fine restaurants, and one of the top small contemporary-art museums in the country. If you're short on time, the Aldrich is a must-see—edgy modern art fills a gem of a building that's part 18th-century farmhouse, part bold architectural wonder. Ridgefield's chic and sophisticated town center bustles with upscale boutiques, art and antiques shops, and jazzy eateries, and you'll find a symphony orchestra, an opera company, and an active community

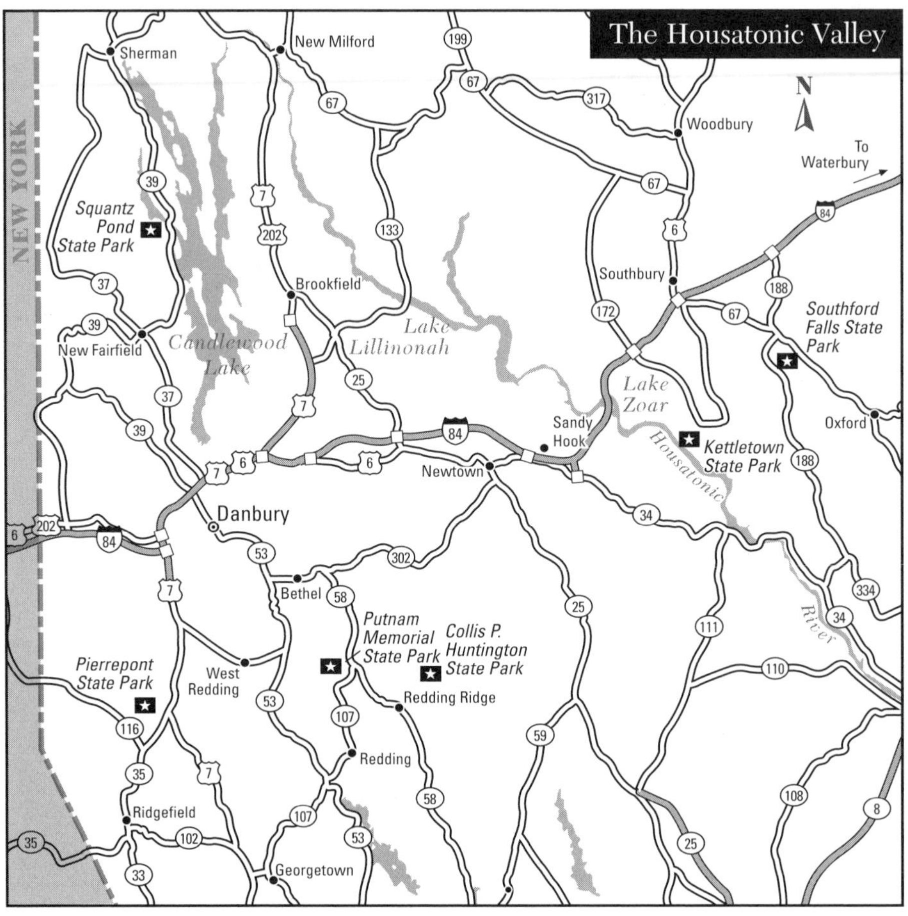

theater residing in a converted dairy barn. No wonder visitors and residents agree that this is Fairfield County with "real" New England flavor, not to mention one of the prettiest towns in Connecticut. Not surprisingly, the area attracts swarms of visitors from New York City, who like the combination of cultural offerings (think symphony, cutting-edge contemporary art, theater), fine cuisine, and laid-back country pace—the perfect antidote to the stresses of urban living.

Redding, Ridgefield's rural neighbor, also has a place in Revolutionary War history. During a break in the hostilities, part of Washington's Northern Army set up quarters here in the frosty winter of 1778–1779. While the army took a hiatus, three brigades under the command of Major General (and Pomfret native) Israel Putnam suffered through biting cold, sickness, and scant supplies—right here in Fairfield County. New Hampshire and Connecticut troops resided in several "hut cities" in Redding; relics of one encampment, known as Little Valley Forge, remain at Putnam Memorial State Park. In addition to being a local hero, "Old Put" was Connecticut's top officer during the Revolution; he and his horse are immortalized in the park's magnificent bronze sculpture, created by local artist Anna Hyatt Huntington when she was 94 years old. If Redding's Spinning Wheel Inn looks as if it has been here forever, it virtually has. The iconic inn has stood in the same spot alongside CT 58 since 1742, decades before the Revolutionary War came to town. Samuel Clemens, aka Mark Twain, arrived from New York City in the early 1900s to build Stormfield, his opulent country retreat styled after an Italian villa. The famous novelist, best known for penning *The Adventures of Huckleberry Finn*, *The Adventures of Tom Sawyer*, and other American classics, was also a well-known travel writer in the day (two new editions of his travel writings were published in 2005); after seeing the world, he decided to live out his last days on a rural hilltop in West Redding. On Labor Day weekend, the town's Mark Twain Library—established with books from his personal library—hosts a used-book sale that lures bookshop owners and bibliophiles from far and wide.

In Brookfield, a crafts center set up shop more than 50 years ago in an abandoned 18th-century gristmill complex, and it has enjoyed prestige and national recognition ever since. The Brookfield Craft Center welcomes visitors into its exhibition gallery and retail shop, a showcase for local and national artists and craftspeople. Newtown is filled with beautifully restored 18th-century homes; a stroll along Main Street might end with ice cream at a 200-year-old general store, or at Rams Pasture, where 18th-century farmers used to graze their sheep, and French troops under the command of Comte de Rochambeau camped in 1781. This is also the birthplace of vulcanized rubber inventor Charles Goodyear and the game of Scrabble. The Revolutionary War–era Meeting House still bears the scars of target practice by Rochambeau's troops. Quiet vineyards with acres of gnarled grapevines dot the countryside in Sandy Hook, Brookfield, and Sherman; visitors can tour the wineries and taste their highly regarded vintages. In Bethel, a town that used to be the outskirts of Danbury, a square at the hub of its old-time downtown of mom-and-pop stores pays homage to infamous 19th-century resident and circus showman P. T. Barnum. Yet another picturesque collection of white-clapboard historic homes can be found in Sherman, an off-the-beaten-path New England village named for Roger Sherman, signer of both the Declaration of Independence and the U.S. Constitution.

Although the valley's main north–south artery, US 7, is fast becoming overbuilt and choked with traffic, much of the surrounding hills and countryside has been set aside as nature preserves and sanctuaries. Rivers and lakes dot the region, including the largest man-made body of water in the state—Candlewood Lake—which provides five Housatonic Valley towns with 60 miles of shoreline. While many associate the Housatonic River as a whitewater hot spot in the state's rugged northwest corner, down here it takes its sweet time, coursing through its namesake valley on the slow journey to Long Island Sound. In wintertime, bald eagles migrate from northern New England and Canada to fish the open waters below the Shepaug Dam. Birders and nature lovers alike come to Southbury in droves for a glimpse at America's winged symbols of freedom. No place in Connecticut has a higher concentration of the majestic birds than this spot in Southbury, and the spectacle of them fishing, roosting, and soaring above the icebound banks of the river is not to be missed.

Entries in this section are arranged in roughly geographic order.

AREA CODES 203 and 860.

GUIDANCE **Northwest Connecticut Convention & Visitors Bureau** (860-567-4506; www.litchfieldhills.com), P.O. Box 968, Litchfield 06759.

State of Connecticut Highway Information Center, Danbury, I-84 eastbound. One of a network of information centers maintained by the state tourism office on interstates, the center is open 24 hours a day, year-round. In addition to rest facilities, there are racks filled with brochures mainly for Litchfield County, but also including the Danbury and Housatonic Valley areas. State guides and maps are a staple. Information on other parts of the state is often available. There's also an information center at the bus terminal in Southbury, at Exit 14 off I-84.

GETTING THERE *By car:* The valley is accessible by car from I-84, east- and westbound, and from US 7, a heavily trafficked, two-lane road that starts at I-95 in Norwalk and runs north through the Housatonic Valley, the Litchfield Hills, and the Berkshires on its way through Vermont.

By air: **Danbury Municipal Airport** (203-748-6375), adjacent to the Danbury Mall, offers a full range of corporate and charter services. **Westchester County Airport** (914-285-4860), in White Plains, New York, serves the area with daily flights by nine airlines, including American, Continental, Delta, Northwest, United, United Express, and US Airways. **Bradley International Airport** (860-292-2000; 888-624-1533; www.bradley airport.com) in Windsor Locks serves the entire state.

By rail: A rail spur from **Metro-North** (800-638-7646; www.mta.info/mnr) connects Danbury to the main line at South Norwalk, with stops in Redding and Bethel. Frequent trains serving New York City's Grand Central Terminal may also be boarded just across the state line in nearby Brewster, New York.

By bus or limo: **Greyhound Lines** (800-231-2222; www.greyhound.com) and **Peter Pan Bus Lines** (800-343-9999; www.peterpanbus.com) offer frequent service to the area, with regular stops in Danbury and Southbury. **Connecticut Limousine Service** (800-472-5466; www.ctlimo.com) serves New York's JFK and LaGuardia airports and Bradley International Airport in Windsor Locks with shuttle buses and vans.

GETTING AROUND **Maffei's Taxi Service** (203-792-0029) and **A Cab Company** (203-792-8294) provide taxi service in the Danbury area.

MEDICAL EMERGENCY The statewide emergency number is **911**.

Danbury Hospital (203-739-7000), 24 Hospital Ave., Danbury. The emergency number is 203-739-7100.

* To See

MUSEUMS

In Ridgefield

Aldrich Contemporary Art Museum (203-438-4519; www.aldrichart.org), 258 Main St. (CT 35). Open year-round, Tue.–Sun. noon–5; closed Mon. and major holidays. Adults $7; seniors and college students $4; children under 19 free; free admission on Tue. This showcase of provocative and cutting-edge works from around the country is one of the finest contemporary-art museums in America and a beloved town landmark. A $9 million makeover has doubled its exhibition space and added a dozen bright and airy galleries. The facility itself is a work of art, in Connecticut granite, soaring glass, and mahogany ceilings mixed with traditional New England design (a nod to the original 1783 clapboard building and its location on Ridgefield's 18th-century Main Street). Fashion designer Larry Aldrich founded the museum in 1964 with his private collection and a vision of making edgy modern art appealing to the masses. Paintings, photography, sculpture, and all forms of mixed media are displayed inside; outdoors, a sculpture garden has its own changing exhibits of contemporary works. Also new: a museum shop, screening room, sound room, and 100-seat performance space for lectures and concerts.

Keeler Tavern Museum (203-438-5485; www.keelertavernmuseum.org), 132 Main St. (CT 35). Open year-round, Wed., Sat., and Sun. 1–4; closed in Jan. Adults $5; seniors and students $3; children under 12 $2. Free admission to the grounds and gardens, which are open daily. Guides in colonial costume recount this building's 300-year history—how it started as a farmhouse, later becoming a hotel and a private summer retreat; but the real story is in its tavern days. It was then, during the Revolutionary War, that it became a rallying place for patriots during the conflict. While retreating to their ships through Ridgefield after torching Danbury, the British fired on the tavern, and a cannonball is still embedded in a corner post. Famed American architect Cass Gilbert—best known for his design of Manhattan's Woolworth building—acquired the property as a summer home in 1907, added a large ell, and planted a formal garden for his wife. He also designed the fountain across the street, a gift to the town.

In Danbury

Danbury Museum and Historical Society (203-743-5200; www.danbury historical.org), 43 Main St. Call for hours. Step back into the days when Danbury

RIDGEFIELD'S NEWLY RENOVATED ALDRICH CONTEMPORARY ART MUSEUM IS KNOWN FOR ITS PROVOCATIVE EXHIBITS OF CUTTING-EDGE MODERN ART.

was America's "hat town." Exhibits tracing the history of men's headwear are on view in the John Dodd Shop of this museum complex. Furnishings from the 18th and early 19th centuries are in the **John and Mary Rider house**, a 1785 Federal structure built on the site of an earlier house burned by the British in a 1777 raid. Don't miss the excellent collection of early carpenter's tools, a one-room schoolhouse, memorabilia of native son and Pulitzer Prize–winning composer Charles Ives, and the **Marion Anderson Studio**, which traces the life of the famous contralto, who lived most of her life in Danbury. The restored **Scott-Fanton house** is open by appointment.

Danbury Railway Museum (203-778-8337; www.danbury.org/drm), 120 White St. Open Nov.–Mar.: Wed.–Sat. 10–4; Sun. noon–4. Apr.–Oct.: Tue.–Sat. 10–5; Sun. noon–5. Adults $6; seniors $5; children 3–12, $4; 2 and under free. Train buffs, children, and others come to this downtown rail yard to take a ride back in time and, if they're lucky, sit in the conductor's seat. A passenger train tours the 6-acre rail yard (weekends Apr.–Nov.; additional charge), home to more than 60 pieces of vintage rolling stock: steam locomotives, rare diesel engines, cabooses, freight cars, maintenance and repair vehicles, passenger coaches, and the only operating turntable in Connecticut. The city's restored 1903 **Union Station** recounts the history of the rails with dioramas, running model trains from the 1920s to the 1960s, and changing exhibits. Hitchcock fans might recognize the historic building: It was a location for his thriller *Strangers on a Train.* Volunteers lead tours of the museum and grounds; the gift shop is stocked with railroad books, toys, clothing, and collectibles.

Military Museum of Southern New England (203-790-9277; www.usmilitarymuseum.org), 125 Park Ave. Open Apr.–Nov., Tue.–Sat. 10–5; Sun. noon–5; closed Mon. and holidays; Dec.–Mar., Fri. and Sat. 10–5, Sun. 1–5. Adults $6; seniors, children, and active military $4; under 5 free. Local military enthusiasts have collected an impressive array of military vehicles representing all branches of the armed services, from tank destroyers to one of the first self-propelled howitzers—and even a 1941 Fiat staff car used by a German officer in the Afrika Korps. But the pride of the museum is the first tank made in the United States—a rare 1917 Renault—as well as tanks from World War II and the Korean and Vietnam War eras. This is the largest private collection of 20th-century military vehicles and tanks in the country. If you come on **Open Turret Weekend**, scheduled once a month Apr.–Oct., you can climb into the tanks for an exciting firsthand experience. A state-of-the-art museum houses U.S. and foreign artifacts, life-sized dioramas depicting combat settings, as well as mess kits and other personal belongings of soldiers.

WINERIES **McLaughlin Vineyards** (203-426-1533; 866-599-9463; www.mclaughlinvineyards.com), Alberts Hill Rd., in the Sandy Hook section of Newtown. Open year-round Wed.–Sun. 11–5 for wine tastings; tours during special events, and for groups by appointment. Tasting fee $5. After tasting a bit of the bubbly—the specialty here is dry table wines—you're invited to discover how this 160-acre estate is much more than a vineyard. In spring, watch as they boil maple syrup in the sugarhouse, using sap from their own sugar maples. In summer, pick heirloom vegetables, picnic, or listen to live jazz, bluegrass, and folk music. Hayrides and pumpkin picking in fall round out the season. Nature trails leading through a wildlife sanctuary to the banks of the Housatonic River are lovely no matter the season.

DiGrazia Vineyard and Winery (203-775-1616; 800-230-8853; www.digrazia.com), 131 Tower Rd., Brookfield. Open May–Dec., daily 11–5; Jan.–Apr., Sat. and Sun. 11–5. Local doctor Paul DiGrazia planted the first vines in 1978; today it's still a family-owned operation using a combination of modern American techniques and traditional winemaking to produce 15 different varieties of medal-winning wines from 50 acres of grapes—some 7,000 cases in all every year. Guided tours explore the production area and bottling facility, and free pourings take place in the cozy, wood-paneled tasting room.

White Silo Farm and Winery (860-355-0271; www.whitesilowinery.com), 32 CT 37, Sherman. Open May–Dec., Fri.–Sun., 11–6. A small, specialty winery producing raspberry, blackberry, cherry, and rhubarb wine from their own farm-grown fruit. Tours, tastings, and art exhibits in the winery's old dairy barn. In Sept. and Oct., the fields are open daily for visitors to pick their own blackberries and raspberries.

HISTORIC HOMES ♿ **Charles Ives Birthplace** (203-743-5200; www.danburyhistorical.org), 5 Mountainville Ave., Danbury. Open by appointment. Winner of the Pulitzer Prize in 1947, native son and composer Charles Ives is considered the father of modern American music. His simple, gambrel-roofed birthplace is now part of the Danbury Museum and Historical Society (see *Museums*). The piano he learned to play on is in the parlor, along with family furniture. (See also *Entertainment—Music.*)

Matthew Curtiss House (203-426-5937; www.newtownhistory.org), 44 Main St., Newtown. Free admission; call for a schedule. One of the many fine restored homes lining historic Main Street, this 18th-century brick-red saltbox is filled with period furniture and preserved architectural features, like the beehive oven in the massive kitchen fireplace. Costumed guides give tours; candle-dipping, blacksmithing, and other demonstrations take place throughout the year.

Northrop House Museum (860-354-3083; www.shermanhistoricalsociety.org), 10 CT 37, Sherman. Open June–Sept., Sat. 2–4, or by appointment. A handsome, 1829 white-clapboard Federal home, once part of a working farm, filled with period furnishings collected from many historic homes in town. Across the street is **The Old Store**, a historic mercantile building with gifts and antiques for sale. Lectures and exhibits—open-hearth cooking, for example—presented by the Sherman Historical Society.

HISTORIC SITES 🖍 **Second Company Governor's Horse Guard** (203-426-9046; www.thehorseguard.com), 4 Wildlife Dr., Newtown. One of the nation's last active cavalry militia units, established in 1808 to escort then–Connecticut governor Jonathan Trumbull between the state's two capitals in New Haven and Hartford. Today the all-volunteer organization serves mostly a ceremonial role, appearing in inaugural parades, state ceremonies, and other events, but it is also used for search-and-rescue. Visitors can come to the stables—home to the unit's 36 horses—to watch fall and winter cavalry military training on Sunday afternoon from mid-October to mid-April; from mid-April to mid-October, drills take place on Thursday evening. Call ahead for drill times and a schedule of free tours. The company hosts an annual summertime horse show (see *Special Events*).

Mark Twain Public Library (203-938-2545; www.marktwainlibrary.org), 439 Redding Rd. (CT 53), Redding. Open daily; closed Sun. in summer. After his daughter Susy died of meningitis in the Hartford mansion, Samuel Clemens—known to the world as Mark Twain—built an Italian villa, Stormfield, in Redding in 1908 (it burned but has been rebuilt). That same year—after learning that his new rural community lacked a library—he founded one with about 3,000 books from his own collection and donations from colleagues in the publishing world, raising funds himself by hosting concerts at his mansion. Annual library fund-raisers include an art show and a gigantic used-book sale that attracts readers and bookshop owners from all over New England (see *Special Events*).

Putnam Memorial State Park Museum (203-938-2285), 492 Black Rock Turnpike, at the junction of CT 107 and 58, Redding. Grounds open daily 8 AM–sunset; museum open Memorial Day–Columbus Day; call for hours, and ask about guided tours. One of only two state parks in Connecticut dedicated to the American Revolution (the other is Fort Griswold in Groton), this one was established in 1887. In the bitter winter of 1779, Connecticut's General Israel Putnam commanded a shivering army of some 3,000 Continental soldiers who set up an encampment, known to Nutmeggers as Little Valley Forge. Replicas of the typical log buildings thrown together by the men hold the meager utensils and implements they used in their struggle for survival; authentically uniformed reenactors stage battle skirmishes in summer and fall. The magnificent statue of "Old Put" astride a horse, at the park entrance, was completed by local sculptress Anna Hyatt Huntington when she was 94. It's an homage to his famous escape from the British by fleeing—according to lore—on horseback down a flight of stone steps in Greenwich.

✷ To Do

BALLOONING ♿ **GONE Ballooning** (203-262-6493), 88 Sylvan Crest Dr., Southbury. Year-round hot-air-balloon rides over scenic countryside in western Connecticut and eastern New York. Flights leave early morning and late afternoon; champagne flights and B&B packages available. Call for reservations.

Steppin' Up Balloons (203-264-0013), 258 Old Woodbury Rd., Southbury. Hot-airballoon trips over the Housatonic River Valley and the Litchfield Hills, weekends year-round. Sunrise, sunset, and champagne flights. Reservations required.

BIRDING **The Audubon Center at Bent of the River** (203-264-5098), 185 East Flat Hill Rd., in the South Britain section of Southbury. Open daily from dawn to dusk. Prime birding on a 700-acre wildlife sanctuary and wildlife education center along the banks of the Pomperaug River. Ask about programs for birders of all skill levels, like bird bandings, predawn owling, and bird counting. This is one of 2,000 counting sites in the Western Hemisphere that participates in the annual Christmas Bird Count, sponsored by the National Audubon Society, the oldest and largest wildlife survey in the world. The Connecticut Audubon Society designated a 66-acre parcel here as an Important Bird Area, or IBA, for its population of nesting blue-winged warblers, indigo buntings, and other species.

♂ ♿ **Shepaug Bald Eagle Observation Area** (800-368-8954) at the Shepaug Hydroelectric Station, River Rd., Southbury. Open late Dec.–mid-Mar., Wed., Sat., and Sun. 9–1. Admission is free, but reservations are required. Wintering bald eagles favor this site on the Housatonic River, thanks to a hydroelectric plant that keeps the churning water below the dam from freezing over, making it easy for them to pluck fish. They usually arrive at their winter feeding grounds in November and December and stay until early spring; peak viewing is in January and February. Visitors watch from large picture windows in a wooden observation hut—complete with high-powered viewing telescopes, eagle photos and facts, and a stove—on a knoll overlooking the river. From there, you can watch the majestic birds perch in the tall trees along the riverbank, forage for fish in the churning waters below the dam, and soar overhead. A unique and wonderful experience, and a popular wintertime destination for birders and nature lovers from around New England to see America's national symbol. Although their numbers are growing, and they were removed from the nation's list of threatened and endangered species in 2007, they are still protected under federal law. Volunteers are on hand to answer questions and point out eagle activity. While more eagles winter on the Connecticut River, the Shepaug observation area has the largest concentration of them in the state.

See also the Saugatuck Valley Hiking Trail System under *Hiking*.

BOATING State boat launches on **Candlewood Lake** include two at **Squantz Pond State Park**. During summer, the 5,420-acre surface of Connecticut's largest man-made lake buzzes with all manner of watercraft. **Echo Bay Marina** (203-775-7077) rents boats for a variety of activities, from waterskiing to fishing. Other places to launch motorized boats include **Huntington State Park Pond** in Redding and Bethel; **Lake Kenosia** in Danbury; **Lake Lillinonah** in Brookfield and Newtown; **Lake Zoar** in Newtown; **Pierrepont Lake** in Ridgefield; and **Squantz Pond** and **Ball Pond** in New Fairfield.

CANOEING AND KAYAKING **Housatonic Valley River Trail** (203-775-6256). A 38-mile river trail on the Still and the Housatonic rivers that offers scenic paddling on a route with diverse birding and wildlife viewing, hiking, and picnicking. Request a trail map, which lists launch sites, river hazards, and portage areas along the trail's route through Danbury, Brookfield, New Milford, Bridgewater, and Newtown.

FISHING Freshwater fishing opportunities are found in **Squantz Pond State Park**, New Fairfield (one of the top bass fishing destinations in the country); **Lake Lillinonah**, Brookfield; **Collis P. Huntington State Park**, Redding; **Putnam Memorial State Park**, Redding; **Pierrepont State Park**, Ridgefield; and **Southford Falls State Park** in Southbury, a trout park that's stocked regularly with fish.

See also *Boating* and *Green Space*.

GOLF **Ridgefield Golf Club** (203-748-7008), 545 Ridgebury Rd., Ridgefield. Par 71, 18 holes, 6,444 yards.

Richter Park Golf Club (203-792-2550; www.richterpark.com), 100 Aunt Hack Rd., Danbury. Rated one of the top 25 public golf courses in America by *Golf*

Digest, a first-rate municipal course on 160 acres near the New York border. Par 72, 18 holes, 6,744 yards.

Sunset Hill Golf Club (203-740-7800), 13 Sunset Hill Rd., Brookfield. Head professional Chet Dunlop, director of the New England School of Golf, is recognized as one of the top 50 golf instructors in the country by *Golf Range Magazine.* Par 70, 18 holes, 4,698 yards.

Gainfield Farms Golf Course (203-262-1100), 255 Old Field Rd., Southbury. Par 28, nine holes, 1,384 yards.

Pomperaug Golf Club (203-264-9484; www.pomperauggolf.com), 522 Heritage Rd., Southbury. Par 35, 9 holes, 3,050 yards.

The Golf Club at Oxford Greens (203-888-1600; www.oxfordgreens.com), 99 Country Club Dr., Oxford. Par 72, 18 holes, 7,147 yards. One of Connecticut's newest golf courses.

HIKING **Collis P. Huntington State Park** (203-938-2285), Sunset Hill Rd. (off CT 58), Redding. Open daily 8 AM–sunset. The lifelike sculptures of wolves and bears at the park entrance indicate where to begin hiking. Most people follow the main 4.5-mile-long loop, but side trails branch out in all directions. In all, close to 8 miles of well-worn, easy to moderate trails pass through 900 acres of dense forest and hills, and ravines thick with mountain laurel. Wooden boardwalks cross over streams, ponds, and bogs that are home to a variety of wildlife.

🐾 **The Saugatuck Valley Hiking Trail System** (203-938-2551), CT 53, Redding. More than 65 miles of trails, some marked, through dense woods and across fields. You get a view of a shimmering reservoir from atop a 200-foot-high cliff. Trails pass through three towns—Redding, Weston, and Easton. Birders, bring your glasses and Roger Tory Peterson bird guides; botanists, your notebooks.

Squantz Pond State Park (203-797-4165), 178 Shortwoods Rd., off CT 39, Sherman. A main trail follows the shoreline of the pond, with lots of side trails branching off. It's hard to get lost; the pond is always in view.

See also *Green Space.*

MOUNTAIN BIKING Popular spots for off-road riding include **Collis P. Huntington State Park** and **Putnam Memorial State Park** in Redding. For more information, contact **Bethel Cycle and Fitness** (203-792-4640), 120 Greenwood Ave. (CT 302), Bethel.

Kettletown State Park (203-264-5169), 175 Quaker Farms Rd., Southbury. Some of the area's first settlers obtained this large tract of land along Lake Zoar from the Pototuck Indians by trading a brass kettle. There are plenty of easy trails suitable for beginning riders; however, the routes are poorly marked.

Other nearby rides include the Steep Rock Reservation in Washington and Litchfield's White Memorial Foundation (see *To Do* in the Litchfield chapter).

Class Cycles (203-264-4708), 105 Main St. North, Southbury, doesn't rent bikes, but it has a repair shop and knowledgeable employees who can offer sound advice on local rides.

SWIMMING 🩹 **Squantz Pond State Park** (203-797-4165), 178 Shortwoods Rd., off CT 39, on the western shore of Candlewood Lake, New Fairfield. A picturesque pond ringed with hills is open to the public for swimming, picnicking, and boating. There's a designated swimming area, and lifeguards are on duty in-season.

Candlewood Lake (860-354-6928), New Fairfield, Danbury, and Brookfield. The dam built by a power company here created the largest constructed lake in Connecticut (5,420 acres), the third largest in the world, and the largest east of the Mississippi. The Connecticut Light & Power Co. pumped in water from the Housatonic River in 1928, flooding abandoned villages and farms in the Rocky River Valley to harness the hydroelectric power and generate electricity. Today it's a major recreation area extending through three towns, 11 miles long and 2 miles across at its widest point. There are many summer cottages and year-round homes, as well as state boat-launching ramps, on the 60-mile-long shoreline. Some town beaches on the lake offer swimming for a fee.

Lake Lillinonah (203-270-2360), CT 133, Brookfield; **Lake Zoar** (203-270-4350), CT 34, Newtown; and **Lake Kenosia** (203-797-4632), Danbury.

✷ Winter Sports

CROSS-COUNTRY SKIING **Collis P. Huntington State Park** (203-938-2285), Sunset Hill Rd., Redding. Cross-country skiing around several ponds.

See also *Green Space.*

ICE SKATING **Danbury Ice Arena** (203-794-1704; www.danburyice.com), 1 Independence Way, Danbury. Public skating daily, as well as family skating programs, and hockey and figure-skating instruction.

See also *Green Space.*

A POPULAR RECREATION AREA, CANDLEWOOD LAKE EXTENDS THROUGH DANBURY, BROOKFIELD, AND NEW FAIRFIELD.

Kim Grant

✱ Green Space

PARKS

In Danbury

✐ **Tarrywile Park & Mansion** (203-744-3130; www.danbury.org/tarry), 70 Southern Blvd. Park open year-round, daily sunrise to sunset; mansion open by appointment. Free admission. This was one of Connecticut's largest dairy farms in its day; today a Victorian mansion and historic gardens are surrounded by 72 acres of meadows, woods, and wetlands. Explore it all on the park's 20-mile trail network, or relax with a picnic by Park's Pond. Call or check online for a schedule of guided weekend hikes, workshops, festivals, events, and children's programs.

In Redding

🐾 **Collis P. Huntington State Park** (203-938-2285, Sunset Hill Rd. Open daily 8 AM–sunset. Free admission. Internationally known sculptress Anna Hyatt Huntington's lifelike wildlife works in bronze grace the entrance to this secluded park, which is off the beaten path but worth finding. Picnicking, hiking, horseback riding, and cross-country skiing on an 878-acre open tract crisscrossed by scenic roads canopied with sugar maples. Five ponds for canoeing and fishing.

Putnam Memorial State Park (203-938-2285), at the junction of CT 58 and CT 107. Grounds open year-round, daily 8 AM–sunset. Free admission. Military history buffs can check out reconstructed soldier huts and ruins from "Connecticut's Valley Forge," when George Washington's Continental army spent the harsh winter of 1778–79 under the command of Pomfret resident Israel "Old Put" Putnam. History aside, this woodsy 232-acre park offers outdoor enthusiasts a lovely rural landscape perfect for hiking, fishing, and picnicking.

In Southbury

Kettletown State Park (203-938-2285), 1400 Georges Hill Rd. Open year-round, daily 8 AM–sunset. A parking fee is charged on weekends and holidays: $7 residents; $10 nonresidents. The name of this park on Lake Zoar dates back centuries. According to legend, the local Pototuck Indians sold the land to European settlers. Their asking price? One brass kettle. Today the 605-acre park offers swimming, fishing, hiking, mountain biking, and camping.

🐾 ✐ ♿ **Southford Falls State Park** (203-264-5169), 175 Quaker Farms Rd. (CT 188). Open daily 8 AM–sunset. Free admission. At the turn of the 20th century, the Diamond Match Company operated next to the scenic waterfalls on the Eight Mile River. Today it's a family-friendly destination for hiking, picnicking, and trout fishing.

In New Fairfield

Squantz Pond State Park (203-797-4165), 178 Shortwoods Rd., off CT 39, New Fairfield. Open year-round, daily 8 AM–sunset. In-season: weekday admission, $7 residents; $14 nonresidents. Weekends and holidays: $9 residents; $14 nonresidents. A small state park on the western shore of Candlewood Lake that's popular among leaf-peepers, who come to admire the foliage around Squantz Pond. Activities include fishing, swimming, hiking, and ice skating.

NATURE PRESERVES ✐ **Highstead Arboretum** (203-938-8809; www.highsteadarboretum.org), 127 Lonetown Rd. (CT 107), Redding. Open by appointment only, Mon.–Fri. 8:30–4; reservations are required for lectures, walks, talks, classes, and educational events. This former farm, now 150 acres of protected native New England woodlands, was established as a woodland sanctuary for people to study and appreciate native New England woodlands. Several miles of hiking paths meander through forest and meadows before climbing to a rugged 758-foot-high outcropping; from here hikers can see Long Island Sound on a clear day. A boardwalk winds through a swamp filled with native calla lily, marsh marigold, and cinnamon fern. In spring, 13 native species of azalea grow in the woods, along with mountain laurel—Connecticut's state flower—witch hazel, and lady's slipper. A serene oasis for nature lovers and expert horticulturalists alike.

Westside Nature Preserve (203-837-8794; www.wcsu.edu/wnp), Westside campus, Western Connecticut State University, Danbury. This 33-acre spread of woods, open meadows, and wetlands serves as an outdoor laboratory for university students, but the public is welcome to enjoy it, too. It doesn't take long to explore, perfect if you're on campus and want to stretch your legs. Pick up the trail at the end of University Blvd. (look for a gate and kiosk). Numbered stations along the nature trail—a mix of boardwalks and dirt paths—point out various plants and trees. In spring, look for woodland beauties like trillium, bloodroot, and jack-in-the-pulpit; more than a dozen species of ferns throughout the season.

The Audubon Center at Bent of the River (203-264-5098; www.ctaudubon.org), 185 East Flat Hill Rd., in the South Britain section of Southbury. Open daily dawn to dusk. Free admission; fee charged for some programs. Fifteen miles of trails lace through 700 acres of meadows and forest along the banks of the Pomperaug River. This wildlife sanctuary is one of the state's significant birding sites, and weekend programs range from bird banding and bird counting to animal tracking. A converted barn houses a nature education and visitor center; in winter, ski, snowshoe, or hike to the barn, where you can enjoy hot cocoa and tea by the woodstove.

See also *Hiking*.

✷ Lodging

RESORT 🐾 ✐ ♿ **Heritage Hotel** (203-264-8200; 800-932-3466; www.heritagesouthbury.com), 522 Heritage Rd., off US 6, Southbury 06488. The rustic wood exterior belies the relatively recent construction of this building, erected on the grounds of the former estate of Danish piano comedian Victor Borge. Recreation, sports, and leisure facilities—including indoor and outdoor pools, golf, tennis, bicycles, racquetball, a day spa, and a health club—entertain guests (if you're traveling with children, there's plenty for them to do). The 163 rooms are standard and on the small side. $139–279.

INNS

In Ridgefield 06877

The Elms Inn (203-438-2541; www.elmsinn.com), 500 Main St. (CT 35). You'd be hard-put to find a 200-year-old colonial-style inn without an array of authentic antiques. The Elms is no exception. Your hosts, the Scala family, will be happy to explain the history and origin of the antiques in each of the 18 rooms and suites, which all have private bath and wireless Internet access. The Elms is just across from Ballard Park and within easy walking distance of Ridgefield's shops, galleries, and restaurants; it also has a highly acclaimed American restaurant and tavern of its own (see *Dining Out*). Continental breakfast is brought to your room. $165–435.

♿ **Stonehenge Inn and Restaurant** (203-438-6511; www.stonehengeinn-ct.com), 35 Stonehenge Rd. (US 7), P.O. Box 667. Situated off the road on a lovely duck pond, Stonehenge, in its garden setting, is the embodiment of country elegance. Since it opened in the 1940s, it has been a magnet for visitors from around the world in search of the perfect "weekend in Connecticut"; among them, newlyweds Elizabeth Taylor and third husband Mike Todd, who spent their honeymoon here. The 16 rooms (two suites) are spread across three buildings; each has luxe linens and classic furnishings. Host Douglas Seville also presides over an exceptional kitchen, which works magic with French Continental cuisine (see *Dining Out*). Continental breakfast. $100–200.

West Lane Inn (203-438-7323; www.westlaneinn.com), 22 West Lane (CT 35). When you step into the hall of this luxurious and intimate country inn, you feel as if you've been invited for a stay at a grand 1849 manor estate. Antiques are in each of the 18 cozy rooms, all with private bath, some with a fireplace—and some with a kitchenette. Ranked among the top inns in the country, it offers a quiet retreat, yet is only a half-mile walk to restaurants, museums, and antiques shops. Continental breakfast. $150–425.

In Newtown 06470

ⓞ **Dana-Holcombe House** (203-426-2000; www.danaholcombehouse.com), 29 Main St. A new inn, catering facility, and conference center near Newtown's landmark flagpole in the historic district. The elegant Federal-style building has six uniquely themed guest rooms and suites. Full breakfast. $175–250.

BED & BREAKFAST In addition to the listing below, B&B reservation services offer access to rooms available in establishments throughout the state. For a list, see *Bed & Breakfasts* in "What's Where in Connecticut."

Cornucopia at Oldfield Bed & Breakfast (203-267-6772; www.cornucopiabnb.com), 782 Main St. North, Southbury 06488. Innkeepers Christine and Ed Edelson offer four beautifully appointed guest rooms in a grand 1818 Georgian Federal homestead surrounded by stone walls and a white picket fence. Guests can explore the perennial and herb gardens and an English maze or relax in the gazebo or by the pool. Inside, the elegant front parlor and an antiques-filled keeping room invite quiet contemplation. All rooms have private bath; some feature fireplace, claw-foot bathtub, or French doors opening onto a private balcony, or a private deck. Outdoor pool, paths meandering through lovely perennial gardens, and grounds with gazebo, lily pond, old-fashioned hammock. Full breakfast in the formal dining room. $150–250.

HOTELS AND MOTELS

In Bethel 06801

🐾 ♿ **Microtel Inn & Suites** (203-748-8318; reservations 800-771-7171; www.microtelbethel.com), 80 Benedict Rd., Exit 8 off I-84. A new hotel with 78 rooms and suites. Continental breakfast. $80–120.

In Ridgefield 06877

♿ **Days Inn** (203-438-3781), 296 Ethan Allen Hwy. (US 7). Conveniently located but in need of an upgrade. Some of the 36 standard rooms and suites have Jacuzzi tubs, others have kitchenettes. An on-site restaurant, Thali (see *Dining Out*), has authentic Indian cuisine. $85–105.

In Danbury

♿ **Ethan Allen Hotel** (203-744-1776; 800-742-1776; www.ethanalleninn.com), 21 Lake Ave. Extension, Danbury 06811-9956, Exit 4 off I-84. A modern, sprawling 193-room inn (including many suites) with classic Ethan Allen interior home furnishings. The location couldn't be more convenient: just off the interstate, near Danbury Fair Mall, and a quick drive to downtown Danbury and the historic towns of Ridgefield and Bethel. Amenities include an outdoor pool, a sauna, and exercise facilities; a lounge and restaurant serve contemporary regional cuisine. $150–265.

🐾 ♿ **Maron Hotel & Suites** (203-791-2200; www.maronhotel.com), 42 Lake Ave. Extension, Exit 4 off I-84, Danbury 06811. A contemporary hotel with 86 clean and comfortable guest rooms and suites, some with whirlpool tubs; others with kitchenettes are designed for extended stays. **Vivo! Bar & Grill** serves Continental cuisine. Continental breakfast. $109–179.

🐾 ♿ **Residence Inn by Marriott Danbury** (203-797-1256; 800-331-3131), 22 Segar St., Exit 4 off I-84, Danbury 06810. The 78 extended-stay suites—with separate living and dining areas and fully equipped kitchens—are clean and comfortable. Indoor pool, spa, and fitness center. Daily continental breakfast and an evening buffet (Mon.–Thu.) is included. $109–169.

🐾 ♿ **Danbury Plaza Hotel** (203-794-0600; www.danburyplaza.com), 18 Old Ridgebury Rd., Exit 2 off I-84, Danbury 06810. The former Sheraton. The 242 rooms and three suites come with standard amenities. Restaurant and pub serve three meals daily plus Sun. brunch. Restaurant, lounge, health club, pool, sauna, tennis. $109–149.

Elsewhere

🐾 ♿ **Southbury Crowne Plaza Hotel** (203-598-7600; reservations: 800-445-8667; www.crowneplaza.com/southbury), 1284 Strongtown Rd., Exit 16 off I-84, Southbury 06488. A comfortable hotel convenient to I-84, with 197 newly renovated guest rooms. Restaurant, health club, indoor pool, sauna, and whirlpool. **Arrowhead Restaurant & Lounge** serves continental cuisine. $99–170.

🐾 ♿ **Newbury Inn** (203-775-0220; www.newburyinn.com), 1030 Federal Rd. (US 7/US 202), Brookfield 06804. A comfortable 47-unit hostelry located on a heavily trafficked stretch of US 7 but close to Candlewood Lake, the state's largest. Formerly Twin Tree Inn & Suites. A hearty continental breakfast is included. $85–125; lower off-season rates.

CAMPGROUND **Kettletown State Park and Campground** (203-264-5678; reservations 877-668-2267), 1400 Georges Hill Rd., Southbury. Campground is open daily, Memorial Day weekend–Sept. Kettletown has 68 open and wooded sites for tents and trailers, many along the edge of Lake Zoar. Amenities include bathrooms, showers, youth-group camping sites. $13.

✷ Where to Eat

DINING OUT

In Ridgefield

♿ **Bernard's** (203-438-8282; www.bernardsridgefield.com), 20 West Lane (CT 35). Open Tue.–Sat. for lunch and dinner; brunch and dinner on Sun.; closed Mon. Reservations suggested. Chef-owners Bernard and Sarah Bouissou (who met as chefs at

Le Cirque) have revamped this landmark 19th-century clapboard inn into a first-class gourmet French restaurant, with touches such as live piano music on weekends and gracious and attentive service. The four elegant dining rooms are filled with tables covered in crisp linens and topped with fresh flowers; the walls are painted in muted shades of yellow and green. If alfresco dining is more your thing, the garden patio is lovely. Both are fitting backdrops for Bernard's innovative modern French cuisine and award-winning cellar of vintage wines. You might begin with baked sea scallops with shaved black truffles. Next, roasted lemon-rosemary loin of lamb, baked monkfish wrapped in bacon, portobello-crusted halibut, or roast free-range chicken with potato-sage gnocchi. Finish with a decadent *fondant au chocolat* or the crème brûlée trio. Bernard's has earned the American Academy of Hospitality Science's prestigious Five-Star Diamond Award, one of only a handful of Connecticut restaurants to do so. The menu may cause sticker shock, but it's worth the splurge. $26–36.

Elms Restaurant and Tavern (203-438-9206; www.elmsinn.com), 500 Main St. (CT 35). Restaurant open for dinner Wed.–Sat.; tavern open for lunch Wed.–Sun.; dinner Tue.–Sun.; closed Mon. Reservations suggested. Chef-owner Brendan Walsh takes traditional New England dishes and applies an innovative twist, creating an American menu lauded by locals and critics. Seafood stew in a fennel-leek broth with tomatoes and herbs, and grilled venison with sweet potato spoon bread might be found on the winter menu. Dinner is served in several intimate candlelit dining rooms with fireplace in this beautifully restored, 200-year-old colonial landmark building. Check out the murals in the entryway that depict the town's famous 1777 battle against British redcoats—Connecticut's only inland battle during the American Revolution. A lighter menu is served in the rustic wood-beamed tavern. $23–29. (See also *Lodging*.)

♿ **La Saliere** (203-438-1976), 3 Big Shop Lane. Lunch Mon.–Sat.; dinner daily; brunch on Sun. A warm and friendly bistro just a stone's throw from Main Street, tucked away in a cozy space that has hosted three other French restaurants in past years. The menu, printed newspaper-style in French with English translations, is a bit tricky to navigate, but the traditional French seafood dishes are expertly prepared. The regular menu and daily blackboard specials might offer baked sole stuffed with shrimp and crabmeat in a champagne sauce; wild striped bass braised and served whole; or salmon *en papillotte* with fresh herbs. Sweet endings like soufflés and profiteroles are homemade. $17–30.

Spagone Ristorante (203-438-5518; www.spagonerestaurant.com), 90 Danbury Rd. (US 7), in Commerce Park. Open for lunch Tue.–Fri.; dinner daily. Regulars rave about chef-owner Michael Spennato's impeccable Tuscan cuisine. Start with the grilled calamari or tomato and mozzarella salad; then try the Mediterranean snapper with capers and fresh tomatoes, lamb osso buco, or one of the homemade pasta dishes. Lively bar. $20–38.

♿ **Stonehenge Inn and Restaurant** (203-438-6511; www.stonehengeinn-ct.com), Stonehenge Rd., off US 7. Open for dinner Mon.–Sat. The Stonehenge has consistently served the finest in French country and Continental cuisine in its quintessential New England country inn setting. The large dining room overlooks the swan and goose pond; a smaller dining room is in the rear. Beef, duck, and lamb are all beautifully executed with a variety of classic French sauces. Begin with smoked salmon stuffed with smoked-trout mousse, then Black Angus steak with Roquefort crust and Bordelaise sauce, and end with pineapple-coconut soufflé. Seasonal specials might include wild game. $22–38. (See also *Lodging.*)

In Danbury

Bangkok (203-791-0640; www.bangkokrestaurant.com), 72 Newtown Rd., in the Nutmeg Square plaza. Open for lunch Tue.–Fri.; dinner Tue.–Sun.; closed Mon. Reservations recommended on weekends. When Bangkok opened in 1986, it was Connecticut's first Thai restaurant. With so many Thai eateries around today, it's hard to imagine a time when people were unfamiliar with staples like pad Thai or chicken satay with peanut sauce. This highly acclaimed family-run place, fans agree, is still the best. Wood booths line a narrow storefront space filled with Asian-inspired decor, where waitresses in traditional Thai dress serve dishes based on family recipes, freshly made with authentic Thai ingredients—lemongrass, coriander, ginger, green chiles, and coconut milk. Start with *tom yum goong*, a traditional Thai shrimp soup, or marinated and broiled pork satay with peanut sauce and fresh cucumber relish for dipping. Move on to pad Thai, the national dish of noodles, shrimp, peanuts, tofu, and bean sprouts; or the house specialty, *ho mook talay*, a fiery Thai curry dish (they'll make it mild, if you wish) with shrimp, lobster, squid, and scallops, steamed in a clay pot. For a sweet ending, the house-made coconut ice cream is refreshingly cool and creamy. $14–24.

Café on the Green (203-791-0369; www.cafeonthegreenrestaurant.com), 100 Aunt Hack Rd. Open daily for lunch and dinner. Northern Italian cuisine overlooking Richter Park Golf Course. There's patio dining in-season, and live music on Friday and Saturday nights. $22–29.

Ciao! Café and Wine Bar (203-791-0404; www.ciaocafetwosteps.com), 2B Ives St. Open daily for lunch and dinner. Visit this delightful place in Danbury's lively entertainment district for innovative Italian cuisine and more than 35 wines available by the glass. $17–24.

♿ **Jim Barbarie's** (203-743-3287; www.jbrestaurant.com), 47 Padanaram Rd. Open for lunch Mon.–Fri.; dinner daily. Loyal patrons, who love the menu of familiar favorites, have flocked to this old-fashioned roadhouse for the past 45 years. To say it's an institution is an understatement. The Barbarie family opened the doors in 1961, and since then Barbarie's has been known as *the* place for steaks, colossal cuts of prime rib, and seafood offerings like 2-pound lobsters and king crab legs. Save room for homey desserts like brownie sundaes, blueberry pie, and chocolate cake. Families usually eat early; the second wave comes for dinner and stays until the tables are pushed aside to make way for live entertainment and dancing, every Friday and Saturday night. $13–37.

♿ **Kabuki Japanese Steak House** (203-744-6885; www.kabuki-house.com), 39 Lake Ave. Extension, across from Maron Hotel & Suites. Open for lunch Mon.–Fri.; dinner is served daily. Guests at this restaurant will enjoy sampling a varied cuisine that includes a sushi bar, teriyaki and tempura dishes, and hibachi-grilled delicacies. The owners defer to more conventional American tastes and serve steaks as tender as any laid on a plate in Omaha. $17–36.

♿ **Ondine** (203-746-4900; www.ondinerestaurant.com), 69 Pembroke Rd. (CT 37). Open for dinner Wed.–Sun.; Sun. brunch; closed Mon. and Tue. Reservations are recommended. A longtime favorite destination for contemporary French cuisine. The ambience is reminiscent of a French country inn, with archways full of flowers and an elegant dining room loaded with art and antiques. On the menu, wild game is a specialty, but also look for fresh foie gras with fig and rhubarb compote, escargots with mushroom ragout, sautéed calf sweetbreads, salmon mousse, and filet mignon in béarnaise sauce. For dessert, the chocolate marquise, raspberry soufflé, and lemon tart will melt in your mouth. Extensive wine list. Entrées $25–36; prix fixe dinner $58.

Elsewhere

♿ **White Horse Tavern at Spinning Wheel Inn** (203-938-2511; www.spinningwheelinn-ct.com), CT 58, Redding Ridge. Open for dinner Wed.–Sun.; Sun. brunch; closed Mon. and Tue. Reservations suggested. Built as an inn in the saltbox style, the Spinning Wheel has been entertaining stage passengers and luminaries, such as former Redding resident Mark Twain, since 1742. It's been a stagecoach stop and tavern since 1806, and the Spinning Wheel Inn since the 1930s. The original saltbox now has big picture windows; a large addition on the northern side opens onto a terrace and a gazebo, popular with wedding couples. In 2008, the inn switched from offering New England fine dining to more casual tavern fare—chicken potpie, braised lamb, crabcakes, and the like. Sunday brunch is an extravagant buffet. The inn stages an annual "theater banquet" around the holidays. $16–24.

Redding Roadhouse (203-938-3388; www.reddingroadhouse.com), 406 Redding Rd., at the junction of CT 53 and CT 107, Redding. Open for lunch and dinner daily; Sun. brunch. A lively local restaurant that is fun and unpretentious. Generous portions of steaks, chicken, pasta, and the like. Would you believe that Mark Twain used to hang out here? It's true; this was a tavern when the novelist lived in Redding in the early 1900s. Live rock, jazz, country, and blues in the Tap Room on Friday and Saturday nights. $14–36.

Clemens Restaurant (203-938-8300; www.clemensrestaurant.com), 4 Long Ridge Rd., West Redding. Open for dinner Wed.–Sun.; closed Mon. and Tue. Across from the train station, named for Samuel Clemens, aka Mark Twain. Gourmet contemporary American cuisine with vegetables, herbs, and fruits from the restaurant's own garden. The creative list of starters might include crabcakes with honey Tabasco rémoulade, or Boursin-stuffed mushrooms with roasted garlic aioli sauce. Entrées may be jumbo shrimp with Maine lobster stuffing and sweet corn risotto; or thyme and paprika crusted wild salmon with tangerine basil beurre blanc. The kitchen's creativity extends to desserts like white nectarine and raspberry crisp with brown sugar ice cream, vanilla cheesecake with fresh peach bourbon sauce, and housemade gingersnap gelato. A lighter menu is served at the bar. $24–29.

The Olive Tree (203-264-4565; www.theolivetreesouthbury.com), 137 East Hill Rd., Southbury. Open for lunch Tue.–Fri.; dinner Tue.–Sun.; closed Mon. A lovely spot overlooking the golf course at the Heritage Village Country Club golf course that offers a convivial bar, an outdoor patio, and three cozy and relaxing dining rooms. Most people come for the steak, seafood, chicken, and pasta. $17–30.

EATING OUT

In Ridgefield

Early Bird Café (203-438-1568), 88 Danbury Rd. (CT 35). This is where locals elbow up to the counter for hearty standard breakfast fare. Comfort food in cozy no-frills surroundings.

J&J's Gathering Place (203-431-3344), Copps Hill Common, CT 35. Open daily. Plan to be here awhile, or come back often. All day, the bakery turns out scones, cookie sandwiches, tarts, muffins, and wraps (try the chicken curry). Afternoon tea is served in the upstairs vintage-style tearoom, with 30 varieties of loose-leaf tea to choose from, brewed in individual china teapots and accompanied by tea sandwiches, scones with imported jams, and desserts. Light lunches like salad, quiche, and sandwiches. Downstairs, a restaurant serves lunch and dinner. There's also a boutique stocked with whimsical clothing and eclectic gifts, and for kids, toys, games, dolls, books, and puzzles.

Thai Pearl (203-894-1424), Copps Hill Common, 113 Danbury Rd. (CT 35). Open daily for lunch and dinner. Good service, authentically exotic and aromatic Thai cuisine at good prices. Tucked away in a shopping center. If you're familiar with Thai cuisine, the menu is fairly standard—satays, pad Thai, and meats and seafood with earthy flavors like lemongrass, chili, cilantro, and ginger. $12–20.

Thali (203-894-1080), 296 Ethan Allen Highway (US 7). Open daily for lunch and dinner; Sun. brunch buffet. Despite the ho-hum locale, critically acclaimed regional Indian cuisine is served up in modern high-tech surroundings, sharing space with a Days Inn. Start with ground lamb kebabs grilled in the tandoor oven, then move on to curries, kebabs, and other traditional dishes or, for something different, braised veal shank, or their signature Colorado lamb chops seasoned with cardamom, nutmeg, and mace. End with rice pudding or chocolate-dipped gelato truffles. The wine list features bottles from around the world, including India. $13–26. Other locations in New Canaan (203-972-8332, and New Haven (203-777-1177).

The Catch (203-438-4422), 967 Ethan Allen Hwy. (US 7). Open daily for breakfast, lunch, and dinner. A family-friendly fish house with a fun menu and beachy decor. Go with the fish-and-chips for a casual meal; seafood is treated with a gourmet touch. $17–25.

♿ **Wild Ginger Café** (203-431-4588; www.wildgingercaferestaurant.com), 461 Main St. Open daily for lunch and dinner. Eclectic pan-Asian cuisine that matches the surroundings: a bustling café reminiscent of a chic SoHo eatery. Grilled-shrimp salad is flavored with lemongrass and lime-miso dressing; sliced flank steak comes with fresh mango, jicama, and crispy vermicelli in a spicy mango sauce; sesame-crusted salmon is paired with sautéed seasoned vegetables. $10–16.

In Danbury

♿ **Cor's** (203-792-9999), 65 West St. Open daily for breakfast and lunch. A great place for breakfast—which is, intelligently, served all day. You can barely get your hands around the bulging deli sandwiches. Check out the impressive collection of celebrity photos filling the walls. Breakfast $4–7.

♿ **Deep's Trellis** (203-792-0494), 49 North St. Open Mon.–Sat. for breakfast and lunch; closed Sun. A modest family-run eatery for more than 20 years. Among the breakfast must-eats: fluffy banana pancakes, stuffed French toast, and colossal muffins in flavors like streusel, peach, and French breakfast. Sandwiches, salads, burgers (more than a dozen varieties), homemade soups and desserts later on, as well as creative daily specials. $4–10.

♿ **Ernie's Road House** (203-790-0671; www.erniesroadhouse.com), 30 Padanaram Rd. Open for lunch and dinner daily. American fare—barbecued ribs, steaks, prime rib, pasta, and seafood—served in a dining room overlooking a waterfall. $10–28.

♿ **Two Steps Downtown Grille** (203-794-0032), 5 Ives St. Open daily. A historic firehouse turned restaurant with a laid-back, eclectic vibe. Kids will love the fire engine on the second floor. Sizzling fajitas and juicy ribs are some of the southwestern favorites here, as is the Sunday brunch buffet. Don't miss the spicy Jamaican jerk chicken with sweet island relish, a standout on the menu of burgers, wraps, quesadillas, and fajitas. $7–18.

In Bethel

Bethel Café (203-790-4433; www.bethelcinema.com/bethelcafe), 269 Greenwood Ave. Open Wed.–Fri. for lunch; daily for dinner; brunch on Sat. and Sun. This storefront eatery in a shopping strip is nonetheless charming, serving salads, paninis, and other light meals, as well as homemade gelato. A good stop for a meal before or after catching a film at the Bethel Cinema right next door. $10–17.

♿ **Biksbee's** (203-744-7368), 211 Greenwood Ave. Open daily for lunch and dinner. Another location at 896 Ethan Allen Hwy. (US 7) in Ridgefield (203-431-4441). A casual and friendly eatery that caters to families with generous portions of well-priced food, even a magician to keep hungry little ones occupied. The something-for-everyone menu ranges from paninis and pizza to chicken potpie and filet mignon. $11–35.

Old Heidelberg German Restaurant (203-797-1860; www.restaurantheidelberg.com), 55 Stony Hill Rd. (US 6). Open for lunch Tue.–Sun.; dinner daily. Authentic German cuisine pairs nicely with the 50 varieties of German *bier*—if you order it on tap, it comes in a hefty 1-liter ceramic stein. German specialties are robust and hearty—bratwurst, sauerbraten, Wiener schnitzel, and späetzle with red cabbage. Desserts are what you'd expect in a German restaurant: Black Forest cake and apple strudel. Saturday night in the Bavarian beer garden means lively German music; many special events throughout the year; the lively Oktoberfest celebration takes place in September and October. $14–20.

Rizzuto's Wood-Fired Pizza Kitchen & Bar (203-790-4444; www.rizzutos.com), 6 Stony Hill Rd. Open daily for lunch and dinner. The kitchen is known for putting a gourmet spin on smoky wood-fired pizzas. Gourmet toppings run the gamut from goat cheese and roasted garlic to broccoli rabe and vodka sauce. There's also a decent selection of pastas and other Italian dishes; the garlic-rosemary focaccia is made here and worth every carb. New: The Bar @ Rizzuto's. $12–24.

Elsewhere

♿ **Julio's** (203-264-7878; wwwjulioswoodfiredpizzagrill.com), 220 South Main St., Southbury. Open for lunch Tue.–Fri.; dinner Tue.–Sun.; closed Mon. Locals love Julio and Maria Duque's charming eatery, with its wood-fired oven that turns out innovative pizzas with a hint of smoky flavor. One is topped with mussels, garlic, parsley, and olive oil; one with grilled vegetables; and another with prosciutto, artichoke hearts, plum tomatoes, and boiled egg. Handmade pasta—cavatelli with grilled chicken, spinach, Marsala, and cream, for example—and a selection of chicken, beef, and seafood entrées rounds out the menu. The Italian staple dessert tiramisu is popular, as is the ricotta cheesecake. $9–26.

Leo's (203-264-9190), Bennett Square, Main St. South, Southbury. Open daily for breakfast, lunch, and dinner. Extremely popular at breakfast, when you can choose from the usual morning meal standbys or go for it with the "Wheel of Fortune," a fluffy Belgian waffle topped with homemade raspberry sauce, whipped cream, and fresh fruit. $5–15.

Down the Hatch Restaurant (203-775-6635), 292 Candlewood Lake Rd., Brookfield. Open Apr.–mid-Oct., daily for lunch and dinner. A casual and friendly seasonal spot on the water; popular with locals and summer visitors, and a great place to bring the kids. For a casual meal and a great view, sit out on the deck—the perfect vantage point for watching the goings-on on the lake. There's a no-frills menu of satisfying favorites—burgers, sandwiches, seafood, and pub-style appetizers—that will please everyone in the family. Inside, the menu runs the gamut, from stuffed lobster tails and grilled salmon to baby back ribs and filet mignon. $14–20.

American Pie (860-350-0662), 29 Sherman Rd. (CT 37), at the junction of CT 39, next to the post office, Sherman. Open daily for breakfast, lunch, and dinner. A restaurant and bakery that draws a regular crowd of locals and weekend residents who come for the 20 varieties of made-from-scratch pie. If you're around in fall, pick up a Harvest Fruit Pie, chock-full of apples, walnuts, cranberries, and blueberries, perfect for a cold New England night. Breakfast, burgers, salads, pasta, and chicken round out the rest of the menu. $6–15.

Arrivederci Trattoria & Pizza (860-210-1266), 1 CT 37, Sherman. Open Tue.–Sun. for lunch and dinner; closed Mon. An intimate and welcoming trattoria serving flavorful northern Italian cuisine. Chef-owner Sergio Ragosta, who used to run a restaurant in his native Naples, now brings the tastes of his homeland to rural Connecticut. Dishes like bruschetta and *pollo nerone* (chicken stuffed with prosciutto di Parma, mozzarella, and baby spinach) are prepared with the freshest possible ingredients, and an expert hand. *Arrivederci* means "We will see you again"; and the food and ambience certainly draw patrons back. BYOB. $10–17.

♿ **Gail's Station House** (203-938-8933), 3 Sidecut Rd., West Redding. Open daily for breakfast and lunch; Friday-night dinner in spring and summer. Breakfast fans remember Ridgefield's Gail's Station House, the downtown icon destryoyed by fire. This latest incarnation debuted in late 2008; many of the old favorites, such as sweet potato pancakes, appear on the new menu of California-inspired continental cuisine. BYOB.

SNACKS **Chez Lenard** (203-431-6324), Main St., Ridgefield. Is there such a thing as haute road food? With names like Le Hot Dog Choucroute Alsacienne (topped with mustard and sauerkraut), yes. This self-described "French gourmet hot dog stand" is a Ridgefield landmark, even if it is a humble sidewalk cart. These classy dogs are dressed with chili, horseradish sauce, and a fondue-like topping that blends kirsch, white wine, and melted cheese. Eat standing on the sidewalk, or cross the street to Ballard Park. Around $5.

♿ **Marcus Dairy Bar** (203-748-9427), 5 Sugar Hollow Rd., Danbury.

Open daily for three meals. The name says it all: Marcus has every variety of ice cream devised. There's a 1950s Cruise Night most Saturdays, and monthly motorcycle rallies that attract bikers from all over, especially on Sundays. A brand-new building is slated to open on the site in 2009.

Sycamore Drive-In (203-748-2716), 282 Greenwood Ave., Bethel. An old-fashioned drive-in with "French-cooked" burgers, meaning they're flattened on the grill and cooked until they're crispy around the edges. You can still get carhop service, just like the good ol' days; just flash your lights when you're ready to order. The Dagwood Burger sports every topping imaginable.

Mocha (203-364-9200; www.mochacoffeehouse.com), 3 Glen Rd., off CT 34, Sandy Hook. Open daily. Coffee, tea, juice drinks, and a light menu of snacks (soups, salads, quiche, paninis) and sweets (cupcakes, pound cake, pignoli cookies). Tap into the free WiFi, or check out the live music and work by local artists.

Newtown General Store (203-426-9901), Main St., Newtown. Open daily. A 200-year-old general store nestled among preserved homesteads and historic churches on a Main Street that hasn't changed much since the 1700s. Breakfast sandwiches, lunch, snacks, homemade ice cream. A popular spot for coffee and the morning paper.

Denmo's Snack & Dairy Bar (203-264-4626), 346 Main St. South, Southbury. This old-fashioned drive-in clam shack is a happy kind of place, well worth the wait that you'll likely encounter. Whole-belly clams, split-charred hot dogs, and hot lobster rolls are crowd pleasers, as are the fried seafood baskets that come with the works: french fries, coleslaw, tartar sauce, and a wedge of lemon. Order at the window and take your goodies to a picnic table.

♿ **European Shoppe** (203-262-1500), 109 Playhouse Corner (US 6), Southbury, Exit 15 off I-84. Breakfast and lunch daily from 6:30 AM. In the morning, locals and commuters crowd in for freshly baked bagels and pastries. Pair one with a strong cappuccino and you have a satisfying, inexpensive breakfast. If you're not eating on the run, get a café table at the back of the shop. Hearty sandwiches (around $5) for lunch.

ICE CREAM **Ridgefield Ice Cream Shop** (203-438-3094), 680 Danbury Rd. (US 7), Ridgefield. You can still get soft-serve chocolate and vanilla in this former Carvel location, but now it's made fresh every day, which makes it extra-silky and super-creamy. Kids clamor for the cold and melty ice cream atop light-as-air wafer cones; the milk shakes and sundaes are pretty good, too.

Dr. Mike's (203-792-4388), 158 Greenwood Ave., Bethel. Open Tue.–Sun.; closed Mon. Since 1975, locals have been eagerly waiting in line for a scoop or two of pure homemade decadence. Flavors like Chocolate Lace, an overwhelming favorite (maybe it's the locally produced chocolate), will make you swoon, as will the homemade whipped cream that tops the hot fudge sundaes. In fact, this old-fashioned ice cream parlor is so revered that local schoolchildren come here on field trips!

Rich Farm Ice Cream Shop (203-881-1040), 691 Oxford Rd. (CT 67), Oxford. Open mid-Apr.–late Nov. This dairy farm has been in business for more than a century, and the family's own herd provides the fresh cream used to make their oh-so-good ice cream. Kid-pleasing flavors like Razzmanian Devil (chocolate chunks and red-raspberry swirls in vanilla), Cowabunga (coconut with pineapple chunks), and Cookie Monster (chocolate chip cookie pieces in blue vanilla) are big sellers. Order from the window and savor your treats at a picnic table, then stop by the cow barn for a peek at the goings-on inside.

✷ Entertainment

ARTS CENTER **The Ridgefield Playhouse** (203-438-5795; www.ridgefieldplayhouse.org), 80 East Ridge Ave., Ridgefield. Musicals, plays, holiday performances, movies, popular music, and original works staged year-round in a restored 1938 theater. It's also home to the **Ridgefield Symphony Orchestra** and the **Ridgefield Opera Company**.

MUSIC

In Danbury

CityCenter Danbury (203-792-1711; www.citycenterdanbury.com), 186 Main St., on the green. A small city green with a band shell is the setting for a popular, free, summertime festival of the arts that brings nationally known musicians to town. Thursday is family night, with children's performances; concerts on Friday and Saturday nights.

Ives Concert Park (203-837-9226; www.ivesconcertpark.com), on the Westside Campus of Western Connecticut State University. Weekends, Memorial Day–Labor Day. The stage, in an outdoor amphitheater, is set on a small island in a pond. Guests can sit in reserved seats, or on the lawn with blankets or beach chairs, and listen to symphonies, jazz, folk music, blues, and pop stars in a beautiful outdoor setting. **Ives Café** serves refreshments and snacks.

THEATER **Musicals at Richter** (203-748-6873; www.musicalsatrichter.org), Richter Arts Center, 100 Aunt Hack Rd., Danbury. Summer concerts—classical, opera, big band, jazz, folk—in Connecticut's longest-running outdoor theater, which also hosts dance performances, musical theater productions, and arts festivals. This is the longest-running outdoor musical theater in southwestern Connecticut; come early and bring a picnic.

Ridgefield Theater Barn (203-431-9850; www.theaterbarn.org), 37 Halpin Lane, Ridgefield. A converted dairy barn is the setting for comedies, musicals, dramas, and experimental works, in both a theater- or cabaret-style setting, performed by Ridgefield's 45-year-old community theater.

Town Players of Newtown (203-270-9144; www.newtownplayers.org), Orchard Hill Rd., Newtown. The Town Players perform comedies, dramas, and holiday shows in their intimate venue, The Little Theater, from April to December.

♿ **Brookfield Theatre for the Arts** (203-775-0023; www.brookfieldplayhouse.org), 184 Whisconier Rd. (CT 25), Brookfield. A former school for boys, but since 1958 the home of the **Country Players**. Year-round schedule of live performances, from comedy and drama to children's entertainment.

♿ **Sherman Playhouse** (860-354-3622; www.shermanplayers.org), at the junction of CT 37 and CT 39, Sherman. Performances Apr.–Dec. on Fri., Sat., and Sun. **The Sherman Players**, a community theater group together for more than 85 years, presents new and classic musicals, comedies, and dramas in a renovated 19th-century church, where performances have been held since the 1920s.

✷ Selective Shopping

Books on the Common (203-431-9100), Copps Hill Common, 109 Danbury Rd. (CT 35), Ridgefield. A family-owned independent bookshop with unique titles, books on tape, and classical CDs.

Hauser Chocolatier (203-794-1861; www.hauserchocolates.com), 137 Greenwood Ave., Bethel. European techniques and imported Swiss and French chocolate are used to create butter-smooth truffles, chocolate dessert cups, and assorted other confections.

Hazel and Sid (203-431-7747; www.hazelandsid.com), 423 Main St., Ridgefield. Open Tue.–Sat. 10–6; Sun. noon–5; closed Mon. Antiques, chandeliers, furniture, clothing, art, and jewelry, both new and vintage.

Danbury Fair Mall (203-743-3247; www.danburyfairmall.com), 7 Backus Ave., Danbury, Exit 3 off I-84. One of Connecticut's largest shopping malls, with more than 200 retailers, including four major department stores and a variety of food shops. The Venetian-style carousel is the only double-decker carousel in the state. It's on the former site of the Danbury State Fair, what was for many years the second-largest country fair in New England.

Stew Leonard's (203-790-8030; www.stewleonards.com), 99 Federal Rd. (US 7), Danbury. Open daily; closed Christmas Day. This unique dairy-grocery store, sister to the original in Norwalk, is listed in the *Guinness Book of World Records* for the world's fastest-moving stock! It attracts plenty of attention, from the *New York Times* ("the Disneyland of Dairy Stores") to *Ripley's Believe It or Not!* ("The World's Largest Dairy Store"). The vibe is part farmer's market, part amusement park, with fresh made-before-your-eyes meals, free food samples, and entertainment ranging from animated cows to costumed characters roaming the aisles.

Our Green House (203-364-1484), 4 Washington St., Sandy Hook. Open Mon.–Sat.; closed Sun. A unique shop where everything is earth-friendly, from household cleaning supplies and skin care products to accessories for pets. Some items are made with ingredients that are all-natural, while others are toxin-free or organically grown. Baby linens—blankets, crib sheets, diapers—are made with organically grown cotton. Handmade beeswax candles and scented soaps make nice gifts for environmentally conscious loved ones.

♿ **Mother Earth Gallery and Mining Company** (203-775-6272), 806 Federal Rd. (US 7/202), Brookfield. Open Wed.–Mon.; closed Tue. Children can don headlamps and search for sparkling minerals and gemstones in an indoor re-created mining cave. The gallery shop features handcrafted jewelry along with minerals, fossils, crystals, shells, games, and nature toys.

Starlight Baby Boutique (203-264-0588), 33 Bullet Hill Rd., Southbury. Open Tue.–Sat. 10–5; Thu. 11–6; closed Sun. and Mon. All things baby—clothing, furniture, gifts, and gear, beautifully displayed in a converted 18th-century barn.

A Touch of Sedona (203-438-7146), 452 Main St., Ridgefield. Open daily 10–5. A "spiritual boutique" selling equestrian gifts as well as southwestern and Native American paintings, jewelry, crafts, and musical instruments. Ask about the drumming circle that meets here.

ANTIQUES SHOPS **Woodbury** is the acknowledged antiques capital of Connecticut, but Ridgefield comes in a close second, and many other shops are scattered around the Housatonic Valley.

In Ridgefield

Country Gallery Antiques (203-438-2535), 346 Ethan Allen Hwy. (US 7). An 18th-century barn full of European country pine antiques and reproductions. Custom-crafted antique barnwood tables.

The King & I Antiques (203-544-8544), 47 Ethan Allen Hwy. (US 7). Antiques, gifts, and consignment items.

Next Step Antiques (203-431-8083), 199 Ethan Allen Hwy. (US 7). The specialty here is Swedish antiques, furniture, and home accessories.

Red Petticoat (203-431-9451), 113 West Lane (CT 35). Open Tue.–Sun.; closed Mon. A trove of 18th- and 19th-century collectibles, plus larger pieces, such as Early American blanket chests and 18th-century card tables. Ridgefield's oldest and largest antiques shop, in the 1740 Benjamin Rockwell Homestead.

Ridgefield Antiques Center (203-438-2777), 109 Danbury Rd. US 7). Open daily. Close to 25 dealers selling country and formal furniture, paintings, folk art, silver, porcelain, and jewelry.

Silver Lining (203-431-0132), 470 Main St. Antiques and consignment items.

Elsewhere

Time After Time (203-743-2801; www.tatpool.com), 32 Stony Hill, Bethel. Custom-made and antique pool tables, many from the 1800s; billiards memorabilia and accessories.

ART AND ARTISANS **Ironwood Gallery of Contemporary Craft** (203-431-3388; www.ironwoodgallery.com), 103 Danbury Rd. (CT 35), Ridgefield. Open Wed.–Sat. 11–5, or by appointment; closed Sun.–Tue. Fine art and contemporary crafts, from furniture and ceramics to glass, lighting, sculpture, painting, and jewelry, by noted American artists.

Ridgefield Guild of Artists (203-438-8863; www.rgoa.org), 34 Halpin Lane, off Prospect Ridge Rd., Ridgefield. Gallery open year-round, Wed.–Sun. noon–4. A former monastery is the site of 13 exhibitions a year featuring the work of regional and national artists. Galleries, workshops, classes. Call for a schedule. Hosts the town's annual summertime Art in the Park arts-and-crafts show in Ballard Park (see *Special Events*).

Brookfield Craft Center (203-775-4526; www.brookfieldcraftcenter.org), 286 Whisconier Rd. (CT 25), Brookfield. Gallery and retail shop open Mon.–Sat. 10–5; Sun. noon–5. Free admission. A sprawling crafts center and school for fine contemporary

BROOKFIELD CRAFT CENTER

Scott Miles

craftsmanship in a historic complex of red colonial buildings—including a gristmill dating from 1780—and a restored 1917 train station overlooking the Still River at Halfway Falls. Visitors can roam the grounds (studio buildings not open to the public) or participate (preregistration required) in the 400 classes and workshops offered every year. You can take up boatbuilding, guitar making, weaving, woodworking, trompe l'oeil painting, glassblowing, or blacksmithing, to name just a few. Two galleries showcase the work of craftspeople from around the country; there's also a gift shop and bookstore. The center's annual holiday crafts sale attracts throngs of shoppers looking for one-of-a-kind handcrafted holiday gifts (see *Special Events*).

Art Center Sculpture Barn (203-746-6101; www.sculpturebarn.com), 3 Milltown Rd., on the Danbury city line at the junction of CT 39, New Fairfield. Open Apr.–Dec., Wed.–Sun. 10–6; Jan.–Mar., open by appointment. Visitors can browse the gallery, sculpture field, and working studios. Want to try your hand? Master sculptor David Boyajian teaches classes on how to create works in stone and metal.

FARMS AND GARDENS

In Bethel

Blue Jay Orchards (203-748-0119; www.bluejayorchardsct.com), 125 Plumtrees Rd. Farm market open daily Aug.–Dec., 10–5:30. Loyal patrons come to the retail market for the homemade chunky applesauce, apple butter, and cider doughnuts; you can also get fresh pies, breads, and muffins baked in their ovens. Summertime means fresh peaches, corn, and tomatoes; crisp autumn days are time to head for the fields and orchard for apple (Rome Beauty, Greening, Macoun, Winesap, and Empire among dozens of varieties) and pumpkin picking as well as cider pressing. Thousands make the pilgrimage every year to experience the old-fashioned rural atmosphere. Take your children on a hayride or to a storytelling session.

Hollandia Nurseries (203-743-0267; www.hollandianurseryct.com). The

INVENTED IN CONNECTICUT

Submarine (1775)
Cotton gin (1794)
Shelf clock (1814)
Colt revolver (1836)
Portable typewriter (1843)
Sewing machine (1846)
Ice-making machine (1853)
Can opener (1858)
Tape measure (1868)
Pay phone (1877)
Collapsible toothpaste tube (1892)
Hamburger (1895)
Electric light socket with pull chain (1896)
Lollipop (1908)
Erector set (1911)
Raggedy Ann doll (1915)
Frisbee (1920)
Mounds bar (1920)
Electric shaver (1931)
Vacuum cleaner (1933)
Polaroid camera (1934)
Helicopter (1939)
Color television (1948)
Silly Putty (1950)
Sunfish (1951)
Nuclear submarine (1954)
Wiffle ball (1956)

nurseries are at 103 Old Hawleyville Rd.; the gift and garden shop is at 95 Stony Hill Rd. (US 6). To find Fairfield County's largest nursery and garden center, look for the half-mile-long border of colorful bulbs and annuals that leads to a gardener's haven. Flowers bloom year-round under the glass of 24 greenhouses; in-season, 5 acres of display gardens showcase shrubs, perennials, and vegetables. Garden ornaments, tools, holiday plants. Friendly and knowledgeable staff.

Sunrise Herb Farm (203-794-0809; www.sunriseherbfarm.com), 35 Codfish Hill Rd. (CT 302). Open Mon.–Sat. 9–5; closed Sun. The state's only herb farm that specializes in medicinal blends—more than 120 of them. Valerie Hoffman's herb shop is a replica of George Washington's Mount Vernon; her herbal remedies are made daily by certified herbalists. Call or check online for a schedule of gardening and herb lectures, cooking classes, and workshops on herbal medicines, stress, wellness, and other topics.

Holbrook Farm Market & Bakery (203-792-0561; www.holbrookfarm.net), 45 Turkey Plain Rd. (CT 53). Open Apr.–Dec., Mon.–Sat. 10-6; closed Sun. This family-run organic farm has been in operation for 30 years; today a farm stand sells veggies, cut flowers, herbs, berries, free-range eggs, and homemade baked goods.

Elsewhere

Warrup's Farm (203-938-9403), 51 John Read Rd., West Redding. Free maple sugaring demonstrations in early spring on the Hill family's 300-acre organic farm. In the log-style sugarhouse, visitors can watch as sap is boiled down over a wood fire into a thick, sweet syrup, known as "liquid gold." Later in the growing season, cut your own flowers and pick your own veggies and pumpkins. The seasonal farm stand is stocked with fresh-from-the-fields organic salad greens, vegetables, and herbs. Kids love the resident barnyard animals and antique-tractor-drawn hayrides in autumn.

Catnip Acres Herb Nursery (203-888-5649), 67 Christian St., Oxford. Browse in the herb gardens, the greenhouse, and the herbal gift shop. The nursery grows 400 varieties of herbs and flowers and is noted for its scented geraniums. Year-round classes and workshops in growing, harvesting, preserving, and using herbs medicinally.

Paproski's Castle Hill Farm (203-426-5487; www.castlehillfarm.net), 40 Sugar Lane, Newtown. Open in Oct., Sat. and Sun. 11–5. Pick your own pumpkins, roam the 6-acre corn maze, or take a hayride; pony rides are available for youngsters.

Larson's Farm Market (203-740-2790; www.larsonsfarmmarket.com), 401 Federal Rd. (US 7), Brookfield. The farm stand is open Mon.–Sat. 10–7, and Sun. 10–6, during the growing season. Four generations of the Larson family have been growing sweet corn since 1901; today, the farm stand sells a huge variety of fresh produce, plus locally produced specialty foods. In fall you can lose yourself in the labyrinthine maze carved out of a 7-acre cornfield.

✳ Special Events

March: **NCAA Division III Women's National Basketball Championship** (203-837-9015), O'Neill Center, Western Connecticut State University, Danbury. **Home and Leisure Show** (203-743-5565), Danbury Fair Mall, Danbury. The oldest and biggest home show in the region.

May: **Colonial Day** (203-438-5485), at the Keeler Tavern Museum, Ridgefield. Fife-and-drum corps, live music, demonstrations of blacksmithing, open-hearth cooking, and other 18th-century tasks; colonial games for children.

Summer: **Summer Concert Series** (203-792-1711; www.citycenter danbury.com), City Center green, Danbury.

June: **Ridgefield Outdoor Antiques Market** (203-438-6962), on the grounds of the Lounsbury Mansion, 316 Main St., Ridgefield. More than 125 East Coast dealers have been exhibiting at this show for more than 45 years.

July: **Second Company Governor's Horse Guard Show** (203-426-9046), 4 Wildlife Dr., Newtown (see *Historic Sites*).

Labor Day weekend: **Mark Twain Library Book Fair** (203-938-2545), Redding. For more than 40 years, this huge used-book sale has attracted bibliophiles from all over New England.

September: **Taste of Danbury** (203-792-1711). Chefs from the area's best restaurants entice you to their booths to sample their specialties. Live music and children's entertainment.

October: **Bethel Film Festival** (203-790-4321; www.bethelfilmfestival.com), Bethel Cinema, Bethel. A weeklong event showcasing more than 50 new and independent films, including documentaries, shorts, features, animation, and student films. **Great Danbury Antiques Fair** (914-273-4667), Danbury. More than 50 antiques dealers.

Mid-November through December: **Brookfield Craft Center Holiday Craft Exhibition and Sale** (203-775-4526), 286 Whisconier Rd. (CT 25), Brookfield. More than 300 local and national artisans offer their works for sale in the valley's largest show of American handcrafts. The sale is held on three floors of a restored 18th-century gristmill at the crafts center.

December: **First Night Danbury** (203-792-1711; www.firstnightdanbury .org). New Year's Eve nonalcoholic, midtown entertainment-go-round. One ticket admits you to a wide variety of family-friendly events, including ice skating, music, entertainment, and dancing, in theaters, schools, galleries, and libraries. Modeled after Boston's First Night, the first such celebration in the country.

The Litchfield Hills

LITCHFIELD AND
SURROUNDING TOWNS

Barnett D. Laschever

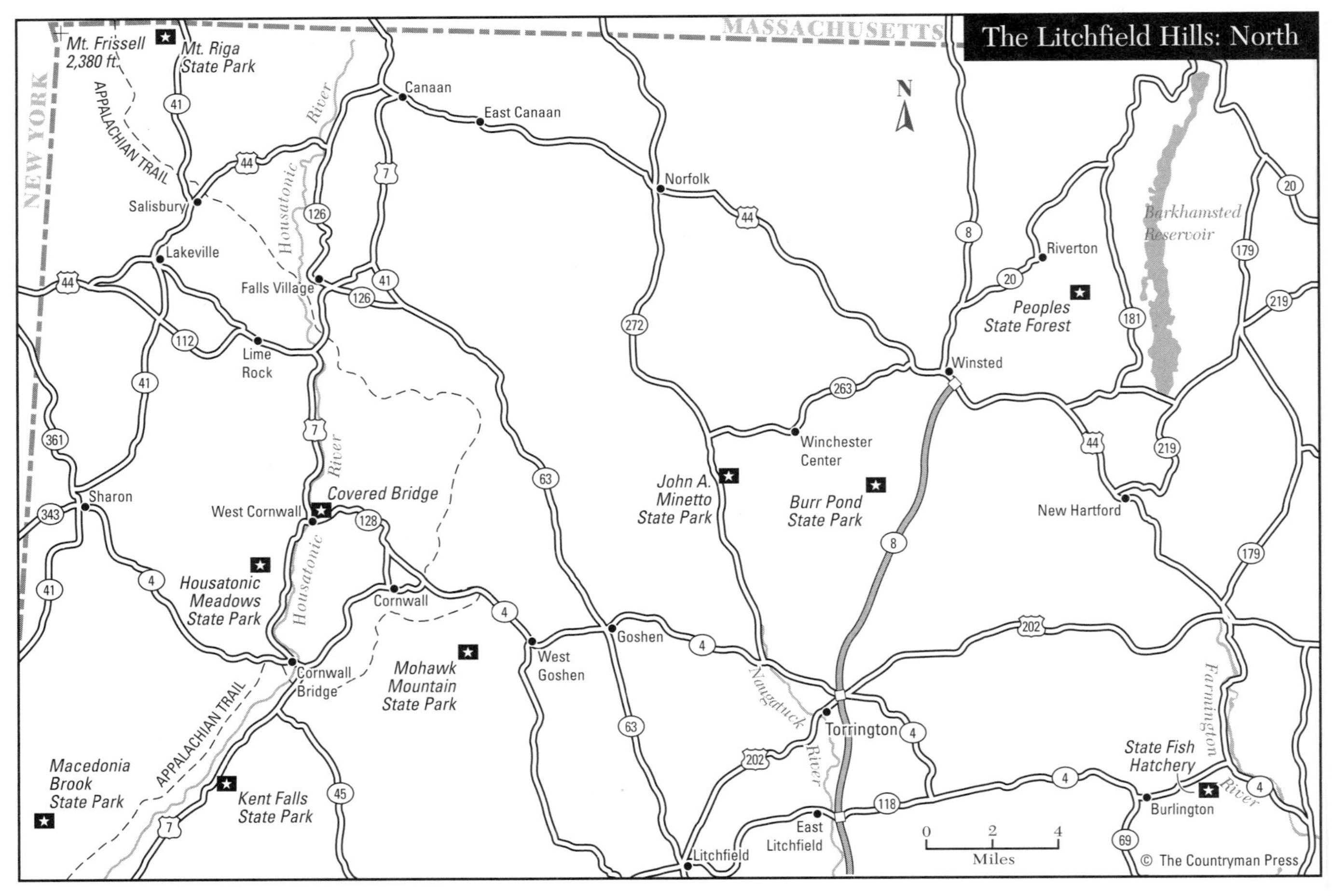
The Litchfield Hills: North
MASSACHUSETTS
NEW YORK
N
Mt. Frissell
2,380 ft.
Mt. Riga
State Park
APPALACHIAN TRAIL
Salisbury
Lakeville
Canaan
East Canaan
Norfolk
Falls Village
Lime
Rock
Housatonic
River
Sharon
West Cornwall
Covered Bridge
Housatonic
Meadows
State Park
Cornwall
Cornwall
Bridge
Mohawk
Mountain
State Park
West
Goshen
Goshen
Macedonia
Brook
State Park
Kent Falls
State Park
John A.
Minetto
State Park
Winchester
Center
Burr Pond
State Park
Winsted
Riverton
Peoples
State Forest
Barkhamsted
Reservoir
New Hartford
Naugatuck
River
Torrington
East
Litchfield
Litchfield
Farmington
River
State Fish
Hatchery
Burlington
0 2 4
Miles
© The Countryman Press

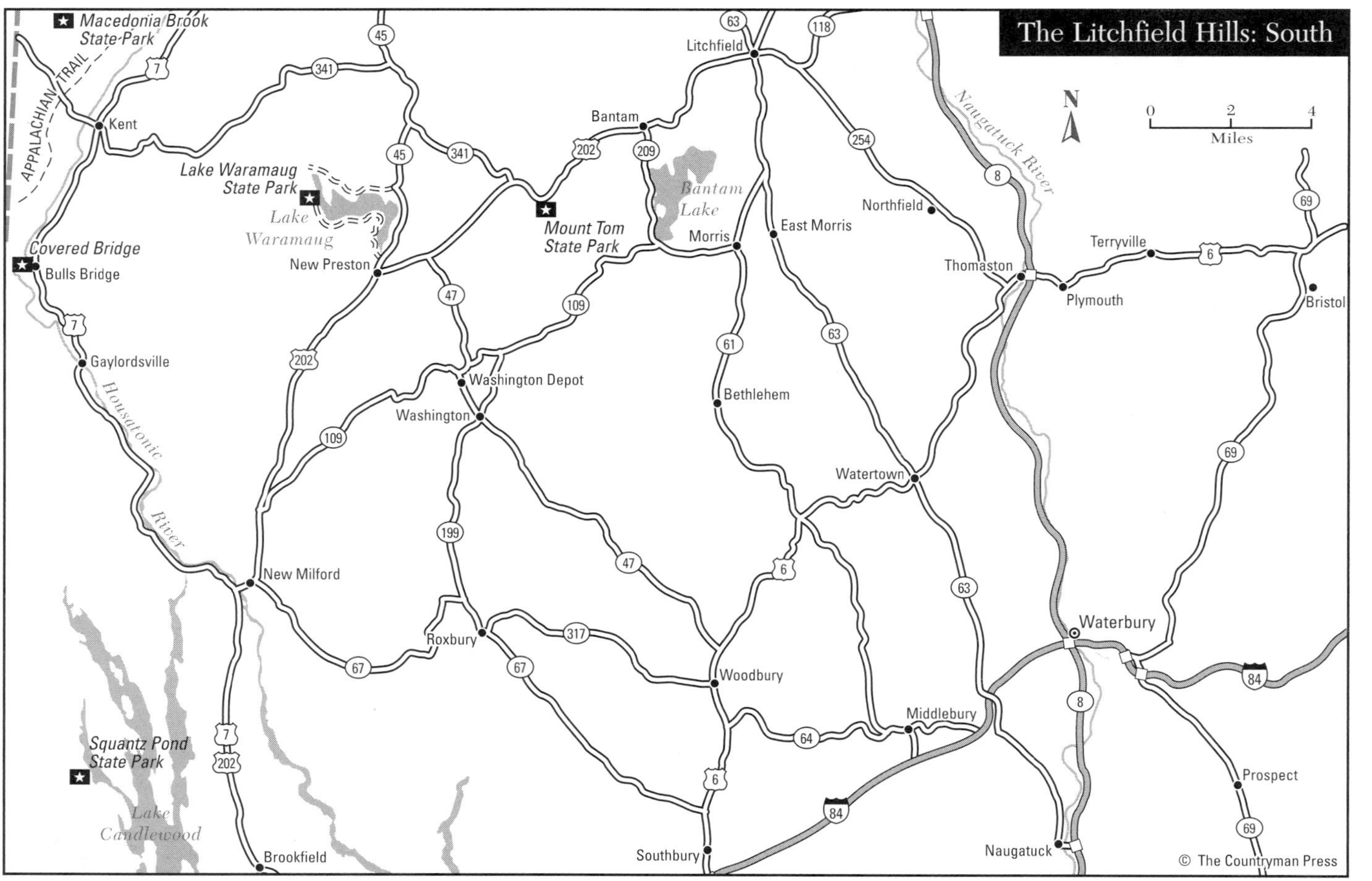
The Litchfield Hills: South
N
0
2
4
Miles
Macedonia Brook State Park
Appalachian Trail
Kent
Lake Waramaug State Park
Lake Waramaug
Covered Bridge
Bulls Bridge
New Preston
Gaylordsville
Housatonic River
Mount Tom State Park
Bantam
Bantam Lake
Litchfield
Morris
East Morris
Northfield
Thomaston
Naugatuck River
Terryville
Plymouth
Bristol
Washington Depot
Washington
Bethlehem
Watertown
New Milford
Roxbury
Woodbury
Middlebury
Waterbury
Prospect
Naugatuck
Southbury
Brookfield
Squantz Pond State Park
Lake Candlewood
© The Countryman Press

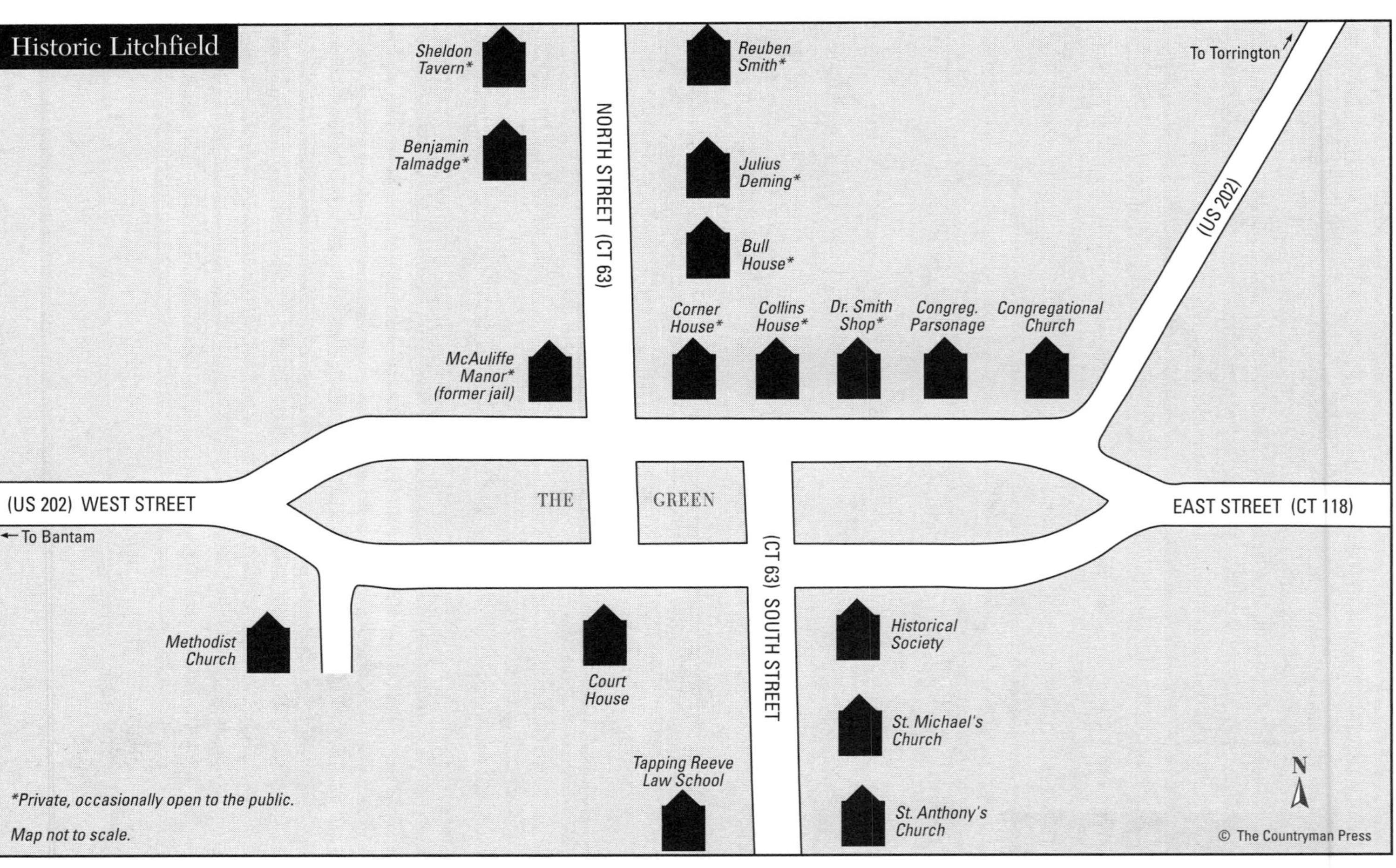
Historic Litchfield
Sheldon Tavern*
Benjamin Talmadge*
McAuliffe Manor* (former jail)
NORTH STREET (CT 63)
Reuben Smith*
Julius Deming*
Bull House*
Corner House*
Collins House*
Dr. Smith Shop*
Congreg. Parsonage
Congregational Church
To Torrington
(US 202)
(US 202) WEST STREET
← To Bantam
THE
GREEN
EAST STREET (CT 118)
(CT 63) SOUTH STREET
Methodist Church
Court House
Tapping Reeve Law School
Historical Society
St. Michael's Church
St. Anthony's Church
N
*Private, occasionally open to the public.
Map not to scale.
© The Countryman Press

LITCHFIELD AND SURROUNDING TOWNS

The diversity of the country's third-smallest state is nowhere so striking as in Connecticut's northwestern corner. Here time has dramatically stood still, leaving the treasured image of quintessential colonial America almost intact. Indeed, in the verdant Litchfield Hills, the village of Litchfield itself has been hailed as picture-postcard New England and attracts thousands of visitors annually who come to walk historic North and South streets and admire the spectacular mansions. In July, many of the great homes are opened to the public for a day. In December, historic houses in Litchfield are draped with understated strings of white Christmas lights. Red neon, in a word, is gauche. The Congregational church on the corner of one of the nation's largest greens (or commons, as they were first called) is arguably the most photographed colonial-style church in New England.

At this point we would be remiss if we failed to let the reader in on a little secret: The great houses of Litchfield in the main are not of the colonial era. While they are nearly all sheathed in clapboard and look like colonial houses, most were built after the American Revolution and are an eclectic mix of Greco-Roman, Colonial Revival, Federal, Victorian, and five modernist structures designed by the Hungarian architect Marcel Breuer. But to the eye unschooled in architecture, Litchfield has a symbiotic unity. Another oddity: Several of the grand homes on North Street have "widow's" walks crowning their roofs. Why, is still a matter of conjecture. Some argue that early Litchfield entrepreneurs were ship owners whose vessels sailed out of New Haven; others contend it was just a fad with no defensible reason or that maybe it had something or other to do with chimney fires.

The southern border of Litchfield's West Street runs along the Litchfield green and hosts an eclectic collection of restaurants, women's clothing stores, art galleries, antiques shops, and a tawny-colored Methodist church. It closely resembles the better-known Main Street just up the road in Stockbridge, Massachusetts, recognized throughout the country from the famous painting by Norman Rockwell. Many stores on West Street in Litchfield glow in-season with myriad blossoms carefully tended in window boxes.

Although the grand homes are not museums, Litchfield does boast several other unique attractions worth visiting. On South Street, a New Jersey judge with the unlikely name of Tapping Reeve founded America's first law school, now a National Historic Site. The Litchfield History Museum traces Connecticut history from the early settling of what was then Connecticut's western frontier to more recent days, when a vicious tornado unexpectedly savaged the western part of the state on a hot July day. The White Memorial Foundation will lure you to its 4,000 acres of forests, lakes, and ponds.

Other villages in the county would meet a movie-set designer's dreams. Washington, which claims it is the first municipality in the country named for the Father of His Country, is a lovely collection of white-clapboard homes set around a green square dominated by the Congregational church. A short jaunt into the nearby woods brings you to the Institute for American Indian Studies, a museum and teaching facility that concentrates on the unique lifestyle of the forest-dwelling Native Americans, who did not live in tepees or hunt buffalo.

The beautiful Battell Stoeckel estate in Norfolk is the home of the Yale University Summer School of Music, which stages a world-renowned annual summer festival of chamber music in an acoustically perfect redwood music shed. A host of artists have gravitated to Kent, on the banks of the Housatonic River, turning this once sleepy town known only for its prestigious Kent prep school into a leading center of art and culture. The hand tools that shaped the dwellings and furniture of colonial Americans are displayed in the Sloane-Stanley Museum. It's on the outskirts of Kent, just below Kent Falls State Park. Kent Falls isn't exactly Niagara, but it is picturesque enough to attract hundreds of visitors daily.

The Litchfield Hills, just south of the Berkshires over the Massachusetts border to the north, contain Connecticut's highest mountains, in the Mount Riga area; its longest river (the Housatonic); and, at West Cornwall, its most beautiful covered bridge.

During the spring thaw, the whitewater of the Housatonic challenges kayakers and canoeists. In summer, less intrepid boaters can venture out on calmer waters. In autumn, when the foliage catches fire, the drive from West Cornwall down US 7 along the river to Kent is a leaf-peeper's paradise. Campers vie for sites in the

KENT FALLS

Cory Mazon

state park on the banks of the Housatonic, while backpackers and hikers slog, happily we can only assume, along the section of the Appalachian Trail that slices through the region. For 5 miles the AT runs alongside the Housatonic, the longest stretch of river walk on the trail between Georgia and Maine. Indeed, while the Connecticut River is the longest in New England, the Housy, as it is called locally, is the longest within the borders of Connecticut.

Barnett D. Laschever

HISTORIANS STILL PONDER WHY WIDOW'S WALKS TOPPED THE ROOFS OF SOME LITCHFIELD MANSIONS.

At the time of the American Revolution, the village of Litchfield was a major manufacturing center, producing supplies for Washington's army. Pig iron was forged from 40 mines dug into the hills around Mount Riga and Kent for cannons and for the huge iron chain that the Continentals strung across the Hudson to block British warships from sailing up the river. (It didn't work.) Several forges have been restored as tourist attractions and educational tools. A leaden statue of King George III was pulled down in New York, cut up, and taken by wagon to Litchfield, where the ladies melted it down and produced more than 40,000 musket balls for Washington's army. The Continental soldiers dubbed them "Melted Majesty" when they left the barrels of their weapons.

At war's end, towns such as Torrington, Winsted, and Naugatuck, sitting on the banks of the Naugatuck River almost at sea level, attracted the major industries, particularly brass, copper, and rubber. Consequently, Litchfield went to sleep. Its little factories withered and died, and the hill country regained its trees.

Before World War II, a few train spurs penetrated the hills, bringing vacationers with steamer trunks who settled into lakeside country inns for the summer. After the war, fast and comfortable cars, new roads, and the dismemberment of the railroads led to new tourists: the day-tripper and the short-term visitor. This advantageous combination of reliable cars and roads also caught the eye of New York celebrities. It was like the famous Oklahoma Land Rush.

Today the woods and hills of Litchfield County have become a refuge for internationally famous playwrights, authors, musicians, artists, sculptors, fashion designers, movie directors, politicos, and even world-class tennis players. Arthur Miller, one of America's most acclaimed dramatists, lived and wrote in Roxbury until his death in 2005. Skitch Henderson, conductor and composer, lived and worked into his 80s in New Milford. Paul Newman raced at the Lime Rock Park track almost until the day he died in 2008. Though they keep mainly to themselves, the presence of celebrities has spawned the growth of restaurants that cater to sophisticated tastes. Hospitable B&Bs sit behind every stone wall. Children and pets are usually welcome, but not always. Best to check.

Native sons and daughters include John Brown, the abolitionist, who was born in Torrington; Ethan Allen, of Litchfield, a Revolutionary War hero; Harriet Beecher Stowe, also of Litchfield and "the little lady who started this big war," as

Lincoln remarked about the Civil War when he met her; and General Benjamin Tallmadge. The chief of intelligence for the Continental army, he won Washington's undying gratitude for capturing Englishman Major John André and uncovering traitor Benedict Arnold's plot to sell plans of West Point to the British. Another notable was Gail Borden, of nearby Bakerville, the man who invented the "milk that won the Civil War"—canned condensed milk that could be carried for weeks and not spoil. Only the stone foundations remain of both Brown's house in Torrington and of the Borden condensary in the Burrville section of Torrington.

The Stowe house for many years was on the campus of Litchfield's Forman School, one of the numerous excellent private secondary schools that help make Connecticut "Schoolmaster to the Nation." The house has since been gutted and dismantled; it is packed away in several trailers, and at press time its location and future were unknown.

Because of the rocky soil and the relatively short growing season, agriculture has mostly been limited to dairy farming, corn, pumpkins, and tomatoes. Even those activities, however, are on the decline, and haying, specialty nurseries, and

THE GREAT FLOOD OF '55: CONNECTICUT'S "KATRINA"

Unlike California, Louisiana, and Florida, Connecticut doesn't suffer massive natural disasters every two weeks, or even once a year. But memories of the Great Flood of 1955 are still alive in the valley of the Naugatuck River. Hurricanes had been moving up the coast in mid-August, but weathermen predicted they would lose their punch before reaching the state. They were wrong. First, the midtown of Winsted was flooded, destroying almost all the factories on one side of US 44. The rains continued, and water from overflowing feeder rivers smashed into Torrington, destroying its brass factories and the bridge across the Naugatuck River, sending a million and a half board feet of lumber down toward Waterbury. Once an industrial giant, Waterbury was crippled for years by the flood, now 20 feet deep. Governor Abraham Ribicoff immediately declared martial law and sent National Guard helicopters to snatch people clinging to rooftops. The Sikorsky Aircraft Company likewise dispatched its entire fleet of helicopters to the rescue. Some 100 people died, and losses to the communities were in the mega-millions. Today, except for some excellent restaurants, Winsted and Naugatuck are not prime tourist destinations. However, there's good reason to visit Torrington and Waterbury. Note of irony: The night before the flood, all of Waterbury turned out to welcome native daughter Rosalind Russell, in town for the premier of one of her movies. Dave Garroway on the nationally broadcast *Today* show covered the showbiz glitz—and the next day's flood—from the high floors of Waterbury's Elton Hotel.

The disaster was not confined to the Naugatuck Valley. The Housatonic, Mad, Still, and Farmington rivers all overflowed, sending their watery destruction halfway across the state to Hartford.

wineries have taken over. Vineyards in Litchfield and New Preston bottle award-winning vintages. More recently grapes have been planted in Goshen, where two vineyards have opened wineries.

Scenic US 7 winds down from Massachusetts through scenery that rivals the Green Mountains of Vermont. The route has earned for itself the sobriquet "Antiques Alley" for the plethora of old homes that peddle antiques from front parlors. But it is Woodbury, with 40 antiques stores, that justifiably is the "antiques capital" of western Connecticut. In recent years antiques dealers have clustered in New Preston, the Bantam section of Litchfield, Norwalk, and en masse in and around Putnam, making it the "antiques capital of eastern Connecticut."

A final word: The Litchfield Hills, and indeed, all the hardwood forests of Connecticut, burst into flame during the remarkable fall foliage season. It's as spectacular a display as any in New England. Book early; the inns, B&Bs, and other lodgings in the hills are packed with happy leaf-peepers.

Entries in this section are arranged in roughly geographic order.

AREA CODES 203 and 860.

GUIDANCE **Northwest Connecticut Convention & Visitors Bureau** (800-663-1273; www.litchfieldhills.com) (mail or phone inquiries only). Call the phone number listed here, or the state office in Hartford—**Connecticut Commission on Culture and Tourism** (888-CT-VISIT or www.ctvisit.com)—for the latest information. Ask for the bureau's *Unwind* publication and/or brochures of individual attractions. The Litchfield office operates an information booth in-season on the Litchfield Borough green.

State of Connecticut Highway Information Center, Danbury, I-84 eastbound. One of a network of highway centers maintained by the state tourism office on superhighways, the center is open 24 hours a day, year-round. In addition to rest facilities, there are racks filled with folders and brochures mainly for Litchfield County, but also including the Danbury and Waterbury areas. State guides and maps often also are available. There's also an **information center** in Southbury, at Exit 14 off I-84.

GETTING THERE *By bus:* **Peter Pan Bus Lines** (888-751-8800; www.peterpanbus.com) serves Waterbury, from Boston or New York City, and from various New England cities. Schedules and municipalities served change so frequently that we can only advise you to call or check Peter Pan's Web site. Waterbury is the southern gateway to the hills and is only 20 miles south of Litchfield.

By rail: A spur of the coastal commuter line **Metro-North** (800-638-7646; www.mta.info/mnr) provides limited rail service from New York City, via Bridgeport, to the Waterbury station.

GETTING AROUND Public transportation is practically nonexistent. Private car is the vehicle of choice. In the last few years, however, a new mode of getting around has become popular, albeit expensive: limousines and taxis. **Executive Livery Service** (860-491-3955) picks up at airports and train and bus stations and will take people to cultural and tourist events, daily. Others are **Ellis Limousines** (860-567-1114) in Morris and **Kelley Transit Company** (860-489-9243) in Torrington.

MEDICAL EMERGENCY The statewide emergency number is **911**.

Charlotte Hungerford Hospital (860-496-6666), 540 Litchfield St., Torrington. The emergency number is 860-496-6650.

Sharon Hospital (860-364-4141), 50 Hospital Hill Rd., Sharon. The emergency number is 860-364-4111.

St. Mary's Hospital (203-574-6000), 56 Franklin St., Waterbury. The emergency number is 203-574-6002.

Waterbury Hospital (203-573-6000), 64 Robbins St., Waterbury. The emergency number is 203-573-6290.

Winsted Health Center (860-738-6600), 115 Spencer St., Winsted. Limited range of hospital services but does include emergency services provided by the Charlotte Hungerford Hospital in Torrington.

New Milford Hospital, affiliated with Columbia University College of Physicians and Surgeons (860-355-2611), 21 Elm St., New Milford. The emergency number is 860-350-7222.

* Villages

The Other Cities, Towns, and Villages of Litchfield County

Torrington, straddling the Naugatuck River at barely 80 feet above sea level, was in a favored position to be come a manufacturing city. Water was plentiful and was quickly harnessed to power the machines in the factories as they arose and attracted workers from other American cities and from overseas. When they first arrived in Torrington, the English settlers found the hills covered with long straight white pine trees, ideal for the masts of His Majesty's Royal Navy. Hence Torrington's first name, Mast Swamp. The trees were marked for the king's axmen; today a conservation agency still in existence is called King's Mark and recalls that little tidbit of history. Woolen and brass factories thrived, and the Torrington Company became world famous for inventing and developing industrial needles. In the 1930s, when Hollywood built lavish palaces throughout the country to showcase its magical moving pictures, the Warner brothers erected the Warner Theatre in Torrington, one of the finest examples of art deco architecture. It has been lovingly restored, at enormous cost, and is a showcase for traveling theatricals, popular musical groups, symphony, and ballet. Although most of the big metal fabricators have moved away, Torrington is still home to numerous small high-tech companies and has also become a bedroom community for commuters. The eastern gateway to the Litchfield Hills, the town is the shopping center of the region. Mall sprawl in the form of Wal-Mart and other giant-box stores has taken root at the

COE PARK IN CENTER OF TORRINGTON IS NOW A MINI THREE-SEASON BOTANICAL GARDEN.

Barnett D. Laschever

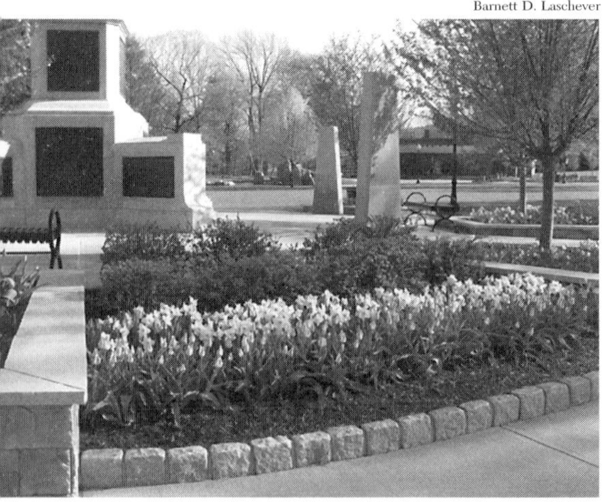

eastern entrance to the city but is not likely to spread into the colonial towns in the hills with their strict zoning regulations. The Nutmeg Conservatory, a recognized international ballet company with a music school, is Torrington's cultural center. Historically, Torrington was the birthplace of John Brown, the violent abolitionist whose exploits inevitably are included in any story of what finally ignited the Civil War. And it was here that Gail Borden devised the process of canning milk. Unlike most American manufacturing towns, Torrington has no slums. Today it is a pleasant middle-class city with an outstanding variety of Victorian architecture. Until 2008 Coe Park, a pleasant little park close to the center of the city, was a pleasant patch of greensward of no particular distinction. Using interest generated by a grant left years ago by the Coe family whose house was on the land, a major landscaping operation took place. The park is now a botanical treasure with plants coming into bloom with the changing seasons and benches for the foot-weary. It's a source of local pride and a destination for visitors.

Goshen. Bordering Litchfield to the north and suited mainly for dairy farming, Goshen early on became America's first center for cheesemaking. In 1792, Alexander Norton carved a wooden pineapple mold and started shipping out his famous "pineapple" cheese. After the Revolution, Goshen cheesemakers shipped out, too, mainly to Wisconsin, which has four cheesemaking towns named Goshen. At an altitude of 1,400 feet, Goshen shares with Norfolk—its immediate neighbor—the unenviable reputation as the "Ice Box of Connecticut." A long-standing aphorism proclaims: "In Goshen, we don't use our snow until it's two years old!" A variety of events are staged on the spacious fairgrounds, from dog shows to hot-air- balloon fairs, grange fairs, Native American powwows, Scottish games, and, of course, the statewide famous Goshen Fair over Labor Day weekend. And Goshen is now home to a live-animal farm. Thanks to acquisitions by the Goshen Land Trust, plus a recent purchase of a large tract by the state that will forever be an undeveloped state park, Goshen now has more protected open space than any other municipality in the state. This is conservation with a vengeance! Goshen's most notable native-born son carried the biblical name of Asaph Hall. He spent his early years as a carpenter, studied at a small New York college, and then attended the University of Michigan, where he came under the tutelage of an outstanding astronomer. From there it was on to Harvard and then the U.S. Naval Observatory in Washington, where he discovered two moons on Mars and became internationally famous. During the Civil War, he was Lincoln's personal meteorologist. His story is told at the observatory—now the official residence of the vice president—and in the Smithsonian Institution's National Air and Space Museum. And finally, joining so many other communities in the state, Goshen is now home to two vineyards and wineries.

Norfolk. As in Goshen, only dairy farming is practical on this cold, rugged land. Because this has discour-

THE LAST OF A CHAIN OF 16 ONE-ROOM SCHOOL HOUSES IN GOSHEN REMIND US THAT EARLY SETTLERS IN THE LITCHFIELD HILLS PRIZED EDUCATION FOR THEIR CHILDREN.

Barnett D. Laschever

DUDLEYTOWN: THE ULTIMATE GHOST TOWN

(Dark Entry Rd., Cornwall Bridge). A tangled, overgrown dirt lane leads up from the state road to the barely visible remains, mostly broken foundations, of what was once a thriving community. Settled in the mid-1700s, it became home to the Dudley family, whose forebears in England lived cursed lives. Although many of Dudleytown's progeny went on to success and fortune, most ended up mad, or worse. The wife of a New York doctor, who set up housekeeping in Dudleytown, went mad nearly 80 years ago—another victim, say locals, of "the Dudleytown Curse." In recent years several families have moved into Dudleytown undeterred by its depressing history. The area is now a private gated compound closed to tourists but still open to ghouls.

aged condo and development growth, Norfolk probably retains more restored and beautifully maintained homes dating from colonial days than any other Connecticut town. Its quiet beauty and cool summers attracted prosperous businessmen from New York in the 1850s, who built large estates. Most notable among them is Whitehall, now home of Yale University Summer School of Music and the nationally known Norfolk Music Festival. More recently, the former Greenwoods Theatre has become the Infiniti Hall & Bistro, a music hall. The village green is a gem. For such a small village, too, Norfolk has an unusually opulent library. Two wealthy families, competing with each other to do good for the town, did very well indeed, pouring money into the library—which now attracts visitors to lectures, poetry readings, and other cultural events.

Riverton. This town's claim to fame was the Hitchcock Factory, established in the 1800s, which until a few years ago was still producing the prized hand-stenciled furniture that graces so many New England homes. Alas, the factory has completely shut down operations, despite efforts to sell the Hitchcock name. Located on the banks of the Farmington River, Riverton is a visual feast in spring and fall, and a mecca in spring when the fishing season opens. The Old Riverton Inn fronts the banks of the river just across the bridge. Connecticut's smallest country fair winds up the fair season in October.

Salisbury and **Lakeville**, twin towns separated by less than a mile, boast some of New England's most authentic colonial buildings, which now serve as inns and B&Bs. The Lime Rock section is home of the Lime Rock Race Track, the most beautiful racetrack in America. Olympic hopefuls hone their skills on the downhill ski jump in Salisbury. Gourmet dining caters to the sophisticated tastes of its summer visitors—and of resident luminaries such as actors Meryl Streep and Michael J. Fox, among others. The famed Hotchkiss prep school was favored by the Rockefellers.

Sharon was founded in 1738. Farming kept the early settlers of this border town busy, but Sharon is famed for the invention of a notable mousetrap. A widely used rifle-cannon explosive shell was invented here, too, by two brothers, Andrew and Benjamin Hotchkiss. Quiet, semi-rural, and still nearly 50 percent forested, Sharon is now a haven for retirees, summer vacationers, and weekenders. The Sharon Audubon Center and the Tri-Arts Sharon Playhouse are its principal attractions.

The Cornwalls. Great Britain has one Cornwall, Connecticut has six: Cornwall, Cornwall Bridge, West Cornwall, Cornwall Hollow, East Cornwall, and North Cornwall. Secluded by high hills, the early settlers of Cornwall (1740) engaged mainly in logging. Today the villages are home to celebrities—actor Sam Waterston among them—weekenders, summer residents, and teachers at the many private schools in the area. Waterston lives in James Thurber's last home. The state's largest ski area swoops down through Mohawk State Forest; the once towering giants of the Cathedral Pines, battered by a tornado, lie tumbled one upon another. Nature, as is its wont, has taken over; the sun on the fallen logs has stimulated a wild growth of shrubs and bushes, almost hiding the damage. Visitors come from miles around to hike, to fish and boat on the beautiful Housatonic River, and to photograph the classic covered bridge at West Cornwall. Advisory to tourists: The covered bridge is in West Cornwall, not Cornwall Bridge.

Washington and **Washington Depot**. The first municipality in the country named for the Father of His Country, Washington is nestled in an upland area of hills and forests, high above the Shepaug River Valley. Because of the steep hills, agriculture was impractical. Instead, starting in 1872 the Shepaug Railroad brought in summer folk. Nowadays, theatrical and communications celebrities spend quiet weekends in opulent colonial homes clustered around the classic green. Deep in the woods, The Institute for American Indian Studies maintains a unique museum that portrays 10,000 years of Native American life in the woodlands of Connecticut. In late winter, nesting American bald eagles can be viewed from a nature preserve blind on the Shepaug Dam in nearby Southbury on the Housatonic River. Down in the valley, at Washington Depot, the Art Association is a beehive of cultural activity; and the famous and busy authors who call the Litchfield Hills home hold frequent book signings in the unusually well-appointed Hickory Stick Bookshop.

Kent. US 7, the main north–south artery in this part of the Hills, is also the Main Street of what was once a sleepy town—first settled by Native Americans—on both sides of a flat alluvial plain of the Housatonic River. Catering for years mainly to the needs of the prestigious Kent School, it was "discovered" in the mid-1980s. New York City designers, artists, and politicos converged on Kent. Main Street is now lined with trendy boutiques, art galleries, and shops selling exotic clothing. When Henry Kissinger bought a sprawling estate here, his security team advised him to uproot a grove of blueberry bushes on his property that had for years kept townspeople in pies and cobblers during the winter. There was an immediate outcry. Local folk and Kent School students descended upon the bushes and transplanted them to the campus, where the berries can still be picked by anyone with a basket or pail. Kent Falls and Bull's Covered Bridge are natural attractions. The *Boston Globe* ranks Kent as one of the prettiest villages in New England. A host of special events are boosting its reputation as a major cultural center, including a recent film festival, art shows, galleries, lectures, athletic competitions, and dramatic events. Add a variety of eateries—and the town has even lured the Litchfield Jazz Festival and Litchfield Jazz Camp from their longtime homes in Litchfield and Goshen.

Waterbury. Once the center of huge brass and copper factories, which became world famous for military brass buttons, watches, and then—during World War II—brass casings for artillery shells, the city has now become a center of small businesses. Its statuary and well-preserved architecture are of prime interest as well. A statue of Father McGivney honors the native son who founded the international Catholic fraternal order Knights of Columbus. The Waterbury Republican building, formerly the town's main railroad station, is an architectural gem, modeled after the Palazzo Publico (city hall) in Siena, Italy. Its soaring tower is a Waterbury landmark. The city hall is widely regarded as one of the most attractive municipal buildings in New England. Along with five other midtown buildings, it forms the Cass Gilbert Historic District; all the buildings are listed on the National Register of Historic Places, and the district itself honors Gilbert, one of America's outstanding architects. Waterbury's green is a 2-acre oasis in the center of the city with a statue of a horse at one end. Ask any local to tell you the story of the horse. And don't miss the Mattatuck Museum and Timexpo Museum. A former brass mill that stretched for a mile along the river was bulldozed to the ground. Arising from the site like a phoenix is the Brass Mill Mall, one of the largest, longest, and most diverse malls in the state. It recalls the huge factory only by name. What promises to put Waterbury on everyone's tourist map is the Co Co Key Water Resort, an indoor water theme park that has been erected next to the Holiday Inn Waterbury.

* To See

SPECIAL ATTRACTIONS **Litchfield History Society** (860-567-4501; www.litchfieldhistoricalsociety.org), corner of East and South streets (CT 63 at the Litchfield green), Litchfield. Open Apr. 15–Oct., Tue.–Sat. 11–5; Sun. 1–5. Adults $5 (includes admission to the **Tapping Reeve House**; see below); children free. The society has collected examples of Early American paintings and furniture, and a photographic history of the town. Changing exhibits are mounted in seven galleries. Lectures by experts in colonial history and culture are perennial attractions.

Tapping Reeve House and Law School, 82 South St. (CT 63), Litchfield. Open mid-May–Nov., Tue.–Sat. 11–5; Sun. 1–5. Adults $6, includes admission to the law school and history museum; children free. An adjunct of the historical society,

AMERICA'S FIRST LAW SCHOOL WAS FOUNDED IN LITCHFIELD BY A NEW JERSEY LAWYER, JUDGE TAPPING REEVE. TWO VICE PRESIDENTS AND OTHER LEGAL DIGNITARIES STUDIED HERE.

Kim Grant

Barnett D. Laschever

TIBETAN MONKS ON PARADE ARE AMONG THE DIVERSE SIGHTS IN LITCHFIELD'S SUMMERTIME. TIBETFEST IS HELD ON THE GROUNDS OF THE GOSHEN FAIR..

these two buildings constitute America's first law school. A permanent exhibit, The Noblest Study, tells how the fundamentals of American jurisprudence, as it differs from British common law, evolved here, including the first moot court in law education. Judge Reeve came to Litchfield from the College of New Jersey (which changed its name in 1890 to Princeton) and trained in the law two vice presidents—Reeve's brother-in-law, Aaron Burr, and John Calhoun; numerous Supreme Court justices; and 130 members of Congress—1,000 students in all. A series of exhibits and interactive stations on the first floor of the home tell the story of the law school from the students' point of view with videos and state-of-the-art displays. One section tells the story of the girls of nearby Pierce Academy, America's first private school for girls. (More than a few of the young ladies found husbands at Judge Reeve's.) The adjacent law school building displays early law books, journals, notebooks, and dissertations. It is also used to discuss the learning of the law. Special lectures are held on an irregular schedule. On the National Register of Historic Places.

Cobble Court, Litchfield. Behind Litchfield's West Street shops on the Litchfield green, in a cobblestone square resembling a British mews, you'll find a custom furniture shop and a stone bench for a moment of rest and meditation.

White Memorial Foundation and Conservation Center (860-567-0857), US 202, Litchfield. Open spring through fall, Tue.–Sat. 9–5; winter 8:30–4:30. This private, unique 4,000-acre tract of lakes, woods, bogs, and fields, established by conservationist and chess expert Alain White, is the largest nature preserve in Connecticut. Other tracts of land, totaling 11,000 acres, gifts of the foundation, formed the basis of the state park system. White Memorial features a nature museum; a library; nature, hiking, and cross-country-ski trails; camping; swimming; sailing; boating; fishing; and special lecture programs for adults and children. Visit the new

Children's Room, which features a live snake habitat, a beaver dam, and books, among other attractions. Modest admission to the museum.

Lime Rock Park (860-435-0896), CT 112 (off US 7), Lime Rock Village. Open Apr.–Oct., Sat. and holidays. When he was an active racer, this was the favorite track of actor Paul Newman, who died at 83 in the fall of 2008. Now watch today's top stock-car superstars as they speed around America's most beautiful racetrack. Regular events: vintage and historic automobile races and the NASCAR season finale.

MUSEUMS **The Institute for American Indian Studies** (860-868-0518), 38 Curtis Rd. (off CT 199), Washington. Open year-round, Mon.–Sat. 10–5; Sun. noon–5. Adults $5, seniors $4.50, children 6–16 $3. A relatively modern museum building that houses a unique collection of artifacts of the northeastern Native Americans—Pequots, Iroquois, Algonquins, Mohawks—who tended gardens, hunted for small game, fished, and in summer migrated to the shore, where they gorged themselves on lobsters and oysters—and left behind mounds of shells. Changing exhibits. Weekly lectures and films, not limited to Native American topics. An unexpected highlight: the almost complete skeleton of an extinct American mastodon elephant. Outside, wander through a reconstructed replica of an Algonquin village, an example of an archaeological dig. When a garden with typical Indian vegetables—corn, squash, and beans—is growing, a teenage Indian boy sits and chases away birds and other predators, as was the custom when English settlers arrived.

Sloane-Stanley Museum (860-927-3849), US 7, Kent. Open mid-May–Oct., Wed.–Sun. 10–4. Adults $3; children and seniors $1.50. Americana artist and author Eric Sloane collected authentic hand tools when he was writing and illus-

SKITCH HENDERSON, AMERICA'S MUSIC MAN

Lyle Cedric Henderson was one of the most remarkable men in American music. Born in 1918, he flew fighter planes both for the RAF and the U.S Army Air Force. At the end of World War II, Henderson, now known as "Skitch," studied music at the University of California and at the Juilliard School, and with preeminent composers. Although he spent most of his musical career as a conductor—for more than a decade with *The Tonight Show*, starring Johnny Carson, where he organized one of the last of the big-band orchestras—he has also been recognized for his compositions. A friend and supporter of performing celebrities, he appeared in numerous movies and on other television shows. Founder and conductor of the highly praised New York Pops orchestra, he still had time to organize an art gallery and cooking school with his wife, Ruth, on their farm in New Milford, known to all who passed by on CT 202 as the Silo.

That too has changed. Skitch and Ruth converted their estate to the Silo/Hunt Hill Farms Trust Inc. The cooking school is still an integral part of the project, but preservation was the goal of the Hendersons. The land and

trating his popular books on colonial life. They are on view in a museum on land donated by the Stanley Tool Company, once the most important hand-tool manufacturer in America. The collection, along with a reproduction of Sloane's Connecticut studio, a replica of an early log cabin, and the remains of an early iron forge, constitute this unique museum. The forge, in operation for 70 years, was recently reconstructed by the state. *The Diary of an Early American*, written by a 15-year-old boy, was Sloane's inspiration for the cabin. Sloane's books and prints are on sale. Among Sloane's favorite subjects were cloud-studded skies. At the onset of World War II, he was hurriedly summoned by the Army Air Corps to paint pictures of cloud formations with possible dangerous thunderheads. They were shown to our fighter pilots to help them navigate safely during their flights over the Pacific. The sky mural across the ceiling of the Smithsonian Institution's National Air and Space Museum in Washington, DC, was painted by Eric Sloane.

Beckley Furnace, Lower Rd. (US 44), East Canaan. From June to September, Saturday 10–1, members of Friends of the Furnace lecture, conduct tours, and answer questions about the 191-year history of the manufacture of pig iron in northwestern Connecticut. In ruins since it stopped operating after World War I, the furnace was restored in 1996 with a $250,000 state grant. It is now the state's only official Industrial Monument. Visit the hearth in what is one of the largest of the 43 blast furnaces in the Salisbury region alone. Across the Blackberry River are giant slag piles from the furnace. Picnic tables. Information kiosks. Restoration of other buildings and machinery is ongoing.

✐ **New England Carousel Museum** (860-585-5411), 95 Riverside Ave., Bristol. Open year-round, Mon.–Sat. 10–5; Sun. noon–5; Nov. 1–Mar. 31, closed Mon. Adults $5; seniors $4; children 4–13 $3. Largest collection of carousel horses in the country. This museum traces the history of the once-popular merry-go-round

its 10 historic buildings, including two barns, date back to the 1700s and are listed on the National Register of Historic Places. Skitch apparently didn't know—or certainly didn't act like—he was 86 years old. He died in mid-2005.

Most important, however, is the **Skitch Henderson Living Museum**, an affiliate of the Smithsonian Institution. In it are myriad collections highlighting Skitch's incredible career, from the Steinway piano he played for years as NBC's main musician to an old-fashioned drugstore soda fountain that recalls his friendship with Ginger Rogers. Instead of the usual booze served at Hollywood parties, Ginger dished out ice cream cones and sodas only to friends who won the approval of her mother.

Other programs at the revamped Silo estate include changing exhibits in the Gallery. The cooking-class curriculum has been expanded. Preservation-minded men and women may learn their crafts as interns and docents through the Hendersons' masterful preservation project.

The Silo/Hunt Hill Farm Trust Inc. is located at 44 Upland Rd., New Milford, CT 06776 (860-355-0300; www.hunthillfarmtrust.org).

through displays of antique wooden carousel horses and carriages. There's a replica of an old carving shop and occasional demonstrations by visiting artisans. Reproductions for sale, and on one floor an extensive exhibit of historical firefighting equipment.

American Clock and Watch Museum (860-583-6070), 100 Maple St. (off US 6), Bristol. Open Apr. 1–Nov., daily 10–5; closed Thanksgiving. Adults $5; seniors $4; children 8–15, $2. America once kept time by the clocks and watches invented and manufactured in Bristol and elsewhere in Connecticut. The factories are gone, but the memories are timeless in the only museum in the country devoted entirely to clocks and watches. Many of the 3,000 instruments that keep time are on display in an 1801 house. Museum shop and sundial garden.

Timexpo Museum (203-755-8463; 800-225-7742; www.timexpo.com), Exit 22/23 off I-84, 175 Union St., in the Brass Mill Commons, Waterbury. A 40-foot-high replica of an Easter Island head stands in front of the building. Open Tue.–Sat. 10–5; closed major holidays. Adults $6; seniors $5; children 5–12 $4. No admission fee to the museum store. Not just a museum of clocks and watches but an opportunity to step into the world of anthropology. The Waterbury Clock Company, now Timex, was contracted in 1890 by the Ingersoll Company to mass-produce watches that could be sold for $1. Mark Twain's letter ordering one of "the watches that made the dollar famous" is on display. In the early 1930s the company introduced the Mickey Mouse watch, which became an instant nationwide success. In 1950 the durable Timex watch was put on the market. Various galleries trace the development of keeping time, while in the Coincidences of Connections gallery visitors learn about such anthropological phenomena as the huge Native American burial mounds in Ohio, the giant sculpted heads on Easter Island, and the voyages of discovery of Thor Heyerdahl. A large museum store sells watches, reproductions of historical watches, and other souvenirs.

Lock Museum of America (860-589-6359), 230 Main St. (US 6), Terryville. Open May–Oct., daily 1:30–4:30; closed Mon. Adults $3; seniors $2.50; children free. The invention and making of locks is another example of Yankee ingenuity. The industry has all but vanished in Connecticut, but here in eight rooms you can view the largest collection of locks, keys, and Victorian hardware in the country.

Mattatuck Museum (203-753-0381), 144 West Main St., Waterbury. Open year-round, Tue.–Sat. 10–5; Sun. noon–5; closed Sun. in July and Aug. and on major holidays. Modest admission. The premier attraction in the former Brass City, this unique museum, installed in spacious quarters in the old Masonic Temple building, has mounted impressive exhibits that chronicle the industrial history of this once-thriving manufacturing city. Period rooms illustrate the social and cultural lives of both the vast numbers of industrial workers and their bosses. The principal art gallery is devoted to works of Connecticut artists and Connecticut scenes. Changing exhibits and special programs related to the art and history of Connecticut. Online exhibits. Acclaimed café; museum shop.

✐ **Golden Age of Trucking Museum** (203-577-2181; fax: 203-577-2404; www.goldenagetruckmuseum.com), 1101 Southford Rd., Middlebury. Open Thu.–Sat. 10–4; Sun. noon–4. Adults $5; everyone else less. If you like surprises, this museum, opened in 2002, will make professional truckers and children gasp with delight. Everything on wheels, from huge 18-wheelers to toy trucks, is on display. In Memory Lane is a display of antique pedal cars and collectibles. There are movies, a library with a comfortable reading area and computers, and puzzles and games in the Interactive Interstate for children. Some displays are rotated, but antiques of the late Richard Guerrera Sr. of Middlebury, the founder, are on permanent display. Indoor picnic area.

Connecticut Antique Machinery Association Museum (860-927-0050; www.ctamachinery.com), US 7, just north of Kent. Open May–Oct., Wed.–Sun. 10–4. Working steam engines, a mining exhibit, a large collection of gas tractors, and an old-fashioned steam locomotive, on the tracks, also in working condition. The Cream Hill Agricultural School, one of the pioneering institutions in the study of agriculture and threatened by the bulldozer, was moved here from Cornwall. It's the precursor to the Agricultural Experimental Station in New Haven, oldest in the country. Annual fall festival, when steam burps out of every engine.

WINERIES **Haight-Brown Vineyard and Winery** (860-567-4045), Chestnut Hill Rd. (off CT 118), just east of the Litchfield green, Litchfield. Open year-round. First of the modern wineries now dotting the state, the Haight-Brown Vineyard is open to guided tours. The winemaking process is explained inside the Swiss-style winery building. Gift shop. The annual Taste of the Litchfield Hills festival is held here in spring, and another wine-tasting festival in midwinter (see *Special Events*).

Hopkins Vineyard (860-868-7954), Hopkins Rd., New Preston. Open daily May–Dec.; Fri.–Sun., Jan.–Apr. Overlooking Lake Waramaug, this 30-acre vineyard welcomes visitors. The winery is in a weathered old red barn. There are tastings and a gift shop. Picnic area. Next to The Hopkins Inn.

Jerram Winery (860-379-8749), 535 Town Hill Rd. (CT 219), New Hartford. Open Apr.–Dec., Wed.–Sun. Sunday sales are permitted. Tour the vineyards, enjoy the wine tasting, learn how wine is made. Perennial gardens in-season. A relative newcomer in a burgeoning agricultural activity in the state.

GRAPES RIPEN IN NEW PRESTON'S 30-ACRE HOPKINS VINEYARD.

Land of Nod Vineyard and Winery (860-824-8225), 99 Lower Rd., East Canaan. Open Sat. and Sun.; closed Jan.–Mar., Thanksgiving Day, and Christmas Day. Self-guided tours encouraged. In the same family for more than 200 years, the farm has been designated a Connecticut Farm of Distinction. In early spring, maple syrup is boiled and sold in the sugarhouse and vineyard shop. The winery is close to hiking, skiing, and picnicking areas. History buffs will want to explore the nearby Beckley Furnace, under continuous reconstruction.

SMV Sunset Meadow Vineyards (860-201-4654; www.sunsetmeadowvineyards .com, Old Middle St. (US 63), Goshen 06756. Open Thu.–Sun. One of two vineyards and wineries that harvest their own grapes set up shop in Goshen toward the end of 2006. SMV's 40 acres of vines are spread over sloping westerly exposed fields. Wine lovers are already flocking to the tasting-room-cum-shop. Offering a variety of reds and a bronze medal White. Vineyard hayrides and wine production tour.

Miranda Vineyard (860-491-9906, www.mirandavineyard.com, 42 Ives Rd., Goshen 06756. Tasting room/purchasing shop open Fri. and Sat. noon–7, Sun. noon–5. Manny Miranda, a retired construction worker, grew up in Portugal, working in vineyards. In his retirement he has returned to his earlier avocation and together with his wife, Maria, a retired school principal, has planted and harvested grapes; the two are now operating a popular and successful winery. Their Woodridge White won a Gold Medal at the Eastern States Exposition. To suit every taste they bottle Cabernet Sauvignon, Merlot, a Chardonnay, and others. Take your shoes off at the annual Harvest Festival and join in the Grape Stomping Contest. Given that at 1,400 feet Goshen, one of the coldest towns in the state, supports two flourishing vineyards, local wags are dubbing it "the Napa Hills of the East."

There are 19 vineyards and wineries on the state's **Wine Trail**. They have been divided into two sections, East and West. Visiting each trail should take a day. See *Trails, Tourism*, in "What's Where in Connecticut."

HISTORIC HOMES **Hotchkiss-Fyler House** (860-482-8260), 192 Main St., Torrington. Open Apr.–Oct., Tue.–Fri. 10–4, Sat.–Sun. noon–4. House museum $5, history museum $2. This is one of the most spectacular Victorian mansions in the state, built in 1900 by one of Torrington's leading industrialists. Original family furnishings, decorative art, superb woodwork. Rare paintings by American artists Ammi Phillips (six portraits of Hotchkiss family members), Winfield S. Clime, and others. An adjoining building with working Hendley machinery tells the story of Torrington's Industrial Revolution. There is also an extensive permanent exhibit covering local history. A small section is devoted to the life of the fiery abolitionist John Brown, a Torrington native. The three-building complex is the home of the Torrington Historical Society. At an annual Christmas party, the mansion is decked out in the holiday style of its original occupants.

Bellamy-Ferriday House and Gardens (203-266-7596), 9 Main St. North (CT 61), Bethlehem. Open mid-May–Oct., Wed. and Fri.–Sun. 11–4. Adults $7; seniors, students, and teachers $6; children $4. Group tours by appointment. This outstanding estate, built by the Reverend Joseph Bellamy (who also founded the first theological seminary in America), was opened to the public in mid-1994 following the death of the last member of the Bellamy family and after extensive restoration work. A 13-room white-clapboard house with Litchfield green shutters, it's a treasure trove of Asian art, Delftware, candlesticks, and furniture. Although the house and formal gardens sit on 9 acres, the nature trails of an adjoining 80 acres left to the Bethlehem Land Trust may also be visited. Lilacs, heirloom roses, peonies, and topiary yews are the highlights of the gardens. Here is a unique opportunity to step back in time. Deeded to the Connecticut Landmarks Society, formerly the Antiquarian and Landmarks Society, the estate is listed on the National Register of Historic Places. The society preserves eight historic properties, including the **Nathan Hale Homestead**, throughout the state. Monthly exciting programs are being held at each of the buildings in-season.

Sheldon Tavern, North St. (CT 63), Litchfield. Now a private home, this beautiful colonial mansion was first an inn, then a residence. Washington records in his diary that he slept here while en route from West Point to Wethersfield to confer with his ally General Rochambeau, commander of the French expeditionary army based in Rhode Island. Together they plotted the campaign that led to the battle of Yorktown, the decisive victory of the American Revolution that sent the redcoats packing.

The Bull House, North St. (CT 63), Litchfield. An imposing mansion built by Ludlow Bull, the American explorer and Egyptologist who participated in one of history's most astonishing discoveries: the tomb of Egyptian king Tutankhamen, completely intact with all its gold treasures. A private home, the Bull House occasionally is opened for the annual Litchfield House Tour (see *Special Events*).

Solomon Rockwell House (860-379-8433), 225 Prospect St., Winsted. Open June–Oct., Sun. 2–4. Free admission. Original Hitchcock chairs and Thomas and Whiting clocks greet you upon entering this magnificent, antebellum-style home built by an early industrialist. There's memorabilia from both the American Revolution and the Civil War. Don't miss the collection of wedding gowns. Headquarters of the Winchester Historical Society. Victorian doll house and toy room. On the National Register of Historic Places.

Glebe House (203-263-2855), 49 Hollow Rd., Woodbury. Open Apr.–Nov., Wed.–Sun. 1–4. House and garden, $5; garden only, $2. This 1740 farmhouse off US 6 is of special interest to gardeners and religious history buffs. Here in 1783 the Episcopal Church in America selected Samuel Seabury as its first bishop. Surrounding the front yard is the only garden in America created by the legendary English artist and garden designer Gertrude Jekyll. It's 600 feet of a typical English "country garden" with a mixed border against a square fence, foundation plantings, and a stone terrace. Neglected for many years, the garden was restored and is now maintained by skilled plantsmen. It is probably the smallest of the 400 gardens designed during Ms. Jekyll's productive life. Period furnishings in the house and a gift shop where you can acquire a plot plan of the garden.

HISTORIC SITES **McAuliffe Manor**, on the Litchfield green, corner of CT 63 and US 202, Litchfield. A state prison since colonial days, the jail was converted in 1994 into a halfway house for drug-addicted women. Benjamin Franklin's illegitimate son, William, was incarcerated here and in a North Street home during the American Revolution. A royal governor of New Jersey, William refused to join the American cause. Harassed in New Jersey prisons, he was removed for his safety to Litchfield. His disconsolate father had him in confinement for more than three

JOHN BROWN, SATAN OR MESSENGER OF GOD?

Connecticut-born abolitionist John Brown is probably the state's most controversial son. His failed attack on the federal arsenal at Harpers Ferry, West Virginia, so scared the Southern plantation slave masters that it stiffened their resolve to secede and go to war. Even today Brown, born on a farm in the backwoods of Torrington, is regarded as either a murderous madman or a messenger from God, ordered to deliver the slaves from bondage.

Russell Banks, historian on opposing views of John Brown, said on a PBS show, "I think the reason white people think he was mad is because he was a white man and he was willing to sacrifice his life in order to liberate Black Americans. . . ."

Americans today who literally hate John Brown inevitably recount the Potawatomi Massacre (five killed) as proof that he was a raving maniacal murderer. They conveniently forget the massacres of hundreds of abolitionists who were settling in "bloody Kansas." Visitors to Torrington can visit the remains of Brown's homestead. When Brown was hanged, Henry Thoreau said, "First there was Christ, now there is John Brown."

years. At the end of the war, William sailed to England. Father and son never again communicated with each other. The village's infamous "hanging tree" stood on the front lawn.

Obookiah Burial Site, CT 4, Cornwall. Hawaiian-born Henry Obookiah swam to a New Haven–bound seal-hunting ship after his family was killed in a tribal war in Hawaii. In New Haven, he became a convert to Christianity and spent many days preaching in the Litchfield Hills. He was buried in the Cornwall cemetery after he died at the age of 26 from typhus. His journal inspired the American Missionary Board to organize and send to Hawaii the now legendary first group of missionaries, led by the Reverend Hiram Bingham. The saga was fictionalized in James Michener's book *Hawaii.* Obookiah's grave was a pilgrimage site among Hawaiians for years. In 1993 the Hawaiians wanted Henry back because Cornwall wouldn't put up a sign on the road. His bones were dug up and shipped back to the islands. The inscribed sarcophagus still attracts visitors. (See also Congregational Church under *Special Churches.*)

Indian Missionary School Marker, Cornwall center, across from the church. After independence, the local Congregational church opened a missionary school for "Indians and heathens." Henry Obookiah (see above) studied here. The school was closed and torn down when two local maidens fell in love with and married two of the Native American converts.

Holy Land Cross. You may wonder as you drive through Waterbury on I-84 why a large rock outcropping is topped by a cross, lit and visible for miles at night. It marks the location of Holy Land, a miniature of Jerusalem that has deteriorated and is closed to the public. In mid-2001 a dedicated group convened in Waterbury, determined to raise money and restore the theme park, which in its halcyon days attracted 40,000 people annually. Meanwhile, the cross is all that remains. At press time, the restoration was still in the planning stage.

All Wars Memorial, CT 202, Bantam. The American Legion Post 44 of Bantam has erected a memorial to all American servicemen and servicewomen who served the United States, from the American Revolution to our latest conflicts. Every month another veteran who is deceased and nominated by a member of the post is honored in a special ceremony. The memorial is easily identifiable from the highway by the circle of flags that surrounds it. No charge.

Wall of America, Main St. (US 44), Winsted. A Sharon artist, Ellen Griesedieck, has for seven years been fabricating a mural that honors the workers of America, from miners to farmers, assembly-line workers, steelworkers, and even surgeons. When finished the extraordinary mural will be 48 feet high and 120 feet wide and will be mounted in a former hosiery factor in Winsted. "Large enough to fill the Parthenon," as the artist told a reporter. Some 15,000 workers from all over the country have contributed to this monumental project. Most unusual for a mural: It will be three-dimensional, so children will be able to wander in and out of the pieces. Construction in the factory is scheduled to start early in 2009; the mural should be open to visitors later in the year. Check with Litchfield or state tourism officials for practical details. A once-bustling industrial town, Winsted lost half of its factories during one of the great floods of the 1940s. It never recovered. The Wall of America will put Winsted on everyone's tourist map. *Note:* The husband of the muralist, also an artist and race car driver, met Paul Newman at the Lime Rock Race Track. He ended up designing the label for Newman's salad dressing bottle!

SPECIAL CHURCHES **Congregational Church on the Green**, US 202, Litchfield. Pictures of this much-photographed church, a classic of its kind, appear on calendars, on postcards, and in photo files of countless visitors. In 1898 the congregants didn't think much of their architectural treasure, for they picked it up and moved it 300 yards down the road, where it served as an armory, a recreation hall, and a movie house. In 1929 the parishioners came to their senses and moved the building back to its present spot at the gateway to the village. It was only then that the pillars and the steeple were added. Acoustically perfect, it's often used as a concert hall.

Lourdes in Litchfield Shrine (860-567-1041), CT 118 just east of the Litchfield green, Litchfield. A noteworthy attempt to replicate, on a lovely tract of land, Bernadette's famous

GOSHEN CONGREGATIONAL CHURCH IS HIGHEST IN CONNECTICUT—ABOVE SEA LEVEL!

Barnett D. Laschever

French grotto. There is a rugged uphill Stations of the Cross trail, and Masses are held daily in the grotto. Once a year the peace of the county is rent by the roar of the big bikes when the Montford Missionary priests perform the Blessing of the Motorcycles. Picnic grounds and gift shop.

Congregational Church, CT 63 and CT 4, Goshen. Hiram Bingham (see Obookiah Burial Site, above) was ordained and married in this church before setting out as head of the first group of U.S. missionaries to Hawaii. A picture of Bingham and his bride and the route their little ship took to what were then called the Sandwich Islands can be seen in the vestry. The church is only one of two on the mainland that hang the Hawaiian flag year-round. Locals like to say that the church steeple is "the highest in the state of Connecticut." It is—from sea level! Bingham's grandson, also named Hiram, after graduating from Yale called on hiking skills acquired while climbing Hawaii's mountains as a youth and discovered Machu Picchu, the lost city of the Incas in Peru. After returning home he became Connecticut's governor, and then its U.S. senator.

Faith Church (www.faithchurch.com), US 7, southern New Milford. In Europe, tourists are escorted from one huge medieval cathedral to another; in New England, visitors lift their praise for our Congregational churches. Add to them an awesome new $15 million megachurch dedicated in July 2005 on busy US 7. In addition to an enormous main sanctuary, the church has planned a four-lane bowling alley, a 200-seat theater, a television studio, a computer lab, a children's arcade, an ice cream and cappuccino bar, baseball and soccer fields, and a 400-seat children's church. Architecturally the church is undistinguished—a long rectangular box that could be mistaken for a shopping mall if three crosses had not been embedded in the front wall. Visitors are welcome.

COVERED BRIDGES **West Cornwall bridge**. The bright-red-painted covered bridge spanning the Housatonic at West Cornwall links CT 128 with US 7. Built in 1837 by famous bridge architect Ithiel Town, it incorporated strut techniques that

THE ELMS' LEAVES ARE LONG GONE. BUT THE MAPLES' FIERY FOLIAGE ENHANCES THE BEAUTY OF THE LITCHFIELD HILLS COUNTRYSIDE WELL INTO THE FALL.

Kim Grant

were later copied by bridge designers around the country. Restored by the Connecticut Department of Transportation, it won a national prize for bridge restoration. The setting is spectacular and attracts thousands of photography fans annually. Experienced sports enthusiasts maneuver canoes and kayaks over the turbulent waters that flow under the bridge.

♿ **Bulls Bridge**. The only other historic covered bridge in Connecticut open to vehicular traffic also spans the Housatonic near Gaylordsville, a short way south of Kent on US 7. Weather-beaten gray, it attracts more artists than photographers. Plans are under way to provide more parking, install informational kiosks, add slopes down the steep bank to improve boater access, provide a designated handicapped parking area, and install a barrier-free portable toilet adjacent to the scenic overlook. Legend has it that the hoof of George Washington's horse broke through one of the bridge's boards as he was crossing the river. Horse and general were immediately hauled out with no lingering damage.

SCENIC DRIVES Three state agencies—transportation, parks, and tourism—joined in driving the highways and byways of Connecticut and designating certain stretches as official scenic roads. Watch for the signs. Goshen's Conservation Commission has laid out a 5-mile trail through woods and across streams and creeks. A map is available from the town clerk. The map also contains a trail mapped by the Goshen Historic Trust.

CT 4, from its intersection with US 7, is among the official scenic drives.

US 202 as it goes east through the center of Litchfield past the stores, restaurants, and shops on West Street and the spacious Litchfield green on the north side offers a rare glimpse of a preserved New England rural town—though the original green had neither grass nor trees.

US 7 is an unofficial scenic drive. From West Cornwall south through Kent and on to New Milford, US 7 is as pretty a road as you can find anywhere in New England. Along the Housatonic River, high cliffs remind you of Vermont. In fall they are ablaze with color.

CT 63. A pleasant, bucolic road as it meanders north out of Litchfield. From Goshen, just before you start to descend to the North Canaan plain, you come upon a breathtaking mountain vista not dissimilar to those on the high roads of the Great Smokies of North Carolina.

✱ To Do

AMUSEMENT PARKS 🖍 **Quassy Amusement Park** (800-367-7275), CT 64, Middlebury. Open Memorial Day–Labor Day 10–10. Free admission, $5 parking fee. More than 30 rides and a sandy swimming beach on Lake Quassapaug will keep the family occupied all day. Boat rides, petting zoo, food concessions, but plenty of picnic tables if you want to bring your own vittles. The 20-acre playground is the state's largest amusement park.

🖍 **Lake Compounce Theme Park** (860-583-3300; www.lakecompounce.com), 822 Lake Ave., Bristol, just across from the world headquarters of ESPN. Open May–Oct. on varying days. Call for hours and prices. America's oldest amusement park in continuous operation is now New England's newest park with the addition of 20 exciting rides, many of them high-tech, that will more than satisfy families in search of fun, excitement, and relaxation. On the shores of a beautiful swimming pond, the park now has one of the most unusual roller coasters in the country, the mile-long Boulder Dash, the world's largest roller coaster and the first to be built entirely on the side of a mountain. There's more: a whitewater raft ride, a mountain sky ride, a 12,000-square-foot Wave Pool, and Circus World Kiddieland. The miniature railroad that originally puffed its way around the estate of actor William Gillette—whose castle is now a state park on the Connecticut River—is on exhibit here. One of the two engines has been returned to Gillette park in East Haddam, where it can now be seen.

♂ ♿ **Action Wildlife Foundation** (860-482-4464), Torrington Rd. (US 4), Goshen. Summer, Tue.–Fri. 10–7; weekends 12:30–7; closed Mon. Adults $7, children under 12 $5. The first major theme park in the Litchfield Hills is a unique collection of mounted and live animals. The live animals are on view in two series of outdoor pens; another section has been described as a *Jurassic Park* setting with a mixture of animals, including bison and other rare species. The entire complex is set behind New England–style stone walls that are so extensive they have been dubbed the Great Walls of Goshen. James Mazzarelli, founder of the park, plans educational programs on wild animal conservation throughout the year. You may walk around the extensive grounds; the handicapped may drive.

♂ **Co Co Key Water Resort**, attached to the Holiday Inn Waterbury (203-706-1000), 3558 East Main St., Waterbury. First in a national chain of indoor water amusement parks to spring up in Connecticut. In 55,000 square feet of space, the kids can enjoy tube rides, water cannons, giant whirlpools, lily pads, water basketball, animated coral reefs, raft waterslides, Parrot's Perch, and more. Suddenly Waterbury has a full-fledged tourist attraction that will witness the kids dragging their parents away from their weekend TV NFL battles.

BALLOONING **Aer Blarney Balloons** (860-567-3448; www.aerblarney.com), P.O. Box 1528, Litchfield 06759. Weather permitting, which means no high winds, balloon flights over Litchfield and central Connecticut. Reservations are recommended, but required during spring and particularly the fall foliage season. First-timers are greeted with champagne upon landing. It's a tradition.

BICYCLING **The Bicycle Tour Company** (860-927-1742;www.bicycletours.com), 15 North Main St. (US 7), Kent. Professional guides will lead you through some of the Litchfield Hills' most stunning country. You set the pace and tell the guide whether you prefer flat roads or biking up and down hills. Be advised, however, that it will be difficult to avoid a hill or two in the Hills.

See also *Mountain Biking*.

BOATING Dotted with lakes and crisscrossed by two major rivers—the **Housatonic**, longest in the state, and the **Farmington**—the Litchfield area is a natural for boating: canoeing, kayaking, sailing, rowing, rafting, tubing, even crew racing and, in winter, iceboating. Launching ramps are maintained by the state on Dog Pond in Goshen, Bantam Lake in Morris, and Lake Waramaug (the state park).

Clarke Outdoors (860-672-6365), on the banks of the Housatonic, 163 US 7, West Cornwall. Canoe, kayak, and raft rentals, Mar. 15–Dec. 2. Instruction and guided trips are available. During the spring thaw, whitewater rafting in Bull's Bridge Gorge.

O'Hara's Landing (860-824-7583), Twin Lakes Rd., Salisbury. Launch your own or rent a rowboat, canoe, pontoon boat, or motorboat. Water skis are also available, with all safety accessories for children. There's a lakeside restaurant and a snack bar for a pick-me-up after a day on one of the state's prettiest small lakes. Anglers take notice: Connecticut's largest brown trout was hooked in these waters!

Farmington River Tubing (860-693-6465), US 44, New Hartford, in Satan's Kingdom State Recreation Area. Open Memorial Day–Labor Day 10–5. Individual river tubes, specially designed, take you on a thrilling 2½-hour ride through three churning rapids. For safety, you must be at least 10 years old and stand 4 feet, 5 inches tall.

FISHING **Housatonic Meadows Fly Shop** (860-672-6064), 13 US 7, Cornwall Bridge. Orvis-trained guides know the pools and inlets where the brown, rainbow, and brook trout are keeping a low profile. Smallmouth bass don't have a chance either with the resident veteran guides. Equipment for rent in the shop.

Housatonic River Outfitters (860-672-1010; www.dryflies.com), 24 Kent Rd. (US 7), Cornwall Bridge. If you're an experienced fly-angler, the Outfitters have 50,000 flies to choose from for your next cast. Novice fisher folk can take classes. Fishing in the Housatonic or full-day trips with gourmet meals can be arranged to the Farmington River or almost any fishable stream open to the public. State license required for freshwater fishing.

See also O'Hara's Landing under *Boating*.

GOLF **Stonybrook Golf Club** (860-567-9977), Milton Rd., Litchfield. Par 35, 9 holes, 2,902 yards. The exquisitely manicured grounds provide a unique challenge to the beginner as well as the more accomplished player.

Eastwood Country Club (860-489-2630), 1301 Torringford West St., Torrington. Par 36, nine holes, 3,105 yards. A pleasant little course in a suburban neighborhood. Much favored by local business duffers.

Fair View Farms (860-689-1000), 300 Hill Rd., Harwinton. Par 72, 18 holes. Beautiful new championship layout, with a driving range, two-tiered putting green, instruction, restaurant with outdoor patio overlooking pond with fountain. Voted one of four best courses to play in Connecticut by *Golf Digest*.

Crestwood Park (860-945-3054), Northfield Rd., Watertown. Par 71, 18 holes, 6,376 yards.

East Mountain (203-753-1425), East Mountain Rd., Waterbury. Par 68, 18 holes, 5,720 yards.

Western Hills (203-756-1211), Park Rd., Waterbury. Par 72, 18 holes, 6,246 yards.

HAYRIDES AND SLEIGH RIDES ✎ **Wood Acres** (860-583-8670), Griffin Rd., Terryville. Horse-drawn hayrides, carriage rides, and sleigh rides.

Loon Meadow Farms' Horse and Carriage Livery Service (860-542-6085), 41 Loon Meadow Dr., Norfolk. Take a nostalgic sleigh or carriage ride ($120–160) through the historic village of Norfolk, past Revolutionary War–era homes and the encampment where General Burgoyne's English army rested after its defeat at Saratoga. Enjoy a picnic along the trail or arrange for a stop at The White Hart Inn for a romantic dinner. After dinner, take in a Yale University Summer School of Music concert at the Music Shed at the Battell Stoeckel estate.

✎ **Bob Ellis Coach and Carriage Service** (860-567-1114; www.ellislimousines.com), 62 Deer Lane, Morris. Genial Bob Ellis retired as proprietor of the country store in Goshen and became operator of a full-fledged carriage and coach service. In addition to the usual sleigh rides and horse-drawn hayrides, he has a Concord stagecoach for special occasions. First designed in the late 1800s in Concord, New Hampshire, the classic Concord (remember John Wayne in *Stagecoach*?) knit the West together until the last spike was driven, uniting the country with iron rails. Ellis also has pony rides for your kids' birthday parties.

HORSEBACK RIDING **High Lonesome at Rose Hurst Farms** (203-758-9094), CT 188, Middlebury. Scenic trail rides across open fields and through the woods, by appointment only. No ponies for the youngsters.

H.O.R.S.E. of CT (860-868-1960), 43 Wilbur Rd. (off US 202), Washington. Principally devoted to caring for neglected and abused horses, this unique facility also offers trail rides for beginners and advanced riders Fri.–Sun. Helmets are supplied. Riders and horses get "acquainted" in a 15-minute riding session in the ring. Adults only. $50 for a 90-minute trail ride, $75 for a 2½-hour ride with a picnic lunch on the trail.

✎ **Lee's Riding Stable, Inc.** (860-567-0785), 57 East Litchfield St. (just off CT 118), Litchfield. English and Western saddles for the equestrian or cowboy in you. Ponies for the kids. Walking trails only, mostly in the woods (wide-open spaces for flashy galloping are hard to come by in Connecticut). Indoor ring for rainy days. No bronco busting; these Yankee horses know their English riding manners.

KAYAKING See *Boating*.

MOUNTAIN BIKING Off-road terrain in Litchfield County is generally rugged and hilly, but suitable trails can be found for riders of all abilities. **White Memorial Foundation and Conservation Center** in Litchfield (see *To See*) offers 35 miles of trail through pine forests laced with ponds, streams, and swamps. Trails can be reached from the several trailheads on CT 63. The **Steep Rock Reservation** (860-868-9131), Washington Depot, can be accessed by two trailheads: one on CT 47, another on River Road. Riders are allowed on the dirt roads and trails—including a former railroad bed—that follow the Shepaug River. Call ahead in early spring. Trails are sometimes closed during the spring thaw.

See also *Bicycling*.

SELF-IMPROVEMENT VACATIONS **The Silo Store, Gallery, and Cooking School** (860-355-0300), Upland Rd. (off US 202), New Milford. In a school started by the late conductor Skitch Henderson and his wife, Ruth, world-famous chefs from New York City along with cookbook authors and local professionals visit the school and guide you through the intricacies of the culinary arts in classes held in an old barn Mar.–Dec.

Skip Barber Racing and Driving Schools (800-221-1131), Lime Rock Park, CT 112 (off US 7), Lime Rock Village. If you have aspirations to become a stock-car racer, former champion Skip Barber and his team of veteran instructors will put you behind the wheel of a souped-up stock car and teach you the ropes. He was Paul Newman's racing mentor.

SWIMMING Freshwater beaches abound on secluded ponds and lakes in many state parks, in addition to town beaches that are open to the public for a fee.

Sandy Beach, on the western end of Bantam Lake, is operated by the town of Litchfield. Lifeguard; concession. Daily fee for nonresidents.

♿ **Mount Tom State Park**, US 202 southwest of Litchfield. The best swimming in the cleanest waters of the Litchfield Hills. The beach is sandy, the lifeguards alert. Rustic dressing rooms, rustic picnic tables, and a rustic food stand. The mile-long hike to the top of Mount Tom rewards the vigorous with a stone tower and a great view of the hills. Parking fee. Handicapped accessible.

Lake Waramaug State Park, Lake Waramaug Rd./West Shore Rd., New Preston. Waramaug recalls the mountain lakes of Austria and Switzerland. Eighty-eight campsites (see *Lodging*). Fishing and scuba diving, and paddleboats for rent. State boat-launching ramp.

✐ **Burr Pond State Park**, 5 miles north of Torrington on old CT 8. A popular family swimming area. Lots of splashing kiddies shouting, nonstop, "Mommy, look at me." Rustic dressing facilities. At the entrance to the park are the ruins of the condensary where Gail Borden invented condensed milk.

Northfield Dam Recreation Area, CT 254, south of Litchfield. The federal government operates this nicely landscaped beach in a flood-control area—that is, on

LAKE WARAMAUG IN NEW PRESTON OFFERS FISHING, BOATING, SWIMMING, AND CAMPING.

Kim Grant

a pond behind a dam that protects Thomaston and Waterbury during spring-thaw floods. It's well equipped, with solid picnic tables and dressing rooms. No need to worry about floods during July and August, when the flow from the river is only a trickle.

Lake McDonough (860-379-3036), Beech Rock Rd. (CT 219), Barkhamsted. Open weekdays 1–8; weekends and holidays 8–8. A beautiful swimming beach on a lake created by overflow from the huge Barkhamsted Reservoir. Rowboats and paddleboats for rent, picnic tables, hiking trails, fishing in-season. Parking $5.

TRAIN RIDE **Naugatuck Railroad/Railroad Museum of New England** (860-283-7245; www.rmne.org), 242 East Main St., Thomaston. A tourist train (nicknamed "the Naugy") and a rail museum have been established in Thomaston. The trains operate scheduled one-hour rides on weekends May–Oct. Round-trip: adults $10; seniors 62 and older $9; children 3–12 $7; age 2 and under, free. There also are special excursions during the fall foliage season and on major holidays. The museum has 70 pieces of historic New England rolling stock for display. The train runs up alongside the Naugatuck River and onto the Thomaston Dam in Black Rock State Park, highlighting the history of this important industrial valley. It's the only tourist train in the country that rides across a dam! Diesel engines will pull the cars until the line's steam locomotives are restored.

✷ Winter Sports

CROSS-COUNTRY SKIING Equipment rental is usually available at areas that emphasize cross-country skiing. Bring your own skis to the trails in state parks and forests, and to the White Memorial Foundation trails.

White Memorial Foundation (860-567-0857), 71 Whitehall Rd., US 202, Litchfield. Thirty-five miles of trails through pine forests and open fields, and around frozen brooks, ponds, and lakes. One of the most beautiful and popular ski-touring areas in the state.

Mohawk Mountain Ski Area (860-672-6464), Great Hollow Rd. (off CT 4), Cornwall, offers 5 miles of cross-country trails in addition to downhill runs.

SNOWMAKING MACHINES, NOW USED WORLDWIDE, WERE INVENTED MORE THAN 30 YEARS AGO AT MOHAWK MOUNTAIN SKI AREA IN CORNWALL.

Barnett D. Laschever

Blackberry River Ski Touring Center (860-542-5100), US 44, Norfolk. Fifteen miles of groomed trails.

Woodbury Ski Area (203-263-2203; 203-263-2213), CT 47 (north off US 6), Woodbury. Twenty miles of trails in addition to downhill runs.

See also *Green Space* for the many state parks that allow cross-country skiing.

DOWNHILL SKIING **Mohawk Mountain Ski Area** (860-672-6464), Great Hollow Rd. (off CT 4), Cornwall. The largest ski resort in the state and the birthplace of the world's first snowmaking machine, with 23 slopes and trails and five lifts. There's a Swiss-style base lodge with cafeteria, rental shop, and ski and snowboard instructors. Near major metropolitan centers. No overnight facilities, but there are inns and B&Bs close by. Open most nights until 10; Sun. until 5.

Woodbury Ski Area (203-263-2203; 203-263-2213), CT 47 (north off US 6), Woodbury. Downhill skiing on 14 trails, day and night—and a lot more. Groomed cross-country trails, tobogganing, sledding, ice-skating rink. If you're a fan of skateboarding, you'll take to snowboarding in the half-pipe, a huge, U-shaped wall much like a toboggan run. In summer you'll find concerts, tennis courts, and a skateboard park. Rentals and lessons. Base lodge and ski shop.

Ski Sundown (860-379-9851), Route 219, New Hartford. A 65-acre winter wonderland of 15 groomed downhill trails for novices and advanced skiers. Refreshments in the cozy base lodge. Rentals and lessons. Overnight facilities in the vicinity. This is the second-largest ski resort in Connecticut. Night skiing. Snowmaking.

OTHER WINTER RECREATION Because of their higher elevation, the Litchfield Hills are colder than the rest of the state. When the deep freeze settles in, **iceboaters** whip around Bantam Lake in Morris and Tyler Lake in Goshen at breakneck speeds. Closer to shore, demented **ice anglers** set up their little huts, drill holes in the ice, and patiently shiver, waiting for a nibble. Limited **winter camping** is permitted in selected state parks. Check with the Bureau of Parks and Forests of the Connecticut Department of Environmental Protection (860-566-2305), 79 Elm St., Box 5066, Hartford 06106-5066. Most state parks and forests in Connecticut also allow cross-country skiing. The very hardy can hike or snowshoe the many trails that crisscross the county.

Norfolk Curling Club (860-542-5579), Golf Dr., Norfolk. For more than 30 years, the locals have been whirling heavy round stones down an ice rink, then running backward in front of the stones and frantically sweeping the ice with little brooms to reduce friction. Occasionally, visiting teams from Scotland and Holland pop over for some friendly competition. A Scots curler, looking for trouble, said on a recent visit: "The Dutch claim they invented curling. We *know* we did!"

* Green Space

Topsmead is located 1 mile east of Litchfield Center on Buell Rd., off CT 118, the 511-acre former estate of the wife of a Waterbury bronze tycoon. The grounds are open only for picnicking, hiking on nature trails, and cross-country skiing. Tours of the estate's Tudor house and gardens are available.

Mohawk State Forest, CT 4 in Cornwall just over the Goshen town line. Park your car in the small lot at the entrance to the forest, which extends southward along a high ridge. Hike through the woods to the state police radio antenna tower for a magnificent view down the mountainside of the Mohawk Mountain Ski Area to Cornwall Village. In fall this spot becomes a ringside seat for some of the brightest foliage in all of New England.

Follow US 7 a mile north of Cornwall Bridge to **Housatonic Meadows State Park**. Stretching 2 miles along the Housatonic River, this mainly wooded area is popular with campers, hikers, and picnickers. Chemical pollution from Massachusetts, now stopped, restricts anglers to catch-and-release fishing. Surprisingly, this restriction has increased the river's popularity because a fish, once caught, is thrown back for another day and another Izaak Walton. The Housatonic is also a magnet for canoeists, kayakers, artists, and photographers. No swimming.

Macedonia Brook State Park was created by another major bequest of Alain White, father of Connecticut's state park system. This 2,300-acre tract, 4 miles north of Kent off CT 341, winds its way up to an elevation of 1,400 feet and attracts the more rugged outdoor enthusiasts. Campsites and stream fishing. In winter, there's challenging cross-country skiing (more like downhill skiing on cross-country slats).

The gurgling waters of the Farmington River lap the shores of **Peoples State Forest**, 10 miles north of Litchfield Center in Pleasant Valley on CT 181. To this rugged setting, bring a book (this one) or the Sunday *Times* and a picnic, and spend a meditative day under the branches of 200-year-old pines in **Mathies Grove**. Fish, hike, bird-watch.

Hollenbeck Preserve, Page Rd. and US 7, Canaan. This 182-acre preserve of The Nature Conservancy is open for hiking and other recreational activities. View rare plants and animals. Bordered by the Hollenbeck and the Housatonic Rivers, this is one of 57 preserves in Connecticut owned and operated by the Conservancy.

Mount Riga State Park is located in the farthest northwestern corner of the Litchfield Hills, just above Salisbury and off CT 41. The highest point in the state, at 2,380 feet, is **Mount Frissel**. Rustic hiking trails, including a section of the **Appalachian Trail**, snake upward through the woods. Rugged hiking boots, a stout heart, and sturdy legs are requisites, along with a small backpack with water and refreshments.

NATURE CENTERS AND FARMS Several nature centers complement the state parks in the Litchfield Hills. All feature interpretive buildings with a variety of nature displays, guided and/or self-guided tours, wildflowers, and gift shops.

Flanders Nature Center (203-263-3711), Church Hill and Flanders Rd., Woodbury. Open year-round daily, dawn to dusk. Offers programs for adults and children and invites you to explore its unique nut tree arboretum, bogs, and geological sites. Maple-syrup-making demonstrations in March.

Sharon Audubon Center (860-364-0520), CT 4, Sharon. The interpretive building is open year-round, Mon.–Sat. 9–5, Sun. 1–5. Adults $3; seniors and children $1.50. Eleven miles of trails are open daily, dawn to dusk. Watch for beavers, muskrats, ospreys, even the elusive otter—and, of course, myriad birds. Exhibits, programs, annual festival, and classes are available at this 684-acre sanctuary of the

National Audubon Society; also herb and wildflower gardens, the **Children's Discovery Room**, and a gift shop.

H. C. Barnes Memorial Nature Center (860-585-8886), 175 Shrub Rd., Bristol. Trails open daily, sunrise to sunset. Center hours: Sat. 9–4:30; Sun. 1–5. Call for weekday hours. Self-guiding trails wind through 70 acres of a variety of natural habitats. Nature library for children, special animal exhibits, games, and educational programs. Gift shop.

Nature's Art and Dinosaur Crossing (860-443-4367; www.enaturesart.com), 1650 CT 85, Oakdale. A new family-operated interactive science, nature, and shopping center on 60 acres of pristine wetlands and woodlands. Youngsters react with amazement as they roam any one of three trails—Raptor, Connecticut, and Mesozoic—and encounter full-scale replicas of the huge animals that once roamed the Connecticut River Valley. Picnic area and snack bar.

The Pratt Center (860-355-3137), 163 Papermill Rd., New Milford. Trails open dawn to dusk. Bird-watching on hiking trails through woods, across fields, and up and down hills on a 193-acre preserve.

Cathedral in the Pines, Cornwall. Pass through the village of Cornwall to a beautiful field at the eastern end of town. You might fancy that you've entered a hidden mountain pass and come upon Shangri-la. Turn left, and in moments you're at a 47-acre tract of what once were towering virgin pines, protected by The Nature Conservancy as a shaded "Cathedral in the Pines"—until a rogue tornado smashed most of these giants to the ground on an oppressively hot day in July in the late 1980s. The Conservancy has let them lie, a lesson in the enormity of the forces of nature. More than a decade later, exposed to the sun, a new growth of shrubs and seedlings has emerged, obscuring the fallen logs.

Sessions Wildlife Management Area (860-675-8130), CT 69, Burlington. Kept open year-round, sunrise to sunset, by the state's wildlife management agency. Free admission. Two self-guided hiking trails—one 0.6 mile long, the other 3 miles—take you alongside a beaver marsh and a small waterfall. From the observation tower you can glimpse other wildlife busy making a living. Youngsters will enjoy the backyard habitat demonstration. They may even learn something.

Burlington Trout Hatchery (860-673-2340), Beldon Rd. (off CT 4), Burlington. Open daily 8–3:30. Some 90,000 trout are raised here each year to stock state fishing streams.

Labyrinth (860-567-3163), 229 East Litchfield Rd., Litchfield. While it's not exactly a nature center, the state's first outdoor labyrinth has been opened at Wisdom House, a quasi-monastery at the edge of the borough that is both a retreat and a center for inspirational programs, most of them more expensive than those offered by other groups. Call ahead to schedule your try at winding your way through the intricate greenery that is a feature at Hampton Castle and other great houses in Britain.

Southwind Farms (860-274-9001), 223 Morris Town Line Rd., Watertown. Flexible schedules. Home to a herd of gentle alpacas. Special tours include spinning demonstrations of prized alpaca fleece.

NURSERIES AND GARDENS **White Flower Farm** (860-567-8789; www.whiteflowerfarm.com), CT 63, East Morris (the mailing address is Route 63,

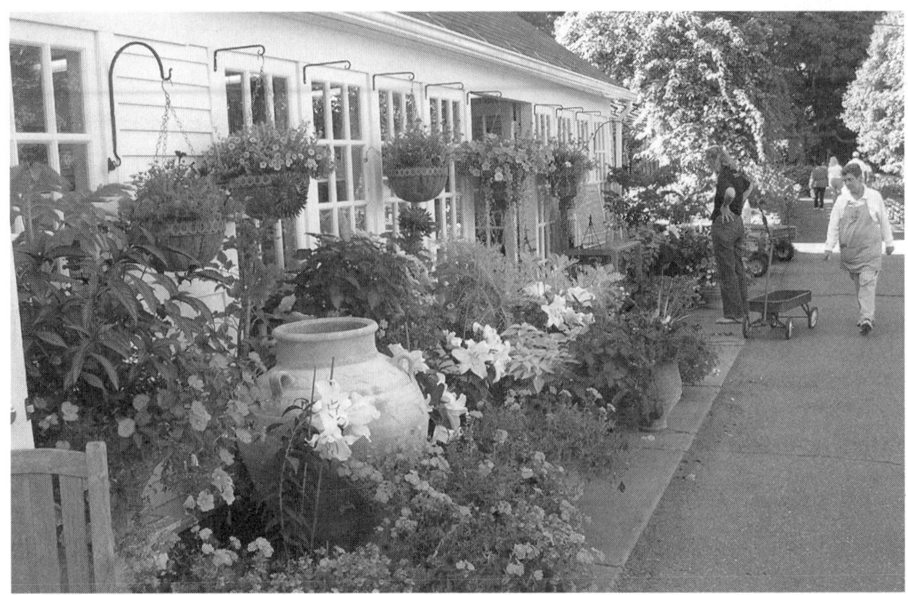

Barnett D. Laschever

A VARIETY OF PERENNIALS ENTICE SERIOUS GARDENERS TO WHITE FLOWER FARM IN EAST MORRIS.

Litchfield 06759-0050). Open 10–5 Thu.–Mon.; closed for the season Dec. 24–early spring. To visit this nationally known garden-cum-nursery, proceed south out of Litchfield on CT 63 and continue a few hundred yards past the sign marking the Morris town line. Ten acres of perennial gardens are spread out on each side of the sales area. Plantings have been designed to greet you with dazzling color from early May to fall. Depending on the time of your visit, you'll see in bloom perennial borders of spring bulbs; tree peonies, Oriental poppies, herbaceous peonies, and tuberous begonias; or mums, asters, and fall foliage. White Flower is famed for its rare plants, many imported. It's the only nursery in the United States that propagates and sells the spectacular English Blackmore and Langdon tuberous begonias, on view in their own special greenhouse. Guided tours of the farm may be arranged four weeks in advance. To order a beautifully illustrated catalog, visit their Web site.

Sweethaven Farm (860-824-0761; www.sweethavenfarmct.com), 70 Weatogue Rd., Salisbury 06068. Open Mon., Wed., Fri., and Sat. 10–5. Herb farm with fresh herbs and herb seedlings in-season. You'll also find a large retail shop with fresh and dried botanicals, unique plants and containers, gifts, a greenhouse, an unusual variety of annuals for cut flowers, and the popular Peter Rabbit Garden.

Lauray of Salisbury (660-435-2263), 432 Undermountain Rd. (CT 7), Salisbury 06068. Open by appointment or by chance. If you're into succulents, make an appointment—this is the nursery for you. The pleasant greenhouse is home to a wide variety of orchids, cacti, begonias, and succulents. You won't leave empty-handed. Offers excellent advice on how to address the needs of desert plants in the confines of a region known for the blasts of winter winds.

Kent Greenhouse and Garden Center (860-927-3480), US 7, just south of Kent Center. Open 9–5:30 Mar.–Jan. You will be instantly compelled to stop and browse this sprawling 33-year-old garden center anchored by a large greenhouse. Dally in the well-mannered display gardens but then turn your attention to the racks and racks of annuals in-season and perennials for all seasons. Bulbs for spring flowers; mums for fall. Lost your favorite trowel or cultivator? Kent has garden accessories to satisfy every need. There's also a staff of trained landscape designers if you live close enough. Christmas shop.

Litchfield Hills Nurseries (860-567-9374), US 202, just east of the Litchfield green, Litchfield. Open year-round. For the gardener in the family who can't resist bringing home another begonia or African violet to add to the collection. This popular nursery has an excellent variety of bedding plants in-season; shrubs, perennials, trees, vegetable flats, seeds, garden books; and, all year, dried floral and evergreen arrangements for Christmas. Comprehensive collection of sturdy garden tools. No outdoor gardens.

Litchfield Horticultural Center (860-567-3707), 258 Beach St., Litchfield. Open Mon.–Sat. 9–5, Sun. noon–4. Under new management. A retail store with a variety of annuals and perennials in its spacious greenhouse, including houseplants and tropicals that you can set outside in summer. Fine-quality trees, shrubs, and exotic and dwarf conifers in elegant display gardens. The center's owners contend that "Anytime is right for planning." Custom holiday wreaths and decorations. Landscape designs are a specialty. A private enterprise, not an official Litchfield town outlet.

Cricket Hill Garden (860-283-1042), 670 Walnut Hill Rd., Thomaston. David Furman and his wife, Kasha, contend that they have "30 children and love them all equally." The "children" are 30 species of classical tree peonies, imported from China and descendants of plants developed more than 1,000 years ago in the Sui dynasty. The Furmans are among the few gardeners in the United States to propagate these rare and beautiful plants.

✷ Lodging

The Litchfield Tourist District was enlarged late in 2003 when, in an effort to economize, the state reduced the number of districts from 11 to 5. Waterbury and Danbury, in the northwest, have became part of the state's new enlarged Litchfield district. In this book, we have continued to divide the state into six distinct vacation destinations. For more information on lodgings in Litchfield, contact the **Northwest Connecticut Convention & Visitors Bureau** (800-663-1273; www.litchfieldhills.com), Box 968, Litchfield, CT 06759-0968. The bureau has a group tour office in Waterbury; its principal tourism information office is in Litchfield, where it also staffs an information booth full of folders on the Borough Green, in-season.

You will find more than 100 places to put in for the night in the northwest corner of the state, the bulk of which are beautifully appointed B&Bs. Some of the most famous country inns and resorts overlook the area's sparkling lakes; others are hidden in the woods or front colonial village greens. Mainline chain hotels are located in Waterbury, Danbury, and Torrington; motels are scattered about. Don't look for the typical family cottages in the woods that you'll find in the more rural New England states. Summer vacation cottages for rent in Connecticut are, for the most part, in the shoreline towns.

Note: Some "inns" are really hotels or motels; others are more like resorts. And an occasional B&B even calls itself an inn. We've tried to sort them out for you. Prices do not include taxes and gratuities. And be advised that they inevitably go up over time, for which we take no responsibility. Most establishments nowadays have Internet and wireless access; if that is important to you, ask when making reservations.

RESORTS ♿ **Interlaken Inn, Resort and Conference Center** (860-435-9878; 800-222-2909; fax 860-435-2980; www.interlakeninn.com), CT 112 (off US 7), Lakeville 06039. In a country setting across the state road from the prestigious Hotchkiss prep school and on the banks of Connecticut's deepest lake—with its most unpronounceable name: Wononskopomuc. The Interlaken offers 82 rooms—including seven duplex suites with fireplaces and kitchens—a complete health center with sauna and massage, and fine dining open to the public (see Morgan's Grill and Café under *Dining Out*) in a relatively modern building. Swimming, boating, and fishing in the lake are available, or you can bathe in the heated outdoor pool. Tennis, chip-and-pitch golf. Inn guests can also tee off on the challenging Hotchkiss course. The inn is close to Lime Rock Park and the music festivals of the Litchfield Hills and Berkshires. Two rooms in the main building are handicapped accessible. $149 double; $399 suites. Two-night minimum in-season. Winter rates. The adjacent **Sunnyside B&B** (same phone number as the inn) is a 12-room house with wraparound porch; $269.

♿ **Club Getaway** (860-927-3664; reservations 212-935-0222; out-of-state 800-643-8292; www.clubgetaway.com), 59 South Kent Rd., South Kent 06757. Open May–Oct. Modeled after Club Med, this 300-acre resort provides a wide range of sporting activities, from tennis to waterskiing on a private lake, windsurfing, volleyball, archery, swimming, mountain biking, in-line skating, sailing, technical rock climbing, and more. Instruction in all of the above. Evening entertainment. Eighty-four cabins. Weekend average $369, including six meals. Golf carts are available for the disabled.

INNS **The Mayflower Inn & Spa** (860-868-9466; www.mayflowerinn.com), 118 Woodbury Rd. (CT 47), Washington 06793. A century-old country inn was razed to the ground, a few timbers were saved, and a beautiful new inn arose in its place on 30 tranquil acres of woods, ponds, and fields. Spectacular gardens have been carved into the hillside. Some of the 30 rooms and suites have working fireplaces. Outdoor heated pool, tennis. Health club with sauna, indoor pool, fitness advisers, plus Special Spa Weekends. A deserved international reputation as the place for a romantic, relaxing getaway in Connecticut. Arguably the premier deluxe resort in the state, rivaling the great resorts elsewhere in New England. Three dining rooms (see *Dining Out*). Double $520–750; suites $700–1,500 per night. Two-night minimum on weekends.

The Litchfield Inn (860-567-4503; 800-499-3444; www.litchfieldinnct.com), US 202, Litchfield 06759. An attractive building in the colonial style, The Litchfield Inn is southwest of the Borough Green on the main state highway. Thirty-two nicely decorated rooms all have private bath. There are eight theme rooms and a formal parlor with baby grand piano and roaring fireplace. Continental breakfast for guests. A new restaurant, which will be open to the public, is under construction. Standard rooms $150; junior deluxe $145;

deluxe $175; theme rooms $250; lower off-season.

Toll Gate Hill Inn & Restaurant (860-567-1233; 866-567-1233; www.tollgatehill.com), 571 Torrington Rd. (US 202), on the eastern outskirts of Litchfield 06759. On the National Register of Historic Places, the inn has been welcoming visitors since 1745. Set back from the highway in a grove of white birch trees, this quiet historic hostelry is just the place for romantic lovers, young and old, or for settled folk hoping to stir the embers of a marriage grown too familiar. The 18th-century paneling, floorboards, and fireplaces have been meticulously restored. Sixteen exquisitely furnished rooms, many with canopy beds; four suites. Continental breakfast; gracious dining Thu.–Sat. in two colonial-style dining rooms: the **Formal Room** and the **Captain William Bull Tavern**. Sample entrée: pan-seared Irish salmon with exotic fixin's, $25. Extensive wine cellar. Double rooms $115; deluxe rooms $170; suites with working fireplace to $195.

🐾 ✐ **Yankee Pedlar Inn** (860-489-9226; 800-777-1891; www.pedlarinn.com), 93 Main St., Torrington 06790. In the heart of downtown Torrington and a short drive to two major ski slopes, this century-old inn is across from the Warner Theatre and in the midst of antiques shops, ballet schools, a library, and places of worship. Four-poster beds, Hitchcock furniture, private bath in each of the 60 rooms, wireless Internet. Paneled dining room with an in-house **English-style tavern**. Rates start at $229 per room ($20 less on weekends) and include a continental breakfast. Senior discount. Children under 12 free. Well-behaved pets are welcome.

♿ **Old Riverton Inn** (860-379-8678; 800-378-1796; fax 860-379-1006; www.rivertoninn.com), CT 20 just north of Winsted, Riverton 06065. Open year-round. An inn since 1796 on what was then the Post Road between Hartford and Albany, the Old Riverton still welcomes the hungry, the thirsty, and the sleepy. Your hosts, Mark and Pauline Telford, invite you to climb into a canopy bed in one of the 12 comfortable guest rooms, all with private bath, and listen to the murmur of the Farmington River meandering past the front door. Sip your cocktails at the historic bar or on the patio. On the National Register of Historic Places. Award-winning dining. Handicapped accessible. Some years ago, a Riverton waiter won $10,000 in the state lottery. He

THE MAYFLOWER INN IN WASHINGTON

Kim Grant

said it was "the biggest tip I've ever received!" $85–180.

Winvian (860-567-9600; www.winvian.com) Alain White Rd., Morris. What do you do with 113 acres of empty prime land lying fallow next to a nature preserve of 4,000 acres? Lash 15 architects together and direct them to come up with a super-extraordinary resort! And that's what they did. For $1,450–1,950 a night (for two), you can pamper yourself in one of 19 very, very special cottages. One is a tree house that you must climb up into like Tarzan; in another the living room is the cabin of a dismantled helicopter. You get the idea: out of this world! All meals, snacks, beverages, and amenities—too many to list—are included, except the spa services are extra and there's a $23 charge to cover myriad taxes. But then that's small change if you can afford an off-the-radar-screen cottage. The dining facilities are open to the public for dinner; reservations are a must. This is a gated community. Sightseers not welcome. Initial reports are putting Winvian in a league with the most prestigious resorts in California and Las Vegas. The West comes East!

Holiday Inn Waterbury, 3580 East Main St., Waterbury 06705. One of only a few main-line chain hotels in Waterbury that we have included in this guide. It has more than 200 rooms, including suites, an indoor pool, a fitness center, and wireless Internet. Rooms range $126–159. The kicker, however, is a new attached building encompassing 65,000 square feet and home to a Co Co Key Water Resort; see *Amusements*.

The Inn at Iron Masters (860-435-9844; www.innatironmasters.com), 229 Main St. (US 44), Lakeville 06039. Recalls the days when iron forges belched forth flames in the woods and produced the cannons for Washington's army. Twenty-eight rooms with Ethan Allen furniture. Chat by the large fieldstone fireplace in the Hearth Room; stroll in the gardens. Outdoor pool. $142–165 includes continental breakfast. Restaurant on premises. Limited handicapped accessibility. Basically a deluxe motel. Skiing packages are available.

Wake Robin Inn (860-435-2000; www.wakerobininn.com), CT 41, Lakeville 06039. Barely visible from the highway, this former school for girls has been converted into a dramatic colonial-style inn. Ideal for weddings, birthday parties, or a romantic weekend. The main building contains 23 year-round guest rooms with an additional 38 rooms in a motel unit in back during the summer months. The back rooms look out into the woods. A deluxe restaurant, **Michael Bryan's Irish Pub**, is open to the public. Average $209.

🐾 🍼 ♿ **The White Hart Inn** (860-435-0030; 800-832-0041; www.whitehartinn.com), CT 41 and US 44, Salisbury 06058. All 26 guest rooms at this restored 19th-century inn have private bath, cable TV, and air-conditioning. One room is equipped for the handicapped. Some suites. From the wide porch or from your canopy bed, you can look out on the village green. There's a historic tavern, the Riga Room dining room, and the Garden Room (see *Dining Out*). Another favorite for romantic getaways. $195–255. Pets $25. Cots and cribs available. Senior discount.

The Curtis House (203-263-2101; www.thecurtishouse.com), 506 Main St. (US 6), Woodbury 06798, is Connecticut's oldest inn—built before 1736. On the main street, it's in the heart of Woodbury's myriad antiques shops and near the Glebe House.

Canopy beds add to the charm of the 18 guest rooms in the main house. Eight have private bath. Four additional rooms in the former carriage house are connected to the main grounds by a footbridge. There's a popular dining room (see *Dining Out*); spa and babysitters are also available. $40 for shared bath; $60–134.40, all double.

🐾 **The Cornwall Inn and Lodge** (860-672-6884; 800-786-6884; www.cornwallinn.com), US 7, Cornwall Bridge 06754. Playing host to travelers since 1871, this gracious inn has six rooms in the main building, all with private bath. An eight-room country motel is adjacent. All rooms have cable TV and wireless Internet service. This family-oriented inn also offers a swimming pool and hot tub. Excellent restaurant and tavern. Pets are welcome. $155–270 in-season includes continental breakfast.

The Boulders (860-868-0541; 800-455-1565; fax 860-868-1925; www.bouldersinn.com), East Shore Rd. (CT 45), New Preston 06777. A charming mansion overlooking Lake Waramaug serves as the centerpiece for this country retreat, which includes four rooms and two suites in the main house, eight guest houses with fireplaces, and a carriage house with three rooms. All rooms are furnished with antiques or in traditional country style. Private beach and boathouse; tennis, bicycling, and a hiking trail up Pinnacle Mountain. With its superb dining room (see *Dining Out*), the Boulders has been garnering superlative reviews from the country's top food and travel writers. Honeymooners should put this inn on the top of their list. Double $350–595, MAP (includes breakfast and dinner).

The Hopkins Inn (860-868-7295; www.thehopkinsinn.com), 22 Hopkins Rd. (off West Shore Rd.), New Preston 06777. Best known for its restaurant's Austrian haute cuisine (see *Dining Out*), this attractive, 19th-century Federal-style country inn high above Lake Waramaug opens its 11 small guest rooms and two apartments from late March through January. Private beach. Myriad sports and cultural activities in nearby towns. Double $110–140. No pets.

THE BOULDERS INN IN NEW PRESTON

Kim Grant

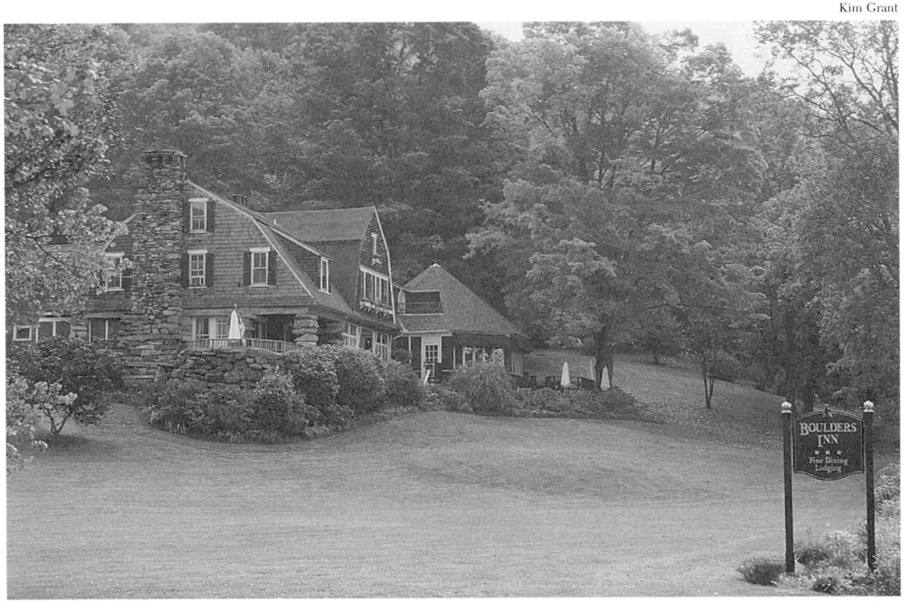

🐾 **The Homestead Inn** (860-354-4080; www.homesteadct.com), 5 Elm St., in the heart of New Milford 06776. The innkeepers have furnished the eight rooms in the 140-year-old main house and six in the adjacent **Treadwell House** with country antiques and reproductions. All guest rooms have private bath, TV, wireless Internet service, and air-conditioning. An antique Steinway in the common room invites the talented to tinkle the keys. Relax on the front and back porches, or stroll in the perennial gardens. $105–160, breakfast included. AAA approved. Pets are welcome.

Mountain View Inn (860-542-6991; www.mvinn.com), CT 272, Norfolk 06058. This gracious 1875 Victorian house overlooks the picture-postcard village of Norfolk. Owners Dean and Jean Marie Johnson invite guests to choose from among seven intimate rooms, most with private bath, some with four-poster bed, others opening onto an enclosed porch or an adjoining study. Includes an art gallery and a vintage boutique, **Gilded Peacock**. The oak-paneled Great Room accommodates private parties and events. Enjoy a full, hearty American breakfast. Weekends $110–155.

BED & BREAKFASTS In addition to the listings below, a number of B&B reservations services offer access to rooms available in establishments throughout the state. For a list, see *Bed & Breakfasts* in "What's Where in Connecticut."

🐾 🖍 **Mary Stuart House Bed and Breakfast** (860-491-2260), 160 Sharon Turnpike (US 4), Goshen 06756. Open year-round. Step back in time in this comfortable 1798 historic country house restored by hostess Mary Orlando. Five rooms are available in the main house; there's also a two-bedroom cottage with kitchen and private bath. A walk through fields and orchards takes you to a quiet brook. After a day of activity—the house is close to Mohawk Mountain Ski Area, Goshen Fairgrounds, Lime Rock Race Track, and the village of Litchfield—a mug of hot chocolate awaits you in front of a warm, cozy fire. $85–160. Children and pets welcome.

Sachem Farmhouse B&B (860-868-0359: www.sachemfarmhouse.com, 15 Hopkins Rd., Warren 06777. Time was six elegant country inns lined the shores of Lake Waramaug. Folks came up with steamer trunks and settled in for the summer. Except for the Boulders and Hopkins, however, the classic inns have now become private homes, and vacationing visitors enjoy the hospitality of such premier bed & breakfasts as the Sachem. Four guest rooms in this newly restored 1870 farmhouse have been beautiful decorated with antiques. A garden hammock overlooks the pristine lake where a private beach awaits you in-season, unless you are a member of the Polar Bears. Organic eggs are collected from the farmhouse's own heritage-breed chickens for a memorable breakfast. Picnic baskets can be arranged. May–Dec. $195–295.

Constitution Oak Farm (860-354-6495), 36 Beardsley Rd., Kent 06757. Four guest rooms, two with bath, in an 1830s house on 90 acres, all furnished in period pieces. Open year-round. A mile from Lake Waramaug State Park. Breakfast included. $75–95.

♿ **Fife 'N Drum** (860-927-3509; www.fifendrum.com), 53 North Main St. (US 7), Kent 06757. An eight-room bed & breakfast in a Victorian house across the parking lot from the restaurant of the same name (see *Dining Out*). Closed Tuesday (except to Monday-night guests who request to stay another day by special reservation). Each nonsmoking room features a private bath and independent heating and air-conditioning controls. Complimentary juice and coffee in the room. Gift shop. $135–150.

The Gibbs House (860-927-1754), 87 North Main St., Kent 06757. Two bright and sunny rooms with color TV and coffeemaker are within walking distance of Kent's prestigious art galleries and international boutiques. The suite has a private bath. Continental breakfast. Single $75; double $85. Children and pets welcome.

The Inn at Kent Falls (860-927-3197), 107 Kent Cornwall Rd., Kent 06757. Set on 2.5 acres, this 1741 inn is located between Kent Falls State Park and the town of Kent. The six guest rooms feature three suites and three queen-sized rooms; one, the Meadows Room, has a large dormer window that reminds us of Paris. You have to imagine the Eiffel Tower yourself when you look out and see maple trees. All rooms have private bath, Frette linens, and Aveda bath products. There's a pool, and you can relax with a spa treatment. Scan the morning paper or catch up on your reading in a screened-in porch. The bountiful breakfast caps off a romantic visit with choices of fresh-baked croissants, scones, salmon, quiches, waffles, fruit, granola, and yogurt. (For bagels, stop at a Dunkin' Donuts on your way to the inn.) $195–350 Apr.–Dec.; less off-season. No smoking.

Hilltop Haven B&B (860-672-6871; www.hilltopbb.com), 175 Dibble Hill Rd., West Cornwall 06796. Open year-round. Expect breathtaking views of the Housatonic Valley, Berkshire foothills, and Taconic Mountains from this 64-acre scenic hilltop estate. Two rooms are furnished with antiques, each with a private bath and private phone. Full country breakfast served beside the stone library fireplace. Owner Everett Van Dorn proudly tells you how his father, a Yale University professor, built the house by hand, stone by stone. In-season, break your morning fast on the flagstone terrace. No smoking. Double $165 per night; two-night minimum. Widely recommended.

Cathedral Pines Farm (860-672-6747; www.cathedralpinesfarm.com), 10 Valley Rd., Cornwall 06753. One big beautiful room in an 18th-century-style farmhouse overlooking some of the most beautiful scenery in the Litchfield Hills. Relax under the stars in the outdoor hot tub. Roam in the gardens and greet the llama babies playing in the pastures. Convenient to fine dining, skiing, antiquing, and music festivals. $235. Full breakfast.

Blackberry River Inn (860-542-5100; 800-414-3636), US 44, Norfolk 06058. This charming 1763 inn, located in the rural foothills of the Berkshires, boasts 20 guest rooms and suites, many with Jacuzzis or working fireplaces. Guests can relax by the fireplace in one of the three parlors or in the wood-paneled library. National Historic Landmark. Complimentary gourmet breakfast and afternoon tea. $135–249.

Manor House (866-542-5690; fax 860-542-5690; www.manorhouse-norfolk.com), 69 Maple Ave., Norfolk 06058. Tiffany windows and a paneled cherry staircase are only some of the architectural delights of this elegant Victorian Tudor estate built in 1898 by the architect of London's subway system. Each of the nine guest rooms has its own distinctive touch, whether it's a four-poster bed, fireplace, or balcony. Three guest rooms have Jacuzzis. The living room is truly baronial. The innkeeper, Michael Dinsmore, invites you to enjoy the perennial gardens and stroll the 5-acre park. The tantalizing smells of the full country breakfast will lure you out of bed. Picnic baskets for two, $30. No pets or smoking. A romantic setting in a quintessential New England village. $130–255; inquire about special rates.

B&B by the Lake (860-738-0230; 914-438-7895; www.bythelakebb.com), 19 Dillon Beach Rd., Barkhamsted 06063. Open year-round for rental by the week only. Excellent for family reunions or friend vacations in groups of up to 10. Four rooms with additional pull-outs. The historic 100-year-old house, once a magnet for New York singers, overlooks West Hill Lake, one of the cleanest in Connecticut and a favorite with anglers (there's a public boat launch in Barkhamsted's town park). Private beach; canoe available for guests. Co-innkeeper Anastasio Rossi, a busy musician, occasionally stops by and entertains on the piano; he loves to play Gershwin. Welcomes couples off-season. Full house rental $2,175.

🐾 **The Rose and Thistle** (860-379-4744), 24 Woodland Acres, Barkhamsted 06063. There are four rooms with private bath in this secluded English Tudor home, set in a 10-acre landscape that offers myriad outdoor pastimes. Additional activities such as skiing, tubing, and kayaking are available nearby. Swim or skate in-season on the spring-fed pond; play badminton or croquet on the large open lawn; relax beside the huge stone fireplace in the living room under a beamed cathedral ceiling; hike into the adjoining woodlands to a wildlife and bird sanctuary. Warning: Don't disturb the nests of the great blue herons! Game room; large fenced-in area for dogs. Pets are welcome with prior arrangements. Full breakfast and afternoon tea. Double $155.

Abel Darling Bed & Breakfast (860-567-0384; cell 860-480-1711; www.abeldarling.com), 102 West St. (US 202), Litchfield 06759. Wide floorboards and exposed beams attest to the authenticity of this 1782 colonial in Litchfield's borough section. It features a spacious, private green backyard. Historic North and South streets—with their impressive mansions and expansive green rimmed with trendy restaurants, art galleries, and a mini shopping center—are within easy walking distance of this charming old home. Wireless Internet, continental breakfast. Two pleasant rooms, with private bath, are priced at $150 and up. Possible full-house rental with six bedrooms, by special arrangement.

Tir' na nóg Farm Bed & Breakfast (860-283-9612), 261 Newton Rd., Northfield 06778. Two rooms and an adjoining sitting room in a 1775 farmhouse with stunning views of the southern hills overlooking Litchfield. Hearty continental breakfast. Convenient to the area's outdoor sports activities. If by the wildest chance you are arriving by helicopter, the farmstead has a private heliport. The Celtic name means "land of the young." $110–150.

Chimney Crest Manor (860-582-4219; fax 860-584-5903; www.chimneycrest.com), 5 Founders Dr., Bristol 06010. A large cut above your typical B&B, the manor will take your breath away. Guests driving up to this 32-room Tudor mansion overlooking the Farmington hills fancy they've been invited to a weekend in an English castle. You walk to the cherry-paneled library through a beautiful 40-foot-long, glassed-in arcade. Each of the five guest suites has a private entrance. Two have working fireplace. A canopy bed graces another. One has a Jacuzzi. Terry-cloth robes and cable television are standard. Some rooms include kitchens. The Rose Garden Suite, with a 40-foot salon, is ideal for family groups. Hosts Dante and Cynthia Cimadamore serve piping hot, full breakfasts on the grand patio off the salon. The ultimate B&B experience! Double occupancy $135–195; senior discount.

Tucker Hill Inn (203-758-8334; fax 203-598-0652; www.tuckerhillinn.com), 96 Tucker Hill Rd., Middlebury 06762. Ancient oaks and maples shade this gracious colonial home. The three rooms—with private bath—are bright and spacious. There is also a family suite. The public rooms feature an extensive library of books, videos, and CDs. Quassy, one of the state's major amusement parks, is nearby. A full breakfast is served in the dining room or, in-season, on the patio. $115–200.

Longwood Country Inn (203-266-0800; www.longwoodcountryinn.com), 1204 Main St. South (US 6), Woodbury 06798. Four rooms and luxury suites, each with its own decor, welcome guests to this simple, rambling colonial house. Large covered porch, wide oak floorboards, and fireplaces. Some rooms have whirlpools. A large, homemade country breakfast is served, while complimentary tea, coffee, and biscuits are available all day. Situated on 4 wooded acres on the Pomperaug River. A highly regarded restaurant is on the premises (see *Dining Out*). $250–350.

Golden Pear at Grandview B&B (203-266-7070; www.goldenpearbb.com), 111 Carmel Hill Rd. South (CT 132), Bethlehem 06751. An elegant 1790s country farmhouse in the foothills of the Litchfield Hills (which are in the foothills of the Berkshires). A covered porch gives you a vantage point to watch the myriad birds and butterflies that visit the farm. Close to antiquing in Woodbury. Three guest rooms and one suite. All rooms have refrigerator, hair dryer, private telephone line, Internet hookup, private en suite bathroom, robes, television with VCR, desk and/or vanity. Spa services and personal trainer are available upon request. The Vintage Suite has a queen-sized four-poster bed and an adjoining sitting room. Full breakfast and afternoon tea. Not handicapped accessible. No pets; leave children under 10 at home. $125–225.

CAMPGROUNDS The Litchfield Hills are ideally suited for camping vacations. Campgrounds are nestled alongside the region's beautiful rivers, on lakeshores, and in scented pine forests. There's a mix of both private and public camps. By design, state facilities are minimal and set up for return-to-nature tenting or very small RVs. Private campgrounds, on the other hand, have become almost complete resorts, with sports fields, food shops, recreation halls, and entertainment. They can accept and service the largest RVs. Without exception they also have electric hookups, and at some you can connect RVs with sewer lines. Rates run from $26 to $53 per night per site. Reservations are strongly suggested, particularly for holiday weekends. Otherwise, call around; usually you can find an opening. All of the state park campgrounds in this region, except one, charge $11–15 per night plus a processing fee. Pets are not permitted at state park campgrounds but are welcome in state forests. See *Camping* in "What's Where" for more details or e-mail dep.stateparks@ct.gov.

Burr Pond (860-379-0172), 385 Burr Mountain Rd., Torrington 06790; just off old CT 8 north of the city. Swimming at a public beach is available to campers staying at the 40-site state campground, which is heavily wooded.

Dumping station but no concession. Fishing. The foundation of Gail Borden's condensary—where he invented condensed milk at the time of the Civil War—is found at the entrance to this campground.

Housatonic Meadows (860-672-6772), River Rd. (US 7), Cornwall Bridge 06754. One of thé prettiest state campgrounds in Connecticut. The 104 sites are strung along the banks of the beautiful Housatonic River, most in the woods but some in open fields. Dumping station, flush toilets, and showers. Alas, beneath the waters of the river lurk chemicals dumped into it years back from an industrial plant up in Pittsfield, Massachusetts. Swimming is thus out, and only catch-and-release fishing is suggested. But it's a great river for kayaking and canoeing, photographing, painting, contemplating. No concession.

Lake Waramaug (860-868-2592), 30 Lake Waramaug Rd., New Preston 06777. Strung along the banks of a spectacular lake that reminds world travelers of Switzerland or Austria, this premier state campground offers 88 wooded and open sites. Swimming and fishing, and you can launch a light canoe or kayak into the water. Dumping station, flush toilets, showers, concession.

Macedonia Brook (860-927-4100), 159 Macedonia Brook Rd., Kent 06757. Just west of the Kent School, this 84-site state area runs uphill into the woods along a stream ideal for fishing. No swimming, but bring your hiking boots. No concession. $9 per night.

🐾 **American Legion State Forest** (860-379-0922), West River Rd., Pleasant Valley 06063. Pine woods shelter 30 sites alongside the Farmington River. No swimming, but great fishing, steep hiking trail. Dumping, flush toilets, showers. No concession. Pets welcome.

Black Rock (860-283-8088), US 6 west out of Thomaston 06787; Exit 38 off CT 8. Swimming at a pleasant pond, fishing, and hiking are the principal activities for campers on 96 wooded and open sites run by the state. Dumping station, flush toilets, showers, concession.

Branch Brook (860-283-8144), 435 Watertown Rd. (US 6), Thomaston 06787. Pool, laundry room, game room, playground, fishing pond. Offers 68 sites; also trailer sales. Bills itself as a quiet campground. Senior discount on seasonal sites. Fully stocked store.

Lone Oaks Campsites (800-422-2267), US 44, East Canaan 06024. The largest private camping area in the state, with 200 wooded sites and 300 open in grassy fields on 180 acres of rolling hills. Hookups, free cable TV, laundry, flush toilets, store, nightclub specializing in country-western and 1950s and '60s bands. Recreation hall and special events.

Mohawk (860-491-2231), CT 4, Goshen 06756. Fifty sites with a swimming pool on a main state road. Ideal for RVs. Easily accessible to other sightseeing and recreational attractions in the area. Not your typical romantic hideaway in the woods.

Valley in the Pines (800-228-2032), Lucas Rd., Goshen 06756. Twenty- to 30-foot-high trees shade the 33 sites. Pool, recreation hall, electric hookups, store. Really in the woods, but surprisingly close to Litchfield, historic sites, ski area, rivers and lakes.

🖉 **Hemlock Hill** (860-567-2267), Hemlock Hill Rd., Litchfield 06759. Children and adult pools, outdoor Jacuzzi, duck pond, 125 sites in the woods. Daily and seasonal camping.

Point Folly Family Campground (860-567-0089), North Shore Rd., Bantam Lake, Litchfield 06759. Operated by the White Memorial Foundation, this 47-site campground is on a peninsula jutting out into the state's largest natural lake. Swimming, fishing, and boating. A tents-only area called **Wind Mill Hill** has 28 sites.

White Pines Campsites (800-622-6614), 232 Old North Rd., Barkhamsted 06063. Complete family vacation on 206 sites. Children's playground, fishing pond, basketball, volleyball, pool, snack bar, planned activities.

✱ Where to Eat

DINING OUT

In Litchfield

West Street Grill (860-567-3885), West St., overlooking the Litchfield green. Open for lunch Mon.–Fri. 11–3; Sat. and Sun. 11–3:30; dinner 5:30–9:30, Fri. and Sat. until 10. Dinner reservations required. Constantly changing menu with innovative touches that have won raves from dining connoisseurs and the travel and cooking media, NBC, QVC, Litchfield resident Susan Saint James, and scads more stars of stage and screen. Owner James O'Shea introduces touches of Irish cuisine when he returns from regular visits to his native Ireland, and he often adds an Asian touch to some of his specialty entrées. We're not going to list the fabulous dinners that await your pleasure, just tease you with one of Shea's favorites: grilled shrimp salad with tomatoes and a citrus vinaigrette. Shea's tomatoes are specially grown for him on a farm in nearby Bethlehem, where we can only assume they have been blessed. Outdoor dining in-season. Pricey.

The Village Restaurant (860-567-8307), 25 West St.; on the Litchfield green. Restaurant open 11:30–9 Mon.–Thu., until 10 Fri. and Sat.; pub bar open until 1 or 2 AM. Reservations suggested for dinner. New York sirloin, sausage-stuffed chicken breast, grilled salmon, and several homemade pasta entrées attract locals and knowledgeable visitors to this village landmark. The pub menu stars spicy Buffalo wings, fried calamari, salmon crabcakes, and a Classic Village Burger that the bartender says lures burger fans from all over the county. Wraps, salads, and ribs complete the pub fare. The "fun" place to be. The chef has been featured in statewide cooking contests. $15–20.

@ the Corner, Restaurant & Pub (860-567-8882), 3 West St.; across from the Litchfield green and the anchor of shops along the street. Open daily, lunch 11:30–3:30, dinner 4:30–9:30. Bakery hours are 7–5. The formerly gussy interior is now spare and clean, with white uninteresting walls. But the menu includes a variety of soups and salads, from sturdy New England clam chowder, to pea and bean chili, to classic Caesar salad. Among the unusual appetizers is the Litchfield Hills lobster mac and cheeese, which weighs in at $14. Sea scallops, crabcakes, et al., are among the other starters. These bring you to such main-course goodies as the Black Angus or White Flower Farm beef burger. (Yes, White Flower Farm is embellishing its reputation with premium cattle.) Krazy Ketchup Meatloaf fetches $16, while lobster and shrimp pappardelle extracts $26 from your pocketbook.

Aspen Garden Restaurant (860-567-9477), 51 West St.; at the south end of the Litchfield village green. Open daily for lunch and dinner. Pleasant atmosphere; you'd never guess this was a Ford showroom for years. As in many "Italian" restaurants in Connecticut, the chefs are talented Greeks. It's no surprise then that, in addition to the Italian specialties, you'll find on the menu gyros and bountiful Greek salads garnished with feta cheese. Try the mussels. Specialty pizzas; seafood and veal dishes. Clams in their half shells decorate the tasty linguine with clam sauce. Fish-and-chips with a delicate crust. Popular three-season heated terrace with umbrella-shaded tables. $11–25.

Litchfield Saltwater Grille (860-567-4900), 26 Litchfield Commons (US 202). In Litchfield, evolution is the norm. What started out as an extensive bicycle shop, then morphed into a steak house, has in a short time become one of the best seafood restaurants in the state. Open seven days a week for lunch and dinner; closed for lunch Mon. Make your choice from bluepoint oysters, Maine lobsters, Rhode Island littleneck clams, and almost anything in between that swims. Patrons in one of the three dining rooms can watch the chef prepare their repasts on an open fire. And of course, there is prime sushi. The wine loft, once the storage room for bicycle parts, is home to 1,200 bottles. On Thursdays, you will be entertained by a live jazz and a guitar player; a fiddle player strolls on Friday nights. $16–25.

da Capo Brick Oven Pizza and Italian Restaurant (860-482-6246), 625 Torrington Rd., US 202, east of the Litchfield green. Open Sun.–Thu. noon–11 PM, Fri.–Sat. noon–midnight. Just when locals thought they didn't need another pizza restaurant, two friends took over the longtime Main Course, knocked down the walls, opened up the space, and brought to Litchfield what they claim is "Manhattan meets Mediterranean" style. This translates into a brick oven with New York thin-crust pizza and a complete Italian menu, with some Greek influences. Why not—both restaurateurs are skilled chefs of Greek descent. Spaghetti *pomodoro* is $9.95 and veal Milanaise, $17.95. Seafood, chicken, and paninis join other specialties on the bountiful menu.

The Market, Organic & Natural Foods (860-567-1900), 55 Village Green Dr. *Note:* Not in the Borough Green, but in the satellite green known locally as Dunkin' Donuts Plaza. Open daily 7:30–7:30. This indeed is a full-service market with organic vegetables, breads, and bulk cheeses, not presliced and interred in plastic—if you are cooking in a RV and need gourmet provisions. But it also specializes in hot meals—take out or eat in a cute little dining room at the side entrance. The deli sandwiches are superb, as are the soups. Coffee, tea, breakfast, lunch, and dinner. Not an overwhelming menu, but the hungry will find enough to satiate them. Discounts off selected purchases—say, $10 off a total purchase of $50 or more.

La Cupola (860-567-3326), 637 Bantam Rd. (US 202). Open Tue.–Sun. year-round for lunch and dinner. On the southern approach to Litchfield, an imposing landmark old stone mansion, overlooking the Bantam River, is a handsome restaurant serving a full range of innovative Italian cuisine, from chicken Piccata and veal Genovese to *tutto mare*, half a dozen antipasti—try the mussels in garlic and herbs—and pastas of your choice. Extensive wine list. Full bar. Dining alfresco in-season. Menu and hours subject to change. $20–25 for dinner. Eight comfortable guest rooms, too.

Zini's Ristorante (860-567-1613), 938 Bantam Rd. (US 202). Open for dinner only, daily 4–10. The daughter of Tom the stonemason, restorer of numerous stone walls throughout Litchfield, has won a reputation for her exquisite presentation of Italian specialties.

Unlike so many Italian restaurants, here the plates are not overflowing with food. Especially delicate is the linguine with white clam sauce. Other specialties: grilled salmon, delectable veal chops, and authentic Caesar salads. For dessert: the crème brûlée. Father Tom has decorated the walls completely with artfully cut stones. Full-service bar. $18–35.

Bantam Inn (860-567-1770), US 202, in the Bantam section of Litchfield. Call for hours. A charming and attentive Balkan couple lovingly operate this venerable inn, whose walls are decorated with advertising flyers of our favorite romantic movies from the 1930s and '40s. The Hungarian-style roast duck is a standout. Sizzling steaks, prime rib, rack of lamb, and seafood round out the menu. $26.

Patty's Restaurant (860-567-3335), 499 Bantam Rd. (US 202). Breakfast until noon on Sun., plus lunch weekdays until 2. Everyone raves about Patty's, and who are we to buck the crowd? Go for the Belgian waffles, raisin French toast, and corned beef hash. But be forewarned: Twice my hash browns have come out hash burned. Nicely ask the server for freshly cooked hash browns, or enjoy breakfast without them. Patty's has won awards, so there.

In New Preston

Oliva (860-868-1787), CT 45; in the center of New Preston, at the southern end of Lake Waramaug. Open for lunch Sat. and Sun.; dinner Wed.–Sun. Closed Mon. and Tue. Reservations recommended. Chef Riad Aamar, formerly of the well-known Doc's, serves Italian and Mediterranean specialties in a popular restaurant that features dining on two levels and on the terrace in-season. Try the stuffed eggplant with prosciutto and Fontina, white beans, and sage, or the gnocchi *à la Romano.* Salmon is often on the menu, as is osso buco. BYOB. $13.25–25.

🏵 🖋 ♿ **The Hopkins Inn** (860-868-7295), 22 Hopkins Rd. (off Lake Rd.). Hours so varied we don't dare try to tackle them here. It's safer to call ahead off-season. Continental cuisine with an Austrian flair. Reserve a table on the lovely, tree-shaded terrace overlooking the north end of beautiful Lake Waramaug. Guests rave about the view as much as the food. Best roast duck à l'orange in the Litchfield Hills. Wiener schnitzel, *backhendl* with lingonberries, escargots, sweetbreads, and for dessert apple strudel and creamy cheesecake. Fresh trout from the restaurant's fish tank. Take home a bottle of the inn's own Caesar or spinach salad dressing. Lunch $10–18, dinner $20–28.

The Boulders (860-868-0541), East Shore Rd. (CT 45). Open year-round, except Tue. in winter. Fresh vegetables, soups garnished with edible flowers and seasoned with herbs—all grown in the inn's garden by co-owner Ulla Adema. Home-baked rolls have guests clamoring for the recipe. Start your dinner with asparagus and wild rice soup with toasted pecans, followed by an herb-grilled veal chop on toasted wild rice, or roasted Alaskan halibut, pan-seared pearl salmon, or a pan-roasted mignon of beef "Benedict." In 1991 the Boulders was hailed as one of the "ten best country inns of the year." It still is. $29–36. Guest rooms (see *Lodging*).

In and around Washington

♿ **G. W. Tavern** (860-868-6633), 20 Bee Brook Rd. (CT 47), Washington Depot. Open for lunch and dinner daily; brunch and dinner Sat. and Sun. American and English favorites from meat loaf and chicken potpie to fish-and-chips and duck with apple chutney. Thick juicy burgers. Start your meal with that traditional Anglo-Indian favorite, mulligatawny soup. Fireside dining in winter, outdoors in summer. $10–36.

The Mayflower Inn (860-868-1497), CT 47, Washington. Open daily for the ultimate in dining in the Litchfield Hills, if not the entire state. Tables are set with Limoges china, crystal, and silver. Gourmets enjoy inspired meals that include house-smoked salmon, game sausage, and seafood from the fishing banks of New England. The chef need go no farther than the inn's organic gardens for the freshest vegetables. Crabcakes are the inn's signature dish. Breads, pastas, and pastries flow from the inn's own bakery. $28–40.

In Woodbury

♿ **Carole Peck's Good News Café** (203-266-4663), 649 Main St. (US 6). Open for lunch 11:30–2:30; dinner 5–10, except Tue. Reservations are recommended. Carole Peck, one of the first female graduates of the Culinary Institute of America, has created a combination restaurant, bar, and art gallery in a former steak-and-potato house. Peck was chosen by *Eating Well* magazine as one of the 10 best chefs in the country for her preparations of healthy gourmet food. The café is eminently accessible, on US 6, just off I-84. On the edge of one shopping mall and across the road from another, it's hardly dining among the honeysuckles. No matter; the café has become a magnet for celebrities and lovers of fine food. You enter the rather undistinguished, rambling clapboard building from the rear. To your right is a take-out bar offering gourmet delights such as peppered pappadam, buckwheat kasha cakes, sun-dried cherry splash, and a comprehensive list of vegetarian specialties. Directly in front is a bar, popular at happy hour. The more casual café anchors the south end of the building; the trendy dining room is on the north. For an entrée, try the wok-seared shrimp with garlic, herb potatoes, and olives. The crispy fried onion bundle is a popular appetizer. Take-out sandwiches $12; dinner $25–40.

The Longwood Country Inn (formerly Coriander) (203-266-0800), 1204 Main St. South (US 6); at the Longwood Country Inn. Open Tue.–Sat. for lunch 11:30–2:30; dinner 5:30–9. Once just a B&B (Merryvale), now serving dinner under the tutelage of a chef from the world-class Copper Beech Inn. Specialties range from stuffed Atlantic salmon to Dover sole, and farm-raised venison (with all the marauding deer in Connecticut, you wish someone would just poke a gun out the window) to slices of roast duck breast with rice fritters. Salads with flower petals (in-season). Save room for dessert. $25–45.

♿ **The Curtis House** (203-263-2101), 506 Main St. (US 6). Open for lunch Tue.–Sat.; dinner daily. Dependable American cuisine in the oldest inn in the state. The owners boast that they offer 38 entrées ($16–22), ranging from roast turkey, trout, bluefish, and shrimp to lamb chops, prime rib, and chicken. Enjoy happy hour in the **City Hall Pub and Tavern**. Guest rooms (see *Lodging*).

In Bethlehem

The Woodward House (203-266-6902), 4 The Green, in the center of Bethlehem. Open Wed.–Sat. 6-9, Sun. brunch 11–3 and Sun. dinner 5–9. Closed Mon. and Tue. Only a little more than two years old, the co-owners have already been named Connecticut Restaurateurs of the Year. And they were among the winners of an "Iron Chef" competition at the Mohegan (Casino) Sun. Their prizewinning restaurant was established in an old house that has served a multitude of purposes during its long life. Now diners can sample the best of the best in four delightful dining rooms. Prix fixe, three courses per person, $50.

In New Milford

♿ **Palma** (formerly Rudy's) (860-354-7727), 122 Litchfield Rd. (US 202); on the main road on the outskirts of town. Rudy has departed, but a semblance of his Swiss menu remains: Holstein schnitzel and sauerbraten with red cabbage and spätzle. The menu then goes Mediterranean in a big way (not the new "healthy" Greek mode, but more French and Italian). For appetizers, salade Niçoise is graced with grilled tuna, hard-boiled egg, string beans, olives, anchovies, and mixed greens with garlic lemon dressing. A hearty paella (for two) is a combination of clams, mussels, squid, shrimp, chicken, chorizo, and veggies simmered in saffron rice. Wow! You can also choose stuffed jumbo shrimp, or chicken *alla Palma*—boneless breast of chicken, battered, layered, and baked. Next comes duck à l'orange, and then the ravioli of the day. One concession to the watchers of the waistline: low-carb scallops. You are advised that the house specialty dessert, Fruit Puff, takes 30 minutes for cooking but is well worth the wait. $15–22.

The Cookhouse (860-355-4111; www.cookhouse.com), 31 Danbury Rd. (US 7), just south of New Milford. A huge red barn that's full of surprises. Inside there's room for everyone in the family, from the toddler to the grandpaw and grandmaw. Regulars claim this is the place in Connecticut for ribs and any other comestible that lends itself to barbecuing. You wonder where some bikers get oversized paunches? From the oversized servings in The Cookhouse. $15–25.

Adrienne (860-354-6001), 218 Kent Rd. (US 7). Open for dinner Tue.–Sat.; brunch on Sun. An acclaimed restaurant in an 18th-century house offers fine dining in the Litchfield Hills. Salmon is always on the menu, but seared Maine diver scallops are a specialty, as are good old-fashioned American lamb chops with no sauce, no glazes, and no reductions. The chef follows the seasons when selecting vegetables. Venison is another specialty. And don't miss the crème brûlée or apple-almond crêpe cake for dessert. Outdoor terrace. Dinner $19.95–25.50; Sun. brunch $18–22.

In New Hartford

Chatterley's (860-379-2428), 2 Bridge St. Open for lunch and dinner. Small musical combos on weekends in the back room. Located in the landmark former New Hartford Hotel in the center of the village, Chatterley's features an ambience that's pure Victorian—but its food is artful 21st century. The Caesar salad, for example, is garnished with shrimp. A sweet-and-sour sauce enhances the grilled medallions of pork loin. Hefty burgers are listed under the "Lighter Side of the Menu." Save space for cheesecake. Chatterley's is popular in winter with athletic folk just off the slopes of nearby Ski Sundown. $17.

In Kent

♿ **Fife 'N Drum** (860-927-3509), 53 North Main St. (US 7). Open year-round for lunch and dinner; Sun. brunch; closed Tue. Just inside the door is a grand piano. It's not for decoration—Dolph Traymon, the genial founder, still plays while you enjoy French and Italian specialties in a barn-like setting. Rack of lamb, steak au poivre, roast duck flambé prepared tableside. Potato-crusted shrimp in Thai sauce. All topped off with the queen of desserts, crème brûlée. Rustic taproom. Popular with Kent School faculty and visiting parents of students. A distinctive gift shop across the parking lot offers cards, gift wraps, candles, and jewelry. $11.95–31.95. Eight comfortable guest rooms (see *Lodging*).

Doc's (860-927-3810; www.docs trattoria.com), Village Barn Shops, 9 Maples St., Kent. Open for lunch and dinner Tue.–Sun. until 10 PM; Fri. and Sat. until 11. Moved from an unprepossessing building at the tip of Lake Waramaug to large quarters in Kent. The patio seats 40 in-season; the dining room has small bistro tables covered with white linen for 80 diners. Large portions of a variety of meticulously prepared Italian specialties crowd the menu that made Doc's a shining light at the lake. Pizzas are still given extra attention, inviting you to choose from seven toppings. Shrimp, mussels, calamari-and-scungiili puttenesca over linguine, veal. Most popular entrées: *penne vessuviana*, *vitello saltimbocca*, and *zuppa di pesce*. These and beef entrées make you glad this popular eatery didn't stray far. Classic Italian desserts and—at last—a full bar. Leave the brown paper bag at home. $18–30.

Blu Grill (860-927-1881; www.theblu grill.com), 14 North Main St., Kent. 06757. Lunch, dinner, and weekend brunch. The new 50-seat Blu Grill has a bar and, in the words of its co-owner Jake Cerrone, offers "a world grill with an American base, a mix of New England sensibility and New York sophistication." The emphasis is on offering a seasonal menu dependent on what's fresh in the local farm markets each day, along with the usual staples. Be a true adventurer, in keeping with the theme of this book, and do a bit of exploring next time you are in Kent, one of the state's premier towns. Moderately priced.

Bulls Bridge Inn (860-927-1000; www.bullsbridgeinn), 333 Kent Rd. (US 7, 4 miles south of Kent Center. Dinner Mon.–Fri. 5–9:30, Sat. 5–10, Sun. 4–9. A historic restaurant with a taproom, offering a complete complement of steaks, bratwurst over braised red cabbage, shrimp scampi, swordfish, and Jamaican jerk chicken. And if you recall your mother's meat loaf kindly, the Bulls Bridge version will stir happy memories. There's an inviting leafy green salad bar. Combine a visit to the covered bridge with dinner in friendly surroundings. History records that when Washington was en route to Hartford to confer with Rochambeau, the bridge was under repair and his horse fell through the boards. He was pulled out unharmed! The general put the rescue on his expense account.

In Norfolk

The Speckled Hen Pub (formerly The Pub) is closed, but at press time negotiations were under way for another enterprising chef to pick up the spatulas. Meanwhile, grab a bite in the new bistro in the new Infiniti Hall music theater just around the back of the building complex.

In Salisbury/Lakeville

✿ ✐ ♿ **The White Hart Inn** (860-435-0030), CT 41 and US 44, Salisbury. Open daily for breakfast, lunch, and dinner. Known locally as the Porch because of the wide, old-fashioned veranda that fronts the Salisbury green. Its restaurant, the **Riga Room**, and its well-prepared seafood dishes are earning additional praises for this charming 19th-century wayside inn. Lunch in the **Garden Room**; or visit the **taproom** for lunch and dinner or for a lively happy hour. Entrées range from Atlantic salmon fillet grilled with whole-grain mustard and caramelized red onions to tournedos of beef and traditional chicken potpie. Innovative sandwiches and salads. Award-winning wine list. $17–27.

The Boathouse in Lakeville (860-435-2111), 349 Main St. (US 44), Lakeville. A less-than-adequate Chinese restaurant has been converted into a versatile American Mediterranean eatery with well-prepared cuisine from a raw bar, a sushi menu, maki rolls, unique pasta creations, sandwiches, and salads to more conventional entrées such as sea scallops, grilled salmon, lamb loin chops, porterhouse steak, baby back ribs, Long Island duck breast, and tenderloin of beef. Entrées are all served with a choice of mashed red-skin potatoes, baked sweet potato, or a rice blend and a vegetable. The new Boathouse was an instant success with the locals and is now attracting discriminating diners from all over the Litchfield Hills. $15–32.

Morgan's Grill and Café at the Interlaken Inn (860-435-9878), CT 112, Lakeville. Open daily except a few holidays; call for hours. Dine overlooking flower beds and artfully landscaped grounds. Chef Vick Beni and his talented staff know how to cut a Black Angus to serve you the most tender steaks, and they do wonders with seafood. The listing of hors d'oeuvres, from butternut bisque to lentil sausage soup, is longer than the menus in most other restaurants. Though Morgan's is self-styled as a "country kitchen," you can dine on such un-country items as a complete Tex-Mex array of foods. The inn (see *Lodging*) also serves house guests and visitors in a penthouse dining room with a fabulous view of the twin lakes. $16–26.

♿ **Pastorale Bistro & Bar** (860-435-1011; www.pastoralebistro.com), 223 Main St., Lakeville. Open for dinner Tue.–Sat.; Sun. lunch and dinner combinations; closed Mon. This relative newcomer to the charming village of Lakeville has the reservation phone bouncing off the hook. The first floor of this 18th-century house has a sophisticated bar—no loud singing or waving steins of beer—and a dining area. The main dining room on the second floor tempts with such specialties as curried carrot and yogurt soup, the house Caesar salad, ahi tuna, and a grilled prime soft-shell crab, to mention only a few items listed on the menu. The chef, Frederic Faveau, should be familiar to Litchfield Hills gourmets from his years masterminding inn kitchens on the shores of Lake Waramaug. And we discovered a dish here that can employ the lemongrass we've been growing all summer: ginger-lemongrass crème brûlée. Wheelchair accessible only to the first floor. Entrées $9.50–18.

China Inn (860-435-6888), 343 Main St., Lakeville. Open daily, Mon.–Thu. 11 AM–10:30 PM; till 11:30 PM on weekends. Standard Chinese fare, fresh food well prepared to your order in a neat dining room with attentive, friendly wait staff. No surprises; a family restaurant offering a satisfying lunch or a comfortable evening out with a familiar menu. $8–12.

In Winsted

The Tributary (860-379-7679), 19 Rowley St. This renovated 1860s warehouse sits on the banks of the Mad River, just off Main Street. Open Tue.–Sun. for lunch and dinner. Reservations are suggested. Awards for its fresh seafood since 1979 have made The Tributary one of the most popular restaurants in northwestern Connecticut. Usually a fresh-grilled fish highlights the three daily specials; or choose fresh veal, chicken, beef, or a vegetarian dish from the full menu. Children's menu. Chocolate cakes, pies, and bread puddings flow from the in-house oven, along with seasonal fruit breads and low-fat options. $15.95–21.95 includes salad, bread, vegetable, and starch.

In Riverton

Sweet Pea's Restaurant, Antique Gallery and Catering (860-379-7020), 6 Riverton Rd. Open year-round for lunch and dinner; on Sun., open only 2:30–8; closed Mon. It's no joke when the waiter asks if you want to start lunch or dinner with fried spinach. Fried what? It's a light, crispy delight, and you'll be asking for the recipe. If you are wondering what happened to the Yellow Victorian restaurant, this is it. Same house, new owners, new approach to gourmet food. For the appetizer, choose the pan-seared Maryland crabcakes. There's a soup of the day, but there's also always French onion soup for $8.95. The dinner entrées run the gamut from shrimp, tuna, and grilled rack of lamb to Steak in the Grass (a center-cut filet mignon served with frizzled onions, whipped potatoes, and veggies). That will relieve your wallet of $22.95. Riverton is one of the state's prettiest towns, bordering the Farmington River.

In Torrington

The Venetian (860-489-8592), 52 East Main St. (US 202). Open year-round 11–10, except Sun. noon–9; closed Tue. Genial host Michael DiIullo greets visitors in what is arguably the county's temple of Italian cuisine. That said, if you tend to go out of your way for thick, juicy lamb chops, this is the place. For years, the house salad dressing was a well-kept secret; now you can pick up a bottle, along with other homemade foods, on the way out after your meal. If you give credence to current medical advice about garlic, the Venetian's linguine with white clam sauce affords a month's ration of the heart-sustaining bulb of believers, mostly Italian. Fresh seafood daily. Veal and chicken specialties. Rum cake. All this and the friendliest waitresses in town. $12.50–26.

Marino's Restaurant (860-482-6864), 12 Pinewoods Rd. Open for lunch and dinner; closed Sun. Family restaurant serving Old World Italian cuisine for nearly 50 years, including

SWEET PEA'S RESTAURANT IN RIVERTON IS IN A LOVELY VICTORIAN HOME.

Barnett D. Laschever

fresh seafood and chicken. Wood-grilled steaks and chops, veal entrées, and the whole gamut of pasta dishes. Regulars boast of the Italian pastries and the authentic cappuccinos and espressos. Bring the kids; they get special attention. $16.

In Watertown

Golden Palace (860-274-6779), 544 Straits Turnpike. Open daily. Well-prepared favorites from two of China's classic cuisines: the better-known Cantonese and the more highly spiced Szechuan. The chef also recommends Polynesian duck, and chicken fingers fried in egg batter on a bed of vegetables. Pleasant Old World atmosphere. $14.50.

In Waterbury

Diorio Restaurant and Bar (203-754-5111), 231 Bank St. Open Mon.–Fri. for lunch 11:30–2:30; dinner 5:30–9 or 10; Sat. for dinner only; closed Sun. Italian and Greek cooking combined with a happy hour make dining here a very pleasant experience. Linguine topped with fish in a red sauce and ravioli with vegetable fillings give you an idea of the pasta treats that await you. Veal is a favorite. Pasta dishes $16.95–25.95; meat dishes $17–31.95.

♿ **Drescher's** (203-573-1743), 25 Leavenworth St. Open for lunch and dinner; closed Sun. A venerable eatery that has been pleasing local and visiting palates since 1868, which makes it older than probably half the states in the Union. High, old-fashioned metal ceiling; polished wooden bar. Vintage photographs on the walls tell the story of Waterbury. The menu offers a wide array of Italian and American dishes such as shrimp with fettuccine, grilled chicken, veal, and lobster combinations. And as befitting its name and origin, German entrées: sauerbraten, Wiener schnitzel, beef goulash, and

Barnett D. Laschever

THE VENETIAN MAY BE THE COUNTY'S TEMPLE OF ITALIAN CUISINE.

stuffed pork chops—surprisingly not up to the standards you'd expect in an eatery of Teutonic origin. Daily specials. $13.95–18.95.

Carmen Anthony Steakhouse (203-767-3040), 496 Chase Ave. An upscale chain of steak houses (and fish restaurants), with outlets in Woodbury and throughout the state. In Waterbury, open for lunch Mon.–Fri.; dinner Mon.–Sat., and on Sun. 4–9. In the steak houses, the emphasis, naturally, is on thick Black Angus steaks, but the seafood menu is just as tempting; ditto in the fish houses. Mr. Anthony's sophisticated guests can also choose from a nearly endless variety of wines. Devoted guests order the crabcakes and the clam chowder without looking at the menu. $16.

EATING OUT

In Litchfield

D'Amico's Pizzeria (860-567-1754), CT 202; Village Green (aka Dunkin' Donuts Plaza). Open Tue.–Thu. 11–8; Fri. and Sat. 11–10; Sun. 3–8. To his wife and four children, Signore D'Amico is Gioso. To his new patrons and friends, he's Joe. A former consultant to computer wizards, Joe found good reason in the recent past to choose a new avocation. He opted for Litchfield's first pizzeria. Not a restaurant that also serves pizza, but a pizzeria that prepares and serves almost only pizza from scratch. He throws the round dough in the air in full view of diners, smooths out the disk of dough, decorates it with sauce and toppings, and slips it into a superheated oven. Opened in the winter of 2005, D'Amico's is becoming a cult. While pizza here is king, New York–style thin crust with your choice of toppings, Joe accommodates non-pizza folk with three choices of grinders, stuffed breads, and a few salads. Joe's wife, Mary Ellen, was the inspiration for the career change, and she's on hand to

DRESCHER'S RESTAURANT HAS BEEN FEEDING FOLKS IN WATERBURY FOR MORE THAN A CENTURY. SAUERBRATEN IS A SPECIALTY.

Barnett D. Laschever

serve and chat with the guests. The decor is decidedly muted: plain-colored walls, no clichéd murals of Mount Vesuvius doing its thing. $6.75–19.

Kawasaki Japanese Restaurant (860-361-6142), 8 Village Green, US 202. Open Mon.–Thu. 11–10, Fri. and Sat. till 10:30; Sun. 2–10. The venerable Ming's Chinese restaurant has finally thrown in the hot towel and left Litchfield without one eatery from the Middle Kingdom. But the Japanese have taken their place. The formerly dull interior has been rearranged and redecorated—and it's like stepping into an upscale fantasyland. Main attractions are the sushi bar and hibachi dinners. Or you can order yaki soban/udon, sashimi, soups, salads, hot noodles, and other hot appetizers. It's like going to Manhattan without the drive. Hibachi dinners range from $15 for chicken to $18 for steak or shrimp.

Common Ground Café and Tea House (201-5138), 250 West St., Litchfield. Open Mon.–Sat. at 6 AM, Sun. at 7 AM. When it first opened, this comfortable teahouse—which suggests the ambience of Vienna's formerly famous coffeehouses—was playing hide-and-seek with its patrons with no sign in front. It is attached to but directly *behind* a relatively new, big Irving gas station. Drive around to the back; there's plenty of parking. You can relax at comfortable small tables or take out specialty coffee, tea, smoothies for breakfast and lunch. A different pot of soup simmers daily. Pastries you can't resist and paninis, gelato, and gift baskets. Wireless.

Hibachi Steak House Sushi & Liquor Bar ((860-482-9308), 1883 East Main St. (US 202), Torrington. Lunch and dinner Mon.–Sat. 11:30 AM–11 PM. Chinese eateries are no novelty; Japanese flashing blades that end with the cook picking up a piece of cooked food off the big table hot plate and sailing it in an arc right over into your mouth is new, and a fun experience. Or you can sneak into a booth and order off a menu that includes steaks, seafood, a variety of vegetables, and great sushi. And all with a happy smile. $12–30.

Stefano's Pizzeria (860-567-2556), 490 Bantam Rd. (CT 202). Open for lunch and dinner daily. And another pizza vendor has joined the ranks of Italian eateries that have diluted (in a nice way) the colonial ambience of Litchfield. Wide, smart dining room with no frills. Full range of the pizza and grinder specialties you would expect, plus cannelloni and other dishes that fill the tummy. Reasonable prices.

DiFranco's Restaurant and Pizzeria (860-567-8872), 19 West St.; on the Litchfield green. Open daily 10:30 AM–11 PM. A popular family restaurant, in the center of the village, that doesn't pretend to be anything but a satellite of Naples in a colonial setting. The decor needs updating, but the food is good and plentiful. Most of the entrées—veal, chicken, and seafood—are sautéed or fried. The pasta dishes are particularly flavorful. Ample children's menu. $5.50–16.

Cinema Cafe (860-567-3282), 8 Village Green Dr. (US 202). A theme delicatessen for visitors and locals who want a quick lunch (but not fast food) or early supper. Open Mon.–Fri. 10–7, Sat. 10–4. There is no cinema in town, so this inauspicious luncheonette shows classic movies on a TV monitor. The menu has expanded, and the wide variety of deli sandwiches, soups, and salads makes this an ideal stopover for the family. The "Now Playing" theme sandwiches run the gamut, from the Ten Commandments (corned beef with melted Swiss) to the Godfather (prosciutto, *capicolo*, and provolone topped with veggies). $4.50–7.95.

Señor Pancho's (860-567-3663), 7 Village Green Dr. (off US 202). Open daily for lunch and dinner. A Mexican eatery that wasn't quite up to par has been replaced by a Mexican family restaurant that has won the approval of the locals. Most entrées still bear a strong resemblance to the standard fare of a good Tex-Mex joint, from tacos to tamales; but several authentic Mexican specialties also are on the menu, including grilled chicken and beef bare of heavy layers of melted cheese. The decor is bright and colorful, and a live mariachi band will serenade you at your table Thu.–Sun. evenings. Look for the Double X—as in Dos Equis, for Mexico's premier beer—neon sign in the window. September 15, Mexican Independence, is always celebrated with a bang. $8–16.

In Torrington

In addition to the eateries described below, visitors with children in tow should know that Torrington now has several chain restaurants where the service is fast and the food predictable. Entering town from the east on East Main St., you will find a bustling **Applebee's** (860-489-8690). Across the street is a **Wendy's**, whose salads and chili make for an inexpensive meal. **Twin Colony Restaurant and Diner** (860-482-5346), 417 East Elm St., is open 24 hours and serves mammoth portions of pasta, meat dishes, Greek specialties, and great salads. It's packed Sunday morning when the churches let out and parishioners scramble in for the incomparable pancakes. Breakfast 24 hours. Senior discount. **Ninety Nine** occupies the midtown restaurant space vacated when Red Lobster picked up its aquariums and swam away. Among the ubiquitous pizza parlors, the **Berkshire**

Barnett D. Laschever

GRAND MANSIONS ON NORTH STREET IN LITCHFIELD EXPANDED, BACKWARD, AS THE FAMILIES WHO LIVED IN THEM GREW AND SET UP HOUSEKEEPING WITH THEIR PARENTS.

Café (860-489-0600), 71 Albert St., has been serving grinders and pizzas to appreciative Torringtonians and visitors for 30 years. It has an old-Irish-pub ambience and an exuberant crowd. If you can't get into the highly regarded Venetian restaurant (see *Dining Out*) in the center of town, try **Dick's** (860-489-7917) or **Bachi's** (860-482-9508), sitting close by on East Main St. **Two Guys Pizza** (860-482-3318), opposite the police station in an unprepossessing store, puts together our favorite Genoa salami grinders. And if you are desperate for a caffeine fix, the city (and all of New England) has more than its share of **Dunkin' Donuts**. (There's even one in Litchfield!)

Northern Galapagos (860-795-0030), 281 Winsted Rd., Torrington. South American fare mixed with traditional American food. Specialties include braised monkfish in a tomato and saffron-lime broth, served with rice and vegetables ($14), and the Galapagos combo—chicken cordon bleu or pan-seared salmon with a peppercorn cream sauce ($15). Other exotics crowd the menu. Interesting breakfast choices. $9–24.

George's Restaurant (860-626-1512), 1203 East Main St. (US 202). Open Tue.–Fri. 6:30 AM–3 PM; Sat. to 1 PM; Sun. 7 AM–noon; closed Mon. Killer breakfasts. A variety of fresh salads, some with fruit, others with chicken, tuna, or crab. All served with pita bread. Big burgers, plain and garnished. Yummy sandwiches. Very safe environment: In addition to attracting town office workers and shopkeepers, it's the favorite eatery of Torrington's police officers and firefighters.

Moon Star Chinese (860-489-8225), Stop & Shop mall, High St. Typically we have not urged readers to "Explore" a Chinese take-out restaurant; however, Moon Star has won enough plaudits from folks who claim this is the best Chinese food they've enjoyed almost anywhere. We agree. We take out, or occasionally eat at one of the five tables. If you eat in, be advised: You'll watch a parade of "Taker Outers" who have phoned in their orders. Steamed specialties if you are on a fat-free diet. Agreeable prices.

We would be remiss if we didn't mention that Chinese food has won a wide following in Torrington. In addition to Moon Star there are now two big **Chinese buffet restaurants**, located on either side of Kmart in the Kmart Plaza. Frequent guests suggest visiting on weekends, when the trays turn over faster—so the food is fresher and hotter.

✐ **Cristy's** (860-496-7330), 545 Winsted Rd. (Old CT 8). Open Tue.–Thu. 7:30 AM–9 PM; Fri.–Sun. to 9:30 PM; closed Mon. Conveniently located in the north end of town across from a major shopping center. A roadside restaurant with faux wood paneling and comfortable booths, Cristy's is a cut above the typical family eatery. The lavish menu runs the gamut from specialty salads such as the California (three garden greens, mandarin oranges, walnuts, and cukes) to "Extraordinary Sandwiches." How about Hot Turkey Supreme? Pastas, burgers, grinders, and a typical children's menu round out your choices. Easy on the pocketbook: $5.75–12.

Cambridge House Brew Pub, 84 Main St. On the second floor of a new addition to the Warner Theater. The longtime Mertz Department store, where everyone in Torrington shopped before the "boxes" were planted on the east end of town, is enjoying a rebirth. Now attached to the Warner, the insides of old Mertz have been ripped out and replaced by an exhibition hall, a small theater on the first floor, and the Brew Pub on the second. Yes, pizzas are mentioned on the menu, but only in passing. You'll want to nosh on the spinach, cheese, and artichoke dip, the pulled pork sliders, or the stout chicken quesadilla. An ale chili highlights the soup section; then you are on to to specialty salads and finally the CBH Classics: five varieties of burgers, stout steak, beer battered fish-and-chips or lobster macaroni-and-cheese. Great place to catch a quick meal before a Warner show. CBH is a welcome addition to a town where pizzerias have ruled! $2.99–7.99.

Prime Steak & Seaford (860-202-4646; www.primesteakandseafood.com), 1435 East Main St. Open Tue.–Thu. 5–9, Fri. and Sat. 5–10. Good news: Here's another new entry in the Pizza NIMBY category. Start with shrimp and mussels, or with a few specialty pastas. The turf department has already won raves from the Big City (read: Hartford) foodies. Bring a big appetite for the 12-ounce New York steak with three rubs. Rib eyes are honored with a seven-spice rub, as are the Angus filet and boneless center-cut pork chops. Swordfish, diver scallops, and salmon Cajun-style highlight the surf menu. What's in the spice rubs? Chef's secret. Nightly specials. Bring the family. Appetizers $9, steaks $19–34, other entrées $16.

In Waterbury

Tower Grill (203-753-0522), 185 Freight St. Celebrating its 50th anniversary, Tower Grill dates from the days when diners were ubiquitous and open 24 hours a day. It still has a loyal clientele for early breakfast starting at 6 and lunch ending at 3 on weekdays, 2 on Sat., and 1 on Sun. The menu has barely changed over time. Coffee is king throughout the day, along with juicy hamburgers, mashed potatoes, and chicken salad sandwiches. The neighborhood is old industrial, but the wife and son of the founder are on hand to tend the grill and welcome you with classic comfort food.

Elsewhere

Jesse Camille's Restaurant (203-723-2275; fax: 203-723-1052), 615

North Church St. (CT 63), Naugatuck. Open daily for lunch and dinner. Overlooks Hop Brook Golf Course. Attractive family-owned Italian eatery with outdoor covered deck and spacious indoor dining room. Extensive menu, from classic Caesar salad, antipasto, chicken cordon bleu, prime rib, and scrod Française to typical European desserts of fresh fruit and cheese. The special meat loaf will remind of Mama's and the fish-and-chips, your first trip to London Town. There's also a variety of pastas and sandwiches to make this a complete dining experience. You'll recall meals you've had in the Old Country, if you have been fortunate enough to have included Italy as one of your vacation destinations. $17.

Painted Pony (203-266-5771), CT 61, Bethlehem. Open daily 11–11. This inauspicious eatery in the center of a sleepy colonial town should be approached with caution: Eat lightly the day before—portions are enormous. Would you believe a baked potato the size of a small football, fillets of sole that cover a huge platter, 20-ounce prime ribs? Oh, if you insist, you can order a 12-ounce cut. Pastas, chicken, and seafood round out the menu. Happily, all this food is expertly prepared. But be ready to take home a doggie bag. Salads are a nice mix of greens, onions, and peppers. Scrumptious desserts in the event there's still room in your tummy. Children's menu. $15–20.

♿ **Wood's Pit B.B.Q. and Mexican Café** (860-567-9869), 123 Bantam Lake Rd. (CT 209), next to the Bantam Cinema, in Bantam. Open for lunch and dinner, Mon.–Fri. and Sun. 11:30–9; Sat. until 10. In the extensive menu that samples the cattle ranges of Mexico and the Southwest, owner-chef Paul Haas takes pains to warn that outdoor "grilling New England–style" is not the same as Texas barbecuing, which is the very slow cooking of meat. (He explained that until southern and western barbecue chefs set up their wood-burning ovens in the region, "You Yankees threw some meat on an open grill, drizzled on barbecue sauce from a bottle, and called it barbecue!") The results speak for themselves: Wood's pulled pork sandwich is a classic. Choose from a variety of other sandwiches or platters. A full-service restaurant, Wood's also offers great catfish, crabcakes, and fish specials on Friday night. White shrimp pizzas and smoked chicken Caesar salads are popular. Mexican, Canadian, and Dutch beers. Shelves on the walls are lined with 50 bottles of varying hot sauces! Sandwiches $6.50; entrées $10–25, $15–32 for two, for the sampler ribs. A family place.

Bantam Pizza (860-567-3357), US 202; in the center of Bantam. Open for lunch and dinner daily until 10. The Greek families that operate this small pizza house have one aim: please the guest. Their pizzas rank with the best in the state; roast half chicken, pasta dinners, and grinders will make you a confirmed client. Friendly waitresses. The tossed dinner salad is a favorite, while others swear by the Greek salad topped with creamy feta cheese. $4–12.

Jackie's (860-567-0770), 920 Bantam Rd. (US 202), Bantam. Open Mon.–Wed. 6 AM–2 PM; Thu.–Sat. 6 AM–9 PM; Sun. 7 AM–3 PM. Family-oriented restaurant with old-fashioned home cooking. Good stop for the usual breakfast or lunch favorites, with dinner options ranging from steak to homemade Italian specialties. Check out the dinner specials. The prices are reasonable; the portions tend to be hefty. $2.95–18.95.

Salsa (860-350-0701), 54 Railroad St., New Milford. Open for lunch and dinner Tue.–Sat.; Sun. dinner only; closed Mon. A southwestern restaurant with authentic regional specialties developed by chef-owner Bill Thomas. Choice of four homemade salsas served with warm tortilla chips, overstuffed burritos smothered in red or green chile sauce, fajitas in a special marinade, soups and tangy salads, classic huevos rancheros. Kids' plates. Moderate prices.

The Upper Crust (860-350-0006), 373 Litchfield Rd. (US 202), Northville. Open daily noon–9; Fri. and Sat. to 10. In a vintage home perched on an uprise, The Upper Crust is carrying on the tradition of Carole Peck (see *Dining Out*), who made her reputation here before moving to larger quarters in Woodbury. The emphasis is on specialty pizzas that would be completely unrecognizable in Naples, the birthplace of pizza. You can ask for almost any topping, from figs to Gorgonzola. Dinner plates, and salads with homemade dressings. $10–17.

Caralee's (860-927-1555), 28 North Main St. (US 7), Kent. Open for breakfast and lunch. The ambience can only be described as "crowded and busy." Caralee's popularity rests on the variety and virility of its sandwiches, bagels, burgers, and croissants. The chili burger is topped with cheddar cheese, chili, and sour cream. House specialty sandwiches run from deli combinations, wraps, and quesadillas, to ingenious salads, and much more. Half sandwiches for the youngsters. For locals, it's the "breakfast place." And Caralee's will do almost anything with an egg except give you an egg shampoo. $4–11.

Higby's Family Restaurant (860-824-4440), 85 Main St., Canaan 06018. Mon.–Tue. and Thu.–Sat., lunch and dinner until 9 or 10; Sun. 11:30–8, brunch 11:30–4:30. Closed Wed. Traditional menu in a neat restaurant established in 2008 by Barb and Charlie Sherman. Seared scallions with soy, ginger, and Thai chile drizzle is a surprise appetizer. Soups include cheddar-topped chili. Caesar salad or mixed greens with a choice of grilled chicken breast or shrimp. For lunch try the Berkshire Blue, an Angus burger topped with melted blue cheese and caramelized onions. As popular food traveler Rachael Ray would say, "Yummy." Our favorite appetizer: potato-wrapped shrimp! Kid-friendly with a healthy choice of fruit. More than affordable: a grilled New York strip steak with baked potato and vegetables runs $17.

Chaiwalla (860-435-9758), Main St., Salisbury. Open 10–6, daily in summer; Wed.–Sun. in the off-season—except March, when it's closed. Owner Mary O'Brien has gathered unblended teas from around the world for sale in, what else, the tearoom. Homemade soup, exotic sandwiches, tomato pie, crumpets, and scones. Moderate prices.

Log House Restaurant (860-379-8937), US 44, Barkhamsted. Open daily, starting with breakfast at 6 and serving dinner until 9:15; Sun., open 7 AM–8:15 PM. Antlers on the wall, rustic furniture, a fast-food counter, and two spacious dining rooms, plus an all-American menu, make this one of the most popular roadside eateries on the Albany Turnpike. Specialties range from corned beef or turkey-pastrami Reuben sandwiches to Yankee pot roast, and from seafood specials, steaks, and chops to grinders and ubiquitous pasta dishes. And the most you can spend on an entrée is $15, except for the Alaskan king crab legs, which are priced to market. A favorite with traveling families.

Monaco's Ristorante (860-379-6648), 380 Main St., Winsted. Open for lunch and dinner; closed Mon. and Tue. Don't pass up this ordinary-looking storefront restaurant; it was the favorite of former governor Lowell Weicker and his wife, Claudia. They made the trip out from Hartford for the ziti in cognac sauce. Spaghetti puttanesca is another specialty among the pasta favorites. Mingle with the locals at the popular bar. Dinner $13–20.

Collin's Diner (860-824-7040), US 44, Canaan. Extended hours. Full breakfast is served all day. One of five classic diners in the United States to be listed on the National Register of Historic Places. Traditional, down-to-earth American food: thick steaks, juicy burgers, shrimp, meat loaf with rich mashed potatoes. An MIT geology professor has been trying for years, in vain, to buy the marble countertop streaked with fossils. Diner prices.

The Pantry (860-868-0258), 5 Titus Rd., Washington Depot. Just behind The Hickory Stick Bookshop. An eclectic mix of yummy sandwiches, unique salads, and exotic soups served beneath walls hung with kitchen accessories. Once a favorite of travelers looking for an inexpensive lunch. No more. Sandwiches average $12. The trinkets are even more expensive. But The Pantry is a refuge for the well heeled, and tables are mostly filled with groups of handsome, well-dressed women.

ICE CREAM AND CANDY It seems hard to believe, but it appears that some of the folks in Litchfield have just discovered ice cream. But then there's Popey's, the pioneer. Read on.

🖉 ♿ **Popey's Ice Cream Shoppe**, at the junction of CT 61 and CT 109, Morris. Open daily, Mar. 15–Oct. 10, for lunch and dinner. When the kids' tummies are growling after a day of swimming and boating at nearby Bantam Lake or Mount Tom State Park, this is the place to stuff them with bulging burgers and fries, clams, sandwiches, ice cream, and ice cream cakes. The ice cream is a better choice than the clams. A popular Litchfield Hills pit stop for nearly half a century.

In addition to the well-known creameries listed below, the quiet village of Goshen recently saw its first ice cream parlor, **Nellies** (860-491-2222), on CT 4 just east of the traffic roundabout. It's popular with residents and folks driving one way or the other on the busy state road. Open generally Memorial Day–Labor Day.

Panini Café & Gelateria (860-927-5083), 7 Old Barn Rd., Kent (CT 341); in the Village Barn Shops, back off the road. Open daily 7 AM–8 PM Memorial Day–Labor Day; 8–6 the rest of the year; closed Easter, Thanksgiving, Christmas, and New Year's Day. Anne McAndrew and Dave Fairty, the owners, daily concoct trays of authentic Italian gelato, denser than American ice cream and, so its devotees say, more flavorful. Starting at 7 AM, the café also serves bagelinis at breakfast; salads and a variety of other sandwiches are offered until closing. Rosemary Brennan, the gelato maven, was trained in the art of making these Italian delicacies and immediately won the hearts and stomachs of residents, Kent School students, and tourists. From $2.50 for a single serving to $20 for a half gallon.

Peaches 'n Cream (860-496-7536), US 202, Litchfield. Open year-round. Well into the evening this parlor, located in an unpretentious building on the eastern outskirts of Litchfield, dishes up 50 flavors of rich, luscious ice cream concoctions—cones, sodas, sundaes, ice cream bars, ice cream cakes, milk shakes, banana splits. Also yogurt, and sugar- and fat-free desserts. Indoor and outdoor tables.

Litchfield Candy Company (860-567-1500), 245 West St. (US 202), Litchfield; next to Señor Pancho's Mexican restaurant. Open daily 10–6, except Sun. at 11; and Sat., when it closes at 7. A deluxe candy store offering special handmade truffles. Large assortment of candies from the prestigious Sweet Shop of Dallas, Texas. Also a complete line of sugar-free candies. (The only other candy available in Litchfield is in limited quantities at **Murphy's Drug** and two large box pharmacies.) (See also Belgique Pâtisserie Chocolatier, in Kent, under *Selective Shopping.*)

SNACKS **Stroble Baking Co.** (860-927-4073), 14 North Main St., Kent. Open daily 8–6. Famed far and wide for its fresh breads, pastries, scones, and cakes, but this is more than an exemplary bakery. You may be standing next to or in line behind one of the local artists waiting for a slice of quiche or one of Patsy Stroble's salads or sandwiches that will handily handle your lunch. Friendly patio with six tables for people-watching in-season. Indoors, only one small table. Every town should have a Stroble's.

Gooseboro Drive-In (860-567-9356), 1293 Bantam Rd. (US 202), Bantam 06750. Housebound residents in the Litchfield Hills know that winter has beat its last retreat when this popular snack bar opens on April 1. Hours are 11–9 seven days a week during the busy spring and summer season. It generally closes 7 or 8 in autumn when business falls off, and then pulls down the shutters at the end of October. Order inside but eat outside at picnic benches—or take out and enjoy great hot dogs and hamburgers with a variety of spices at nearby Mount Tom Beach or Lake Waramaug State Park. Equally popular are the fried seafood baskets. Finish off your picnic with ice cream that complements the delicious dogs.

✷ Entertainment

MUSIC AND THEATER **Warner Theatre** (860-489-7180), 68 Main St., in the heart of Torrington. Open year-round. One of the state's few remaining grand old art deco movie theaters. A $2 million restoration was completed in 2003. Showcases Broadway musicals, top solo artists, and the internationally renowned local Nutmeg Ballet.

Palace Theater (203-755-4700), 100 East Main St., Waterbury. Open year-round, this 1920 Renaissance Revival theater sparked a cultural revolution in midtown after undergoing a massive and extremely expensive renovation—from the top of the ceiling to all-new, comfortable seats—supported by state and foundation funds. Broadway's best and America's newest and oldest offerings in entertainment, classic and popular, are showcased here.

Thomaston Opera House (860-283-6250), Main St., Thomaston. Open year-round. A classic community opera house, once slated for the wrecking ball but restored by state and local funding. Family fare, highlighting seasonal holidays, with local and traveling drama troupes.

Litchfield Performing Arts (860-567-4162). A homegrown management group, without a theater of its own, that stages classical music series, piano competitions, selected readings, jazz, and a variety of outreach cultural programs in regional theaters, auditoriums, schools, and churches.

Litchfield Jazz Festival (860-567-4162). After many years on the Goshen Fairgrounds, the festival and its

Barnett D. Laschever

THE COUNTY COURTHOUSE ON THE GREEN IS A LITCHFIELD LANDMARK.

adjunct summer jazz camp have moved to the grounds and buildings of the Kent Preparatory School in Kent. The three-day festival presents America's top jazz artists. Among recent headliners were the legendary Dave Brubeck and Nicholas Payton's big band in a Louis Armstrong Centennial Celebration. Performances are under a tent. Or you can enjoy the music while sitting on a blanket on the lawn. Gourmet food vendors. Ranked with the Newport Jazz Festival. Sponsored by Litchfield Performing Arts.

Norfolk Music Festival (860-542-3000), US 44 and CT 272, Norfolk. What Tanglewood is to the Berkshires, Norfolk is to the Litchfield Hills, with a few differences: size and the scope of music. Where 25,000 souls can crowd the lawn in front of the Tanglewood Shed, the Music Shed at Norfolk entertains only 1,000 music lovers. And here the repertoire is limited to chamber music, an annual choral concert, and an occasional jazz concert. The Music Shed, an acoustically superb hall lined with redwood from California, was built in 1906. Prior to that, Ellen Battell Stoeckel and her husband, Carl, held musical gatherings in Whitehouse, their estate's 35-room mansion. They brought to Norfolk on specially chartered trains such luminaries as Fritz Kreisler, Rachmaninoff, Caruso, Paderewski, and violinist Efrem Zimbalist and his wife, Metropolitan Opera star Alma Gluck (cousins of one of the authors of this book). Jean Sibelius made his only visit to the United States in 1914 at the request of the Stoeckels and, while a guest at Whitehouse, composed his tone poem *The Oceansides.* In 2005 the estate was left to the Yale University Summer School of Music, which now sponsors chamber music, jazz, and choral music concerts from June to August. Concertgoers enjoy picnic suppers on tree-shaded grounds beside a gurgling brook.

Music Mountain (860-824-7126), Falls Village off US 7. From June to early September, 16 string quartet concerts are presented in the oldest continuing summer chamber music festival in the country, in a specially designed hall (air-conditioned at long last). U.S. and international artists are featured; Saturday-night jazz festivals. Picnic and stroll in the woods on this 120-acre hilltop aerie. Take a good look at the houses on the grounds. They were purchased sight unseen years ago through Sears-Roebuck catalogs! These unique architectural oddities now house staff and visitors. Concerts are broadcast on 125 American stations and over the air in 35 other countries. $25 for single weekend seats; discounts for students and lawn seating.

Tri-Arts Sharon Playhouse (860-364-6066), CT 343, just west of the center of the village of Sharon. Summer season of Broadway family musicals are staged in a revitalized and renovated traditional summer theater. Children's theater series, live one-hour musicals in the morning and early afternoon, and a theater workshop for youngsters. $18–22.

The Nutmeg Conservatory for the Arts in downtown Torrington has a worldwide reputation for developing top performers. Nutmeg's ballet dancers, trained under the overall direction of Sharon Dante, have won international competitions and have been invited to join European companies. A state-of-the-art addition to a historic building has provided the Nutmeg with more dance rooms, and facilities to also offer instrumental training. Dormitories house dancers enrolled in the summer program. Watch local papers for performances. At Christmas, folks from near and far gather to see the Nutmeg's acclaimed *Nutcracker Suite* in the art deco Warner Theatre.

In addition, the Litchfield Hills are alive with the declamations of amateur actors, expressing themselves year-round in a variety of local theater groups. The **Goshen Players**, with year-round offerings of Broadway musical and plays, is the granddaddy of the area's thespian groups. **Seven Angels** brings top theatricals to Waterbury most of the year. Check listings in local papers for current offerings.

Litchfield Community Center (860-567-8302; www.thecommunitycenter.org), 421 Bantam Rd. (US 202); just southwest of the historic borough. A combined effort by most of the folks in Litchfield, from the moneyed rich to craftspeople, yielded gifts of land, money, and architectural designs to produce a clean, white building that offers myriad activities. You can take a class in watercolor, tai chi, or yoga; watch a movie; listen to lectures; get married; or give blood to the Red Cross. Free admission to most activities; some fees. Everyone is welcome.

✷ Selective Shopping

THE "VILLAGE GREEN" SHOPPING CENTER Before we share with you the plethora of antiques shops in the northwest corner, a word about a recent development on the edges of the historic borough. A fairly sizable tract of land between the elementary school and Stop & Shop supermarket, lying fallow for many years, was bought at the end of the last millennium. The bulldozers followed, and two mini shopping centers greet visitors to Litchfield coming in from the west. The buildings, all commercial, have been covered with early American siding.

Signs carry either the words THE LITCHFIELD COMMONS, or THE VILLAGE GREEN. Not true. The real Litchfield green/commons is more than 100 yards farther up the road. Some of the entrepreneurs even give their address as Litchfield Plaza. All in the same complex and with made-up names. Locals are now advising visitors who are looking for an address in either section to go to "Dunkin' Donuts Plaza"!

But to show the reader that we are aware of this not-very-welcome addition to the town—but aren't really mad—let us list what you will find in the Green, aka the Commons, aka the Plaza:

Litchfield Saltwater Grille, **Robertson Jewellers**, **Headlines Hair Salon**, a radio station, a state office, a liquor store, **Dunkin' Donuts**, **Señor Pancho's**, **Cinema Cafe** (a luncheonette), and the **Kawasaki Japanese Restaurant**. Stores come and go, so we lay down no warranty that any of the above will be there when you arrive.

ANTIQUES SHOPS What cars are to Detroit, jetliners are to Seattle, and jazz is to New Orleans, antiques are to the Litchfield area. New Preston was once a sleepy little town whose grocery store served summer residents and campers on nearby Lake Waramaug. Today it is a major antiques center, with 10 dealers offering everything from kerosene lamps to Native American rugs from Santa Fe. All are on CT 45 (Main St.), off US 202. Woodbury has long held the title of "antiques capital" of the state, but in recent years antiques dealers have opened shops in almost every village and town, including Norwalk, the Bantam section of Litchfield, and clear across the state in the Quiet Corner, particularly in Putnam and Pomfret Center. Herewith, we offer only a selection. Have fun and explore others on your own.

In and around Litchfield

Tillou Antiques (860-567-9693), 39 West St. on the Litchfield green, Litchfield. Open Mon. and Wed.–Sat., 10:30–5; Sun. 11–4:30. Rare, quality 18th- and 19th-century American antiques are gathered for connoisseurs who prize authenticity above all else. Paintings, furniture, dinnerware, decorative art, clothing, and accessories are displayed on three floors.

Lindsley Antiques (860-567-4245; 800-572-2360; www.homepagemac.com/linsleyantiques), 725 Bantam Rd. (US 202), Bantam. Open daily 11–5; closed Wed. Located in a building housing several antiques shops. Featuring an unusual collection of fine English antiques and accessories, some dating from the 16th century.

The Old Carriage Shop Antiques (860-567-3234), 920 Bantam Rd. (US 202), Bantam. Open Wed.–Sun. 11–5. One of the largest antiques centers in the region: Some 20 dealers offer for sale an eclectic array of antiques and collectibles ranging from silver to furniture, from glassware to pottery, mirrors to accessories—and even this guidebook! (If they are out, ask.)

Black Swan Antiques (860-567-4429), 710 Bantam Rd. (US 202), Bantam. Open Thu.–Sun. 11–5. Country English, American, and European furniture from the 17th and 18th centuries crowds the floors of this popular dealer. Specialist in large antique tables. Accessories and prints. There is another outlet in the town of Washington.

Robertson Jewellers (860-567-8486), Litchfield Commons, Litchfield; and 43 Main St., New Milford. Large collection of gems, Waterford crystal, Movado watches, and antique and estate jewelry. The premier jewelry dealers in the Hills. Batteries for your ailing wristwatches.

Les Plaisirs de la Maison (formerly French Country Antiques) (860-567-2555), corner West and Meadow streets, Litchfield; just behind Aspen Garden Restaurant. Open Mon. and Thu.–Sat. 10:30–5:30; Sun. noon–5. Also open by appointment. Features 18th- and 19th-century French country antiques, including pottery, Oriental rugs, paintings and prints, old copper and brass. The shop is small; the selections are choice.

Bradford House Antiques and Lawrence Jeffrey Estate Jewelers (860-567-0951), 33 West St., on the green. Open daily. If you're looking for jewelry for your sweetie, you will find here a large selection of antique, period, and signed jewelry including works by Tiffany, Cartier, et al. Choose fine crystal, porcelain, or objets d'art in the downstairs section of the gallery.

Four Winds, Cultural Antiques (860-567-5607, 931 Bantam Rd. (US 202), in the Old Switch Factory, Bantam. Open Thu.–Sun. 11–5. Other days by chance or appointment. Specializing in rustic Chinese country antiques, but the owners have also collected gifts and accessories from around the world.

In and around Kent

The Bittersweet Shop (860-354-1727), US 7 at the junction of CT 55 south of Kent, Gaylordsville. Open daily noon–6; closed Wed. and holidays. You're certain to find something to your taste. A consortium of 14 dealers who have pooled the choice pieces they've collected in their world travels, from portrait and landscape paintings to prize quilts, along with traditional antique formal and country furniture.

The Village Barn and Gallery (860-868-0501), Main St. (CT 45); off US 202. Closed Tue. and Wed. Their specialty is lighting; and they make as well as repair lighting pieces. If it can't be found in a catalog, they will create it for you.

Foreign Cargo, Main St., Kent. An unbelievable treasure trove of handicrafts, unique clothing—you can stage *Kismet* in your living room—antiques, art, and jewelry collected by the owners during their many years of travel, often in the Far East. Two floors of authentic museum-quality artifacts in a large 19th-century house in the center of town. Husbands be warned: You may have to drag your wife screaming out of this house of too many surprises.

In Woodbury

Woodbury has so many antiques shops that we can give only a sampling here. The bible of the antiques shops is a newspaper, the *Newtown Bee.* Its listings are comprehensive, and it's always on top of the latest news. If you are a fan of *The Antiques Road Show* on public television, you will occasionally see Woodbury experts on the screen, examining and giving their opinion on treasures brought in by the hopeful public.

Monique Shay Antiques and Design (203-263-3186), 920 Main St. (US 6). Open daily. The focus is on country antiques, tables, armoires, chairs, and cupboards from Canada. Six showrooms in a New England barn.

Robert S. Walin American Antiques (203-263-4416), 547 Flanders Rd. Folk art along with 18th- and 19th-century American furniture.

West Country Antiques (203-263-5741), US 6; off Main St. Open Wed.–Sat. 11–5; Sun. noon–5. Two barns bulging with 18th- and 19th-century French and English furniture. Design service available.

Antiques On The Green (203-263-3045, 6 Green Circle, North Green. Open daily by chance or appointment. Formal and country antiques from the late 17th to the early 20th century are attractively displayed in a converted 1823 two-story barn. Silver, china, and other accessories. Licensed firearms liquidator. Depression glass (from the first Great Depression!).

Salisbury

Creative Hands ((860-435-8255),17 Main St., in the Eliza Peet Building. Open Mon.–Sat., 10–5, Sun. 11–4. A not-for-profit gallery celebrating the creativity of local artisans, such as potters, weavers of sweaters, quilt makers, soap makers, card makers, jewelry makers, and others who produce works of arts with their hands. Changing assortments and monthly exhibits.

Buckley & Buckley, Antiques, c. 1680–1860 (860-435-9919), 84 Main St. Open 10–noon, 2–5, except Tue. and Sun. mornings. The name tells it all. The dealers regularly tour the eastern seaboard and the other early American states seeking treasures of colonial America. They are specialists in William & Mary, country Queen Anne, painted furniture, and paintings and lighting. New collectors, this is the place for you. Teaching you what to look for when shopping for Americana is one of their pleasures. The three-room gallery is a National Historic Site.

John Spencer Antiques (860-435-1099; www.johnspencerantiques.com), 92 Canaan Rd. Open weekends and by appointment. Specialist in American Federal furniture. This is also the gallery where you will find an excellent selection of American 19th- and 20th-century paintings. After 26 years of buying and selling American furniture, you will agree that John Spencer is one of the foremost experts on this genre. Some of the pieces he has acquired are in museum and corporate collections.

Elsewhere

Remember When (860-489-1566), 111 Main St., Torrington. Wed.–Sat. 10:30–6, Sun. noon–5. Two floors of almost anything from the 1920s to the 1950s: jewelry, lamps, linen, furniture, china, pottery. Large selection of lighting fixtures and remnants from estate sales.

Kathy's Cupboard (860-738-7663), 406 Main St., Winsted. Open Wed.–Sun. 10–5, Sat. 10–7. Vintage furniture, including Hitchcock chairs and tables—prized now that the factory has shut down for good—lighting fixtures, and a variety of collectibles.

SPECIALTY STORE In the Silo, in New Milford, in the same complex as the teaching kitchen, is a store still run by the late Skitch Henderson's wife, Ruth. It has a wide variety of premium kitchen utensils and other useful items to make life easier around the house, or around the farm, if you happen to live on one. A new Skitch Henderson Museum is on the premises.

ART GALLERIES **P.S. Gallery** (860-567-1059), West St., on the Litchfield green, Litchfield. Open May–Dec., daily 11–4; weekends off-season. One of the first galleries to feature paintings, sculpture, and prints by Connecticut artists. Changing shows. Watch for the paintings of Richard Derwitch of Torrington. Framing available.

Renaissance Artisan Center (860-567-9894), 387 Torrington Rd. (US 202); just east of the borough, next to the Litchfield Nursery. A variety of art, sculpture, and crafts from all over the country. Classes in all media offered. In a separate section of the building, **Susan Wakeen** now teaches art and sculpture. Noted for her dolls, which she still sells here, she has also achieved a reputation for her portraits.

Artwell Gallery (860-482-5122), 51 Water St., Torrington. Open Thu.–Sun. A well-concocted Russian salad of art exhibits, classes, lectures, poetry readings, and musical and theatrical performances. Check area newspapers for happenings when you're in town.

Bachelier-Cardonsky Art Gallery (860-927-3357), Main St. (US 7), Kent, atop the House of Books. Open Sat. and Sun. 11–5 and by appointment. Contemporary and Connecticut artists displayed in a charming setting. Ranks with the most attractive galleries in New England.

Kent Caboose Gallery (860-927-3357), Kent Station Square, US 7, Kent. Formerly Paris–New York–Kent Gallery. One of New York's foremost furriers, Jacques Kaplan, persuaded by his conservation-minded children to abandon the sale of animal pelts, established an art gallery based in Kent that had an "international reputation." Jacques then persuaded 10 other outstanding artists to set up their easels in Kent, making the town a major art center. Jacques, a decorated fighter in General de Gaulle's Free French Army, died late in 2008. The gallery, in a retired red railroad caboose, fittingly just behind the former railroad station, is still serving artists and art lovers under new owners.

Carol Wallace Fine Art Studio (860-379-4286), 437 Main St., Barkhamsted. Open by appointment. Carol Wallace has achieved a reputation for her watercolor paintings and pen-and-ink sketches of American and regional scenes, particularly landscapes of the Litchfield Hills and the Berkshires. She takes commissions.

ARTISANS **Cornwall Bridge Pottery Store** (860-672-6545), CT 128, West Cornwall. A hop, skip, and jump from the covered bridge that spans the Housatonic. Award-winning pottery designed by Todd Piker and fashioned in his huge Korean kiln down the road. The store also sells works of other local artisans—plates, mugs, tiles and lamps, toys, glassworks, containers for indoor bulbs, and a variety of Australian outerwear.

Ingersoll Cabinetmakers (860-672-6334; www.ianingersoll.com), CT 128, West Cornwall. Ian Ingersoll, son of the late, famed journalist Ralph Ingersoll, meticulously crafts replicas of the famous furniture made in New England and New York in once-thriving Shaker villages. Tables, chairs, and benches, simple but just as functional as the day they were designed. Also in the inventory are sideboards, chests, period chairs, beds, and clocks and grandfather clocks.

Guy Wolff Pottery (860-868-2858), US 202, in the Woodville section of Washington. This talented potter copies the designs of clay flowerpots from 17th- and 18th-century paintings. He also incorporates into his work shards sent to him by archaeologists. He "antiques" the pots with leaf mold and other natural stains. From his "little shop by the road," long a favorite of a select group of local pottery fans, Wolff has been discovered and now has an international clientele. Pots now range from $3 to $5,000! Wolf also has erected a new larger studio.

BOOKSTORES What with superstores and online shopping for books threatening the existence of small independent bookstores, a quiet revolution has taken place. More than 60 Connecticut dealers of antiquarian and used books have taken to cyberspace. Online sales of old rare books now make up half the business of these retailers. One of the most successful in the Litchfield Hills is Bill Goring, who owns **Nutmeg Books** (860-482-9696; www.nutmegbooks.com; 354 New Litchfield St., US 202, Torrington) and says business is booming on the Web. Meanwhile, we also suggest the following bookstores for your perusal:

The Hickory Stick Bookshop (860-868-0525), Green Hill Rd. (CT 47), in the center of Washington

THE CORNWALL BRIDGE POTTERY STORE IN WEST CORNWALL

Kim Grant

Depot, Washington. Open Mon.–Sat. 9–6; Sun. 11–5. An attractive full-service bookstore with an unusually large section devoted exclusively to children's books. At Hickory Stick's frequent book signings, you can meet and buy signed copies of the books of the famous and not-so-famous authors who labor over hot computers in their Litchfield Hills farmhouses.

House of Books (860-927-4104), Main St. (US 7), Kent. Open daily 10–5; Sun. noon–5. A midtown landmark, this cozy shop stocks cards, CDs, tapes, maps, and calendars to complement its comprehensive selection of the latest books.

Barbara Farnsworth, Bookseller (860-672-6571), 407 CT 128, West Cornwall. Open Sat. 9–5 or by appointment. If you can't find it here, you can't find it anywhere. Ms. Farnsworth bids you to browse among 40,000 used books, most out of print, some rare. Major emphasis on horticulture.

The John Bale Book Company (203-757-2279; 888-268-2984; www.johnbalebooks.com), 158 Grand St., Waterbury. Open Mon.–Sat. 10–5. Specializing in upscale antiquarian books but also has a selection of new books. Does much of its business on the Internet but has a huge eclectic inventory in the shop. Breakfast and lunch are served in a small café.

FACTORY OUTLET **Woodbury Pewterers** (203-263-2668), 860 Main St. South (US 6), Woodbury. Open daily 9–5. Museum reproductions and factory "seconds." Dinnerware, lamps, and accessories. For the visitor, pewter spells New England.

SPECIALTY FOODS **Dutch Epicure** (860-567-5586), US 202, southwest of Litchfield. Closed midwinter. Pastries, cakes, muffins, cookies, and a huge inventory of imported European cheeses. The cook is a miracle worker, with chocolate you would kill for.

Nodine's Smokehouse (800-222-2059), North St. (CT 63), Goshen. Retail store in the rear yard. Open Mon.–Sat. 9–5; Sun. 10–4. One of two smokehouses in the state. Smoked chicken, turkey, beef, andouille and other sausages; bacon without nitrites. Supplier to major New York City gourmet food stores and international airlines. Join the parade of Yale University professors and their wives who make monthly pilgrimages to Goshen for the Cajun chicken.

Belgique Pâtisserie Chocolatier (860-927-3681), corner of US 7 and CT 341, Kent. Open Mon., Thu., Fri. 8–6; Sat. 9–6; Sun. 10–6. If I say chocolate, you say Swiss. Right? Not always. Belgium, like its small Alpine neighbor, has an international reputation for gourmet food and great chefs—and once you have tasted Belgique's (*Belgique* is French for "Belgium") chocolates, you will agree that they rank with the best in the world. The enticing display of chocolate-based goods here ranges from layered cakes to a mousse flavored with Jamaican rum to fruit tarts with dark Belgian chocolate to confections and breakfast pastries. This is the place for the chocolate lover. Tables outside in the summer; otherwise, it's take-out.

SPECIAL SHOPS **Kitchenworks and Gourmet Gifts** (860-567-5011), 23 West St., on the Litchfield green, Litchfield. Open Mon.–Sat. 10–5; Sun. noon–5. Garlic peelers, sturdy whisks, and a variety of other cookware, bakeware, and tableware, all designed to take the work out of cooking and serving family and friends.

The Workshop (860-567-0544), West

St., on the Litchfield green, Litchfield. Open Mon.–Sat. 9:30–5:30, Sun. 11–5. If you're furnishing your home or looking for the dress or ensemble that matches your sophisticated tastes, don't pass up this outstanding boutique. Glassware, rugs, pottery, and handmade furniture, plus elegant women's clothes.

J. Seitz & Co. (860-868-0119), Main St. (CT 45), New Preston. Open daily. Distinctive furniture, men and women's accessories. The store overlooks New Preston Falls in the heart of the town's antiques center.

✷ Special Events

Note: As early as weather permits, homeowners all over the state empty their attics and garages and proudly invite passersby to garage or "tag" sales on their front lawns. You can usually count on finding just what you've been looking for. In addition to the events listed here, many churches, museums, historical societies, and libraries schedule special events throughout the year. All-you-can-eat pancake, sausage, and egg breakfasts are ubiquitous. The times and events vary, of course, so for a full listing of the latest events when you plan to visit, check www.litchfieldhills.com and click on "Events."

Late January: **Woodbury Antiques Show**, Woodbury. **Medieval Banquet & Concert**, Episcopal Church, Torrington.

Mid-February: Olympic hopefuls vie for berths on the U.S. team during the annual **U.S. Eastern Ski Jumping Contest** in Salisbury on one of the most beautiful ski jumps in the country. **Ice Fishing Derby**, Bantam Lake, Bantam.

Mid-March: **Maple-Syrup-Making Demonstration** at Flanders Nature Center, Woodbury. **Maple Sugaring Festival** in Norfolk. **Connecticut Antiquarian Book Fair**, Litchfield Community Center.

Early April: **Connecticut Cactus and Succulent Society Show & Sale**, Naugatuck Community College, Waterbury.

May: Three crew races attract visitors to the shores of Lake Waramaug: the **Connecticut State Rowing Championships**, featuring competitions among crews from all prep schools in the state; the **Connecticut Public School Champions** race; and a few days later the Gunnery prep school sponsors champion races of the "4s": Regular shells are crewed by eight rowers; only four rowers compete in the small shells. All of these events take place within a 10-day period, after ice-out.

Mid-May: **Blessing of the Motorcycles**, Lourdes Shrine, Litchfield.

End of May: ✐ **Traditional Memorial Day parade** in Litchfield winds down historic North Street and around the southern part of town, then back to the Litchfield green for patriotic oration. The parade is kicked off with cannon blasts by colorfully garbed troopers of the 1st Litchfield Artillery Regiment. Advise your children to put their hands over their ears. **Fireworks** at night at the community field off US 202. Bring a picnic supper and blankets or lawn chairs. (Most towns in the state stage Memorial Day parades, so be advised you may run into a short wait in traffic almost anywhere in the state during the three-day holiday. **Taste of Bridgewater**, Congregational Church, Bridgewater.

Early June: **Laurel Festival** in Winsted, celebrating the state flower. This three-day festival features the crowning of a queen, who rides a float in the parade. Laurel ball; sidewalk café. For more information and a road map of the best viewing areas of the thousands of bushes in bloom in the surrounding hills, call 860-379-1652.

Mid-June: **Gallery on the Green**, Litchfield. Watercolors, oils, drawings, and crafts for sale in booths that cover the Borough Green for one day.

June: **Litchfield 10K Road Race**—this annual race starting in the center of the village now attracts the best runners in the world. Festive social event on the Litchfield green. **Taste of the Litchfield Hills**—a two-day celebration, at Litchfield's Haight-BrownVineyard and Winery, of the distinctive culinary creations of the region's best restaurants, bistros, gourmet food shops, and caterers. Country and classical music, and demonstrations. Hayrides for the children.

Mid-June through early September: **Music Mountain**, Falls Village off US 7. Chamber music concerts (see *Entertainment*).

Late June through mid-August: **Norfolk Music Festival** (see *Entertainment*) in an acoustically perfect redwood shed on the beautiful grounds of the Battell Stoeckel estate in Norfolk. Jazz concerts and chorales.

Midsummer: **Lime Rock Race Track**—varied schedules of weekend stock-car races on one of the country's most beautiful racetracks.

Early July: **Litchfield House Tour**—unique, elegant estates and gardens are opened to visitors as a benefit for the Connecticut Junior Republic.

August: **Bridgewater Country Fair**, Bridgewater. Sponsored by the Volunteer Fire Department, the three-day fair begins with a parade of firefighters and engines from fire departments around the state. Meals focus on "famous" roast beef sandwiches, chicken, and hot dogs. There is also a midway with rides and competitions. **Connecticut Agricultural Fair**, Goshen Fairgrounds, Goshen.

Mid-August: **Litchfield Jazz Festival**, Kent School, Kent. **Sharon Audubon Festival**, Sharon. Educational and fun day full of nature activities.

Labor Day weekend: **Goshen Fair**—tiny, rural Goshen hosts 60,000 visitors for three days at one of the state's top 10 old-fashioned country fairs. Ox pull, wood-cutting contests, children's midway with a variety of rides, competitions for vegetables, flowers, baked goods, arts and crafts. Enough food to feed the 82nd Airborne for a week.

Saturday after Labor Day weekend: **Salisbury and Lakeville House Tour**.

Second week in September: **Bethlehem Fair**—Bethlehem stages the second-largest fair in the county during the week following the Goshen Fair.

Last week in September: **Connecticut Antique Machinery Fall Festival**, Kent.

Fourth Saturday in September: **Family Nature Day**, White Memorial Conservation Center, Litchfield.

Autumn: **Crew races** on the Housatonic at Kent by the champion rowers of the private Kent School.

Early October: **Scottish Games** on the Goshen Fairgrounds, CT 63, Goshen. Tossing the caber, bagpiping, the clans marching in their colorful tartans, Scottish souvenirs, and plenty of food. Sorry, no haggis. **Riverton Country Fair**, Riverton, the last of the season. **Yankee Invention Expo**, Fri. and Sat., Waterbury Armory. Some 80 inventors from 20 states display their works of genius in the largest nonprofit annual invention exposition in the nation. Ideas on making life easier, healthier, and even more profitable for all of us on display. Featured regularly on *The Tonight Show with Jay Leno*.

Mid-October: **Witches Dungeon—A Horror Festival**, Bristol. **Great Teddy Bear and Doll Jamboree**, Senior Center, Bristol.

Thanksgiving: **Turkey Trot**—a grueling 6-mile road race up hill and down dale, starting at 10 AM on the Goshen Fairgrounds, Goshen. Runners and spectators work up a great appetite for the big bird.

Late November: **Festival of Traditions**, Mattatuck Museum, Waterbury.

Early December: Carol singing, a visit with Santa, and browsing for collectible treasures displayed by 75 craftspeople at the annual **Christmas Town Festival** in Bethlehem. Thousands annually have their holiday greeting cards stamped in the village post office with the Bethlehem postmark.

Mid-December: **The Christmas House**, a private home on Main Street in Torrington, is annually decorated inside and out with an overwhelming display of colored lights and animated figures. Model trains. Hot chocolate for the kids. A donation is suggested for an indoor visit.

December: Annual performance of *The Nutcracker* by the **Nutmeg Conservatory for the Arts, Warner Theatre**, Main St., Torrington. Children can pet the reindeer and give Santa their wish list in the **Torrington Christmas Village**, Torrington, from the second Sunday of December to December 24.

Hartford and Central Connecticut

THE CITY OF HARTFORD

WEST OF THE RIVER

EAST OF THE RIVER

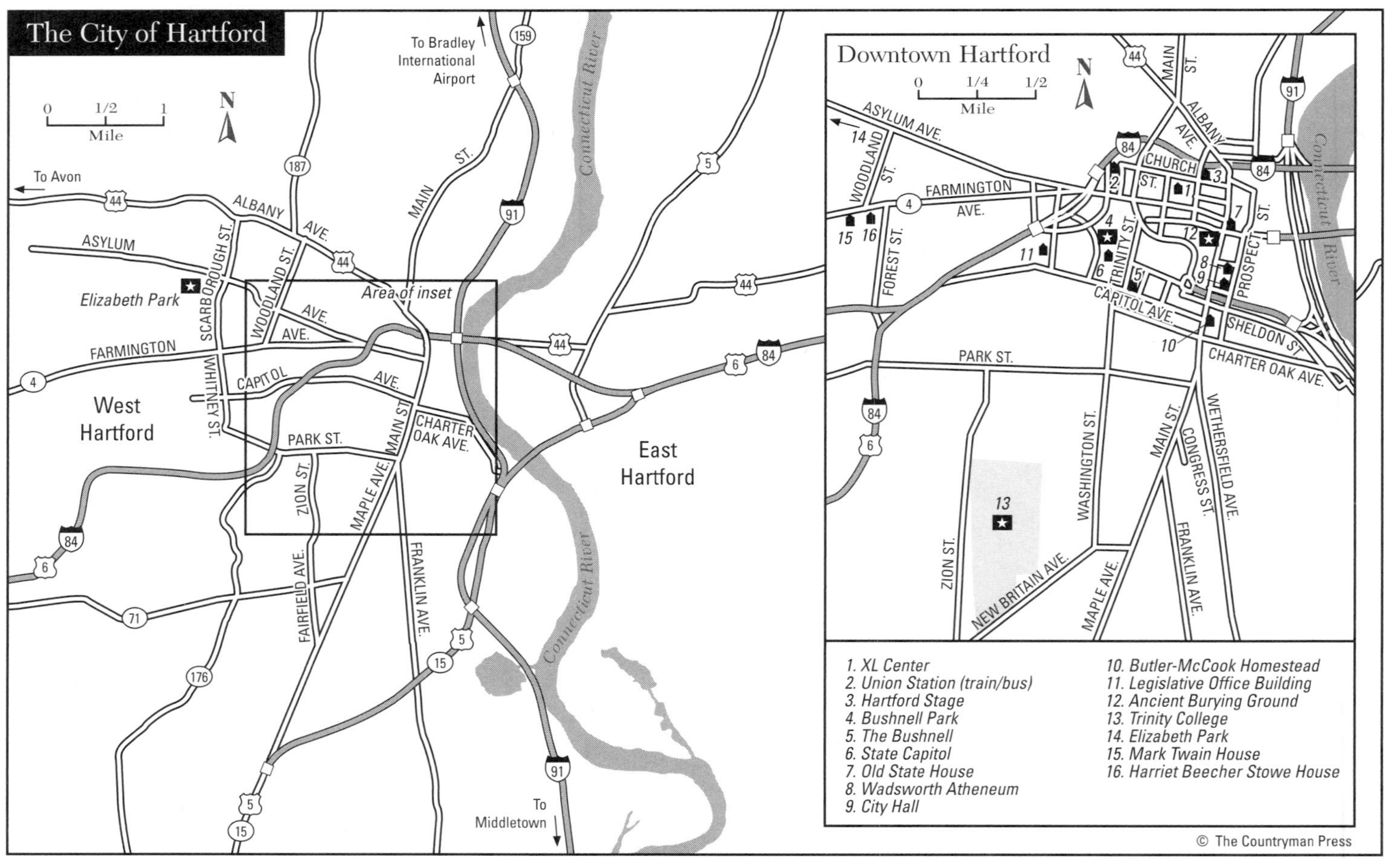
The City of Hartford
0 1/2 1
Mile
N
To Avon
To Bradley International Airport
ALBANY AVE.
ASYLUM
Elizabeth Park
SCARBOROUGH ST.
WOODLAND ST.
AVE.
FARMINGTON
WHITNEY ST.
CAPITOL AVE.
PARK ST.
MAIN ST.
CHARTER OAK AVE.
ZION ST.
MAPLE AVE.
FAIRFIELD AVE.
FRANKLIN AVE.
Area of inset
West Hartford
East Hartford
Connecticut River
To Middletown
Downtown Hartford
0 1/4 1/2
Mile
N
ASYLUM AVE.
WOODLAND ST.
FARMINGTON AVE.
FOREST ST.
ALBANY AVE.
MAIN ST.
CHURCH ST.
TRINITY ST.
PROSPECT ST.
CAPITOL AVE.
SHELDON ST.
CHARTER OAK AVE.
PARK ST.
WASHINGTON ST.
ZION ST.
NEW BRITAIN AVE.
MAPLE AVE.
CONGRESS ST.
WETHERSFIELD AVE.
FRANKLIN AVE.
Connecticut River
1. XL Center
2. Union Station (train/bus)
3. Hartford Stage
4. Bushnell Park
5. The Bushnell
6. State Capitol
7. Old State House
8. Wadsworth Atheneum
9. City Hall
10. Butler-McCook Homestead
11. Legislative Office Building
12. Ancient Burying Ground
13. Trinity College
14. Elizabeth Park
15. Mark Twain House
16. Harriet Beecher Stowe House
© The Countryman Press

THE CITY OF HARTFORD

Connecticut's capital city is one of the oldest in New England, so it naturally boasts an impressive roster of firsts: the country's first public art museum, its oldest public park, oldest statehouse, and first municipal rose garden. Lately it has become a city of dynamic changes: a new convention center, jazzed-up hotels, buzz-worthy restaurants, historic landmarks turned upscale condos. It seems as though everywhere you look in Hartford these days, buildings are coming down and going up. The reason? A downtown renaissance, the likes of which Hartford has never seen, is under way. For years Hartford has struggled with a reputation as a sceneless city, where the sidewalks are rolled up at 5 o'clock when the workforce heads home to the suburbs. These days, a mammoth building blitz is sparking life in the state's second-largest city and turning around its 9-to-5 image. Case in point: the new $160 million Hartford 21 building; at 36 stories, it's the loftiest apartment tower in New England, and just one of many downtown residential developments in progress. Cranes and scaffolds have been dotting the city's skyline and sidewalks for the past several years, proof that the biggest effort Hartford has ever expended to rehabilitate itself is taking shape along the Connecticut River. A once-beleaguered city is on its way to becoming a comeback capital.

The much-anticipated centerpiece of Hartford's "Six Pillars of Progress" revival centers on a link between the city's future and its historic ties to the river: an ambitious $775 million revitalization project called Adriaen's Landing, named for 17th-century navigator Adriaen Block, whose exploration of the Connecticut River led to the Dutch trading post that would eventually become Hartford. The project's cornerstone debuted in 2005: the $271 million Connecticut Convention Center, the largest meeting facility of its kind between New York and Boston. Its soaring glass atrium is a new downtown landmark. The brand-new 22-story Marriott next door is the first full-service hotel to come to Hartford in two decades. And there's more to come: the $150 million state-of-the-art Connecticut Center for Science and Exploration is expected to open in 2009 and, later on, a new-from-the-ground-up shopping, entertainment, and housing district linking downtown to the riverfront. Even the Connecticut-based ESPN sports news giant is in on the action, slated to build an "interactive sports museum" here. The hoped-for net result is a cosmopolitan, 24/7 city, where a mix of new urbanites—empty nesters, families, and young professionals—not only work but also live, shop, and dine. Expectations are as big as the project's cost and scope.

Those early Dutch traders would hardly recognize their Fort New Hope today. Neither would the Reverend Thomas Hooker, who, with a following of Puritan dissenters from the Massachusetts Bay Colony, settled here on the banks of the Connecticut River. They built a meetinghouse in 1636 at the site of the 1706 Old State House, a grand Federal-style brownstone. Visitors can tour the magnificent legislative chambers where Connecticut's government resided for nearly a century, until an ornate gold-domed capitol was built in 1878. The new colony's Fundamental Orders of 1638 is regarded as the world's first written constitution, lending Connecticut its moniker, the Constitution State, and paving the way for American democracy.

For centuries Hartford has been reinventing itself: from trading post to agricultural economy, industrial ingenuity to insurance. When a city resident had his home insured against fire in 1794, a nationwide industry was born. This first written policy led to the establishment of the Hartford Fire Insurance Company (1810), whose reputation soared after a devastating New York City fire in 1835. Policies covering shipping were followed later in the century by automobile and home insurance policies; hence, Hartford became known worldwide as the Insurance City. A reminder of the city's ties to the industry is the Travelers Tower, once the tallest building in New England, which still offers a spectacular view of the countryside in all directions. On Constitution Plaza, the Phoenix Home Life Mutual Insurance Company inhabits a two-sided (designed with curves) green-glass wonder—the first of its kind in the world—known locally as the Boat Building. Across town, Aetna is headquartered in what is considered the world's largest Federal-style building, across the street from Saint Joseph's Cathedral.

Hartford was the hometown of notables, from J. P. Morgan in the 19th century to Katharine Hepburn in the 20th. Its distinguished sons include the inventor of anesthesia and the founder of the world's first permanent school for the deaf. Frederick Law Olmsted, the father of American landscape architecture, lived here for a time and designed the state capitol grounds; his son mapped the city's string of parks. Its manufacturing heyday produced the pay telephone, the Columbia bicycle, the Pope Motor Car, and the Colt revolver. In the 19th century, gunsmiths were producing the Old West six-shooter in the city's venerable Colt factory, whose distinctive blue onion dome has been a beacon to travelers since the 1850s. With National Historic Landmark status on the horizon, the building that once produced firearms now houses artists and local entrepreneurs.

The proximity of its larger neighbors, New York and Boston (each less than two hours away), keeps Hartford abreast of urban trends, but the city has an identity and a charm of its own. Downtown is the best place to begin exploring, where vestiges of the past stand proudly amid skyscrapers. There's the Ancient Burying Ground, where city founders are memorialized; a 1914-vintage carousel in Bushnell Park that spins to the tunes of a 1925 Wurlitzer organ; and the Old State House, whose Museum of Natural and Other Curiosities makes for an offbeat adventure. Fans of American literature should keep in mind that the writer who penned *The Adventures of Tom Sawyer*, *The Adventures of Huckleberry Finn*, and other classics, as well as the author of the seminal antislavery novel *Uncle Tom's Cabin*, called Hartford home. Samuel Clemens, better known as Mark Twain, built himself a grand Victorian mansion in Hartford and lived there during his most prolific years. Harriet Beecher Stowe resided nearby; you can wander through both homes for a peek at how two of the most influential voices of the 19th century

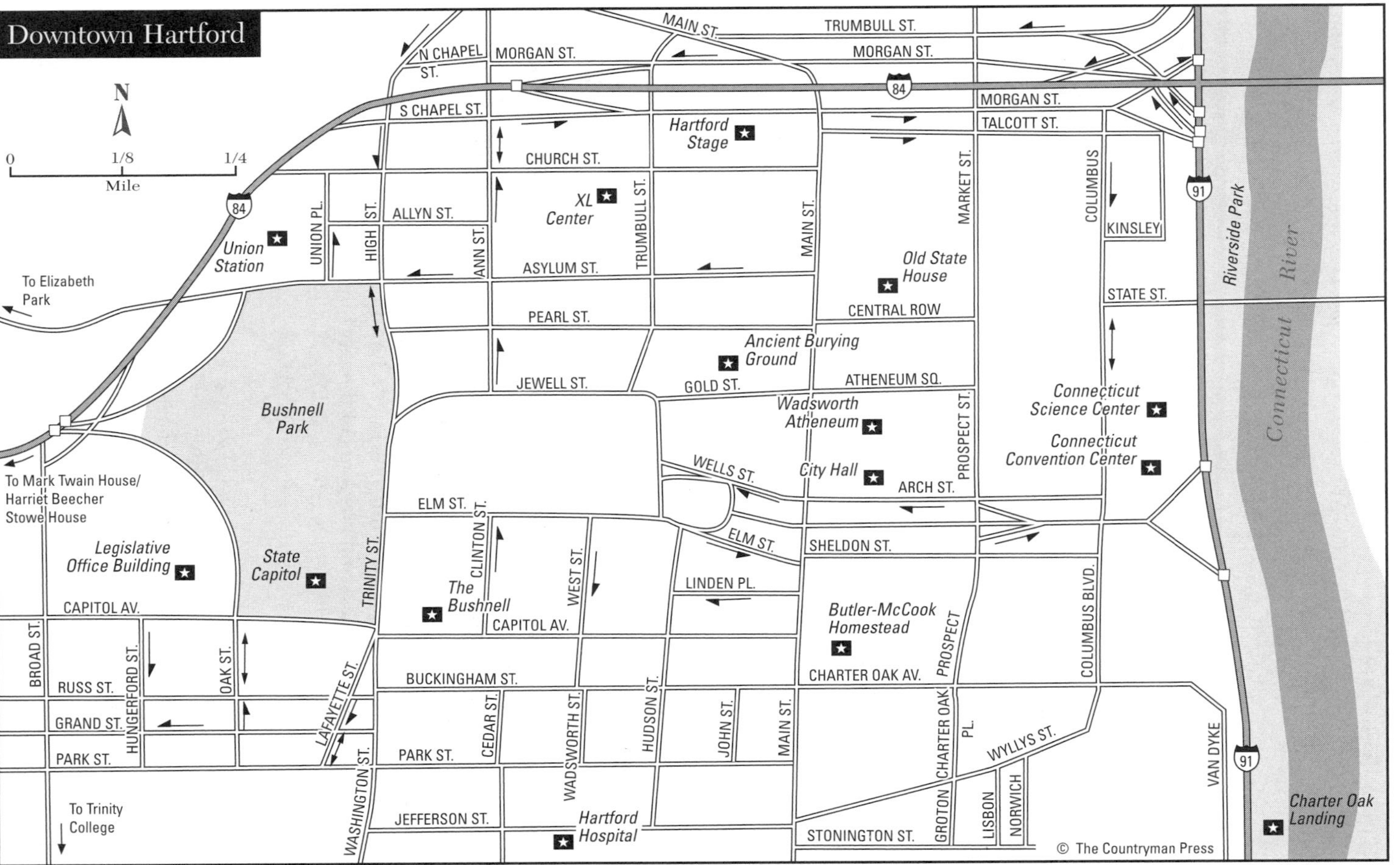

Downtown Hartford
N
0
1/8
1/4
Mile
To Elizabeth Park
To Mark Twain House/ Harriet Beecher Stowe House
To Trinity College
Union Station
Bushnell Park
Legislative Office Building
State Capitol
The Bushnell
XL Center
Hartford Stage
Old State House
Ancient Burying Ground
Wadsworth Atheneum
City Hall
Butler-McCook Homestead
Connecticut Science Center
Connecticut Convention Center
Hartford Hospital
Charter Oak Landing
Riverside Park
Connecticut River
84
91
N CHAPEL ST.
MORGAN ST.
MAIN ST.
TRUMBULL ST.
S CHAPEL ST.
TALCOTT ST.
CHURCH ST.
ALLYN ST.
ASYLUM ST.
PEARL ST.
JEWELL ST.
GOLD ST.
ATHENEUM SQ.
CENTRAL ROW
UNION PL.
HIGH ST.
ANN ST.
MARKET ST.
COLUMBUS
KINSLEY
STATE ST.
PROSPECT ST.
ARCH ST.
WELLS ST.
ELM ST.
SHELDON ST.
CLINTON ST.
WEST ST.
LINDEN PL.
CAPITOL AV.
TRINITY ST.
BROAD ST.
RUSS ST.
HUNGERFORD ST.
OAK ST.
GRAND ST.
PARK ST.
LAFAYETTE ST.
WASHINGTON ST.
BUCKINGHAM ST.
CEDAR ST.
WADSWORTH ST.
HUDSON ST.
JOHN ST.
JEFFERSON ST.
CHARTER OAK AV.
PROSPECT
CHARTER OAK PL.
WYLLYS ST.
COLUMBUS BLVD.
VAN DYKE
GROTON
LISBON
NORWICH
STONINGTON ST.
© The Countryman Press

lived during the Gilded Age. For jazz aficionados, summertime means the Greater Hartford Festival of Jazz, when local and national artists perform in parks, clubs, and historic sites around the city. Arts lovers take note: The Wadsworth Atheneum Museum of Art is a national treasure; the Tony Award–winning Hartford Stage Company is a downtown icon; and the Real Art Ways, a funky arts venue housed in a former Underwood Typewriter factory, offers cutting-edge fare, as does TheaterWorks.

The city's restaurant-coffeehouse-bar scene has been experiencing a renaissance of its own. The result is a dynamic juxtaposition of been-here-forever favorites and bright new hot spots. You'll find sleek (Max Downtown) and sophisticated (Firebox), old-school (Carbone's) and ultra-hip (Koji), eclectic (Trumbull Kitchen) and organic (Alchemy). In ethnic neighborhoods, like the largely Italian section around Franklin Avenue, grocery stores, bakeries, and restaurants maintain Old World traditions, while exciting new bars and eateries are lighting up downtown, giving it a much-needed shot of youthful energy and big-city buzz.

Check the mileage scale on your map: Hartford makes an excellent base for exploring the whole state, but do take a good look at the city itself—the local events, the neighborhoods, and the people. It's a city on a path of self-improvement, say city leaders, who believe that all of the optimistic talk of "New England's Rising Star" has a core of reality. With fingers crossed, they're hoping that Connecticut's capital city will, at last, shine brightly.

Entries in this section are arranged in alphabetical order.

AREA CODE 860.

GUIDANCE For information on attractions, events, lodgings, and more in Hartford and surrounding towns, contact the **Central Regional Tourism District** (860-244-8181; 800-793-4480; www.enjoycentralct.com); the **Greater Hartford Convention & Visitors Bureau** (860-728-6789; 800-446-7811; www.enjoyhartford.com), 31 Pratt St., fourth floor, Hartford 06103; or stop in at the **Greater Hartford Welcome Center** at 45 Pratt St. The **Connecticut Commission on Culture & Tourism** (860-256-2800; 888-288-4748; www.ctvisit.org), 1 Financial Plaza, 755 Main St., Hartford 06103, can also offer guidance.

Connecticut Heritage Discovery Tours (860-247-8996; www.hartnet.org/als), 255 Main St., fourth floor. The **Antiquarian & Landmarks Society** offers a variety of guided walking tours and bus tours of the city's historic homes, churches, parks, neighborhoods, and the historic sites along Main Street. Reservations required.

GETTING THERE All train and bus lines, including local buses and **Connecticut Limousine Service** airport transportation (800-472-5466; www.ctlimo.com), connect downtown at **Union Station** (860-247-5329), 1 Union Place, Exit 48 off I-84. This is the city's transportation hub, and a dependable place to pick up a taxi (see *Getting Around*, below).

By car: Hartford is accessible by car from I-91 north- or southbound, and I-84 east- or westbound. Indoor parking is available at the Connecticut Convention Center, the XL Center (formerly known as the Hartford Civic Center), the Morgan Street Garage, and the Church Street Garage.

By air: **Bradley International Airport** (860-292-2000; 888-624-1533; www.bradleyairport.com), Windsor Locks, 12 miles north of Hartford off I-91, serves the region with daily flights scheduled by major airlines, including American Airlines, America West, American Eagle, Continental, Continental Express, Delta, Northwest, Southwest, United, United Express, US Airways, and US Airways Express.

By rail: **Amtrak** (800-872-7245; www.amtrak.com) serves Hartford and connects at Union Station. Amtrak's Regional line—which links Washington, DC, Philadelphia, New York, and Boston—provides service to Hartford via New Haven.

By bus or limo: **Greyhound Lines** (800-231-2222; www.greyhound.com) and **Peter Pan Bus Lines** (800-343-9999; www.peterpanbus.com) operate from Union Station. **Connecticut Limousine Service (CT Limo)** (800-472-5466; www.ct limo.com) serves Bradley International, JFK, Newark, and LaGuardia airports.

GETTING AROUND *Taxi service:* **United Cab Co.** (860-547-1602), **A-1 Taxi Service** (860-944-0911), **Yellow Cab Co.** (860-666-6666), and **Central Connecticut Taxi** (860-833-6949) serve the city. Taxis are available at Union Station and on call.

City bus service is available and reliable in Hartford; most routes operate during daytime only. **CTTRANSIT** (860-525-9181; www.cttransit.com) operates from the Old State House and connects downtown to Bradley International Airport as well as the surrounding suburbs. (*Note:* Unless you plan to limit your visit strictly to downtown Hartford, you will need a car.)

The **Hartford Star Shuttle** (860-522-8101) is a free downtown bus service that makes more than a dozen stops on its route between the Connecticut Convention Center and the riverfront. Look for the blue-and-gold buses and coordinating shuttle stop signs near hotels, restaurants, and attractions. Buses operate Mon.–Fri. 7 AM–11 PM, and Sat. 3–11; no service on Sun.

MEDICAL EMERGENCY The statewide emergency number is **911**.

Connecticut Children's Medical Center (860-545-9954), 282 Washington St. (next to Hartford Hospital). The emergency number is 860-545-9200.

Hartford Hospital (860-545-5000), 80 Seymour St., off Washington St. The emergency number is 860-545-0000.

St. Francis Hospital & Medical Center (860-714-4000), 114 Woodland St. The emergency number is 860-714-4001.

✷ To See

THE CONNECTICUT RIVER Hartford has a new attraction, one that has been there all along—the Connecticut River. New England's longest river courses and curls through the city; but in the grip of progress, Hartford abandoned its waterway in favor first of the railroads and later of the interstates. Today, however, all that is changing. A string of parks and walkways has been created along both banks of the Connecticut, and excursion boats are back in business. There are picnic areas and playgrounds, quiet spots for reflection, and, on the East Hartford side, an amphitheater. Trails for walkers, joggers, and cyclists make use of two bridges, and a landscaped plaza leading from downtown Hartford to the riverfront. For information on facilities, activities, and special events, call **Riverfront Recapture** (860-713-3131; www.riverfront.org), the nonprofit group that brings regattas, concerts, and festivals that keep the riverfront bustling with activity. The Connecticut River thrives once again!

MUSEUMS ✐ **Connecticut Historical Society Museum** (860-236-5621; www.chs.org), 1 Elizabeth St. Open year-round, Tue.–Fri. noon–5; Sat. 10–5; closed Sun. and Mon. Its library is open Tue.–Sat. 10–5. Adults $6; seniors and students $3; children 6 and under free. A comprehensive museum, library, and education center with outstanding collections: three million manuscripts, more than 200,000 photographs and prints, and nearly 35,000 relics of Connecticut's cultural, political, social, and military history, including Civil War–era letters and a costume collection that dates from the 17th century. Changing exhibits—some hands-on and kid-friendly—focus on selected topics in state history: Recent ones explored colonial Connecticut, Connecticut River Valley furniture, and the state's link to the revolt aboard the 19th-century slave ship *Amistad.* The library specializes in history and genealogy. Musical events, lectures, and family programs are scheduled throughout the year. The museum shop has books, reproduction prints, T-shirts, and gifts.

✐ ♿ **Connecticut Science Center** (860-727-0457; www.ctsciencecenter.org), 50 Columbus Blvd., Hartford. Slated to open in 2009; call or check the Web site for hours and admission prices. As of press time, the new Connecticut Science Center was nearly finished, its dramatic profile rising high above the Connecticut River in downtown Hartford. The real showstoppers, however, will be the innovative, hands-on exhibits and programs for children and their families. Topics run the gamut from space and earth scienes to the Connecticut River and Connecticut inventors; in all, 200 exhibits in 10 galleries.

THE WADSWORTH ATHENEUM MUSEUM OF ART, FOUNDED IN 1842, IS THE NATION'S OLDEST CONTINUOUSLY OPERATING PUBLIC ART MUSEUM.

Courtesy Central Regional Tourism District

Hartford Police Museum (860-522-0855), 101 Pearl St. Open Mon.–Fri. 9–4; closed Sat. and Sun. Call about group tours. Exhibits document the history of the Hartford police department (from 1870) with photographs and memorabilia on local law enforcement and the city.

Menczer Museum of Medicine and Dentistry (860-236-5613), Hartford Medical Society Building, 230 Scarborough St. Open year-round, Mon.–Fri. 10–4:30. Adults $2; children free. A one-of-a-kind museum with exhibits of instruments, equipment, and medications used by doctors and dentists over the past three centuries. Exhibits also trace the career of Horace Wells, the Hartford dentist who pioneered the use of nitrous oxide as an anesthetic. An excellent aid to appreciation of modern methods and technology. A comprehensive medical library is on the premises.

The Museum of Connecticut History (860-757-6535; www.cslib.org), 231 Capitol Ave., in the Connecticut State Library/State Supreme Court complex. Open year-round, Mon.–Fri. 9–4; Sat. 9–3; closed Sun. Free admission. Facing the ornate state capitol across the street, this striking example of Beaux-Arts architecture adds to the monumental aspect of the neighborhood. The main reading room of the library is a handsome hall with a spectacular ceiling. Downstairs, the nationally known history and genealogy collection attracts researchers from all over. Changing exhibits are devoted to aspects of state history, economic life, Connecticut products, and events of note. Permanent displays include the Colony of Connecticut Royal Charter of 1662, portraits of state governors, and a collection of more than 300 artifacts covering the state's political, military, and industrial history, including Colt firearms and uniforms, from the Civil War through the Gulf War, worn by Connecticut soldiers.

The Trash Museum (860-757-7765; www.crra.org), 211 Murphy Rd. Open Sept.–June: Wed.–Fri. noon–4. July and Aug.: Tue.–Sat. 10–4. Guided tours by appointment. Free admission. See what happens to your trash and recyclables after you leave them at the curb. Hands-on exhibits and games reinforce the importance of recycling. Visitors can watch as bottles, cans, paper, cardboard, and plastic items are sorted, crushed, baled, and shipped away to become something new. The Temple of Trash exhibit illustrates the evils of old-fashioned garbage dumping. The gift shop features items made of recycled materials.

Wadsworth Atheneum Museum of Art (860-278-2670; www.wadsworthatheneum.org), 600 Main St. Open year-round, Tue.–Fri. 11–5; 11–8 on the first Thu. of each month; Sat. and Sun. 10–5. Adults $10; seniors $8; students $5; children under 13 free. The country's oldest continuously operating public art museum (since 1842) is nationally recognized for the excellence and scope of its collections, which include 45,000 works covering 5,000 years of art. Specialties include Hudson River School paintings, European Old Masters, French and German porcelain, handcrafted New England furniture, rare 19th-century French sculpture, English and American silver, costumes and textiles, and contemporary art (including Sol LeWitt wall drawings). In addition to the permanent collection, there are world-class changing loan exhibitions. The Aetna Theater presents foreign films (see *Entertainment*), and the **Museum Café** serves light fare at lunch. Of course there's a quality museum shop.

CHURCHES AND CEMETERIES **Ancient Burying Ground** (860-561-2585), at the corner of Main and Gold streets. Call for hours. Hartford's oldest historic site remains a remarkably peaceful enclave next to the historic Center Church (see below) even though it's in the middle of the city. In use from 1640 to the early 1800s, it is the resting place of the city's founders, and of many who came after. The carvings and inscriptions on a number of the headstones and monuments—about 415 gravestones remain—have been restored or replicated. A sober epitaph found on several stones is typical of the Pilgrim fathers' views: "Behold my friend as you pass by, / As you are now so once was I / As I am now, so you must be / Prepare for death and follow me."

Cedar Hill Cemetery (860-956-3311; www.cedarhillcemetery.org), 453 Fairfield Ave. Open year-round, daily 7 AM–dusk; special events and tours May–Oct.; call or check the Web site for a current schedule. Cedar Hill is an example of the possibilities of the picturesque in landscaping. Founded in 1864, it is a premier example of the American "rural" cemetery that became popular in the Victorian era and is the last resting place for many of the city's important citizens, including the elite of Hartford's Gilded Age. Financier J. P. Morgan, Samuel and Elizabeth Colt, Isabella Beecher Hooker, the poet Wallace Stevens, James G. Batterson (founder of the Travelers Insurance Company), and actress (and Hartford native) Katharine Hepburn are among the notables buried here. Burial areas are planted with more than 2,000 trees and filled with imposing monuments designed by noted 19th-century architects and artists. Its 270 secluded acres—meadows, woodlands, and a pond—attract wildlife and provide a pleasant place to walk, despite the reminders of mortality. However, a note of hope is inscribed on the tombstone of Horace Wells, the local dentist who pioneered the use of nitrous oxide as a surgical anesthetic: "There shall be no pain."

Center Church (860-249-5631; www.centerchurchhartford.org), 60 Gold St., at the corner of Main St. Open May–Oct., Wed. and Fri. 11–2, and by appointment. This is the church that Thomas Hooker began when he brought his band of dissenters from Massachusetts in 1636 to found Hartford. The first meetinghouse was on the site of the Old State House, across Main Street. The church site was moved in 1737, and the present church, patterned after St. Martin in the Fields in London, dates from 1807. The elegant barrel-vaulted ceiling and the remarkable stained-glass windows—six of them by Louis Tiffany—would no doubt surprise Thomas Hooker, whose original meetinghouse was a simple square wooden building. Visitors are welcome to attend services, and tour the church and the adjacent Ancient Burying Ground (see above), where Hooker is buried. Concerts are often held here; call for information.

Christ Church Cathedral (860-527-7231; www.cccathedral.org), 45 Church St., at the corner of Main St. This imposing beauty, built in 1828, is one of the oldest Gothic-style churches in America. The elegant stained-glass windows are styled after those in a church in Oxford, England; inside an ornate barrel-vaulted ceiling soars above an altar inspired by a tomb in England's Canterbury Cathedral. Today it's a National Historic Landmark, where visitors are welcome to attend services, or concerts and choral performances in the cathedral theater.

Church of the Good Shepherd (860-525-4289), 155 Wyllys St. Open by appointment. Edward Tuckerman Potter designed this Victorian Gothic church of red and yellow sandstone, with intricate carvings, stained-glass windows, and a decorative motif of crossed pistols. It was commissioned by Mrs. Colt as a tribute to her entrepreneur and gun-manufacturer husband, Samuel Colt, and to their three children who died in infancy.

HISTORIC HOMES **Butler-McCook House & Garden/Main Street History Center** (860-522-1806), 396 Main St. Open year-round, Wed.–Sat. 10–4; Sun. 1–4. Adults $7; seniors and students $6; children $4; children under 6 free. Though the home dates from 1782, it was expanded, "improved," and finally "Victorianized" by successive generations of the same extraordinary family, which included educators, doctors, artists, and social reformers among its members. It thus recorded a living history and is indeed one of a very few surviving historic homes in the city. Formal Victorian ornamental gardens designed by Jacob Weidenmann in 1865 are maintained out back, and mementos of the Reverend Mr. McCook and his large and active family—they lived here for 189 years—enliven the tour. Among the treasures are a collection of Japanese samurai armor, a Bierstadt landscape, Connecticut-made colonial furniture, Victorian-era toys, and period clothing. The **Main Street History Center** has exhibits on the city's evolution into a modern urban center. The house is a property of Connecticut Landmarks, which restores and maintains a number of historic buildings throughout the state.

Governor's Residence (860-566-4840), 990 Prospect Ave. Open for guided tours by appointment. Free admission. Visitors are guided through the carefully restored first-floor public rooms in the 1909 Georgian Revival home where the state's first families have resided since 1945. Special events, including the annual holiday open house, take place here throughout the year; call for a schedule.

Harriet Beecher Stowe Center (860-522-9258; www.harrietbeecherstowe.org), 77 Forest St., at Farmington Ave. (CT 4). Open year-round, Tue.–Sat. 9:30–4:30; Sun. noon–4:30. Also open Mon., Memorial Day–Columbus Day; closed major holidays. Adults $8; seniors $7; children $4; 4 and under free. Across the way from Mark Twain's mansion, the Victorian Gothic "cottage" of the Stowes was home to the "little lady who started this big war"—in the words of Abraham Lincoln. The author of the 1852 antislavery classic *Uncle Tom's Cabin* was one of a group of literary and social activists who settled in the city's Nook Farm neighborhood in the latter part of the 19th century, when it was a semi-rural area, nearly a mile from the crush of downtown Hartford! Stowe's views on housekeeping and decorating

FOUR GENERATIONS OF THE BUTLER AND MCCOOK FAMILIES RESIDED IN HARTFORD'S OLDEST SURVIVING HOUSE.

Courtesy Central Regional Tourism District

Courtesy Central Regional Tourism District

THE 19TH-CENTURY VICTORIAN HOME OF ABOLITIONIST AND AUTHOR HARRIET BEECHER STOWE RESIDES IN HARTFORD'S WEST END.

are evident in the house, which is quietly Victorian and comfortably human-scaled. The center's grounds include lush Victorian-era gardens (guided tours June–Oct.); the **Katharine S. Day House** (itself a striking example of Victorian architecture) features a library (open by appointment) and is a treasure trove of materials about Stowe, the Beecher family, abolitionism, suffrage, African American history, 19th-century theater, Hartford architectural history, and more. The **Stowe Visitor Center** features a museum shop and changing exhibitions.

Isham-Terry House (860-522-1984), 211 High St. Open year-round by appointment. Adults $4; children $2. This dignified Italianate 1854 mansion—property of the Antiquarian and Landmarks Society—was purchased in 1896 by Dr. Oliver Isham, whose sisters Charlotte and Julia lived there well into their 90s (the second died in 1979). The sisters left the house in mint condition, complete with ornate Victorian gaslight fixtures, stained-glass panels over the French doors, a mammoth carved mirror, a heavy carved mantel, and coffered ceilings. Collections include rare books and paintings, Dr. Isham's untouched medical office, Connecticut-made clocks, and automobile memorabilia.

HISTORIC SITES **Charter Oak Cultural Center** (860-249-1207; www.charteroakcenter.org), 21 Charter Oak Ave. Gallery is open Sept.–June, Mon.–Fri. 10–4. Admission $5. Listed on the National Register of Historic Places, this Romanesque Victorian brick building was Connecticut's first synagogue, built in 1876. Irish-born Hartford architect George Keller used rounded arched windows to echo its domed twin towers, and the restored interior features remarkable stenciling and other ornate touches. Today it's a multicultural arts venue, presenting a variety of performances, exhibitions, and concerts featuring local artists and musicians.

Mark Twain House & Museum (860-247-0998; www.marktwainhouse.org), 351 Farmington Ave. at Woodland St. Open Mon.–Sat. 9:30–5:30; Sun. noon–5:30; closed Tue., Jan.–Mar., and major holidays; open on Mon. holidays. Adults $13; seniors $11; students $10; children $8 (under 6 free). Determined to live up to the standards of the Gilded Age, Mark Twain moved to Hartford with his new wife and in 1874 built this flamboyant, many-gabled mansion, which added his own unique whimsy to the quirkiness of the era. He spared no expense in building his 19-room Victorian manse—interiors are by Louis Comfort Tiffany. His specifications included a room shaped like a pilot's house and a kitchen at the front of the house, so servants could view the goings-on in the street. The mansion has been restored with great care—artisans were brought here from Germany for the project—and docents are prepared with anecdotes to help you imagine a time when Sam Clemens's world was a happy one. He composed some of his greatest masterpieces in the Billiard Room, including *The Adventures of Tom Sawyer*, *The Adventures of Huckleberry Finn*, and *A Connecticut Yankee in King Arthur's Court*. Check out the new $17 million **Museum Center**, a state-of-the-art facility with films, lectures, and family programs in two auditoriums, and permanent exhibits not just on Twain but also on the history of the Gilded Age during which he lived and worked.

MARK TWAIN COMPOSED SOME OF HIS GREATEST MASTERPIECES WHILE LIVING IN HARTFORD.

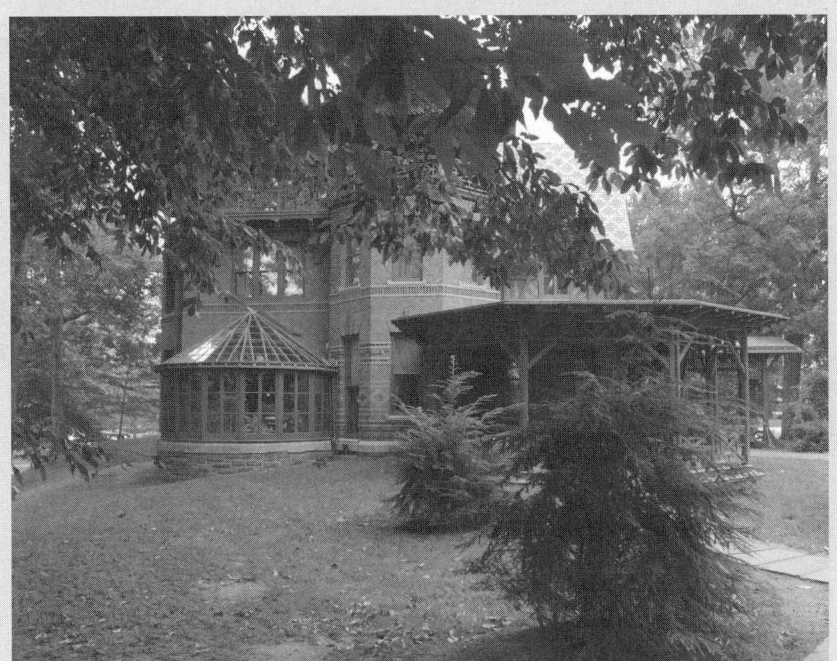

Courtesy Central Regional Tourism District

Charter Oak Marker. Not many cities boast a legend featuring a tree, but as mentioned earlier, Hartford has its own character. Charter Oak Place is near the spot where the Charter Oak stood. Strictly undocumented legend says that when the mother country sent a new governor, Edmund Andros, to take control of the New England colonies in 1687, the Connecticut colony balked. Still, Hartford city fathers gathered, on Andros's command, in Joseph Wadsworth's tavern to turn over their original and very generous charter, thus relinquishing their freedom to govern themselves. At the moment of transfer, however, the lights were extinguished and confusion set in; when the candles were relit, the charter was gone. It had been concealed—by Wadsworth, it is said—in the hollow of an enormous oak. By the time the tree blew down in 1856, it was 33 feet in circumference and had become an icon of state history. Objects made, or said to be made, from its wood were considered precious, and they proliferated. Mark Twain remarked, typically, that he himself had seen "a walking-stick, dog collar, needle-case, three-legged stool, bootjack, dinner table, tenpin alley, toothpick, and enough Charter Oak to build a plank road from Hartford to Salt Lake City."

♿ **Old State House** (860-522-6766; www.ctosh.org), 800 Main St. Open Tue.–Fri. 11–5; Sat. 10–5; closed on Sun. and major holidays. Free admission. The nation's first statehouse built specifically for that purpose, the 1796 Federal-style Old State House was the first public building designed by Boston's Charles Bulfinch. Today it's run by the Connecticut Historical Society, and careful renovations have not only saved the building from collapse but also added features that bring its history to life—including costumed guides playing historical roles. This is the site of the first written constitution, as well as the *Amistad* and Prudence Crandall trials. Inside, visitors can follow the building's changing role in Hartford: The elegant Colonial Revival–style Court Room looks as it did in 1796; the upstairs chambers show where the city council met in the early 19th century. Upstairs, the **Museum of Natural and Other Curiosities** features relics of the late 1800s that are most unusual, such as a two-headed calf, a wall-mounted crocodile, and similar oddities. The Old State House is the scene of public meetings, official and private events, arts-and-crafts shows, and performances of all sorts. An exceptional **museum shop** features Connecticut goods and local artwork. A new hands-on permanent exhibit is devoted to the history of the statehouse and the city.

Stegosaurus is a monumental and unmistakable work of the sculptor Alexander Calder, in the center of downtown Hartford on Main Street. The gigantic red structure perches between the Hartford Municipal Building, a 1915 Beaux-Arts beauty with a grand atrium that runs the length of the building, and the Wadsworth Atheneum Museum of Art. This metal monster dominates **Alfred E. Burr Memorial Mall**, a vest-pocket park with plantings and benches where you can sit and watch the birds that nest on the giant creature's infrastructure. The eccentric artist, who lived and worked in Roxbury until his death in 1976, was known for his kinetic art, from small modern mobiles to the mammoth metal sculptures, like *Stegosaurus*, known as stabiles. Calder's installations reside in museums and parks around the world.

St. Paul Travelers Tower (860-277-4208), 1 Tower Square. Free tours, weather permitting, May–Oct., Mon.–Fri. 10–3. Group tours by appointment. Once the tallest building in New England, the 34-story tower in the heart of downtown still offers a spectacular view of the countryside in all directions. *Caution:* After you get off the elevator, you still have 70 steps to climb.

Trinity College (860-297-2000; www.trincoll.edu), 300 Summit St. A compact and self-contained 100-acre campus located at the city's highest elevation, Trinity (founded in 1823) is a good browsing ground for architecture buffs. The Long Walk comprises three connected brownstone buildings in the Victorian Gothic style. The college chapel, considered by many to be the finest example of collegiate Gothic architecture in America, is the setting for organ and chamber concerts. The college sponsors showings of films both old and new and presents lectures, dance programs, and other performance events open to the public (see *Entertainment*).

✷ To Do

AIRPLANE RIDES **Metro Flight Services** (860-722-9667; www.metroflightct.com), Hartford-Brainard Airport, 20 Lindbergh Dr., Exit 27 off I-91. Sightseeing flights over Hartford and the surrounding countryside.

BOAT EXCURSION **Lady Katharine Cruises** (866-867-4837; www.ladykatecruises.com), Riverfront Plaza (300 Columbus Blvd.) and Charter Oak Landing (Reserve Rd., under the Charter Oak Bridge). Public cruises May–Nov. The *Hartford Belle* takes passengers on scenic cruises up and down the Connecticut River. Some trips offer Sunday brunch or jazz; others, dinner and dancing, fall foliage, karaoke, and holiday celebrations. Named for Connecticut's own Katharine Hepburn.

FISHING There are public boat-launching sites on the Connecticut River at **Charter Oak Landing** (860-713-3131), Reserve Rd., Exit 27 off I-91; and at **Riverside Park** (860-293-0130), 300 Columbus Blvd., Exit 33 off I-91. Just across the river in East Hartford, there's a boat launch at **Great River Park** on East River Dr. Anglers can also cast their lines from the riverbanks. The area's largemouth and smallmouth bass populations are thriving, and **Riverfront Recapture** (860-713-3131; www.riverfront.org) hosts weekly amateur fishing competitions at these sites, as well as top-level professional bass tournaments; call for a schedule. A license is required to fish on the Connecticut River; for information, contact the **Fisheries Division** of the **Department of Environmental Protection** (860-424-3474; www.ct.gov/dep).

GOLF **Goodwin Park Golf Course** (860-956-3601), 1130 Maple Ave. Two courses: one has 18 holes (par 70, 6,015 yards); the 9-hole course (par 35, 2,544 yards) is ideal for beginners.

Keney Golf Course (860-525-3656), 280 Tower Ave. Par 70, 18 holes, 5,969 yards.

ROWING **Riverfront Recapture Community Rowing** (860-713-3131; www.riverfront.org), at Riverside Park, Exit 33 off I-91. Open June–Sept.; call for a schedule. Recreational rowing on the Connecticut River for rowers of all abilities. There are short introductory sessions and summerlong programs on sculling (using two oars in a single-person shell) and sweep rowing (using one oar with a four- or eight-person crew). The rowing program is based at the Greater Hartford Jaycee's Victorian-style community boathouse. In late September, Riverfront Recapture hosts the Head of the Riverfront Regatta, a major fall event.

SPECTATOR SPORTS **Hartford Wolf Pack Hockey Club** (860-548-2000; www.hartfordwolfpack.com), XL Center (formerly the Hartford Civic Center), 1 Civic Center Plaza. Games mid-Oct.–mid-Apr. Call or check online for a schedule. The American Hockey League's Wolf Pack, an affiliate of the New York Rangers, takes to the ice at the downtown civic center. Home games feature a fun variety of kid-friendly contests, giveaways, and theme nights.

* Green Space

Bushnell Park (860-232-6710; www.bushnellpark.org), one block west of Main St., at Elm and Jewell streets. Hartford's downtown green space—the oldest public park in the nation—is named for the Reverend Horace Bushnell, who advocated creation of the park to counter the rapid urbanization of the city—in the 1850s. Its 37 acres are embellished with bridges—although the streams no longer flow under them—a pond, varied plantings (call for tours of Memorial Arch and guided tree walks), a playground, and benches. The performance shell hosts summer concerts of all sorts. The **Pump House Gallery** (860-543-8874), on the park grounds, is open year-round, Tue.–Fri. 11–2. To the west of the gallery, on Jewell St., is the handsome pavilion that houses **The Carousel** (860-585-5411; www.thecarousel museum.org), an authentic 1914 Stein and Goldstein merry-go-round with antique hand-carved horses prancing to the music of a 1925 Wurlitzer under hundreds of twinkling lights. It operates mid-Apr.–mid-Oct., Tue.–Sun. 11–5. The park extends north of the state capitol, where the dominant feature is the Corning Fountain, memorializing the Native Americans who were the original inhabitants of the region. The handsome brownstone Soldiers and Sailors Memorial Arch, designed by local architect George Keller, frames the entrance to the park on Trinity Street and honors the 4,000 city residents who served in the Civil War. The outdoor Performance Pavilion, just below the state capitol, is the site of theatrical, dance, and musical shows by local artists and performance groups.

Charter Oak Landing, **Riverside Park**, **Riverwalk Downtown**, and **Riverfront Plaza** (860-713-3131; www.riverfront.org), in the downtown area along the river. These parks—148 acres in all—are strung along the banks of the Connecticut River, set with picnic benches, walkways, a gazebo, playgrounds, a sculpture walk, and boat launches. Fishing tournaments and athletic contests, from swimming meets to rowing regattas, take place from spring to fall. The parks also serve as departure points for boat ridesthat further open up Hartford's landmark waterway.

Elizabeth Park (860-231-9443; www.elizabethpark.org), 915 Prospect Ave. Open year-round, dawn to dusk. Greenhouses open Mon.–Fri. 8–3. This 102-acre park, straddling the Hartford–West Hartford town line, has many features—vistas, plantings, and activities—to recommend it but is best known as the site of the nation's first municipal rose garden. Upward of 15,000 rosebushes (900 varieties!) grow in beds and over archways, on fences, and up around a perfect wedding-picture gazebo. If you're lucky enough to visit this National Historic Landmark in late June or

Kim Grant

ELIZABETH PARK IN HARTFORD IS THE NATION'S FIRST MUNICIPAL ROSE GARDEN.

early July, you'll catch these beauties at their peak (see Rose Weekend under *Special Events*). Other features are the Perennial Garden—designed by Frederick McGourty, a nationally known gardener based in Norfolk—the Rock Garden, and the Annual Garden, as well as some 120 varieties of trees. Lunch is served at The Pond House Café (see *Eating Out*).

✷ Lodging

HOTELS 🐾 ♿ **Crowne Plaza Hartford Downtown** (860-549-2400; reservations 888-444-0401), 50 Morgan St., Exit 50 off I-84, 06120. Hartford's Crowne Plaza is on the opposite side of I-84 from downtown, yet it's an easy walk to the XL Center, the Wadsworth Atheneum Museum of Art, and other historic and cultural venues. The hotel has 350 guest rooms, including five suites; a fitness center and seasonal outdoor pool with sundeck round out the amenities. Multilingual (French, German, Arabic, Portuguese, and others) staff are friendly and helpful; shuttles run to and from Bradley International Airport on a regular basis. **Bristol Bar & Grill** serves American fare for breakfast, lunch, and dinner. $169–199.

🐾 ♿ **Hilton Hartford** (860-728-5151; reservations 800-325-3535; www.hartford.hilton.com), 315 Trumbull St. 06103. Most people think of Paris when they hear the word *Hilton* these days, but in Hartford it refers to downtown digs fresh off a $34 million facelift. This is one of the most convenient of the city's hotels—a block from the Hartford Stage Company and linked directly to the Civic Center via an enclosed skywalk—with a comfortable, deeply upholstered lobby and a pair of hot new places to eat and drink. **M&M Coffee Shop** is a unique eatery that's half Jewish delicatessen, half Chinese restaurant, which means you can nosh on beef brisket or shrimp fried rice, depending on your mood. **Elements 315** is an upscale, ultracool lounge. There are 392 guest rooms and 11 suites, plus a fitness center, whirlpool, and sauna, and an indoor pool. $119–199.

Courtesy Connecticut Convention Center

HARTFORD'S NEW CONVENTION CENTER IS THE LARGEST MEETING FACILITY BETWEEN NEW YORK CITY AND BOSTON.

🐾 ♿ **Holiday Inn Express** (reservations 800-315-2621; www.hiexpress.com) hotels operate two downtown locations; one (860-525-1000), near the Connecticut Convention Center at 185 Brainard Rd., Exit 27 off I-91, 06114, has 150 rooms, free high-speed Internet access, a fitness center, and an outdoor pool. $99–149. The other lodging (860-246-9900) is across from the Bushnell Center for the Performing Arts, at 440 Asylum St. 06103. It offers similar amenities—minus the pool and fitness center—but there's a lounge, and pets are welcome. Both offer continental breakfast and shuttles to downtown locations. $119–149.

♿ **Homewood Suites** (860-524-0223; www.homewoodsuites.com), 338 Asylum St. 06103. Hartford's newest hotel occupies a grand old historic building on Asylum St., next to Bushnell Park. The former Bond Hotel, which first opened in 1913, has 116 suites designed for extended stays. Walk to restaurants, Union Station, the XL Center, and the state capitol. Continental breakfast. $119–159.

♿ **Marriott Hartford Downtown** (860-249-8000; reservations: 800-228-9290; www.hartfordmarriott.com), 200 Columbus Blvd., Exit 29A off I-91, 06103-2807. This $81 million, 22-story downtown hotel overlooking the Connecticut River and connected to the new Connecticut Convention Center is a key piece of the city's huge ongoing riverfront development project. The August 2005 opening, on the heels of the convention center grand opening, was big news: Hartford got its first new full-service hotel in 20 years. There are 409 smartly decorated guest rooms and eight suites, each with high-speed Internet access. The spa and fitness center comes with a rooftop pool, which comes with an eye-popping, bird's-eye view. Vivo is a dynamic, city-slick trattoria (see *Dining Out*); Crush is the hip lounge across the hall (see *Entertainment*). $199 and up.

🐾 ♿ **Residence Inn by Marriott** (860-524-5550; reservations 800-331-3131), 942 Main St. 06103. A handsome 1876 brownstone—the city's historic Richardson Building—offers 100 rooms and suites designed for extended stays. Health club, continental breakfast. Close to downtown shops, restaurants, and businesses. Shuttles whisk guests to and from Bradley International Airport. $129–229.

✱ Where to Eat

DINING OUT **bin 228** (860-224-9463; www.bin228winebar.com), 228 Pearl St. Open for lunch Mon.–Fri.; dinner Mon.–Sat.; closed Sun. Food-savvy locals adore this urbane and classy wine bar and bistro off Bushnell Park, the perfect spot to catch a meal or drink before a show at the nearby Bushnell Performing Arts Center. As the name suggests, vino is serious business here. The walls are lined with it, and the wine list is loaded with offerings from around the world, including daily blackboard specials and many by-the-glass choices. The sophisticated Italian menu includes creative salads and pressed panini sandwiches at lunch; later on, a menu of excellent small plates like beef carpaccio with arugula and Parmesan, and bruschetta topped with fresh tomatoes and basil, is a real treat. $11–20.

Carbone's Ristorante (860-296-9646; www.carbonesct.com), 588 Franklin Ave. Lunch Mon.–Fri.; dinner Mon.–Sat.; closed Sun. Reservations recommended. Three generations of the Carbone family have run Hartford's best-known Italian restaurant since 1938. This old-school landmark—the king of Franklin Avenue's Italian dining scene—also happens to be one of Connecticut's all-time great Italian restaurants (think Boston's North End, or New York's Little Italy). Service is masterful; menu choices, elegant. Tableside preparation; pasta (of course) and veal, but they also have inventive ways with fresh fish, poultry, and beef. $19–32.

♿ **Churrascaria Braza** (860-882-1839), 488 Farmington Ave. (CT 4). Open for lunch Mon.–Fri.; dinner daily. Reservations recommended. Tired of been-there-done-that dinners out? This West End hot spot, known around here as "Braza," really jazzed up the neighborhood when a stunning $5 million makeover turned an abandoned neoclassical theater into a dramatic setting for authentic Brazilian-style steak house fare. A meal here is far from ho-hum, especially if you opt for the grilled and slow-roasted rotisserie meats, which offer the festive experience that most diners come here for. Choose your meat, such as beef short ribs or spicy chorizo, from the wait staff parading around with skewers and knives, ready to carve you a sample—you set the pace with a color-coded chip—while traditional sides like Brazilian cheese bread and crisp yucca fries are served family-style. Finish your feast with *bunuelos* (fried pastries filled with melted bitter chocolate), a classic Brazilian dessert. The lively bar is known for its cool mojitos and energetic 30-something crowd. Prix fixe $30.

Dulce Restaurant (860-756-0988; www.dulcerestaurant.com), 100 Trumbull St. Open for lunch Mon.–Fri.; dinner daily; late-night menu on Fri. and Sat. until 1 AM. A stylish new Portuguese restaurant (pronounced *duel-say*) with lofty windows and an outdoor patio overlooking Bushnell Park. Steaks, chops, seafood, pasta, and Portuguese dishes, with an extensive wine list. Live music, from acoustic to jazz, on weekends. $19–32.

Feng Asian Bistro (860-549-3364; www.fengrestaurant.com), 93 Asylum St. Open for lunch Mon.–Fri.; dinner daily; sushi bar stays open late. Never mind the sleek and sexy decor and energetic vibe; this is the city's new go-to spot for top-notch sushi. For a full meal, the Asian pear and beet salad with lemongrass vinaigrette is a fine start; then try the dry-aged rib eye with ginger salad and fried potatoes, or the Thai-spiced lamb chops with roasted fingerling potatoes and lavender jus. The Fuji apple tart with cinnamon ice cream is decadent, the lychee sorbet a lighter ending. $24–38.

Firebox (860-246-1222; www.firebox restaurant.com) 539 Broad St. Open for lunch Mon.–Fri.; dinner daily. The *New York Times* and *Gourmet* magazine have taken note of this sophisticated high-ceilinged restaurant. It's one of the newest players in Hartford's culinary scene, featuring astronomically good contemporary American cuisine with ingredients from local farms and purveyors. Start with the asparagus salad with duck prosciutto, then try the Stonington flounder with fava beans and smoked olive tapenade. End with a fig and rhubarb cobbler with vanilla ice cream from Simsbury's Tulmeadow Farms. $21–33.

♿ **Hot Tomato's** (860-249-5100; www .hottomatos.net), 1 Union Place. Open for lunch Mon.–Fri.; dinner daily. Reservations recommended. A lively Italian restaurant adjacent to the train station offers two distinct venues for dining. The main dining room is an open and airy see-and-be-seen spot decorated in tomato-inspired pop art. For a more intimate vibe, head for the wine room out back, with stone walls and vintage French winemaking equipment. The exposed kitchen puts out innovative Italian dishes: grilled chicken, sun-dried tomatoes, and house-made ricotta gnocchi with pesto cream sauce; salmon osso buco over garlic mashed potatoes; and lobster, portobello mushrooms, and asparagus in a lobster cream sauce atop tagliatelle are standouts. There's also a good selection of grilled seafood and chops. The garlic bread, stuffed with four cheeses and loaded with garlic, is to die for. In summer, patio dining comes with views of Bushnell Park. $17–33. There's an equally popular spin-off location in New Haven.

♿ **Max Downtown** (860-522-2530; www.maxrestaurantgroup.com), 185 Asylum St., in City Place, opposite the Civic Center. Open for lunch Mon.–Fri.; dinner daily. Reservations suggested. Internationally inspired cuisine is served at this sleek downtown hot spot that melds hip with good taste. The high-ceilinged dining room is decked with white linen and chandeliers, and chef Hunter Morton's cooking more than matches the sophisticated surroundings. On the lighter side is pan-seared shrimp with gnocchi and roasted eggplant; more filling entrées include the date and almond crusted rack of lamb with chanterelle mushrooms, caramelized celery root, and red wine curry jus; and the chipotle-marinated "cowboy cut" beef rib chop, with chili onion rings. For dessert, the warm chocolate tart with espresso ice cream and cocoa syrup, and the mascarpone cheesecake with citrus consommé are standouts. An urbane crowd packs the bar, which has killer martinis and its own menu of cool bar bites. $21–35.

♿ **Peppercorn's Grill** (860-547-1714; www.peppercornsgrills.com), 357 Main St. Lunch Mon.–Fri.; dinner Mon.–Sat.; closed Sun. An established spot on downtown's dining scene, full of up-and-comers. They call it Nuova Italian, and that means stylish pasta combinations, with broccoli rabe pesto, say, and scallop-and-lobster ravioli. Risotto, pizza, veal, seafood, and lots more to choose from. Waiters are friendly and helpful; the surroundings are cozy: white linen, hand-painted wall murals, soft lighting. The Cialfi family run an equally fine Italian restaurant in the suburbs (see "West of the River"). $17–28.

ON20 (860-722-5161; www.ontwenty .com), 1 State St., 20th floor. Open for lunch Mon.–Fri. Reservations are required. Formerly The Polytechnic Club, this elegant dining room in the Hartford Steam Boiler building offers the same stellar cuisine and magnificent wraparound city views from 20 floors up. This is a quiet and gracious retreat, where classical music and fine paintings (and that view) provide a fitting backdrop to chef Noel Jones's expertly prepared classic and contemporary American cuisine. His multicourse fixed-price menu offers seasonally changing food that looks beautiful and tastes wonderful. There might be petit filet mignon with golden mushroom sauce; poached red snapper with artichoke puree; or wild mushroom risotto with shaved truffles. Wave away the dessert cart at your own peril. Most people might not equate fine dining with daytime, but here it's well worth the splurge. Ask about special evening events like seasonal dinners and wine tastings. Prix fixe $35; à la carte $8–20.

Sally's Fish Camp (860-278-8852; www.sallysfishcamp.com), 201 Ann St. Open for lunch Tue.–Fri.; dinner Tue.–Sat.; closed Sun. and Mon. For years this was Pastis, the city's first authentic brasserie. Today a fish-centric menu that includes fried fish platters and lobster potpie has replaced the coq au vin and *pomme frites.* $16–28.

♿ **Spris Restaurant & Bar** (860-247-7747; www.sprishartford.com), 10 Constitution Plaza. Open for lunch Mon.–Fri.; dinner Mon.–Sat.; Sun. brunch. Open for dinner on Sundays in December. Spris (pronounced *sprees*) is named for a well-known Italian aperitif; here well-known northern Italian cuisine is done exceptionally well. It's a great place for traditional dishes of Treviso: marinated sardines, veal liver, or a variety of tasty pastas and pizzas. A stylish, modern dining room, with soaring windows overlooking the plaza; alfresco dining when the weather allows. $15–34.

♿ **Trumbull Kitchen** (860-493-7412; www.trumbullkitchen.com), 150 Trumbull St. Open for lunch Mon.–Fri.; dinner daily. Reservations suggested. Part of the venerable Max restaurant group, Trumbull offers an extensive, something-for-everyone menu that follows the retro-comfort-food trend. Like the menu, the decor is part sleek (leather-upholstered walls and floor-to-ceiling mirrors), part homey (family-style long communal tables). An excellent case in point is Hilda's Meatloaf, which is paired with garlic mashed potatoes and roasted shallot sauce. Or try the dim sum, tapas, stone pies, or fondue. The real fun, though, comes with the dessert menu, especially the sweet potato pie with cranberry pomegranate sauce and caramel whipped cream. $16–25.

Vivo (860-760-2333), in the Marriott Hartford Downtown, 200 Columbus Blvd. Open Mon.–Fri. for breakfast, lunch, and dinner; Sat. and Sun. for breakfast and dinner. This better-than-usual hotel restaurant bills itself as a "seasonal trattoria," which translates into fresh local ingredients, from baby arugula in spring to butternut squash in autumn. You might start with seared beef carpaccio with lemon Parmesan aioli, then try pork loin with caramelized apples and Gorgonzola roasted potatoes; or manicotti stuffed with tofu, spinach, and basil with sautéed fennel and a sherry-infused marinara sauce. Desserts are traditional and satisfying: cheesecake, bread pudding, *panna cotta*. $23–43.

EATING OUT **Agave Grill** (860-242-3344; www.agavehartford.com), 100 Allyn St. Open for lunch Mon.–Sat.; dinner daily; seating until midnight on

Fri. and Sat. Agave is one of the new kids on the block that has breathed new life into Hartford's nighttime scene. Here Tex-Mex standards are given a contemporary spin and are accompanied by more than 30 tequilas. Guacamole is prepared tableside; corn tortillas are stuffed with roasted pork loin in a pineapple-chile sauce, then topped with manchego cheese; shrimp comes skewered on sugarcane, brushed with a chipotle passion fruit glaze, and served atop roasted pineapple and black bean salad. For traditionalists, there are enchiladas, burritos, burgers, and *chili con queso.* The young and lively crowd comes for the laid-back vibe reminiscent of a breezy beach cantina. $12–21.

The Asylum Café (860-524-8651; www.theasylumcafe.com), 253 Asylum St. Open for lunch and dinner daily. This used to be the über-popular Red Plate, and signature dishes like pizza and cheesecake are still on the menu. There's also homey Italian comfort food (eggplant parmigiana, spaghetti and meatballs, lasagna), plus entrées that are dressed up a bit (tilapia Piccata; yellowfin tuna; grilled Angus ribeye steak). Save room for the must-try cheesecake: individual creamy portions are wrapped in a cookie crust, then drizzled in raspberry sauce. A late-night crowd packs the bar. $13–25.

♿ **Black-Eyed Sally's BBQ and Blues** (860-278-7427; www.blackeyedsallys.com), 350 Asylum St. Open for lunch Mon.–Fri.; dinner Mon.–Sat.; closed Sun. A little slice of Memphis in New England, serving up food that is as red-hot as the blues musicians who heat up the stage. Cajun and Creole cuisine—gumbo, jambalaya, and fried crawfish tails, to name a few—with such classic southern accompaniments as collard greens, black-eyed peas, and corn bread. Live blues in the evening, Wed.–Sat. (see *Entertainment*). $15–23.

City Steam Brewery Café (860-525-1600; www.citysteambrewerycafe.com), 942 Main St. Open for lunch Mon.–Sat.; dinner daily. An eclectic yet casual menu served in an ornate 1877 Romanesque Revival gem, the former Brown Thompson building. A full menu of classic American fare, but best known for its award-winning handcrafted brews that are available only here. Live music and weekend comedy acts (see *Entertainment*). $11–23.

♿ **First and Last Tavern** (860-956-6000), 939 Maple Ave. Open daily for lunch and dinner. A 70-year-old tavern that's got an appealing neighborhood-joint feel and a wood-burning oven that turns out justly famous brick-oven Neapolitan pizzas. There's also a raw bar and Italian specialties. The long wooden bar bustles with an after-work crowd. Check out the montage of celebrity photos on the dining room wall. $8–20.

Mayor Mike's (860-522-6453; www.mayormikes.com), 283 Asylum St. Open for lunch Mon.–Fri.; dinner daily. Yes, Mike was a mayor. Mike Peters is a firefighter turned four-term Hartford mayor, in fact. Until his death in 2009, friends still called him "Mayor," but his real job was as co-owner of this friendly American tavern that seems well on its way to becoming a city institution. The menu of seafood, steak, pasta, and other American and Italian favorites is given a southwestern spin. Solid and dependable pub-style appetizers lead to generously portioned plates of meat loaf, barbecued pork, grilled seafood, and robust pasta dishes. The ales are locally brewed; the old framed photos are of important Hartford folks. $12–18.

Polish National Home (860-247-1784), 60 Charter Oak Ave. Open for lunch and dinner Mon.–Sat.; call ahead about Sun. hours, which vary. This eatery in a longtime Polish American club is the kind of place that most people have heard of, yet haven't been to themselves. Thus it remains a somewhat hidden gem, and a local favorite for authentic Polish food in a no-frills, nostalgic setting. The bottles of horseradish on each table, and the live radio broadcasts of polka tunes (on Sunday), are signs that this place is different. Satisfyingly hearty meals come with modest prices. Kielbasa, pierogi, potato pancakes, and stuffed cabbage are all available, as are homemade sauerkraut and cabbage soup, expertly cooked by Polish immigrants. For the indecisive, there's a sampler of favorites called the Polish Plate. $7–15.

The Russell (860-727-4014), 103 Pratt St. Open daily for lunch and dinner; Sun. brunch. This casual storefront café and bar at the busy corner of Trumbull and Pratt streets is good for grabbing a quick bite or whiling away a couple of hours, if your schedule allows. Curry Cajun shrimp salad and the jerk chicken sandwich are standouts on the Caribbean-inspired menu, which features desserts like gelato and key lime cheesecake. $8–15.

Tapas on Ann (860-525-5988; www.tapasonline.com), 126-130 Ann St. Open Mon.–Sat. for lunch and dinner; closed Sun. A busy, noisy, and energetic café known for its Mediterranean-inspired dishes. Depending on when you're here, you'll rub elbows with the mad lunch rush, the afterwork crowd, or those grabbing a quick bite before a game or concert at XL Center. Here, *tapas* refers to flatbread pizzas rather than Spanish-style small plates; gyros, falafel, souvlaki, and kebabs are equally good. $10–15.

Trinity Restaurant (860-728-9822), 243 Zion St. Open Mon.–Sat. for breakfast, lunch, and dinner; brunch on Sun. Reservations suggested on weekends. For years this was Timothy's, known by students and professors for its huge portions of comfort food. It's just across the street from the Trinity College campus, in the area known as Back of the Rocks. Casual American cuisine means inventive soups (a specialty) and unusual treatments of standard entrées (sweet potato enchiladas, chicken tacos) using locally grown organic ingredients. Service is known to be slow, but for the promise of a decent meal within walking distance of campus, loyal patrons let it slide. $9–15.

Tisane Euro-Asian Café (860-523-5417), 537 Farmington Ave. (CT 4). Open daily 7 AM–1 AM; open until 2 AM on Fri. and Sat. Everyone knows this West End fixture as a coffeehouse (see below) and a martini bar, but there's also a full menu that takes its inspiration from virtually every corner of the globe. Start off by sampling the appetizers, which include *steak frites*, edamame hummus, and grilled portobello bites. Move on to shrimp pad Thai or a hearty sandwich on grilled flatbread. Dessert is where things really get going: fresh fruit and bite-sized chunks of cake come with a pot of luscious melted chocolate for dipping. This is a dawn-to-dusk operation: You can begin your day with a latte here at 8 AM and wind things up with martinis at midnight. $11–16.

COFFEEHOUSES **La Paloma Sabanera Coffeehouse and Bookstore** (860-548-1670; www.lapalomasabanera.com), 405 Capitol Ave. Open Mon.–Fri. 7–6; Sat. 10–6; closed Sun. This friendly community gathering spot attracts a mix of college students, insurance workers, artists, and families with youngsters, who love the upstairs room just for them. The deliciously robust coffee comes from fair-trade organic beans grown in Puerto Rico and Central and South America; the bookshelves feature titles by Latino authors. Ask about their schedule of live-jazz evenings, book readings, independent films, and art exhibits.

Jojo's Coffee Roasting Company (860-524-1488), 22 Pratt St. Open daily. A busy downtown coffee shop with a relaxing feel (think comfy couches and local artwork). More than a dozen coffee blends are crafted from roasted-right-here beans; sandwiches, homemade soups, desserts, and other quick bites go nicely with them.

Tisane Euro-Asian Café (860-523-5417), 537 Farmington Ave. (CT 4). Open daily from 7 AM. Gourmet coffee, eye-popping espresso drinks, 100 teas and 80 specialty coffees, and a creative international menu (see above). The artsy vibe and laid-back atmosphere make this a beloved retreat among the Starbucks-weary.

SNACKS **Alchemy Juice Bar Café** (860-246-5700; www.alchemyjuicebar.com), 203 New Britain Ave. Open Tue.–Sat. 11:30–8:30; Sun. 10–6; closed Mon. "Changing the world one juice at a time." That's the mantra at this vegetarian/vegan eatery across from the Trinity College campus. Good-for-you juice drinks come jam-packed with amino acids and antioxidants, by way of ginger, garlic, beets, kale, wheatgrass, and goji juice, which Himalayans believe contains antiaging properties. Of the organic nondairy milk shake smoothies, the Peanut Butter Cup exudes dessertlike decadence. The menu is 99 percent organic, from the tofu scrambles and homemade granola in the morning to the soups, sandwiches, wraps, and salads later on. Feeling stressed? Pull up a stool at the oxygen bar, where you can take a hit of pure oxygen scented with clove, eucalyptus, lavender, and other organic essential oils. A yoga studio, eco-boutique, and film series round out the offerings. $5–12.

♿ **First & Last Bakery and Café** (860-956-7000), 920 Maple Ave. Open daily for breakfast and lunch. A new South End bakery and café resides in a renovated 1920s-era brick factory building with vintage-style lighting and green canvas awnings. Homemade European-style pastries, handcrafted artisan breads, deli sandwiches, grilled panini, and salads are all available to go. If you stay, kick back on the brownstone patio or inside the café, which also sells white truffle olive oil and other gourmet specialty foods.

Franklin Giant Grinder Shop (860-296-6574), 464 Franklin Ave. Open Tue.–Sun.; closed Mon. A local favorite in Hartford's Italian district for authentic Italian fare, but it's the generous amounts of quality meats and cheeses stuffed into freshly baked breads that most people make the trip for.

Mozzicato–De Pasquale Bakery & Pastry Shop (860-296-0426; www.mozzicatobakery.com), 329 Franklin Ave. Bakery and café open daily 7 AM–9 PM. Traditional Italian pastries, each more sinfully tempting than the next, fill gleaming glass cases in this tidy South End shop that has been run by the same family since 1908. Cannoli, biscotti, éclairs, marzipan, cookies, cakes, and imported Italian confections. They also make stuffed breads and pizza slices mounded with toppings, creamy gelato, and in the summertime, cool granita. Next door, the **Mozzicato Caffe** is a real-deal Italian coffee bar, with pastries, gelato, cappuccino, and espresso.

Roscoe's Big Dog (860-296-2867), 24 Temple St. Open Mon.–Sat. 11–3; closed Sun. Roscoe's is giving the region's hot dog hot spots a run for the money. The first-rate grilled franks are served in split-top buttered and grilled buns and can be topped with your choice of 14 condiments, from classic mustard to homemade chili meat sauce and coleslaw. The burgers are steamed to perfection, but the dogs rule. Big appetites should order the quarter-pounder with a side of crunchy hand-cut Belgian fries. $3–7.

Woody's Hot Dogs (860-278-5499), 915 Main St. Open for lunch Mon.–Sat.; open Sundays during football season. It's all about dogs at Woody's, a longtime downtown favorite. Hot dog aficionados who don't go to Roscoe's (see above) will likely be found here, noshing on grilled, foot-long, all-beef dogs on toasted buns. Go ahead and order them smothered in the usual toppings, but they're also good enough to enjoy plain. $3–8.

Entertainment

Before going out, pick up a free copy of the *Hartford Advocate*, available at stores and restaurants all over the city, for listings of concerts, exhibits, films, and events. The **Greater Hartford Arts Council** (860-525-8629; www.letsgoarts.org), 45 Pratt St., promotes the city's cultural scene and is a good resource for what's going on in the arts and entertainment community. Check their online calendar of events, exhibitions, performances, festivals, and concerts.

The XL Center (860-249-6333; box office: 860-525-4500; www.hartfordciviccenter.com), 1 Civic Center Plaza, Trumbull and Asylum streets. Formerly the Hartford Civic Center, this is the venue for sports contests, popular and rock concerts, and trade shows of all sorts.

ARTS CENTERS **Aetna Theater** (860-278-2670), 600 Main St. This attractive little theater on the lower level of the Wadsworth Atheneum Museum of Art presents a variety of live entertainment and films, including innovative concerts and programs designed to illuminate current exhibits; family activities that combine theater and artworks for parents and children together; film festivals; and live drama by local theater companies.

The Artists Collective (860-527-3205; www.artistscollective.org), 1200 Albany Ave. An arts and cultural center supporting African American musicians hosts year-round jazz performances, dance and theatrical productions, gospel singers, and art exhibits; call or check online for a schedule.

♿ **Austin Arts Center** (860-297-2199; www.austinarts.org), 300 Summit St., on the campus of Trinity College. Performances during the academic year, Sept.–Apr. Musical, dramatic, and dance performances, as well as art exhibits, by college faculty, students, and guest artists.

Bushnell Center for the Performing Arts (860-987-5900; 888-824-2874; www.bushnell.org), 166 Capitol Ave. The Bushnell is the city's premier center for both local and touring performance artists and companies, and the performance home of the **Hartford Symphony Orchestra** (www.hartfordsymphony.org). The building, with its distinctive art deco auditorium, is a National Historic Landmark. Free tours of the hall are offered; call 860-987-6033 for a schedule.

Charter Oak Cultural Center (860-249-1207; www.charteroakcultural

Courtesy Central Regional Tourism District

HARTFORD'S BUSHNELL CENTER FOR THE PERFORMING ARTS IS THE CITY'S PREMIER VENUE FOR CONCERTS, MUSICALS, DANCE PERFORMANCES, AND HOLIDAY SHOWS.

center.org), 21 Charter Oak Ave. A variety of concerts and performances mounted year-round in the city's oldest synagogue. Call for a schedule.

Hartford Conservatory of Performing Arts (860-246-2588; www.hartford conservatory.org), 834 Asylum Ave. A top-notch school for emerging performance artists. For the public, a year-round schedule of concerts as well as dance and theatrical performances at various venues.

Real Art Ways (860-232-1006; www.realartways.org), 56 Arbor St. Open throughout the year, with gallery hours Tue.–Thu. and Sun. 2–10; Fri. and Sat. 2–11; closed Mon. Admission $3; films $9. An old typewriter factory turned art gallery and performance space is one of Connecticut's most innovative arts centers. Real Art Ways is devoted to new and experimental art in exhibits, concerts, performances, and spoken-word and video presentations. A 153-seat cinema showing first-run independent and foreign films, and a café, are on the premises.

MUSIC **Concerts and recitals** are held in many of the city's churches and public buildings; check local newspaper listings for more information.

Outdoor concerts are held during the summer in **Bushnell Park**, **Elizabeth Park**, and elsewhere around the city (see *Green Space*). A music series is featured at **Riverfront Plaza** downtown (www.riverfront.org) on summer weekends.

Dodge Music Centre (860-525-4500; box office: 203-265-1501; www.live nation.com), 61 Savitt Way. Formerly the Meadows Music Theater, this is the state's most popular outdoor amphitheater, designed to allow both indoor seating (for 7,500) and outdoor seating (for 18,000) at performances. The schedule includes pop, rock, blues, country, and classical artists, as well as comedy and family shows.

Webster Theater (860-525-5553; www.webstertheater.com), 31 Webster St. National and regional rock, blues, jazz, and other acts take the stage in this well-preserved 1937 art deco movie house turned rock club known simply as "The Webster." The original movie screen is still here; five bars have been added. Call or check online for a schedule.

NIGHTLIFE **Arch Street Tavern** (860-246-7610; www.archstreettavern

.com), 85 Arch St. A favorite institution on the city's bar scene with a menu of sandwiches, salads, and other pub fare. DJs, karaoke, and acoustic performances during the week; rock bands on weekends.

Black-Eyed Sally's BBQ and Blues (860-278-7427; www.blackeyedsallys.com), 350 Asylum St. Live music Wed.–Sat. nights. When nationally known blues artists come to Hartford, this is where they play. Also a good restaurant, with New Orleans and Cajun specialties (see *Eating Out*).

Brick Yard Café (860-249-2112), 111–113 Allyn St. Live bands Thu., Fri., and Sat. nights. A sprawling multilevel nightclub—live bands and a lounge on the first floor; DJ and dancing on the second floor; pool tables and 27 televisions on top.

City Steam Brewery Café (860-525-1600; www.citysteambrewerycafe.com), 942 Main St. A many-level restaurant (see *Eating Out*) and gathering spot, in a landmark Romanesque brownstone. Blues, jazz, and DJs most nights. Home of the **Brew Ha Ha Comedy Club**. Pool room and outdoor beer garden.

Crush (860-760-2340), in the Marriott Downtown, 200 Columbus Blvd. The business-as-usual hotel bar gets a shot of stylish, youthful energy at Crush, where a crowd of conventioneers, dressed-up locals, and martini-sipping hipsters come for the ultrasleek surroundings (white leather banquettes and cool-hued glass walls), killer house cocktails, DJ-spun house music, and New York ambience. Live jazz on Tuesday and Wednesday nights.

The Half Door (860-232-7827; www.thehalfdoor.com), 270 Sisson Ave. Lunch and dinner served daily; breakfast on Sat. and Sun. A traditional Irish pub featuring live Irish and American music, authentic Irish fare, and an extensive list of lagers, ales, stouts, porters, and pilsners.

♿ **Joe Black's** (860-524-0796; www.joeblacksbar.com), 31 Pratt St. Open daily for lunch and dinner. The gorgeous marble-and-wood interior of this former bank is reminiscent of a Dublin pub. There's a convivial crowd, live music, and lots of beers on tap. The traditional Irish fare ranges from lamb stew and fish-and-chips to brown-bread-and-butter pudding.

Koji (860-247-5654), 17 Asylum St. One of downtown's sleekest watering holes; this one specializes in sake, and lots of it—more than 100 varieties of the Japanese rice-based drink. Saki-based cocktails, called saketinis, come with lychee, coconut, and other exotic flavors. A full roster of sushi, tempura, and *yakitori* (Japanese-style skewered grilled meats and veggies) comes in small-plate portions.

Pig's Eye Pub (860-278-4747), 356 Asylum St. A no-frills wood-paneled beer joint upstairs from Black-Eyed Sally's (see above), with pool tables and video games. In summer, the outdoor rooftop bar offers reggae and other live music. The crowd is a mix of youngsters out for the night and business types just out of work.

Room 960 (860-522-9960), 960 Main St. Longtime Connecticut residents know this place as the historic G. Fox department store building. Today DJs spin house music in this modern and minimalist dance club and lounge, where a hip, young crowd dresses to see and be seen.

Vaughan's Public House (860-882-1560; www.irishpublichouse.com), 59 Pratt St. Pints of ale, pub-style grub, and Irish standards (Guinness, shepherd's pie, corned beef and cabbage) are served until late; games are broadcast on big-screen TVs. The black-and-white photos, jukebox out back, and long stool-lined bar lend an old-school vibe to this new place.

Wood-n-Tap Bar & Grill (860-232-8277; www.woodntap.com), 99 Sisson Ave. A local favorite just off I-84 (Exit 46). College students and locals come for the late-night menu of pub appetizers, pizza, and burgers, as well as the live entertainment.

THEATER ▼ ♿ **Cinestudio** (860-297-2544; showtimes 860-297-2463; www.cinestudio.org), 300 Summit St., on the Trinity College campus. An old-fashioned one-screen theater, founded by Trinity students in 1970, showing first-run, foreign, and classic films. The theater hosts the annual **Connecticut Gay & Lesbian Film Festival**.

Hartford Stage Company (860-525-5601; box office 860-527-5151; www.hartfordstage.org), 50 Church St. Downtown Hartford's prestigious Tony Award–winning theater, at home in a Venturi and Rauch–designed redbrick block of a building, slashed with bold zigzags of darker brick. The three-quarter-thrust stage in a 489-seat auditorium provides flexibility for a wide range of offerings: Shakespeare, Molière, and other classics, along with new plays and cutting-edge experiments. The season is late Sept.–June, with summer stage productions in July and Aug. Call for a schedule.

TheaterWorks (860-527-7838; www.theaterworkshartford.org), 233 Pearl St. New and edgy contemporary works presented by a local professional company at this intimate, 200-seat Off-Broadway-style venue. Several productions a year. Call for information.

✷ Selective Shopping

ART GALLERIES **Artworks Gallery** (860-247-3522; www.artworksgallery.org), 233 Pearl St. Open Wed.–Fri. 11–5; Sat. 12:30–3:30; other times by appointment. Exhibitions by local and regional contemporary artists, as well as lectures, workshops, and performances. This is Greater Hartford's first artists' cooperative, founded in 1976.

Paesaggio at 100 Pearl (860-680-3596), 100 Pearl St. Open Mon.–Fri. 9–8; Sat. 9–3. Changing exhibitions focus on works of contemporary regional, national, and international artists.

Pump House Gallery (860-543-8874), 60 Elm St., near Pulaski Circle, in the southeast corner of Bushnell Park. Open year-round, Tue.–Fri. 11–2. Works of Connecticut artists are shown in this charming 1947 Tudor-style stone (still functioning) pump house, and in summer there is a music series.

BOOKSTORES **Gallows Hill Book Store** (860-297-5231), 300 Summit St., on the Trinity College campus (use the Broad St. entrance). A former maintenance building has been transformed with carpets, woodwork, and taste into a book lover's paradise. An exhibit is devoted to works by Trinity faculty, and the general level of offerings, befits a college campus. There's a good children's section and good travel coverage; coffee and cookies are available, as are comfortable chairs to sit in.

Hartford Seminary Bookstore (860-509-9527), 77 Sherman St. In the pristine and unusual white building that houses the seminary, the bookstore serves those interested in religion, theology, and related fields.

SPECIAL SHOPS **Kolo Boutique** (860-293-0624; www.kolo.com), 241 Asylum St. This photo album giant is based in Hartford and has a small retail shop downtown where you can browse their stylish, archival-quality photo albums that come in an eclectic variety of colors and materials. Ask about special events like album design workshops, perfect for organizing all those family photos in style.

Stackpole, Moore & Tryon (860-522-0181), 242 Trumbull St. An upscale men's clothier and a venerable Hartford institution for more than a century, selling top-of-the-line suits, ties, and clothing to the city's business and political community since 1909.

Tuesday's (860-247-1999), 257 Asylum St., at the corner of Ann St. Open Tue.–Sat.; closed Sun. and Mon. Traditional and trendy fashions for men and women; custom-designed shirts, suits, sport jackets, and outerwear.

✷ Special Events

January: **Boar's Head and Yule Log Festival** (860-278-0785), Asylum Hill Congregational Church, 814 Asylum Ave. Music, dance, medieval pageants and costumes. ♿ **Hartford Boat and Fishing Show** (860-767-2645; www.hartfordboatshow.com), Connecticut Convention Center, 100 Columbus Blvd. Boats of all sizes, from recreational and fishing boats to personal watercraft. A full schedule of seminars and professional speakers.

February: ♿ **Connecticut Flower and Garden Show** (860-529-2123; www.ctflowershow.com), at the Connecticut Convention Center, 100 Columbus Blvd. Display gardens by the area's top landscape designers; fresh flowers and herbs, gardening products, advice, seminars, and workshops.

March: **Connecticut Spring Antiques Show** (860-493-1300; www.ctspringantiquesshow.com), Connecticut Expo Center, Weston St. Nationally recognized event with more than 16 dealers. **Spring Home Show** (860-563-4565), at the Connecticut Convention Center, 100 Columbus Blvd. Hundreds of the newest products and services to enhance your domain. **Greater Hartford St. Patrick's Day Parade**, downtown. The parade, which starts at the state capitol and ends at Bushnell Park, is preceded by a 5K road race.

Summer: The **Hartford Regional Market** (860-713-2503), 101 Reserve

CONNECTICUT'S ORNATE 19TH-CENTURY GOLD-DOMED STATE CAPITOL BUILDING STANDS SENTINEL OVER DOWNTOWN HARTFORD.

Courtesy Connecticut General Assembly and the League of Women Voters of Connecticut

Rd., Exit 27 off I-91. Those in the know get up bright and early and head to this vast 32-acre outdoor market selling fruits, vegetables, perennials, trees, and other farm products. **Laurel Street Farmers Market** (860-296-9325), 75 Laurel St. Held on Saturdays from mid-June through September. A popular West End farmer's market offering fresh fruits, vegetables, herbs, and cut flowers from local farms, as well as jams, honey, eggs, and homemade breads and pies.

June: **Rose Weekend** (860-242-0017; www.elizabethpark.org), in the Rose Garden at **Elizabeth Park** (860-242-0017), celebrates the park's more than 15,000 rosebushes in the height of bloom.

July: **Riverfest** (860-713-3131), Hartford's regional Fourth of July celebration. A traditional community gala in Hartford and East Hartford, with events, performances, food, and fun on either side of, and even in, the water. Fireworks launched above the Connecticut River. **Greater Hartford Festival of Jazz** (866-843-5299; www.jazzhartford.org), Bushnell Park. Free three-day weekend of live outdoor concerts in the city's iconic green space, featuring local and nationally known small ensembles and big bands, even students from area schools' jazz programs.

Late September/early October: **Head of the Riverfront Regatta** (860-713-3131), Charter Oak Landing. Thousands of high school, college, and masters rowers compete on a 2.5-mile course up the Connecticut River.

October: **Fall Hartford Antiques Show** (207-767-3967), Connecticut Expo Center, Weston St. American pieces dating from the early 1600s. **Greater Hartford Marathon** (860-652-8866; www.hartfordmarathon.com), Bushnell Park. Marathon, half marathon, and kids' race through the area. **Hartford International Jazz Festival** (860-524-9094; www.hijf.com), Columbus Day weekend. A three-day festival with jazz, Latin, blues, and world music at parks, restaurants, clubs, and other venues around the city.

November: **Open Studio Weekend** (860-371-3924; www.open-studio.com), various locations. Artists across the city open their galleries, studios, and shops to the public. **Fall Hartford Home Show** (860-563-2111), Connecticut Expo Center, Weston St.

November through early January: **Festival of Light** (860-525-8629), on Constitution Plaza downtown, celebrates the holiday season with thousands of tiny white lights on trees, buildings, and fountains, with silhouetted angels in midair. **Holiday Lights Fantasia** (860-343-1565), Goodwin Park, 1192 Maple Ave. A leisurely 2-mile drive through a display of twinkling lights and animated holiday scenes. The spectacular show kicks off at Thanksgiving and lasts for 40 days, celebrating Christmas, Hannukah, Kwanzaa, Three Kings Day, and New Year's.

December: **Christmas Crafts Expo** (860-653-6671), Connecticut Expo Center. More than 250 crafters display their holiday wares during the first two weekends in December. **The Governor's Residence** (860-566-4840), 990 Prospect Ave., and **Mark Twain House & Museum** (860-247-0998), 351 Farmington Ave. at Woodland St., are both decorated for the holidays; call for a schedule.

December 31: **First Night Hartford** (860-722-9546; www.firstnighthartford.org), a downtown celebration to greet the new year with music, theater, art, dancing, and children's entertainment, including a parade and early fireworks.

WEST OF THE RIVER

The region west of the Connecticut River, just out the back door of Connecticut's capital city, is a study in contrasts. Seen from the air, it's a patchwork of wooded hills, suburban neighborhoods, and commercial strips, not to mention a surprising amount of farmland. It isn't as rural as it was, say, in the 19th century, when shade tobacco was a major cash crop. At first blush, today's visitor might see little more than a string of upscale suburbs and shopping centers, but a closer look reveals something quite different. It's a mecca for travelers looking to divide their time between history and shopping, art and antiques, and it boasts some of the brightest stars on the state's culinary scene. Today's visitors follow a long line of travelers—farmers and statesmen, artists and architects—who've been drawn to the valleys of the Connecticut and Farmington rivers for nearly 400 years, ever since Windsor's founding in 1633, which makes Windsor arguably the oldest town in the state. The natural beauty of the countryside, and its proximity to Hartford, have attracted many who work in the city to establish their homes and develop community life in the region's well-tended towns. Those in the know recognize it as one of Connecticut's best areas for living and dining.

Hartford's neighboring towns have preserved much of their New England flavor, thanks to the foresight of tradition-conscious citizens. While many have been transformed from sleepy farm villages into upscale enclaves of high-priced real estate, they tread a careful path between commercialism and historic integrity that stretches their small-town labels. There is no truer emblem of New England than the lovingly preserved homes that capture the feel of the colonial era, as in Windsor; or the grand clapboard mansions—some house museums, others B&Bs—that allow travelers a glimpse into the past, as in Suffield. Also in the mix are exclusive private schools, polo grounds, working farms that date back centuries, and industrial centers that stand as a testament to Connecticut's manufacturing heyday. Farmington is perhaps best known as the site of Miss Porter's School, where young women are prepared for college, life, and, in many cases, celebrity. Avon was a longtime farming town until the Farmington Canal and Albany Turnpike crossed paths in the 18th century and a commercial center blossomed. In Simsbury a complex of historic buildings dates from the earliest contacts between colonists and Native Americans. On the Farmington River, Collinsville is a quintessential 19th-century one-mill town and home to the former Collins Co., the world's first ax factory. Today a lively community of commuters, artists, and outdoorsy types call the leafy postcard village home.

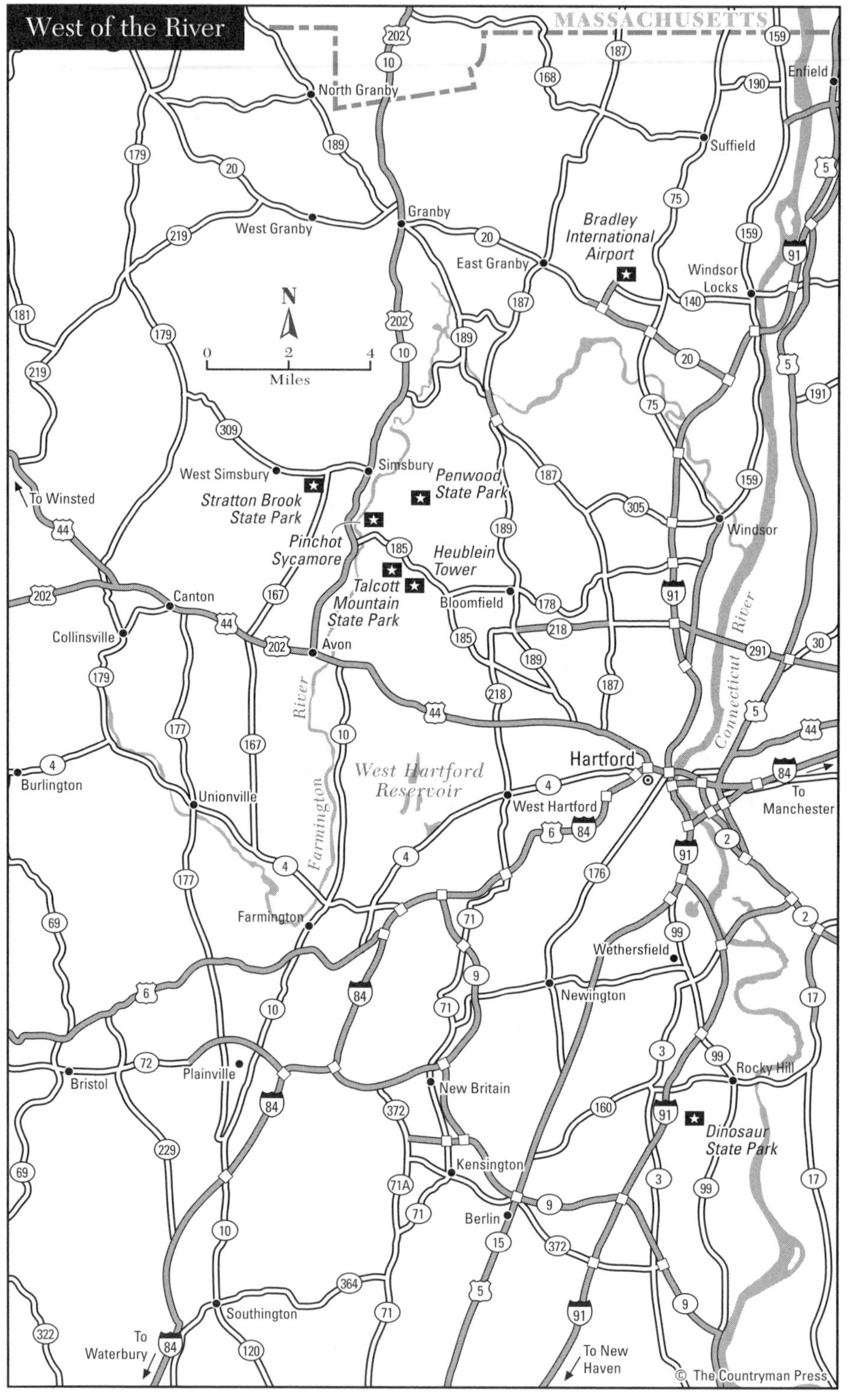
West of the River
MASSACHUSETTS
North Granby
Enfield
Suffield
Granby
West Granby
East Granby
Bradley International Airport
Windsor Locks
Miles
West Simsbury
Simsbury
Penwood State Park
Stratton Brook State Park
Pinchot Sycamore
Heublein Tower
Talcott Mountain State Park
To Winsted
Windsor
Canton
Collinsville
Avon
Bloomfield
Connecticut River
Farmington River
West Hartford Reservoir
Hartford
Burlington
Unionville
West Hartford
To Manchester
Farmington
Wethersfield
Newington
Rocky Hill
Bristol
Plainville
New Britain
Dinosaur State Park
Kensington
Berlin
Southington
To Waterbury
To New Haven
© The Countryman Press

If history is your fancy, you can't do any better than Wethersfield, which claims the state's largest historic district with more than 200 buildings predating 1850. It boasts the house where George Washington not only slept but also planned, along with Rochambeau, the campaign that ended the Revolutionary War. A number of homes—one open as a museum—date from the Pilgrim century, and a pre-1691 warehouse on the cove harkens to the town's long-ago importance as a shipping port. Wethersfield was once dubbed Oniontown because the pungent scent of the town's famous red bulbs pervaded the air; in the town center stands the handsome redbrick church funded by the sale of locally grown red onions. In his diary, John Adams describes the view from its steeple as "the most grand and beautiful prospect in the world." A vestige of Wethersfield's agricultural past is Comstock, Ferre & Co., the oldest continuously operating seed company in the United States and a Main Street landmark since 1820.

New Britain belongs to another age, the industrial 19th century. It's known as the Hardware City, where the Stanley Works, P. and F. Corbin, North and Judd, and New Britain Machine Company distributed hardware, builders' tools, locks, ball bearings, and much more worldwide. The city began to decline as industry departed for the south, and the factories are less of a presence in town these days; but New Britain points to other attractions: minor-league baseball, a top-notch art museum, the Central Connecticut State University campus—home to one of the country's largest public telescopes—and myriad Polish bakeries, cafés, and groceries that celebrate the city's rich ethnic heritage.

If traffic makes you cringe, stay away from US 44, the Berlin Turnpike, and other commercial strips similarly lined with national big-box behemoths. Go instead for the quiet back roads that wend their way through a far more satisfying landscape. A good place to start is the rural towns (Granby, Suffield, Windsor) just below the Massachusetts border, then head south to cross the Connecticut River via the nation's oldest continuously operating ferry service; fortunately, the ferry still keeps time, at a 17th-century pace. Along the way, apple orchards and roadside produce stands speak of simpler times.

Tobacco Valley is the local name for the land alongside the Connecticut River. Native Americans were cultivating it when the first English settlers arrived, and by 1640 the skill had been passed on to the newcomers. This is Connecticut's tobacco country, where many entrepreneurs made their fortunes by peddling tobacco products. Later it was discovered that the climate in the river valley was similar to that of Sumatra, where broadleaf tobacco—used for cigar wrappers—originated. The nation's first cigar factory opened in West Suffield in 1810; by the Civil War, the majority of the town's 316 working farms were growing the cash crop. The Phelps-Hatheway House on Suffield's historic Main Street is the grandest, its architecture a testament to tobacco's riches. Much less tobacco is raised nowadays, but in summer you'll still see fields covered with billowy white cloth—a puzzling sight to visitors. Today the land has been claimed for other uses, but agriculture still helps define the region, from small dairy operations to pick-your-own fields—even a farm devoted to garlic.

For a more trendy experience, head to West Hartford, whose hip see-and-be-seen downtown known as West Hartford Center is filled with more than 140 cafés, boutiques, and galleries that offer unparalleled people-watching. The $160 million Blue Back Square retail, residential, and entertainment complex debuted in 2007, changing the face of it all with upscale condos, a hotel, an art cinema, trendy restaurants, and high-end shops (think Crate & Barrel, REI, Ann Taylor), all named for the *Blue-backed Speller*, a 19th-century grammar text written by local-boy-made-good Noah Webster, who also penned America's first dictionary. The junction where Farmington Avenue and Main Street meet is now one of the most vibrant downtowns in the state.

The Farmington River Valley is filling up with new culinary hot spots: In Canton, Simmer is as hot a restaurant as you're likely to find in the suburbs, but eclectic gourmet experiences are popping up everywhere, it seems. Want a little culture? In Farmington, the elegant turn-of-the-20th-century Hill-Stead mansion is a virtual museum of fine arts, while the polo grounds host the largest outdoor antiques show in Connecticut on Labor Day weekend. In Avon, cubicles of a former explosives plant have been turned into a series of artists' and crafts workers' studios. The New Britain Museum of American Art, fresh off a $26 million makeover, is a treasure trove of impressionism and Hudson River School paintings. For your listening pleasure, the Hartford Symphony Orchestra plays its summer concert series in Simsbury, and community theaters provide a delightful spectrum of entertainment, from first-rate original productions to Broadway musicals.

This is the suburbs, true; but there are plenty of places for locals to take off the Brooks Brothers suit and tie and venture outdoors. Green space comes by way of state parks and nature centers, rivers and rail-trails, ideal for a picnic, a spin on a bike, a paddle or float downstream, or a quiet hike through the woods. The Farmington River, which stakes out a generous loop of territory west and north of Hartford, offers whitewater sports during the spring thaw, as well as a cool venue for kayaking, tubing, and canoeing in summer. Cyclists and solitude seekers love the Farmington Valley Greenway, a multiuse recreational trail that cuts a quiet path through neighborhoods and along the old Farmington Canal. A wilderness experience it's not, but Talcott Mountain State Park offers a woodland getaway that will satisfy most outdoors enthusiasts, not to mention unparalleled panoramas from the top of Heublein Tower. From there you can see that this is a region of hills and valleys rolling endlessly in all directions, and the traprock ridge lends variety to the landscape.

However you decide to spend your time, don't miss the must-dos: In East Granby, visitors can explore the cold underground caverns of America's first copper mine, from the early 1700s, which became Old New-Gate Prison, Connecticut's first state jail, later that century. On the grounds of Bradley International Airport, the New England Air Museum has an impressive array of aircraft—historic to ultramodern—to see, and a cockpit simulator to climb into. The state's largest tree, the massive Pinchot Sycamore, stands proudly on the banks of the Connecticut River, not far from the ice rink where Olympic skaters train. And in Avon, you can watch the nation's oldest cavalry unit practice its drills, as it has since 1778.

Entries in this section are in roughly geographic order.

AREA CODE 860.

GUIDANCE **Central Regional Tourism District** (860-244-8181; 800-793-4480; www.enjoycentralct.com), 31 Pratt St., Hartford 06103, can provide brochures, events listings, maps, and answers to questions about travel and lodging in the area.

The **Greater Hartford Convention & Visitors Bureau** maintains a tourist information center stocked with travel literature at the **Windsor Chamber and Visitors Center** (860-688-5165), 261 Broad St., Windsor 06095. Open Mon.–Fri. 9–3.

Farmington Valley Visitors Association (860-676-8878; 800-493-5266; www.farmingtonvalleyvisit.com), 33 East Main St. (US 44), Avon 06001. This local organization can supply information on special seasonal promotions as well as visitor attractions and lodgings in Avon, Canton, Simsbury, Farmington, Granby, East Granby, and New Hartford.

Wethersfield Visitor's Center (860-529-7656), at the Keeney Memorial, 200 Main St., Wethersfield 06109. Open Mon.–Sat. 10–4; Sun. 1–4. Brochures and maps, as well as information on museums, historical sites, and shopping in town.

GETTING THERE *By car:* I-84 and I-91 intersect in Hartford, providing access from all directions. CT 9 is a divided, limited-access route connecting I-84 in Farmington with I-91 in Hartford and continuing south to I-95 in Old Saybrook. US 44 and CT 4 are good routes heading west from Hartford.

By air: **Bradley International Airport** (860-292-2000; 888-624-1533; www.bradleyairport.com) serves the entire state.

By train: **Amtrak** (800-872-7245; www.amtrak.com) stops at Windsor, Windsor Locks, and Berlin.

By bus: **Greyhound Lines** (800-231-2222; www.greyhound.com) and **Peter Pan Bus Lines** (800-343-9999; www.peterpanbus.com) stop in Farmington and New Britain.

GETTING AROUND For sightseeing or traveling in this area, a car is necessary.

By limo: **Connecticut Limousine Service (CT Limo)** (800-472-5466; www.ctlimo.com) serves Bradley International Airport in Windsor Locks with shuttle buses and vans.

By taxi: In Windsor Locks: **AAA Cab & Livery** (860-623-8888), **Best Cab** (860-623-0200), and **Airport Service Cab** (860-623-0333). In Plainville: **Valley Cab** (860-673-4250). In West Hartford: **Royal R's Inc.** (860-236-6000). In Farmington: **Suburban Livery Services** (860-284-0508). In Bloomfield: **Airport Taxi Service** (860-726-9400).

MEDICAL EMERGENCY The statewide emergency number is **911**.

The Hospital of Central Connecticut: Bradley Memorial Campus (860-276-5000), 81 Meriden Ave. (CT 120), Southington. The emergency number is 860-276-5200.

University of Connecticut Health Center (860-679-2000), 263 Farmington Ave. (CT 4), Farmington. The emergency number is 860-679-2588.

The Hospital of Central Connecticut: New Britain General Campus (860-224-5011), 100 Grand St., New Britain. The emergency number is 860-224-5671.

✷ To See

MUSEUMS See also *Historic Homes.*

In Farmington

Day-Lewis Museum (860-677-2754), 158 Main St. Open Mar.–Nov., Wed. 2–4; closed Aug., Dec.–Feb. Call for admission prices. At the site of an archaeological dig in the 1970s that turned up evidence of more than 10,000 years of human habitation, this Yale-owned archaeology museum specializes in Native American artifacts. The house itself, with its gambrel roof and clapboard siding, is an example of the post-and-beam construction used in colonial times.

In New Britain

Copernican Observatory and Planetarium (860-832-3399; 860-832-2950), Copernicus Hall, 1615 Stanley St., campus of Central Connecticut State University. Call for hours and admission prices. The observatory has one of the largest telescopes in the country. Friday- and Saturday-night shows on constellations, stars, planets, and other astronomical topics, followed by a session in the observatory, weather permitting; imaginative programs for all age groups scheduled year-round.

♿ **New Britain Industrial Museum** (860-832-8654; www.nbim.org), 185 Main St., second floor. Open year-round, Mon.–Fri. 2–5; Wed. noon–5. Free admission. Still known as the Hardware City, New Britain commemorates its industrial giants with changing exhibits devoted to Stanley Works, Fafnir Bearing, American Hardware, and other manufacturers that brought prosperity and jobs to the city in its heyday. Local residents have contributed thousands of items that their fathers and grandfathers helped make, from saddle hardware to art deco kitchenware. There are also glimpses of the future, focusing on electronics and new technologies.

New Britain Museum of American Art (860-229-0257; www.nbmaa.org), 56 Lexington St. Open Tue., Wed., and Fri. 11–5; Thu. 11–8; Sat. 10–5; Sun. noon–5; closed Mon. and major holidays. Adults $9; seniors $8; students $7; children under 12 free. This art museum is a treasure: It's an impressive collection devoted exclusively to American artworks, and its conception in 1903 makes this the oldest such collection in the country. There are more than 5,000 pieces in all, with an emphasis on American impressionism, Hudson River School paintings, and colonial portraiture. Among the noteworthy: Thomas Hart Benton murals, Borglum bronzes, and Sol LeWitt line drawings; Copley, Stuart, Whistler, Sargent, Wyeth, Cole, and Church are also well represented. For more than a century, the museum was housed in a stately 19th-century mansion on the city's historic Walnut Hill Park; a brand-new building and a $26 million makeover doubled the size of the museum and added a café, a museum shop, and studio art classes.

New Britain Youth Museum (860-225-3020; www.newbritainyouthmuseum.org), 30 High St. (behind the public library). Open year-round, Tue. 10–5; Wed.–Fri. noon–5; Sat. 10–4; closed Sun. and Mon.; extended summer hours. Admission is free. A small but winning hands-on spot for children and their families, founded in 1956, with exhibits and events that focus on the history, art, and cultural heritage of central Connecticut. Explore the Dinosaur Room, the puppet theater, construction toys, the outdoor garden, and fossils and artifacts from Connecticut's prehistoric days. On Saturday, there's always a special crafts- or art-related activity planned.

♿ **Hill-Stead Museum** (860-677-4787; www.hillstead.org), 35 Mountain Rd., Farmington. Open May–Oct., Tue.–Sun. 10–5; Nov.–Apr., Tue.–Sun. 11–4; closed Mon. and major holidays. Grounds open daily, 7:30–5:30. Adults $9; seniors $8; students $7; children 6–12 $4; 5 and under free. This 1901 Colonial Revival mansion, home of industrialist Alfred A. Pope, was designed by his daughter, Theodate Pope Riddle. As a student at Miss Porter's School, she fell in love with Farmington and prevailed upon her parents to move to Farmington from Cleveland. One of the country's first female architects, she designed and built her family's elegant home—inspired by George Washington's Mount Vernon—with noted architect Stanford White. Subsequently, she designed two of Connecticut's private schools and other private homes. In 1915, she was a passenger on the *Lusitania*, bound for England when the torpedo struck. As the ship sank, she refused to leave without her friends and wound up in the water, clinging to an oar. Naturally, she was rescued; Theodate survived several other brushes with death. William and Henry James were among the distinguished visitors she entertained at her Farmington home. The interior remains as it was when lived in, with exceptional European and American furnishings and an outstanding collection of impressionist paintings—by Monet, Manet, Degas, Cassatt, and Whistler—as well as exquisite 16th- and 17th-century Italian majolica, Japanese prints, Chinese ceramics, and family memorabilia. You can explore the grounds (pick up a trail map at the visitor center), paint en plein air, or take one of the many tours on offer; check the Web site for a schedule. The Beatrix Farrand–designed sunken garden is the site of an acclaimed summertime poetry festival (see *Special Events*).

THE HILL-STEAD MUSEUM'S BEATRIX FARRAND–DESIGNED SUNKEN GARDEN IS THE SITE OF AN ACCLAIMED SUMMERTIME POETRY FESTIVAL.

Kim Grant

In Windsor and Windsor Locks

Luddy/Taylor Connecticut Valley Tobacco Museum (860-285-1888; www.tobaccohistsoc.org), 135 Lang Rd., in Northwest Park, Windsor. Open Mar.–mid-Dec., Tue.–Thu., and Sat. noon–4; closed Mon., Fri., and Sun.; closed mid-Dec.–Feb. Free admission. A barn where tobacco was once cured today houses exhibits explaining how the crop was cultivated, harvested, and subsequently prepared for use in cigars. A separate modern building supplies additional background photos and documents on the history of Tobacco Valley. Tobacco was once the chief agricultural product of the Connecticut River Valley, from central Connecticut north through Massachusetts and into southern Vermont. Visitors can watch a short film on tobacco growing.

♿ **New England Air Museum** (860-623-3305; www.neam.org), 36 Perimeter Rd., off CT 75 at Bradley International Airport, Windsor Locks. Open year-round, daily 10–5; closed Thanksgiving and Christmas. Adults $9; seniors $8; children 6–11 $6; 5 and under free. This largest museum in the Northeast devoted to aviation is a virtual treasure trove. When you walk through the hangars, you walk into aviation history: trainers, gliders, fighters, bombers, helicopters—more than 80 U.S. aircraft dating from 1909 to the present. The showpiece of the 58th Bomb Wing Memorial Hangar is a meticulously restored B-29 Superfortress, along with related memorabilia. For a multimedia experience, climb into the jet fighter cockpit simulator (Sundays in summer; call or check the Web site for a schedule). Aviation films are shown—ask about special events like open-cockpit days and antique auto shows. Gift shop.

Elsewhere

Canton Historical Museum (860-693-2793; www.cantonmuseum.org), 11 Front St., Collinsville. Open Apr.–Nov., Wed.–Sun. 1–4; Thu. until 8. Dec.–Mar., Sat. and Sun. 1–4; closed Mon. and Tue. Adults $3; seniors $2; children 6–15 $1; children under 6 free. On the site of the world's first ax factory, established in 1826 (until then, blacksmiths made axes to order), are three floors filled with 19th-century memorabilia. John Brown, the fiery abolitionist, brought the pikes he used at Harpers Ferry to this location. Museum exhibits cover various aspects of Victorian life, from firefighting equipment and farm implements, to locally produced machetes, to the gown milady wore to tea and the teapot she poured from. There's also a re-created blacksmith shop, and a 19th-century general store, post office, and barbershop.

THE WORLD'S FIRST AX FACTORY WAS BUILT ON THE BANKS OF THE FARMINGTON RIVER IN COLLINSVILLE IN 1826.

© S. Wacht, GeminEye Images

The Children's Museum (860-231-2824; www.thechildrensmuseumct.org), 950 Trout Brook Dr., West Hartford. Open year-round, Tue.–Sat. 10–5; Sun. noon–5; closed Mon. and major holidays. Admission $8; children under 2 free. Additional charge for planetarium and laser shows. On the grounds is Conny, the popular, life-sized, walk-in replica of a sperm whale (Connecticut's state animal). Inside, for the younger set, the Discovery Room is devoted to hands-on exhibits. Besides a live animal center, there are displays on the wonders of physics, electricity, electronics, and technology. Daily star shows in the planetarium and laser light demonstrations.

HISTORIC HOMES

In Wethersfield

Buttolph-Williams House (860-529-0460; 860-529-0612), 249 Broad St. Open May–Oct., Wed.–Sat. and Mon. 10–4; Sun. 1–4; closed Tue. Adults $4; children $2. Built in 1700, this is one of the area's truly early homes; it has dark clapboards and small casement windows, and inside are period furnishings, a collection of wooden kitchenware, and an enormous fireplace. Exposed beams upstairs show the solid framing methods of the first settlers. If the houses didn't catch fire, they could last virtually forever. A property of Connecticut Landmarks, it is a compelling introduction to life in early Connecticut.

Webb-Deane-Stevens Museum (860-529-0612; www.webb-deane-stevens.org), 211 Main St. Call or check the Web site for admission rates, as they vary. The museum consists of three 18th-century houses, side by side, each telling a different story. Properties of the National Society of Colonial Dames in Connecticut, they are open May–Oct., Wed.–Mon. 10–4; Nov.–Apr., Sat. and Sun. 10–4; open daily in Dec. Guided tours of the three properties leave on the hour; last tour at 3 PM. The **Joseph Webb House**, built in 1751 and expanded as Webb's business prospered, is an example of the mid-18th-century style known as Connecticut River Valley. The wide central hall, well-proportioned rooms, and interior paneling are typical. This is where George Washington, in 1781, met with Rochambeau and others of his staff to plan the campaign that led to the battle of Yorktown—a restoration of the house uncovered murals depicting the conflict. Another chapter concerns Mrs. Webb, who rose to the challenge of a visit from the commander of the Continental armies by selecting, buying, and hanging fancy new French flocked wallpaper in an upstairs bedroom for his gratification—all on very short notice. The paper is still on the walls for our gratification. The **Silas Deane House**, dating from 1766, was home, at least for a time, to a lawyer who quickly moved into circles of power in the emerging United States. He served as a member of the First Continental Congress and in 1776 went to Paris to negotiate with the French government for help for the Revolutionary forces. The **Isaac Stevens House**, a Georgian-style home built in 1789, belonged to a leatherworker and saddler who built it for his bride, Sarah. Of interest to gardeners is a period herb garden behind the house.

In Windsor and Windsor Locks

Oliver Ellsworth Homestead (860-688-8717), 778 Palisado Ave. (CT 159), Windsor. Open mid-May–mid-Oct., Wed., Thu., and Sat. noon–4; open on the last Sun. of the month, 1–4. Admission $4; children under 13 free. This 1780 Georgian manse was the home of one of the state's most distinguished public figures: Oliver Ellsworth was a delegate to the Constitutional Convention, a chief justice of the Supreme Court, Connecticut's first senator, and minister plenipotentiary to France. George Washington and John Adams both visited him here. Inside are many of Ellsworth's personal belongings and a piece of a Gobelin tapestry presented to him by Napoleon Bonaparte. In a state blessed with a bounty of historic house museums, this was the first.

Pinchot Sycamore, the largest tree in Connecticut (and southern New England's largest sycamore), is worth a stop just to contemplate what nature can accomplish in the way of size. In a tiny park on the banks of the Farmington River in the rural Weatogue section of Simsbury, the Pinchot Sycamore is visible as you cross the steel bridge over the river on CT 185 south of Simsbury center. The massive tree is named for local conservationist Gifford Pinchot, who headed the U.S. Division of Forestry under Teddy Roosevelt, cofounded the Yale School of Forestry, and later served as governor of Pennsylvania. At last measurement, its gnarled and noble trunk had a circumference of 25 feet, 8 inches. It stands 93 feet high, and its average branch spread (the diameter of the canopy formed by its branches) is 138 feet. Depending on the size of your family, you may be able to join hands around its huge base.

WHILE IN SIMSBURY, STOP TO CONTEMPLATE THE PINCHOT SYCAMORE, THE LARGEST TREE IN THE STATE.

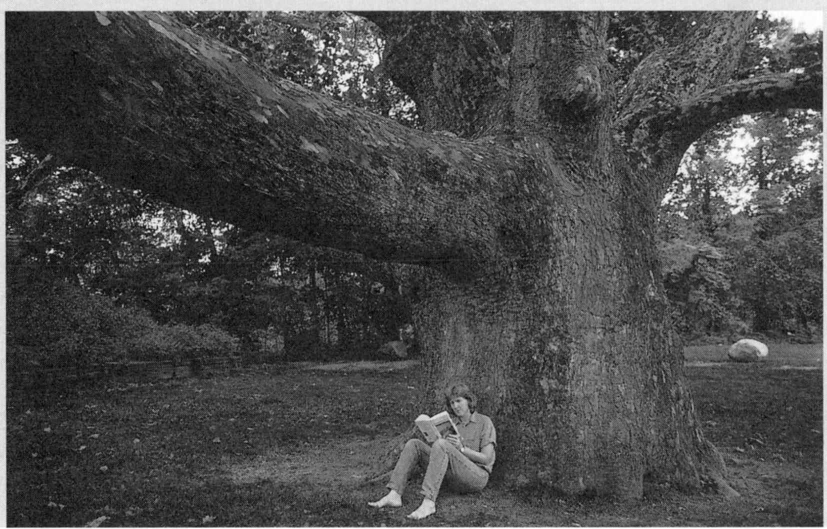

Kim Grant

Noden-Reed House & Barn (860-627-9212), 58 West St., Windsor Locks. Open May–Oct. and by appointment; call for hours. Free admission. The period artifacts housed in the 1840 early-Victorian home and the 1826 brick barn are of considerable interest, but the real attraction here is a story: According to legend, the first Christmas tree in Connecticut—perhaps in the country—was set up at the Noden-Reed house by a Hessian soldier captured during the Revolutionary War. He remembered, it's said, the customs of his homeland and introduced what became a lasting practice in this country.

Windsor Historical Society (860-688-3813; www.windsorhistoricalsociety.org), 96 Palisado Ave., Windsor. Open Tue.–Sat. 10–4; closed Sun. and Mon. Adults $5;

seniors and students $4; children under 13 free. Admission includes the museum, library, and a guided tour of both houses. The society headquarters and museum are in the **Lieutenant Walter Fyler House**, built in 1640, seven years after Windsor's first settlers arrived. One of New England's oldest survivors, the Fyler House is an oxblood, clapboard-sided house with gables, a distinctive broken roofline, and fairly ornate pediments over the windows—clearly the home of an important citizen. There are nine antiques-furnished rooms, a small "fancy goods" shop, and a vest-pocket post office. You can also arrange a walking tour of the adjoining Palisado (palisaded against the Pequots) area and the settlers' burying ground. The society also manages the **Dr. Hezekiah Chaffee House** (circa 1765), a Georgian, brick-sided, three-story house; and the **Strong House** (circa 1758), a modest dwelling containing Windsor's first post office, a general store, and a Victorian parlor. Both are enhanced with period furnishings. Changing exhibits are devoted to local history; there is a library for genealogical and historical research, as well as a museum shop.

In Suffield

King House Museum (860-668-5256), 232 South Main St. (CT 75). Open May–Sept., Wed. and Sat. 1–4, and by appointment. Adults $1; students free. A 1764 center-chimney mansion noted for its long porch, the King House is an upscale colonial: ornate mirrors, crewel-embroidered bed linens, a shell corner cupboard in the dining room. Of special note are the exhibits on the local cigar and tobacco industry, the collection of Bennington pottery and early Connecticut Valley furniture, and an antique flask and bottle collection.

Phelps-Hatheway House & Garden (860-668-0055), 55 South Main St. (CT 75). Hours limited; phone ahead. Adults $7; seniors and students $6; children $4; 5 and under free. One of the prime properties of Connecticut Landmarks, this commodious white-clapboard early colonial (1761) with a later neo-Classical wing (1794)—the first of this style in the river valley—was in its day the most opulent house in the state and provides a quick tour of 18th-century Connecticut. The midcentury parlor is sparsely furnished with elegantly simple tables and chairs; the parlor's wide-board floor is bare, and the curtains are plain white hangings. In the later section of the house, there's a lavish look to the rooms, as no expense was spared. The French wallpaper—reproduced in all its elaborate splendor—heavy red window hangings, damask-covered wing chairs, and intricately designed Oriental rugs stand in striking contrast to the original section. On the grounds, enjoy a formal garden, 19th-century barns, and a carriage house. Pick up a walking tour pamphlet and check out the centuries-old architecture of Suffield's Main Street, most of which is a National Historic District.

In West Hartford

✐ **Noah Webster House** (860-521-5362; www.noahwebsterhouse.org), 227 South Main St. Open Thu.–Mon. 1–4; closed Tue., Wed., and major holidays. Adults $6; seniors $5; students $4; children 5 and under free. The restored colonial farmhouse where Noah was born in 1758 is a saltbox with an added-on lean-to that sports proper period furnishings and an especially good hearth restoration. His *Blue-backed Speller*, published in 1783, sold 24 million copies in his lifetime. His groundbreaking *American Dictionary* was published in 1828, when he was 70. The museum, with guides in colonial garb, mounts changing exhibits related to local history as well as excellent programs—notably Noah's birthday party each September, featuring a hard-fought, herculean spell-down for local students, and a holiday open house in December. Check out the re-created colonial herb garden outside the kitchen door.

Sarah Whitman Hooker Homestead (860-523-5887; 800-475-1233), 1237 New Britain Ave. Hours limited; phone ahead. This house started out simply as one room with a chamber above. Like many colonial homes, this Connecticut River Valley saltbox underwent a series of changes, serving as an inn for a time, and ended as a large and sturdy representative of the period 1720–1807. The meticulous restoration traces changes in the size and appearance of the house, with ingenious "windows" enabling the visitor to see construction details ordinarily out of sight. Look for reproductions of original wallpapers and fabrics, a good collection of Staffordshire, and a tale of Tories quartered here while under house arrest during the Revolutionary War.

Elsewhere

Barnes Museum (860-628-5426), 85 Main St. (CT 10), Southington. Open Mon.–Wed., and Fri., 9–5; Thu. 11–7; first and last Sat. of the month 1–5; closed Sat. in summer. Adults $2; children $1. The building is the 1836 **Amon Bradley house**, home of a distinguished local family for more than a century. Many of the original furnishings remain, with collections of antique toys, glassware, and furniture.

Newington Historical Society (860-666-7118; www.newingtonhistoricalsociety.org), Newington. The society has two properties that offer special insights into early times, when Newington was an outpost of nearby Wethersfield. Both are open Apr.–Nov. on the first Sun. of the month for guided tours 1–3. Admission $2. **The Enoch Kelsey House**, 1702 Main St., was saved from demolition when valuable trompe l'oeil floral wall paintings were discovered and identified as authentic period decorations. Fireplaces, a beehive oven, and paneling are all original to this 1799 home built by Enoch Kelsey, an affluent farmer and tinsmith. The **Kellogg-Eddy Museum**, 679 Willard Ave., is an 1808 three-story Georgian-style home with furnishings from local collectors, a changing display of quilts, noteworthy mantelpieces, and a ceiling frieze.

✐ **Stanley-Whitman House** (860-677-9222; www.stanleywhitman.org), 37 High St., Farmington. House tours May–Oct., Wed.–Sun. noon–4; Nov.–Apr., Sat. and Sun. noon–4; and by appointment. Adults $5; seniors $4; children 6–18 $2; children under 6 free. Built in 1720, the post-and-beam saltbox in Farmington's historic center retains some of the very early medieval characteristics of colonial architecture: for example, narrow casement windows with small diamond panes, an 18-inch overhang in front (embellished with four pendant drops), and a lean-to in back that creates the classic saltbox. A restoration project provided for hinged panels, which allow examination of construction details. Period furniture and an exhibit outlining the results of an archaeological investigation show what life was like in the Connecticut River Valley in the 1700s. In addition to the historic house, centuries-old burying ground, and period gardens, a new education and research center contains a gift shop, exhibit space, a library, and a welcome desk. Special programs for adults and children on spinning, weaving, open-hearth cooking, and colonial crafts are held periodically; call for a schedule.

In Wethersfield

First Church of Christ, Congregational (860-529-1575), 250 Main St. Connecticut's only remaining brick colonial meetinghouse, completed in 1764. Funded by the sale of red onions—Wethersfield's principal crop and main claim to odorous fame in early times—it's a noble example of church architecture. The cupola is an exact replica of that on Boston's fabled Old North Church. George Washington and John Adams appear on the roster of worshipers here.

Trinity Episcopal Church, 300 Main St., may seem a stranger among all the colonial-era saltboxes and hewn overhangs; it came into town with the Victorian age, in 1871–74. Designed by Edward Tuckerman Potter, architect of Mark Twain's Hartford mansion, it's of Portland (Connecticut) brownstone and enhanced by three Tiffany windows.

Wethersfield Historical Society (860-529-7656; www.wethhist.org) manages the following: **The Old Academy**, 150 Main St. Open Tue.–Fri. 10–4; and by appointment. You can pick up information on museums and historic sites either here or at the Keeney Memorial down the street. The academy houses research archives and a library of local and state history, specializing in genealogy and architecture. **Wethersfield Museum at Keeney Memorial**, 200 Main St. Open Mon.–Sat. 10–4, Sun. 1–4. Admission to the galleries: adults $3; children under 17 free. An 1893 structure, clearly designed to be a school, served first as a high school and later as a location for elementary classes. It's now a museum and lecture-recital hall, with a permanent exhibit of local history and changing displays, generally of arts and crafts by local artists, as well as special events throughout the year. Visitor information on area events and attractions is available. **Hurlbut-Dunham House**, 212 Main St. Open mid-May–mid-Oct., Sat. 10–4; Sun. 1–4. Adults $3; children under 17 free. A resplendent brick Georgian mansion with a Palladian window, marble fireplaces, a painted ceiling, chandeliers, furnishings, and artwork reflecting three centuries of its inhabitants. The **Cove Warehouse**, at the north end of Main St. Open mid-May–mid-Oct., Sat. 10–4; Sun. 1–4. Adults $1; children under 17 free. Built around 1690, the warehouse was used to store goods brought upriver by seagoing merchant vessels. What's now the cove was just a bend in the river until the flood of 1692, which swept away the other warehouses and left this lone survivor.

Elsewhere

First Company Governor's Horse Guards (860-673-3525; www.govhorseguards.org), 232 West Avon Rd. (CT 167), Avon. Drills every Thu. at 7:30 PM. Special weekend events, including open houses and horse shows; call for a schedule. Free admission. Watch the nation's oldest cavalry unit in continuous service (since 1658) practice its precision maneuvers. Now serving primarily a ceremonial function, the unit has a noble history, from acting as an honor guard when President Washington visited town to service in the War of 1812, the Spanish-American War, and the two world wars.

National Iwo Jima Memorial Monument (860-666-5521), Ella Grasso Blvd. (CT 175), at Exit 29 off CT 9, Newington–New Britain town line. Open daily; free admission. A simple park just off the highway honors the 6,821 American soldiers killed on the island of Iwo Jima. The bronze and granite sculpture is inspired by Joe Rosenthal's photograph of six Marines raising the U.S. flag on Mount Suribachi on February 23, 1945. Special memorial events are held on national holidays.

Phelps Tavern Museum (860-658-2500; www.simsburyhistory.org), 800 Hopmeadow St. (CT 10), Simsbury. Open for guided tours year-round, Tue.–Sat. noon–4; closed Sun., Mon., and major holidays. Adults $6; seniors $5; children $4. This village complex, home to the **Simsbury Historical Society**, covers some 300 years of local history: a replica of the 1683 meetinghouse; museum exhibits in the 18th-century **Phelps House** that include rare Higley coppers, the first coins struck in the colonies; a tin peddler's cart that represents the heyday of the Yankee trader; and a one-room schoolhouse and Victorian carriage house that bring visitors into the 19th century.

Old New-Gate Prison and Copper Mine (860-653-3563), 115 Newgate Rd., off CT 20, East Granby. Open mid-May–Oct., Wed.–Sun. 10–4:30. Adults $5; seniors $4; children 6–17 $3; under 6 free. The first chartered copper mine in North America (1707) did not produce much copper. Perhaps the Pilgrim fathers were just trying, in Yankee style, to make use of the tunnels when they converted it into the colonial government's first prison in 1773. During the Revolutionary War, Tories were housed here. Walking through the underground caves, hearing the water dripping on the stones, imagining the prospect of spending time there in the damp darkness, is enough to make you think twice about wanting to live in the Pilgrim century. Guides tell fascinating tales of escapes and of prison life in colonial times.

Salmon Brook Historical Society (860-653-9713; www.salmonbrookhistorical.org), 208 Salmon Brook St., Granby. Open June–Sept., Sun. 2–4; research library open Tue. 9–noon. Admission $2. Visitors can explore a collection of buildings on the National Register of Historic Places that date from Salmon Brook, a British settlement founded in 1680, which later became Granby. The complex includes the 1790 **Weed/Enders House**, a saltbox-style farmhouse that houses the historical society's research library and museum store; the **Cooley School**, a 19th-century one-room schoolhouse, complete with woodstove, writing slates, and the requisite portrait of George Washington; the 1914 **Colton/Hayes Tobacco Barn**, filled with historical displays and artifacts; and the 1732 **Abijah Rowe House**, the oldest remaining building from the original Salmon Brook settlement.

✷ To Do

BALLOONING **Berkshire Balloons** (203-250-8441; www.berkshireballoons.com), P.O. Box 706, Southington 06489. Open year-round; reserve in advance. Available daily for one-hour rides. Specializing in foliage tours and overnight bed & breakfast packages.

CT Ballooning (860-209-0351; www.ctballooning.com), P.O. Box 177, Kensington 06037-0177. Year-round flights over central and eastern Connecticut.

KAT Balloons (860-678-7921), 40 Meadow Lane, Farmington. Champagne charter flights over the Farmington River Valley at dawn and before sunset. Call for a brochure.

A Windriders Balloon (860-677-0647), 314 South Rd., Farmington. Hot-air balloon tours and champagne charter flights over the Farmington and Connecticut River Valleys. Reservations required.

Sky Endeavors Hot Air Balloons (860-242-0228), 4 Brown St., Bloomfield. Champagne flights over the Farmington River Valley. Reservations required.

♿ **Airvertising and Airventures** (860-651-4441; 800-535-2473), P.O. Box 365, West Simsbury 06092. Balloons that are handicapped accessible, others that hold up to 20 people. Year-round, weather permitting.

Livingston Balloon Company (860-651-1110), 70 West St., Simsbury. Champagne flights over the Farmington River Valley.

© S. Wacht, GeminEye Images

A SCENIC NETWORK OF RECREATIONAL PATHS LINKING SEVERAL FARMINGTON VALLEY TOWNS IS POPULAR WITH WALKERS AND CYCLISTS.

BICYCLING The **Farmington Valley Greenway** (860-658-4065; www.fvgreenway.org) is a don't-miss cycling destination, perfect for an afternoon outing with the kids. The 26-mile-long paved and gravel recreational trail (completed in sections) cuts a flat and easy path through the central Connecticut suburbs. Among the highlights: the Flower Bridge, a 19th-century iron footbridge in Simsbury that blossoms in an explosion of color in summer; and a bridge set with benches high above the Farmington River in Unionville. The **Farmington River Trail** is a spur trail passing through Collinsville, Unionville, and Simsbury on an abandoned railbed along the winding Farmington River. It's all part of the **Farmington Canal Heritage Trail**, a multiuse path along a historic system of 19th-century canals and railbeds that, when completed, will stretch 60 miles from New Haven to the Massachusetts border. The trail can be picked up in a number of locations; popular ones include the parking area in Unionville at the junction of CT 4 and CT 179; in the center of Avon near Sperry Park, off CT 10; and another off CT 10 in the center of Simsbury.

Suffield–Windsor Locks Canal Trail, from the CT 140 bridge in Windsor Locks north to the CT 190 bridge in Suffield. Parking on Canal Rd. in East Windsor and in Suffield. A 4.3-mile-long towpath follows the Connecticut River and the historic canal, dug by hand in the 19th century by Irish immigrants. Boats traveling along the Connecticut River were pulled by oxen, mules, and horses through the canal to avoid the dangerous rapids and falls in Enfield. Today it's used by runners and walkers as well as cyclists.

BOAT EXCURSION **Glastonbury–Rocky Hill Ferry** (860-563-9758; 860-443-3856), CT 160, either town. May–Oct., Mon.–Fri. 7 AM–6:45 PM; Sat. and Sun. 10:30–5. Car and passengers $3; pedestrians and bicyclists $1. The nation's oldest ferry in continuous operation, in business since 1655. Drive your car onto the barge and get out to watch the towboat pull you across the Connecticut River. It's a short trip, but the views are lovely.

CANOEING, KAYAKING, AND TUBING **Collinsville Canoe & Kayak** (860-693-6977; www.cckstore.com), 41 Bridge St. (CT 179), Collinsville. Open Wed.–Sun.; closed Mon. and Tue. Canoe and kayak rentals for flatwater sections of the Farmington River, as well as for area ponds and lakes. Customized group outings and instructional programs available; call for information.

Farmington River Tubing (860-693-6465; www.farmingtonrivertubing.com), 92 Main St. (US 44), in Satan's Kingdom State Recreation Area, on the Canton–New Hartford town line. Rentals daily, Memorial Day weekend–mid-Sept.; call daily for times and conditions. Specially designed river tubes are available for the 2.5-mile ride downstream through three sets of rapids. The ride back is provided.

♿ **Huck Finn Adventures** (860-693-0385; www.huckfinnadventures.com), P.O. Box 137, Collinsville 06022. Canoe and kayak instruction, and guided trips for groups and families, on a scenic, wooded, flatwater section of the Farmington River. Services available for wheelchair-bound passengers. Whitewater instruction is also available.

FISHING **Connecticut River** shad fishing is permitted, in-season, in Suffield along the Windsor Locks Canal below the Enfield dam (there's no fishing in the canal, however). This is a controlled area, and posters mark the limits within which fishing is allowed. Boaters can access the river at state launch sites in **Windsor** and **Rocky Hill**.

CALM FLATWATER STRETCHES ALONG THE FARMINGTON RIVER ARE PERFECT FOR A SCENIC PADDLING EXCURSION.

Kim Grant

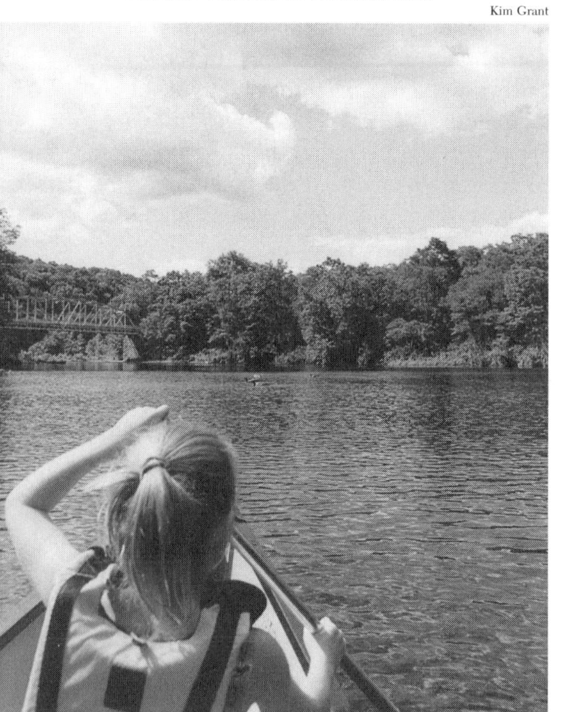

The **Farmington River** winds through the area, replete with brown, brook, and rainbow trout; large- and smallmouth bass; pickerel; yellow perch; and other species. For specifics, contact the **Farmington River Anglers Association** (P.O. Box 177, New Hartford 06057; www.fraa.org). The river's western branch, from Hogback Dam to Riverton, is one of state's most popular spots for trout fishing.

Rainbow Reservoir, in Windsor, is recommended for largemouth bass, and you can also expect sunfish, chain pickerel, and brown bullheads. Access is on foot through **Northwest Park** (see *Green Space*) or, if you have a boat, at the state boat launch off Merriman Rd. In Simsbury, **Stratton Brook State Park** is stocked with trout.

GOLF **Hawk's Landing Country Club** (860-793-6000; www.hawkslandingcc.com), 201 Pattonwood Dr., Southington. Par 71, 18 holes, 5,650 yards.

Pine Valley Golf Course (860-628-0879; www.pinevalleygolfct.com), 300 Welch Rd., Southington. Par 71, 18 holes, 6,325 yards.

Timberlin Golf Club (860-828-3228; www.timberlingolf.com), 330 Southington Rd. (CT 364), Berlin. Par 72, 18 holes, 6,733 yards. A longtime favorite course in central Connecticut.

Stanley Golf Course (860-827-8570; www.stanleygolf.com), 245 Hartford Rd. (CT 71), New Britain. Par 72/35, 18/9 holes, 6,553/3,048 yards. A top-notch municipal course with a 19-hole driving range and golf school.

Tunxis Plantation Golf Course (860-677-1367; www.tunxisgolf.com), 89 Town Farm Rd., off CT 4, Farmington. Par 72/70/35, 18/18/9 holes, 6,638/6,354/2,999 yards.

Buena Vista Golf Course (860-521-7359), 56 Buena Vista Rd., West Hartford. Par 31, nine holes, 1,977 yards. A short course that's good for beginners.

Rockledge Golf Club (860-521-6284; www.golfrockledge.com), 289 South Main St., West Hartford. Par 72, 18 holes, 6,436 yards.

Blue Fox Run Golf Course (860-678-1679; www.bluefoxent.com), 65 Nod Rd., off US 44, Avon. Par 71, 18 holes, 6,536 yards.

Wintonbury Hills Golf Course (860-242-1401; www.wintonburyhillsgolf.com), 206 Terry Plains Rd., Bloomfield. Par 70, 18 holes, 6,623 yards. A top-notch municipal course on the banks of the Tunxis Reservoir.

Simsbury Farms Golf Course (860-658-6246; www.simsburyfarms.com), 100 Old Farms Rd., West Simsbury. Par 72, 18 holes, 6,454 yards.

Fox Run at Copper Hill (860-653-6191), 20 Copper Hill Rd., East Granby. Par 36, nine holes, 5,761 yards.

Airways Golf Course (860-668-4973; www.airwaysgolf.com), 1070 South Grand St., West Suffield. Par 71, 18 holes, 6,000 yards.

MINI GOLF ✐ There are two outstanding family-friendly venues in the Farmington River Valley for miniature golf. In Farmington, **Farmington Miniature Golf & Ice Cream Parlor** (860-677-0118), 1048 Farmington Ave. (CT 4), has a driving range and a traditional mini golf course. A few miles down the road, **Riverfront Miniature Golf & Ice Cream Parlor** (860-675-4653), 218 River Rd., at the junction of CT 4, in the Unionville section of Farmington, resides in a scenic spot on the banks of the Farmington River.

HAYRIDES AND SLEIGH RIDES ✐ **DeMaria Family Farm** (860-828-6724), 1165 Edgewood Rd., Kensington. Reservations are required. Horse-drawn hayrides on weekends, year-round, plus cut-your-own Christmas trees.

✐ **Flamig Farm** (860-658-5070; www.flamigfarm.com), 7 Shingle Mill Rd., West Simsbury. Open year-round. A working farm in the Farmington River Valley for nearly a century; today it offers horse- and tractor-drawn hayrides, weekend pony rides, sleigh rides (by appointment only), and a petting zoo with geese, goats, bunnies, and other cuddly creatures.

✐ **Brown's Harvest** (860-683-0266; www.brownsharvest.com), 60 Rainbow Rd. (CT 75), Windsor. Six generations of the Brown family have been in Windsor since the 1800s. Today the farm specializes in pumpkins, shade tobacco, and mums.

Free tractor-drawn hayrides venture out to the pumpkin patch in October, daily 10–6.

HIKING **Lamentation Mountain**, off Spruce Brook Rd., which abuts the Berlin Turnpike (US 5 and CT 15) in Berlin. Part of the traprock ridge that runs down the center of the state, the 720-foot mountain is named for an early settler who, lamentably, was lost here for two days. The blue-blazed **Mattabesett Trail** takes you up the rise through hardwoods and hemlocks—to views that include the so-called hanging hills of Meriden, to the west; and to the Connecticut River and its gorge at Middletown to the east. Another part of the trail intersects the loop around 761-foot **Ragged Mountain** on the Berlin–Southington town line. The loop is accessible from either West Lane or Reservoir Rd., both of which run west from CT 71A.

Heublein Tower (860-667-0662), Talcott Mountain State Park, Hartford Rd. (CT 185), on the Bloomfield–Simsbury town line. Park open daily 8 AM–sunset; tower open Memorial Day weekend–Labor Day, Thu.–Sun. 10–5; Labor Day–last weekend in Oct., daily 10–5. Free admission. The 1.25-mile Tower Trail follows traprock ridges to the prominent Heublein family's former summertime retreat: a Bavarian-style 1914 tower, whose red-tile cupola is a venerable icon in the Farmington River Valley. Climb the 120 steps to the glass observation room for a spectacular bird's-eye panorama that stretches from Long Island Sound to the Berkshires on a clear day. The trail and tower are jam-packed with leaf-peepers on fall weekends; come during the week for relative solitude.

McLean Game Refuge (860-653-7869), Salmon Brook Rd. (CT 10 and US 202), Granby. Open daily 8 AM–sunset. Free admission. This spot has been set aside to preserve the trees and flowers, and to safeguard the wildlife that lives here or migrates through. Hiking, birding, cross-country skiing, and general nature lore are what the McLean is for. You have the **Barndoor Hills** to climb, excellent views, a picnic grove and recreation field, and some 2,400 acres in all to explore.

Metacomet Trail runs from Sleeping Giant State Park (see the New Haven chapter) in Hamden up to **Mount Monadnock** in New Hampshire, with just one break in Massachusetts. A good entry point is in Granby at CT 20. Watch for the blue oval sign that marks Connecticut's spectacular network of blue-blazed hiking trails. If you hike north, the trail goes near **Old New-Gate Prison**; if you turn south, it takes you to the dramatic **Tariffville Gorge** of the Farmington River and on down through Penwood State Park in Simsbury.

See also *Green Space*.

MOUNTAIN BIKING Despite their proximity to Hartford, the suburbs to the west offer riders plenty of trails to explore. The terrain is generally challenging but doable; local bike shops will steer you toward the best of it.

West Hartford Reservoir (860-231-9023), 1420 Farmington Ave. (CT 4), on the West Hartford–Farmington town line. This 3,000-acre suburban oasis will satisfy riders of all abilities with a 3.5-mile paved loop, an extensive network of fire roads, and—for the adventurous—challenging singletrack trails on Talcott Mountain. Bikes are not permitted on the blue-blazed Metacomet trail. *Tip:* Come during the week, when most of the park regulars are at work or at home; weekends are mobbed.

Central Wheel (860-677-7010), 62 Farmington Ave. (CT 4), Farmington (near West Hartford Reservoir, rents mountain bikes and has an extensive line of cycling equipment and accessories.

Benidorm Bikes and Boards (860-693-8891), 247 Albany Turnpike (US 44), Canton. Full-service bike shop with knowledgeable staff. Ask about local rides.

SIGHTSEEING TOUR ***Amistad* Tour** (860-677-8867; www.charteroaktree.com), P.O. Box 138, Farmington 06034-0138. Farmington's role in African American history is explored in a tour available by special arrangement. The connection has to do with the takeover of the ship *Amistad* by the slaves on board. After a series of trials, 38 members of the Mende tribe were declared freemen and came to stay in Farmington while funds were raised to return them to their homes in Sierra Leone. The quarters where they lived, their school, and their farmlands are now privately held but are available to interested visitors. Also included on the tour are authenticated stops on the **Underground Railroad**, the network of safe houses run by pre–Civil War abolitionists to assist runaway slaves on their way north to freedom.

SPECTATOR SPORTS ✐ **New Britain Rock Cats** (860-224-8383; www.rockcats.com), Willow Brook Park Complex, South Main St., New Britain. Games Apr.–Sept.; call for a schedule and prices. Class AA minor-league baseball (the Rock Cats are an affiliate of the Minnesota Twins), which takes family fun seriously. Furry mascots like Rocky and Ball D the Eagle, as well as fireworks, contests, and giveaways, keep the fans entertained between innings. Kids run the bases after every Sunday home game.

Bradley Teletheater (860-623-0380), 11 Schoenphoester Rd. (near Bradley International Airport), Windsor Locks. Open daily year-round. Live simulcasts of jai alai, and horse and greyhound racing.

✱ Winter Sports

CROSS-COUNTRY SKIING **Winding Trails Cross-Country Ski Center** (860-674-4227; www.windingtrails.com), 50 Winding Trails Dr., off CT 4, Farmington. Open mid-Dec.–mid-Mar., 9 AM–dusk, depending on snow conditions. This touring center offers 20K of track-set and groomed trails in a 350-acre wooded recreation area. Rentals, lessons, and food service available in the ski shop. Wide, groomed trails on gently rolling terrain; ice skating, sledding, and snowshoeing also available.

DOWNHILL SKIING ✐ **Mount Southington Ski Area** (860-628-0954; 800-982-6828; www.mountsouthington.com), 396 Mount Vernon Rd., in the Plantsville section of Southington. Modest mountains characterize Connecticut's ski areas; Mount Southington offers good, easily accessible family skiing, with snowmaking capability to extend the season. There are 14 trails, three chairlifts and five surface lifts, a ski shop, lessons, food service, and night skiing.

ICE-SKATING ✐ **Newington Arena** (860-665-7825; www.newingtonarena.com), 300 Alumni Rd., Newington. Public skating sessions, hockey leagues, lessons, and world-class ice shows at a state-of-the-art facility. Pro shop, café, and fitness center.

Veterans Memorial Ice Skating Rink (860-521-1573; www.skatevmsr.com), 56 Buena Vista Rd., West Hartford. Public skating sessions; skate rentals and snack bar.

International Skating Center of Connecticut (860-651-5400; www.isccskate.com), 1375 Hopmeadow St. (CT 10), Simsbury. Visitors are admitted daily 6 AM–midnight. In 2007, *Forbes* magazine rated this one of the top 10 rinks in the country. And it's a first for Connecticut: a world-class twin-rink ice-skating facility for learners and pros. One rink is Olympic-sized; the other meets National Hockey League specifications. If you're lucky, you may see Olympic medalists practicing and/or legendary hockey stars on the ice. Restaurant/coffee shop allows visitors a view of both rinks. Ask about the current schedule for public skating; skate rentals are available.

✷ Green Space

NATURE CENTERS **New Britain Youth Museum at Hungerford Park** (860-827-9064), 191 Farmington Ave. (CT 372), Kensington. Open year-round, Tue.–Fri. 1–5; Sat. 10–5; closed Sun., Mon., and holidays. Adults $4; seniors $3; children $2; under 2 free. Hiking trails are free. Operated by the New Britain Youth Museum, the family museum and nature center offers activities year-round, with animal programs on Saturday. Attractions include animals both familiar and exotic, hiking trails, flower and vegetable gardens, a pond with an observation station, a puppet theater, and changing exhibits on natural history, geology, science, and architecture. There's also a gift shop and an old-fashioned ice cream parlor.

Tomasso Nature Park (860-747-6022), Granger Lane, Plainville. Open daily mid-Mar.–mid-Nov. Free admission. An 11-acre home to nearly 600 painted turtles, as well as other animals, which can be viewed from trails, bridges, and observation areas. Prime area for birding.

♿ **Westmoor Park** (860-232-1134), 119 Flagg Rd., off US 44, West Hartford. Grounds open daily, dawn to dusk. Demonstration farm open daily 9–4. Education center open Mon.–Fri. 9–4:30; Sat. and Sun. 9–4. Closed major holidays. Free admission. A 162-acre educational park with an emphasis on the environment, agriculture, and horticulture. The demonstration farm has barnyard animals. Also on-site are herb, perennial, and organic gardens; an education center with a heated greenhouse; exhibits; and a nature discovery room. And visitors will find 3 miles of trails, including a 0.5-mile nature discovery trail through a variety of natural habitats.

Roaring Brook Nature Center (860-693-0263; www.roaringbrook.org), 70 Gracey Rd., Canton. Open year-round, Tue.–Sat. 10–5; Sun. 1–5; open Mon. July and Aug. Hiking trails are open daily, dawn to dusk. Adults $4; seniors and children $3. Native American exhibits, including a longhouse, nature displays, live animals, self-guiding nature trails, and wildlife-attracting areas. With 115 acres of natural terrain and woodland trails, this is an inviting place (a stream runs through it) to visit, especially with children. Call for information about the many tours, guided walks, and family activities. Live entertainment by renowned national and international acoustic folk musicians; call for a schedule.

Northwest Park & Nature Center (860-285-1886; www.northwestpark.org), 145 Lang Rd., Windsor. Open daily, dawn–dusk. A town park, these 473 green acres border the Farmington River's Rainbow Reservoir. It's a good place for birders: Bluebirds and other species are encouraged to settle here. There are 12 miles of walking trails, a nature center with live animals, maple sugaring demonstrations, and a series of live concerts. On-site is the Luddy/Taylor Connecticut Valley Tobacco Museum (see *To See*).

🐾 ✐ **Holcomb Farm Learning Center** (860-844-8616; www.holcombfarm.com), 113 Simsbury Rd., West Granby. Open Mon.–Sat. 8:30–4:30; closed Sun. A family farm turned learning center, with educational, arts, and environmental programs focused on the natural environment. Check out the live animals inside and outside, and explore the network of trails for hiking, horseback riding, snowshoeing, and cross-country skiing. Festivals and outdoor sculpture exhibits are on the roster of special events; arts and crafts, jewelry, and unique gifts in the gift shop.

PARKS ✐ ♿ **Dinosaur State Park** (860-529-8423; www.dinosaurstatepark.org), 400 West St., Rocky Hill. The exhibit center, a geodesic dome enclosing a museum and some footprints, is open Tue.–Sun. 9–4:30. Grounds open daily 9–4:30. Adults $5; children $2; 5 and under free. The feature of this 70-acre park is the treasure trove of some 2,000 Jurassic-era footprints embedded in the ancient sandstone, one of the largest dinosaur track sites in North America. A dramatic discovery by a bulldozer operator in 1966 resulted in the establishment of this park, where about 500 of the prehistoric three-toed tracks—believed to be made by the carnivorous *Dilophosaurus* about 200 million years ago—are on display. Although no dinosaur bones were ever uncovered in the area, the park is unique due to the sheer number of footprints found here. You can make a plaster cast to take home. Special programs are offered; call for a schedule. Outside are 2.5 miles of nature trails through an arboretum, and areas for picnicking.

Walnut Hill Park (860-826-3360), West Main St., New Britain. Open daily. A historic 90-acre retreat designed by Frederick Law Olmsted—Manhattan's Central Park is another of his claims to fame. Walking and exercise paths, a band shell, a World War I monument, and rewarding vistas at the crest of the hill. The park is next to the city's first-rate New Britain Museum of American Art.

🐾 **Penwood State Park** (860-242-1158), 57 Gun Mill Rd. (CT 185), Bloomfield, on the Simsbury town line. Open 8 AM–sunset. Free admission. Curtis H. Veeder, industrialist, outdoorsman, and inventor, originally developed this 787-acre paradise as his own estate. His home no longer stands, but the park is a tribute to his love for the woods. Roads, small lakes, shelters, picnic areas, a bikeway, trails (part of the blue-blazed Metacomet Trail comes through), small bridges, scenic overlooks. *Veeder* is Dutch for "pen," and Veeder's ancestors came from Pennsylvania—the official explanation for the name of the park.

🐾 ♿ **Stratton Brook State Park** (860-242-1158), 149 Farms Village Rd., off CT 309, Simsbury. A small park—148 acres—where you can swim in the brook, hike, fish for trout, bike along a former railway, and picnic. There are facilities for changing clothes, as well as a concession, drinking water, and flush toilets.

Talcott Mountain State Park (860-242-1158), CT 185, south of Penwood State Park (see above), on the Bloomfield–Simsbury town line. Open daily 8 AM–sunset. The main attraction here is what many consider the state's best viewing spot: Talcott Mountain is 1,000 feet above the valley of the Farmington River. On the mountain, accessible by a 1.25-mile walking path, is the **Heublein Tower**, built as a summer place by the family that owned Heublein Liquor Distributors. The four-story square white tower is visible from up to 50 miles away. A society dedicated to its preservation opens it to visitors on a seasonal basis, and it attracts more than 100,000 people a year, mostly to view fall foliage. It's a good climb, and worth it—your reward at the top is an eye-popping panorama of four states.

✱ Lodging

INN ⚭ 🐾 ♿ **Simsbury 1820 House** (860-658-7658; 800-879-1820; www.simsbury1820house.com), 731 Hopmeadow St. (CT 10), Simsbury 06070. A spacious manor house of early-19th-century vintage—before Victorian tastes took over. The elegant former home of local conservationist Gifford Pinchot is a sought-after venue for weddings, corporate functions, and romantic weekends. The common rooms are classic, with creamy walls and white woodwork, leaded-glass windows, fine paintings, authentic antiques, and reproductions throughout. The huge, open porch makes you want to linger. The rooms are up to the same standards: the charm of an old-fashioned country inn, with down comforters, Belgian sheets, and marble baths, plus modern amenities such as TV. There are 34 rooms, all with private bath and continental breakfast. Outstanding café (see *Dining Out*). $119–249.

BED & BREAKFASTS In addition to the listings below, a number of B&B reservation services offer access to rooms available in establishments throughout the state. For a list, see *Bed & Breakfasts* in "What's Where in Connecticut."

Chester Bulkley House (860-563-4236; www.chesterbulkleyhouse.com), 184 Main St., Wethersfield 06109. This elegant 1830 Greek Revival home is a perfect base from which to explore the historic district in Old Wethersfield. Common space includes working fireplaces, wide-pine floors, hand-carved woodwork, and period antiques. There are five rooms, three with private bath; guests are served a full breakfast. Innkeeper Tom Aufiero is a gracious host and will arrange for special needs. $95–145.

Silas W. Robbins House (860-571-8733; www.silaswrobbins.com), 185 Broad St., Wethersfield 06109. The area's newest B&B is a meticulously restored 1873 Victorian mansion overlooking the green in the historic district. Innkeepers John and Shireen Aforismo offer five elegant guest rooms (all with private bath) filled with antiques and period details; air-conditioning, flat-screen TVs, and WiFi keep them firmly rooted in the present. A full breakfast is served fireside in the tearoom; there's also a parlor and formal dining room. $195–325.

The Linden House (860-408-1321; www.lindenhousebb.com), 288/290 Hopmeadow St. (CT 10), in the Weatogue section of Simsbury, 06089. A beautifully restored Victorian home close to many of the area's shops, cafés, and private schools. There are five comfortable and tastefully decorated guest rooms; each has a private bath, and four feature working fireplaces. Continental breakfast. $140–150; reduced off-season and corporate rates.

Merrywood (860-651-1785; www.merrywoodinn.com), 100 Hartford Rd. (CT 185), Simsbury 06070. Michael and Gerlinde Marti's elegant Colonial Revival home, set on 6 wooded acres, has a pleasing mix of period antiques, Oriental carpets, and original artwork.

Guests can explore hiking trails, stroll through the garden, or relax on the sunporch, in the library, or by the fire in the living room. There are two guest rooms and one suite, each with private bath. Breakfast at Merrywood is splendid, with candlelight, handmade linens, and antique English porcelain. $165–195.

Dutch Iris Inn Bed and Breakfast (860-844-0262; 877-280-0743; www.dutchirisinn.com), 239 Salmon Brook St. (CT 10), Granby 06035. This lovely 1812 colonial in the historic district is a gem. Innkeepers Vicky and John Freeman offer six elegant and tastefully decorated guest rooms, all with private bath, most with working fireplaces and whirlpool tubs. It's the unique touches that make this place so special: Where else does a guest room feature an antique piano from the 1830s? In the living room, guests can relax by a fireplace used for cooking in the 1800s. The perfect romantic retreat; ask about their special packages. A full breakfast is served by candlelight. $109–159.

The Lily House B&B (860-370-9701; www.thelilyhouse.com), 13 Bridge St., Suffield 06078. A restored butter-yellow Victorian home in Suffield's historic district, tucked behind a tidy white picket fence. Three guest rooms are nicely furnished with antiques and unique decor; all have private bath. They occupy the second floor and share a cozy common area that's well stocked with books, games, and puzzles, plus a refrigerator filled with complimentary snacks and beverages. Guests can also relax on the inviting wraparound porch. Full breakfast is served in the formal dining room. Victorian teas are held at the house every month. In-house massages are available on request. Suffield Academy and Bradley International Airport are nearby. $95–140.

Spencer on Main (860-668-5862; www.spenceronmain.com), 264 South Main St. (CT 75), Suffield 06078. An elegant and beautifully restored 1871 Second Empire–style mansion offers picture-perfect accommodations in gracious surroundings. There's one twin room and two suites, each with private bath and Italian marble fireplace, some with claw-foot bathtubs and towel warmers. A screened porch, an outdoor pool, and 8 acres of gardens and grounds invite relaxation. Inside, paintings, local memorabilia, and historic photographs decorate the inn for good reason: Hostess Caroline d'Otreppe has family ties to Suffield's founding fathers. Host Etienne d'Otreppe is Belgian and likes to cook full gourmet European-style breakfasts. Guests can be picked up at Bradley International Airport or the Windsor Locks train station—a nice touch for a small B&B. $119–219.

HOTELS

In Farmington 06032

🐾 ♿ **Centennial Inn Suites** (860-677-4647; 800-852-2052; www.centennialinn.com), 5 Spring Lane (US 6 and CT 177). Popular with relocating families and business travelers who prefer to settle into a homelike arrangement, the inn has 112 suites, some with fireplace in the living room, each with a kitchen. Other amenities include an exercise room, an outdoor pool, a whirlpool, barbecue grills, evening social gatherings, and continental breakfast. $127–252.

♿ **Farmington Inn** (860-677-2821; 800-648-9804; www.farmingtoninn.com), 827 Farmington Ave. (CT 4). There are 72 rooms and suites featuring original paintings by area artists, fresh flowers, and luxury amenities—same-day valet service, covered parking. Also a gourmet Italian restaurant on the premises (see *Dining Out*). This is an excellent base for a Farmington River Valley visit, or for business travelers. Continental breakfast. $139–169.

♿ **Marriott Hotel Farmington** (860-678-1000; reservations 800-228-9290; www.farmingtonmarriott.com), 15 Farm Springs Rd. With 381 rooms, six suites, a parklike setting, and a jogging trail, this is a model of a suburban hotel. Restaurant, lounge, coffee shop, health club, indoor and outdoor pools, tennis, and easy access to the interstate. $109–209.

Elsewhere

♿ **West Hartford Inn** (860-236-3221; 877-782-2777; www.westhartfordinn.com), 900 Farmington Ave. (CT 4), West Hartford 06119. Just two blocks from West Hartford center and Blue Back Square, with their chic shops and restaurants, this 50-room in-town accommodation offers laundry and room service, an exercise room, free enclosed parking spaces, and continental breakfast. $99–139.

Avon Old Farms Hotel (860-677-1651; 800-836-4000; www.avonoldfarmshotel.com), CT 10 and US 44, Avon 06001. The hotel has 157 rooms and three suites. At the foot of Avon "Mountain," this is a 20th-century Georgian colonial with a spectacular lobby and curved staircases leading to mezzanines. Mindful of its New England past, it's furnished with antiques, embellished with traditional architectural touches, and thoroughly comfortable. Rooms are in the main building and in the outbuildings on the 20-acre site. Amenities include an outdoor pool and a health club. **Seasons Restaurant & Tap Room** offers excellent food. $149–229.

🐾 ♿ **Marriott Residence Inn** (860-678-1666; reservations 800-331-3131; www.marriott.com/bdlha), 55 Simsbury Rd. (CT 10), Avon 06001. An all-suite hotel for travelers who require the comforts of home: 100 studios and one- and two-bedroom suites designed for extended stays. All have dining and living areas, fully equipped kitchens, and free high-speed Internet access; some come with a fireplace. Avon's restaurants, shops, and bike path are close by. Continental breakfast is included, as are complimentary evening snacks during the week. $129–219.

♿ **The Simsbury Inn** (860-651-5700; 800-634-2719; www.simsburyinn.com), 397 Hopmeadow St., Simsbury 06070. This full-service hotel looks like a resort: a redbrick, white-trimmed central building with wings on either side, a circular drive, and flags flying at the entrance. Besides a restaurant (see Evergreens Restaurant under *Dining Out*) and 100 guest rooms, there are tennis courts, an indoor pool, health club facilities, and a cozy lounge with a crackling fire when the weather turns cold. $169 and up.

Sheraton Bradley Hotel (860-627-5311; reservations 877-422-5311; www.sheratonbradley.com), 1 Bradley International Airport, Windsor Locks 06096; located between two terminals. While many lodgings ring the airport, this is, no contest, the most convenient; it's the only one right there, with 237 units, one suite, and a host of amenities: coffee shop, lounge, entertainment, fitness center, sauna, and indoor pool; **Concorde's Restaurant** specializes in grilled meats and seafood. $119 and up.

While the **Sheraton Hotel** is the only lodging right at Bradley International Airport, the Ella Grasso Turnpike (CT 75) in Windsor Locks offers a plethora of lodging options that are minutes away from the terminals; most provide free airport shuttle service and offer park-and-fly packages. They include **Homewood Suites by Hilton** (860-627-8463; 800-225-5466), **Doubletree Hotel** (860-627-5171; 800-631-0019), **Ramada Inn** (860-623-9494), **Fairfield Inn by Marriott** (860-627-9333), and **Days Inn** (860-623-9417).

MOTELS

♿ **Hawthorne Inn** (860-828-4181; www.hawthorne-inn.com), 2387 Wilbur Cross Hwy. (US 5 and CT 15), on the Berlin Turnpike, Berlin 06037. Open year-round; 68 rooms, all with private bath. Managed by the Grelak family for nearly 60 years, the Hawthorne is known for quality service. Recently renovated, its amenities include high-speed wireless Internet access, an outdoor pool, an exercise room, miniature golf, shuffleboard, volleyball, and horseshoes. The Grelaks run a well-regarded traditional restaurant next door, known for its prime rib, seafood, and other American specialties. Continental breakfast. $79–175.

Iron Horse Inn (860-658-2216; 800-245-9938; www.ironhorseinnofsimsbury.com), 969 Hopmeadow St. (CT 10), Simsbury. Clean, simple, no-frills accommodations. The 27 rooms have kitchenettes and private balconies; a two-bedroom suite has a living room and full-sized kitchen. Outdoor pool, laundry room, and free Internet access. $75–170.

✷ Where to Eat

DINING OUT

In Farmington

♿ **Apricots** (860-673-5405; www.apricotsrestaurant.com), 1593 Farmington Ave. (CT 4). Open for lunch and dinner daily. Despite the Farmington River Valley's paucity of restaurants coming and going, loyal fans stand by this venerable establishment, where views of the Farmington River—floodlit at night—are the icing on an elegant dining experience. There's an English-type pub downstairs, with piano Wed.–Sat. Upstairs are three dining rooms with formal lighting, crisp white linen, and contemporary American and Continental cuisine, all under the management of Ann Howard—a respected name among Connecticut gourmets. You may find such temptations as baked Maine crabcakes with a mango glaze (as an appetizer), pan-seared rack of spring lamb with ratatouille and lamb jus, or grilled swordfish dressed with an asparagus vinaigrette and accompanied with rösti potatoes. The menu changes seasonally and mixes gourmet standards with trendy dishes that show the kitchen is not resting on its laurels. Exquisite desserts, including the signature apricot mousse. $18–35.

♿ **Cugino's of Farmington** (860-678-9366), 1053 Farmington Ave. (CT 4). Open for lunch Sun.–Fri.; dinner daily. Northern Italian cuisine in elegant Old World surroundings. Start with lightly fried calamari, or the portobello mushroom stuffed with shrimp, smoked prosciutto, and Gorgonzola. Huge plates of fish, steak, veal, chicken, and pasta are authentic and expertly prepared. Extensive wine list. Endings like tiramisu, gelato, and espresso will satisfy the most die-hard Italophiles. The bar is intimate and cozy, with live guitar and jazz. $16–32.

♿ **The Grist Mill Restaurant** (860-676-8855; www.thegristmill.net), 44 Mill Lane. Open daily for lunch and dinner. Reservations suggested. Dine on northern Mediterranean seafood and pasta specialties in this converted 17th-century flour mill, where there is a view of the Farmington River from every table. Outdoor patio and specialties like Dover sole and lobster beggar's purse. $22–32. Millrace Books, an inviting bookshop, is upstairs.

Piccolo Arancio (860-674-1224; www.piccoloarancio.com), 819 Farmington Ave. (CT 4), next door to the Farmington Inn. Open for lunch Mon.–Fri.; dinner Mon.–Sat.; closed Sun. An award-winning list of wines (more than 120) complements hearty, elegant Italian cuisine, from veal osso buco to porcini-crusted chicken breast. Gourmet pizza, homemade pasta, and other Italian staples round out the menu. The surroundings are at once elegant and welcoming; tables are in constant demand. $19–29.

In West Hartford

Fleming's Prime Steakhouse & Wine Bar (860-676-9463; www.flemingssteakhouse.com), 44 South Main St., in Blue Back Square. Open daily for dinner. Reservations are recommended. Feeling carnivorous? *Meat* is the word at this urbane chophouse and bar that stands out in an upscale town rich in upscale restaurants. It's pricey, to be sure, but the prime meats are top-notch. Other dishes come with their own unique touches: seared tuna mignon with poppy seed au poivre; seared scallops in a lobster cream sauce; and chicken baked with white wine, mushrooms, shallots, and thyme. Save room for chocolate lava cake, a wedge of silky chocolate with a molten center. This upscale nationwide chain is known for its creative takes on American standards; at the bar, a hip crowd favors the roster oF 100 wines by the glass. $19–42.

♿ **Barcelona Restaurant & Wine Bar** (860-218-2100; www.barcelonawinebar.com), 971 Farmington Ave. (CT 4). Open for lunch Mon.–Sat.; dinner daily. One of West Hartford center's hippest eateries is also a sibling of a Fairfield County chain. The patio's overhead awning and heated floor help extend New England's relatively short outdoor-dining season. Hot and cold tapas come in little-plate portions designed for sharing and sampling. Heartier appetites should consider the entrées, from paella and grilled lamb chops to New York strip steak and a good selection of seafood. A decent list of well-chosen and reasonably priced wines. $20–27.

♿ **Grants** (860-236-1930), 977 Farmington Ave. Open for lunch Mon.–Fri.; dinner daily. Reservations suggested. The city-chic feel and seasonally changing creative American cuisine with Italian and French influences are why this restaurant/bar/patisserie is often touted as the best place to dine in West Hartford's center. The mantra on the menu says it best: "Eat and live well always." Patrons achieve this end with chef Billy Grant's dressed-up comfort food: Baked macaroni is crafted with goat, cheddar, and Gruyère cheese with roasted mushrooms—no "processed cheese food" here. Other standouts are the rack of Australian lamb, steamed Pacific salmon, porcini-rubbed pork tenderloin, and the signature filet mignon with melted Gorgonzola. White chocolate cheesecake brûlée, fallen chocolate-cherry soufflé cake, Italian plum cobbler, and rich, silky truffles are among the patisserie offerings. In warm weather, tables are set up right on the sidewalk. $19–40; three-course, prix fixe menu $29.

♿ **Max's Oyster Bar** (860-236-6299; www.maxrestaurantgroup.com), 964 Farmington Ave. (CT 4). Open for lunch and dinner daily; Sun. brunch. You'll feel like you're in a big-city fish house in this sleek and sophisticated eatery in the center of town, with its art-clad dining room and bustling sidewalk tables. It's often packed with stylish young locals and dressed-up suburbanites, particularly at the bar. The kitchen does wonders with modernized American bistro fare, but as the name implies, seafood rules. For drama, the Hi-Rise of Shellfish tops it all: an impressive vertical tower of scallops, mussels, oysters, and the like, on a mountain of shaved ice. $20–39.

♿ **Restaurant Bricco** (860-233-0220), 78 LaSalle Rd. Open for lunch Mon.–Sat.; dinner daily. A chic establishment serving creative American cuisine with Italian and Mediterranean influences. The seasonal menu might include wood-oven-baked mushroom and spinach lasagna, mustard BBQ cedar-planked salmon, or fennel- and pepper-crusted tuna. Pasta selections range from spaghetti with fava beans, prosciutto, and white truffle oil to veal and spinach ravioli with sage butter. The wood ovens turn out imaginative pizzas. $18–28.

In Avon

♿ **Avon Old Farms Inn** (860-677-2818; www.avonoldfarmsinn.com), 1 Nod Rd., at the junction of CT 10 and US 44. Open for dinner Mon.–Sat.; brunch on Sun. The Avon Old Farms Inn looks the way you expect a historic inn to look—low, rambling, and comfortably colonial (a 1757 core building)—and it houses one of the oldest restaurants in the country. Several additions over the years have produced a series of dining spaces, most with exposed beams, wide-board floors, and New England memorabilia. In winter you'll welcome a seat in the Forge Room, under wagon-wheel light fixtures and near the fireplace, or across the room in the booths that were once horse stalls. The award-winning cuisine is New American—pan-seared sea bass with a spicy citrus sauce, and portobello mushroom tempura with kalamata olive dip are examples—and tried-and-true: baked stuffed shrimp, pan-seared sirloin steak, and other classics. Across the street from Avon Old Farms Hotel. $17–28.

Bosc Kitchen & Wine Bar (860-676-2672; www.boscwinebar.com), 136 Simsbury Rd. (CT 10), in the Riverdale Farms shopping center. Open for lunch and dinner Mon.–Sat.; closed Sun. This relative newcomer to the local dining scene was an instant hit, thanks to its polished cuisine and intimate and sophisticated vibe. The terrace is a prime spot in warm weather, with its magnificent view of Talcott Mountain, as are the dining rooms inside, made cozy with banquettes lined with throw pillows, and walls in pearlike hues of gold and green. The menu delivers on its promise of "creative contemporary American cuisine." For openers, try foie gras with bee pollen and toasted brioche; the signature salad of Bosc pear, Gorgonzola, pecans, and fresh herbs and field greens topped with a chai tea vinaigrette; or tuna tartare in a black sesame soy glaze. Then choose from entrées like grilled tandoori rack of lamb with roasted-shallot puree; fresh ravioli stuffed with mushrooms, asparagus, and roasted red pepper; or pan-seared duck breast with toasted barley and a black fig reduction. Desserts are flawless, and the wine bar features a long list of vintages from around the globe. $22–31.

♿ **Max a Mia** (860-677-6299; www.maxrestaurantgroup.com), 70 East Main St. (US 44). Open for lunch and dinner daily. Reservations suggested. A roadside restaurant with a superior northern Italian menu. Popular with the boomer set, and a gathering place both at lunch and in the evening. The dozens of varieties of "stone pies"—pizzas baked in a stone wood-burning pizza oven—are worth a trip. The menu also features Tuscan-style fare: grilled-salmon risotto, ricotta gnocchi, seafood, and chicken, along with distinctive and tasty vegetarian concoctions. Desserts are sublime, from tiramisu to apple tart with puff pastry. $12–27.

In Simsbury

♿ **Amelia's American Bistro** (860-408-1234; www.ameliasamerican bistro.com), Fiddler's Green, 2 Wilcox St. Open for lunch Tue.–Sat., dinner Tue.–Sun.; Sun. brunch; closed Mon. Reservations are recommended. The fact that this bistro is named for chef-owner Anthony Camilleri's grandmother only adds to its charm. His sit-up-and-take-notice cooking doesn't hurt, either. You can start with icy shellfish from the raw bar, or an appetizer like jumbo lumb crabcake fritters, then try the smoked pork chop with housemade sausage and seared foie gras; lamb osso buco with goat cheese grits; or the signature monkfish schnitzel, panko-crusted and topped with lobster meat. Live jazz on Friday and Saturday nights. $16–30.

♿ **Evergreens Restaurant** (860-651-5700), at the Simsbury Inn, 397 Hopmeadow St. (CT 10). Open for lunch Tue.–Fri., dinner Tue.–Sat.; Sun. brunch; closed Mon. Linen on the tables, carpeting underfoot, greenery throughout, and tall windows to bring in the light. Continental fare: bourbon and brown sugar sirloin, arctic char, creative pasta dishes, a good hand with herbs. $22–30.

♿ **Maeda Sushi** (860-651-4100; www .maedasushi.com), 530 Bushy Hill Rd., in the Simsbury Commons Shopping Center. Open for lunch and dinner Tue.–Sun.; closed Mon. Reservations are recommended for the sushi bar. Sushi lovers love this chic storefront Japanese restaurant run by chef-owner Yasuo Maeda, who earned his stripes in Tokyo and Manhattan before heading to the suburbs. Grab a seat at the sushi bar to watch him at work. $14–35.

♿ **Metro Bis, An American Bistro** (860-651-1908; www.metrobis.com), in the Simsburytown Shops, 928 Hopmeadow St. (CT 10). Open for lunch and dinner Mon.–Sat.; closed Sun. Reservations suggested. This small, casual bistro is a local culinary darling, with a dynamic husband-and-wife team at the helm. Chef Chris Prosperi lures foodies to the suburbs with exceptional cuisine; sometimes the accent is French, other times Asian. You might start with crispy marinated calamari with tamarind-miso dipping sauce, then try pan-seared salmon with sweet potato vegetable hash and red wine cream sauce. Another winner is the ricotta cavatelli with wild mushrooms and porcini broth. Must-have desserts include maple and white chocolate bread pudding with white chocolate crème Anglaise; or hazelnut, green tea, or chocolate gelato. Courtney Febbroriello is the author of *Wife of the Chef*, a witty exposé about being a chef's wife. $21–25.

♿ **Simsbury 1820 House Café** (860-658-7658), 731 Hopmeadow St. (CT 10). Open for dinner Mon.–Fri.; closed Sat. and Sun. for private functions. Reservations suggested. Set in a New England manor house that has been transformed into a country inn (see *Lodging*), an intimate (read: tiny) café where the decor is dignified, and the dining room has a working fireplace and is softly lit. Dishes are imaginatively prepared: You might begin with roast duck atop a bed of fennel and oranges, then dine on salmon stuffed with spinach, sun-dried tomatoes, and Parmesan cheese; or grilled chicken breast sauced with a peach and jalapeño glaze. For dessert, try dark rum chocolate bread pudding or a triple chocolate terrine. $18–25.

Elsewhere

Great Taste (860-827-8988; www.greattaste.com), 597 West Main St., New Britain. Open daily for lunch and dinner. After more than 20 years of serving traditional Chinese favorites, this establishment has it down pat. It's off the beaten path, and locals like it that way, but the top-notch fare makes it well worth finding. The menu mixes what you'd expect—tangerine beef, General Tso's chicken, wonton soup—with nice surprises like pan-seared Chilean sea bass or a flavorful duck wrap. Decor is smart and tasteful, complete with Asian art and crystal chandeliers. Certainly not your average take-out Chinese spot. $14–25.

Cottage Restaurant and Café (860-793-8888; www.cottagerestaurant andcafe.com), 427 Farmington Ave., Plainville. Open for lunch Tue.–Fri.; dinner Tue.–Sat.; closed Sun. and Mon. Reservations are recommended for dinner. Three generations of the Queen family have run this beloved local gem with a creative seasonal menu. Crispy swordfish nuggets with lobster aioli dipping sauce make a fine appetizer; must-try entrées include grilled hanger steak with truffle fries, and crêpes stuffed with goat cheese and summer vegetables. Avocado cheesecake is a pleasurable end to everything. $18–28.

J. Timothy's Taverne (860-747-6813; www.jtimothys.com), 143 New Britain Ave. (CT 372), Plainville. Open daily for lunch and dinner. This rambling colonial structure, with its wide-plank floors, wall sconces, and fireplaces, harks from 1789, the year President Washington was inaugurated and the tavern first opened for business. Traditional American fare is served in several hushed, softly lit dining rooms. The lunch menu offers hearty sandwiches and salads; the dinner menu includes satisfying and well-prepared steak, chicken, and seafood dishes. Lively pub. $14–27.

Buon Appetito (860-693-2211), Gateway Office Park, 50 Albany Turnpike (US 44), Canton. Open for dinner daily. The aroma of garlic greets you at the door of this bustling trattoria with its open kitchen, and garlic infuses many of the excellent dishes: crusty bread topped with a pungent garlic spread, dressings and sauces flavored with minced garlic—even a simple dish of asparagus sautéed with diced garlic is sublime. Expect hearty food, with lots of fresh herbs and, of course, garlic. The extensive menu is complemented each night with a list of specials—many featuring seafood, and seafood is prepared especially well here. Among the many pasta dishes, a standout is made with sweet sausage, artichokes, basil, and, naturally, garlic. BYOB. $13–26.

Tuscan Twins (860-243-2757; www .tuscantwins.com), 39 Jerome Ave., Bloomfield. Open for lunch Mon.–Fri.; dinner Mon.–Sat.; closed Sun. Generous portions of gourmet Italian fare are served up in bright and airy upscale surroundings. Some dishes are familiar—lobster risotto, pasta Bolognese, fried calamari—while others boast an adventurous spin. Be sure to save room for chocolate Chambord crème brûlée; you'll be sorry if you don't. $19–30. Upstairs, **Red** has style aplenty. Expect a cocktail lounge with hip Moroccan-style decor (plush pillows, Persian rugs, mosaic tiles, jewel-toned tapestries); it's a good stop for an after-dinner martini or live jazz.

Ginza (860-242-8289; www.ginza cuisine.com), 14 Wintonbury Mall Rd., Bloomfield. This newer restaurant offering authentic Japanese cuisine, fresh sushi, and live hibachi shows is a rising star on Connecticut's diverse culinary scene. A standout among the growing number of sushi places in the region. $14–26.

♿ **Tosca** (860-668-0273; www.toscact.com), 68 Bridge St., in Suffield Village Plaza, Suffield. Open for dinner Mon.–Sat.; closed Sun. Reservations recommended. An intimate, candlelit eatery that prepares familiar Mediterranean dishes—carbonara, seafood penne, even seared tuna with olive tapenade or grilled chicken with wild mushrooms and roasted peppers in a Gorgonzola cream sauce. The romantic ambience—couples are known to get engaged here—makes this little gem a good pick for a date. The menu changes with the seasons but always has an Italian flair. Outdoor patio. $17–30.

♿ **Bonterra Italian Bistro** (860-426-2620; www.bonterraitalianbistro.com), 98 Main St., Southington. Open for lunch Tue.–Sat.; dinner Tue.–Sun.; closed Mon. Reservations are recommended, especially on weekends. *Bonterra* is Italian for "good earth," a nod to the homemade pastas and sauces, organic wine, and fresh-squeezed juices this bistro on the town green is known for. Mediterranean cuisine translates into pork shank osso buco, grilled scallop risotto, and fennel-crusted salmon. Extensive wine and martini list. $12–27.

EATING OUT

In New Britain

Cracovia (860-223-4443), 60 Broad St. In a city with a rich Eastern European heritage and generous numbers of restaurants offering the cooking of that region, this place is a standout. When it comes to serving traditional Polish fare, the kitchen has it going on. Start with cabbage soup and move on to kielbasa and sauerkraut, potato pancakes, stuffed cabbage, or pierogi stuffed with potatoes and cheese. $5–11.

East Side Restaurant (860-223-1188; www.eastsiderestaurant.com), 131 Dwight St. Open daily for lunch and dinner. Satisfying the appetite of locals for more than 60 years, the East Side is a great place to sample authentic and hearty German cuisine. Start with corn fritters, marinated herring, or potato pancakes, followed by bratwurst, knockwurst, Hungarian goulash, or Wiener schnitzel, all served by friendly waitresses in traditional German attire. There are also steak, chicken, seafood dishes. The list of German beers is extensive, and on weekends accordion players in Tyrolean costume entertain. $24–31.

Staropolska Restaurant (860-612-1711; www.staropolska.net), 270 Broad St. Open daily for lunch and dinner. This is the read deal: pierogi, red borscht with dumplings, blintzes, and potato pancakes. Casual and friendly, authentic Polish home cooking. $10–17.

In West Hartford

The Cheesecake Factory (860-233-5588; www.cheesecakefactory.com), 71 Isham Rd., in Blue Back Square. Open daily for lunch and dinner; Sun. brunch. A perpetually packed upscale chain restaurant with a huge something-for-everyone menu (nine pages of entrées). It's been a hit since opening day and they don't accept reservations, so be prepared to wait. If everyone in your party is in the mood for something different, don't fret: They try to make everyone happy here, and according to regulars, they pull it off. The namesake dessert, of course, is a must-have. $11–30.

♿ **The Corner Pug** (860-231-0241; www.tapasonline.com), 1046 New

Britain Ave., in the Elmwood section. Open daily for lunch and dinner. Irish nachos, St. Louis ribs, fish-and-chips, and the Zen burger are favorites among the well-prepared, hearty tavern fare. The bar is lively and fun; the tall wooden booths in back are more intimate. A dozen beers on tap (local brews like Hartford's Thomas Hooker Blonde Ale and East Hartford's Burnside Tenpenny Ale), plus Irish and English ales and more than 20 bottled beers. $9–26.

The Elbow Room (860-236-6195; www.americanjoint.com), 998 Farmington Ave. (CT 4), in West Hartford Center. Open daily for lunch and dinner. If the wait for tables is long (and it may be), pass the time at the rooftop bar and check out the scene below. It's packed up there during the warmer months, a reminder of how aptly named an eatery this place is. The menu hits mostly high notes with chicken, steak, pasta, and seafood. $12–20.

Harry's Pizza (860-231-7166; www.harryspizza.net), 1003 Farmington Ave. (CT 4), in West Hartford Center. Open for breakfast Sat. and Sun.; lunch Thu.–Sun.; dinner daily. Here is a place where foodies and families are equally happy. The thin-crust Neapolitan-style gourmet pizza is to die for; we love the signature summer pie topped with local organic tomatoes and fresh basil. Snow peas, whole belly clams, capers, and cilantro are other toppings not often seen on pizza house menus. $12–20.

Lemon Grass (860-233-4405), 7 South Main St. Open for lunch Mon.–Sat.; dinner daily. In the center of West Hartford, this storefront oasis manages to create a calm spot in a busy shopping area. It serves Thai cuisine, as hot as you can stand it or serenely mild if you prefer. The house specialty is Lemongrass Treasure, combining shrimp, scallops, squid, and fish with hot chiles, mushrooms, onions, green peppers, and mysterious spices and herbs on top of steamed clams. There are simple salads, fiery curries, barbecued chicken dishes, and pad Thai—the classic noodle dish with shrimp, tofu, ground peanuts, and vegetables. $8–18.

Pond House Café (860-231-8823; www.pondhousecafe.com), 1555 Asylum Ave. Open for lunch and dinner Tue.–Sat.; Sun. brunch; closed Mon. This quaint BYOB café, actually part of Hartford's historic Elizabeth Park, draws both locals and travelers, not the least for its lovely surroundings (request one of the prized patio tables) and its terrific menu of creative comfort food. On the lighter side, the grilled chicken over ratatouille is superb; the hearty Tuscan-style stew (a winter offering) is also a standout. Elizabeth Park is America's oldest public rose garden, so try to plan a visit to the café when the 15,000 thorny beauties are in full dazzling bloom. $12–23.

Tapas (860-521-4609; www.tapasonline.com), 1150 New Britain Ave., in the Elmwood section. Open daily for lunch and dinner. A local institution for 25 years, serving Greek and Mediterranean food to a seemingly perpetually packed house. Try Greek salad topped with "almost famous" dressing, then the falafel platter or some of the namesake tapas, which here are more Spanish-style pizzas than appetizers. Great vegetarian dishes, especially the spanakopita. $8–17. Other locations in Hartford (860-525-5988) and Bloomfield (860-882-0756).

In Simsbury

Maple Tree Café (860-651-1297; www.mapletreecafe.com), 781 Hopmeadow St. (CT 10). Hearty American fare—chicken, steak, seafood, pasta—

in a center-of-town eatery recognized far and wide for the live local and nationally known blues acts that grace the stage on weekends. $11–20.

The Perfect Pear Café (860-651-7734), 532 Hopmeadow St. (CT 10), in Simsmore Square. Open for lunch Mon.–Fri.; dinner Wed.–Sat.; brunch on Sun. A cozy neighborhood café known for its deliciously creative specialty sandwiches. Lunch is a fabulous reward after a hike up the Heublein Tower atop nearby Talcott Mountain. The pastry case at the front door teases with freshly baked desserts. $6–15.

Plan B Burger Bar & Tavern (860-658-4477; www.planbtavern.com), 4 Railroad St. Open Mon.–Sat. for lunch and dinner; closed Sun. Other locations in West Hartford (860-231-1199) and Glastonbury (860-430-9737). Craving beef? You can't do much better than this convivial neighborhood pub, where the menu is long on burgers. Caramelized onions, bourbon sauce, and truffle mayo are among the creative toppings on America's favorite sandwich. Fresh beef is ground here daily; the handcrafted American ales are ice cold. $10–20.

Elsewhere

Pagliacci's Restaurant (860-793-9241; www.pagliaccisrestaurant.com), 333 East St. (CT 10), Plainville. Open daily for lunch and dinner. The heady aroma of garlic and fresh-baked bread is the first thing you notice as you enter this bustling restaurant. Generous portions of traditional Italian specialties—veal scaloppine, chicken parmigiana, and shrimp scampi, to name a few—impossibly huge bowls of house-made pasta, hearty pizzas, and calzones. Be prepared to wait for a table, especially on weekends—Pagliacci's has a loyal following. $10–22.

Olympia Diner (860-666-9948), 3413 Berlin Turnpike (US 5 and CT 15), Newington. Open daily 5:30 AM–midnight. The diner of your dreams: Bright neon guides you to the super-long, silver-bullet core car with added-on dining rooms. Since 1952, the Olympia has been a venerable icon on the Berlin Turnpike for dependable diner fare—burgers and dogs, home fries, rice pudding. Booths with slick plastic, Formica tables, a voluminous menu offering serious food dished out in generous portions, or just that quintessential diner order—hot coffee and a slab of pie. $8–15.

Toshi Japanese Restaurant (860-677-8242; www.toshirestaurant.com), in the Riverdale Farms Shopping Plaza, 136 Simsbury Rd. (CT 10), Avon. Open daily for lunch and dinner. A favorite spot with area sushi and sashimi lovers. Well-prepared authentic Japanese cuisine that successfully blends flavors, textures, and colors. $13–25.

Bamboo Grill (860-693-4144; www.bamboogrillcuisine.com), 50 Albany Turnpike (US 44), Canton. Open for dinner Tue.–Sun.; closed Mon. Reservations suggested on weekends. Behind its small, plain storefront—not easy to find—the Bamboo Grill dazzles with variety. Vietnamese to take out or eat in, totaling more than 70 choices. Rice-batter crêpes, flan caramel, or this satisfying one-dish concoction: grilled chicken (or beef or pork) on rice noodles with lettuce, fried onions, peanuts, and house sauce. BYOB. $9–16.

Crown and Hammer (860-693-9199; www.crownandhammer.com), 3 Depot St., Collinsville. Open Wed.–Sun. for lunch and dinner; closed Mon. and Tue. A lively pub in an old train depot is a neighborhood favorite for the better-than-usual pub fare and live acoustic music. $13–24.

The Cambridge House (860-653-2739; www.cbhbrew.com), 357 Salmon

Brook St. (CT 10), Granby. Open for lunch and dinner Tue.–Sun.; closed Mon. A restaurant and brewpub that gets packed, a testament to its popularity with locals. The menu revolves around American tavern classics; starters are decidedly pubby—wings, chili, beer-battered onion rings—while dinner means pizza, pasta, ribs, burgers, and steak, with a few Asian-fusion-style dishes thrown into the mix. There's a handful of brewed-on-site ales, and desserts are the usual suspects: tiramisu, brownie sundaes, and pie. $8–23.

♿ **Union Street Tavern** (860-683-2899; www.unionstreettavern.com), 20 Union St., Windsor. Open daily for lunch and dinner. A bar and grill on Windsor's historic green, featuring pub standards (wings, skins, burgers), seafood, steak, and ribs in a renovated historic firehouse on Windsor's historic green. $14–19.

COFFEE- AND TEAHOUSES

Mainly Tea (860-529-9517; www.mainlytea.com), 221 Main St., Wethersfield. Open Thu.–Sat. for lunch and afternoon tea. Reservations are recommended. A delightful gourmet tea parlor that makes a perfect stop during a day spent wandering through Wethersfield's historic district. The traditional tearoom menu has tea sandwiches, homemade soup, scones with cream and jam, and 80 varieties of premium teas from around the world, served in individual pots. A shop selling teas, tea accoutrements, and other gifts beckons to be browsed. Ask about special seasonal events.

The Coffee Trade (860-676-2661; 800-764-5282; www.thecoffeetrade.com), 21 West Main St. (US 44), Avon. Open daily. In this old farmhouse turned coffeehouse, the coffee beans are freshly roasted, and the heavenly scent literally fills the air. Browse the assortment of antiques and collectibles (they're all for sale) that fill a trio of quiet and cozy sitting rooms, stocked with newspapers to encourage lingering. Baked goods pair well with a huge selection of flavored coffees that features the usual suspects, plus unique varieties: chocolate-covered graham cracker, apricot, and Island Mist, an exotic combination of pineapple, chocolate, and coconut. Gift baskets come with coffee beans, biscotti, gourmet chocolates, and specialty teas.

59ers Café (860-231-9390; www.59erscafe.com), 984A Farmington Ave. (CT 4), West Hartford. Open daily. An ice cream shop and espresso bar named for the owner's restored '59 Chevy (check out the vintage car ads on the walls). Besides the University of Connecticut's main campus, this is the only place in the state to serve UConn Dairy Bar ice cream.

It's a Grind (860-761-3290), 51 Memorial Rd., Blue Back Square, West Hartford. Open daily. A small coffeehouse in West Hartford's chic new shopping district. Sure, it's a chain, but the coffee is good (try the Aztec Café Mocha), there's free WiFi, and the baristas are friendly and enthusiastic.

♿ **The Beanery Bistro** (860-688-2224; www.thebeanerybistro.com), 25 Central St., Windsor. Open Mon.–Sat.; closed Sun. A likable little place with seating outdoors on the patio in warm weather. The menu includes desserts and "savory sandwiches"—for example, one with artichoke hearts, Parmesan cheese, and mild chiles in a spread. The specialty is a sandwich made with roast turkey and stuffing, tomato, and Swiss on crispy French bread. Pastries, breads, and muffins are baked on the premises. As for the coffee, choose espresso or one of several flavored brews. There's a gift store as well, with gift baskets to give (or keep and enjoy). $4–7.

ICE CREAM **Main Street Creamery & Café** (860-529-0509), 217 Main St., Old Wethersfield. Open daily 10–10. Right in the heart of town, this is a great place for sweet tooths to pop in for a cone after exploring the historic district. Frozen yogurt and sorbet, too.

A. C. Petersen Farms (860-233-3651), 240 Park Rd., West Hartford. Half a century ago, their milk trucks were a familiar sight around town. Today this is one of West Hartford's most revered sweet spots, a nostalgic, turn-back-the-clock, casual family-style restaurant known for old-fashioned homemade ice cream. Old-time indulgences like banana splits and Belgian waffle sundaes are topped with their signature hand-whipped cream.

Tulmeadow Farm Store & Ice Cream (860-658-1430; www.tulmeadowfarmstore.com), 255 Farms Village Rd. (CT 309), West Simsbury. In-season, the ice cream window is open Sun.–Thu. noon–8; Fri. and Sat. noon–9. Maybe they weren't making ice cream when the farm was founded in 1768, but many locals are glad they picked up the practice somewhere along the way. The ice cream is made right here, from old-fashioned favorites to seasonal flavors made with fresh peaches. Enjoy a cone, dish, or sundae on the hay bales out front, or take some home by the pint or quart. Pick up some fresh produce while you're here.

See also Farmington Miniature Golf & Ice Cream Parlor and Riverfront Miniature Golf & Ice Cream Parlor under *To Do.*

SNACKS **Capitol Lunch** (860-229-8237), 510 Main St., New Britain. Open daily. Do as the locals do at this longtime institution: Order a couple of chili dogs at the counter and grab a table in the lunchroom-style eatery. You'll be sure to rub elbows with a coterie of regulars. $4–9.

Atlanta Bread Company (860-667-7759), 3243 Berlin Turnpike, Newington. Open daily. Bread is the forte, but you can also pick up light meals that revolve around bread. Some of the made-right-here soups, for example, come in a hollowed-out sourdough bread bowl; many of the gourmet sandwiches are made with warm focaccia. Biscotti, pastries, and other desserts pair nicely with specialty coffees, smoothies, cappuccino, and espresso. In cold weather, enjoy your treats in front of the fireplace. $4–7.

Doogie's (860-666-1944), 2525 Berlin Turnpike, Newington. Look for the mustard-yellow sign. This hot dog joint is a Connecticut favorite for top-notch frankfurters; home of the "two-footer"—a 2-foot hot dog on a special 2-foot-long, breadstick-style bun. Philly steaks, fried dough, milk shakes, and lobster rolls are on the menu, but everyone comes to this 1950s-style diner for the char-cooked Grote & Weigel dogs, served plain or topped with sauerkraut, bacon and cheese, or chili. Serving about 2,000 hot dogs a week makes them truly worthy of the moniker *institution*.

Carmela's Pasta Shop (860-529-9533), 338 Silas Deane Hwy., Wethersfield. There's a small dining area, but most folks come to this little pasta shop to take home fresh pasta, cheese, and containers of homemade sauce. Regulars rave about the ravioli, which comes stuffed with cheese, meat, seafood, roasted eggplant, lobster, pumpkin, and mushrooms.

The Spicy Green Bean Deli (860-563-3100; www.spicygreenbean.com),

285 Main St., Wethersfield. Open Mon.–Fri. 7:30 AM–3 PM; open Sat. in summer; closed Sun. This cheery little deli in the historic district is the perfect respite before or after touring Wethersfield's many notable homes and sites. Offerings are simple yet satisfying: breakfast sandwiches in the morning; soups, salads, and sandwiches for lunch; cookies, tarts, muffins, and other sweets for a snack. Indoor seating can feel cramped; take your meal to an outdoor table, in-season. $4–8.

AS'n Delicatessen (860-676-2253), in the Riverdale Farms Shopping complex, 136 Simsbury Rd. (CT 10), Avon. Open daily. A New York–style deli menu so authentic, you'll swear you're in Manhattan. Breakfast means omelets, pancakes, and corned beef hash. Later on, oversized sandwiches piled high with deli standards—corned beef, pastrami, brisket, knockwurst—are on the menu; the homemade chicken matzo ball soup will cure whatever ails you. $6–15.

LaSalle Market & Deli (860-693-8010; www.lasallemarket.com), 104 Main St., in the Collinsville section of Canton. Open daily. A friendly neighborhood market and deli smack in the middle of Collinsville's old-fashioned downtown. It's the perfect stop for a bite before or after biking the Farmington River Trail or paddling the Farmington River, both of which cut through town. French toast, pancakes, and egg sandwiches for breakfast; later on, New York–style pizza, soups, specialty sandwiches, and wraps. Friday open-mike nights draw a colorful crowd of local musicians. $4–8.

Front Street Sweets (860-233-3535; www.frontstreetsweets.com), 35A LaSalle Rd., West Hartford. Open daily. In the morning, made-from-scratch scones, muffins, and croissants; later on, salads, soups (mulligatawny is a specialty), and sandwiches. Bakery goodies—cookies, cakes, cannoli—are good anytime.

Bittersweet Bakery (860-413-9602; www.bittersweetbakery.info), 32 Rainbow Rd. (CT 20), East Granby. Open Mon.–Sat.; closed Sun. A few minutes' drive from Bradley International Airport. Artisan breads, panini sandwiches, espresso, breakfast sandwiches, pies, cakes, and cookies. $6–8.

Bart's Drive-In (860-688-9035; www.bartsdrivein.com), 55 Palisado Ave. (CT 159), Windsor. Open daily year-round for breakfast, lunch, and dinner. For more than 60 years, this has been the place to nosh on fried clams and chili dogs along the Farmington River, just outside the center of town. $2.50–8.50.

Entertainment

MUSIC AND THEATER **Miller Band Shell** (860-826-3360), Walnut Hill Park, New Britain. A long-standing summer music festival featuring jazz, blues, country-western musicians, and other performers. Concerts every Mon. and Wed. evening during July and Aug. Call for a schedule and information.

Hole in the Wall Theater (860-229-3049; www.hitw.org), 116 Main St., New Britain. This local theater group takes its unusual name from the bookstore where they debuted their first show more than 35 years ago. Ambitious amateur productions are performed year-round; call or check online for information.

Repertory Theatre of New Britain (860-223-3147; www.nbrep.org), 23 Norden St., New Britain. "The Rep" is Connecticut's largest community theater—and the first in the state to own its own facility. Year-round performances at the 4,300-seat

Norden Street Lodge include Shakespeare's works, Broadway and Off-Broadway comedies and musicals, children's productions, playwright competitions, and other events.

Connecticut Cabaret Theatre (860-829-1248; www.ctcabaret.com), 31–33 Webster Mill Plaza, Webster Square Rd., Berlin. Live Broadway-style musicals and comedy shows on Friday and Saturday nights. Patrons are welcome to bring their own dinner, drinks, and snacks.

Carol Autorino Center (860-231-5555; www.sjc.edu/arts), St. Joseph College, 1678 Asylum Ave., West Hartford. Opera, ballet, art exhibitions, and performances by Hartford Symphony.

Lincoln Theater and **Handel Performing Arts Center** (860-768-4228; 800-274-8587; www.hartford.edu/hartt), University of Hartford, 200 Bloomfield Ave., West Hartford Together, these two facilities showcase performances by students, faculty, and guest artists at the university's Hartt School of Music. Call for schedules—chamber and orchestral concerts, recitals, opera, musical comedy, and more.

Park Road Playhouse (860-586-8500; www.parkroadplayhouse.org), 244 Park Rd., West Hartford. A talented community theater group presents Broadway musicals and contemporary dramas and comedies.

✳ Selective Shopping

ANTIQUES SHOPS

In Canton

Antiques at Canton Village (860-693-2715), 220 Albany Turnpike (US 44). A multidealer shop featuring 18th- and 19th-century furniture, along with home accessories.

The Balcony (860-693-6440), 81 Albany Turnpike (US 44). Open Mon.–Sat. 10–5; Sun. noon–5. Connecticut's oldest group shop in continuous operation. Some 60 dealers offer accessories, antique and custom furniture, fine art, jewelry, silver, and home accessories. Some pieces are the work of local artisans, others are Asian and European imports.

Canton Barn (860-693-0601; www.cantonbarn.com), 75 Old Canton Rd. Year-round Saturday auctions begin at 7:30 PM. Antiques, with an emphasis on Victorian- and colonial-era pieces, as well as collectibles that date up to the 1950s. The auction hall is housed in a charming circa-1820s barn. When the weather turns cold, a 19th-century woodstove provides old-fashioned warmth.

Antiques on the Farmington (860-693-0615; www.antiquesonfarmington.com), 10 Depot St., at CT 179, in the Collinsville section of Canton. Open daily 10–5. A new locale—the old Collinsville ax factory—for a longtime multidealer business on the Farmington River. You'll still find the same nice variety of quality goods: art, linens, silver, furniture, sports memorabilia, and collectibles.

Elsewhere

Antiques at Old Avon Village (860-677-1150; www.oldavonvillage.com), 1 East Main St. (US 44), Avon. Open daily. A multidealer shop in the charming Old Avon Village shopping complex, featuring early American and Victorian furniture, jewelry, china, glassware, art, and vintage memorabilia.

Farms Village Antiques (860-651-9599; www.farmsvillageantiques.com), 250 Farms Village Rd. (CT 309), West Simsbury. Open Wed.–Mon.; Tue. by chance. Antiques and collectibles in a post office turned multidealer shop, from furniture and garden accessories to pottery and glass.

ART GALLERIES

In West Hartford

Brick Walk Fine Art (860-233-1730; www.brickwalkfineart.com), 322 Park Rd. Open Tue.–Sat. 10–5; closed Sun. and Mon. A contemporary fine arts gallery featuring paintings, mixed media, and other works by regional and national artists.

♿ **St. Joseph College Art Gallery** (860-231-5399; www.sjc.edu/art gallery), 1678 Asylum Ave. Open during the academic year, Tue.–Sat. 11–4 (until 7 on Thu.); Sun. 1–4; closed Mon. The college's collection of fine art—more than 1,200 objects, with a special emphasis on American art—is on display. Changing exhibitions feature contemporary and traditional works by national and international artists. **The Bistro** café serves light meals, refreshments, and snacks.

Saltbox Gallery (860-521-3732), 37 Buena Vista Rd. Call for exhibition schedules. Home of the West Hartford Art League, which also maintains the **Clubhouse Gallery** (860-521-1138) and **Chimney Gift Shop** (860-521-3732), both adjacent. Outstanding works by local artists in various media.

Elsewhere

✐ **Art League of New Britain** (860-229-1484; www.alnb.org), 30 Cedar St., New Britain. This 1870 Victorian carriage house with horse stalls is a center for area artists and has been affiliated with the New Britain Art School since 1928. Exhibits, and classes for adults and children.

Farmington Valley Arts Center. See *Artisans*.

Petrini Frame & Art (860-677-2747), Old Avon Village, 35 East Main St. (US 44), Avon. Nationally known fine art and custom framing.

Gallery on the Green (860-693-4102; www.galleryongreen.org), on the town green, US 44, Canton. Open Fri.–Sun. 1–5. Exhibits of work by members of Canton Artists' Guild, one of the longest-running artists' cooperatives in the state, with three galleries in a circa-1790 schoolhouse and an outdoor sculpture garden. The gallery also schedules invitational and open shows.

Arts Exclusive Gallery (860-651-5824; www.arts-exclusive.com), 690 Hopmeadow St. (CT 10), Simsbury. Open Tue.–Sun. and by appointment. Exhibits of work in a variety of media by 30 artists from around the country.

ARTISANS **Farmington Crafts Common** (860-674-9295), 248 Main St., Farmington. Some 200 artists and craftsworkers. Café and gift shop.

Farmington Valley Arts Center (860-678-1867; www.fvac.net), 25 Arts Center Lane, off US 44, Avon. Open Wed.–Sat. 11–5; Sun. noon–4. A stretched-out 19th-century brownstone, formerly an explosives plant, makes an ideal studio complex: Each artisan has a private space, with access provided by an exterior walkway. The 20-odd studios are open at varying times at the artists' discretion, and visitors are invited to come in and watch, and to ask questions. Workers in ceramics, stone, textiles, wood, metal; portrait and landscape painters, water colorists, and photographers. The center also offers classes in arts and crafts; the **Fisher Gallery** exhibits the work of resident artisans, and the **Visitors' Gallery** features American-made arts and crafts for sale.

BOOKSTORES ✐ **Bookworm** (860-233-2653), 968 Farmington Ave. (CT 4), West Hartford. A full-service, locally owned bookstore (since 1972) at the heart of West Hartford center and known throughout the area. Book signings, special orders, advice, suggestions, and a play area for children.

Leaves and Pages (860-224-4414), 59 West Main St., New Britain. A friendly, locally popular bookstore with a coffee shop. Gifts, cards, and city memorabilia.

Millrace Books (860-677-9662; www.millracebooks.com), 40 Mill Lane, Farmington. Set in a former mill building, the store consists of a succession of large and small rooms that are quirky and comfortable; located above the very good Gristmill Restaurant. Accommodating, knowledgeable staff. Iin an era of book superstores, this independent shop is a welcome throwback.

On the Road Bookshop (860-693-6029; www.ontheroadbookshop.com), 163 Albany Turnpike (US 44), Canton. A comfortable storefront place, excellent for browsing and specializing in fine used, rare, and out-of-print books. Titles run the gamut, from popular paperbacks to collectible literary works. They also buy books in most subject areas, as well as book-related items.

FARMS AND FARM STANDS

In Canton

Applegate Farms (860-693-8428), 39 Lawton Rd. Open daily June–Oct. Maple syrup, honey, jams, and farm-fresh produce at a family-run farm stand.

Bristol's Farm (860-693-8965; www.wildcarrotfarm.com), 541 Albany Turnpike (US 44). Open in May, Fri.–Sun.; Memorial Day–Sept., open daily; Oct., Thu.–Sun. A certified-organic farm where, in addition to the usual fruits and vegetables, you can pick up fresh eggs, honey, herbs, specialty foods, even compost and organic potting soil.

Leonard's Sugarhouse (860-693-8514), 555 Cherry Brook Rd., North Canton. Watch maple syrup production from late winter to early spring, depending on conditions, or stop by year-round to buy maple syrup and other maple products. Call for a schedule of sugarhouse tours.

Elsewhere

Karabin Farms (860-620-0194; www.karabinfarms.com), 894 Andrews St., Southington. In Sept. and Oct., take a weekend tractor-drawn hayride to the fields and orchards to pick pumpkins and apples; you can also cut your own Christmas tree. The country store sells locally made honey and maple syrup, cider doughnuts and pies, specialty foods, and holiday items. Kids love the barnyard, home to pygmy goats, Scottish Highland cows, and more.

The Pickin' Patch (860-677-9552), 276 Nod Rd., Avon. Open daily, May–Dec. Woodford Farm is Connecticut's 10th-oldest family farm, in operation since 1666. You can pick your own fruits and veggies in summer; later in the season, tractor-drawn hayrides head to the pumpkin patch. Christmas trees in-season; bedding plants in spring.

Rosedale Farms (860-651-3926), 25 East Weatogue St., off CT 185, Simsbury. Open daily June–Oct. Locals come to this farm—established in 1920—for fresh-cut flowers, sweet corn, and vegetables. Their latest venture is a vineyard; call for details.

Tulmeadow Farm Store & Ice Cream (860-658-1430; www.tulmeadowfarmstore.com), 255 Farms Village Rd. (CT 309), West Simsbury. Open daily 9–7. A working dairy farm (family run since 1768) with a popular farm stand selling farm-made ice cream (they provide the hay bales to sit on), just-picked veggies and herbs, perennials, and Connecticut-made specialty foods; pumpkins and Christmas trees in fall. Also see *Where to Eat—Ice Cream*.

✐ **Bushy Hill Orchard** (860-653-4022; www.bushyhill.com), 29 Bushy Hill Rd., off CT 20, Granby. Open daily May–mid-Dec.; call or check online for hours. Something for everyone: Pick your own raspberries in summer; take a wagon ride to the apple orchard in the fall; buy freshly baked doughnuts and pies in the Apple Barn Farm Store.

The Garlic Farm (860-653-0291; www.garlicfarmct.com), 76 Simsbury Rd., West Granby. Farm stand open July–Oct., daily 10–7. Garlic lovers, rejoice: Here's an organic farm devoted almost entirely to the pungent bulb. Many varieties, but mostly German White, which has intense flavor and plump cloves. The bulbs are harvested by hand, then hung from the rafters in the old tobacco barn to cure—or dry—for a month or so until the flavor is fully developed. Fresh garlic is available starting in July; dried bulbs are usually ready by August. The farm stand also sells onions, shallots, tomatoes, and other veggies, as well as herbs and flowers.

✐ **Lost Acres Orchard** (860-653-6600; www.lostacres.com), 130 Lost Acres Rd., off CT 189, North Granby. The farm store is open year-round; apple picking on weekends in Sept. and Oct. A tractor-drawn wagon takes visitors to the orchard, where they can pick their own apples. The farm store is full of good stuff—freshly baked breads and pies, and Connecticut-grown specialty foods. Ask about cider-pressing demonstrations and quilting programs.

SHOPPING CENTERS **West Farms Mall** (860-561-3024), 500 West Farms Mall, Exit 40 off I-84, on the West Hartford–Farmington town line. A 1.3-million-square-foot indoor shopping center with the usual lineup of national and regional retailers, from A (Abercrombie) to Z (Zales Jewelers), plus eateries, salons, and the first Nordstrom department store to open in New England.

Blue Back Square, West Hartford. The much-heralded $160 million combination retail-residential and entertainment district connected to the West Hartford center downtown area debuted in 2008. It's an upscale open-air complex that includeS super-fancy condos, high-end shops (including Connecticut's first Crate & Barrel home furnishings store), hip cafés and restaurants, and a cinema. It's named, humbly enough, for West Hartford's distinguished son Noah Webster, who penned America's first dictionary as well as the *Blue-backed Speller*, an 18th-century grammar textbook.

Old Avon Village Market Place (860-678-0469; www.oldavonvillage.com), East Main St. (US 44), Avon. One-of-a-kind shops and boutiques—64 in all—in a charming complex of early-1900s barns, houses, and farm buildings, originally the center of the village of Avon. Jewelry, antiques, crafts, salons, eateries, and day spas. Look for the giant rocking chair.

Riverdale Farms Shopping (860-677-6437; www.riverdalefarmsshopping.com), 124 Simsbury Rd. (CT 10), Avon. It's a quarter mile north of busy US 44, but it feels like the country. A restored 19th-century dairy farm turned into an unusual shopping complex—a series of buildings inhabited by 50 or so gift and specialty shops (clothing, gifts, jewelry, kitchenware, furnishings), along with boutiques and restaurants.

The Shoppes at Farmington Valley (860-693-3059), 110 Albany Turnpike (US 44), Canton. Central Connecticut's newest shopping complex, with upscale national chains (think Ann Taylor, Nine

West, Talbots), the requisite Barnes & Noble, an interesting mix of independent shops.

Old Mill Pond Village Shops (860-653-3433; www.oldmillpondvillage.com), CT 10/US 202, Granby. Open Tue.–Sun.; closed Mon. Eight historic New England buildings surrounding a millpond host shops selling gifts, country furniture, and Christmas items.

SPECIAL SHOPS ✐ **Avery Beverages** (860-224-0830; www.averysoda.com), 520 Corbin Ave., New Britain. Open Tue.–Sat.; closed Sun. and Mon. A vintage red barn houses one of New England's oldest beverage companies. Since 1904, they've been bottling and selling handcrafted soda, and they still use the recipes and small-batch methods developed by Sherman Avery a century ago. Today two dozen varieties come in old-fashioned glass bottles that are washed, filled, and capped using 1950s-era bottling equipment, then shaken by hand to blend syrup and seltzer. On Saturday, visitors can tour the soda factory and mixing room, then make their own soda, from measuring syrup to hand shaking the bottles and creating their own labels. Kids love the new line of flavors like Bug Barf and Monster Mucus, while older fans lean toward lime rickey, birch beer, and other nostalgic varieties.

Artisan's Marketplace (860-747-4121; www.artisansmarketplacect.com), 120 East St. (CT 10), Plainville. Open daily; closed Sun. in July and August. American crafts, gifts, pottery, furnishings, and jewelry fill handcrafted display cases in a cheery Victorian house.

✐ **Stew Leonards** (860-760-8100; www.stewleonards.com), 3475 Berlin Turnpike, Newington. Open daily; closed Christmas Day. The newest outpost of this dairy turned superstore has all the usual offerings, plus cooking demonstrations and classes for adults and children. Sister stores operate in Danbury and Norwalk.

Comstock, Ferre & Co. (860-571-6590; www.comstockferre.com), 263 Main St., Wethersfield. Open Mon.–Sat. 9–5; Sun. 10–5. The oldest continuously operating seed company in the United States (since 1820); the late-1700s chestnut post-and-beam structure is a National Historic Landmark. In addition to purchasing seeds, gardeners come for 2,000 varieties of perennials and annuals, not to mention good, reliable advice.

O'Reilly's Irish Gifts (860-677-6958; 866-384-7474; www.gotirish.com), 248 Main St., Farmington. Open Tue.–Sun.; closed Mon. Billed as the largest Irish store in the United States. Fine Irish and Celtic china, jewelry, pottery, clothing, and gifts come directly from top-quality manufacturers in Ireland.

Comina (860-233-9726; www.comina.com), 982 Farmington Ave. (CT 4), West Hartford. Open Mon.–Sat. 10–5:30; Sun. noon–4. Comina is known for its handcrafted and stylish home furnishings, decor, and accessories from around the world. This location, in West Hartford Center, was the first of what is now half a dozen stores around New England.

Homeward Bound (860-233-9500; www.homewardboundstyle.com), 77 Isham Rd., in Blue Back Square, West Hartford. Right across from the mammoth Crate & Barrel store is this stylish little enclave, selling chic gifts, eco-friendly furniture, and upscale accoutrements for the home.

Ten Thousand Villages (860-233-5470; www.tenthousandvillages.com), 967 Farmington Ave., West Hartford. Another location in New Haven. Their motto is "Fairly traded handicrafts from around the world," and that's what you'll find in this eclectic shop, whether it's pottery from Bangladesh or a holiday ornament made in Kenya. The company—a not-for-profit Mennonite organization founded in 1946—works with artists' cooperatives in third-world countries around the globe, paying fair market value for their products, which range from jewelry and handmade papers to musical instruments and stone sculpture.

Three Dog Bakery (860-232-6299; www.threedog.com), 967 Farmington Ave., West Hartford. An upscale bakery and boutique for the most pampered of canines. Freshly baked treats artfully created with natural ingredients, including peanut butter, carob, and vanilla. Dog-style truffles, pizza, cookies, and, for the ultimate splurge, celebration cakes big enough for Fido and all his friends. Naturally, your pooch is welcome to shop with you.

The Spirited Hand (860-693-3300; www.spiritedhand.com), in the Shoppes at Farmington Valley, 110 Albany Turnpike (US 44), Canton. Open daily. A gift gallery widely known for contemporary American handcrafts, plus essentials in ceramic, glass, wood, and more.

Say Cheese! (860-658-6742; 888-243-3373; www.saycheese-lgp.com), in the Simsburytown Shops, 924 Hopmeadow St. (CT 10), Simsbury. Cheese, of course, more than 125 varieties of it, from French Brie to Canadian cheddar, plus coffee and tea, gourmet gift baskets, kitchen gadgets, and specialty foods.

SPORTING GOODS **Eastern Mountain Sports** (860-561-4302; www.ems.com), 1459 New Britain Ave., West Hartford; and in Simsbury (860-651-8031) on US 44. Equipment and clothing for hiking, kayaking, climbing, skiing, and other outdoor pursuits.

REI (860-233-2211; www.rei.com), 71 Raymond Rd., in Blue Back Square, West Hartford. Open daily. The outdoor recreation behemoth's first Connecticut outpost is the go-to place for hiking, paddling, camping, climbing, skiing, and cycling gear.

Ski Market (860-677-2186; www.skimarket.com), 195 West Main St. (US 44), Avon. It isn't all about skiing here, although downhill and cross-country winter sports are certainly their specialty. They also sell and rent bikes (the Farmington River Greenway bike path is close by) and carry a full line of outdoor clothing.

Special Events

May: **Shad Derby Festival** (www.windsorshadderby.org), Windsor. Various events throughout the month include a parade, and a fishing tournament on the Farmington River. **Quinnipiac Downriver Classic** (203-237-2237; www.qrwa.org), CT 322, Southington. Scenic 5-mile canoe and kayak race down the river to Hanover Pond in Meriden.

June: **Farmington Antiques Weekend** (317-598-0012; www.farmington-antiques.com), Farmington Polo Grounds, Farmington. The state's largest antiques event, with more than 400 dealers, is considered one of the top open-air antiques shows in the Northeast. **Berlin Blues Festival** (877-828-0063; www.berlinmusicfest.com), Berlin Fairgrounds, 430 Beckley Rd., East Berlin. National and local bands, car show, children's activities. **Celebrate! West Hartford** (www.celebratewesthartford.com), various locations, West Hartford. Something for everyone: a 5K road race, an arts-and-crafts show, rides, and a food court.

Summer: **Sunken Garden Poetry & Music Festival** (860-677-4787; www

.hillstead.org), at the Hill-Stead Museum, Farmington. Local and world-renowned poets read their works in this popular summerlong event; live jazz. **Talcott Mountain Music Festival** (860-244-2999; www.hartfordsymphony.org), Simsbury. The Hartford Symphony Orchestra performs its summer series in the Performing Arts Center at Simsbury Meadows.

July: **Bloomfield Sheep Dog Trial**, Samuel Wheeler Reed Park, Bloomfield. More than 100 working dogs hustle sheep around a half-mile course in this entertaining canine competition.

August: ✐ **Plainville Fire Company Hot Air Balloon Festival** (860-747-0283; www.plainvilleballoonfestival.com), Norton Park, South Washington St. (CT 177), Plainville. Balloon "night glow," arts-and-crafts show, car show, family entertainment.

Labor Day weekend: **Farmington Antiques Weekend** (317-598-0012; www.farmingtonantiques.com), Farmington Polo Grounds, Farmington. One of the top open-air antiques shows in the Northeast, and the largest in Connecticut, featuring more than 600 dealers outdoors and under tents.

September: **American Arts & Crafts Show** (860-223-6867), Walnut Hill Park, New Britain. An annual gathering of artisans and craftspeople, sponsored by the New Britain Museum of American Art. **New Haven Underground Film Festival** (860-768-4951; www.nhuff.com), University of Hartford, West Hartford. Daylong celebration of independently produced feature films and short subjects by American filmmakers.

October: ✐ **Berlin Fair** (860-828-0063), Berlin Fairgrounds, 430 Beckley Rd., East Berlin. This longtime event marks the end of Connecticut's agricultural fair season. ✐ **Apple Harvest Festival** (860-276-8461), downtown Southington. A festival honoring the apple crop that has been Southington's main product since the 1700s. Still one of the state's top apple growers. Food, crafts, a parade, and a road race round out the festivities on and around the town green. **Open Studios** (860-844-0277; www.granbyartists.com), Granby. A weekend of artist studio tours, sponsored by the Granby Artist's Association.

November through December: ✐ **Webb-Deane-Stevens Museum** (860-529-0612), 211 Main St., Wethersfield, decorates its historic homes for the holidays. **Hill-Stead Museum** (860-677-4878) in Farmington decorates its period rooms with early-20th-century holiday finery. ✐ **Simsbury Celebrates!** (860-658-3200), Hopmeadow St. (CT 10), Simsbury. A new community celebration that kicks off the holiday season with a fire truck parade, community carol sing, and fireworks.

EAST OF THE RIVER

The Connecticut River effectively divides the state—east and west. To get from Hartford to East Hartford, Windsor to East Windsor, Rocky Hill to Glastonbury, you need a bridge or a ferry. And that may be why the communities east of the river have developed an identity all their own, distinct from those west of the river. Around here, in the northern half of the state, the barrier is spanned, so to speak, by a ferry and five bridges—three of them in Hartford. Most people cross the river—New England's longest—to go home to the suburbs from their jobs in Connecticut's capital city.

The east-of-the-river character was built on industrial development as much as on agriculture. In the 1600s, farming plantations were set up by some of the settlers who followed Hartford founder Thomas Hooker from Massachusetts to establish a colony on the opposite side of the Connecticut River. The area was home to the native Podunk tribe, Algonquin Indians who migrated up and down the river to fish for sturgeon, shad, and salmon (East Hartford's annual bluegrass festival is named in their honor). The many swift streams encouraged farmers to turn to water-powered milling operations instead of plowing Connecticut's notoriously rock-filled hills. By the 19th century, industrialization had come to the region, and the many textile mills attracted workers from Ireland, Germany, Britain, Sweden, Canada, and elsewhere, to find themselves part of what was called the nation's melting pot. Up until 1783, East Hartford and Hartford were the same city.

Today East Hartford is a blue-collar, working-class town, home to the world-renowned Pratt & Whitney aircraft jet-engine manufacturer; but it has its share of remembrances of earlier times, including 18th-century gunpowder factories, a possibly haunted house, and a one-room school built in 1820. Rentschler Field Stadium, the $92 million, 40,000-seat stadium across the Connecticut River from downtown Hartford, is home turf for the University of Connecticut's Big East football team, and a destination for big-name entertainers like Bruce Springsteen as well as the rabid Huskymania that seems to have swept up every resident of the state, whether they can claim actual ties to UConn or not. The new Cabela's outdoor superstore next to the stadium draws huge crowds of its own. Hartford's mega-million-dollar downtown revitalization across the river has not left East Hartford out. The capital city's string of riverfront parks, joined by bridges and walkways, includes East Hartford's Great River Park, linked to Hartford's Riverfront Plaza by the Founder's Bridge.

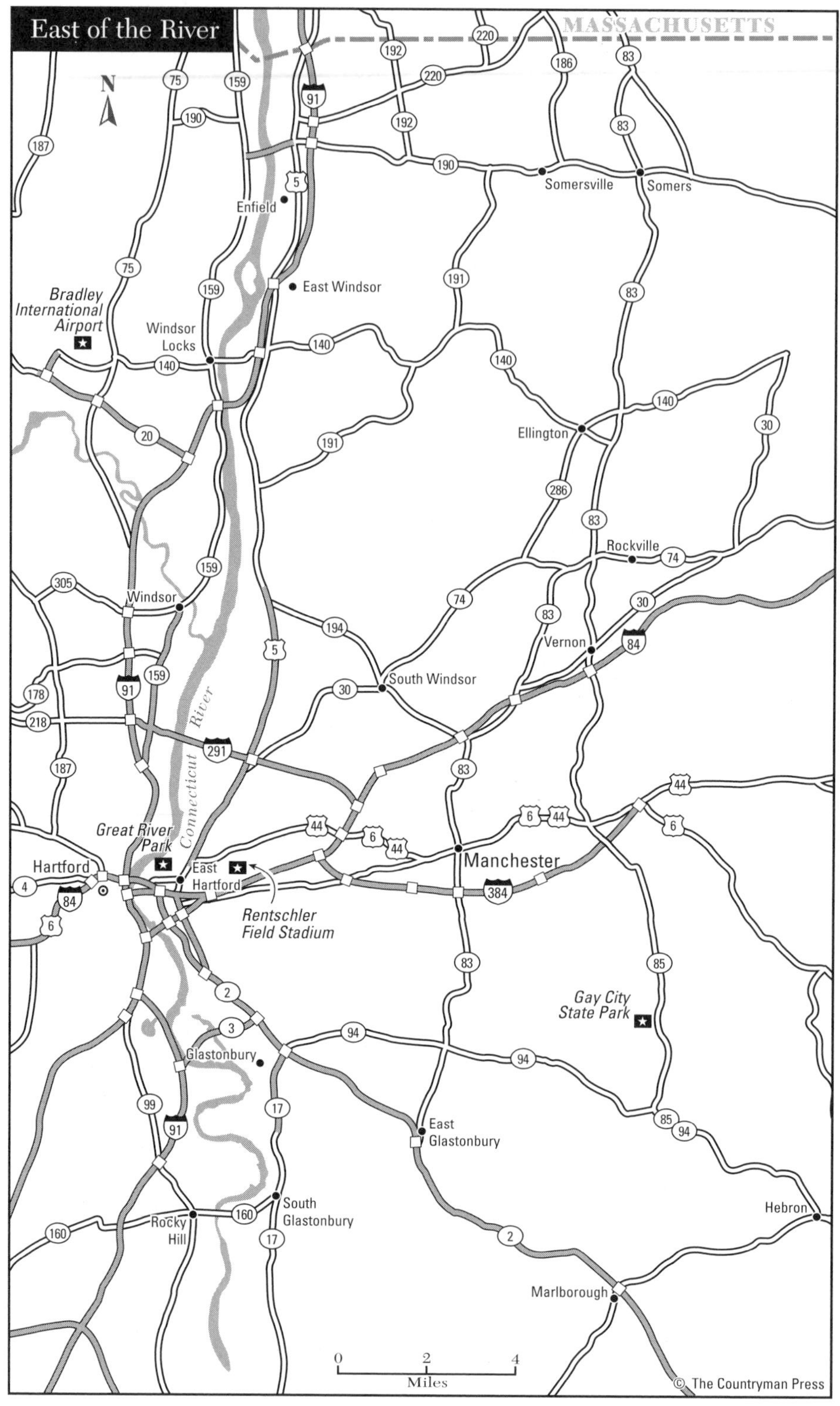

East of the River
MASSACHUSETTS
N
Enfield
East Windsor
Somersville
Somers
Bradley
International
Airport
Windsor
Locks
Ellington
Rockville
Windsor
Vernon
South Windsor
Connecticut River
Great River
Park
Hartford
East
Hartford
Manchester
Rentschler
Field Stadium
Gay City
State Park
Glastonbury
East
Glastonbury
South
Glastonbury
Rocky
Hill
Hebron
Marlborough
0
2
4
Miles
© The Countryman Press

Neighboring Manchester was settled by English colonists in 1672 as an agricultural community, but it was the Cheney brothers who put the town on the map in 1838, when they opened what would become the largest silk mill on the planet. These two silk barons at one time imported silkworms in order to control the means of production; indeed, Cheney was one of the most renowned silk-manufacturing empires in the world. Today the mill buildings, modest workers' houses, and owners' mansions are part of the Cheney National Historic District. For the visitor, Manchester offers a delightful children's museum, summertime band-shell concerts, community theater in historic Cheney Hall, a gourmet French restaurant that's considered one of the state's best, and a Thanksgiving Day road race that attracts thousands of runners from around the country. The Buckland Hills area on the South Windsor town line, meanwhile, draws thousands of shoppers from around the state. The Buckland Hills Mall is surrounded by an ever-growing number of shopping plazas and big-box stores (think Target, Wal-Mart, Best Buy).

South Windsor, just above East Hartford, and its neighbor East Windsor were major tobacco-farming areas when the whole region was called Tobacco Valley. Earlier, it was the site of fierce battles during the Mohawk and Podunk Wars. The first settlers built no homes here and used the fertile land only for hay and pasture crops because of the danger from unfriendly Pequots. South Windsor was the birthplace of Jonathan Edwards, a leader of the 18th-century religious revival known as the Great Awakening. His fire-and-brimstone sermon "Sinners in the Hands of an Angry God," delivered in an Enfield meetinghouse in the summer of 1741, stands as a statement of the beliefs of New England's founding fathers. Today South Windsor is a leafy shopping and bedroom community, home to The Shoppes at Evergreen Walk, a popular venue for upscale shopping. East Windsor's popular attraction is the Connecticut Trolley Museum, where you can climb aboard a vintage electric streetcar and take a ride along the tracks.

Continuing east, you'll find the town of Vernon, named for George Washington's Virginia home. Vernon's textile mills were the first to weave satinet, a fabric developed to simulate satin. Both here and in Rockville the mill buildings, as well as much of the workers' housing, remain. Enfield, settled in the 17th century by colonists from Salem, Massachusetts, was home to a 19th-century Shaker community, which resided on a 3,000-acre spread before disbanding in 1917.

Glastonbury, south of East Hartford along the Connecticut River, is accessible from the western side of the river by the Putnam Bridge or by the nation's oldest continuously operating ferry service, in operation on the river between Rocky Hill and Glastonbury since 1655. It's now powered by a small tug that surpassed the small raft propelled by wooden poles, and a horse-powered treadmill later modernized with a steam engine in 1876. Out of the manufacturing mainstream, Glastonbury ran more to orchards than to industry, and it has blossomed into an upscale suburb with designer homes, trendy bistros, and boutiques supplanting the apple and peach trees of earlier times. Still, enough farms and tobacco fields remain to serve as reminders of the town's rural beginnings.

Entries in this section are arranged in alphabetical order.

AREA CODE 860.

GUIDANCE **Central Regional Tourism District** (860-244-8181; 800-793-4480; www.enjoycentralct.com), 31 Pratt St., Hartford 06103, can provide brochures, events listings, maps, and answers to questions about travel and lodging in the area.

On request, the **Greater Hartford Convention & Visitors Bureau** (860-728-6789; 800-446-7811; www.enjoyhartford.com) will send you a visitor's guide to the area.

GETTING THERE *By car:* I-84, I-384, I-91, and CT 2 are the major interstates and highways through this region.

By air: **Bradley International Airport** (860-292-2000; 888-624-1533; www.bradleyairport.com) in Windsor Locks serves the whole state as its major airport.

By bus: **Peter Pan Bus Lines** (800-343-9999; www.peterpanbus.com) and **Greyhound Lines** (800-231-2222; www.greyhound.com) stop in Enfield and Manchester.

GETTING AROUND *By taxi:* In East Hartford: **Dial-A-Ride Taxi Services** (860-528-7433) and **Khan's Taxi** (860-290-8976). In Manchester: **AAA Cab & Livery** (860-645-1999), **Ace Taxi** (860-244-9999), and **Manchester Cab & Livery** (860-966-8888). In Vernon: **Ace Transportation Service** (860-870-0418).

MEDICAL EMERGENCY The statewide emergency number is **911**.

Manchester Memorial Hospital (860-646-1222), 71 Haynes St., Manchester. The emergency number is 860-647-4777.

Rockville General Hospital (860-872-0501), 31 Union St., Vernon. The emergency number is 860-872-5291.

✷ To See

MUSEUMS ✐ **Connecticut Fire Museum** (860-627-6540; www.ct-trolley.org), 58 North Rd. (CT 140), at the Connecticut Trolley Museum, East Windsor. Open July and Aug.: Wed.–Sat. 10–5; Sun. noon–5. May and June: Sat. 10–5; Sun. noon–5. Sept.–Oct.: Sat. and Sun. noon–5. The museum is on the grounds of the Connecticut Trolley Museum (see *To Do* for admission prices). A century's worth (1850–1950) of fire trucks and other historic firefighting apparatus and memorabilia are displayed in a hangarlike building. You might see a 1927 "Bull Dog" Mack, a 1928 American LaFrance pumper, a 1943 GMC airport crash truck, a 1930 Maxim hose wagon, or a 1934 Seagrave ladder truck, as well as fire truck models, fire alarm equipment, and other memorabilia.

Edward E. King Museum (860-289-6429), 840 Main St., at the East Hartford Public Library, East Hartford. Open Mon.–Thu. 9–9; Sat. 9–5; closed Fri. and Sun. Extended summer hours. Free admission. Exhibits in this small museum trace the history of local tobacco and aviation industries.

✐ **The Fire Museum** (860-649-9436; www.thefiremuseum.org), 230 Pine St., Manchester. Open Sat. and Sun. noon–4; closed weekdays. Adults $4; seniors and children 12–16 $2; children 6–11 $1; 5 and under free. Who can resist the lure of the fearless firefighter, the trucks and sirens, dangers and rescues? Hand-pulled and horse-drawn wagons and early motorized apparatus are on display, as are leather fire buckets, helmets, tools, badges, and lanterns, all in a restored 1901 firehouse.

Lutz Children's Museum (860-643-0949; www.lutzmuseum.org), 247 South Main St. (CT 83), Manchester. Open Tue.–Fri. 9–5; Sat. and Sun. noon–5; closed Mon. Admission $5. It's busy inside this schoolhouse turned children's museum, where the watchwords are "Do touch." The exhibits cover science, history, and natural history, with live animals to visit in the wildlife rehabilitation room and hands-on displays geared to catch and hold youngsters' interest. They love the 1950s gas station and 1910 schoolhouse. This happy place was founded with the personal collection of local art teacher Hazel Lutz. Ask about concerts and other special programs. The museum operates the nearby Oak Grove Nature Center (see *Green Space*).

Museum on the Green (860-633-6890; www.glasct.org), 1944 Main St., at the corner of Main and Hubbard streets, Glastonbury. Open Mon., Tue., and Thu. 10–4; third Sun. of the month 1–4; and by appointment. Free admission. The former circa-1840 town hall is a museum of local history, with artifacts from area Native Americans and memorabilia of local industry—soap, glass, silver plate. Changing exhibits, a costume collection, and other displays. The ancient burial ground for this 300-year-old town is adjacent.

HISTORIC HOMES AND SITES **Cheney Homestead** (860-645-5588; www.manchesterhistory.org), 106 Hartford Rd. (US 44), Manchester. Open year-round, Fri.–Sun. 10–3, and by appointment. Adults $2; children under 12 free. Farmer-clockmaker Timothy Cheney built this relatively modest home in 1785; the furnishings and paintings date from the 18th and 19th centuries. Cheney's sons, born here, launched the silk industry that put Manchester on the world map in the 1800s. Also on the grounds is a restored schoolhouse built in the 18th century.

Makens Bemont House, **Goodwin Schoolhouse**, and **Burnham Blacksmith Shop** (860-568-6178; www.hseh.org), Martin Park, 307 Burnside Ave. (US 44), East Hartford. Open Memorial Day–Sept.; call for hours. Free admission. A concentration of local history. The Makens Bemont House, constructed circa 1761, is atypical of the homes built by the English and their descendants; it stands out with its gambrel roof and vaulted dormer windows. Furthermore, there's a ghost story connected to the builder, a colonial saddler. The school is of later vintage, 1820; and the blacksmith shop dates from about 1825, when horses were used in the region's tobacco fields.

Jonathan Edwards Marker, next door to the Montessori School at 1370 Enfield St. (US 5), Enfield. In a church that stood on this site, the legendary preacher delivered his blistering sermon "Sinners in the Hands of an Angry God" in 1741, giving new strength to the Great Awakening. Edwards's father, the Reverend Timothy Edwards, was pastor there, at what was Enfield's second meetinghouse.

Martha A. Parsons House Museum (860-745-6064), 1387 Enfield St. (US 5), Enfield. Open May–Oct., Sun. 2–4:30, or by appointment. Free admission. Built in 1782 and lived in by the same prominent local family, the Parsons, for more than 180 years, the house neatly covers most of the country's lifetime. Rare "George Washington Memorial" wallpaper (this is one of only two homes in the country where it has been found) was installed in the front hallway by a sea captain who resided here. Run by the **Enfield Historical Society**. Martha Parsons, a wealthy businesswoman—an unusual status for a woman at the turn of the 20th century—

filled the family home with antiques, from Chippendale chairs and family silver to furnishings from the West Indies.

Shaker Monument, Shaker Rd. and CT 220, Enfield. The Enfield Shaker community that flourished here in the 19th century is no more, although some of the buildings remain.

Welles-Shipman-Ward House (860-633-6890), 972 Main St. (CT 17), South Glastonbury. The house is open one Sunday a month, Apr.–Nov., 1–4; call for a schedule. Admission $2. Built in 1755 and cited by the Department of the Interior for "exceptional architectural interest," it also incorporates much local history. Children's animal drawings from the 19th century are preserved on a chamber wall, and the kitchen fireplace and elaborate paneling are among points of interest. There's an 18th-century herb garden on the grounds, as well as a 1790 post-and-beam barn housing a collection of horse-drawn vehicles.

SCENIC DRIVE For a little over a mile—from Roaring Brook Bridge to Ferry Lane, then to the banks of the Connecticut River—**CT 160** in Glastonbury is one of the state's official scenic roads. You'll travel through low-lying bottomland set with houses built two centuries ago for farms—some of them still in operation—and open land. The ride ends at the dock, where you drive onto the ferry for the short trip to Rocky Hill. This is the operation that began in 1655, propelled by a hardworking ferryman pushing a long pole.

✱ To Do

AMUSEMENTS ✐ **Connecticut Golf Land** (860-643-2654; www.ctgolfland.com), 95 Hartford Turnpike (CT 83), Vernon. Open daily, weather permitting. Go-carts, bumper boats, miniature golf, arcade, batting cages, a nine-hole golf course, and more; enough to amuse the entire family.

BOAT EXCURSION ✐ **Glastonbury–Rocky Hill Ferry** (860-443-3856; 860-563-9758), CT 160, Glastonbury. Operates daily May–Oct.; Mon.–Fri. 7–6:45; Sat. and Sun. 10:30–5. Car, driver, and passengers $3; walk-on pedestrians and cyclists $1. The nation's oldest continuously operating ferry: Drive onto the open three-car barge—the *Hollister III*—and watch as the diesel-powered towboat, the *Cumberland*, pulls you across the sometimes mighty Connecticut River. It's difficult to describe how satisfying this simple trip can be. People have been making this river crossing since 1655, when a ferryman shuttled his craft by pushing a long pole.

FISHING There's a boat-launching site on the Connecticut River at Great River Park (860-713-3131), East River Dr., East Hartford, Exit 53 off I-84 East. Anglers can also cast from the docks on shore. Another boat launch on the Connecticut River, on Parson's Road in Enfield, is popular during the springtime shad season. There's pond fishing in **Gay City State Park** (860-295-9523), CT 85, Hebron; and in Glastonbury at **Angus Park Pond**, in the town park off Manchester Rd. (CT 83).

GOLF **Blackledge Country Club** (860-228-0250; www.blackledgecc.com), 180 West St., Hebron. Par 72, 36 holes, 6,537/6,787 yards.

Cedar Knob Golf Course (860-749-3550; www.cedarknobgolfcourse.com), Billings Rd., Somers. Par 72, 18 holes, 6,734 yards.

Kim Grant

THE ROCKY HILL–GLASTONBURY FERRY ON THE CONNECTICUT RIVER IS THE OLDEST CONTINUOUSLY OPERATING FERRY SERVICE IN THE UNITED STATES.

East Hartford Golf Course (860-528-5082), 130 Long Hill St., East Hartford. Par 71, 18 holes, 6,186 yards.

Grassmere Country Club (860-749-7740; www.grassmerecountryclub.com), 130 Town Farm Rd., Enfield. Par 35, nine holes, 3,031 yards.

Manchester Country Club (860-646-0226; www.mancc.com), 305 South Main St., Manchester. Par 72, 18 holes, 6,167 yards.

Minnechaug Golf Course (860-643-9914), 16 Fairway Crossing, off CT 83, Glastonbury. Par 35, nine holes, 2,668 yards.

Rolling Meadows Country Club (860-870-5328; www.rollingmeadowscountryclub.com), 76 Sadds Mill Rd. (CT 140), Ellington. Par 72, 18 holes, 6,818 yards.

Tallwood Country Club (860-646-1151), 91 North St. (CT 85), Hebron. Par 72, 18 holes, 6,353 yards.

Topstone Golf Course (860-648-4653; www.topstonegc.com), 516 Griffin Rd., South Windsor. Par 72, 18 holes, 6,549 yards.

Willow Brook Golf Course (860-648-2061; www.willowbrookgc.com), 124 Brookfield St., South Windsor. Par 60, 18 holes, 2,985 yards.

HIKING **Lookout Mountain**. The trailhead is on Spring St., in the Rockville section of Vernon. A gated, paved road becomes a gravel path, then a well-worn trail leading to the 744-foot summit. Depending on visibility, you can see the Hartford skyline and beyond to Heublein Tower on Talcott Mountain.

In Somers, several routes lead to the 1,075-foot summit of **Soapstone Mountain** in Shenipsit State Forest. One is the blue-blazed **Shenipsit Trail**; park at the trailhead on Gulf Rd., off CT 190. From the observation tower, views of north-central Connecticut's ridges and valleys are spectacular. Another trail, shorter and steeper, is maintained by a local running club and marked with white dots. From the summit, a yellow-blazed path leads back to the trailhead, while the blue-blazed trail—part of the statewide system maintained by the Connecticut Forest and Park Association—continues north to the Massachusetts border, about 6 miles away.

MOUNTAIN BIKING A 10-mile network of well-groomed fire roads is open to riders at **Gay City State Park** (860-295-9523), CT 85, Hebron. Some dirt roads and trails in **Shenipsit State Forest** (see *Green Space*) are open to mountain bikes. You can also cruise along the **Charter Oak Greenway** (860-647-3084), a 9.8-mile paved bike path that follows I-384 from Bolton to East Hartford. A parking lot and trailhead are located at Charter Oak Field in Manchester. The adjoining **Captain John Bissell Greenway** (860-647-3084) runs 8 miles through South Windsor, Manchester, East Hartford, and across the Connecticut River on the Bissell Bridge to Windsor. Parking is available in Wickham Park in Manchester. **The Bike Shop** (860-647-1027), 681 Main St., and **Manchester Cycle Shop** (860-649-2098), 178 West Middle Turnpike, both in Manchester, have a repair shop on the premises and carry a complete line of cycling accessories. Ask them about off-road riding on Manchester's **Case Mountain**, whose trails offer what many consider some of the best mountain biking in the state.

SKYDIVING **Connecticut Parachutists Inc.** (860-871-0021; www.skydivect.com), Ellington Airport, CT 83, Ellington. Open Apr.–Nov., Thu.–Mon. Reservations recommended. It's fun to watch, and if you yearn for adventure, this may be it. Since 1962, the club has been taking novice and experienced jumpers on tandem skydives with certified instructors. The journey back to earth from 14,000 feet starts with a free fall; then you drift gently back to the ground.

SPECTATOR SPORTS **Rentschler Field Stadium** (860-610-4700; 877-288-2666; www.rentschlerfield.com), 615 Silver Lane, East Hartford. The state's newest sports and entertainment stadium is the 40,000-seat home to the University of Connecticut Big East Huskies football team but also hosts professional soccer and rugby. Call or check their Web site for game and event schedules.

Shallowbrook Equestrian Center (860-749-0749; www.shallowbrook.com), 247 Hall Hill Rd. (CT 186), Somers. A family-owned complex of stables, rings, arenas, and polo fields, this 50-acre compound also contains one of the world's largest indoor hippodromes. Primarily a training school for riding and polo, Shallowbrook presents a year-round schedule of spectator events: ASHA horse shows, carriage shows and sleigh rallies, dressage and three-day events, and polo tournaments—national and international, collegiate, and professional. Check their Web site for a schedule of events.

TROLLEY RIDE **Connecticut Trolley Museum** (860-627-6540; www.ct-trolley.org), 58 North Rd. (CT 140), East Windsor. Open mid-June–Labor Day: Mon., and Wed.–Sat. 10–5; Sun. noon–5; Labor Day–Oct., and Mar.–mid-June: Sat. 10–5; Sun. noon–5. Closed Tue. Ask about seasonal and holiday programs. Adults $8; seniors $7; children $5; 2 and under free. Admission includes a ride on antique trolley cars. More than 70 trolley cars, elevated railway cars, electric locomotives, freight cars, and other rolling stock from 1869 to the 1970s have been restored or are in the restoration process; visitors can watch. Three miles of track allow for a taste of old-time fun. Trolleys were the mass transit of the late 19th century, and tracks crisscrossed New England and many other parts of the country. The wheels still clack along the rails, and the conductor-engineer still keeps that guide wheel on the overhead wire. Bumping along, you can sit and read the period advertisements on the curve between the windows and the roof on the narrated 20-minute round-trip on the Connecticut Electric Railway. Displays in the visitor center, deli, picnic area, and a gift shop stocked with books, toys, and wooden trains. The complex also includes a collection of motorcoaches and is located next to the Connecticut Fire Museum (see *To See*), which is included with admission to the trolley museum.

✷ Green Space

NATURE CENTERS ✐ **Connecticut Audubon Center at Glastonbury** (860-633-8402; www.ctaudubon.org), 1361 Main St., Glastonbury. Open year-round, Tue.–Fri. 1–5; Sat. 10–5; Sun. 1–4; closed Mon.; closed Sun. in Jan. Of the state's five Audubon centers, this is the only one in central Connecticut. It overlooks the Connecticut River next to 48-acre Earle Park, where there is a trail system for hikers, equestrians, and skiers to explore. The area is known for its scenic views—especially of Tom's Pond—soft hills, meadows, and rural feel. The museum building has exhibits on the Connecticut River ecosystem and local plant and animal life; also a shop catering to naturalist interests. The Discovery Room has hands-on exhibits and activities, live animals, wildlife mounts, and natural history exhibits. Outdoors, check out the four-season gardens and bird-feeding station. Educational nature programs for kids and families, and annual special events ranging from wine tastings, to fiddle contests, to a live music series.

Oak Grove Nature Center (860-647-3321), 269 Oak Grove St., Manchester. Open daily year-round, dawn to dusk. Free admission. A 53-acre, soul-soothing park operated by the town of Manchester, complete with ponds and streams, fields, and nature trails.

PARKS AND FORESTS **Gay City State Park** (860-295-9523), CT 85, 3 miles south of Bolton center in the town of Hebron. Open daily 8 AM–sunset. Weekend and holiday parking fee $7 residents; $10 nonresidents. The ruins of an abandoned 18th-century mill village are concealed by the second-growth forest. Some 1,569 acres in all, with lots of hiking opportunities, swimming, picnicking, fishing, cross-country skiing, and mountain biking.

✐ **Great River Park** (860-713-3131; www.riverfront.org), East River Dr., East Hartford. A small, grassy retreat—one link in the chain of parks along the Connecticut River—with walking paths, picnic areas, a boat launch, and a fishing dock, across the river from Samuel Colt's 19th-century arms factory. A 350-seat amphitheater hosts children's entertainment and concerts. The park's walkways include a path along the river connecting the Bulkeley Bridge to the Charter Oak Bridge, where pedestrians can cross over to Charter Oak Landing, a park on Hartford's riverbank.

Shenipsit State Forest (860-684-3430), off CT 190, in Ellington, Stratford, and Somers. Open daily, sunrise to sunset. More than 30 miles of trails crisscross this 6,126-acre forest, but most popular is the hike up Soapstone Mountain (see *To Do*), named for the talclike stone quarried long ago by Native Americans and the region's earliest settlers. There's also fishing, hunting, cross-country skiing, and picnicking.

Wickham Park (860-528-0856), 1329 West Middle Turnpike, Manchester. Open Apr.–Oct., 9:30–sunset. Weekday admission $3, $4 on weekends. Formerly The Pines, the estate of a prominent Manchester industrialist, this 250-acre park straddles the East Hartford–Manchester border, with wooded areas, ponds, a picnic area, playgrounds, an aviary, sports facilities, walking trails, and more than 20 acres of themed ornamental gardens.

* Lodging

BED & BREAKFASTS In addition to the listings below, a number of B&B reservation services offer access to rooms in establishments throughout the state. For a list, see *Bed & Breakfasts* in "What's Where in Connecticut."

Butternut Farm (860-633-7197; www.butternutfarmbandb.com), 1654 Main St., Glastonbury 06033. Welcome to the 18th century at this 1720 homestead furnished with period antiques. Host Don Reid (a superb cook and model innkeeper) will give you a tour of the livestock—prizewinning goats, pigeons, chickens, ducks, geese, and pheasants—if you wish. There are four guest rooms, including one apartment and one suite (some with fireplace), all strictly New England in character and appearance. An herb garden is a highlight of the imaginatively landscaped grounds. A full breakfast is served, featuring homegrown eggs and other specialties, in the original colonial kitchen. $95–120.

The Mansion Inn B&B (860-646-0453; www.themansioninnct.com), 139 Hartford Rd., Manchester 06040. The gracious old house, built for the silk barons who put Manchester on the world map, is now a historic retreat welcoming a new generation of guests. The nostalgic style evokes a more romantic time, when the Cheney family was running the largest silk mill in the world and living the good life in the mansion. Common rooms—library, dining room, parlor—are formal yet comfortable. Three rooms and two suites, each with working fireplace and private bath, are furnished with antiques, floral wallpaper, and hand-embroidered linens; the master suite has a wicker-filled sunporch. Outdoors, a walled garden is robed in flowers. Bruce and Marianne Hamstra are the resident innkeepers; Marianne is a justice of the peace and performs ceremonies here. A full breakfast, which might include jam made from the inn's own arbor, is served at the antique dining room table or outdoors on the piazza. $95–145.

HOTELS ♿ **Courtyard Hartford Manchester** (860-533-8484; reservations 800-321-2211), 225 Slater St., Exit 63 off I-84, Manchester 06040. This newly renovated Marriott is convenient both to downtown Hartford (10 miles) and to the University of Connecticut (18 miles). The 90 rooms—including three suites and four spa rooms with Jacuzzi tub—have all the usual amenities, plus free high-speed Internet access; there's also a restaurant, a fitness center, and an indoor pool. $109–179.

♿ **Sheraton Hartford Hotel** (860-528-9703; 888-537-9703), 100 East River Dr., Exit 53 off I-84, East Hartford 06108. A 215-room hotel in a corporate office park 0.5 mile from downtown Hartford. There's a restaurant and lounge, fitness center, gift shop, business center, and indoor pool.

Shuttle vans to Bradley International Airport, which is 12 miles away. A bit run down and in need of updating, but generally more reasonable than newer downtown hotels just across the river. $99–219.

South of downtown Hartford (Exit 6 off CT 2), **Hilton Garden Inn** (860-659-1025), 85 Glastonbury Blvd., Glastonbury 06033 and, right next door at 65 Glastonbury Blvd., a new **Homewood Suites** (860-652-8111) both have standard chain hotel amenities.

✱ Where to Eat

DINING OUT

In Glastonbury

♿ **Glas** (860-657-4527; www.glas-restaurant.com), 2935 Main St., Glastonbury. Open for lunch Mon.–Fri.; dinner daily. Reservations recommended. This lively restaurant recently morphed from Latino fusion to modern American. It retained the drama: The dining room has an electrified neon sculpture at its dramatic centerpiece, and the food (pepper-crusted beef carpaccio, grilled rib eye with melted Gorgonzola) keeps pace with bold ingredients and presentations. $19–32.

2hopewell American Bistro & Bar (860-633-9600; www.2hopewell.com), 2 Hopewell Rd., South Glastonbury. Serves dinner Tue.–Sun.; closed Mon. This friendly, casual bistro occupies a corner of Main Street. It's one of those 200-year-old structures (this one, a former bootery) that conveys authentic New England—candles on the tables, exposed hand-hewn beams overhead in the upstairs dining room. novel but sound treatments of both meat and seafood. There's also a menu of homey tavern fare (not available on Sat. night): Think burgers, sandwiches, salads. Live entertainment on weekends, and patio dining in-season. $18–33.

♿ **Max Amore** (860-659-2819; www.maxrestaurantgroup.com), 140 Glastonbury Blvd. (Somerset Square), Glastonbury. Open for lunch and dinner daily; brunch on Sat. and Sun. One of a family of Max restaurants in central Connecticut, all loosely Italian but each with its own flair. This one features stone pies with inventive toppings—for instance, oven-dried tomatoes, roasted cremini mushrooms, and smoked mozzarella; or wood-grilled chicken with caramelized onions and rosemary; another is dotted with pancetta, wild mushrooms, Asiago, and mozzarella. Salads are equally creative, like the *insalata di Toscana*, with roasted garlic, fresh mozzarella, kalamata olives, and polenta croutons. For dinner, the seared scallops with spicy caper sauce makes a fine appetizer; follow it with herb-crusted filet mignon and garlic mashed potatoes with artichoke aioli. For a sweet finale, try the flourless chocolate cake with milk chocolate and caramel ganache, and Tahitian vanilla gelato. An *in mezzo* menu offers light meals and stone pies between lunch and dinner. Good wine list and specialty martinis. $16–32.

♿ **Max Fish** (860-652-3474; www.maxrestaurantgroup.com), 110 Glastonbury Blvd., Glastonbury. Open for lunch Mon.–Sat.; dinner daily. Reservations are strongly recommended. Fun, energetic, often packed, and all about fish. It's also two restaurants in one: an upscale dining room and a more casual Shark Bar. Their extensive menus revolve around fish and shellfish from New England and around the world. $17–33.

Min Ghung Asian Bistro (860-659-2568; www.minghungcuisine.com), in the Glen Lochen plaza, 39 New London Turnpike, Glastonbury. Open for lunch Mon.–Fri.; dinner daily. The suburbs get a shot of stylish, youthful energy at Min Ghung. There's midnight sushi, live jazz, art exhibits, and Asian fusion cuisine as sleek as the bold crimson walls and cushy silk upholstery. It's a scene straight out of SoHo (maybe it's the subway signs), but this subterranean spot manages to be comfortable as well as trendy. More than 50 top-shelf imported cold sakes are dramatically displayed in a backlit wall. The traditional Japanese rice-based drink pairs nicely with a menu that leans toward Korean dishes. Try egg rolls stuffed with fresh avocado, cilantro, and sun-dried tomatoes with a tamarind-cashew dipping sauce; salmon tartare with wasabi soy sauce, topped with osetra caviar; or a simple plate of steamed edamame and sea salt. $13–24.

Elsewhere

Burton's Grill (860-432-4575; www.burtonsgrill.com), 100 Evergreen Way, in the Shops at Evergreen Walk, off CT 194, South Windsor. Open daily for lunch and dinner. Caters to legions of hungry shoppers with contemporary American dishes heavy on steak and seafood. $18–33.

♿ **Cavey's** (860-643-2751; www.caveysrestaurant.com), 45 East Center St., Manchester. Open for dinner Tue.–Sat.; closed Sun. and Mon. Reservations recommended. Founded in 1934, Cavey's is a local institution that's ambitious and successful on two levels—northern Italian cuisine upstairs, contemporary French downstairs. Many believe this is the best: The service is authoritative, the food exquisite, the surroundings suitably tasteful. The French restaurant is the more expensive, considered among the best in the state, although neither is cheap. In the French venue, the changing menu (à la carte or prix fixe) might feature lobster with black truffle vinaigrette, or house-smoked salmon with caper coulis. In the more casual Italian restaurant upstairs, equally creative cuisine can be found—northern Italian staples like risotto, veal, and game; the menu changes seasonally. À la carte entrées $20–38; prix fixe $35–62.

♿ **Jonathan Pasco's** (860-627-7709; www.jonathanpascos.net), 31 South Main St., East Windsor. Open for dinner daily; brunch on Sun. Reservations recommended. Named for a captain in Washington's army in the Revolutionary War, Pasco's house, a late-18th-century brick structure, has been refurbished but preserved. The bar and half a dozen dining rooms in the original house are cozy and intimate. You can dine fireside in winter or on the patio in summertime. The menu includes steaks from the grill, Cajun-inspired pork chops, seafood in many presentations, grilled duck with apricot coulis, and blackened mahimahi with mango salsa. The convivial bar is cozy and friendly and offers a casual pub menu. $19–31.

ꝏ ♿ **The Mill on the River** (860-289-7929; 888-344-4414; www.themillontheriver.com), 989 Ellington Rd. (CT 30), South Windsor. Open Mon.–Fri. for lunch; daily for dinner; brunch on Sun. Reservations recommended. A big, sprawling building—indeed, once a gristmill—with choice seating overlooking the Podunk River. A local favorite for romantic dining, there's also a greenhouse overlooking the millpond. Specialties from the extensive menu include pecan-crusted salmon; wood-grilled pork topped with sun-dried cherry sauce; and redfish nouvelle, blackened and topped with Mornay sauce, shrimp, scallops, and spinach—the house signature dish. There are chicken, beef, and pasta entrées as well. Chocolate mousse cake and a classic tiramisu are among the desserts. $16–32.

♿ **The Nutmeg Restaurant** (860-627-7094; www.nutmegrestaurant.com), 297 South Main St. (CT 5), East Windsor. Open daily for lunch and dinner; Sun. brunch. Reservations suggested. The Nutmeg has a distinctly elegant tone: part New England manor house, part American cuisine. The menu offers solid favorites like New Zealand rack of lamb with mint demiglaze, along with some unusual creations, such as honey nut encrusted salmon with mint risotto, or a variety of Asian fusion dishes like hoisin-rubbed pork tenderloin with sesame crispy vegetables. Appetizers include lobster bisque and grilled bruschetta with mozzarella and basil. Outdoors, bubbling fountains and tables on brick patios, bloom-clad trellises. $16–33.

♿ **Somers Inn** (860-749-2256; www.somersinn.com), 585 Main St., Somers. Serves lunch Wed.–Fri.; dinner Wed.–Sun., as well as Sun. brunch; closed Mon. and Tue. Reservations suggested. Facing a major intersection in the center of Somers, the inn announces its existence since 1769: It looks important, and in this part of the state it is. No longer offering lodging, it comforts the traveler with good familiar food. The menu is comprehensive if not lengthy, featuring all-American favorites—stuffed mushrooms and bourbon-glazed scallops for starters; twin lobster tails, baked stuffed shrimp, and other seafood; also veal, duck, beef, and chops. $22–30.

EATING OUT **Ambassador of India** (860-659-2529; www.ambassadorofindia.com), 2333 Main St., Glastonbury. Open for lunch Sun.–Fri.; dinner daily; Sun. brunch. Don't be dismayed by the unassuming storefront; better-than-usual Indian cuisine is expertly prepared inside. Regulars pack the place for the authentic tandoori dishes (the salmon is especially good), *biryanis*, traditional breads like naan and *poori*, fiery chicken tikka masala, and cool mulligatawny. Other locations in Hartford (860-727-1092) and New Haven (203-848-2290). $11–20.

Char Koon (860-657-3656; www.charkoon.com), 882 Main St., South Glastonbury. Open for lunch and dinner daily. Traditional dishes of the Pacific Rim, from Indian curries to traditional Chinese noodle dishes, and others influenced by Thai and Vietnamese cooking. There's not much in the way of seafood, but you can't go wrong with the chicken, lamb, or duck. Start with chicken satay, and you'll be pleasantly surprised to find the traditional peanut sauce flavored with lemongrass. All the traditional pan-Asian flavors—tamarind, curry, ginger, garlic, coriander—are well represented. The dining room is small, so be prepared to wait. $12–20.

The Cookhouse (860-289-0053; www.thecookhouse.com), 221 Governor St., East Hartford. Open daily for lunch and dinner. Traditional southern-style favorites—brisket, fried catfish po'boys, pulled pork, and country biscuits smothered in creamy gravy—in a casual, family atmosphere. Connecticut diners have voted their ribs and barbecue the state's best for several years running. The secret, some say, is in the slow smoking and in Fat Tommy's special sauce. $12–23.

The Cosmic Omelet (860-645-1864), 485 Hartford Rd., Manchester. Open Tue.–Sun. for breakfast and lunch; closed Mon. As at all popular breakfast places, be prepared to wait on weekends. As for the omelets, more than 20 appear on the regular menu, and specials are picked from another

50 selections. It's quirky, friendly, and families love it, which should guarantee the future of this homey spot. $4–8.

Country Kitchen (860-654-1726), 75 South Main St. (CT 5), East Windsor. Locals pack this nostalgic place for hearty breakfasts (pancakes are a must) and lunches (burgers, dogs, Philly cheese steak sandwiches). Staff are friendly and efficient. $5–10.

Frank Pepe Pizzeria Napoletana (860-644-7333; www.pepespizzeria.com), 221 Buckland Hills Dr., Manchester. Open daily for lunch and dinner. The newest outpost of the legendary New Haven pizzeria ensures that, finally, Pepe fans don't have to trek to the shoreline. Favorites include the plain pie (sauce only, no cheese) and the white clam pie, topped with fresh clams. $6–28.

♿ **The Hungry Tiger Music Club & Cafe** (860-649-1195; www.thehungrytiger.com), 120 Charter Oak St., Manchester. Open for lunch and dinner daily; kitchen open until 11 PM on Fri. and Sat.; Sun. brunch. This is one of the best places in the state to hear live music, but it's also a laid-back and friendly café serving all-American pub fare. The turn-of-the-20th-century building housed an ice cream shop, a soda fountain, and an iron forge before opening as a tavern in the 1930s. Hungry? Go for the chicken, steak, ribs, and Mexican dishes; on the lighter side are salads and specialty sandwiches. Back to the music: Local and national acts—jazz, blues, acoustic, you name it—take the stage every night (see *Entertainment*). $7–16.

♿ **John Harvard's Brewhouse** (860-644-2739; www.johnharvards.com), 1487 Pleasant Valley Rd., Manchester. Open daily for lunch and dinner. This is the Connecticut version of an English pub, complete with a vague allusion to a beer recipe connected with William Shakespeare. Legends aside, the food is sturdy, tasty, and traditional: bangers and mash even, with homemade sausages and chicken pie. Entrées are in the realm of grilled meat loaf, pan-seared Atlantic salmon, and baked lasagna, mixed with pub favorites like burgers, nachos, and quesadillas. Wash 'em down with a seasonal brew or one of their own nut brown ales, Irish stouts, or light lagers. $10–19.

♿ **Lotus Restaurant** (860-871-8962), 409 Hartford Turnpike (CT 30), Vernon. Open Tue.–Sat. for lunch 11:30–2; dinner 5–9; closed Sun. and Mon. Reservations suggested. In a suitably serene dining room, Vietnamese cuisine is presented in impeccable style. Chicken is surrounded by freshly cooked onions, carrots, green peppers, and lemongrass, and zinged with chile peppers. The seafood basket contains shrimp, scallops, and crabmeat stir-fried with vegetables and served in a basket of deep-fried matchstick potatoes. $12–18.

The New Brass Key Restaurant (860-643-8609), 829 Main St., Manchester. Open for lunch and dinner Tue.–Fri.; breakfast, lunch, and dinner on Sat. and Sun.; closed Mon. Why travel to Dixieland for southern-style home cooking when you can chow down on barbecue and soul food in an old-fashioned luncheonette in downtown Manchester? The perfume of slow-cooked barbecue fills the air from the smoker out back. Slabs of barbecued ribs, smoky pulled pork, and fried chicken come with traditional southern sides like fried okra, collard greens, and hush puppies. The kitchen also turns out Jamaican dishes like goat curry. For dessert, sweet potato pie and bread pudding are a couple of house favorites. Live music on Fri.

night—think reggae and Bob Marley classics. BYOB. $6–20.

Pazzo Italian Cafe (860-657-3447; www.pazzoitaliancafe.net), 60 Hebron Ave., Glastonbury. Open for lunch and dinner Mon.–Sat.; closed Sun. The Italian word *pazzo* means "crazy," and that's how loyal fans feel about this laid-back neighborhood café, which serves up hearty portions of creative Tuscan cuisine. At lunch they come for the chicken tortellini soup and hot panini sandwiches; at night, entrées like fettuccine with pancetta, shrimp, and cream sauce, and filet mignon, dress things up a bit. Creamy gelato imported from Milan and their own tiramisu shine on the dessert menu. Bring along your own beer or wine. $15–24.

♿ **Rein's Deli Restaurant** (860-875-1344; www.reinsdeli.com), 435 Hartford Turnpike (CT 30), in the "Shops at 30" plaza, Vernon. Open daily 7 AM–midnight for breakfast, lunch, and dinner. They seat and serve you in a New York minute and start you off with crisp garlic pickles. At a word from you, they pile savory pastrami or corned beef on rye, layer hand-cut lox onto cream-cheese-laden bagels, and tempt you with blintzes until you think you're in Manhattan. The menu at this New York–style Jewish deli is long and lighthearted: borscht, chopped liver, *rollmop* herring, noodle pudding, knishes; also tuna melts and peanut butter and jelly. Famous for breakfast combos served all day. Be prepared for a line if you go at mealtime (regulars travel across the state to dine here), but it moves fast. The cheesecake and cold cuts are top-notch. $5–15.

Ted's Montana Grill (860-648-1100; www.tedsmontanagrill.com), at The Shoppes at Evergreen Walk, 500 Evergreen Way, South Windsor. Open daily for lunch and dinner. "Ted" is Ted Turner. The media mogul and Montana rancher also has a nationwide chain of western-style steak houses, and this is the first to open in the Northeast. The decor is Craftsman-inspired and reminiscent of a mountain lodge. The menu of traditional bar-and-grill-style American fare emphasizes fresh ingredients and homemade dishes. Beef and bison steaks are hand-cut, as are the chunky golden french fries; meat loaf, soups, and cookies fall under the made-from-scratch category. $10–24.

SNACKS **Augie & Ray's Drive-In** (860-568-3770), 314 Main St., East Hartford. Open Mon.–Sat. for breakfast, lunch, and dinner; closed Sun. This no-frills take-out spot—named for the two police officers who founded it in 1946—is a local landmark where grilled hot dogs, chili dogs, onion rings, and whole belly clam strips are whipped up behind the counter. A popular stop for workers from Pratt & Whitney, which manufactures commercial and military jet engines at a nearby plant.

Collins Creamery (860-749-8663), 9 Powder Hill Rd., Enfield. Open mid-Mar.–mid-Oct., daily noon–9. The Holsteins at the Collins family's Powder Hill Farm provide the fresh milk that's churned into homemade ice cream daily at the creamery. Flavors are yummy and traditional; they also make sugar-free and fat-free varieties, as well as frozen yogurt.

Daybreak Coffee Roasters (860-657-4466; www.daybreakcoffee.com), 2377 Main St., Glastonbury. Open daily; closed Sun. in July and August. In good weather, the outdoor tables are packed and are more of a landmark than the café's crimson awning. A bustling gourmet coffee joint whose brew is fair trade, meaning the beans are organic and purchased from small-scale farmers who receive a fair price. Try one of the espresso drinks or a freshly baked pastry; then browse the shop's coffee and tea gifts and gourmet gift baskets.

Great Harvest Bread Company (860-647-8837), 809 Main St., Manchester. Several varieties of bread are baked on the premises every day.

Mickey's Oceanic Grill (860-528-6644), 119 Pitkin St., East Hartford. Open Mon.–Fri. for breakfast, lunch, and dinner; closed Sat. and Sun. Road food at its finest with a lean on seafood: fried clams, lobster rolls, chowders; burgers and dogs, too.

Shady Glen Dairy Store (860-649-4245), 840 East Middle Turnpike, Manchester. In fall, in-the-know regulars flock into this friendly, old-fashioned shop for the homemade pumpkin ice cream. Year-round, though, folks come for the cheeseburgers. The place seems like stepping into a bygone era: Maybe it's the 1950s attireor the creamy milk shakes.

Entertainment

In Manchester

MUSIC AND THEATER **The Hungry Tiger Music Club & Cafe** (860-649-1195; www.thehungrytiger.com), 120 Charter Oak St. This is one of the hottest small venues in the state if you'd like to check out national and local bands—be it blues, folk, rock, or open-mike night—and they take the stage just about every night of the week. Unfussy, hearty pub fare served for lunch and dinner (see *Eating Out*).

♿ **Little Theater of Manchester at Cheney Hall** (860-647-9824; www.cheneyhall.org), 177 Hartford Rd. This elegant French Second Empire monument, with mansard roof, circle windows, arches, and fancy cornices, has an equally fine interior, resplendent with carved oak and chestnut woodwork and paneling. Listed as a National Historic Landmark, it was built in 1867 for the Cheney family of silk industrialists as Manchester's theater and cultural center. The building serves the same function today, part of the legacy of the silk mills that employed, housed, educated, and watched over 19th-century Manchester. Connecticut's oldest operating community theater presents a year-round performing arts series featuring plays, jazz, folk, world music, dance, art exhibitions, and family and holiday programs. More than 1,000 nonprofessional actors have performed on the boards here since 1960. Call or check online for a schedule.

Manchester Bicentennial Band Shell (860-432-7728; www.manchesterbandshell.com), Manchester Community College, 60 Bidwell St. Mid-June–Aug., performances begin at 7 PM; call or check online for schedules. A summertime series of free concerts and presentations by a wide variety of instrumentalists and singers, with programs several nights a week. Performers run the gamut: bluegrass, big band, soul, country, traditional Irish music, a barbershop chorus, Dixieland jazz. Bring a chair or blanket.

Selective Shopping

ART GALLERIES **Christopher Gurshin Studio & Gallery** (860-633-7707; www.christophergurshin.com), 1313 Main St., Glastonbury. Open Sat. 10–3 or by appointment. The specialties in this barn studio are contemporary folk art, murals, and old New England–style paintings.

Hartford Fine Art and Framing (860-528-1409; www.hartfordfineart.com), 80 Pitkin St., East Hartford.

Open Mon.–Sat.; closed Sun. The area's oldest art gallery, showcasing the work of artists from Connecticut and across the country.

FARMS AND GARDENS South Glastonbury is known as a prime spot for raising fruit, and many orchards and berry patches remain, despite the encroachment of suburbia into this once-agricultural community. Visitors who come from around the state to pick their own veggies, apples, berries, peaches, pumpkins, and Christmas trees are keeping a handful of local farmers in business. Below are just a few. Generally, crop fields and orchards are open for picking from June to October; many farms also have markets selling everything from local honey and homemade fruit pies to their own just-from-the-fields produce.

Belltown Hill Orchards (860-633-2789; www.belltownhillorchards.com), 483 Matson Hill Rd., South Glastonbury. Pick your own blueberries, raspberries, pears, peaches, apples, cherries, and peaches. Before heading into the orchard, stop by the farm market and bakery for freshly baked pies, local honey, or the farm's homemade applesauce.

Dondero Orchards Farm Stand & Bakery (860-659-0294; www.donderoorchards.com), 529 Woodland St., South Glastonbury. Open daily mid-Apr.–Dec. Since 1911, this farm has been run by four generations of the Dondero family. Today visitors are welcome into the fields to pick strawberries, blueberries, raspberries, and blackberries, and into the orchards for apples, peaches, and pears. The farm stand and bakery have ice cream, wreaths, gift baskets, pies, and pumpkins.

Easy Pickin's Orchard (860-763-3276; www.easypickinsorchard.com), 46 Bailey Rd., off CT 191, Enfield. Open daily July–Nov. It seems like just about every crop imaginable grows here. In the fields, visitors pick their own blueberries, raspberries, and all manner of veggies, from beets and broccoli to carrots and cauliflower. In the apple orchard, 20 varieties grow on easy-to-reach dwarf trees; you can also pick pears, or peaches that come in 13 varieties. Don't forget the pumpkins, flowers, and herbs. All told there are 100 types of fruits, vegetables, and flowers, all for the picking. In fall, there's a flurry of family activities, from wagon rides to gourd hunts.

River View Farms (860-657-9197), 1287 Main St. (CT 17), South Glastonbury. Open Sept.–Oct., daily 9–6. The farm stand at Connecticut's oldest cider mill is stocked with apples, made-right-here cider, flowers, and local fruits and veggies. There are hayrides and, for the kids, a petting zoo.

Rose's Berry Farm (860-633-7467; www.rosesberryfarm.com), 295 Matson Hill Rd., South Glastonbury. The Rose family has been farming in Glastonbury since 1910; today they run Connecticut's largest berry farm, where you can pick your own strawberries, raspberries, blueberries, and, later in the season, pumpkins and Christmas trees. From June through October there are baked goods, cider, and farm-fresh pies in the country store, and hayrides to the pumpkin patch on fall weekends. They pack 'em in for the popular Sunday-morning breakfast, served alfresco on the deck from June through October. Pancakes, Belgian waffles, and French toast come topped with blueberries or apples and cider, depending on the season. From May to October, the Rose family also runs a farm stand in town at 1200 Hebron Ave. (CT 94), with fresh produce, cut flowers, cider, mums, and homemade baked goods.

Scott's Orchard & Nursery (860-633-8681; www.scottsorchardand nursery.com), 1838 New London Turnpike, Glastonbury. The roadside market has operated here for 60 years; you can also pick apples, pears, plums, and peaches in the orchard. There are horse- and tractor-drawn hayrides, family activites, an apple festival in September, and a harvest festival in October.

Udderly Woolly Acres (860-633-4503), 581 Thompson St., Glastonbury. An 1820 homestead on 20 pastoral acres with farm-fresh organic produce, milk, eggs, meat, cheese, and hand-knit wool products for sale at the farm stand. Visitors can pick raspberries in July and August. Kids will love the sheep, goats, and geese. (See also *Lodging.*)

SHOPPING CENTERS **The Shoppes at Buckland Hills** (860-644-1450), Buckland St., Exit 62 off I-84, Manchester. A traditional enclosed mall with the usual suspects: Filene's, JCPenney, American Eagle Outfitters, Bath & Body Works, Victoria's Secret, and Starbucks.

The Shoppes at Evergreen Walk (860-432-3398), Evergreen Way, Exit 62 off I-84, South Windsor. Open daily. This isn't your usual ho-hum shopping center. One of Connecticut's newest shopping venues features the state's first **L.L. Bean**, as well as upscale stores (think Brooks Brothers, Anthropologie, Pottery Barn, Banana Republic) in an outdoor villagelike setting, complete with old-fashioned streetlights and piped-in music.

The Shops at Somerset Square (203-861-9000; www.theshopsatsomerset square.com), 140 Glastonbury Blvd., Exit 6 off CT 2, Glastonbury. Open daily. An upscale retail center with Georgian colonial-style shops housing the likes of Smith & Hawken, Ann Taylor, Coldwater Creek, and Talbots.

SPECIAL SHOPS **Cabela's** (860-290-6200; www.cabelas.com), 475 East Hartford Blvd. North, East Hartford. Open daily. When Cabela's opened in 2007, it was the first New England outpost of the venerable hunting/fishing/camping/outdoor gear superstore. All the hallmarks are here: wildlife dioramas, huge aquariums, hundreds of big-game trophies, a gun library, an indoor archery range, a trophy deer museum, and a centerpiece two-story mountain with waterfalls, stream, a trout pond, and wild game mounts.

Cape Cod Crafters (860-648-9277), 120 Hale Rd., Manchester. Open daily. Hundreds of local artists and craftspeople ply their wares.

Marlborough Barn (860-295-8231; 800-852-8893; www.marlborough barn.com), 45 North Main St., Marlborough. Open Tue.–Sat. 10–5; Sun. noon–5; open until 8 PM on Fri.; closed Mon. Longtime patrons refer to this furniture emporium simply as "The Barn." It has been known for more than 40 years as much for its handcrafted furniture as its old-fashioned New England–style village setting. Inside a lovely complex of restored and reproduction barns and country buildings, furniture is arranged in attractive, professionally styled "rooms." Separate galleries display rugs, quilts, and curtains; the **Country Store** sells unique home accessories; the **Holiday Shoppe** is the place to go for seasonal items.

Broad Brook Books & Stuff (860-623-5100; www.broadbrookbooks .com), 100 Main St. (CT 191), in the Broad Brook section of East Windsor. Open daily. One of Connecticut's newest independent bookstores, in

East Windsor's quiet downtown, is packed with an interesting selection of new and used titles, as well as gifts.

Village Wool (860-633-0898), 2279 Main St., Glastonbury. Open Tue.–Sat.; closed Sun. and Mon. Skeins upon skeins of wool, yarn, ribbon, and other knitting supplies. Lessons and weekend workshops.

✷ Special Events

April: ✐ **Connecticut Sheep, Wool and Fiber Festival** (www.ctsheep.org), Tolland Agricultural Center, CT 30, Vernon. Since 1910: Connecticut Sheep Breeders Association, live sheep, goats, alpacas, and other animals that are part of the state's fiber industry. Sheepdog trials, fleece-to-shawl competition, sheep shearing.

June: **Show in the Park** (860-995-0511), Center Park, Manchester. A huge arts-and-crafts festival, sponsored by the Manchester Art Association for the past 30 years. Professional and amateur artists and craftspeople.

July: ✐ **Fourth of July Town Celebration** (860-749-1820), on the Enfield town green (CT 5), Enfield. An old-fashioned Independence Day celebration with a parade, 5K road race, family activities, live entertainment, a crafts fair, and fireworks. ✐ **Riverfest** (860-713-3131), Great River Park, East Hartford. A July 4 celebration in the riverfront parks on both sides of the Connecticut River, here and in Hartford. An evening of live entertainment and family activities is capped with a fireworks display over the river.

August: ✐ **Tolland County 4-H Fair** (860-875-3331), 24 Hyde Ave. (CT 30), Vernon. Livestock shows, entertainment, baking contests, and exhibits featuring canning, produce, photography, and collections. **Podunk Bluegrass Music Festival** (860-528-1458; www.podunkbluegrass.net), Martin Park, East Hartford. Four days of live music, named for a 17th-century local Native American tribe. ✐ **Hartford County 4-H Fair** (860-570-9074), Four Town Fairgrounds, 56 Egypt Rd., off CT 83, Somers. Livestock judging, dog show, homemaking exhibits, live music, and children's entertainment.

September: **Chili Festival** (860-749-6527), Four Town Fairgrounds, 56 Egypt Rd., off CT 83, Somers. **Four Town Fair** (860-749-6527; www.fourtownfair.com), Four Town Fairgrounds, 56 Egypt Rd., off CT 83, Somers. A country fair established in 1838. ✐ **Wapping Fair** (www.wappingfair.org), Rye Street Park, South Windsor. Know what a wapping is? Find out here. Arts and crafts, entertainment, fireworks, exhibits, rides, and lots of fair food. ✐ **Hebron Harvest Fair** (860-228-0892; www.hebronharvestfair.org), Hebron Lions Fairground, 347 Gilead St. (CT 85), Hebron. Tractor pulling, Wild West show, carnival, children's games, livestock shows, and live entertainment.

October: **Apple Harvest Festival** (860-659-3587), on the Hubbard green, Glastonbury.

Thanksgiving Day: **Manchester Road Race** (860-649-6456; www.manchesterroadrace.com), downtown Manchester. Free for spectators. More than 14,000 runners in the second-oldest race in the East. The 4.75-mile race, which features live bands along the course, has been a tradition for nearly 75 years.

Cory Mazon

The Quiet Corner

THE VILLAGES OF
NORTHEASTERN CONNECTICUT

Kim Grant

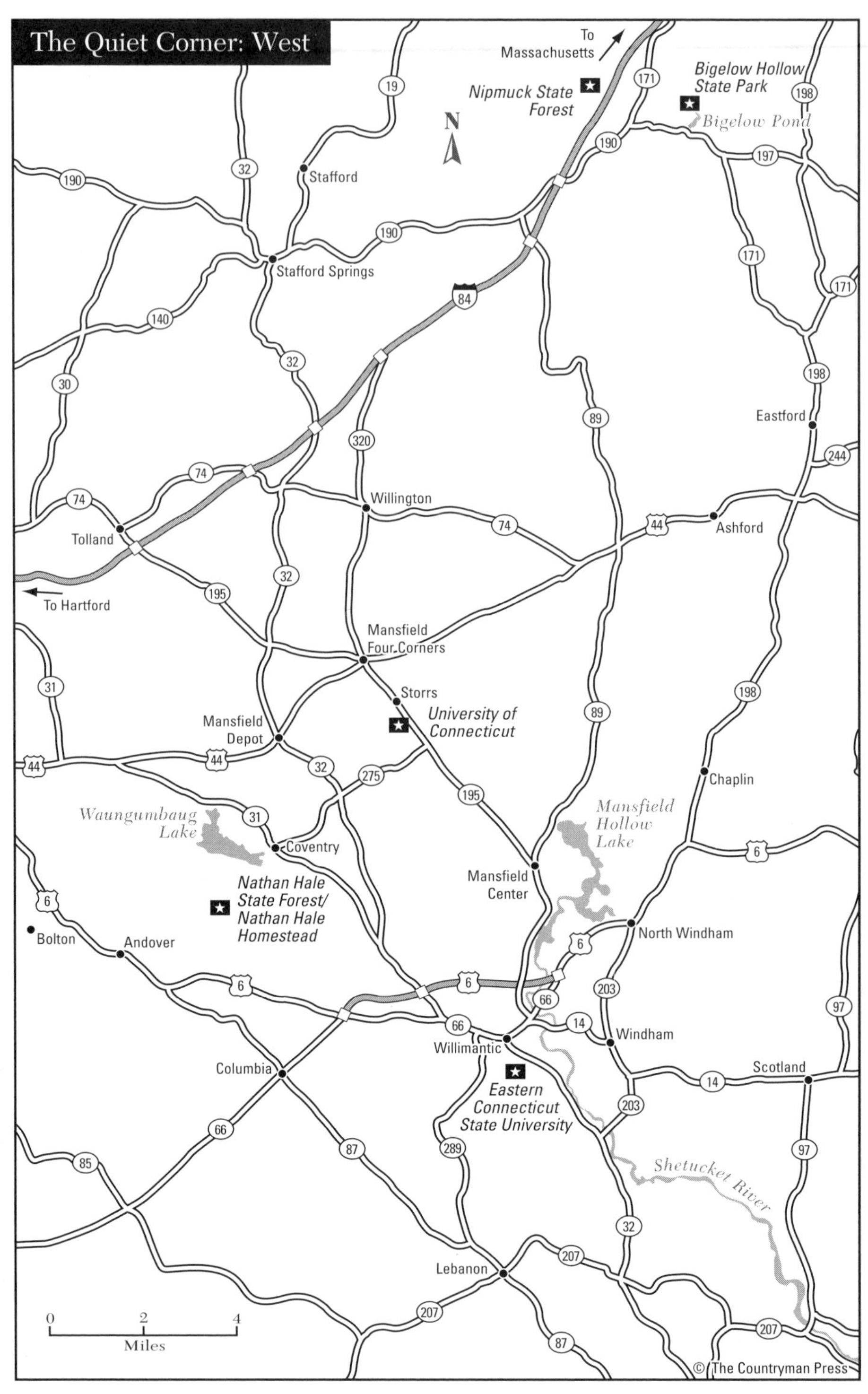
The Quiet Corner: West
To Massachusetts
Nipmuck State Forest
Bigelow Hollow State Park
Bigelow Pond
N
Stafford
Stafford Springs
Eastford
Willington
Tolland
Ashford
To Hartford
Mansfield Four Corners
Storrs
University of Connecticut
Mansfield Depot
Chaplin
Waungumbaug Lake
Coventry
Mansfield Hollow Lake
Mansfield Center
Nathan Hale State Forest/ Nathan Hale Homestead
Bolton
Andover
North Windham
Windham
Willimantic
Columbia
Eastern Connecticut State University
Scotland
Shetucket River
Lebanon
0
2
4
Miles
© The Countryman Press

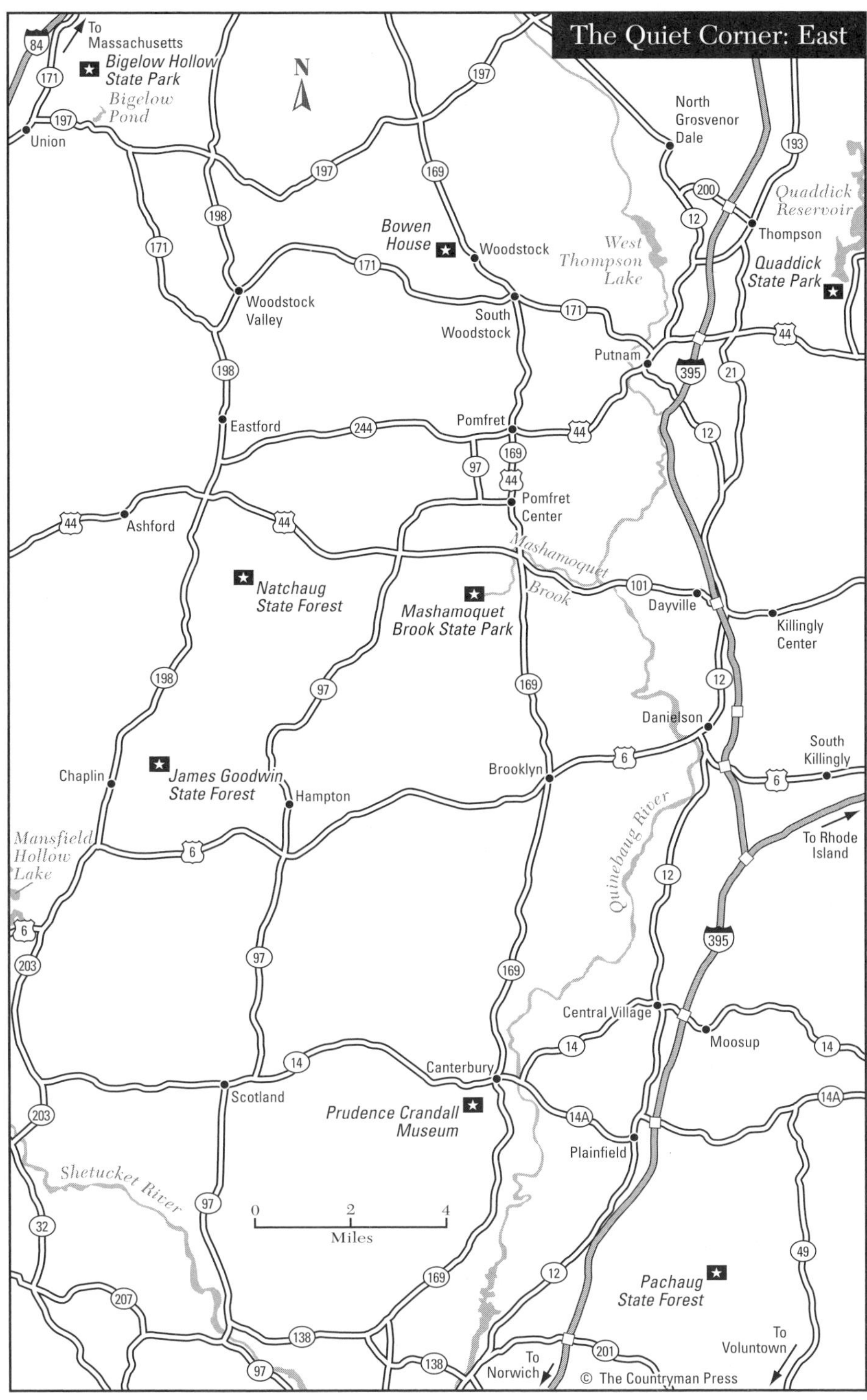

The Quiet Corner: East
To Massachusetts
Bigelow Hollow State Park
Bigelow Pond
Union
N
North Grosvenor Dale
Quaddick Reservoir
Thompson
Quaddick State Park
Bowen House
Woodstock
West Thompson Lake
Woodstock Valley
South Woodstock
Putnam
Eastford
Pomfret
Pomfret Center
Ashford
Natchaug State Forest
Mashamoquet Brook
Mashamoquet Brook State Park
Dayville
Killingly Center
Danielson
South Killingly
Chaplin
James Goodwin State Forest
Hampton
Brooklyn
Mansfield Hollow Lake
Quinebaug River
To Rhode Island
Central Village
Moosup
Canterbury
Scotland
Prudence Crandall Museum
Plainfield
Shetucket River
0 2 4
Miles
Pachaug State Forest
To Norwich
To Voluntown
© The Countryman Press

THE VILLAGES OF NORTHEASTERN CONNECTICUT

If there's a part of Connecticut that can be considered far from the madding crowd, the aptly named Quiet Corner is it. And quiet it is. Country lanes and a National Scenic Byway link pockets of rolling farmland to 200-year-old villages, with forested ridges wedged between. The state's extreme northeast corner is arguably away from the action, nestled alongside Massachusetts and Rhode Island; but the location is more serene than remote. Only lately have newcomers discovered that it's within easy commuting distance of Hartford, Worcester, and Providence. Yet thanks to the dual forces of foresight and preservation, it remains a rural landscape that contains some of the prettiest scenes in all of New England, neighborly villages, and plenty of open space seemingly untouched by the hand of the 21st century, all with a laid-back and unpretentious identity. This spot is far enough from the interstates and cities to exist quietly under the radar, yet close enough to provide visitors a quintessential country weekend.

The region is also known as the Quinebaug and Shetucket Rivers Valley National Heritage Corridor, a 1,085-square-mile area protecting the "last green valley" in the sprawling megalopolis between Boston and Washington, DC, the most heavily urbanized region in America. The federally designated area, comprising 35 towns in the Quiet Corner and nearby south-central Massachusetts, is one of the only significant green (or black, at night) swaths on the East Coast that can be seen from aircraft or by satellite. One way to savor the quiet is by exploring CT 169, the National Scenic Byway that runs through orchards and farm fields that speak to the region's agrarian roots, and through villages that seem frozen in the 18th and 19th centuries. Places like Woodstock, Pomfret, and Brooklyn—from their requisite red barns and rambling stone walls to the tidy clapboard homes fronting colonial greens—distill rural New England's history and character. These features keep the area rather sleepy and attract history buffs, outdoorsy types, and solitude-seeking urbanites from far and wide. Woodstock was once dubbed "inland Newport" for the elegant summer retreats built by wealthy Manhattanites in the grand Victorian era, while the oldest agricultural fair in the nation, dating from 1849, can be found in Brooklyn, a town where you might spot shaggy bison grazing alongside Holsteins. Pomfret is a bucolic hilltop village with an ivied private school and the Vanilla Bean Café, a crossroads social hub that's popular with both locals and out-of-towners, who come for poetry readings and folk music. Farming lives on in vineyards, nurseries, and orchards, while much-photographed National Historic Landmarks stand proudly along country lanes and village greens.

This is the Connecticut of long ago—its big events date from Revolutionary War era, when settlers drifted here from Massachusetts, looking for elbow room and an escape from Puritanism. The local hero was Israel ("Don't fire until you see the whites of their eyes") Putnam, the plucky old general who left his plow in the furrow in Brooklyn when news came of Lexington and Concord. After Bunker Hill, Old Put evaded the redcoats in Greenwich, survived a brutal winter with his colonial troops at the Redding encampment known as Putnam's Valley Forge, and finally retired to run a tavern back at home. And all of this happened long after he famously crawled into a dark cave to kill the she-wolf that was decimating local herds of sheep. Speaking of history, the Quiet Corner has the distinction of serving as home for both the state hero, Coventry's Nathan Hale, the patriot-spy whose only regret was that he had but one life to lose for his country; and the state heroine, the abolitionist and schoolteacher Prudence Crandall. In Canterbury, 30 years before the start of the Civil War, Miss Crandall defied popular opinion by admitting a young black woman to the school she ran in her home. Crandall was arrested and run out of town, but a series of legal actions ultimately vindicated her.

Lebanon's past is decidedly patriotic; in fact, 2006 marked the 225th anniversary of the town's participation in the French-American campaign that ultimately led to British defeat at Yorktown, Virginia, and the end of British colonial rule. It was Lebanon where General George Washington and the Comte de Rochambeau planned military strategy while some 220 French cavalry troops conducted daily drills in the winter of 1780–1781. The home of Connecticut governor Jonathan Trumbull, who provided the Continental army with soldiers, food, and munitions during the American Revolution, stands sentinel on Lebanon's mile-long green, along with several other colonial-era house museums and the stable where Washington's horse spent the night.

Still more pictures from the past: In a scene played out all over New England, prosperity visited northeastern Connecticut in the 19th century by way of the Industrial Revolution, as textile manufacturers found ways to harness the region's abundant waterpower. Blue-collar mill towns like Putnam, Killingly, Stafford, and Willimantic sprang up along ponds and rivers, turning out cotton and silk thread in abundance. As immigrants poured in from Europe to work the looms, mill owners built grand Victorian mansions—monuments to their success. By the 1970s, most mills had closed or moved south, challenging developers to find new uses for the abandoned industrial buildings scattered around the rural landscape. Many of the brick and granite mills are getting a new lease on life, imaginatively converted into housing and office space; others remain vacant, broken-down vestiges of the Quiet Corner's long-ago golden days. In Willimantic, nicknamed Thread City, a museum devoted to the city's industrial heyday resides in the historic mills of the old American Thread Company. On a lighter note, check out the city's downtown bridge, where 12-foot-high bullfrogs—four in all—are perched atop massive sculpted spools of thread above the Willimantic River. According to 18th-century legend, townspeople mistook the persistent nighttime croaking of bullfrogs for an Indian attack and prepared themselves for battle. Today bullfrogs can be seen, it seems, all over Willimantic—even on the municipal seal. The bullfrog is, after all, the city's mascot.

The manufacturing interests are long gone, for the most part, and the towns no longer tell time by the mill whistle. Putnam was a virtual ghost town until a decade or so ago, when antiques dealers moved in and revived its shuttered downtown. Now it's a New England hot spot for things past, drawing buyers and sellers to shops jammed to the rafters with treasures from the past three centuries. Artists and craftspeople quietly hone their skills in studios scattered throughout the region, and twice a year many take part in a local tradition of inviting the public to tour their workspaces. For a dose of collegiate vitality, head to Storrs, where the University of Connecticut, founded in 1881 as an agricultural school for boys, is now the top public university in New England, according to *U.S. News & World Report*. Activity stirs all around the rural campus; for the visitor, there are musicals and plays at the Connecticut Repertory Theatre, concerts at the Jorgensen Center for the Performing Arts, world-class paintings at the William Benton Museum of Art, basketball by the championship Huskies, and fresh ice cream at the iconic UConn Dairy Bar. And everyone should get outdoors for at least one up-close, out-of-car experience: Opportunities for hiking, biking, camping, and fishing are plentiful.

In the end, though, it's all about the quiet. The hills and valleys are more charming than chic, the sort of place where attractions are subtle in nature. Visitors come here for rural scenes and small-town friendliness rather than tourist haunts, and these traits help the region maintain its modest, almost self-effacing character. The classic Quiet Corner weekend is a laid-back affair, and the basic formula doesn't show signs of changing. Stroll along nature trails, browse for antiques, visit a farm stand, dine in a gourmet outpost or a homey local joint, and spend the night in a colonial-era homestead turned B&B, where antiques and fireplaces keep things cozy. It's impossible not to relax here, which is precisely why it's cherished by so many who discover it. The Quiet Corner hangs on to history yet mixes old with new as it moves, ever so quietly, forward.

Entries in this section are arranged in alphabetical order.

AREA CODE 860.

GUIDANCE The towns of Andover, Tolland, and Stafford are part of the **Central Regional Tourism District** (860-244-8181; 800-793-4480; www.enjoycentralct.com), 31 Pratt St., Hartford 06103. This district publishes informative materials and will supply them on request.

Eastern Regional Tourism District (860-444-2206; 800-863-6569; www.mysticcountry.com), 32 Huntington St., New London 06320. This district, which includes *most* of the towns discussed in this section, publishes guides to lodgings, attractions, restaurants, events, and antiques and crafts shops.

Coventry Visitor Center (860-742-1085), 1195 Main St. (CT 31), Coventry. Open Mar.–Nov.: Wed.–Sun. 10–2; Thu. 4–8 during warm-weather months. Dec.–Feb.: Thu.–Sun. 10–2. Housed in a picturesque 1876 redbrick building, first a post office and later the local probate court, the center is a must-stop for Quiet Corner visitors. There are local maps, travel brochures, information on the Quinebaug and Shetucket Rivers Valley National Heritage Corridor, and directions and suggestions provided by friendly staff.

Lebanon Historical Society Museum and Visitor Center (860-642-6579; www.lebanoncthistsoc.org), 856 Trumbull Hwy. (CT 87), Lebanon. Open year-round, Wed.–Sat., noon–4; closed Sun.–Tue. Self-service information center open 24 hours. The local historical society operates this visitor center at the edge of Lebanon's historic mile-long green; there is also a comprehensive museum (see *To See*).

Quinebaug-Shetucket Heritage Corridor, Inc. (860-963-7226; 866-363-7226; www.thelastgreenvalley.org), 107 Providence St., Putnam. A nonprofit grassroots organization that promotes tourism in the Quinebaug and Shetucket Rivers Valley National Heritage Corridor. On request, they will send free brochures on self-guided walking, driving, and biking tours, as well as area attractions, wildlife, and the Quiet Corner's popular Walking Weekends events. All of this, as well as a calendar of events, links to area attractions, and other information of interest to visitors can be downloaded from their Web site.

GETTING THERE *By car:* Major routes into the area are I-395, which runs north–south through eastern Connecticut and connects I-95—the shoreline route—with the Massachusetts Turnpike (I-90); and I-84, which links New York (through Hartford) with the Massachusetts Turnpike in Sturbridge, Massachusetts, running in a northeasterly direction along the western edge of the district. US 6 and US 44 are major two-lane highways between Hartford and Providence, Rhode Island, US 44 being the more northerly route.

By air: **Bradley International Airport** (860-292-2000; 888-624-1533; www.bradleyairport.com) in Windsor Locks serves the whole state as its major airport. The Quiet Corner is also convenient to **T. F. Green Airport** (401-737-8222; 888-268-7222; www.pvdairport.com) in Warwick, Rhode Island.

By bus: **Peter Pan Bus Lines** (800-343-9999; www.peterpanbus.com) makes scheduled stops in Willimantic, Storrs (UConn), and Danielson on runs connecting Providence, Rhode Island, and New York City. The same locations are also served by **Greyhound Lines** (800-231-2222; www.greyhound.com).

GETTING AROUND **Thread City Cab** (860-456-2227) serves the Willimantic area.

MEDICAL EMERGENCY The statewide emergency number is **911**.

Day Kimball Hospital (860-928-6541), 320 Pomfret St. (US 44), Putnam. The emergency number is 860-928-7503.

Johnson Memorial Hospital (860-684-4251), 201 Chestnut Hill Rd. (CT 190), Stafford Springs. The emergency number is 860-684-8111.

Windham Hospital (860-456-9116), 112 Mansfield Ave., Willimantic. The emergency number is 860-456-6715.

* Villages

The Cities, Towns, and Villages of the Quiet Corner

Coventry benefits from both history and geography: You can visit the home of Nathan Hale's family and walk in the neighboring forest named for the official state hero. There is open space and farmland here, the scenic interest of New England hills, and a lake with an ancient name, Waungumbaug. To help you find your way around, a Visitor Information Center is staffed by the local historical society. If you explore the historic village area, nearly 200 buildings on the National Register, you'll discover the streams and falls that powered the mills here, and, at Patriot's Park, an impressive monument to hometown patriot Nathan Hale.

Lebanon has as long a green as any town can seriously claim—a country mile top to bottom, along CT 87. If you're a walker, go ahead and stretch your legs on the walking path around the green; it's the way to get acquainted with Lebanon's New England identity. The historic expanse can also claim more Revolutionary War significance than any other town common in Connecticut. The green was the site of an encampment of Hussars under the Duc de Lauzun in the winter of 1780–1781, awaiting Rochambeau and his troops for the final push of the Revolutionary War. The reason they picked Lebanon was not so much the size of the green as the fact that facing it was the home of Jonathan Trumbull, royal governor of the colony during the Revolution, who sided with the Continentals. He was, in fact, the only colonial governor to do so, and to remain in office when the war began. Referred to as "Brother Jonathan" by Washington, Trumbull proved a valuable source of supplies, which made Connecticut Washington's "Provision State." During the winter of 1780, Connecticut sent some 3,000 barrels of pork and 1,500 barrels of beef to feed the starving troops. Washington wrote in his diary, "No other man than Trumbull would have procured them and no other state could have furnished them." In the War Office, a modest two-room frame building, Washington, Lafayette, Rochambeau, Adams, Franklin, and other dignitaries gathered to plan strategy and decide on ways and means. The artist John Trumbull, whose paintings of historic Revolutionary War scenes grace not only the halls of Congress in Washington but also the nation's one-dollar bills, was a son of Governor Trumbull. The Trumbull homes and the War Office are open to visitors, as are other historic sites in town. William Williams, one of the signers of the Declaration of Independence, was also a native of Lebanon. The museum and visitor center on the green tell Lebanon's story.

Putnam, one of the area's busier towns, was named for Revolutionary War general Israel Putnam and reportedly served as a stop on the Underground Railroad prior to the Civil War. When the Industrial Revolution crept into this isolated corner of the state, it brought wealth and success as water-powered textile mills sprang up along the Quinebaug River. One of the largest silk thread factories in the country operated here on into the 1940s. Cargill Falls in the center of town, and the railroad station up the hill, now serve only as reminders of an industrial past; but new interests have seen Putnam's potential. In the 1990s, downtown morphed into an antiques lover's paradise, with storefronts housing hundreds of dealers peddling goods ranging from elaborate silver tea sets and ornate stained-glass windows to Victorian furniture and vintage toys. This plethora of dealers attracted a string of eateries—many tucked into the heart of town along Main Street—to encourage the dedicated browser to settle in. In recent years (not coincidentally, local dealers lament, coinciding with the advent of online auctioning on eBay and other Web sites), many shops have shut down or now keep irregular hours. These days it's best to phone ahead to be sure the shops you wish to visit are open.

Tolland presents the visitor with an idyllic green ringed by the white-clapboard houses associated with New England towns, as well as some striking Victorian gems. Among them are the Congregational church, a pair of historic homes open to visitors, a souvenir and gift shop, the old jail museum, the town library, an active art association, and a charming B&B. Throughout the summer and into fall, the green—less than a mile from the interstate—is the setting for crafts shows, pancake breakfasts, and other town events.

Woodstock has a quiet presence, with most of its area devoted to farms. As you drive north on scenic CT 169, look sharp and you'll see, on your right, close to the road, a one-room stone schoolhouse that operated from 1745 to 1946—the longest run in the country. In the mid–19th century, when wealthy city dwellers began to look for summertime respite from the heat and bustle, northeastern Connecticut became a resort area. Henry Bowen, publisher of the *Independent*—an influential abolitionist weekly edited for a time by Henry Ward Beecher—chose Woodstock as the site of his summer "cottage." Roseland, now open to the public, appears frequently in guidebooks on American domestic architecture as an outstanding example of the Carpenter Gothic style. The scenic road also takes you past antiques shops, a grand country inn, several orchards, and the local fairgrounds, where one of the state's best-known and best-attended country fairs is held each Labor Day weekend.

✷ To See

COLLEGES AND UNIVERSITIES **Eastern Connecticut State University** (860-465-5000; www.ecsu.ctstateu.edu), 83 Windham St., Willimantic. A small and friendly campus that offers concerts and theater productions, sporting events, lectures, and art exhibits throughout the academic year. Call or visit their Web site for information.

University of Connecticut (860-486-2000; www.uconn.edu), main campus, CT 195, Storrs. Spread over more than 4,000 acres—including the campus, fields, and barns—and offering a full range of academic study, UConn appeals to visitors as well as students and scholars. While 75 percent of the 15,000-plus undergrads are from Connecticut, the rest come here from 109 nations. Stop in at the **Lodewick Visitor Center** (860-486-4900; www.visitors.uconn.edu) on Hillside Rd. for general information or to schedule a guided campus tour. Student-led tours are held daily year-round, and reservations are required (weekend tours, and those during school holidays, fill up fast—it's best to call about two weeks ahead). Visitors can park in metered spots or in the two parking garages on campus. Highlights include **Gampel Pavilion**, where the basketball Huskies have been generating excitement in the Big East—capturing multiple NCAA championships, most recently in 2004, when the men's and women's teams both took home top honors. Longtime men's basketball coach Jim Calhoun was inducted into the Basketball Hall of Fame in 2005. The **J. Robert Donnelly Husky Heritage Sports Museum** is chock-full of UConn sports memorabilia, and is open weekdays 8–5 and before home basketball games. For information on sports events, call 860-486-5050, or check www.uconnhuskies.com. Football games are played at **Rentschler Field Stadium** in East Hartford. A short distance east of Gampel is the **Homer Babbidge Library**, with close to three million volumes. The **UConn Co-op** is the source of books of all sorts, and campus souvenirs: T-shirts, sweats, baseball caps, mugs, totes. Next door is the **Connecticut State Museum of Natural History**, a must-see, especially if you've brought along youngsters. The **Connecticut Archaeology Center** houses an extensive collection of Connecticut Native American, colonial, and industrial artifacts. For art, head to the **William Benton Museum of Art** for changing exhibits devoted to American art, the **Ballard Institute and Museum of Puppetry** for more than 4,000 puppets on display, and the **Contemporary Art Galleries** in the Fine Arts Building for cutting-edge modern art. You may want to inquire about what's on at the **Jorgensen Center for the Performing Arts** or the **Connecticut Repertory Theatre**, which present programs throughout the year in music, dance, and drama.

On the other side of CT 195 you'll find the **Floriculture Greenhouses**, a wonderland of plants and flowers, and the **Ecology and Evolutionary Biology Conservatory**, where more than 3,000 plant species from around the world are grown and studied. On down the road you can take the children to visit the **UConn barns** (with sheep, horses, and cows), as well as the **Kellogg Dairy Center** (there's a short video on milking and cow tending). Last, but often foremost on visitors' must-stop lists, is the **Dairy Bar**, with ice cream that is simply the best, according to on-campus experts. See the appropriate listings below for details on all these campus attractions.

The university that began as a rural 19th-century agricultural school continues to evolve: In the works for the School of Fine Arts is a $90 million Frank Gehry–designed arts center, which will include a concert hall, theaters, recital halls, art galleries and studios, and a bold exterior typical of Gehry's world-famous architectural style.

MUSEUMS ✐ **Ballard Institute and Museum of Puppetry** (860-486-4605; www.bimp.uconn.edu), School of Fine Arts, Depot Campus, off US 44, Storrs. Open late Apr.–mid-Nov., Fri.–Sun. noon–5. Admission by donation. Connecticut's official state museum of puppetry houses a remarkable collection of more than

THOUSANDS OF PUPPETS ARE ON DISPLAY IN THE BALLARD INSTITUTE AND MUSEUM OF PUPPETRY AT THE UNIVERSITY OF CONNECTICUT IN STORRS.

Kim Grant

Prudence Crandall House Museum (860-546-7800; www.cultureandtourism.org), 1 South Canterbury Rd., at the junction of CT 14 and CT 169, Canterbury. Open Apr.–mid-Dec., Wed.–Sun. 10–4:30; open Jan.–Mar. by appointment. Adults $3; seniors and children 6–17, $2; 5 and under free. This was New England's first academy to accept African American women, in 1833–1834. A handsome 1805 structure—a National Historic Landmark—fronted with a fine Palladian window, the house is famous as the site of a dramatic confrontation over racial issues some 30 years before the Civil War. Prudence Crandall, a Baptist schoolmistress, opened a school here in 1831 for the daughters of local white families who could afford the $100 tuition. She later accepted among her students a young black woman, 19-year-old Sarah Harris, precipitating an angry response from both townspeople and the families of her students. When Miss Crandall stood her ground, the school was stoned and finally closed, and she was arrested and held overnight in prison. Released the next day on a technicality, she and her husband left the state and settled in Kansas. When Miss Crandall was in her old age, Mark Twain, then a resident of Hartford, urged her to return to Connecticut. She declined. The Connecticut Legislature thereupon awarded her a lifetime $400 annual stipend, which was paid until her death in 1890.

A portion of the house is furnished as it would have been in the 1830s, and a permanent display covers the story of the woman who has been named State Heroine. Changing exhibits cover topics suggested by Prudence Crandall's struggle: African American history, women's history, and local history; there's also a small research library.

CANTERBURY'S PRUDENCE CRANDALL HOUSE MUSEUM, A NATIONAL HISTORIC LANDMARK, IS THE SITE OF THE FIRST ACADEMY IN NEW ENGLAND TO ACCEPT AN AFRICAN AMERICAN WOMAN.

Kim Grant

4,000 puppets and puppetry-related items from around the world. Renowned puppeteer Frank Ballard started the nation's first college degree program in puppetry at UConn. Many of the shadow puppets, marionettes, glove puppets, and body puppets, displayed in rotating exhibits (and used in theatrical productions), were designed and crafted by either Ballard or students in the Puppet Arts Program. Visitors can create their own puppet in the museum's hands-on room to take home.

Brayton Grist Mill and Marcy Blacksmith Museum (860-928-0304), US 44 at the entrance to Mashamoquet Brook State Park, Pomfret. Open June–Sept., Sun. 2–5. Free admission. The Pomfret Historical Society cares for this 1890s structure, the town's sole remaining mill, complete with the original machinery that milled grain into flour for our forebears. The humble red building on Mashamoquet Brook housed a one-person operation. In addition to the gristmill, there's an exhibit of antique tools used by three generations of a local blacksmithing family.

Connecticut Eastern Railroad Museum (860-456-9999; www.cteastrrmuseum.org), 55 Bridge St. (CT 32 at the railroad crossing), Willimantic. Open May–Oct., Sat. and Sun. 10–4. Adults $5; seniors $4; children 8–12 $1; 7 and under free. Vintage railcars and railroad buildings in various stages of restoration are displayed on the grounds of Willimantic's old Columbia Junction Freight Yard. The collection includes locomotives, boxcars, stainless-steel Pullman coaches, and a wrought-iron turntable. Kids can operate a replica of an 1850s-style pump car on a section of track once part of the Air Line railway between Boston and New York City. The museum, which also houses exhibits and historical archives, is run by members of the Connecticut Eastern Chapter of the National Railroad Historical Society.

♿ **Connecticut State Museum of Natural History and Connecticut Archaeology Center** (860-486-4460; www.cac.uconn.edu), University of Connecticut campus, 2019 Hillside Rd. (CT 195), Storrs. Open year-round, Tue.–Sat. 10–4; closed Sun. and Mon. Free admission. Learn about Connecticut's natural and cultural history, or take part in lectures, family programs, workshops, and other activities. The Connecticut Archaeology Center has programs and exhibits, and houses a collection of some 600,000 state artifacts documenting 11,000 years of colonial, industrial, and Native American history.

♿ **Lebanon Historical Society Museum and Visitor Center** (860-642-6579; www.lebanoncthistsoc.org), 856 Trumbull Hwy. (CT 87), Lebanon. Open Wed.–Sat. noon–4. Adults $3; students $2; children under 12 free. Outside is classic colonial; inside is a modern museum, the newest addition to Lebanon's mile-long village green steeped in Revolutionary War history. Stop by to view the orientation video that highlights the historic sites around the Lebanon green; there's also a historical research center, changing exhibits, a museum shop, and a hands-on history room for children.

Mansfield Historical Society Museum (860-429-6575), 954 Storrs Rd. (CT 195), Mansfield. Open June–Sept., Thu. and Sun. 1:30–4:30. Admission $2; children 12 and under free. Mansfield's former (1843) Town Hall and adjacent office building now house the museum and library facilities of the historical society. Changing exhibits showcase clothing, furnishings, and various items such as vintage photographs and decorative objects. In the library are hundreds of books and documents on local history and genealogy, emphasizing 19th-century town life.

The museum is about a mile from the University of Connecticut's main campus at Storrs.

♿ **New England Center for Contemporary Art** (860-774-8899; www.museum-necca.org), 7 Putnam Place, at the junction of US 6 and CT 169, Brooklyn. Open Sat. and Sun. noon–5. Free admission. A contemporary art gallery in a refurbished colonial on Brooklyn's quaint village green is devoted to 20th-century modern painting and sculpture and a fine collection of contemporary Chinese art. Several changing exhibits are mounted each year.

♿ **Northeast States Civilian Conservation Corps Museum** (860-684-3430), 166 Chestnut Hill Rd. (CT 190), at the entrance to Shenipsit State Forest, Stafford. Open Memorial Day–Oct., Sun. noon–4; other times by chance or appointment. Free admission. Photographs and exhibits document the handiwork of the Civilian Conservation Corps (CCC), President Roosevelt's initiative to create jobs during the Depression. The CCC helped build and maintain state and national parks around the country, and the museum resides in a camp headquarters building the CCC constructed in 1935. An interesting collection of memorabilia, from uniforms and equipment to tools and documents, is on display, as are a re-created barracks and work camp, and old photos and films of CCC camps around Connecticut.

Old Tolland County Jail Museum (860-870-9599), 52 Tolland Green, junction of CT 74 and CT 195, Tolland. Hours limited; phone ahead. Admission by donation. The iron bars still clang shut on this 19th-century stone jail (in use until 1968), and the form of a prisoner under the gray blanket on a narrow cot lends authenticity. Other displays in the attached 1893 jailer's residence feature the local historical society's large collection, including furniture, children's toys, farm tools, and Native American artifacts. Next door, the **Old Tolland County Courthouse** is a beautiful 1822 building with a furnished courtroom as well as exhibits relating to Tolland's role as county seat and the growth of this prosperous rural community in the 19th century. A new exhibit space is devoted to farm implements and other outdoor tools.

♿ **William Benton Museum of Art** (860-486-4520; www.thebenton.org), University of Connecticut, 245 Glenbrook Rd. (CT 195), Storrs. Open Tue.–Fri. 10–4:30; Sat. and Sun. 1–4:30; closed Mon. Free admission. A space whose new look (thanks to a $3.2 million face-lift) is bright, airy, and stylishly minimalist is the scene of excellent contemporary and historical exhibits in a trio of galleries. The permanent collection of more than 5,000 works includes European and American paintings, drawings, prints, and sculptures from the 16th century to the present, including the work of Connecticut artists such as American impressionist Childe Hassam. A variety of programs are open to the public, from docent tours and lectures to live music and art discussions. The museum shop is well stocked with books, toys, jewelry, and gifts, and **Café Muse** serves coffee drinks and light snacks.

♿ **Windham Textile and History Museum** (860-456-2178; www.millmuseum.org), 411 Main St. (CT 66), at the corner of Union St., Willimantic. Open Memorial Day–Columbus Day, Wed.–Sun. 1–4:30; at other times, Fri.–Sun. 1–4; and by appointment. Adults $5; seniors and students $3.50. An interesting local museum telling the story of the textile industry that gave Willimantic its nickname: Thread City. The museum occupies a pair of 1877 buildings that belonged first to the

Willimantic Thread Company, later the American Thread Company, once the state's largest employer. In one building, changing exhibits on three floors include re-creations of millworkers' housing, a manager's mansion, and a company store, where immigrant millworkers would purchase groceries and other household items. Dugan Mill houses the vintage textile machinery (wooden spools, skein winders, cotton bales) once used to make thread. The gift shop sells items reminiscent of 19th-century life and the textile industry that once flourished here.

HISTORIC HOMES **Daniel Benton Homestead** (860-974-1875), Metcalf Rd., Tolland. Hours limited; phone ahead. Admission by donation. A well-preserved 1720 center-chimney colonial cape, complete with low ceilings, five fireplaces, original paneling, a history of Hessian prisoners kept in the cellar during the Revolutionary War, and tales of spirits still roaming the house. Not only is this the oldest surviving house in Tolland, but six generations of Benton's descendants lived and farmed here until 1932.

Dr. William Beaumont Birthplace (860-642-6579), 169 West Town St., on the Lebanon green, Lebanon. Open May 15–Columbus Day weekend, Sat. noon–4. Admission $1. This 18th-century farmhouse was the childhood home of Dr. William Beaumont, known as the "father of the physiology of digestion." While caring for soldiers during the War of 1812, Beaumont conducted cutting-edge research in the science of human digestion. Today the house contains period furnishings that reflect Lebanon's agrarian roots, and a re-created doctor's examination room with 18th- and 19th-century surgical instruments on display that instill an appreciation of current medical practice.

THE JONATHAN TRUMBULL HOUSE ON THE GREEN IN LEBANON

Kim Grant

Governor Jonathan Trumbull House (860-642-7558), 169 West Town St., Lebanon. Open mid-May–mid-Oct., Wed.–Sun. noon–4. Admission $3; children under 6 free. In 1776, at the outset of the Revolutionary War, Jonathan Trumbull had been governor of the colony of Connecticut for seven years. He was the only colonial governor to defy the Crown and support the American War of Independence. He continued in office until 1784. His home is listed on the National Register of Historic Places as the birthplace, in 1756, of America's patriot artist, Jonathan Trumbull, his youngest son (see below). While here, check out the Wadsworth Stable (see *Historic Sites*).

Hicks-Stearns Museum (860-875-7552), 42 Tolland Green, Tolland. Hours limited; phone ahead. Recording changes in taste, this house was originally a colonial and over time was transformed into a Victorian home with such improvements as taller windows, a wide veranda, and an ornamental turret. Furnishings are family heirlooms, mostly 19th-century pieces. Summer concerts are held on the lawn.

Huntington Homestead Museum (860-456-8381; www.huntingtonhomestead.org), 36 Huntington Rd. (CT 14), Scotland. Open May–Oct. on the first and third Sat. of the month, 10:30–3:30. Not only did Samuel Huntington sign the Declaration of Independence, he also served as president of the Continental Congress and as governor of Connecticut for 10 terms until his death in 1796. His birthplace, an 18th-century saltbox-style colonial surrounded by farmland, includes the original rooms that date from the 1720s and more than a century's worth of additions and renovations.

♿ **Jillson House Museum** (860-456-2316; www.windhamhistory.org), 627 Main St., at the foot of the frog bridge, Willimantic. Open on the second and third full weekend of the month, Sat. and Sun. 1–4. Free admission. Built circa 1825 of granite quarried from the nearby Willimantic River, this was the home of a mill owner and is furnished in keeping with his position. Besides changing exhibits, the house contains local memorabilia and period artifacts, and it headquarters the Windham Historical Society.

Jonathan Trumbull Jr. House (860-642-6100), 780 Trumbull Hwy. (CT 87), on the Lebanon green, just down from the Trumbull homestead. Open mid-May–mid-Oct., Sat. and Sun. noon–4; or by appointment year-round. Admission by donation. Built circa 1769, this is a foursquare example of a Georgian-style center-chimney farmhouse, boasting eight corner fireplaces and elaborate paneling carved by Isaac Fitch, Lebanon's master joiner. General George Washington was an overnight guest in March 1781; Trumbull was Washington's military secretary and later served as governor for more than a decade.

Nathan Hale Homestead (860-742-6917; www.ctlandmarks.org), 2299 South St. (off US 44), Coventry. Open May–mid-Oct., Wed.–Sun. 1–4. Adults $7; seniors and students $6; children $4; 5 and under free. Ironically, Connecticut's state hero never lived in the house, although the Revolutionary War captain was born on this site in 1755. Nathan, whose five brothers also fought in the war, was already in the Continental army in 1776 (the year he was hanged by the British as a spy) when the present Georgian house—quite fashionable in its day—was built by his father, Deacon Richard Hale, on his 450-acre livestock farm. Period furnishings include memorabilia of the schoolteacher turned patriot, whose only regret was that he had but one life to lose for his country. A full roster of special programs at the homestead includes tours of the heirloom gardens, guided nature walks, colonial cooking demonstrations in the re-created period kitchen, and fall lantern tours (see *Special Events*). The property, which also includes a gift shop in a restored 18th-century barn, is surrounded by 1,219-acre Nathan Hale Forest.

♿ **Roseland Cottage–Bowen House** (860-928-4074), 556 CT 169, Woodstock. Open June–mid-Oct., Wed.–Sun., plus July 4 and Columbus Day, 11–5. Tours on the hour; last tour at 4. Adults $8; seniors $7; children 5–12 $4; under 5 free. A perfect gem of the Carpenter Gothic Revival style, with crockets, pointed arches, and stained-glass windows. Built in 1845 by wealthy New York publisher, merchant, and avid abolitionist Henry Bowen as a summer home, it shares the property with formal boxwood parterre gardens, a summerhouse, a vintage bowling alley—one of the oldest in the country—an icehouse, and an aviary. Bowen loved roses: The cottage is painted a wild and rosy salmon-pink, and the garden between the residence and the carriage house features his beloved blooms. Bowen also loved the Fourth of July: His annual celebrations included fireworks and refreshments for the town, and visits by every U.S. president from Grant through McKinley.

Strong-Porter House Museum (860-742-1419; www.coventrycthistoricalsociety.org), 2382 South St., Coventry. Open May–Oct., first and third weekend of the month, Sat. and Sun. 1–4. Free admission. A staff of volunteers maintain this near neighbor of the Nathan Hale Homestead (see above) and home of the Coventry Historical Society. Half of the large frame farmhouse dates from circa 1730 and was built by a great-uncle of Nathan Hale, Aaron Strong. The house was renovated and expanded by the Porter family, who would reside here for more than 170 years. On the grounds and open to visitors are a carpenter's shop, carriage sheds, and a barn. The house museum was revamped and reopened in 2005 with brand-new exhibits and displays.

Waldo Homestead (860-456-0708), 96 Waldo Rd., Scotland. Open year-round by appointment and for special events. Free admission. A restored 1714 saltbox-style home, in the Waldo family until 1975, now maintained by the Scotland Historical Society with an extensive collection of 18th-century farming tools and equipment, as well as books and early American antiques. A well-attended Scottish Highland Festival is held here in fall (see *Special Events*).

HISTORIC SITES **Daniel Putnam Tyler Law Office** (860-774-7728), 25 Canterbury Rd. (CT 169), Brooklyn. Open mid-May–Columbus Day, Wed. and Sun. 1–5. Free admission. The restored circa-1820 office of country lawyer Daniel Putnam Tyler is furnished as it would have been in the mid–19th century. The lawyer, a great-grandson of local Revolutionary War hero General Israel Putnam, became clerk of the county and superior courts and a county court judge, and he also held state elective offices. Tyler practiced law in this modest white-clapboard building for more than 50 years until his death in 1875. There are changing displays and a permanent exhibit on "Old Put."

Frog Bridge, Bridge St., at the junction of CT 32 and US 66, Willimantic. You'll definitely want your camera when you visit what's quite possibly New England's quirkiest bridge. It's presided over by a quartet of bronze Volkswagen-sized amphibians perched atop concrete spools, a nod to both a popular 18th-century local legend about frogs and the city's long-ago thread industry.

♿ **Gurleyville Grist Mill** (860-429-9023), Stone Mill Rd., Storrs. Open late May–Columbus Day, Sun. 1–5; also by appointment. Free admission. A mill has stood at this site on the Fenton River since 1720. The existing structure and machinery are of 19th-century vintage; the mill is believed to be the state's only remaining stone gristmill. The miller's nearby house is open as a museum of local history. Wilbur Cross—author, Yale professor of literature, and governor of the state during the 1930s—once lived here.

Garden on the Bridge (860-465-3048; www.gardenclubofwindham.org), US 66, Willimantic. This historic stone arch bridge, built in 1857, no longer carries autos; instead, it's lined with native trees and 25 lushly planted flower beds.

Revolutionary War Office (860-916-1804), 149 West Town St., on the Lebanon green, Lebanon. Open Memorial Day–Labor Day, Sat. and Sun. noon–4. Admission by donation. General Washington, Governor Trumbull, the Comte de

Rochambeau, Lafayette, and other key officials in the Council of Safety met here periodically to coordinate supplies and plan military strategy. Before the war, this two-room circa-1730 structure served as the Trumbull family store. Nutmeggers call it the "Pentagon of the Revolution."

Wadsworth Stable (860-642-7558), on the Lebanon green, Lebanon, near the Governor Jonathan Trumbull House Museum (see *Historic Homes*). A rare example of Palladian-style architecture, and surely the only structure to claim that George Washington's *horse* slept there. In 1953, the stable was brought to Lebanon from Hartford, where the stable's owner, Revolutionary partisan Jeremiah Wadsworth, lived. He and Trumbull managed Connecticut's major contribution to the war effort—the supply of provisions to Washington's Continental troops. Washington referred to Trumbull as "Brother Jonathan" and to Connecticut as the "Provision State." For admission, inquire at the Governor Jonathan Trumbull House Museum.

TROUT HATCHERY ♿ **Quinebaug Valley Trout Hatchery** (860-564-7542), 141 Trout Hatchery Rd., off CT 14, in the Central Village section of Plainfield. The visitor center and hatchery is open daily 9:30–3:30. Free admission. At a glass wall, visitors can glimpse the scale (no pun) of the job of making sure there will be trout in the state's rivers and ponds for all fishing enthusiasts. This is one of the largest fish hatcheries in the East, producing 600,000 rainbow, brook, and brown trout—that's 320,000 pounds—every year for recreational fishing.

WINERIES **Sharpe Hill Vineyard** (860-974-3549; www.sharpehill.com), 108 Wade Rd., Pomfret. Open year-round, Fri.–Sun. 11–5. Tour this scenic vineyard, then sample award-winning wines in the early-American-style tasting room. Sharpe Hill has won 58 medals, but don't miss their signature Ballet of Angels. Visitors can also make advance reservations for gourmet French-influenced dining in the fireside tavern or seasonal outdoor wine garden (see *Dining Out*).

Taylor Brooke Winery (860-974-1263; www.taylorbrookewinery.com), 848 CT 171, Woodstock. Open May–Dec., Fri. 11–6; Sat. and Sun. 11–5. Specialty and top-notch vinifera wines are made from the grapes of 2,000 vines of Cabernet Franc, Riesling, and other varieties on Dick and Linda Auger's family farm. There are tours and tastings, and a shop selling gifts by local artisans and Connecticut-made gourmet foods.

SCENIC DRIVE: NATIONAL SCENIC BYWAY **CT 169**, the rolling two-lane highway along the spine of eastern Connecticut, takes visitors through farmland and hilly wooded areas interspersed with exclusive private schools, quaint inns, and villages seemingly untouched by time—Canterbury, Brooklyn, Pomfret, and Woodstock, to name a few—each with its historic landmarks and all with an air of another era. The 32-mile section of road from Lisbon north to Woodstock, near the Massachusetts border, is one of the prettiest drives in New England, among only 98 federally designated National Scenic Byways in the country, and one of only two in the state (the other is southeastern Connecticut's Merritt Parkway) chosen for their historical and cultural value, as well as unparalleled loveliness. The scenic route passes through what Congress has designated the **Quinebaug and Shetucket Rivers Valley National Heritage Corridor**. The 1,085-square-mile region of rural villages, farmland, historic mill towns, and scenic country lanes is considered the "last green valley" in the urban sprawl between Boston and Washington, DC, and includes 35 communities in northeastern Connecticut and south-central Massachusetts.

✷ To Do

BALLOONING **Brighter Skies Balloon Company** (860-963-0600; www.brighterskies.com), P.O. Box 158, South Woodstock 06267. Open year-round, daily—depending on conditions, of course. Reservations are required. Balloon flights at sunrise and just before sunset over Connecticut's rural northeastern hills, with breakfast or the traditional champagne toast.

ViewPoint Balloons (860-428-6769; www.cthotair.com), 690 Wrights Mill Rd., Coventry. Champagne flights over eastern and central Connecticut offered year-round.

BICYCLING **Air Line State Park Trail**, a shady 50-mile multiuse recreational path, is a cyclist's dream—a place to enjoy the Quiet Corner's rural beauty without sharing the road with motorists. The flat, smooth-surfaced (stone dust), and relatively straight route runs through several towns in the region along the path of the former Air Line railway—once the shortest route between Boston and New York City. The abandoned railroad bed passes a bucolic landscape of meadows, stone walls, historic barns, and ponds and streams. Stop and savor the views of Salmon River State Forest from the historic Lyman Viaduct, 137 feet above Dickinson Creek. The trail, which is still under construction, begins in East Hampton and runs north to Thompson. A 10-mile stretch between East Hampton and Hebron on the trail's southern end is complete—the parking area on Smith St. in East Hampton, near Lake Pocotopaug, is a good place to start the ride. There's another trailhead on CT 85 in Hebron. The trail is popular on weekends with walkers, joggers, equestrians, and cyclists; come during the week to enjoy solitude. The pleasant route is ideal for cyclists with young children in tow.

Among the area's helpful and knowledgeable bike shops are **The Silver Bicycle Company** (860-928-7370; www.thesilverbikeco.com) in Putnam, and **Scott's Cyclery** (860-423-8889; www.scottscyclery.com) in Willimantic.

BIRDING See The Connecticut Audubon Society Center at Pomfret under *Green Space*.

BOATING You can launch a boat on Morey Pond at the **Ashford–Union boundary** (CT 171); in **Coventry** on Coventry Lake; in **Hampton** on Pine Acres Lake; in **Mansfield** on Mansfield Hollow Lake; in **Plainfield** on Moosup Pond; in **Thompson** on Quaddick Reservoir and West Thompson Lake; and in **Woodstock** on Black Pond and Roseland Lake. See also *Green Space*.

FISHING This is a prime freshwater fishing area. Streams and lakes abound, and all locals have their favorite spots. In **Eastford** and **Chaplin**, along CT 198, is access to trout fishing areas on the Natchaug River. In **Willington**, a fly-fishing catch-and-release area on the Willimantic River can be reached from either CT 74 or the state welcome center on I-84 between Exit 70 and Exit 69 westbound; trout are stocked. In **Plainfield**, at the trout hatchery off CT 14 (see *To See*), there's access to trout fishing on the Moosup River. In **Mansfield Center**, Mansfield Hollow Lake, in Mansfield Hollow State Park off CT 195, is a favorite spot for bass and northern pike. In **South Coventry**, Waungumbaug (some call it Coventry) Lake off CT 31 has good bass fishing. In **Union**, Mashapaug Lake and Bigelow Pond are two popular trout ponds in Bigelow Hollow State Park, off CT 197. See also *Green Space.*

GOLF **Brooklyn Country Club** (860-779-9333), 170 South St., Brooklyn. Par 35, nine holes, 2,783 yards.

Harrisville Golf Course (860-928-6098; www.harrisvillegolfcourse.com), 125 Harrisville Rd., Woodstock. Par 36, nine holes, 5,830 yards.

Putnam Country Club (860-928-7748), 136 Chase Rd., Putnam. Par 72, 18 holes, 6,169 yards.

Raceway Golf Club (860-923-9593; www.racewaygolf.com), 205 East Thompson Rd., Thompson. Par 71, 18 holes, 6,412 yards.

Skungamaug River Golf Club (860-742-9348; www.skungamauggolf.com), 104 Folly Lane, Coventry. Par 70, 18 holes, 5,785 yards.

Twin Hills Country Club (860-742-9705; www.twinhillscountryclub.com), 199 Bread and Milk St., Coventry. Par 71, 18 holes, 6,274 yards.

Vineyard Valley Golf Club (860-974-2100; www.vineyardvalleygolfclub.com), 34 Brayman Hollow Rd. (CT 244), Pomfret Center. Par 36, nine holes, 3,033 yards.

HAYRIDES AND SLEIGH RIDES **Creamery Brook Bison** (860-779-0837; www.creamerybrookbison.net), 19 Purvis Rd., Brooklyn. Wagon tours every Sat., July–Sept.; ice cream shop open Apr.–Oct., Mon.–Sat., closed Sun.; Nov.–Mar., Wed.–Sat., closed Sun.–Tue. Take a tractor-pulled wagon to the pasture where a herd of more than 100 shaggy bison—also known as American buffalo—roam, and wait for the cows and calves to come over for a nibble of hay. Austin and Debbi Tanner's 120-acre working farm has a collection of resident farm animals, a shop selling homemade ice cream, and a retail store where the Tanners sell various cuts of bison meat, from burgers to steaks.

Edmondson's Farm (860-742-6124; 800-215-1505; www.edmondsonsfarm .com), 2627 Boston Turnpike (US 44), Coventry. Hayrides in Sept. and Oct. This farm is open year-round for all manner of plants, produce, and farm products, but fall means hayrides—via antique tractor or draft horse—around the farm's 32 acres of greenhouses, gardens, fields, and woods.

Palazzi Orchard (860-774-4363), 1393 North Rd., off CT 101, East Killingly. Open daily Sept.–Oct. A hilltop working apple orchard offering spectacular views of three states, and weekend tractor-drawn hayrides through the orchard. Tours of the barn, where there's a cider press and other equipment; a farm stand sells more than 20 varieties of apples, as well as cider and jellies.

HIKING **Mansfield Hollow State Park** (860-928-6121), Bassett Bridge Rd., off CT 195, Mansfield. Open daily 8 AM–sunset. Free admission. The variety of trails makes this park—with its rocky ridges and hilly woodland blanketing 26,000 acres—a favorite among local hikers; its proximity to the University of Connecticut makes it a popular escape from the rigors of academia. A footbridge spans the Fenton River, and 50 Foot Cliff affords views of the Quiet Corner's spectacular woodland and countryside. Intrepid hikers can follow the blue-blazed Nipmuck Trail on its 34-mile course to the Massachusetts border.

Mashamoquet Brook State Park (860-928-6121), 147 Wolf Den Dr., off US 44, Pomfret Center. Open year-round, daily 8 AM–sunset. Seasonal parking fee on weekends: residents $7; nonresidents $10. Of all the hikes in Connecticut, this is the one most fraught with local myth: It takes you to **Israel Putnam's wolf den**. Putnam is an important presence in this part of the state. He saw a good deal of military service—escaped death more than once in the French and Indian War, led the colonial troops at the battle of Bunker Hill, and later in that same war escaped capture by making a daring dash on horseback down a precipice in Greenwich. But it was here in Pomfret that he became truly legendary. According to one interesting tale, an old she-wolf was ravaging local flocks of sheep, and the farmers had no luck catching her. Israel Putnam crawled into her den in the dark of night, shot the wolf, and dragged her out to the cheers of his lantern-lit friends. Various versions of the story elaborate on the struggle and supply details on the roistering, all-night vigil at the mouth of the wolf's lair, but the upshot is that before he was 20 years old, Old Put had manifested the stuff of greatness. To follow in his footsteps, then, take the trail that leads past the campground down to the scene of the struggle. You can continue on a 5-mile loop with some mild climbs, through woodlands and marsh, past the rock formation Indian Chair, across Mashamoquet Brook, and, finally, back to the parking lot.

Rock Spring Wildlife Refuge (CT 97), Scotland. Open year-round, daily dawn–dusk. This little-known gem, managed by The Nature Conservancy, is a 450-acre tract of quiet woodland, home to wild turkeys, black bears, and bobcats. Take the 3.6-mile white-blazed trail that meanders by the Little River and past a multitude of old stone walls, remnants of abandoned colonial farmland. Don't miss the side trail, marked with yellow blazes, that leads to a lookout with a granite bench and lovely views of the Little River Valley, especially in autumn when the changing leaves put on a fiery display.

HORSEBACK RIDING AND HORSE CAMPING **Diamond A Ranch** (860-779-3000; www.daranch.net), 975 Hartford Turnpike (CT 101), Dayville. Reservations are required. Scenic trail rides through woods and fields on a rural 107-acre working farm and equestrian facility. Choose from a variety of trips, from one-hour jaunts to daylong trips that include a picnic or western-style cookout. Overnight expeditions (year-round, if the weather allows) include meals, gear, horses, and shelter; you bring a sleeping bag and pillow.

Silvermine Horse Camp (860-974-1562), Natchaug State Forest, Pilfershire Rd. (CT 198), Eastford. Open Apr. 15–Nov. Sites are free and available on a first-come, first-served basis. This campground is one of two in the state park system designated exclusively for equestrian use. There are 15 rustic sites with basic facilities. Campers must pack out their trash.

MOUNTAIN BIKING **James L. Goodwin State Forest** (860-455-9534), US 6, Hampton. Open year-round, daily dawn–dusk. Pleasant and easily ridable dirt and paved forest roads crisscross this 1,820-acre forest of hardwoods and towering evergreens. Follow the trails to a gravel railbed, which will lead you into the neighboring 12,935-acre **Natchaug State Forest**, where marshes, bogs, and thick stands of white pines are ideal for spotting birds and other wildlife.

The Silver Bicycle Company (860-928-7370; www.thesilverbikeco.com) in Putnam, and **Scott's Cyclery** (860-423-8889; www.scottscyclery.com) in Willimantic are full-service bike shops that can offer advice on riding in these two state forests.

SKYDIVING **Boston-Hartford FunSkydiving** (860-774-5867; 800-928-5867; www.funskydiving.com), Danielson Airport, 41 Airport Rd., Danielson. Open daily Apr.–Oct., weather permitting; reservations recommended. Tandem and solo parachuting starts with a 120-mile-per-hour free fall from 10,000 feet before your chute opens and you drift back to earth. No previous experience is required, but jumpers must be at least 18 years old. There's a picnic area with barbecue grills and picnic tables available for guests.

SPECTATOR SPORTS **Stafford Motor Speedway** (860-684-2783; www.staffordmotorspeedway.com), 55 West St. (CT 140), Stafford Springs. Open Apr.–Sept. NASCAR auto racing on a 0.5-mile paved oval track; modified late-model pro stocks; monster trucks late July, early Aug.

Thompson International Speedway (860-923-2280; www.thompsonspeedway.com), 205 East Thompson Rd., off CT 193, Thompson. Open Mar.–Oct. Professional, sportsman, street, and modified stock-car racing in a NASCAR weekly racing series.

✐ **University of Connecticut** (860-486-2724; www.uconnhuskies.com), main campus, CT 195, Storrs. Athletic events at Gampel Pavilion and playing fields on campus, as well as football at Rentschler Field in East Hartford. Basketball, soccer, football, baseball, men's and women's team events.

SWIMMING The lakes and ponds of the Quiet Corner provide ideal swimming for those who prefer fresh water and minimal wave action. Most of the swimming areas are in state parks, with shelters for changing and lifeguards on duty during the summer. In most cases there's a fee for parking, swimming, or both. Swimming is permitted at Bicentennial Pond, **Mansfield**; Coventry Lake, **Coventry**; Moosup Pond, **Plainfield**; Mashamoquet Brook State Park, **Pomfret**, and Quaddick Reservoir, **Thompson**. See also *Green Space*.

✷ Green Space

Quinebaug and Shetucket Rivers Valley National Heritage Corridor (860-963-7226; www.thelastgreenvalley.org). The National Park Service, together with state and local agencies, has designated an unprecedented 1,085-square-mile region that extends from Mystic, through the Quiet Corner, and into south-central Massachusetts as one of the country's "last green valleys." It is a region of small towns, villages, farmland, and forests in what once was a thriving, bustling complex of towns subsisting on fabric mills. Today it's indeed a green valley, with five state parks, seven state forests, and 16 state wildlife management areas, all dotted with more than 80 lakes and ponds. Its major artery is CT 169, but the full-color illustrated map/brochure published by the National Park Service suggests byways and small highways inviting you to explore at your leisure. The mission is to hold back the developers who would plant their urban malls on this inviting open space. Call for a copy of the brochure and other literature, or check their Web site.

NATURE PRESERVES **Albert E. Moss Forest**, at the junction of CT 195 and South Eagleville Rd., Storrs. Open to the public, this 157-acre wildlife and wildflower sanctuary serves as an outdoor classroom for botany students at the University of Connecticut. Moss, who spent his career studying New England forests, taught forestry from 1914 to 1942, back when UConn was known as an agricultural college.

The Connecticut Audubon Society Center at Pomfret Center (860-928-4948; www.ctaudubon.org), 189 Pomfret St. (CT 169), Pomfret. Open daily, dawn to dusk. Free admission. Some of the best birding in the state is on these 650 acres of former farm fields, a popular habitat for hard-to-spot grassland birds. The adjoining **Bafflin Sanctuary** adds 700 acres of woods, meadows, ponds, streams, hiking trails, and an environmental education facility. Ask about special programs like weekend workshops and guided bird walks. This is a designated Important Birding Area, with 200 feathered species; peak activity is in spring and fall when migrants are en route to and from their winter quarters.

Connecticut Audubon Society Center at Trail Wood (860-928-4948; www.ctaudubon.org), 93 Kenyon Rd. (off CT 97), Hampton. Open daily, dawn to dusk. Four miles of trails on a 168-acre farm, formerly the home of birder, naturalist, and author Edwin Way Teale. Many of Teale's Pulitzer Prize–winning writings on nature were inspired by his beloved Trail Wood, which offers visitors a pleasing mix of fields, forest, ponds, and wetlands to explore. Hikers are welcome anytime; guided walks and other activities are scheduled. A small museum, as well as Teale's writing cabin and study, are open by appointment. Trail maps (and a donation box) are at the information shed.

🐾 **James L. Goodwin State Forest and Conservation Center** (860-455-9534), 23 Potter Rd. (off US 6), Hampton. Trails open year-round, daily dawn to dusk. Formerly a private tree farm owned by noted conservationist James Goodwin, who donated the 1,820 acres of woodland, pine groves, marshes, and ponds to the state in 1964. His white-clapboard farmhouse is now a conservation center. A network of trails is open to hikers and cross-country skiers; cyclists and equestrians can enjoy miles of dirt forest roads. Fishing and boating on the ponds.

PARKS AND FORESTS For more information on these and other parks and forests in the Quiet Corner, contact the **Connecticut Department of Environmental Protection, Bureau of Parks and Forests** (860-424-3200; www.dep.state.ct.us). State parks and forests are open year-round, daily 8 AM–sunset. A parking fee ($7 for Connecticut residents; $10 for out-of-state visitors) is charged at the following state parks on weekends and holidays; there is no fee at state forests.

🐾 **Bigelow Hollow State Park** (860-684-3430), CT 171, Union. Activities include picnicking, fishing, hiking, boating, hunting, and cross-country skiing. Along with the adjoining **Nipmuck State Forest**, there are more than 9,000 acres of protected woodland, making this rural tract one of the largest unbroken forests in eastern Connecticut. The forest is best known for its **Laurel Sanctuary**, which bursts into clouds of pink and white mountain laurel blooms in June and July. The sanctuary entrance is on CT 190 in Union, west of the state park.

🐾 **Mashamoquet Brook State Park** (860-928-6121), 147 Wolf Den Dr., off US 44, Pomfret Center. A good trail system (the park is nearly 1,000 acres) for hikers; picnicking, fishing, swimming; nature trail, concession, and camping sites. Changing houses for swimmers; flush toilets. Follow the Wolf Den Trail (see *To Do*) to the wolf den where Revolutionary War hero General Israel Putnam is purported to have killed Connecticut's last wolf.

🐾 **Natchaug State Forest** (860-928-6121), off CT 198, Chaplin. A large (12,500 acres) forest with several miles of dirt forest roads for hiking, horseback riding, and cycling. Fishing, swimming, and canoeing are popular on the Natchaug River, which cuts through the forest. A scenic hemlock-filled picnic grove along the riverbank is the site of the 18th-century homestead and birthplace of Brigadier General Nathaniel Lyon, the first Union general killed in the Civil War.

🐾 **Quaddick State Park** (860-928-6121), 818 Town Farm Rd. (off US 44), Thompson. Originally a fishing area for the Nipmuck tribe, later Thompson's town farm, this popular 116-acre space contains a reservoir with a separate swimming pond. The sandy beach and cool water are major attractions; activities include hiking, fishing, and boating. There's a concession for food and drink during summer, as well as changing houses, flush toilets, and a boat ramp.

West Thompson Lake Recreation Area (860-923-2982), West Thompson Rd. (CT 193), Thompson. Open daily, dawn to dusk. Fishing and boating on a 200-acre lake. Wooded sites for camping; hiking trails, picnicking, cross-country skiing, snowshoeing, and ice fishing are among the activities available to visitors. The 1,700 acres of woods and open fields surrounding the lake make this a prime area for birding and wildlife viewing. Call for a schedule of interpretive programs. The lake was built by the U.S. Army Corps of Engineers in the 1960s when they dammed the Quinebaug River. Boat launch on the eastern shore.

✷ Lodging

RESORT 🏵 **The Spa at Grand Lake** (860-642-4306; 800-843-7721; www.thespa atgrandlake.com), 1667 Exeter Rd. (CT 207), Lebanon 06249. Open Apr.–Dec. A peaceful, rural retreat on 180 rural acres on Lake Williams. Individualized programs for weight loss and stress reduction: outdoor Olympic-sized pool, sauna, massage, tennis, yoga, Pilates, facials, and body treatments; 50 rooms with private bath. Packages, including lodging, meals, fitness classes, facilities, and a daily massage, $275–375.

INN ♿ **Inn at Woodstock Hill** (860-928-0528; www.woodstockhill.com), 94 Plaine Hill Rd. (off CT 169), Woodstock 06281-2912. This 19th-century Federal- and Georgian-style mansion, surrounded by unspoiled rural Connecticut countryside, has been transformed into a romantic getaway. Of the 21 rooms (18 in the main house, 3 in a guest cottage), some come with four-poster bed; others boast fireplace; all have private bath, TV, air-conditioning, and wireless Internet access. A 1900 shingled cottage on the property has three guest rooms with private bath and a shared sitting area. The main house was built in 1816 for William Bowen, whose grandson, New York publisher Henry C. Bowen, spent summers nearby at Roseland Cottage. Continental breakfast is included; lunch and dinner are served in the restaurant daily; brunch on Sun. (see *Dining Out*). $160–260.

BED & BREAKFASTS In addition to the listings below, B&B reservation services offer access to rooms available in establishments throughout the state. For a list, see *Bed & Breakfasts* in "What's Where in Connecticut."

The bed & breakfasts in this section are listed alphabetically by town and then by the lodging's name.

In Coventry 06238

🐾 **The Daniel Rust House** (860-742-0032; 877-348-0032; www.thedaniel rusthouse.com), 2011 Main St. Long known as the Bird in Hand, this 1731 center-chimney colonial with snazzy red trim opened as a tavern in 1800. Now a tranquil B&B, it still welcomes travelers after more than two centuries. The four guest rooms each have private bath and unique touches—maybe a fireplace, a whirlpool tub, or vintage wide-board floors; there's even a "secret" closet where slaves on the Underground Railroad were believed to have taken refuge. Outdoors, stone walls crisscross a rolling landscape, and perennial flower beds and an apple orchard invite strolling. A full breakfast is served in the formal dining room. $120–185.

Special Joys B&B (860-742-6359), 41 North River Rd. With a hexagonal turret front and slightly off-center, a veranda across the front, and pink as its signature color, all surrounded by gardens, Special Joys makes you smile before you're out of your car. As you enter, you see the doll and toy shop of Joy Kelleher, who, with her husband, runs the comfortable and homey inn. Antique dolls, stuffed animals, and toys of all sorts, sizes, and ages fill the house—some for sale, all for enjoying. B&B guests have their own entrance and a choice of porches and gardens. Two cozy and uniquely decorated guest rooms, each with private bath; a continental breakfast is served in the sunroom. $55–75. (See also *Selective Shopping*.)

In Mansfield and Storrs

The Fitch House (860-456-0922; www.fitchhouse.com), 563 Storrs Rd. (CT 195), Storrs 06250-0163. Massive Ionic columns and a classical pediment announce the Greek Revival taste of the architect-builder of this 1836 home, now an inviting B&B run by innkeeper Kay Holt. Three large guest rooms, named for previous owners of the house, have period antiques, private bath, and either a queen-sized canopy bed or four-poster bed; the Golding Room has a working fireplace. Two rooms can be connected to create a suite, if you require extra space. Common areas include a formal music room complete with Steinway piano, and the living room, where refreshments are always available. A classical garden enhances the experience, as does the elegant breakfast in the two-story solarium. The house is conveniently close to the University of Connecticut. Ask about special packages like Victorian Christmas and 1950s Drive-In Movies. $125–145.

🐾 **Jarnoval Bay B&B** (860-455-1938; www.jarnovalbay.com), 10 Kaya Lane, Mansfield Center 06250. An open and airy three-story contemporary post-and-beam home with lots of soaring glass and native oak makes for a comfortable retreat. Outdoor decks overlook the gardens and the Mansfield Hollow Reservoir beyond. One suite has a private bath and kitchenette; two other guest rooms share a bath and a sitting room with wood-burning stove. Each has a private entrance. Full breakfast. $115–145.

In Pomfret 06259 and Pomfret Center 06259

🐾 ✐ **Chickadee Cottage B&B** (860-870-5065; www.chickadeecottage.com), 70 Averill Rd. (US 44), Pomfret Center. The location, next to a 500-acre Audubon preserve, is perfect if you've come to the Quiet Corner to do some serious birding. A private and spacious carriage house has a kitchenette, gas-log woodstove, and private deck, all on 4 rural acres. The new Lower Nest accommodation sleeps four. In addition to the nature preserve, the B&B also neighbors the Air Line State Park Trail, a scenic hiking and biking path that crosses six towns. Continental-plus breakfast. $210; weekly rates are available.

Cobbscroft (860-928-5560; 800-928-5560; www.cobbscroft.com), 349 Pomfret St. (CT 169), Pomfret. Two artists are at work in this 1780 white-clapboard house, which has been welcoming overnight guests since 1985. The location, just across the street from the prestigious Pomfret School, is ideal for visiting parents. Tom McCobb's oil, water, and acrylic paintings of New England landscapes enliven the walls (and are for sale), and Janet McCobb's bold decorating flair is evident everywhere—in the green-and-white-striped bathroom with gold-footed tub, in the deep red walls of the parlor, as well as in the notecards and other items offered in the studio shop. There are three upstairs guest rooms, all with private bath; there's also a downstairs suite with a private bath and fireplace. Guests are welcome to check out the art gallery, where new works are always in progress, as well as the shop with whimsical painted and stenciled pine furniture. A full breakfast is served in the sunny dining room. $90–125.

Feather Hill Bed & Breakfast (860-963-0522; 866-963-0522; www.featherhillbedandbreakfast.com), 151 Mashamoquet Rd. (US 44), Pomfret. A historic center-hall colonial turned B&B that's nicely furnished and country comfortable, and close to UConn and the area's private schools. Innkeepers Angela and Fred Spring offer three tastefully furnished guest rooms and a suite, all with private bath, some with a Jacuzzi tub. There's also a separate cottage that's roomy and sleeps four. Guests can relax in front of the parlor fireplace or on the enclosed porch. The 8 acres surrounding the house include an expansive lawn and a swimming pool; outdoorsy types will love the Air Line State Park Trail, a popular destination for biking or hiking that runs right behind the property. Full breakfast includes warm fruit compote, the inn's signature dish. $110–225.

In Putnam 06260

Thurber House (860-928-6776), 78 Liberty Way (CT 21). On the village green, this traditional colonial was once the home of artist T. J. Thurber. Two guest rooms with fireplace, private bath, full breakfast. Close to the Putnam antiques district. $80.

Whitehaven (860-367-2064; www.whitehaven-ct.com), 255 East Putnam Rd. A restored 19th-century home—first a stagecoach inn, later a chicken farm—now offers two elegant suites, each with a private bath, one with its own veranda. Future plans for the 5-acre property include a swimming pool and gardens. For now, guests can enjoy the rambling wicker-filled porch, the hammock on the upper porch, and the comfy family room with grand piano and fireplace. Full gourmet breakfast. $150–175.

In Thompson

🏅 ✐ **Corttis Inn** (860-935-5652), 235 Corttis Rd., Thompson (North Grosvenor Dale) 06255. A genuine colonial—1758—that has been in the same family for generations. Outdoors, 900 acres crisscrossed with stone walls are perfect for hiking, biking, cross-country skiing, and viewing the resident wildlife that inhabits the property's woodland and ponds. Indoors, relax by the cozy fireplace. There are six rooms and one suite, all with private bath. The inn is close to Thompson Motor Speedway and the area's private schools. A full breakfast is served. $65–150.

ꝏ ♿ **Lord Thompson Manor** (860-923-3886; www.lordthompsonmanor.com), CT 200, P.O. Box 428, Thompson 06277. It's easy to see why this spectacular 30-room country estate—built in 1917 as a summer retreat for a wealthy industrialist—is a favorite among brides-to-be looking for a romantic spot to say their I dos. The manor, with its dramatic 0.5-mile approach, sits amid 42 acres of grounds designed by iconic landscape architect Frederick Law Olmsted. Common areas boast magnificent touches: Fireplaces carved out of African marble, parquet floors, rich wood paneling, lofty ceilings, and soaring windows—all hark back to the manor's opulent past. Of the six guest rooms, four are spacious luxury suites with fireplaces, antiques, and private baths. Full breakfast. Just down the road, **The Cottage House** (860-923-3886; www.ltmcottagehouse.com), 351 CT 193, has six light and airy guest rooms and a spa. $125–175.

THE TOLLAND INN, ON TOLLAND'S HISTORIC TOWN GREEN, IS ONE OF MANY CHARMING BED & BREAKFASTS SCATTERED AROUND THE QUIET CORNER.

Courtesy Tolland Inn

In Tolland 06084

Tolland Inn (860-872-0800; 877-465-0800; www.tollandinn.com), 63 Tolland Green (CT 74). Standing midway along the town green, this former inn returned to its original calling after a long hiatus. Innkeepers Susan and Steve Beeching have redesigned and expanded, adding a sunroom with a massive fireplace, wraparound porch, and a new Treehouse Suite. There are books everywhere, lovely gardens, and a pair of birds that nest on the front porch. The rooms, individually decorated, are furnished with a combination of antiques and custom furniture designed and built by Steve Beeching. Three rooms, and three suites with sitting rooms; all with fireplace and private bath, most with hot tub. Full breakfast with home-baked Belgian waffles and specialty French toast. $99–239.

In Woodstock 06281 and South Woodstock 06267

Elias Child House B&B (860-974-9836; 877-974-9836; www.eliaschildhouse.com), 50 Perrin Rd., off CT 171, Woodstock. A handsome 18th-century colonial—complete with nine fireplaces, two walk-in cooking hearths, and a beehive oven—set on 47 lovely acres. Three guest rooms (one suite) with antiques, fireplaces, air-conditioning, and private bath. Guests are welcome to stroll the gardens and enjoy the pool. Ask about special programs like hearth-cooked dinners, hikes, and massages. Full country breakfast. $115–145.

The Mansion at Bald Hill (860-974-3456; www.mansionatbaldhill.com), 29 Plaine Hill Rd., off CT 171, South Woodstock. This 21-room mansion offers 21st-century guests a taste of the Victorian-era good life enjoyed by the railroad heiress who once summered here. It manages to be homey and welcoming while retaining its grandeur, from the formal wood-paneled common rooms and 13 fireplaces to the well-manicured perennial gardens. Six guest rooms offer a range of accommodations, from the Garden Room painted in cheery hues and overlooking the perennial beds to the elegant Mrs. Bowen's Suite, with four-poster bed, fireplace, and sitting area. A full breakfast is served in the formal dining room or outdoors on the terrace. New: gourmet dining that's open to the public (see *Dining Out*). $125–210.

In other Quiet Corner towns

These B&Bs are listed alphabetically by the lodging's name.

The Inn Keeper's Place (860-684-7202; www.innkeepersplace.com), 111 Stafford St., Stafford Springs 06076. A charming 18th-century home—part 1778 Federal-style brick, part circa-1732 saltbox—with many period architectural features, from the original hand-carved wood molding, dome window, and plank floors to the exterior bricks from England. The house served as a tavern and meetinghouse before its latest incarnation as a cozy base for exploring the Quiet Corner, or the adjoining 200-acre wildlife refuge. There are two guest rooms (one with private bath) and one spacious suite. Full breakfast. $125–165.

Nathan Fuller House (860-456-0687; www.nathanfullerhouse.com), 147 Plains Rd., Scotland 06264. On a real country road, set on a lot trimmed by a stone wall, its clapboards a reserved beige, the Nathan Fuller House invites getaways. If you crave peace and quiet, it's here in this 1790s Cape attached to an 1820 center-hall colonial. Three rooms, two with fireplace; guests share two baths. A full breakfast is served. Children older than 10 are welcome (they'll love the game room), but the inn can't accommodate pets, as cats reside on the premises. A full breakfast is served. $80–90.

The Pond House Bed & Breakfast (860-684-1644; www.pondhousebb.com), 19 Crystal Lake Rd., Stafford Springs 06076. A rustic wooded retreat, where you can explore 4 acres of quiet woodland with a private pond, brooks, and a waterfall. Two cozy guest rooms with two shared baths are nicely furnished with antiques and views of the pond. A full or continental breakfast is served. An art gallery and an antiques shop across the pond are perfect for browsing. $85.

♿ **Safe Haven Bed & Breakfast** (860-455-1101; www.staywithsafehaven.com), 39 Drain St., off US 6, Hampton 06247. Not your typical Quiet Corner 18th-century accommodations. Here is a dramatic A-frame home reminiscent of a rustic western lodge, built of native fieldstone and timber, complete with soaring ceilings and lots of light. Edie Roxburgh started welcoming overnight guests to her 90-acre alpaca farm in 2005 and has created a warm and friendly destination for people looking to stay someplace unique. Common areas and guest rooms feature artifacts from around the world as well as Edie's own paintings. Guests can stay in the spacious suite with elegant decor and private balcony; or in the two rooms, one with hand-painted garden murals, the other done entirely in soothing white. Outside is a hot tub, a stocked stream for fishing, hiking trails, and pastures where the herd of gentle alpacas roams. Breakfast is served in front of the dining room's massive fieldstone fireplace, in view of the brand-new gourmet kitchen. $150–250.

HOTELS 🐾 ♿ **Holiday Inn Express Hotel & Suites** (860-779-3200; 877-580-7108), 16 Tracy Rd., Exit 94 off I-395, Dayville 06241. This Holiday Inn offers 78 rooms, including 17 suites, as well as a fitness room, restaurant and lounge, and indoor pool. Continental breakfast. Another location in Plainfield (860-564-1010; 800-465-4329) at 18 Pratt Rd. $109–149.

🐾 ♿ **Country Hearth Inn & Suites** (860-928-7961; 800-541-7304; www.countryhearthinnputnam.com), 5 Heritage Rd., Putnam 06260. A clean and comfortable small hotel on 7 landscaped acres, with a pond, outdoor pool, 40 rooms, and one suite. Mexican restaurant and lounge. Near Putnam antiques district and Old Sturbridge Village, just across the border in Massachusetts. Continental breakfast. $62–120.

♿ **Nathan Hale Inn and Conference Center** (860-427-7888; www.nathanhaleinn.com), 855 Bolton Rd., Storrs 06268. A new full-service hotel smack in the middle of the UConn campus, named for Connecticut's state hero who was born in nearby Coventry. The 100 rooms are standard hotel accommodations; some rooms have upgraded amenities such as microwave ovens and refrigerators. **The Blue Oak Restaurant** serves casual American cuisine for breakfast, lunch, and dinner; **True Blue Tavern** has a pub-like feel and an outdoor deck. An indoor pool and a spa, a fitness center, and a business center round out the amenities. $169–219.

CAMPGROUNDS There are numerous places to spend the night outdoors in northeastern Connecticut, from private campgrounds with a wide variety of amenities to rustic and inexpensive campsites in state parks, forests, and recreation areas. Mashamoquet Brook State Park in **Pomfret** has two campgrounds; West Thompson Lake Recreation Area in **Thompson** offers camping in a quiet natural setting; and Natchaug State Forest in **Eastford** maintains a campground just for equestrians (see *To Do*) as well as several primitive backcountry sites and shelters available by reservation only. For information and reservations for camping in state parks and forests, call the **Department of Environmental Protection's State Parks Division** (860-424-3200; 866-287-2757). A selection of Quiet Corner private campgrounds is described below; for a complete listing, obtain a copy of the Connecticut Campground Owners' Association's annual *Connecticut Campground Directory* (860-521-4704; 14 Rumford St., West Hartford 06107) or view it online at www.campconn.com.

🐾 **Beaver Pines Campground** (860-974-0110; www.beaverpinescampground.com), 1728 CT 198, Woodstock 06281. Open mid-Apr.–mid-Oct. A quiet retreat surrounded by 7,500-acre Nipmuck State Forest. The 50 sites range from rustic tent sites to trailer sites with the usual amenities. Facilities include playing fields, hiking trails, a playground, and a pond for fishing. The emphasis here is on quiet, so there are few planned activities. $25–35.

🐾 ✐ **Brialee R.V. and Tent Park** (860-429-8359; 800-303-2267; www.brialee.net), 174 Laurel Lane, off CT 89, Ashford 06278. Open Apr.–Oct. A grassy and shaded family campground with 195 sites on 120 acres in Natchaug State Forest. There's plenty to do for everyone in the family, mostly in the form of planned activities, from games and crafts to mountain bike races, volleyball games, wagon tours, and live music. In 2005, a video arcade, outdoor rides for youngsters, and wireless Internet access were added. $15–55.

🐾 ✐ **Charlie Brown Campground** (860-974-0142; 877-974-0142; www.ctcampground.com), 98 Chaplin Rd. (CT 198), Eastford 06242. Open mid-Apr.–mid-Oct. Outdoor enthusiasts take note: The rural surroundings include fishing on the Natchaug River and hiking and biking in Natchaug State Forest. Of the 128 sites, 5 are just for tents; all are spread across 30 acres. Planned activities include the usual suspects: bingo, crafts, karaoke, and holiday celebrations. $25–57.

🐾 ✐ **Mineral Springs Campground** (860-684-2993; www.mineralspringscampground.com), 135 Leonard Rd., off CT 32, Stafford Springs 06076. Open May–mid-Oct. If you're looking for rustic wilderness-style sites, there are 21 of them; others have hookups for trailer camping. Activities include fishing, mountain biking, and hiking. There's also a pool, an arcade, and special events like bingo and live entertainment. $25–35.

🐾 ✐ **Nickerson Park Family Campground** (860-455-0007; www.nickersonpark.com), 1036 Phoenixville Rd. (CT 198), Chaplin 06235. This is one of the few campgrounds in the Quiet Corner that's open year-round. It's on the banks of the Natchaug River (swimming, tubing, trout fishing), just across from Natchaug State Forest (mountain biking, hiking, hunting). Of the 100 sites, half are along the riverbank. Wireless Internet access is available at most sites. $30–40.

🐾 ✐ **River Bend Campground** (860-564-3440; www.riverbendcamp.com), 41 Pond St. (CT 14A), Oneco 06373. Open mid-Apr.–mid-Oct. As the name suggests, the campground is on a river—the Moosup River, in this case—which offers swimming, fishing, and boating (canoes and kayaks are available for rent). There are 160 sites and lots of activities; kids love to pan for gems in the replicated mine. Campsites $33–45; rental units (log cabins and trailers) $68–128.

🐾 ✐ **Water's Edge Family Campground** (860-642-7470; reservations 800-828-6478; www.watersedgecampground.com), 271 Leonard Bridge Rd., Lebanon 06249. Open mid-Apr.–mid-Oct. Some of the 200 sites are right on the shore of a 10-acre spring-fed lake, perfect for swimming and fishing. Two playgrounds, ball courts, a new swimming pool, and planned activities from family bingo and kids crafts to live entertainment, dancing, pizza parties, and hayrides. $35–45.

✱ Where to Eat

DINING OUT ♿ **Altnaveigh Inn** (860-429-4490; www.altnaveighinn.com), 957 Storrs Rd. (CT 195), Storrs. Lunch served Tue.–Fri.; dinner Tue.–Sat.; closed Sun. and Mon. Reservations suggested. This rambling 1734 farmhouse turned restaurant, which gets its name from the Gaelic word for "hilltop," is fresh off a recent renovation. It's also close to the University of Connecticut campus, making it an ideal place to dine with visiting parents. The kitchen turns out great seasonally changing Continental fare—Maryland crabcakes, grilled New Zealand rack of lamb, pan-fried brook trout. Dine by the fireplace or, in warm weather, on the fieldstone patio. $28–38.

The Courthouse Bar & Grille (860-963-0074; www.courthousebarandgrille.com), 121 Main St., Putnam. Open daily for lunch and dinner. This downtown bar and grill occupies the early-20th-century digs of the historic courthouse in the center of town. The menu has fun with this heritage, organizing dishes into "opening statements" (appetizers), "baliff's beef" (hand-carved steaks), "closing arguments" (desserts) . . . you get the idea. $12–25.

♿ **85 Main Restaurant & Raw Bar** (860-928-1660; www.85main.com), 85 Main St. (off US 44), Putnam. Open for lunch and dinner daily. Among the many antiques shops that have settled in downtown Putnam, here's the perfect storefront restaurant (formerly The Vine Bistro)—offering New American fusion cuisine in casual surroundings. Start with roasted-corn and clam chowder or one of the creative salads tossed with locally grown greens. The seasonally adjusted menu features dishes such as veal meat loaf with red bliss potatoes and caramelized brussels sprouts, lamb osso buco with polenta and broccoli rabe, and the 85 Main seafood bowl, studded with lobster, shrimp, mussels, clams, and whitefish in a saffron, tomato, fennel, and fresh herb broth. The bar has its own lighter menu: think steamers, burgers, pulled pork sandwiches, and crabcakes. $13–25.

The Fireside Tavern at Sharpe Hill Vineyard (860-974-3549; www.sharpehill.com), 108 Wade Rd., Pomfret. Open for lunch Fri.–Sun.; dinner on select Fridays; call for a schedule and reservations, which are required (as much as four weeks in advance). French-accented gourmet meals, a charming hilltop vineyard setting, and spectacular views of three states elevate this restaurant above the ordinary. The changing menu, which specializes in wood-grilled meats and relies on locally grown ingredients, might feature sea bass with rosemary and olive oil, spicy Creole shrimp with mango chutney, or chicken with fresh herbs and lemon-thyme rice. In-season, meals are served alfresco in the wine garden. When the weather turns cold, dining fireside in the cozy tavern is equally charming. Be sure to visit the tasting room, where the vineyard's medal-winning wines are ready for sampling. $24–35.

♿ **The Harvest** (860-928-0008; www.harvestrestaurant.com), 37 Putnam Rd. (US 44), Pomfret. Open for lunch Tue.–Fri.; dinner Tue.–Sun.; Sun. brunch; closed Mon. Fine dining in a 1785 homestead that is a beloved favorite among locals, weekend visitors, and Pomfret School parents: there are four dining rooms dressed in antiques and local art, and a cozy bar and lounge that offers its own bistro menu. The kitchen takes full advantage of the region's seasonal flavors in dishes that blend creative American fare with international flavors, most notably the repertoire of authentic Japanese dishes. To get the full effect, start with sushi (yellowtail and scallion roll), then order salad (poached pears and caramelized pecans with baby spinach) and an entrée (roasted salmon with ginger butter and white wine). Save room for house-made sweet endings like white chocolate bread custard with warm chocolate sauce. Sun. brunch packs 'em in for vanilla crème brûlée French toast and made-to-order omelets. Dedicated oenophiles will appreciate the award-winning 6,000-bottle wine cellar. $16–34.

The Mansion at Bald Hill (860-974-3456; www.mansionatbaldhill.com), 29 Plaine Hill Rd., off CT 171, South Woodstock. Open for dinner Tue.–Sun.; closed Mon. The Mansion is one of the most gracious lodgings in the Quiet Corner (see *Lodging*); now it ups the ante by serving seasonal gourmet cuisine to the public. Standouts on

♿ **Golden Lamb Buttery** (860-774-4423; www.thegoldenlamb.com), 499 Wolf Den Rd. (off CT 169), Brooklyn. Opens sometime in spring and closes in late Dec. The Golden Lamb serves dinner only on Fri. and Sat. at 7. Lunch is served Tue.–Sat. noon–2:30. Reservations are essential, since you're truly treated as a guest. This is more than a restaurant; it is one of Connecticut's most unusual and memorable dining experiences, as it has been for more than 40 years with Bob and Virginia ("Jimmy") Booth at the helm. (In 2008, their granddaughter, Katie, became the new hostess and proprietor.) For dinner, you'll assemble at 7 in Hillandale Farm's vintage red barn, where an assortment of antiques, heirlooms, and whimsical gleanings promote conversation. You're then led through an impossibly tiny kitchen where the legendary gourmet meals are prepared into a trio of dining rooms. On the walls are ecstatic reviews of the restaurant's triumphs. You're invited to go on a hayride to view the 1,000-acre grounds, with grazing sheep, transient deer, and rambling stone walls. Music is provided on the hayride and during dinner by a singing guitarist. Meals are prix fixe and include a choice of soups along with a selection of entrées that might feature sautéed shrimp in puff pastry with creamy lemon-dill sauce, chateaubriand, or the house specialty: roast duckling topped with orange marmalade and served with wild rice. The vegetable courses change with the seasons—peas with mint, tomatoes with basil, and the like, fresh from the garden. The desserts are exquisite: Poppyseed cake with praline frosting, chocolate hazelnut torte, and cheesecake with raspberry sauce are a few of the kitchen's creations. In December, there are special holiday festivities. Prix fixe dinner is $75 per person; à la carte lunch around $25.

THE GOLDEN LAMB BUTTERY IN BROOKLYN

Kim Grant

the exceptional menu include Maine lobster strudel, with sweet tomato relish; New Zealand rack of lamb with roasted turnip and black pepper potato hash; and sage-roasted chicken with Parmesan risotto. $17–31.

♿ **Inn at Woodstock Hill** (860-928-0528; www.woodstockhill.com), 94 Plaine Hill Rd. (just off CT 169), Woodstock. Lunch Tue.–Sat. (Mar.–Dec.); dinner daily; Sun. brunch. Reservations are suggested. The grand piano provides tranquil background music; the pale pink table linen reflects careful service and properly prepared dishes. This is the restaurant of an upscale country inn (see *Lodging*), and the cuisine, described as American Continental, bears out the claim and has captured the attention of travel writers around the country. New England seafood chowder, wild mushroom ravioli, and saffron lobster bisque are among the appetizers. Entrées feature seafood: blackened tuna steak with Creole sauce, seared Atlantic salmon with a honey-mustard glaze, or pecan-encrusted red snapper topped with cranberry salsa. For meat fanciers, there's filet mignon with Madagascar green peppercorn sauce; duck, pork tenderloin, and veal dishes; or rack of lamb. Cap off your meal with a scrumptious caramel chocolate pecan torte. $18–40.

Still River Café (860-974-9988; www.stillrivercafe.com), North Ashford Farm, 134 Union Rd., Eastford. Open for dinner Fri. and Sat.; lunch and brunch on Sun.; closed Jan.–mid-Mar. Reservations are recommended. Everyone is saying it: This sophisticated country bistro on a 27-acre farm is one of the state's rising culinary stars. Urban émigrés and gastronomes happily make the trek to this truly special place for seasonal contemporary American cuisine. Chef-owners Bob and Kara Brooks take the farm-to-table approach, turning out daily-changing dishes using local and organic ingredients. Despite the pastoral surroundings—the café resides in a converted 19th-century barn—the food is anything but rustic. Starters such as house-made gnocchi with polenta-encrusted sweetbreads and squash blossom beignets are followed by equally enticing entrées. The list might offer George's Bank scallops, cranberry and apple stuffed quail, and saffron and golden beet risotto, to name a few. The lemon-thyme crème brûlée is a subtle finish. $24–34.

EATING OUT ♿ **Angellino's** (860-450-7071; www.angellinos.com), 135 Storrs Rd. (CT 195), Mansfield. Open daily for lunch and dinner. A dependable menu of Italian favorites in a friendly place that's popular with families as well as UConn students and their visiting parents. Start with grilled *ciabatta* bread topped with chicken and spicy chipotle pesto, the roasted-pepper antipasto, or mussels steamed in garlic, herbs, olive oil, and chorizo. Meals are equally robust—if you're a fan of Italian specialties like osso buco, eggplant parmigiana, and pasta every which way (you can create your own with a dozen sauces), you'll go home happy. $12–24. Another location at 346 Kelly Rd. in Vernon (860-644-7702).

♿ **Bidwell Tavern** (860-742-6978), 1260 Main St. (CT 31), South Coventry. Open daily for lunch, dinner, and late-night snacks. Built in 1822 as a tavern, the Bidwell has changed and grown into a locally popular café but maintains its historic flavor. Among the latter-day additions is a two-level double porch and garden room, perfect for snacks or mealtimes. Specialties of the house include 26 varieties of chicken wings—Buffalo, garlic pepper, ranch, teriyaki—and the interesting choice: mild, hot, or complicated. They sell more than 3,000 pounds a week that are, more often than not, washed down with their two dozen or so beers on tap. There are 14-ounce steaks to be had, as well as ribs, veal, seafood, and vegetarian dishes. Live music Wed.–Sun. $10–22.

George's Galley (860-774-7111), 55 Main St. (CT 12), Danielson. Open Mon.–Wed. until 5:30 PM (take-out only after 2:30); Thu.–Sat. until 7; closed Sun. When absolutely nothing but breakfast will do, stop in at this in-town restaurant for a morning meal any hour of the day. Otherwise, choose from one of the standard family classics, like a turkey dinner with all the fixings. $5–15.

The Pickled Pepper Café (860-963-0401), 172 Main St., Putnam. Open daily for breakfast and lunch; breakfast served all day. Generous portions of diner fare, from omelets and hot coffee in the morning to soups, sandwiches, and burgers later on. Creative deviations include the fresh grilled tuna salad and Muenster cheese melt, and the baked potatoes stuffed with a variety of toppings. $3–8.

Pyzzz Brick Oven Pizza & Tavern (860-928-7424), 8 Harris St., Putnam. A little hard to find, but this tiny no-frills tavern on the outskirts of Putnam's 19th-century brick downtown makes oh-so-tasty authentic Italian brick-oven pies. The atmosphere is casual and friendly—a nice mix of families, regulars, and devoted patrons who trek across the state on a regular basis to savor no-fuss traditional pizzas and creative specials that celebrate the region's seasonal bounty, like native corn and tomatoes with cilantro in late summer. Others are topped with everything from leeks and chicken to feta, garlic, and spinach. We can't say enough about the dessert pizzas that come with peanut butter, chocolate, and other sinful ingredients. $7–15.

The Desert Café (860-774-3397; www.raindesert.com), 49 Cottage St., Danielson. Open Sun.–Thu. 11:30 AM–1 AM; Fri. and Sat. until 2 AM. In Danielson's downtown is a local treasure: a lively little café with an funky menu and decent live music. The music-inspired menu (Frank Zappa Spinach Salad, John and Yoko Antipasto, Maggie's Farm Turkey Sandwich) certainly has a sense of humor and revolves around pub-style appetizers, salads, and a long list of burgers and sandwiches, including several options for vegetarians. Open-mike nights are popular; other times, bands belt out jazz, rock, folk, blues, and reggae. $7–13.

♿ **Stoggy Hollow General Store and Restaurant** (860-974-3814), CT 198, Woodstock Valley. Opens daily 7 AM–8 PM. Close to the road, rustic, informal, and inviting, with outdoor seating in summer, Stoggy Hollow manages to combine the atmosphere of an old-time general store and bakery with a small down-home café. Breakfast features omelets and buttermilk pancakes; soups, burgers, pizza, and sandwiches later in the day. Dinner entrées might include fish-and-chips or prime rib. Lots of regulars come here just for the homemade pies and other tasty desserts. $3–10.

Thai Basil (860-774-1986), 187 North St., Brooklyn. Open daily for lunch and dinner. Locally adored spot that charms diners the old-fashioned way, with warm service and well-prepared renditions of authentic Thai cuisine. $8–16.

Traveler Restaurant: The Food and Book People (860-684-4920), 1257 Bulkley Hwy. (CT 171), Union.

Open daily for breakfast, lunch, and dinner. The specialty at this casual restaurant on the state line is turkey—white meat, dark meat, or mixed—prepared five ways, but the menu runs the gamut from pasta and chicken to seafood and steak. Homey desserts include hot blackberry cobbler with ice cream. The second specialty, to the delight of many a bibliophile, is free books. The foyer and the interior walls are lined with them; diners are encouraged to find a good one and start right in. Take it along when you leave. You've got to love the "Three Free Books" policy: If you eat here, you're welcome to take three books home, free of charge. With thousands of volumes in the collection, you should have no problem finding some that you like. An added treat: The walls of the restaurant are crowded with autographed photographs of myriad famous authors. $8–15.

The Vanilla Bean Café (860-928-1562; www.thevanillabeancafe.com), junction of CT 169 and US 44 with CT 97, Pomfret. Open for lunch daily; dinner Wed.–Sun.; breakfast Sat. and Sun. This early-19th-century yellow barn is a Quiet Corner icon and a magnet for bikers (astride both Cannondales and Harleys), families, and Sunday drivers who make the pilgrimage to "The Bean" on a regular basis for the creative casual dining and roster of live music, from folk and acoustic to indie and rock. An innovative menu, with daily specials posted on the board, features quesadillas (shrimp and Canadian bacon with watermelon salsa), sandwiches (roast beef and Brie), soups (sesame garlic chicken), and other hearty standbys at lunch. Dinner, which is kicked up a few notches, might be herb-crusted salmon with brown rice and collard greens, chipotle and lime marinated flank steak, or chicken and chorizo with fingerling potatoes in a spicy garlic cream sauce. $12–22.

Willimantic Brewing Company/ Main Street Café (860-423-6777; www.willibrew.com), 967 Main St., Willimantic. Open daily for lunch and dinner. "Beer," Benjamin Franklin once opined, "is living proof that God loves us and wants us to be happy." This lively pub and brewery, housed in a historic former U.S. post office building, sports that famous utterance on its beer-themed menu. You can wash down a Parcel Post flatbread pizza with Address Unknown IPA, or quaff a Rural Route Red while noshing on a Bulk Mail Burrito. House-brewed ales find their way into many dishes, from the steamed mussels to the beer-battered fried cod. Today the pub is in the customer lobby, with gleaming marble and terrazzo floors, and soaring 21-foot ceilings; the dining room is in the employee workroom, where you can feast on generous portions of pub food—as well as pizza, wraps, seafood, steak, pasta, and chicken—and see the kettles where a variety of brews are crafted. Live music, game and movie nights, special beer dinners, and beer tastings are always on tap. Pizza and sandwiches $7–10; entrées $13–19.

Willington Pizza House (860-429-7433; www.willingtonpizza.com), CT 32, 0.5 mile east of the junction with CT 195, Willington. Open daily for lunch and dinner. A sprawling, comfortable place built around a 200-year-old house and decorated with carousel horses. Great for families, it's recommended by the locals. What began as a humble four-seat pizza joint now seats 200 and serves pies with all the old favorite toppings. To broaden your horizons, consider the national-award-winning Red Potato Pizza (featured on network TV), which comes with sour cream, bacon, chives, and cheddar cheese, or the seafood pizza, covered with shrimp, snow crabs, and scallops. Other menu possibilities revolve around Italian standards: spaghetti, ravioli, lasagna, and chicken parmigiana; and there's a kiddie menu. **Willington Pizza Too** (860-429-9030), at the intersection of CT 74 and CT 32 in the Phelps Crossing shopping center, is a branch operation, attesting to the popularity of the original. Pizzas $6–19; entrées up to $14.

SNACKS **Chelle's 50s Car Hop Diner** (860-684-6622), 107 West Stafford Rd. (CT 190), Stafford Springs. The name pretty much says it all. Elvis has his photos on the walls and his tunes on the jukebox; waitresses wear poodle skirts and bobby socks; the menu features 2-foot-long hot dogs and breakfast all day.

Java Jive (860-963-1241), 283 CT 169, Woodstock. Open daily until 6 PM. This friendly coffeehouse next to the Woodstock fairgrounds serves breakfast all day, plus pastries, soups, and sandwiches, making it the perfect stop for a snack or a sandwich to take on the road. $4–8.

Jessica Tuesday's (860-928-5118), 35 Main St., Putnam. Open Mon.–Fri. 9–3:30; Sat. 11–3:30; closed Sun. This upscale deli housed in the former ticket office next to Putnam's vintage train station is the ideal place to recharge during a weekend spent trolling Putnam's antiques shops. The menu features an eclectic selection of homemade sandwiches, wraps, salads, soups, and desserts. $6–9.

Monet's Table (860-896-1709; www.monetscatering.com), 71 Hartford Turnpike, Tolland. Open Tue.–Fri. 11–6. Chef-owner Debra Bahler has scaled down her beloved jewel box of a restaurant into a marketplace, where gourmet take-home foods are homey, seasonal, and fresh. Each dish is more delectable than the next; corn and bacon chowder, pulled pork, sweet mashed potatoes, grilled hazelnut-crusted chicken. Just be sure to leave room for desserts like banana caramel bread pudding. $7–20.

Mrs. Bridge's Pantry (860-963-7040; www.mrsbridgespantry.com), 292 CT 169, South Woodstock. Open Wed.–Mon.; closed Tue. British classics are served in the tearoom of Veronica Harris's and Diana Jackson's quaint shop. The two expatriate Englishwomen recently moved their popular business here from Putnam, but don't worry—you can still have a pot of tea with crumpets, scones, and clotted cream. In addition to tea, the menu delves deeper into British middle-class comfort food. Try the beans or spaghetti on toast, meat pies, or the ploughman's lunch—a plate of cheese, ham, chutney, salad, and bread that's on the menu of every pub in England. Afterward, browse through a delightful selection of British gifts, teas and tea accoutrements, specialty foods, books, and antiques (see *Selective Shopping*). $3–8.

Nikki's Dog House (860-928-0252), 35 Main St., Putnam. Open daily. Kids love the fun train theme and running model trains. Fans of good old-fashioned road food love the Coney Island–style hot dogs and piping hot crispy fries. $3–8.

Victoria Station Café (860-928-2600; www.victoriastationcafe.com), 91 Main St., Putnam. Open daily. Located in Putnam's historic downtown antiques district, this warm and friendly coffee shop serves up freshly baked American (cookies) and Italian (cannoli, biscotti) treats, washed down with espresso, cappuccino, hot apple cider, or fresh lemonade. For lunch, croissants come with fillings like turkey and

Swiss, and Sicilian-style pizza comes by the slice. Bistro tables line the sidewalk in warm weather, and live acoustic music and other entertainment keep things going at night. $4–8.

ICE CREAM **Fish Family Farm Creamery and Dairy Farm** (860-646-9745; www.fishfamilyfarm.com), 20 Dimock Lane, Bolton. Open daily in summer until 8 PM. More than a dozen flavors of homemade ice cream are available by the cone or by the quart at the retail store of this 260-acre family-run dairy farm. Flavors are creamy and satisfyingly traditional: vanilla, chocolate, strawberry, maple walnut, butter pecan. Visitors are welcome in the barns, where they can watch as milk from the herd of Jersey cows is pasteurized and bottled.

UConn Dairy Bar (860-486-2634), on the University of Connecticut main campus, 3636 Horsebarn Rd. Ext., off CT 195, Storrs. Open Mon.–Fri. 10:30–5; Sat. and Sun. noon–5; extended summer hours. There's nothing quite like ice cream to put a smile on your face. Here, 25 homemade flavors, including seasonal additions like pumpkin and cinnamon caramel swirl, or the mascot-inspired Jonathan Supreme (peanut butter and chocolate-covered peanuts swirled into vanilla ice cream), are served up in an old-fashioned 1950s-style soda fountain. The dairy bar has been a campus institution for half a century, and loyal fans insist that this is the state's best ice cream. Be prepared to wait in line.

We-Li-Kit Farm (860-974-1095), 728 Hampton Rd. (CT 97), Pomfret. Ice-cream stand open Apr.–Oct., Mon.–Sat. until 8 PM. Locals flock to this happy, laid-back place in a bucolic setting for the homemade ice cream. The usual crowd-pleasing flavors are here, but you can also get a scoop or two of Road Kill (vanilla ice cream studded with walnuts, white chocolate chips, and cherry swirls), or varieties laced with the farm's own pure maple syrup.

Entertainment

MUSIC AND THEATER **Connecticut Repertory Theatre** (tickets 860-486-4226; information 860-486-1629; www.sfa.uconn.edu), Harriet S. Jorgensen Theatre, University of Connecticut, Hillside Rd. (off CT 195), Storrs. Professional and student actors perform in classic and contemporary musicals and plays during the academic season. Original plays are staged in the **Nafe Katter Theatre**, and the **Studio Theater** offers puppet shows and other lighter fare.

Jorgensen Center for the Performing Arts (860-486-4226; www.jorgensen.uconn.edu), 2132 Hillside Rd. (off CT 195), University of Connecticut, Storrs. During fall, winter, and spring, the campus's 2,630-seat art-deco-style performance hall offers a variety of world-renowned dance companies (Russian National Ballet, Martha Graham Dance Company) and concerts (Tony Bennett, London Philharmonic Orchestra), as well as theater, stand-up comedy, cabaret, and other entertainment.

Mansfield Drive-In (860-423-4441; www.mansfielddrivein.com), 228 Stafford Rd., at the junction of CT 31 and CT 32, Mansfield. Open Apr., May, and Sept.: Fri.–Sun. June–Aug.: daily. A survivor! First-run movies, including family films, are shown on three screens at what's billed as the last remaining drive-in theater east of the Connecticut River. Wed. is family night, and eastern Connecticut's largest flea market takes place here on Sun. from spring to fall (see also *Selective Shopping*).

Quinebaug Valley Community College (860-774-1130; www.qvctc.commnet.edu), 742 Upper Maple St., Danielson. Concerts, art exhibitions, poetry readings, and special events throughout the academic year. Call or visit their Web site for information.

✐ **Theatre of Northeastern Connecticut at the Bradley Playhouse** (860-928-7887; www.bradleyplayhouse.org), 30 Front St. (US 44), Putnam. Amateur productions of musicals, comedies, and dramas are staged by local performers in a 100-year-old former vaudeville theater in Putnam's antiques district. In addition to the seven regular shows mounted every year—which include children's performances—there are classes and workshops in theater arts. Dinner packages are available.

Windham Theatre Guild (860-423-2245; www.windhamtheatreguild.org), Burton Leavitt Theatre, 779 Main St., Willimantic. A nonprofit community theater group run by volunteers and amateur artists from Windham County. Dinner-theater-style shows include musicals, comedies, and murder mysteries; other productions such as dramas, Broadway revues, jazz concerts, and classical recitals.

✷ Selective Shopping

ANTIQUES SHOPS You'll find good antiquing in this section of Connecticut, at both individual shops and multidealer venues. The historic mill town of Putnam has become a major player in New England's antiques scene in the past two decades. Because Putnam's stores are grouped within easy walking distance, we've made a separate listing for your convenience. Antiques shops elsewhere are listed below, alphabetized by name. In recent years, as any shop owner will tell you, Internet sales have affected the antiques business. In Putnam these days, it's best to phone ahead—many have closed their doors or resorted to keeping irregular hours.

In Putnam

Antiques Marketplace (860-928-0442), 109 Main St. Open daily 10–5. This sprawling antiques mall is billed as the largest antiques store in New England, so it's safe to say you should find what you're looking for here. Dealers exhibit their wares in showcases and booths spread across four floors of a renovated historic department store founded by Jerry Cohen, who's credited with starting the antiques boom in town.

The Great Atlantic Company (860-428-3439), 58 Pomfret St. Open daily 10–5. When restaurants want eclectic decor, they come here for architectural salvage, funky items, European pieces, and statues.

Also in Putnam, check out **Jeremiah's Antique Shoppes** (860-963-2671), 26 Front St.; **Palace Antiques** (860-963-1124), 130 Main St.; and **The Little Museum Company** (860-928-2534), 86 Main St.

In other Quiet Corner towns

Cackleberry Farm Antiques (860-546-6335), 16 Lisbon Rd. (off CT 14), Canterbury. FYI: *Cackleberry* is a Briticism for "egg," eggcups being a special interest of the owner.

ANTIQUING IN PUTNAM

Kim Grant

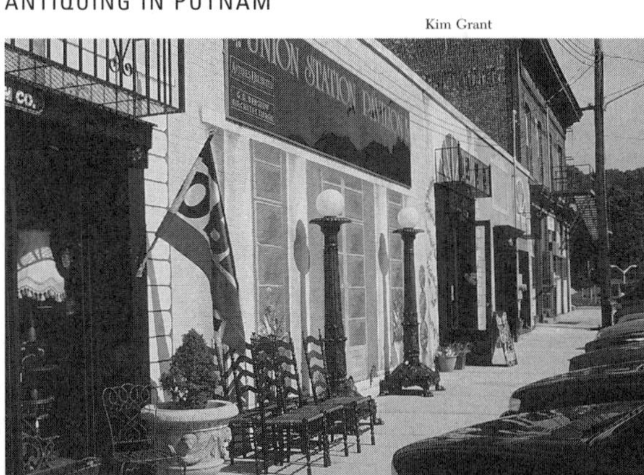

Heirloom Antiques (860-774-7017), 8 Wolf Den Rd., Brooklyn. Fine antiques, including furniture and vintage lamps; lamp and clock repairs. They also carry reproductions.

McClellan Elms Antiques (860-928-0885; www.mcclellanelmsantiques.com), 8 Stone Bridge Rd., at the junction of CT 171 and CT 169, South Woodstock. Open Thu.–Sun. 11–5; closed Mon.–Wed. Historic antiques in equally historic surroundings: the restored 1760 home of General Samuel McClellan. Items range from small accessories to 18th- and 19th-century formal and primitive furniture.

Memory Lanes Countryside Antiques Center (860-742-0346), 2224 Boston Turnpike (US 44), at the junction of CT 31, Coventry. A trio of buildings houses 50 dealers selling all manner of antiques and collectibles, from furniture and lamps to china and artwork. **Memory Lanes Too** (860-742-2865), at 2208 Boston Turnpike (US 44), features 30 additional dealers.

The Old General Store (860-742-7999), 1140 Main St. (CT 31), Coventry. Open Sun. 10–4; other times by chance. A diverse selection of antiques and collectibles, including vintage advertising signs, as well as handcrafted country furniture made by local artisans.

Scranton's Shops (860-928-3738), 300 CT 169, South Woodstock. Open daily 11–5. More than 90 local artisans sell antiques, art, gifts, and crafts jam-packed into renovated early American barn buildings.

ART GALLERIES **Akus Gallery** (860-465-4659), Shafer Hall (lower level), 83 Windham St., Eastern Connecticut State University, Willimantic. Open Tue.–Sun.; closed Mon. Student exhibitions, and group and solo shows, featuring the work of professional contemporary artists.

Arts of Tolland (860-871-7405), 22 Tolland Green (CT 195), Tolland. Open Sept.–Nov. and Mar.–June, Sat. noon–4. Tolland's original 1879 Town Hall—complete with vintage touches like tin ceilings and hardwood floors—was renovated by Arts of Tolland, a local artists' association. It's the scene of a wide variety of art exhibitions, concerts, and literary events.

Birch Mountain Pottery (860-875-0149; www.birchmountainpottery.com), 223 Merrow Rd. (CT 195), Tolland. Open Tue.–Sat. 10–5; or by appointment. A gallery and showroom feature a line of handmade glazed stoneware and one-of-a-kind pieces by potter Susan Gerr. Classes and workshops for adults and children.

Contemporary Art Galleries (860-486-1511), Fine Arts Building, University of Connecticut, 830 Bolton Rd., Storrs. Open during the academic year, Mon.–Fri. 8:30–4:30; call ahead for a schedule of exhibitions. A light and airy gallery space showcasing the work, in all media, of nationally known artists and UConn students.

Middle River Art Gallery (860-684-6226), 58 Main St., Stafford Springs. Fine art by local and regional artists, as well as custom framing.

BOOKSTORES **Great Expectations** (860-564-3584), 20 Railroad Ave., Plainfield. Open Sat. and by appointment. Used books, as well as antiques, furniture, and collectibles, fill a historic 1905 opera house.

UConn Co-op (860-486-3537; www.bookstore.uconn.edu), 2075 Hillside Rd., Storrs. Open daily during the academic year; closed Sun. during summer. In the middle of campus, the co-op has a huge selection of textbooks, general books, stationery,

UConn memorabilia, and dorm needs.

Wonderland Books (860-963-2600), 120 Main St., Putnam. Books, including a wide selection of art books, in a laid-back shop that invites leisurely browsing. Unique cards, prints, jewelry, and gifts.

FARMS AND GARDENS ✐ **Buell's Orchard** (860-974-1150; www.buellsorchard.com), 108 Crystal Pond Rd. (off CT 198), Eastford. Open Mon.–Sat. 9–5; closed Sun. The specialty here is Buell's famous caramel apples, made with just-picked apples from the hundred-acre orchard. The farm store also sells honey, cider, homemade jams, and more, depending on the season. Summer visitors can pick their own strawberries, blueberries, and peaches; apples and pumpkins are ready in fall.

Crooke Orchards (860-429-5336), 317 Bebbington Rd. (1 mile from the junction of CT 44 and CT 89), Ashford. Hours, with seasonal variations, are generally Mon.–Fri. 1–6; Sat. and Sun. 9–6. Head to the fields to pick your own fruits and vegetables, or browse the farm store for fresh apples, peaches, pears, and cider, as well as gift baskets and plants.

✐ **Hurst Farm Country Store & Greenhouses** (860-646-6536), 746 East St., Andover. An old-time country store at the Hurst family farm sells homemade jams and salsas. Outside, there's a sugar shack and lush gardens surrounded by magnificent rural views.

Logee's Greenhouses (860-774-8038; 888-330-8038; www.logees.com), 141 North St., Danielson. Open Mar.–Oct., Mon.–Sat. 9–5; Sun. 11–5; reduced winter hours Nov.–Feb. A family business founded in 1892 and offering delight to the senses. You can stroll through eight greenhouses among thousands of varieties of indoor tropical and subtropical plants: orchids, bougainvilleas, lemon trees, exotic herbs, geraniums, ferns, and hundreds of begonias.

Long Hill Gardens (860-742-2407; www.longhillgardens.com), 167 Long Hill Rd., Andover. Open Thu.–Sun. 10–5; and by appointment. Beautiful display gardens on an 18th-century farm. In the barn shop, browse through perennials, dried flowers, wreaths, and home decor. Gravel pathways meander through lovely display gardens blooming with perennials, roses, herbs, and shrubs, set against a pastoral backdrop of rolling meadows and stone walls.

Meadow Stone Farm (860-617-2982; www.meadowstonefarm.com), US 6, Brooklyn. Farm shop open Mar.–Dec., Thu. and Sat. 1:30–6:30. Health-conscious locals come to this small family farm for cheese, soap, raw goat's milk (must be ordered ahead), honey, eggs, and unique gifts.

Topmost Herb Farm (860-742-8239; www.topmostherbfarm.com), 244 North School Rd., Coventry. Open May–Sept. The greenhouse and display gardens feature primarily organic culinary and medicinal herbs, but garlic, onions, and heirloom tomatoes are grown here as well.

Quintessential Gardens at Fort Hill Farms (860-923-3439), 260 Quaddick Rd., Thompson. This small farm is worth seeking out for its 70 organic gardens. While here, you can also cut your own lavender or pick your own blueberries.

University of Connecticut Greenhouses (860-486-4052), 75 North Eagleville Rd., off CT 195, Storrs. Open Mon.–Fri. 8–4. There are tours for the public on weekends in March and April. Talk about diversity—UConn's internationally recognized

Ecology and Evolutionary Biology Conservatory greenhouses contain more than 3,000 kinds of plants, from aquatic carnivores (yes! underwater meat eaters) to a redwood tree. There are 900 varieties of orchids, as well as ferns, cacti, palm trees, passionflowers, cinnamon, lavender, and violets, and exotic forms, scents, and colors from around the world.

Woodstock Orchards (860-928-2225), 494 CT 169, Woodstock. Pick your own, beginning with blueberries in July and apples in autumn. Sweet cider, honey, maple syrup, and farm-fresh produce are available at the farm stand. The happy placement of an old-time orchard on this scenic routemakes a rewarding stop for hungry, road-weary travelers.

SPECIAL SHOPS **Baker's Country Furniture** (860-684-2256), 42 West Main St. (CT 190), Stafford Springs. Open Tue.–Sat. 9–5; Thu. until 8; Sun. noon–5; closed Mon. The store, known for its top-notch reproductions of 18th-century American furniture, also carries home decor, table linens, window treatments, candles, and seasonal items—all filling a charming Victorian building. In-the-know shoppers scout out deals in the bargain basement.

Celebrations Gallery & Shoppes (860-928-5492; www.celebrationsshoppes.com), 330 Pomfret St. (CT 169), Pomfret Center. Open Wed.–Sun.; closed Mon. and Tue. Gifts, art, pottery, jewelry, tea, exhibits, workshops (woodworking, weaving, photography), demonstrations in a cheery 19th-century Queen Anne Victorian.

Christmas Barn (860-928-7652; www.thechristmasbarnonline.com), 835 CT 169, Woodstock. Open July–Dec., Tue.–Sat. 10–5; Sun. noon–5; closed Mon. Open on Thanksgiving Day; closed Jan.–June. Since 1965, this rustic barn has been *the* place to shop for all things Christmas, no matter what time of year it happens to be. Twelve rooms are packed with seasonal items, country primitives, folk art, home accessories, candles, linens, and gifts.

Mansfield Marketplace (860-456-2578; www.mansfielddrivein.com), at the Mansfield Drive-In Theater, 228 Stafford Rd., at the junction of CT 31 and CT 32, Mansfield. Open Mar.–Thanksgiving, Sun. 8–3. Billed as the oldest and largest indoor/outdoor flea market in eastern Connecticut, on the grounds of one of the last drive-in theaters in the state.

Martha's Herbary (860-928-0009; www.marthasherbary.com), 589 Pomfret St. (CT 169 at its junction with CT 97 and US 44), Pomfret. Open Tue.–Sun. 10–5; closed Mon. This aromatic Victorian shop tucked behind an 18th-century homestead sells fragrant soaps, eclectic home decor, natural-fiber clothing, jewelry, cookbooks, and lots of herbs. Outside, a profusion of herbs and perennials grow in a sunken medicinal garden, a water garden, and raised beds, all connected by meandering paths that invite strolling.

Mrs. Bridge's Pantry (860-963-7040; 888-591-5253; www.mrsbridgespantry.com), 292 CT 169, South Woodstock. Shop open daily 11–5; tearoom open Wed.–Mon. 11–5. This quaint shop filled with British gifts, specialty foods, books, and antiques was a downtown Putnam landmark until it recently moved here. You'll find an extensive range of tea, both loose and bagged, plus everything that goes with it: infusers, pots, delicate cups, and cozies to keep the brew warm. The shop now has a new specialty—yarn—and carries a lot of it, along with knitting and crochet pattern books. A tearoom serves afternoon tea and light lunches (see *Where to Eat*).

Munson's Chocolates (860-649-4332; 888-686-7667; www.munsonschocolates.com), 174 Hop River Rd. (US 6), Bolton. Open Mon.–Fri. 8–8; Sat. and Sun. 10–6. This third-generation candy family has been in the chocolate business since Ben and Josephine Munson founded the Dandy Candy Company in 1946. Today Munson's is Connecticut's largest chocolate retailer, with 10 stores statewide; but this is the headquarters and factory, where you can treat yourself to their delicious handiwork. There are gourmet truffles, chocolate-covered cherries, traditional boxed assortments (think nougats, caramels, crèmes, nut clusters, jellies), peanut brittle made with microbrewed ale, pumpkin pie fudge, ice cream toppings, sugar-free chocolates, even factory seconds (they still taste great). Stop by for a sample, or pick up a bag of Route 6 Toffee Crunch, a luscious blend of butter toffee, pretzels, and peanuts, made fresh daily along its namesake highway.

Quilter's Dream (860-456-7629; www.quiltersdream.com), 1158 Main St., Willimantic. Open Mon.–Sat. 10–6 (until 8 on Thu.); Sun. noon–5. A quilter's supply store with a national reputation; the store is appropriately housed in a Victorian home in the center of Thread City. Some 6,000 bolts of top-of-the-line fabrics, as well as quilting books and patterns.

South River Herbals & Education Center (860-742-1258; www.southriverherbals.com), 140 South River Rd., Coventry. Herbalist and owner Eva Maynard sells more than 250 varieties of herbs from New England organic farms. Her cozy shop is also stocked with earth-friendly treats: teas, tinctures, aromatherapy sprays, and massage oils. Ask about classes on herb gardening and soapmaking.

Special Joys Doll and Toy Shop (860-742-6359), 41 North River Rd., Coventry. Open Thu.–Sun. 11–4:30; closed Mon.–Wed. Antique dolls, dollhouses, miniature kitchens and schoolrooms, stuffed animals, and display-sized mechanicals, all in a unique and whimsical shop inside a Victorian-style B&B. The collection includes rare Steiff dolls, tin windup toys, cloth animals from the 1940s, even dolls that come with their own wardrobe of vintage clothing. Owner Joy Kelleher often travels to doll shows, so it's best to phone ahead to be sure the shop is open.

✷ Special Events

January: **Tolland Antiques Show** (860-870-9599), Tolland. This popular one-day antiques show has been a fixture for more than 40 years. It's hosted by the Tolland Historical Society and specializes in 18th- and 19th-century Americana.

April: **Daffodil Festival** (860-742-9311), Patriot's Park, Lake St., Coventry. A popular arts-and-crafts festival with many horticultural exhibits.

Summer: **Willimantic's 3rd Thursday Street Festivals** (860-456-2188; www.willlimanticstreetfest.com), Main St., Willimantic. May–Oct. Live music on five stages, ethnic food, and vendors line four blocks of Willimantic's Main Street on the third Thursday of the month. Entertainment ranges from bands and clowns to street performers. **Coventry Regional Farmers' Market** (www.coventryfarmersmarket.com), Nathan Hale Homestead, Coventry. Sundays July–Oct.

June: **Victorian Days in Willimantic** (860-456-4476; www.victorianwillimantic.org), Prospect St., Willimantic. The city's beautifully restored Victorian houses and historic buildings are open to the public. Concerts, teas, gallery tours, and museum exhibits round out the events.

July: **Nathan Hale Antiques Festival** (860-742-6917), on the grounds of the Nathan Hale Homestead, Coventry. Sponsored by the Antiquarian and Landmarks Society. The society also hosts a **Revolutionary War Encampment** at the homestead in July.

July 4: **Boom Box Parade** (860-456-3046), Willimantic. Local radio station WILI broadcasts patriotic marching music at 11 AM, and hundreds of marchers decked out in red, white, and blue and carrying radios take to Main Street for a wacky band-free stepoff. The tradition was born in 1986, when the town couldn't find a marching band for its Memorial Day parade. Seeing is believing. **Windham County 4-H Fair** (860-774-9600), Brooklyn Fairgrounds, CT 169, Brooklyn. Tractor pulls and livestock shows featuring horses, goats, sheep, cattle, and poultry.

August: Second weekend: **Lebanon Country Fair** (www.lebanon countryfair.org), Mack Rd., off CT 87 and CT 207, Lebanon. A major Connecticut country fair for half a century. **Brooklyn Fair** (860-779-0012; www.brooklynfair.org), Brooklyn Fairgrounds, CT 169, Brooklyn. This is the state's oldest country fair, and the oldest continuously operating agricultural fair in the country, dating from 1849.

September: **Woodstock Fair** (860-928-3246; www.woodstockfair.com), at the junction of CT 171 and CT 169, South Woodstock. This Labor Day weekend fair has been drawing crowds since the mid–19th century; today it's one of the largest of Connecticut's fairs, and celebrates its 150th anniversary in 2010. **Outdoor Antiques Show** (www.historyoflebanon.org), on the green, Lebanon. Furniture and collectibles from dealers around New England.

October: ♿ **Walktober** (860-963-7226; 866-363-7226; www.thelastgreenvalley.org), throughout the month. More than 100 free guided walks, hikes, and strolls—ranging from farm tours and gentle jaunts to serious treks in the hills—throughout 35 Quiet Corner towns, celebrating the autumn splendor of the Quinebaug and Shetucket Rivers Valley National Heritage Corridor. Some walks cater to people with children or pets; other routes are handicapped accessible. **Highland Festival** (860-456-0708; www.scotlandgames.org), Waldo Homestead, 96 Waldo Rd., Scotland. Scottish dancing, bagpiping, food, and traditional Scottish athletic competitions attract thousands of spectators. **Lantern Tours** (860-742-6917), Nathan Hale Homestead, 2299 South St., Coventry. Space is limited; reservations are required. Spooky tales and evening tours of the old Hale homestead and the nearby Strong-Porter House by lantern light. **Connecticut Renaissance Faire** (860-478-5954; www.ctfaire.com), CT 85, Hebron. **Fine Arts and Crafts Festival** (617-227-3957; www.historicnewengland.org), Roseland Cottage—Bowen House, Woodstock.

November and December: **Artists Open Studios** (www.aosct.org), various weekends and locations. As with the springtime studio tours, dozens of Quiet Corner artists allow visitors into their working studios to view their creative efforts, from contemporary art and sculpture to wood turnings, photography, and pottery. Many studios feature working demonstrations.

Mystic and More

MYSTIC, STONINGTON, AND EAST OF THE THAMES

NEW LONDON, NORWICH, AND WEST OF THE THAMES

Kim Grant

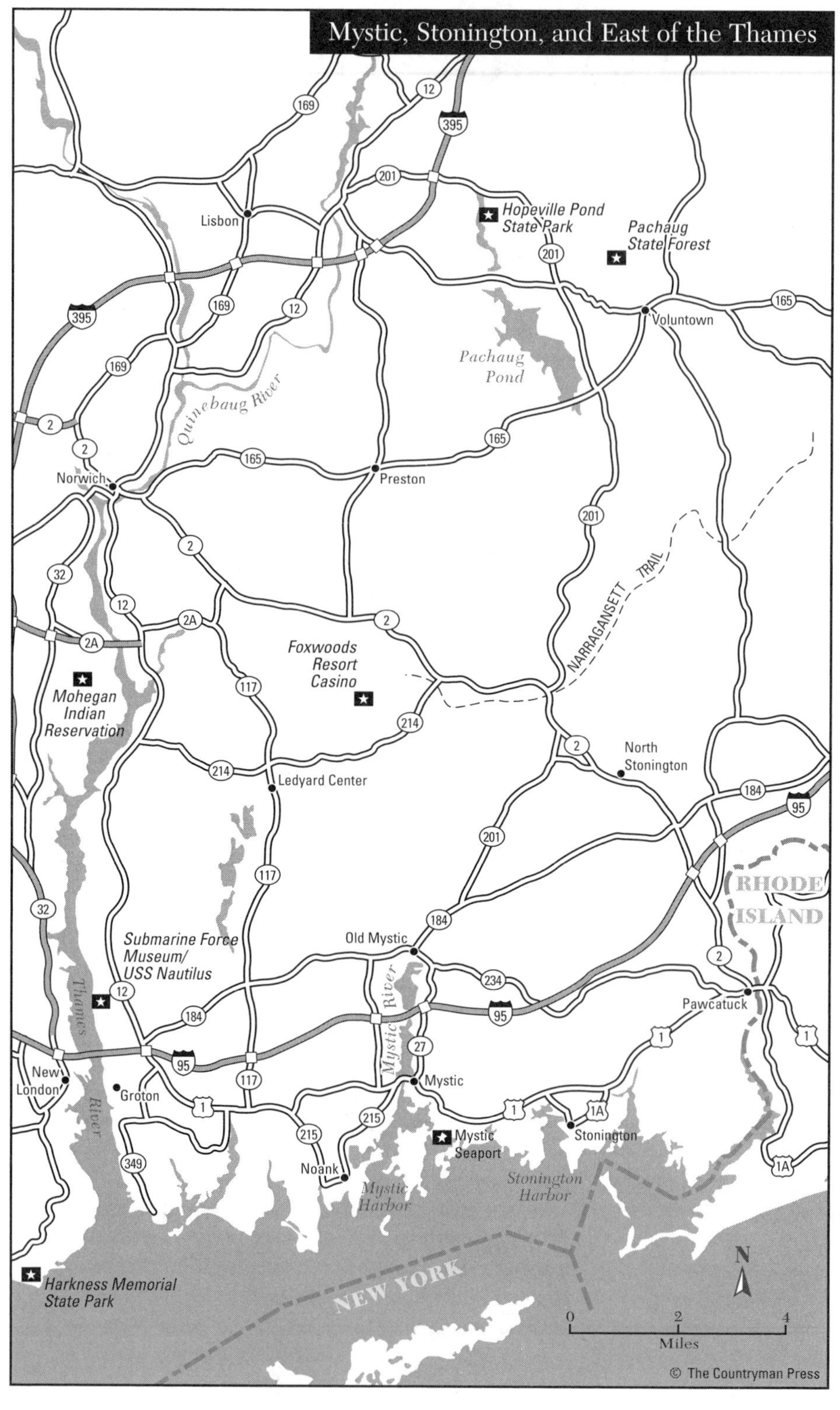
Mystic, Stonington, and East of the Thames
Lisbon
Hopeville Pond State Park
Pachaug State Forest
Voluntown
Pachaug Pond
Quinebaug River
Norwich
Preston
NARRAGANSETT TRAIL
Foxwoods Resort Casino
Mohegan Indian Reservation
Ledyard Center
North Stonington
RHODE ISLAND
Submarine Force Museum/ USS Nautilus
Old Mystic
Thames River
Mystic River
Pawcatuck
New London
Groton
Mystic
Mystic Seaport
Stonington
Noank
Mystic Harbor
Stonington Harbor
Harkness Memorial State Park
NEW YORK
Miles
© The Countryman Press

MYSTIC, STONINGTON, AND EAST OF THE THAMES

It is safe to say that southeastern Connecticut is unlike any other region in the state, and there is no question that it is Connecticut's number one tourist destination. The heritage of its seafaring days lives on in the country's largest maritime museum, Mystic Seaport—The Museum of America and the Sea, and at the U.S. Navy Submarine Base in Groton, the birthplace of the nuclear submarine (the Submarine Force Museum and Historic Ship *Nautilus*), and home to Mystic Marinelife Aquarium and Institute for Exploration, one of the top aquariums in New England.

From the Pequot, Mistick, and Mohegan tribes that inhabited the region for 10,000 years, to the 17th century, when the first permanent English settlers bit their axes into the trees hugging the shores of the Mystic River to build shelters, the people of southeastern Connecticut have turned to the sea for sustenance. The pioneers became fishermen, hunters of whales, and builders of clipper ships that broke speed records while sailing around the tip of South America and across the Pacific to China.

Four lighthouses remain standing along the coast here, sentinels whose lights still arc into the sky and once guided to safety the brave men who launched their ships in search of the denizens of the deep. Visitors can embark on cruises in replicas of authentic tall ships, watch wooden-boat regattas, and dine in scores of extraordinary restaurants where fish, crabs, oysters, mussels, and lobsters are king of the table.

Strictly speaking, Mystic is not a legal entity with its own government. It's a place-name, a postal address spilling halfway into Groton on the west and Stonington on the east. The present Seaport museum was erected on the site of a former major shipbuilding yard. At the shipyards of the so-called Mystic area, numerous ships were built for the navy and for commercial fleets. A world's record, still standing, was set by the *David Crockett*, a clipper ship built by Greenman and Company, on its run around Cape Horn to San Francisco. During the Civil War, 56 transports, gunboats, and other warships went down the ways from Mystic shipyards. But when iron ships came along, shipbuilding declined here. It was only in 1929 that the venerable maritime history museum was founded to preserve the region's maritime heritage. Today it's one of the state's most popular places to sail; yachties come ashore and mingle with tourists for people-watching and window-shopping in downtown Mystic, where restaurants and shops emanate from the famous Bascule (French for "seesaw") drawbridge, which is raised on schedule for tall-masted schooners, yachts, and fishing boats.

Five miles east of Mystic Seaport, in the state's extreme southeastern corner, is the historic fishing village of Stonington, extending along a narrow mile-long peninsula to the sea. It's one of the most charming seaside villages in New England, where fishing is a centuries-old industry and Connecticut's only remaining commercial fleet is alive and well. On weekends, urban sophisticates rub shoulders with yachties who trickle to shore from the marinas for the cafés, galleries, and boutiques that line Water Street, the narrow main artery through the village. During the American Revolution and the War of 1812, courageous villagers with a pair of old cannons chased away attacking British warships that were bent on stealing sheep. Today, visitors to Cannon Square in the village center can see the British cannonballs atop a granite column. Historic house museums tell the story of history of whaling and Arctic exploration. A web of quiet side streets is a delight for strollers. At the Old Lighthouse Museum, you can climb the winding iron stairs for a 360-degree panorama from the lantern room. The last weekend of July features the colorful Blessing of the Fleet parade and festivities, when Stonington prays for its fishermen and celebrates its seafaring heritage while remembering those lost at sea. As in Mystic, you can head north away from the coast to quiet countryside dotted with hiking trails, charming bed & breakfasts, and vineyards nourished by a microclimate of mild coastal temperatures.

The manufacturing town of Groton, on the eastern edge of the wide and tidal Thames River, is steeped in U.S. military and naval history. It's home of the U.S. Navy's major submarine training school, and fittingly is known as the Submarine Capital of America. By no strange coincidence, the Electric Boat division of General Dynamics, the builder of subs, is located downriver. The defense contractor sent diesel subs to the navy during World War II and is the birthplace of the Historic Ship *Nautilus*, the world's first nuclear submarine, now permanentely berthed at the sub base, part of the fine Submarine Force Library and Museum. The USS

THE DRAWBRIDGE AND SAILBOATS ALONG THE MYSTIC RIVER

Kim Grant

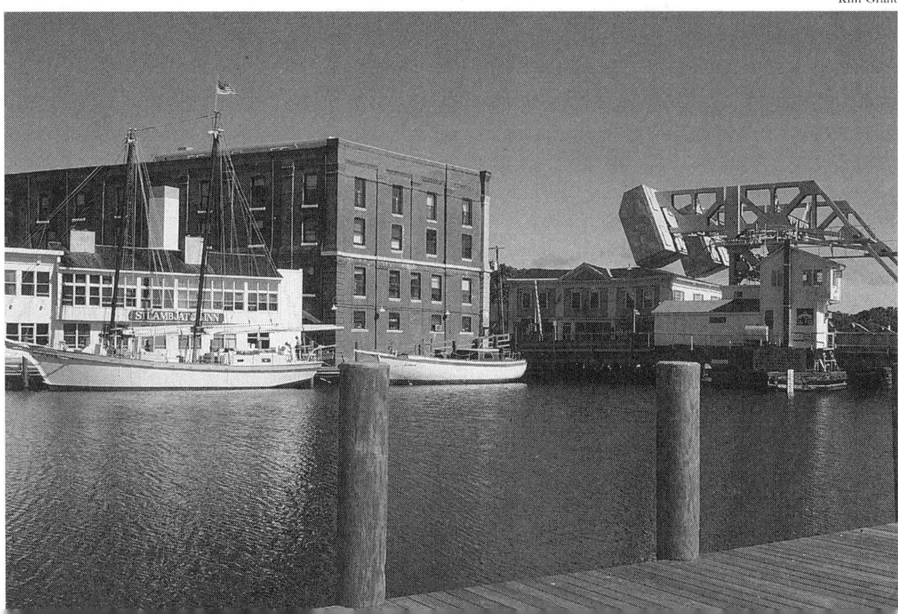

Nautilus, the world's first nuclear sub, was designed at Groton. (Local lore has it that an Italian restaurateur in Groton was the first to slice a long roll in half and stuff it with a variety of Italian deli meats, hot peppers, and vegetables. The creation, dubbed a "submarine sandwich," was popular with sailors.) History buffs shouldn't miss the Revolutionary War–era Fort Griswold, a little-known gem overlooking New London Harbor. This was the site of the battle of Groton Heights in September 1781, when British troops led by the traitorous Benedict Arnold, a native of nearby Norwich, raided the fort. It's now a state park where visitors can see the original earthen ramparts and explore a museum dedicated to the battle. Bluff Point State Park and Reserve, on a high bluff overlooking the Sound, is Connecticut's last remaining undeveloped land along the shoreline. And Noank, a tonier seaside section of town, has several upscale fish and seafood restaurants.

Today this is a region known as much for casino gambling as maritime history and the defense industry: A handful of Mashantucket Pequot Indians, the last descendants of the once mighty tribes that lived in and roamed this area, has made an unexpected comeback. The fierce Pequots, almost wiped out in King Philip's War, are now wealthy and powerful again from an avalanche of casino money. In Mashantucket, on their minuscule reservation in the forests just north of Mystic, the Pequots built a bingo hall in 1986, which evolved into Foxwoods Resort Casino, the largest casino in North America. And it keeps getting bigger: A massive $700 million expansion unveiled in 2008 added the MGM Grand at Foxwoods, a Las Vegas–style casino resort with restaurants, a luxe hotel, a 4,000-seat theater, and more gaming. To their immediate west, the Mohegans, once enemies of the Pequots, have also built a thriving casino, Mohegan Sun Casino. Together these two gambling powerhouses bring in 25 million visitors and $2.2 billion a year.

Entries in this section are arranged in roughly geographic order.

AREA CODE 860.

GUIDANCE **Eastern Regional Tourism District** (860-444-2206; 800-863-6569; www.mysticcountry.com), 32 Huntington St., New London 06320. Write, call, or go online for maps and publications, including the district's *Driving, Biking, and Walking Tours* guide, and calendars of events.

State Highway Information Center, I-95 southbound, North Stonington, just this side of the Rhode Island border. Guides, brochures, pamphlets, and maps. Full rest facilities. Open year-round daily; staffed by tourism specialists in high season.

Mystic Information Center (860-536-1641), I-95, Exit 90 off I-95, at the entrance to Olde Mistick Village shopping complex on CT 27. Maps and information on area attractions.

GETTING THERE *By car:* The Mystic area is accessible by I-95. The region's two casinos, Foxwoods Resort Casino (on the Mystic side of the Thames) and Mohegan Sun Casino (on the New London side) are massive generators of traffic and are best reached via I-395 from the west or CT 2 from the east.

By air: **Groton–New London Airport** (860-445-8549; www.grotonnewlondonairport.com) in Groton serves only corporate and charter aircraft. **T. F. Green Airport** (888-268-7222; www.pvdairport.com) in nearby Warwick, Rhode Island, offers less expensive fares on many routes and is becoming increasingly popular with Connecticut air travelers to the area. **Bradley International Airport** (860-292-2000; 888-624-1533; www.bradleyairport.com), about 1½ hours away in Windsor Locks, is the state's main airport.

By bus: **Greyhound Lines** (800-231-2222; www.greyhound.com) and **Peter Pan Bus Lines** (800-343-9999; www.peterpanbus.com) stop in New London.

By rail: **Amtrak** (800-872-7245; www.amtrak.com) stops occasionally at the Mystic station; it makes frequent stops at New London 7 miles away. High-speed **Acela Express** trains also stop in New London.

By ferry: **Cross Sound Ferry** (860-443-5281; www.foxwoodsferry.com) offers high-speed ferry service from Orient Point, Long Island, to New London, where buses transport passengers to **Foxwoods Resort Casino**.

GETTING AROUND Local taxi service is provided by **Mystic Cab** (860-536-8888) in Mystic and **Yellow Cab Co.** (860-443-6230) in Groton.

MEDICAL EMERGENCY The statewide emergency number is **911**.

Lawrence and Memorial Hospital (860-442-0711), 365 Montauk Ave., New London. The emergency number is 888-777-9539.

William Backus Hospital (860-889-8331), 326 Washington St., Norwich. The emergency number is 860-823-6389.

✷ To See

MUSEUMS ✐ ♿ **Mystic Aquarium & Institute for Exploration** (860-572-5955; www.mysticaquarium.org), 55 Coogan Blvd., Exit 90 off I-95 at the eastern end of Olde Mistick Village. (Friendly tip: Because it's first off the interstate, the

MYSTIC SEAPORT, AMERICA'S LARGEST MARITIME MUSEUM

Kim Grant

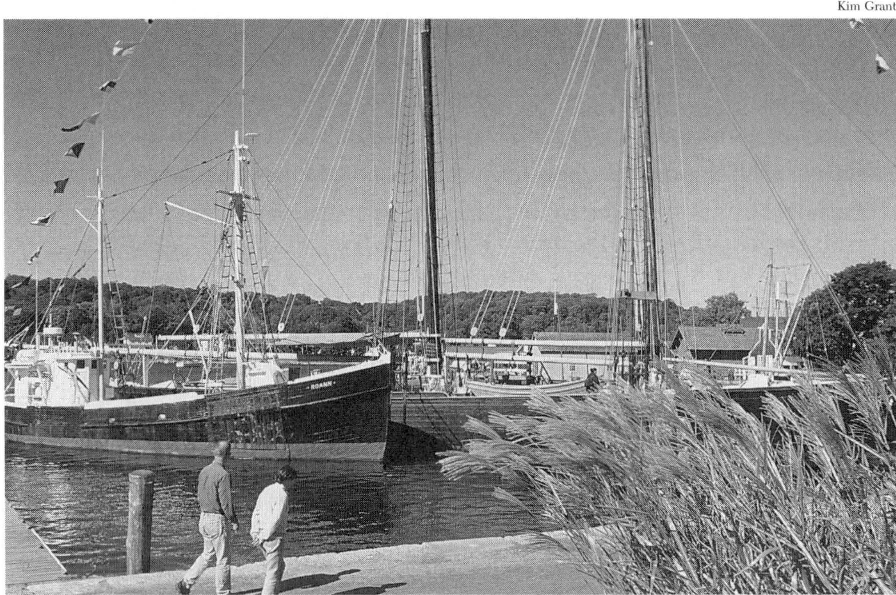

Mystic Seaport—The Museum of America and the Sea (860-572-5315; 888-973-2767; www.mysticseaport.org), 50 Greenmanville Ave. (CT 27), Mystic. Open daily, Apr.–Oct., 9–5; Nov.–Mar., 10–4; closed Christmas Eve and Christmas Day. Adults $18.50; seniors, active military, college students, $16.50; children 6–17 $13; reduced rates off-season and for special events. A typical 19th-century New England whaling village has been re-created alongside the Mystic River on 17 acres of a former shipyard where clipper ships that still hold world speed records were launched. What was founded in 1929 as the Marine Historical Association is now America's largest maritime museum and Connecticut's top tourist attraction, with more than 1,000 volunteers and some 300,000 annual visitors. Original buildings and sailing vessels of all kinds have been gathered to help create the illusion of stepping back in time; for example, a famous cordage factory that produced the hundreds of ropes needed to maneuver a square-rigger was brought down from Plymouth, Massachusetts, and reassembled here.

The Seaport boasts a collection of more than 500 ships and boats, but the focus and pride here is its "tall" ships, all original and all meticulously restored: the 1841 ***Charles W. Morgan***, last of the great wooden whaling ships; the ***Joseph Conrad***, a steel-hulled square-rigger that served for years as a Danish cadet training ship and now hosts a summer school for young sailors; and the 1921 ***L. A. Dunton***, a classic Gloucester fishing schooner. Today you stroll along the rope walk and watch the artisans at work. Planetarium presentations depict the starlit skies over the oceans where Yankee sailors roamed. Paintings with sea-related themes are mounted in an art gallery. Other indoor exhibits are devoted to ship models, ship gear and rigging, rowing, and, in one building, an extended graphic history of seafaring in New England. In another shed, craftspeople fashion replicas of small wooden boats. Tour the ships, see how the crews lived, then board the ***Sabino***, America's last coal-fired steamboat, for a cruise down the river (see *To Do*). Dozens of special activities are staged at the Seaport throughout the year (see *Special Events*). On the Fourth of July, marchers parade in period costumes. The Seamen's Inne (see *Dining Out*) serves traditional American fare; the museum store includes maritime photography and boasts of the largest collection of maritime books in America. Here's a tip: The Seaport receives the bulk of its visitors in summer; come in the off-season for a more intimate look at this special place.

Kim Grant

THE OLD LIGHTHOUSE MUSEUM IN STONINGTON

aquarium is often confused with Mystic Seaport. After seeing the fishes, proceed a mile down CT 27 to the ships.) Open Mar.–Nov., daily 9–6; Dec.–Feb., Mon.–Fri. 10–5, Sat., Sun., and holidays 9–6; closed Christmas and New Year's Day. Last entry is one hour before closing. Adults $24; seniors $21 children 3–17 $18. Ever-changing exhibits on sea life, deep-sea exploration, and marine mammals are at the heart of this nationally recognized center. There are more than 12,000 fish, mammals, and other denizens of the deep, including beluga whales, poison dart frogs, penguins, and Steller's sea lions; in all, they represent 425 species from around the world. They're on view in a 30,000-gallon tank and in 70 re-created indoor and outdoor settings, such as the seal and walrus habitat and the ray touch pool. Dr. Robert Ballard, the famed oceanographer who discovered the wrecks of the *Titanic* and the *Bismarck*, has moved his research facilities from Woods Hole on Cape Cod to the aquarium. The **Institute for Sea Exploration** features relics Ballard has retrieved from the ocean floors and a simulated submarine. In the **Challenge of the Deep** exhibit, visitors can explore shipwrecks and oceans thousands of miles away using interactive satellite and computer technology. Another permanent exhibit is **Return to the *Titanic***. It features videos taken by new sophisticated undersea cameras Ballard uses in his continuing exploration of the "unsinkable" ocean liner; there's also a 25-foot replica of the ship's bow and and a reproduction of the ship's radio room. The **Arctic Coast exhibit**, featuring an 800,000-gallon tank with New England's only beluga whales in a naturalistic setting, is permanent. The new **Fluorescent Coral Exhibit** is a dramatic walk-through display of glowing corals from around the world.

Old Lighthouse Museum (860-535-1440), 7 Water St., Stonington. Open May–Oct., daily 10–5. Adults $5; children 6–12, $3. Includes admission to the Captain Nathaniel Palmer House. The story of the valor of Stonington's patriots is told in this unique museum. Climb the iron steps to the top of the lighthouse tower for great views of Stonington Harbor and Long Island Sound.

✐ **Submarine Force Museum** and **Historic Ship *Nautilus*** (860-694-3174; 800-343-0079; www.submarinemuseum.org), 1 Crystal Lake Rd., at the U.S. Naval Submarine Base, Exit 86 off I-95, Groton. Open May–Oct., Wed.–Mon. 9–5, Tue. 1–5; Nov.–Apr., Wed.–Mon. 9–4, closed Tue.; also closed the third week of Apr. and the first full week of Nov. Free admission. Peer through one of three

Kim Grant

VISITORS TO THE U.S. NAVY'S SUBMARINE FORCE MUSEUM IN GROTON CAN TOUR THE USS *NAUTILUS*, THE WORLD'S FIRST NUCLEAR SUBMARINE.

periscopes in the U.S. Navy's only submarine museum and see simulated battle scenes from World War I to the present. Trace the history and lore of sailing underwater in two mini theaters. Inspect the full-sized model of the *Turtle*; invented by Connecticut's David Bushnell, it was the first sub to attack an enemy battleship—a British man-of-war in New York Harbor in the opening days of the Revolutionary War. Leave the museum and descend into the Historic Ship *Nautilus*, the world's first nuclear submarine, now tied up at the dock in the Submarine Capital of America. Built by Admiral Hyman Rickover and in service for 30 years, the *Nautilus* was the first submarine to cross the geographic North Pole and the first to journey "20,000 leagues under the sea." Visit the control and navigation room, the crew's quarters, and the galley. The *Nautilus* ranks with such other historic navy vessels as the USS *Constitution*; "Old Ironsides," now berthed in Boston Harbor; and the USS *Arizona*, torpedoed and sunk at Pearl Harbor.

Mashantucket Pequot Museum and Research Center (800-411-9671; www.pequotmuseum.org), 110 Pequot Trail, Mashantucket. Open year-round, daily 10–4; closed major holidays. Adults $15; seniors $13; children 6–15 $10; 5 and under free. From the casinos, hop a free shuttle to this extraordinary museum, a gem in Foxwood Resort Casino's entertainment complex and a hidden treasure among Connecticut's trove of museums. It traces the history of the Pequots and other Northeast woodland tribes through historic artifacts, art, films, and interactive computers that tell the frightful story of the 17th-century massacre of the Pequots at Mystic. Four acres of permanent exhibits trace 18,000 years of Native American and natural history; the centerpiece is a collection of stunningly lifelike dioramas, with subjects ranging from the Pequot War to a 16th-century Native American village. A 185-foot stone-and-glass observation tower offers panoramic view of southeastern Connecticut's rolling countryside.

HISTORIC HOMES AND SITES ♿ **National Submarine World War II Memorial/Wall of Honor**, Thames St., Groton. Open year-round; free admission. A conning tower and memorial wall honor the 52 U.S. Navy subs lost at sea during World War II. On the wall are engraved the names of the submariners who died in the line of duty.

Fort Griswold Battlefield State Park (860-449-6877; www.fortfriends.org), 57 Fort St., Groton. Grounds open year-round, daily 8 AM–sunset. Monument and museum open Memorial Day–Labor Day, daily 10–5; weekends 10–5 until Columbus Day. Free admission. September 6, 1781: While Washington and his French allies were marching toward Yorktown, the British launched a diversionary attack against New London under the command of the traitor—and Connecticut native—Benedict Arnold. After burning the city's bulging warehouses, a British force of 800 regulars crossed the Thames and attacked Fort Griswold, defended by only 150 militiamen led by Colonel William Ledyard. In a fierce battle that lasted just 40 minutes, the defenders killed many of the British but were finally overwhelmed. Colonel Ledyard offered his sword in surrender, in keeping with military custom. Instead of accepting the sword, the British commander, enraged at the Americans' temerity in fighting back, plunged the blade into Ledyard's stomach, killing him on the spot. Much of the ramparts of the fort remains, a plaque marks where Ledyard fell, the story of the battle is told in the Monument House museum building, the Ebenezer Avery House is a restored field hospital, and a monument commemorates the bravery of Ledyard and his men. The 134-foot-high granite obelisk, erected in the 1820s, is the earliest patriotic obelisk in America.

Portersville Academy (860-536-4779), 74 High St., Mystic. Open year-round, Tue. 9–noon; Wed. and Thu. 1–4. Free admission; no apple for the teacher is necessary. Step back more than 100 years as you sit at a tiny desk in the restored classroom of this once active 19th-century schoolhouse, now home to the Mystic River Historical Society. Changing exhibits on the first floor.

B. F. Clyde's Cider Mill (860-536-3354), 129 North Stonington Rd. (CT 27), Old Mystic. Open Sept.–Dec., daily 9–5; closed Thanksgiving and Christmas. Free tours. Watch the country's oldest and largest steam-powered cider mill squeeze juice from barrels of apples amid the sweet aroma of newly crushed fruit. Sweet and hard cider, apples, cider doughnuts, honey, maple syrup, gourds, and johnnycake meal are for sale. Bring your camera—and your sweet tooth. The mill has won a National Historic Mechanical Engineering Landmark award. Steam wafts outside this 1898 mill, a family-run operation, and throngs of camera-toting tourists swarm the place on weekends.

Captain Nathaniel Palmer House (860-535-8445), 40 Palmer St., Stonington. Open May–Oct., Thu.–Sun. 1–5; closed Mon.–Wed. Your paid admission at the Old Lighthouse Museum is valid here. The intrepid Captain Palmer and his sturdy crew are remembered and honored for discovering the Antarctic in 1820 on a sealing expedition in the 47-foot sloop *Hero*—and returning to tell about it. A versatile Yankee, the captain also was skilled in architectural and clipper ship design. A docent on the tour of his 16-room Victorian mansion points out Palmer's architectural innovations.

John Bishop Museum (860-376-6866), 11 South Burnham Hwy. (CT 169), Lisbon. Open June–Aug., Sat. 10–2. Donation suggested. Ever wonder why an occasional New England home is painted white on three sides and red on the back?

This circa-1810 farmhouse, now the home of the Lisbon Historical Society, is a good example. Historians explain that red paint was less expensive than white, but white was more prestigious. So many a thrifty Yankee saved a bit of money, showing his white face to the passersby. A unique feature of the Bishop house, a remarkable early Federal structure, is the well shaft in the pantry, allowing residents to fetch water without going outside. Ask about a schedule of hearth cooking demonstrations.

WINERIES AND BREWERY **Stonington Vineyards** (860-535-1222; 800-421-9463; www.stoningtonvineyards.com), 523 Taugwonk Rd., Stonington. Open year-round, daily 11–5; closed major holidays. Free winery tours daily at 2 PM. So much to do: Stroll among the rows of grapevines, picnic in the vineyard, enjoy free wine tasting, or browse in the art gallery and wine shop, where you can buy a bottle of crisp Seaport White or Seaport Blush for your table. Special events include art exhibitions and food and wine festivals.

Jonathan Edwards Winery (860-535-0202; www.jedwardswinery.com), 74 Chester Maine Rd., North Stonington. Open Wed.–Sun.; wine tours at 3 PM. Named not for the singer or 18th-century preacher, but for the family that runs this pretty hilltop vineyard and winery. The cozy tasting room, with stone fireplace and polished wine bar, will transport you to Napa.

Heritage Trail Vineyards (860-376-0659; www.heritagetrail.com), 291 North Burnham Hwy., Lisbon. This 6-acre vineyard on the site of an 18th-century farm is located on CT 169, one of America's most scenic roads. Sample award-winning Cabernet Sauvignon and Chardonnay and French-American hybrids brewed by a native of the wine country in Northern California.

Cottrell Brewing Company (860-599-8213; www.cottrellbrewing.com), 100 Mechanic St., Pawcatuck. Tours by appointment. A microbrewery known for its handcrafted and unpasteurized ales and lagers, including its flagship brew, Old Yankee Ale.

✻ To Do

BIRDING ♿ **Bluff Point Coastal Reserve State Park** (860-444-7591), Depot Rd. (off US 1), Groton. Cars are not allowed in this 800-acre wooded peninsula, so be prepared to explore on foot. This park is a rarity: the last significant tract of undeveloped shoreline in Connecticut. In fall, thousands of warblers, thrushes, vireos, and other migrants pass through, making it one of top shoreline spots for fall birding (don't forget your field guide).

BOAT EXCURSIONS See also *Fishing*.

The Mystic River, barely long enough to show up on a state map, is nonetheless a beehive of maritime activity. Busy private marinas sit cheek by jowl alongside Mystic Seaport, whose own dock accepts reservations from out-of-town yachters in for a visit to the prestigious museum. Three boat excursions embark from the Seaport on 30-minute trips down the Mystic River from mid-May to mid-October; phone 860-572-0711 for information, or click on www.mysticseaport.com. There's ***Sabino*** (860-572-5351), the only coal-fired vessel still in operation; ***Resolute***, a diesel-powered antique wooden launch; and the ***Breck Marshall*** (860-572-0711), a 20-foot Crosby catboat reproduction.

Voyager Cruises (860-536-0416; www.voyagermystic.com), Schooner Wharf, 15 Holmes St., Mystic. Half-day sails and sunset trips aboard ***Argia***, an 81-foot two-masted schooner, a replica of a 19th-century trading schooner. The tall ship ***Mystic*** departs on multiday excursions from late May to early October.

Downeast Lighthouse Cruises (860-460-1802; www.downeastlighthousecruises.com), Pine Island Marina, Shennecossett Rd., Groton. Lighthouse and sunset cruises in New London Harbor and Fishers Island Sound aboard ***Escape***, a working lobster boat.

Project Oceanology (860-445-9007; 800-364-8472; www.oceanology.org), Avery Point campus of the University of Connecticut (I-95, Exit 87), Groton. Oceanographic and lighthouse cruises, mid-June–Aug.; seal watches run Sat. in Feb. and Sat.–Sun. in Mar. The capacity of the floating laboratories is limited to 50, so reservations are a must. Lace up your boat shoes and bring along a sweater or windbreaker for exciting adventures on the 55-foot *Enviro-lab II* or the 65-foot *Enviro-lab III*, two research vessels sponsored by several New England schools and universities. During the summer months, family groups are invited aboard for such hands-on activities as pulling nets and identifying and recording catches of lobsters, crabs, fish, and other marine life. You and your young ones will collect plankton, test the waters of Long Island Sound, and, on the bridge, learn from the captain how to unravel the mysteries of navigation maps and charts. Visit the inside of the famous **New London Ledge Lighthouse** for a 2½-hour tour. On another day, book a 2½-hour **Oceanograhic Tour**; this could be the highlight of your visit to southeastern Connecticut.

FISHING See also *Green Space*.

There are a number of *charter boats* in the Mystic area that may be rented with or without a crew. *In Groton:* ***Capt. Bob II*** (860-434-5681), at Thames Marina; ***Otter*** (860-267-4449), ***Fish Connection*** (860-642-6714), and ***Reel Deal*** (860-861-4193), all at Pine Island Marina. *In Noank:* ***Mataura*** (860-536-6970), Riverview Avenue Dock; ***Magic*** (860-455-9942), at Spicer's Marina; ***First Light*** (860-344-1698), and ***Kingfisher*** (860-573-3614), both at Noank Shipyard. *In Mystic:* ***Benmar*** (860-521-3345), at Mason's Island Marina; ***Lady Adventurous*** (860-381-5074), Seaport Marine; ***Lorna Anne*** (860-423-9121), Mystic Shipyard East. *In Stonington:* ***Blue Heron*** (860-535-3387), at Skippers Dock; ***Compass Rose*** (860-535-3387), Stonington Village Harbor; ***Lauren B*** (860-572-9896) and ***Rum Runner*** (860-886-9212), both at Walker's Dock.

Party boat: ***Hel-Cat II*** (860-535-3200), *Hel-Cat* Dock, 181 Thames St., Groton. New England's largest steel party fishing boat has been in service for more than 60 years. Rental tackle on board; there's a restaurant with hot food and cold beverages, including draft beer. No bottled beer or booze may be brought with you. There's an upper observation deck for sunbathing or bird- and whale-watching if you are half a couple not into fishing. Winter and spring fishing for cod, hake, pollack, mackerel, and sea bass; summer, blues and striped bass; fall, blues, bass, bonita, and false albacore. Night fishing on weekends for ocean blues.

Top spots for inland fishing include Amos Lake and Avery Pond in **Preston**; Glasgo Pond, Hopeville Pond, and Pachaug Pond in **Griswold**; and Beach Pond, Beachdale Pond, and Green Falls Reservoir in **Voluntown**.

GAMING **Foxwoods Resort Casino** (800-752-9244; www.foxwoods.com), 39 Norwich Westerly Rd. (CT 2), Ledyard. Open 24 hours a day, every day of the year. This is where it all began. Ever since Connecticut's first casino opened more than a decade ago, it's given Atlantic City and Vegas a run for their money. More than 425 table games and 8,900 slot machines cater to both high rollers and new gamblers, whose quest to beat the odds keeps time with the perpetual blinking and clanging of the thousands of machines. The slots are decidedly user-friendly—all you need to know is where to insert your money and which button to push. The complex includes four hotels and a large convention center. A $700 million expansion includes the MGM Grand at Foxwoods, a 4,000-seat theater, a massive convention center and ballroom, shops, restaurants, and more gaming; in all, adding 2 million square feet to the resort. See also Mohegan Sun Casino in the New Londonchapter.

GOLF **Elmridge Golf Course** (860-599-2248; www.elmridgegolf.com), 229 Elmridge Rd., Pawcatuck. A challenging hilltop course with lovely views of picturesque Connecticut countryside. Par 71, 27 holes, 6,501 yards.

River Ridge Golf Course (860-376-3268), 259 Preston Rd. (CT 164), Griswold. A championship course overlooking the Quinebaug River. Full pro shop, rentals, and lessons; restaurant and lounge. Par 72, 18 holes, 6,871 yards.

Lake of Isles (888-475-3746; www.lakeofisles.com), 1 Clubhouse Dr., North Stonington. One of Connecticut's newest and most acclaimed golf courses sits across the street from Foxwoods Resort Casino and is owned by the casino. It's the work of legendary golf course designer Robert Jones, and comprises a state-of-the-art golf academy and a pair of 18-hole courses (one of which is private) spread across 900 acres of rolling countryside.

Birch Plain Golf Course (860-445-9918; www.birchplaingolf.com), 119 Highrock Rd., next to Groton Airport, Groton. An 18-hole, par-54 course with driving range. Good course for beginners.

Shennecossett Golf Course (860-445-0262; www.shennygolf.com), 93 Plant St., Groton. Founded in 1898 as a private course, now owned by the town of Groton. Views of the Thames River and Long Island Sound from the 16th and 17th holes. Restaurant and golf shop.

HAYRIDES ✐ **Davis Farm at Osbrook** (860-599-5859), Greenhaven Rd., Pawcatuck. Beautiful big Belgian horses pull hay wagons on hour-long rides.

SCENIC DRIVES **Pequot Trail**, just north of Stonington. The first of 27 official state scenic trails, **CT 234** climbs a steep ridge, plunges into a scenic valley, and winds through colonial villages graced by the famed maple trees whose fiery leaves turn autumn in New England into an artist's palette. The trail follows the warpath blazed by the fierce Pequots. Three other Mystic-area roads have also been designated official state trails: **CT 49 in North Stonington**, **CT 169 in Lisbon**, and **CT 164** beginning at the border of **Preston**. The Lisbon drive runs 32 miles through breathtaking woods and fields and pristine colonial towns and has been named by *Scenic America* as one of the top scenic roads in America. There are also several National Scenic Byways (see the back of the official state map).

SWIMMING ✐ **Esker Point Beach**, CT 215 and Marsh Rd., Noank. Parking fee $10. This picturesque spot has a sandy beach and shallow water, perfect for families with very young children. Food concessions and picnic tables are available.

✱ Green Space

Pachaug State Forest (860-376-4075), CT 49, Voluntown. More than 30 miles of the **Pachaug Trail** snake through this massive, 24,000-acre forest preserve, the largest in the state. Only a short distance from the busy coast, Pachaug also invites visitors to hunt, camp, picnic, and fish. Fishing is available nearby at Beach Pond, north of CT 165 at the Rhode Island border; Beachdale Pond, on the west side of CT 49 at CT 165; Green Falls Reservoir, south of CT 138; and Hodge Pond, on CT 49 south of the village center.

✐ ♿ **Denison Pequotsepos Nature Center** (860-536-1216; www.dpnc.org), 109 Pequotsepos Rd., Mystic. Open May–Oct., Tue.–Sat. 9–5. Shorter hours off-season. Self-guiding trails on a 300-acre wooded nature preserve where your children come face-to-face with great horned owls, toads, bogs of frogs, and lots of turtles. Native wildlife, birds, and small animals are on exhibit and described in a small natural history museum. The gift shop is stocked with an interesting mix of birdhouses, jewelry, games, and books: titles run the gamut from gardening and wildflower identification to birding guides.

♿ **Bluff Point Coastal Reserve** (860-444-7591), Depot Rd. (off US 1), Groton. An 800-acre hot spot for hikers, birders, and other outdoor types, with some of the state's last undisturbed shoreline. The park offers walking and hiking trails, a picnic area, and a beach. Cars are not allowed; be prepared to explore on foot. You can through the 1.5-mile-long wooden peninsula to a windswept headland bluff, or explore a mile-long pebbly tombolo beach. This was the home of Governor John Winthrop, whose family farmed the peninsula in the 18th century.

Barn Island Wildlife Management Area (860-424-3000), Palmer Neck Rd., Stonington. Sea kayakers and canoeists come to explore the placid waters; birders, to spy the winged creatures (hundreds of species of birds and waterfowl) that inhabit it. In all, 1,000 acres of land surrounded by nearly 300 acres of salt marsh.

✱ Lodging

RESORTS 🏵 🐾 **Inn at Mystic** (860-536-9604; 800-237-2415; www.innatmystic.com), US 1 and CT 27, Mystic 06355. The former estate of a local industrialist, this unique 15-acre complex, set on a plateau overlooking Mystic Harbor and Long Island Sound, is a beautiful Russian salad. The first section is an upscale motor inn with 47 rooms, plus four efficiencies and five suites. In the center of the estate, the Georgian colonial mansion of the late owner has five suites, including one in which Humphrey Bogart and Lauren Bacall spent their honeymoon more than 60 years ago. The building is on the National Register of Historic Places. The Gatehouse has five rooms, each with a fireplace and a Jacuzzi. Finally, there's the deluxe East Wing. English gardens, outdoor and indoor pools, tennis, canoeing or kayak sailing in one of the inn's boats, and a fitness room round out the facilities. Afternoon tea is served; the inn's Flood Tide restaurant (see *Dining Out*) is ranked with the best in the state. Your hosts, the Dyers and the Grays, guarantee you a resort experience you won't forget. Featured in *1,000 Places to See Before You Die.* $75–295. All rates include a full buffet breakfast and afternoon tea.

Foxwoods Resort Casino (800-369-9663; www.foxwoods.com), 39 Norwich Westerly Rd. (CT 2), Ledyard 06338. This resort complex just keeps growing. It offers four major hotels, and the end, probably, is not in sight. Newest is the **MGM Grand at Foxwoods** (866-646-0050; www.mgmatfoxwoods.com), an 825-room hotel tower that opened in the summer of 2008 with a 21,000-square-foot spa, a nightclub, restaurants, and a casino. **Grand Pequot Tower**, a deluxe 24-story hotel soaring above the wooded hills, has an indoor pool, a spa, and a gourmet restaurant on the top floor (see Paragon under *Dining Out*). It joins **Two Trees Inn**, which has a country inn feel with hardwood floors, wool scatter rugs, cherry paneling, and custom-made furniture. The fourth, a 312-room luxury hostelry called the **Great Cedar Hotel**, is located right above one of the resort's casinos. For substantial discounts on rooms, you can become a member of the Foxwoods Wampum Club.

INNS ♦ ✐ ♿ **Whaler's Inn** (860-536-1506; 800-243-2588; www.whalersinnmystic.com), 20 East Main St., Mystic 06355. There are 45 rooms spread throughout five buildings in this comfortable and homey inn in the heart of downtown Mystic, next to the historic Bascule bridge. Rooms are decorated with canopy beds, wingback chairs, humpback couches, and rich color schemes. Some are standards; others have whirlpool tub, fireplace, and river views. Restaurant on premises (see Bravo Bravo Restaurant under *Dining Out*). $105–259.

♿ **Steamboat Inn** (860-536-8300; www.steamboatinnmystic.com), 73 Steamboat Wharf, Mystic 06355. The location couldn't be more ideal: This small and intimate luxury inn is right on the banks of the Mystic River but close to the heart of the city and Seaport. In fact, it's the only waterfront lodging in this historic town surrounded by water. The 10 rooms and suites have interiors decorated with antiques and earth tones; most have a working fireplace, whirlpool tub, and windows that frame views of boats plying to and from Long Island Sound on the Mystic River. The larger suites on dock level have wet-bar areas and refrigerators. Continental breakfast and afternoon tea. $140–300.

♿ ✐ **Taber Inne and Suites** (860-536-4904; 866-822-3746; www.taberinne.com), 66 Williams Ave. (US 1), Mystic 06355. A variety of lodging options spread across several buildings: 16 standard guest rooms, and one- and two-bedroom suites with fireplace, Jacuzzi tub, and balcony. There's an indoor pool, and guests can use the facilities of the private health club across the street. Continental breakfast. $110–425.

The Inn at Stonington (860-535-2000; www.innatstonington.com), 60 Water St., Stonington 06378. This three-story, 18-room, elegant Greek Revival–style inn has been widely touted as one of Connecticut's "most romantic hotels." Who can deny it when all rooms have Jacuzzi, Frette robes, and Anachini linens? Some have a gas fireplace, others, decks with water views. Common rooms are bright and sunny, with the work of local artists hanging on the walls. From the windows overlooking Stonington Harbor, watch the sun rise, or the fishermen, lobstermen, and yachtsmen heading out to sea for a day of work or fun. At eventide make your way to the third-floor "Harborview" for the magnificent sunset. There's a 400-foot deep-water dock for visiting yachters, and bicycles and kayaks are available to guests. Continental breakfast, tea in the afternoon. $150–445.

BED & BREAKFASTS In addition to the listings below, a number of B&B reservations services offer access to rooms available in establishments throughout the state. For a list, see *Bed & Breakfasts* in "What's Where in Connecticut."

In Mystic 06355 and Old Mystic 06372

Pequot Hotel Bed & Breakfast (860-572-0390; www.pequothotelbandb.com), 711 Cow Hill Rd., Mystic. A full country breakfast is served by a veteran flight attendant in this restored 19th-century stagecoach inn. The three charming rooms all have private bath, one with whirlpool, two with working fireplace. Guests can stroll around the estate's 23 wooded acres, play horseshoes or badminton, enjoy the well-tended gardens, or relax on the large porch. A dog and a cat are in residence. $95–175.

The Adams House (860-572-9551; www.adamshouseofmystic.com), 382 Cow Hill Rd., Mystic. A little more than a mile from the Seaport. A charming 1750s-era house with six rooms in the main building; the two rooms in the carriage house are an ideal setting for family groups. Full breakfast. $85–175.

🐾 **Harbour Inne & Cottage** (860-572-9253; www.harbourinne-cottage.com), 15 Edgemont St., Mystic. In the heart of downtown Mystic, a short walk from the railroad station, restaurants, and shopping. Overlooks the Mystic River. Each of the four bedrooms has kitchen privileges, cable TV, and air-conditioning. The cottage is decorated in cedar and offers a bedroom with a fireplace; it can sleep six. There's a hot tub on the deck, and an antique piano and fireplace in the social room. Continental breakfast. $70–300.

House of 1833 Bed and Breakfast Resort (860-536-6325; 800-367-1833; www.houseof1833.com), 72 North Stonington Rd., Mystic. A Greek Revival banker's mansion built in 1833 and set in the midst of 3 acres has been lovingly restored. Innkeepers Evan Nickles and Robert Bankel make every effort to create a "romantic hideaway" and have artfully succeeded. All five guest suites have private bath, four with Jacuzzi tub, porch or balcony, and each with a working fireplace. Antiques abound throughout the house. A baby grand piano invites you to tinkle the keys in the music room. Sit before the Belgian fireplace in the large common room or catch up on your reading in the library. Take a dip in the outdoor pool. Lush perennial gardens. There's a gas grill, croquet, a tennis court, and bicycles for touring. Full gourmet breakfast by candlelight. $99–249.

The Old Mystic Inn (860-572-9422; www.oldmysticinn.com), 52 Main St., Old Mystic. This old home and its carriage house welcome guests in eight rooms. Three of the four rooms in the main house have working fireplace; three in the carriage house also have fireplace, and two have whirlpool. Canopy beds add that certain old New England ambience in five rooms. And all of the rooms are named for famous New England authors, from Thoreau to Stowe, and including that Hannibal, Missouri, transplant to Hartford, Mark Twain. Owner Michael Cardillo Jr. is a graduate of the Culinary Institute of America, and his gourmet breakfasts will be the highlight of your morning. $135–215.

In Stonington 06378 and North Stonington 06359

Another Second Penny Inn (860-535-1710; www.secondpenny.com), 870 Pequot Trail, Stonington. Check in at Jim and Sandra Wright's classic 1710 clapboard on a lovely 5-acre farm. The three guest rooms are inviting. All have a private bath, working fireplace, and mini refrigerator; two have claw-foot tubs. Full breakfast. $99–250.

Orchard Street Inn (860-535-2681; www.orchardstreetinn.com), 41 Orchard St., Stonington. Three rooms, one with private bath, in a secluded, small cottage in the rear yard. Nicely decorated, stylish, and comfy. Antique furniture; TV and in-room refrigerator. There are also three new guest rooms in the main building. $160–220.

High Acres Bed & Breakfast (860-887-4355; 888-680-7829; www.highacresbb.com), 222 Northwest Corner Rd., North Stonington. A 100-acre retreat with majestic views and miles of walking trails. All four rooms in this 1740 colonial farmhouse have private bath. Tea and backgammon in the library. A perfect place to relax after a full day of sightseeing. Antiques-filled common rooms are elegant and cozy. Full breakfast. $129–169.

Antiques and Accommodations (800-554-7829; www.antiquesandaccommodations.com), 32 Main St., North Stonington. Hosts Tom and Ann Gray have lovingly restored this yellow-clapboard Victorian home, on the National Register of Historic Places. It feels like a retreat, yet it's near enough to the shore and casino to feel close to the action. There are two rooms with private bath, one with a working fireplace. Full of fine American and English antiques, some for sale. Full breakfast by candlelight. $129–229.

Inn at Lower Farm B&B (866-535-9075; www.lowerfarm.com), 119 Mystic Rd., North Stonington. Four large guest rooms have a sitting area and private bath—most also have fireplace and whirlpool tub—in a restored 1740 center-chimney Georgian colonial farmhouse. Five acres of gardens, marshlands, and woodlands can be explored on easy walking trails. Wooden benches are scattered around so guests can pause, catch their breath, and track the myriad birds. Full country breakfast served by candlelight in front of the large hearth fireplace in the keeping room. $100–175.

Elsewhere

Stonecroft Country Inn (860-572-0771; 800-772-0774; www.stonecroft.com), 515 Pumpkin Hill Rd., Ledyard 06339. This elegant 1807 Georgian Colonial, formerly a sea captain's home, has four guest rooms. In the converted 19th-century barn, called The Grange, six rooms and suites have fireplace, whirlpool tub, and Internet access. Dinner (see *Dining Out*) by the fireside in dining room or on the garden terrace. Full breakfast. $150–300.

The Mare's Inn (860-572-7556), 333 Colonel Ledyard Hwy., Ledyard 06339. A simple and comfy B&B with three guest rooms (fireplace and private bath), plus a suite with a kitchen and its own entrance. Full breakfast. $125–220.

Branch Place Bed & Breakfast (860-376-5885; 866-376-5885; www.thebranchplace.com), 34 Newent Rd., Lisbon 06351-2925. A restored 1790 New England gambrel Cape built by a Revolutionary War veteran in the center of town. In the keeping room you feel the depth of years, with vintage touches that extend to two nicely appointed guest rooms. Full breakfast. $125–145.

Captain Grant's (860-887-7589; 800-982-1772; www.captaingrants.com), 109–111 CT 2A, Poquetanuck 06365. Travelers will do well to book a room at this charming bed & breakfast on the National Register of Historic Places that some believe is haunted. It was built in 1754 by Captain William Grant for his wife; later it was used as a garrison by Continental troops during the Revolutionary War. Lovingly restored historic details, from wide-board floors and a two-story deck overlooking the historic green, to a mural depicting the village in 1825. Of the seven guest rooms, two are in the Avery Home next door. Discounts available for several area restaurants and the Mashantucket Pequot Museum, and guest passes for Mystic Seaport Museum. Full breakfast. $89–169.

The Morgan Inn (860-599-5470; 866-782-9948; www.themorganinn.com), 16 South Broad St., Pawcatuck 06379. A romantic and nostaligic B&B; the five guest rooms, with names such as Thanks for the Memories and Sentimental Journey, are thoughtfully decorated with music themes from the early 1900s. Full breakfast. $109–179.

HOTELS

In Mystic 06355

Hilton Mystic (860-572-0731; 800-445-8667; www.hiltonmystic.com), 20 Coogan Blvd. Unusually attractive for a chain establishment, this rambling redbrick hotel sits on a ledge overlooking the aquarium and Olde Mistick Village, and it's just down the road from the Seaport. You'll find 183 rooms, some suites, an indoor pool, and a fitness room. Golf, tennis, and racquetball are nearby. The hotel caters to children, with special activities including clowns and a kids' barbecue. **The Mooring** is the main restaurant; **Soundings Lounge** is a bit more casual. $119–319.

Best Western Mystic Hotel & Conference Center (800-363-1622; www.bwmystic.com), 9 Whitehall Ave. Great location, within blocks of the seaport, the aquarium, and Olde Mistick Village. Indoor pool and restaurant. Continental breakfast. $99–159.

Hyatt Place Mystic (860-536-9997; reservations 888-492-8847; www.hyattplace.com), 224 Greenmanville Ave. (CT 27). A newly renovated hotel with contemporary decor; guest rooms have flat-panel HD television and free WiFi. The outdoor pool is on the small side, but adequate. Continental breakfast. $139–229.

Residence Inn by Marriott (860-536-5150; www.marriott.com), 40 Whitehall Ave.; just north of Olde Mistick Village on CT 27. **Whitehall Mansion** is a colonial home with five guest rooms. The inn itself features 128 fully equipped suites, all with kitchen. Some suites have Jacuzzi and fireplace. Indoor pool and fitness center. Continental breakfast. $99–219.

Elsewhere

Mystic Marriott Hotel and Spa (860-446-2600; 866-449-7390; www.marriott.com), 625 North Rd., Groton 06340. A Georgian-style hotel with 285 rooms in the state's most popular travel destination. Indoor pool, Elizabeth Arden Red Door Salon, and a full-service spa. **Octagon** features fine dining; **Vines Restaurant** has more casual fare. $169–299.

Groton Inn and Suites (860-445-9784; 800-452-2191; www.grotoninn.com), 99 Gold Star Hwy. (CT 184), Groton 06340. A variety of accommodations, from standard rooms and deluxe suites to apartments and efficiency studios. Clean and comfortably furnished, with coffeemakers, refrigerators, and microwave ovens. $80–233.

♿ **Bellissimo Grande Hotel** (877-700-0079; www.bellissimogrande.com), 411 Norwich Westerly Rd. (CT 2), North Stonington 06359. This Italian-themed all-suite hotel is a popular alternative when Foxwoods Resort Casino is booked; they even run a free limousine service to Foxwoods. Amenities include plasma TVs, ceiling fans, and in-room safes; some of the suites have fireplace. There's a small but well-regarded spa, an indoor pool, a bistro, and a bar. Continental breakfast. $99–259.

♿ **AmericInn Lodge & Suites** (860-376-3200; reservations 800-396-5007; www.americinn.com), 375 Voluntown Rd., Griswold 06351. Standard accommodations that are simple and clean. Suites have microwave oven and mini fridge; some also have gas fireplace and whirlpool tub. Continental breakfast. $89–199.

MOTELS

In Groton 06340

♿ **Flagship Inn and Suites** (860-405-1111; 888-800-0770; www.theflagshipinn.com), 470 Gold Star Hwy. (CT 184). A family-friendly motel with 60 comfortable and simply furnished rooms, some double guest rooms with adjoining rooms for families. Continental breakfast. $99–129.

Hampton Inn (860-405-1585; www.hamptoninngroton.com), 300 Long Hill Rd. (US 1). Convenient location. Of the 80 clean basic rooms, 4 are suites. Indoor pool and fitness room, business center. Continental breakfast. $119–209.

♿ **Sojourner Inn** (860-445-1986; 800-697-8483; www.sojournerinn.com), 605 Gold Star Hwy. (CT 184). Convenient to Mystic, the naval base, and the casinos. Four types of suites to accommodate families or singles, or to provide a deluxe vacation with a Jacuzzi. Each suite has cable TV and kitchenette. Special rooms welcome the tabby or the pooch. $69–259.

Elsewhere

♿ **Days Inn** (860-572-0574; reservations 800-329-7466; www.daysinn.com), 55 Whitehall Ave., Mystic 06355. A pleasant motel near the Seaport, the aquarium, and I-95 with an outdoor pool and 122 rooms that are above average, clean, and well appointed. Continental breakfast. $59–169.

Sea Breeze Inn (860-535-2843), 812 Stonington Rd. (US 1), Stonington 06378. The 28 rooms and two suites are clean, decent-sized, and modern, with standard amenities. Stonington Borough is a short drive away. $55–175.

♿ **Stonington Motel** (860-599-2330; www.stoningtonmotel.com), 901 Stonington Rd. (US 1), Stonington 06378. Each of the 13 simply furnished guest rooms here has TV, air-conditioning, refrigerator, and microwave oven. $59–89.

CAMPGROUNDS

Seaport Campground (860-536-4044; www.seaportcampground.com), CT 184, P.O. Box 104, Old Mystic 06372. Open Apr.–Nov. A family campground about 3 miles from Mystic Seaport with 130 tent and RV sites. A full schedule of events is scheduled from spring to fall; there's also an in-ground pool, mini golf, a fishing pond, and games for children. $33–47.

Mystic KOA Campground (800-562-3451; www.mystickoacampground.com), 118 Pendleton Hill Rd. (CT 49), North Stonington 06359. Open year-round. This new KOA campground, formerly Highland Orchards RV Park, offers fishing, swimming, hayrides, outdoor movies, and full services. On a hilltop with views of rolling hills; ancient apple trees and maples are a clue that this was one of Connecticut's earliest farms. $35–55.

Strawberry Park (860-886-1944; 888-794-7944; www.strawberrypark.net), 42 Pierce Rd., Preston 06365. Open year-round. A full-service family campground on 160 wooded and pleasantly landscaped acres. There's a busy schedule of planned activities in addition to swimming, horseback riding, ball fields, and a popular annual bluegrass festival. $60–90.

Circle C Campground (800-424-4534; www.campcirclec.com), 21 Bailey Pond Rd., Voluntown 06384. Open mid-Apr.–mid-Oct. A family campground near the state's largest forest. There's a swimming pond, a playground, basketball courts, a convenience store, and many other amenities. Indoor accommodations include rustic cabins that accommodate four people. Sites $29–36; cabins $40.

Hopeville Pond State Park (860-376-0313), 193 Roode Rd., Jewett City 06351. Open mid-Apr.–Sept. There are 80 wooded sites in this state park campground that's encompassed by the larger Pachaug State Forest. There's plenty to do here, too, from canoeing and pond swimming to fishing. Sites $13.

Ross Hill Park (860-376-9606; 800-308-1089; www.rosshillpark.com), 170 Ross Hill Rd., Lisbon 06351. Open mid-Apr.–Oct. A 50-acre family campground on the Quinebaug River with sites for tents and RVs, and rustic camping cabins. Amenities include a swimming pond with sandy beach, playgrounds, kayak and canoe rentals, and free WiFi. A full schedule of activities such as live music, karaoke, and fun contests for kids. Sites $38–43; cabins $80.

Pachaug State Forest (860-376-4075), Voluntown 06384. Two camping areas: **Green Falls Campground**, off CT 138, just 3 miles east of town, with 18 sites, pond fishing; and **Mt. Misery Campground**, off CT 49 north of town, with 22 sites, stream fishing, and swimming nearby. **Frog Hollow Horse Camp** is for equestrians. All are first-come, first-served wooded sites and rustic—meaning no concessions. Pets allowed. $11–14.

Where to Eat

DINING OUT

In Mystic

Azu (860-536-6336), 32 Main St. Open for lunch and dinner daily; breakfast on Sat. and Sun. A lively and energetic restaurant and bar in downtown Mystic. The creative menu is evidence that the kitchen is clearly having a ball. The nachos topped with sautéed lobster makes a fine appetizer; must-try entrées include cashew-encrusted pork tenderloin, fish stew over linguine, and—if it's on the specials roster when you're there—lobster risotto. Almond tiramisu is a pleasurable end to everything. $15–30.

♿ **Steak Loft** (860-536-2661; www.steakloftct.com), Olde Mistick Village. Open for lunch Mon.–Sat.; dinner daily. The massive wooden beams have anchored this local favorite for more than 35 years. In-the-know locals come for the steak, chops, seafood, and ligher bar bites. $16–33.

Go Fish (860-536-2662; www.gofishct.com), Olde Mistick Village. Open for lunch Mon.–Sat.; dinner daily. This eclectic eatery just across the road from the aquarium is the go-to spot for fresh seafood in all its incarnations: sushi and sashimi, raw shellfish, chowder, and fish that comes baked, grilled, sautéed, steamed, and fried. $17–27.

Seamen's Inne Restaurant and Pub (860-572-5303), 105 Greenmanville Ave. (CT 27), just outside the north gate of Mystic Seaport. Open daily for lunch and dinner. Tourists and locals love the English-pub atmosphere, from the antique ship figureheads on the wall to the ales on tap. They rave about the menu, too, especially New England classics such as the Old Mystic fisherman's stew and the Seamen's Inne seafood pie. $15–26.

Captain Daniel Packer Inne Restaurant and Pub (860-536-3555, www.danielpacker.com), 32 Water St. Open for lunch and dinner daily. The menu steers diners to standouts like the almond-encrusted goat cheese medallions and Blackjack Sirloin: aged Angus steak seared and grilled, served with a wild mushroom and Jack Daniels demiglaze. The 250-year-old building is on both the national and Connecticut historic registers. $14–26.

Flood Tide (860-536-8140), at the junction of US 1 and CT 27, at the Inn at Mystic (see *Lodging*). Open daily for breakfast, lunch, and dinner; brunch on Sun. Mystic's only restaurant with views of Mystic Harbor and Long Island Sound is set high on a knoll that also overlooks Mystic Railroad Station, which was the model for the station in the Lionel toy train sets. Diners can catch glimpses into the new open-hearth kitchen as they feast on gourmet cuisine. Wait staff are informed and honest, steering diners to standouts like the house-made grilled vegetable ravioli with fennel pollen pasta and fire-roasted tomato coulis, the arctic char en papillote, and the lobster cioppino. For dessert, it's hard not to love the lavender crème brûlée or the decadent chocolate hazelnut torte. $24–39.

Bravo Bravo Restaurant and Bar (860-536-3228), at the Whaler's Inn (see *Lodging*), 20 East Main St. Open for lunch Tue.–Sat.; dinner Tue.–Sun.; closed Mon. Italian fare and fresh seafood at the foot of the Bascule bridge in downtown Mystic. For an appetizer, try the sirloin carpaccio. Choice entrées include champagne risotto with lobster and asparagus, and spicy seafood stew over linguine. $16–25.

Peking Tokyo (860-572-9991; www.pekingtokyomystic.com), 12 Coogan Blvd. (across from the aquarium). Open for lunch Mon.–Sat.; dinner daily. The kitchen produces top-flight sushi and the full range of udon and danburi dishes, as well as a first-class Chinese menu. $12–18.

In Stonington and North Stonington

Noah's Restaurant (860-535-3925; www.noahsfinefood.com), 113 Water St., Stonington. Open Tue.–Sun. for breakfast, lunch, and dinner; closed Mon. A café and lively bar in the heart of Stonington Borough that's casual at breakfast and lunch (a good time to bring the kids), and more dressed up at dinner. Bypass the meats and chops on the regular menu for the exceptionally fresh seafood specials, particularly the local scallops, lobster, and flounder. Some come just for the Boston cream pie and other made-right-here desserts. Dinner reservations are a good idea, especially on weekends when visitors descend on this lovely village. $14–27.

Dogwatch Café (860-415-4510; www.dogwatchcafe.com), Dodson Boatyard, 194 Water St., Stonington. Open daily for lunch and dinner; breakfast on Sat. and Sun. For years this was Boom, sitting virtually in a working boatyard and marina. It's more casual these days, and the name has changed but, happily, not much else.

Masts and crisp white sails provide a fitting backdrop to the blue-water views from the dining room, where you can still dine on incredibly fresh flounder and scallops hauled in by Stonington's fishing fleet, based nearby at the Town Dock. The lively bar remains a hangout for upscale revelers. $12–25.

♿ **Water Street Café** (860-535-2122), 142 Water St., Stonington. Open for lunch Thu.–Mon.; dinner daily. Only 10 tables in a 1900s post-and-beam house, but well worth a wait. Start dinner with tartare of smoked salmon or gravlax or seared shrimp in Pommery mustard sauce. For the main course, you might enjoy seared scallops in a ginger-scallion vinaigrette. Meat lovers rave over the grilled hanger steak (hanger steak is better known as butcher's tenderloin) in a red wine and blue cheese sauce. $17–25.

In Groton and Noank

Olio Restaurant (860-445-6546), 33 Kings Hwy., Groton. Open for lunch Mon.–Sat.; dinner daily. From the same owners as Bravo Bravo Restaurant in Mystic, this sleek and stylish spot attracts a 30-something crowd that comes for the top-shelf martinis and chic surroundings. Contemporary American cuisine translates into grilled fish, gourmet pizza, and fresh pasta. $16–30.

Koto Japanese Steak House (860-445-5686; www.kotoct.com), 527 Long Hill Rd., Groton. Open for lunch Tue.–Sat.; dinner daily. At the hibachi tables, dining is an interactive experience. Watch while your meal is cooked tableside by chefs full of tricks and culinary acrobatics. Start with miso soup, move on to sushi or teriyaki steak, end with fried tempura ice cream. $15–26.

Octagon Steak House (860-326-0360), 625 North Rd., at the Mystic Marriott Hotel and Spa (see *Lodging*), Groton. Most hotels get away with serving solidly mediocre fare; not so at the Mystic Marriott, where sophisticated steak house dishes are accompanied by an extensive wine list. It's named for the massive octagonal open-flame grill, which puts out food that is picture-perfect, and much of it is as good as it looks. Beneath the original painting *Le Sommelier*, diners feast on pistachio-crusted salmon, grilled veal porterhouse, and the signature chili-rubbed Angus rib eye with bordelaise sauce. $27–40; $70 for the Kobe beef.

🖍 **Seahorse Restaurant** (860-536-1670; www.seahorserestaurant.com), 65 Marsh Rd., Noank. Open daily for lunch and dinner. So popular that the line extends out the door, even in midwinter. Clams casino is a Seahorse tradition. Other appetizers range from clams, shrimps, mussels, oysters, and calamari to stuffed quahogs. A variety of salads and sandwiches, along with fish entrées, complete the luncheon menu. Steaks, chops, fish, and seafood are your dinner choices. $13–30.

🖍 **The Fisherman Restaurant and Lounge** (860-536-1717; www.fishermanrestaurant.com), 937 Groton Long Point Rd. (CT 215), Noank. Open daily for lunch and dinner. You'll want to start dinner with such local delicacies as Noank bluepoint oyster or Stonington sea scallops, then plunge into the seafood entrées, from grilled swordfish to bouillabaisse. Beef, poultry, and pasta complete the extensive main menu. The setting, overlooking Palmers Cove and Fishers Island Sound, is lovely. $21–32.

In Mashantucket and Ledyard

♿ **Al Dente** (860-312-2000), Foxwoods Resort Casino, 39 Norwich Westerly Rd. (CT 2), Mashantucket. Open daily for dinner. In the Grand Pequot Tower, fine dining by way of sophisticated Italian cuisine. Signature dishes like lobster tails and grilled veal chops don't disappoint—the former arrives atop linguine with a spicy roasted garlic tomato sauce. For dessert, zuccotto never fails to elicit gasps of wonder. $28–40.

♿ **Alta Strada** (860-312-2582; www.altastradarestaurant.com), MGM Grand at Foxwoods, 240 MGM Grand Ave. (off CT 2), Mashantucket. Open for lunch and dinner daily. Ever since New England's own haute-cuisine chef, Michael Schlow, opened this gem (its name means "high road" in Italian) in 2008, high rollers have had more cause to work up an appetite on the casino floor. Lavish standouts include organic Atlantic salmon with roasted baby beets and salsa verde, and arctic char with leeks and house-cured pancetta. Attentive (but not overly so) staff add to the ambience of this oasis sheltered from the boisterous casino floor. At the bar, 150 Italian wines. $31–50.

♿ **Craftsteak** (860-646-0050; www.craftrestaurant.com), in the MGM Grand at Foxwoods, 240 MGM Grand Ave. (off CT 2), Mashantucket. Open daily for dinner. This is dining as it should be: a feast for all the senses. It's a posh, Manhattan-style affair, with superchef Tom Colicchio (think Bravo TV's *Top Chef*) at the helm. And with entrées in the $50 neighborhood, it's also not for the faint of wallet. Dishes like the braised Maine lobster and hefty dry-aged steaks prove, however, that a truly memorable meal may be worth your very last dime. $25–101.

Paragon Restaurant (860-312-3000), Foxwoods Resort Casino, 39 Norwich Westerly Rd. (CT 2), Mashantucket. Open for dinner Wed.–Sun.; closed Mon. and Tue. Most people come to Foxwoods for the casinos, but on the 24th floor of the Grand Pequot Tower, it's the food that's on display. This is one of only a handful of Connecticut restaurants to earn the AAA Four Diamond Award of Excellence, so expect luxe cuisine in luxe surroundings. Super-high rollers and others with deep pockets dine on Niman Ranch steaks and Asian-influenced continental cuisine. $26–85.

David Burke Prime (800-369-9663), Foxwoods Resort Casino, 39 Norwich Westerly Rd. (CT 2), Mashantucket. Open daily for lunch and dinner; Sun. brunch. David Burke has scored again with this follow-up to his eponymous New York, Las Vegas, and Chicago hot spots. The luxe steakhouse and bar in the Grand Pequot Tower is everything you'd expect from the celebrity chef (including sky-high prices), like steaks from an in-house salt-lined aging room, and more than 5,000 wines on display in a dramatic three-story tower. Save room for the sinful butterscotch *panna cotta*—after a hard day or night on the casino floor, you've likely earned it. The more casual **Burke in the Box** eatery offers sandwiches, salads, pizza, and other simple fare prepared with upscale ingredients. $25–58.

Shrine (860-312-8888; www.shrinemgmfoxwoods.com), MGM Grand at Foxwoods, 240 MGM Grand Dr., Mashantucket. Open daily for dinner; late-night menu. Reservations are strongly recommended, especially on weekends. This stylish Asian-fusion newcomer is truly ahead of the curve. You'll find beautifully plated dishes inspired by virtually every corner of Asia. The East Coast cod is a standout, but perhaps the most delicious of all is the Wagyu rib-eye steak, served with grilled baby shiitake mushrooms and soya onions. The trend factor is high—chic wait staff, sophisticated clientele, over-the-top decor, and food that lives up to the hype. The cavernous space, with the feel of a lushly exotic Chinese nightclub, is part sushi bar, restaurant, and lounge, but morphs into a nightclub later on. Half the menu features sushi and sashimi; the other, pan-Asian cuisine, from Wagyu beef short ribs to panko-crusted calamari. $23–49.

Stonecroft (860-572-0771; 800-772-0774; www.stonecroft.com), 515 Pumpkin Hill Rd., Ledyard. Open for dinner Wed.–Sun.; closed Mon. and Tue. Reservations are essential. Contemporary American cuisine in an elegant 1807 Georgian colonial (see *Lodging*). In warm months, it's a tough choice between the dining room in the converted 19th-century barn and the garden terrace, but you can't go wrong with either. Start with crêpes stuffed with lobster, shallots, and cremini mushrooms in a Madeira wine sauce; then try the roast rack of spring lamb with walnut spearmint pesto, or the pan-roasted red snapper with coriander-scented tomato sauce. $18–36.

EATING OUT

In Mystic

Harp and Hound Pub (860-572-7778), 4 Pearl St. Open daily for lunch and dinner. Duck into this cool and dark pub for a bit of Ireland in New England, not to mention a break from the tourist-thronged sidewalks. Irish and Scottish malts and Irish ales on tap; burgers, bangers and mash, and other light meals. $8–20.

Jamms Restaurant (860-536-2683; www.jammsrestaurant.com), 8 Coogan Blvd., overlooking Olde Mistick Village. Open daily for lunch and dinner; Sun. brunch. Everything from soups—clam chowder, naturally—to light fare, sandwiches, pastas, and complete meals with a varied selection of New England seafood (the stew with scallops, shrimp, clams, mussels, and fish in a tomato broth has a devoted following). Kids can choose off their own menu or opt for one of the signature burgers. $15–24.

Margaritas (860-536-4589; www.margs.com), 12 Water St. Open daily. Tex-Mex specialties with a nautical touch: seafood enchiladas plus the usual American Mexican dishes. Margaritas occupies a converted factory across from the Mystic Arts Center. As befits the establishment's name, the frozen drinks are marvelous. $12–17.

A Taste of India (860-536-8485), 35A Williams Ave. Open for daily for lunch and dinner. A small Indian restaurant that's simply and pleasantly furnished with traditional Indian decor. Tandoori ovens busily churn out the cuisine known for its exotic and earthy spices in varying degrees of intensity. To start, you can try the one of the traditional samosas, stuffed with spicy ground lamb or a filling of potatoes and peas. The extensive menu features chicken korma, tandoori lamb, and a roster of meatless dishes that vegetarians will appreciate. $12–20.

Kitchen Little (860-536-2122), 135 Greenmanville Ave. (CT 27), Mystic. Open for breakfast daily; lunch Mon.–Fri. "Little" it is; more like tiny. Stop for breakfast to fuel up for a day at Mystic Seaport, just down the road. Most come for breakfast: omelets, corned beef hash, scrambled eggs with cream cheese and crabmeat. If you stop by later in the day, the chowder made with fresh clams and herbs, and fried scallop rolls, are hits at lunchtime. $5–13.

Mystic Pizza (860-536-3700; www.mysticpizza.com), 56 West Main St., in the heart of downtown. Open daily for lunch and dinner. More than a few years back, a writer motoring from Maine down along the East Coast stopped here for a pizza. Intrigued by both the food and the name of the restaurant, she wrote a movie script called *Mystic Pizza.* The movie was produced for a measly $9 million on location in Mystic and Stonington, and catapulted one of the three female leads, Julia Roberts, into instant stardom. It didn't hurt the pizza shop, either. You decide whether a slice of Mystic Pizza is "a slice of heaven." Another location at the junction of CT 2 and CT 184 in North Stonington (860-599-3111). $6–17.

♿ **Rice-Spice-Noodles Restaurant** (860-572-8488), 4 Roosevelt Ave. (US 1). Open for lunch Tue.–Fri.; dinner Tue.–Sun.; closed Mon. A tiny Thai restaurant just outside the Mystic train station is a local favorite. Craving the tingling heat of Thai cooking? Try the vegetarian drunken noodles, zapped with the region's signature chili. Pad Thai, soft-shell crab, lemongrass pork, and fried ice cream are equally good. $9–25.

Somewhere in Time (860-536-1985), 3175 Gold Star Hwy. (CT 184), Old Mystic. Open Tue.–Sun. for breakfast and lunch; closed Mon. This homey gem off Mystic's tourist track is a local favorite. Overlook its strip-mall location and you'll be rewarded with satisfying comfort food: pancakes and omelets at breakfast, homemade soups and generous sandwiches made from fresh-roasted turkey at lunch. $5–9.

S&P Oyster Company (860-536-2674; www.sp-oyster.com), 1 Holmes St. Open daily for lunch and dinner. This popular downtown restaurant and bar, whose windows frame views of the Mystic River bridge, is just three blocks from the Seaport museum. Market-fresh seafood means pan-seared Stonington scallops, Alaskan king crab legs, and of course oysters in all their incarnations. $14–30.

Elsewhere

♿ **Abbott's Lobster in the Rough** (860-536-7719; www.abbotts-lobster.com), 117 Pearl St., Noank. Open May–Oct. for lunch and dinner. The ultimate fun place on the Connecticut shore for your lobster experience. Complete lobster meals are served on rustic picnic tables in the sun, beneath a striped tent, or in a closed pavilion on Noank Harbor. Watch the panorama of passing yachts, fishing boats, and windjammers while you enjoy steamers, clam chowder, stuffed clams, and oysters on the half shell. There's lobster, of course, and lots of it: Order it on a roll, steamed in the shell, or in a creamy bisque. $12–16.

ABBOTT'S LOBSTER IN THE ROUGH ALONG THE MYSTIC RIVER IN NOANK

Kim Grant

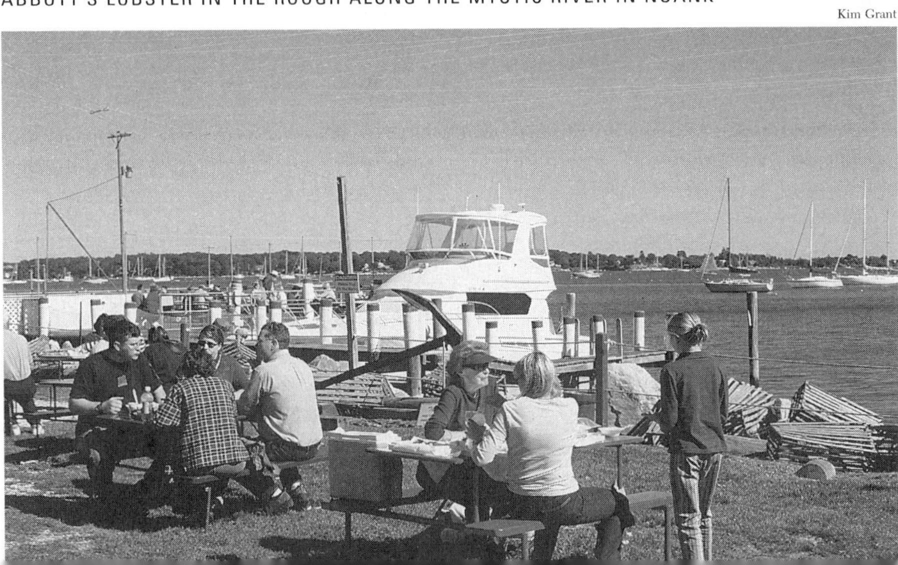

Russell's Ribs (860-445-8849), 214 CT 12, Groton. Open daily for lunch and dinner. Huge portions of southwestern dishes are served family-style. Don't miss the barbecue, particularly the signature baby back ribs. $6–22.

The Blue Door (860-536-5300), 36 Quarry Rd., Stonington. Open Mon.–Fri. for lunch; dinner daily; breakfast on Sat. and Sun. It's worth finding this out-of-the-way waterfront café far from the tourist fray. Creative American dishes blend familiar local ingredients with unique preparations; expect dishes such as lobster rolls, crabcakes, fish-and-chips, and seafood risotto. Grab a table on the deck in-season and enjoy the views of the Mystic River. $8–18.

Skipper's Dock (860-535-0111; www.skippersdock.com), 66 Water St., Stonington. Open daily for lunch and dinner; Sun. brunch in fall. In-season, grab a table on the 600-foot pier for good looks at Stonington Harbor's bustling yachting scene. The menu revolves around fresh-caught native fish and shellfish hauled in by the local fleet. Inside, the dining room and cozy bar are outfitted in nautical decor. Boat-mooring facilities are available for diners arriving by water. $10–18.

Watermark (860-535-2529; www.watermarkcafe.com), 2 Wyassup Rd., North Stonington. Open Tue.–Sat. for breakfast and lunch; closed Sun. and Mon. A former general store is now this café and back-room art gallery. Well-prepared renditions of breakfast and lunch standbys: egg dishes in the morning; salads, wraps, and soups later on. $4–9.

SNACKS

In Mystic

Sea Swirl (860-536-3452; www.seaswirlofmystic.com), 30 Williams Ave., at the junction of CT 27 and US 1. Open Apr.–Columbus Day weekend, daily 10–10. Local foodies agree this seafood shack is *the* spot along the Connecticut shore for fried clams. They caught the attention of Rachael Ray, who filmed a spot here for the Food Network. Besides bivalves, there are juicy hamburgers, hot dogs, rotisserie chicken, sandwiches, soups, and two dozen flavors of ice cream—something for the entire family. Dine outdoors and view the water activity on the Mystic River or, if you're lucky, catch a phenomenal sunset. $6–15.

Sea View Snack Bar (860-572-0096), 145 Greenmanville Ave. (CT 27). Open daily May–Oct. Don't pass up this unprepossessing-looking shanty on the banks of the Mystic River if you have a carful of hungry children. The menu runs the gamut from great chowder to fried clams or clam strips, lobster salad rolls, cheese dogs, juicy burgers, platters, fries, milk shakes, and soft-serve ice cream. $4–11.

Coastal Gourmet (860-572-7992; www.mysticmarket.com), 63 Willliams Ave. (US 1); another location at 375 Noank Rd. (860-536-1500). This upscale market is the go-to place for gourmet groceries, boxed lunches, desserts, snacks, and prepared entrées for a picnic, the beach, or to take on your boat.

Elsewhere

Cove Fresh Fish Market (860-536-0061; www.covefish.com), 20 Old Stonington Rd. (US 1). Open daily. More than 40 years of serving a million bowls of clam chowder and lobster salad rolls has earned this "eat in the rough" market and shack a deserved reputation for fresh, delicious fish. There are lobster rolls and there are lobster rolls, and then there are Cove's. In its March 2008 issue, *Esquire* magazine named the fried cod sandwich on its list of Best Sandwiches in America. Other fish sandwiches are made from flounder right from the Stonington docks.

The Yellow House Coffee & Tea Room (860-535-4986), 149 Water St., Stonington. Open daily. A popular morning stop for coffee, breakfast sandwiches, and baked goods; sandwiches, salads, and homemade soups later on. The breads and desserts reflect the village's Portuguese heritage.

Fun 'n Food Clam Bar, Inc. (860-445-6186), 283 CT 12, Groton. Open daily year-round. Just the place to stuff a hungry teenager. Foot-long hot dogs, chili dogs, clam fritters, whole and strip fried clams, grinders, chowder, and onion rings, all washed down with rich milk shakes.

Paul's Pasta Shop (860-445-5276), 223 Thames St., Groton. This is the kind of local joint that tourists love to find. You can eat in, but most people pick up the made-right-here pastas and pasta dishes (chicken Diablo is a must) to bring home. Watch pasta makers at work through the front window.

Costello's Clam Shack (860-572-2779; www.costellosclamshack.com), in the Noank Shipyard, 145 Pearl St., Noank. Open seasonally; call ahead. Patrons line up at this old-fashioned seafood shack for its delicious to-go menu of fried clams, fried, cod, onion rings, even fried ice cream.

Carson's Store (860-536-0059), 43 Main St., Noank. Open daily. A general store has operated here for more than a century; today locals and summer cottage folks pile in for breakfast, lunch, ice cream, coffee, and penny candy in 1950s-era surroundings.

ICE CREAM **Mystic Drawbridge Ice Cream Shoppe** (860-572-7978), 2 West Main St., Mystic. Nothing says summer at the shore quite like ice cream, and this parlor dishes out cups, cones, and colossal sundaes to a hungry vacation crowd. The shop is tucked next to the historic drawbridge, so take your double scoop of Jamaica Me Nutty (chocolate and coffee ice cream, almonds, pecans, walnuts . . . yum) outside and watch the parade of boats plying the Mystic River.

Buttonwood Farm Ice Cream (860-376-4081; www.buttonwoodfarm icecream.com), 471 Shetucket Turnpike (CT 165), Griswold. Three cheers for this treasure, which not only makes delicious ice cream but also raises money for a great cause. The Button family plant a sea of sunflowers here for their Sunflowers for Wishes fundraiser. In July, they sell bunches of freshly cut blooms ($5); all proceeds benefit Make a Wish Foundation.

Cows and Cones (860-464-2663; www.cowsandcones.com), 39 Military Hwy., at Alice Acres Farm Market, Gales Ferry. When the mercury goes up-up-up, locals line up here for yummy flavors like brownie dough, lemon pie, and white chocolate raspberry. Smoothies, floats, and shakes round out the tempting menu.

✱ Entertainment

Foxwoods Resort Casino (860-312-3352; 800-752-9244; www.foxwoods .com), 39 Norwich Westerly Rd. (CT 2), Mashantucket. Foxwoods offers plenty of what, in casino-speak, is called "nongaming" entertainment. Headliners such as Miley Cyrus and Jerry Seinfeld, plus rock and country music notables appear on a regular schedule in the 4,000-seat **MGM Grand Theater** and the more intimate cabaret-style **Fox Theatre**. There's a rock-and-roll aesthetic at **The Hard Rock Café**, the only one between Boston and New York.

✱ Selective Shopping

The streets of historic downtown Mystic, just south of the Seaport, are lined with gift shops, boutiques, and bookstores, with a heavy emphasis on items nautical.

Olde Mistick Village (860-536-4941; www.oldemysticvillage.com), Coogan Blvd. (CT 27), Exit 90 off I-95. Open Mon.–Sat. 10–6; Sun. 11–5; open until 8 PM summer and holidays. A bustling shopping complex designed to resemble a circa-1720 New England village, with some 60 colonial-style "homes" around a small landscaped green with a creek and waterwheel, and a typical white-clapboard meetinghouse. Specialty shops carry famous-label sportswear, New England collectibles, toys, nautical memorabilia, and the like; the movie theater is a popular attraction on rainy beach days. In-season, outdoor entertainment runs the gamut from concerts and car shows to arts and crafts shows.

Museum Store at Mystic Seaport (860-572-5315; www.mysticseaport.org), 75 Greenmanville Ave. (CT 27), Mystic. Outside the south gate, so a Seaport museum pass is not needed (see the Mystic Seaport sidebar). The emphasis here is on nautical books and paintings, marine artifacts, and ship models. With 6,000 square feet of selling space, if you can't find something to buy, you are not trying.

Company of Craftsmen (860-536-4189; www.companyofcraftsmen.com), 43 West Main St., Mystic. Open daily. Contemporary American artisans: jewelry, hand-blown glass, wood, and pottery are the star attractions.

Boat Stuff (860-536-3422; www.mysticboatstuff.com), Schooner Wharf, 15 Holmes St., Mystic. Whether or not you need stuff for your boat, this is a fun place to browse. Thousands of consignment items, from charts and books to marine hardware and nautical antiques.

Boondocks (860-535-3474; www.boondocksct.com), 417 Norwich Westerly Rd. (CT 2), North Stonington. Freshwater, saltwater, and fly-fishing gear; rods and reels, lures, bait and tackle, apparel. Kids love the 1,500-gallon aquarium.

Luli (860-535-3336; www.lulionline.com), 158 Water St., Stonington. One-of-a-kind women's clothing and accessories.

EARLY AMERICAN HOUSEWIVES SHOPPED IN GENERAL STORES LIKE THESE IN STONINGTON AND OLDE MISTICK VILLAGE.

Kim Grant

OSKA (860-572-8442; oskamystic.com), 24 West Main St., Mystic. This elegant boutique has all you need to outfit yourself in chic and stylish women's fashions.

Stonington Seafood Harvesters (860-535-8342), on the Town Dock, Stonington. Just-caught cod, halibut, shrimp, scallops, and flounder from the *Patty Jo*, docked a stone's throw from the market when not at sea.

ANTIQUES AND ART **Finer Line Gallery** (860-536-8339; www.finerlinegallery.com), 48 West Main St., Mystic. Open daily. Marine art and local scenes depicted in original works, posters, and limited-edition prints. Ask about art classes for all skill levels.

Trade Winds Gallery (860-536-0119), 42 West Main St., Mystic. Open daily 10–6; extended summer hours. Antique maps and prints of New England and the sea are the specialty.

Mystic Arts Center (860-536-7601; www.mysticarts.org), 9 Water St., Mystic. Open year-round, daily 11–5. Suggested donation $2. A sprawling arts center on the west bank of the Mystic River. Changing and permanent exhibits in five galleries, including the works of William North, a modern-day impressionist who painted many local landscapes. Home to the Mystic Art Association, founded in 1913.

Cutwater Gallery (860-572-1576; www.cutwatergallery.com), 14 Holmes St., in the Schooner Wharf complex, Mystic. Open Wed.–Sat. noon–5; and by appointment. Fine art and prints, home decor, gifts, and books.

The Greenwood Gallery (860-535-3997; www.thegreenwoodgallery.com), 77 Main St., Stonington. Paintings, prints, and sculpture, with an emphasis on works that came out of art colonies in Old Lyme and Cos Cob in the 19th and 20th centuries.

Velvet Mill Studios (www.velvetmillstudios.com), 22 Bayview Ave., Stonington. A historic mill converted to studio and gallery space. Artist studios are open for tours on the last Sunday of the month.

Pratt Wright Galleries (860-536-9243), 48 Main St., Noank. Landscapes, seascapes, and American and European art in the center of a picturesque village.

Alexey von Schlippe Gallery of Art (860-405-9052; www.averypointarts.uconn.edu), University of Connecticut, Avery Point campus, Groton. Open Mar.–Dec., Wed.–Sun. noon–4; closed Jan.–Feb. Changing exhibits of regional, national, and international artists in a converted Tudor mansion on UConn's seaside campus.

BOOKSTORES **Bank Square Books** (860-536-3795; www.banksquarebooks.com), 53 West Main St., Mystic. A popular downtown independent shop with thoughtful staff picks, author events, and children's story hour.

Village Booksmith (860-536-6185), Olde Mistick Village, Mystic.

The Book Mart (860-535-0401), 17 High St., Stonington.

FARMS **Allyn's Red Barn** (860-464-7245; www.allynsredbarn.com), 610 Colonel Ledyard Hwy., Ledyard. Farm store open Aug.–Dec., daily 10–5. Pick your own apples in fall; the farm store sells cider, apples, and pies.

Holmberg Orchards (860-464-7305; www.holmbergorchards.com), 12 Orchard Lane, off CT 12, Gales Ferry. Farm market open year-round, daily 9–6. Pick your own berries, cut flowers, and peaches in summer; apples, pears, and pumpkins in fall. The farm market sells their own hard cider, pies, local produce, native honey, and wines from area vineyards.

✷ Special Events

Mystic Seaport: The Museum of America and the Sea (860-572-5215; 888-973-2767; www.mysticseaport.org), 75 Greenmanville Ave. (CT 27), Mystic, hosts dozens of events throughout the year; just a sampling is listed below. Call or check their Web site for a complete listing.

Memorial Day weekend: **Lobster Days** (860-572-5315; 888-973-2767), Mystic Seaport. Old-fashioned lobster bake with corn and baked potatoes in the open-air boat shed on the banks of the Mystic River. Put on a bib and pick the shells clean, accompanied by sea-chantey singing.

Late May through early June: **Strawberry Park Bluegrass Festival** (860-886-1944), Strawberry Park Campground, Preston. An annual festival for more than 30 years.

June: **Sea Music Festival** (860-572-5315; 888-973-2767; www.mysticseaport.org), Mystic Seaport. North America's top sea music festival, with music from oceans around the world—chanteys, forbitters, whaling songs, and more. **House and Garden Tour** (860-536-4779), sponsored by the Mystic River Historical Society, showcases several private homes and gardens. **Wooden Boat Show** (860-572-5315; 888-973-2767; www.thewoodenboatshow.com), Mystic Seaport.

July: **North Stonington Agricultural Fair** (860-535-3956), Wyassup Rd., off CT 2, North Stonington. A traditional country fair with animal shows, tractor pulls, baking contests, and lots of food. **Independence Day Celebration** (860-572-5215; 888-973-2767), Mystic Seaport, Mystic. A traditional 1870s Fourth of July celebration, complete with a children's parade and spelling bee.

Late July: **Blessing of the Fleet** (860-535-3150; www.stoningtonblessing.com), Stonington Harbor. A New England clambake, fishermen's Mass, and parade lead up to a colorful ceremony as the gaily decorated vessels in Connecticut's only commercial fishing and lobster fleet gather in the harbor for its annual blessing, since 1954. ✐ **Antique & Classic Boat Rendezvous** (860-572-5315; 888-973-2767; www.mysticseaport.org), Mystic Seaport. Private owners of pre-1963 classic all-wooden boats, speedboats, sailboats, and yachts, polished to a fare-thee-well, parade down the Mystic River from the Seaport. View the parade from the dockside of the Seaport or from the spacious lawn of the Mystic Art Association Gallery on the southern side of the Bascule bridge.

August: **Melville Marathon**, Mystic Seaport. In Dublin, they read the complete *Ulysses* of James Joyce once a year. Here, Herman Melville's birthday (August 1) is celebrated with a 24-hour reading of *Moby-Dick*—all 135 chapters!—aboard the *Charles W. Morgan*. Call 860-572-5322 to reserve an overnight spot on America's last surviving wooden whaler. **Mystic Outdoor Art Festival** (860-572-9578; www.mysticchamber.org), downtown Mystic. Some 300 artists and craftspeople from around the country take over downtown sidewalks in one of New England's finest outdoor juried shows. **Schemitzun Feast of Green Corn and Dance** (800-322-2676; www.shemitzun.com), North Stonington. Drumming, dancing, rodeo, and singing competitions in the largest Native American powwow on the East Coast, hosted by the Mashantucket

Pequot tribe. **Meet the Artists and Artisans** (860-536-4941), Olde Mistick Village, Mystic. An annual gathering of artists and craftspeople for more than 35 years.

September: **Mystic Weekend of Rowing**, on the Mystic River, Mystic. Two competitions, the Coastweeks Regatta and the Battle of the Bridges, attract rowers from around the country. **Foxwoods Food and Wine Festival** (800-369-9663; www.foxwoodsfoodandwine.com), Foxwoods Resort Casino, Mashantucket. Dinners and tastings featuring gourmet cuisine and fine wines.

Columbus Day weekend: **Chowderfest**, Mystic Seaport. Back to the Seaport again for clam and fish "chowda" and other seafood specialties.

Late November through December: **Holiday Fine Art & Artisan Show** (www.mystic-art.org), Mystic Arts Center, Mystic.

December: **Festival of Lights** (860-536-4941), Mystic. More than 5,000 luminaria illuminate the walkways of the Olde Mistick Village shopping complex and Mystic Aquarium. **Lantern Light Tours**, Mystic Seaport. Call 860-572-5331 to reserve a spot on this popular holiday tradition at the Seaport that brings to life theatrical scenes from Christmas past. A **Community Carol Sing** is also held at the Seaport; bring a canned good for free museum admission.

NEW LONDON, NORWICH, AND WEST OF THE THAMES

One of the finest deep-water harbors along the New England coast, New London has a three-century-long history with the sea. After the Revolutionary War—when this city near Long Island Sound's outer edge was the home port for the largest fleet of New England privateers to prey on British shipping—local mariners set out in pursuit of whales. Museums recall the halcyon days when stout men pitted their individual strength against the leviathans of the deep. At one time, New London was second only to New Bedford, Massachusetts, in the number of whalers seeking the elusive giants in the oceans of the world (Nantucket was third). In 1858, with the discovery of crude oil in Pennsylvania, whale oil to light the lamps of the world was no longer necessary. New London evolved into a major commercial port, and the country's first customhouse is now a museum and a stop on Connecticut's Freedom Trail (the slave ship *Amistad* was brought to port here by the U.S. Navy). The port has since been refurbished, and the historic waterfront district has become a magnet for residents and visitors for sightseeing and fishing. Meanwhile, Royal Caribbean, Holland America, and other major cruise lines now dock at State Pier from May to November, bringing thousands of passengers and crew into downtown to buy souvenirs and postcards. On Pequot Avenue, regal Victorian and Greek Revival homes face the Sound; among them is the Queen Anne where American playwright Eugene O'Neill spent his childhood. A statue of a boy sitting on a rock in New London Harbor, reminiscent of the *Little Mermaid* in Copenhagen's harbor, depicts the young O'Neill. Today the O'Neill center offers theater and contemporary art.

New London's maritime heritage also lives on in the in the classrooms, dormitories, and training ships of the U.S. Coast Guard Academy, one of America's five military academies. Visitors can tour the grounds and the academy's museum, and attend dress parades and free summertime band concerts. For the last several decades, its cadet training barque *Eagle*, a graceful square-rigger, has led the parades of tall ships as they sail majestically into America's ports. Visitors may tour the ship when it is berthed at the Coast Guard Academy's dock. The seventh in a long line of proud cutters to bear the name *Eagle*, the present ship was built in 1936 in Germany and taken as a war prize at the end of World War II. It's not well known, but "Coasties," as they are called, manned the landing craft during the Normandy invasion and suffered heavy casualties. In addition to fighting drugs,

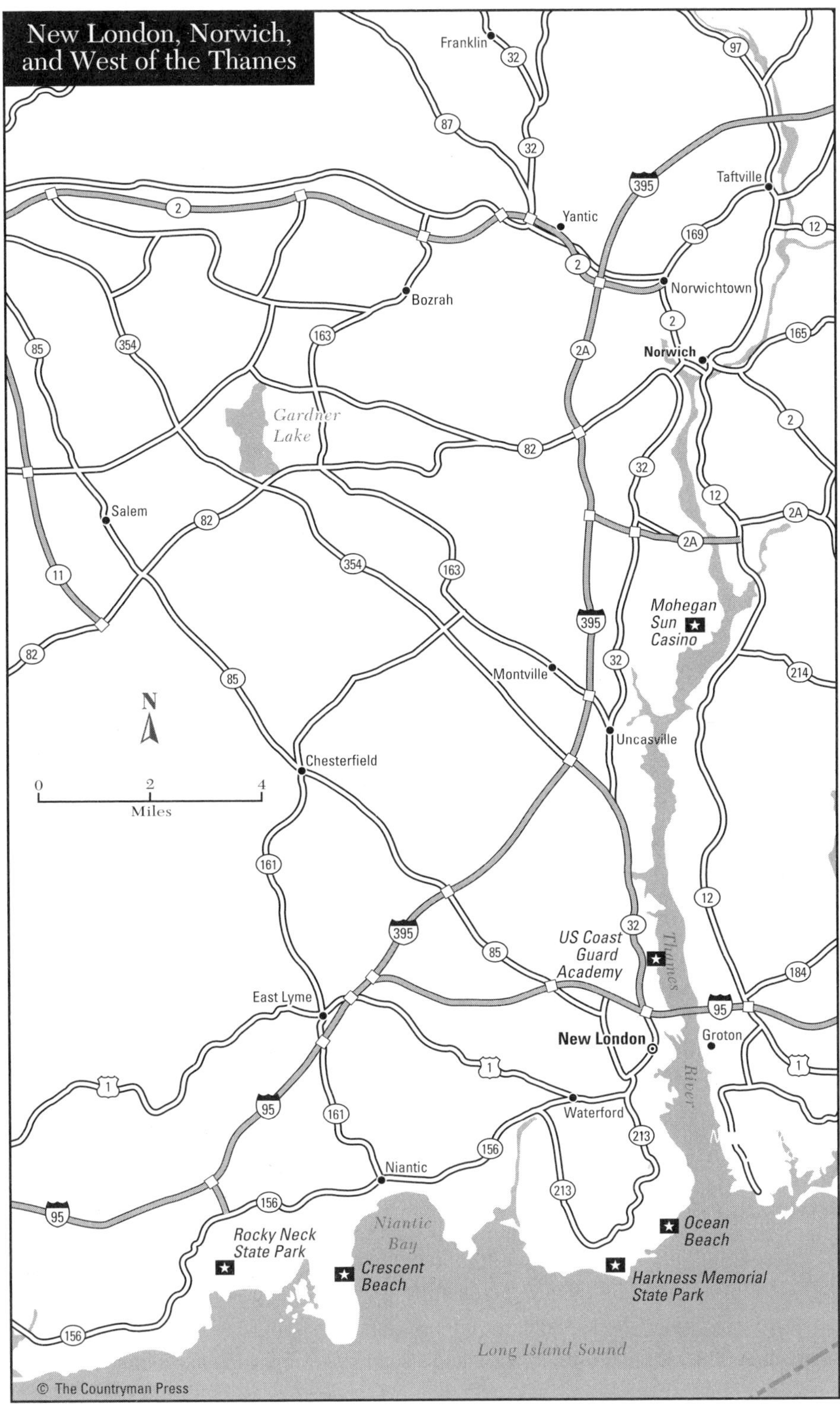
New London, Norwich, and West of the Thames
Franklin
Yantic
Taftville
Norwichtown
Bozrah
Norwich
Gardner Lake
Salem
Mohegan Sun Casino
Montville
Uncasville
Chesterfield
N
0 2 4
Miles
US Coast Guard Academy
Thames River
East Lyme
New London
Groton
Waterford
Niantic
Niantic Bay
Rocky Neck State Park
Crescent Beach
Ocean Beach
Harkness Memorial State Park
Long Island Sound
© The Countryman Press

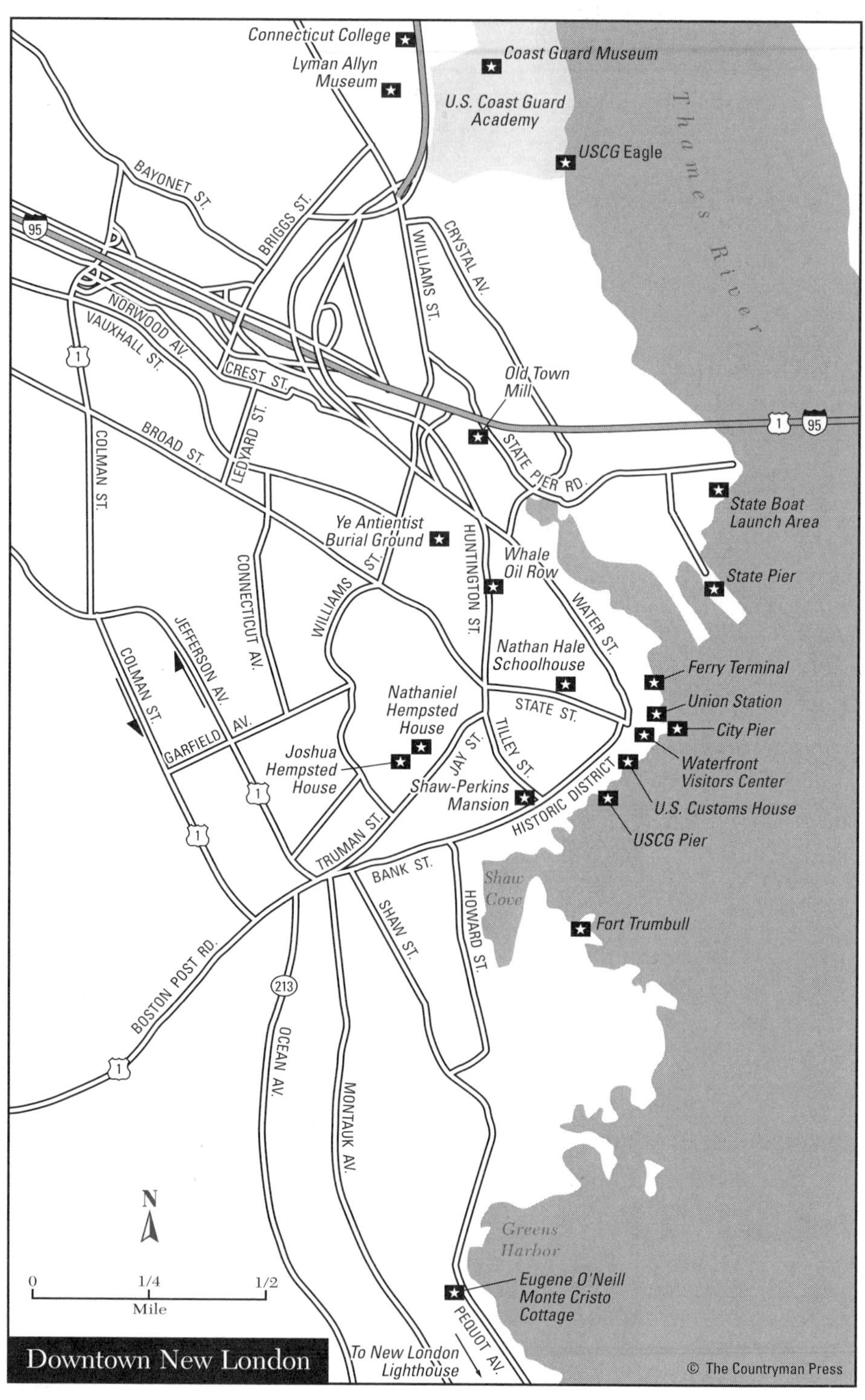
Connecticut College
Lyman Allyn Museum
Coast Guard Museum
U.S. Coast Guard Academy
USCG Eagle
Thames River
BAYONET ST.
BRIGGS ST.
95
WILLIAMS ST.
CRYSTAL AV.
NORWOOD AV.
VAUXHALL ST.
1
CREST ST.
Old Town Mill
1
95
BROAD ST.
COLMAN ST.
LEDYARD ST.
STATE PIER RD.
State Boat Launch Area
Ye Antientist Burial Ground
HUNTINGTON ST.
Whale Oil Row
State Pier
CONNECTICUT AV.
WILLIAMS ST.
WATER ST.
JEFFERSON AV.
Nathan Hale Schoolhouse
Ferry Terminal
Union Station
City Pier
COLMAN ST.
Nathaniel Hempsted House
STATE ST.
Waterfront Visitors Center
GARFIELD AV.
Joshua Hempsted House
JAY ST.
TILLEY ST.
HISTORIC DISTRICT
U.S. Customs House
1
Shaw-Perkins Mansion
USCG Pier
1
TRUMAN ST.
BANK ST.
Shaw Cove
SHAW ST.
HOWARD ST.
Fort Trumbull
BOSTON POST RD.
213
1
OCEAN AV.
MONTAUK AV.
N
Greens Harbor
0
1/4
1/2
Mile
Eugene O'Neill Monte Cristo Cottage
PEQUOT AV.
Downtown New London
To New London Lighthouse
© The Countryman Press

protecting fisheries, battling pollution, and maintaining aids to navigation, the Coast Guard annually responds to some 70,000 search-and-rescue calls, saving thousands of lives. Its motto remains as always: *Semper paratus* (always prepared).

You may reasonably presume that Norwich, an architecturally eclectic city at the head of the Thames River, carries the sobriquet *Rose City* because its hills look like the petals of a rosebud. It was Henry Ward Beecher, a Litchfield native, who declared the city the Rose of New England. So while the city is proud of its municipal garden of prize roses, the entire town is *not* awash in the thorny beauties. Settled 300 years ago, Norwich was home to more millionaires at the turn of the 20th century than any other city in New England. These entrepreneurs accumulated their wealth not from factories in the city, but from textile mills that drew their power from the many rivers in the valleys of southern and northeastern Connecticut. The mills eventually fled south; the legacy of these early industrialists can be seen in the great houses that still dot the city. One of the most interesting buildings is the spectacular city hall, with its ornate Second Empire facade. Built in 1870, it has been restored and still serves as the city's seat of government.

Benedict Arnold, America's best-known traitor, was born in Norwich and was a local pharmacist and merchant before he went off, first to fame and then to infamy. In the 1770s, he used his own ships to smuggle contraband between the West Indies and New England, and his leap to the British side included bringing loyalist troops into New London and burning it. But the city also was the home of Samuel Huntington, a signer of the Declaration of Independence and one of our most influential Founding Fathers.

For the visitor, Norwich offers a cornucopia of activities and attractions, the aforementioned public rose garden, antique auto shows, Harbor Day, historic Norwichtown Days, Italian and Greek food festivals, concerts, musicals, crafts shows, fairs, minor-league baseball, one of the state's premier spas, a unique museum of reproductions of classical statuary—and much more. In 1886, William Albert Slater memorialized his wealthy industrialist father with a museum at Norwich Free Academy. Today Slater Memorial Museum is known for its unique full-sized plaster-cast Renaissance and classical statues, the largest such collection in the country.

In 1996, the tiny Mohegan tribe opened a casino in Uncasville, a quiet blue-collar community between Norwich and New London on the Thames River. Along with Foxwoods Resort Casino across the river, it is one of the world's largest casinos, and continues to grow, thanks to a billion-dollar expansion in recent years. Still to come: A 38-story, 1,000-room hotel that will include a smaller House of Blues–style hotel, another 1,000 slot machines, and a House of Blues music hall. People from around the world and all walks of life are lured to the betting action by the promise of instant fortune.

All the coastal towns in the region offer a plethora of nautical sites and activities: charter fishing boats, whale-watching expeditions, oceanographic floating laboratories. Rocky Neck State Park in East Lyme has a sandy beach, nature trails, fishing, and a campground. Niantic, a village within the town of East Lyme, boasts Connecticut's only oceanfront Main Street, a mile-long boardwalk along Niantic Bay's crescent-shaped shoreline. The village's restaurants and shops include an eclectic bookstore, a stop at which should be on every bibliophile's to-do list. In Waterford, Harkness Memorial State Park is presided over by Eolia, an elegant waterfront mansion surrounded by Beatrix Farrand–designed gardens and a sprawling lawn that is the setting for picnics and kite flying. Finally, a semantic note: The Thames is named for the river that runs through London, where it is pronounced *Tems* by the Brits; in New London it's *Thaymes*.

Entries in this section are arranged in roughly geographic order.

AREA CODE 860.

GUIDANCE **Eastern Regional Tourism District** (860-444-2206; 800-863-6569; www.mysticcountry.com), 32 Huntington St., New London 06320. Stop in, call, or write for brochures, maps, and a calendar of events. Extensive tourism information is also available on the Web site.

Norwich Tourism Office (860-886-4683; 888-466-7942; www.norwichct.org), 77 Main St., Norwich 06360. Local information for visitors by way of brochures, maps, tour guides, and a calendar of special events.

Quinebaug-Shetucket Heritage Corridor, Inc. (860-963-7226; 866-363-7226; www.thelastgreenvalley.org), 107 Providence St., Putnam. A nonprofit organization that promotes tourism in the **Quinebaug and Shetucket Rivers Valley National Heritage Corridor**, a unique project of the National Park System to preserve 850 square miles of what has been called "the last green valley" in the Boston-to-Washington megalopolis sprawl. Most of it lies in the Quiet Corner, but its southernmost borders encompass Norwich. On request, they will send free brochures on area attractions; that information, as well as a calendar of events and other information of interest to visitors, can be downloaded from their Web site.

State Highway Information and Rest Center (860-599-2056), I-95 southbound, North Stonington. Open year-round, daily. Guides, brochures, pamphlets, maps. Full rest facilities.

GETTING THERE *By car:* The New London area is accessible by car from I-95, east- and westbound, and from CT 32 from the north. The Norwich area is accessible by I-395 and CT 32.

By air: The **Groton–New London Airport** (860-445-8549; www.grotonnewlondonairport.com) offers charter flights; no commercial service is available. Visitors can fly into nearby **T. F. Green Airport** (888-268-7222; www.pvdairport.com) in Warwick, Rhode Island, or **Bradley International Airport** (860-292-2000; 888-624-1533; www.bradleyairport.com) in Windsor Locks.

By bus: **Greyhound Lines** (800-231-2222; www.greyhound.com) and **Peter Pan Bus Lines** (800-343-9999; www.peterpanbus.com) stop in New London at **Union Station**, 45 Water St.

By rail: **Amtrak** (800-872-7245; www.amtrak.com), including the high-speed **Acela Express**, stops frequently at New London.

By ferry: (*Note:* Most, but not all, boats are handicapped accessible. Ask when calling for a reservation.)

Cross Sound Ferry Services (860-443-5281; www.longislandferry.com), 2 Ferry St., New London. Vehicle and passenger ferries leave from the Ferry Street dock for the 80-minute trip to Orient Point, Long Island. Free shuttle-bus service is available to Mohegan Sun and Foxwoods Resort Casino.

Fishers Island Ferry District (860-442-0165; www.fiferry.com), State St., New London. Auto ferries depart from Ferry District Landing to Fishers Island, New York.

Block Island Ferry Express (860-444-4624; www.goblockisland.com), 2 Ferry St., New London. A high-speed catamaran carries foot passengers and bicyclists to Block Island from the New London Ferry Dock.

Viking Ferry (631-668-5700; www.vikingfleet.com), Cross Sound Ferry Dock, New London. A high-speed passenger ferry links New London to Montauk, Long Island.

GETTING AROUND For sightseeing or traveling in this area, a car is necessary. *By taxi:* **Yellow Cab** (860-536-8888), **Port City Taxi** (860-444-9222), and **Red & White Taxi** (860-443-2255) serve the New London area.

MEDICAL EMERGENCY The statewide emergency number is **911**.

Lawrence and Memorial Hospital (860-442-0711; 888-777-9539), 365 Montauk Ave., New London.

William Backus Hospital (860-889-8331), 326 Washington St., Norwich. The emergency number is 860-823-6389.

✷ To See

U.S. Coast Guard Academy (860-444-8444; 800-883-8724; www.cga.edu), 15 Mohegan Ave. (CT 32), New London. Open daily 9–4:30 for self-guided tours (walking maps available in the admissions office); cadet-led tours on Mon., Wed., and Fri. at 1 PM. Free admission; a photo ID is required for entry. Closed on federal holidays and weekends during academic breaks. Although Connecticut is the country's third-smallest state, it is proud to be home to one of America's five military academies. The nation's smallest service academy sits on the banks of the Thames River. Cadets are trained to command ships in what is probably the true "multimission service." In addition to performing rescue missions at sea and interdicting drug and customs violators, Coast Guard personnel have served in all of this country's major conflicts. When in port, the beautiful cadet training barque USCG *Eagle* is open to visitors. The *Eagle* is an icon

THE BARQUE *EAGLE*, TRAINING SHIP OF THE U.S. COAST GUARD ACADEMY, MAY BE VISITED WHEN IT'S IN PORT.

Kim Grant

of New London's maritime heritage, and the only square-rigger in active service. Dress parades occur in spring and fall on Friday afternoons at 4, and free summertime concerts are held by the Coast Guard band. Visitors can eat at the Dry Dock snack bar. The **U.S. Coast Guard Museum** (860-444-8511) houses some 6,000 works of Coast Guard–related art and artifacts, including a 13-foot first-order lighthouse lens from the Cape Ann Lighthouse; signatures of Presidents Washington, Lincoln, and Kennedy; and 200 ship models.

MUSEUMS ✐ ♿ **Lyman Allyn Art Museum** (860-443-2545; www.lymanallyn.org), 625 Williams St., New London. Open Tue.–Sat. 10–5 and Sun. 1–5. Adults $5; seniors and students $4; children 8 and under free. A part of the Connecticut College campus, the museum has more than 10,000 works of art from Asia, Europe, and America. The neoclassical "temple" was designed by Charles A. Platt. Best known for its outstanding collection of 18th- to 20th-century American art, particularly impressionist paintings and Connecticut decorative art, as well as European works on paper, sculpture, furniture. On the third Sunday of every month, visitors can check out the museum's unique doll collection, housed in the **Deshon-Allyn House**, on the grounds of the museum, which also feature sculpture gardens. Children will revel in the unique collection of antiques, dolls, dollhouses, antique toys, and miniatures from the 19th and 20th centuries.

♿ **Slater Memorial Museum** (860-887-2506), 108 Crescent St., on the campus of Norwich Free Academy, Norwich. Open Tue.–Fri. 9–4; Sat. and Sun. 1–4; closed Mon. and major holidays. Adults $3; seniors and students $2; under 13 free. Packed into the Slater's relatively small space is an astonishing collection of 150 full-sized, plaster-cast replicas of the most famous statuary of ancient Egypt, Rome, and Greece—from Zeus to Athena, Michelangelo's *Pietà*, Donatello's *David*, Apollo, Perseus, Julius Caesar, Medusa, and Amenhotep the Magnificent. It's one of the largest such collections in the country, and the grand building, a Romanesque Revival brownstone, has housed it since 1888. The **Converse Art Gallery** mounts changing exhibits.

✐ **Tantaquidgeon Indian Museum** (860-862-6144), 1819 Norwich–New London Turnpike (CT 32), Uncasville. Open May–Oct., Mon.–Fri. 10–3; closed Sat. and Sun. Admission by donation. Literally the home of the "Last of the Mohegans." A large collection of artifacts made and used by the Mohegan tribe; exhibits focus on tribes of the eastern forests. The museum is run by the Tantaquidgeon family, which included Gladys Tantaquidgeon, the venerable Medicine Woman of the Mohegan nation, who died in 2005 at the age of 106. She had lectured on the Mohegans all over the country and is credited with earning the tribe federal recognition.

✐ ♿ **Children's Museum of Southeastern Connecticut** (860-691-1111; www.childrensmuseumsect.org), 409 Main St. (CT 156), Niantic. Tue.–Sat. 9:30–5 (Fri. until 8); Sun. noon–5; open Mon. in summer and during school vacations. Admission $6; children under 1 free. Science, arts, history, and health are illustrated in unique, interactive displays for children ages 1–12. There is also an art table, a pipe organ, a replica of a submarine, a climbing wall, a kids' clubhouse, and an outdoor learning garden.

✐ **Blue Slope Country Museum** (860-642-6413; www.blueslope.com), 138 Blue Hill Rd., Franklin. Open by appointment. More than 4,000 farm tools and implements are on display in a rustic, barn-like structure on a 380-acre working dairy farm. Educational programs include blacksmithing and woodworking, spinning and weaving, basketmaking, butter making, soil tillage and planting, and special activities geared to children. Hayrides and sleigh rides in-season.

Kim Grant

THIS STATUE OF YOUNG EUGENE O'NEILL OVERLOOKS NEW LONDON HARBOR.

HISTORIC HOMES **Monte Cristo Cottage** (860-443-5378), 325 Pequot Ave., New London. Open Memorial Day–Labor Day, Thu.–Sat. noon–4, Sun. 1–3; Labor Day–mid-Oct., Thu.–Sun. 1–5; closed major holidays. Adults $7; students and seniors $5; children under 2, free. Eugene O'Neill, America's only dramatist to be awarded the Nobel Prize and four Pulitzer Prizes, spent his first 26 summers here when the area was a fashionable resort. The cottage is named for a character in a classic play, *The Count of Monte Cristo*, a part performed endlessly by O'Neill's actor-father. O'Neill fans will recognize the living room: the setting for two of his most famous plays—his greatest tragedy, *Long Day's Journey into Night*, and his only comedy, *Ah, Wilderness!* For visitors, there is a permanent collection of portraits, posters, and writings on the life and work of the playwright, as well as literary readings. (See also *Entertainment*.)

Shaw-Perkins Mansion (860-443-1209), 11 Blinman St., New London. Open Wed.–Fri. 1–4; Sat. 10–4; closed Sun.–Tue. Adults $5; seniors $4; students $3; children 12 and under free. Changing exhibits, tours, and interpretative programs occur here, in Connecticut's Revolutionary War Naval Office. Washington, Lafayette, and top commanders of the fledgling Continental navy met in this

MONTE CRISTO COTTAGE IN NEW LONDON, THE BOYHOOD HOME OF EUGENE O'NEILL

18th-century granite mansion, home of Captain Nathaniel Shaw, to plot strategies. Today displays of regional art, furniture, and artifacts, as well as an outstanding collection of manuscripts, fill the house; outside are attractive colonial-style flower gardens.

Hempsted Houses (860-443-7949), 11 Hempsted St., New London. Open daily, except Mon., May–Oct. Adults $5; seniors and students $3; children 5 and under free. Here are two important colonial houses that survived the burning of New London by Benedict Arnold. The 1678 Joshua Hempsted House is one of the oldest frame buildings in New England, and the oldest house in New London. The adjoining stone house was built by a grandson in 1759, constructed with a gambrel roof and an exterior projecting beehive oven. Both have been restored with family artifacts, and both are on the National Register of Historic Places. Seasonal programs on colonial life.

Whale Oil Row, 105–119 Huntington St., New London. Unique row of four nearly identical magnificent Greek Revival houses built in the 1830s for captains or merchants who made their fortunes from whaling. Each two-story portico is supported by fluted Ionic columns.

Leffingwell House Museum (860-889-9440; www.leffingwellhousemuseum.org), 348 Washington St., Norwich. Open mid-Apr.–mid-Oct., Sat. and Sun. 1–4, and by appointment. Adults $5; seniors $3; children under 13 $2. Started in 1675 and expanded over the years, the inn was the home of Colonel Christopher Leffingwell, deputy commissary to the Continental army, who did yeoman service rounding up food, arms, and clothing for Washington's troops, earning Connecticut the title of Provision State. It's owned and operated by the Descendants of the Founders of Norwich, and furnished with local antiques and art, from clocks and firearms to silver.

Smith-Harris House (860-739-0761; www.smithharris.org), 33 Society Rd., Niantic. Open for guided tours in June, Fri.–Sun. noon–4; July and Aug., Thu.–Sun. noon–4. Admission by donation. A Greek Revival farmhouse, a popular style in America from 1820 to 1850, has been renovated with the help of local

WHALE OIL ROW WAS NAMED AFTER FOR THE COMMODITY THAT ENRICHED ITS BUILDERS.
Kim Grant

schoolchildren as a learning project. Annual Wassail Party in December (see *Special Events*). The last member of the family died in 1973, so visitors can view authentic furnishings. Picnic facilities available.

HISTORIC SITES **Custom House Maritime Museum** (860-447-2501; www.nlmaritimesociety.org), 150 Bank St., New London. Open July–Dec., Tue.–Sun. 1–5; Apr.–June, Tue.–Sat. 1–5; other times by appointment. Free admission. The first customhouse in the United States and the oldest continuously operating customhouse in America is now a museum and home to the New London Maritime Society. It tells the story of the customs service as well as 300 years of the city's maritime history. Collecting duty on imported goods was the way the fledgling United States first raised funds to run the federal government. The grand Federal-style granite building was designed by Robert Mills, who also designed the Washington Monument. A bronze sculpture, *First Step to Freedom*, honors Joseph Cinque, leader of the revolt of African captives aboard the Spanish slave ship, the schooner *Amistad*, which was brought into New London port. Former President John Quincy Adams fought for and won their freedom. The doors of the Custom House came from planks torn off the USS *Constitution* during a renovation of the famed warship. The site is on Connecticut's Freedom Trail (see *Trails, Tourism* in "What's Where in Connecticut").

County Courthouse, 70 Huntington St., at the top of State St., New London. An architectural treasure that escaped the torches of the British marines, this beautiful Georgian building has been a courthouse for more than 200 years. When the siege of New London Harbor was lifted at the end of the War of 1812, the citizenry staged a "Peace Ball" in this hall for the British officers.

Nathan Hale Schoolhouse (860-443-7949), 35 State St., New London. Open May–Oct., Wed.–Sun. 11–4; closed Mon. and Tue. Adults $2; children free. Moved from its original site, this is one of two schoolhouses in which Connecticut's state hero, a Yale graduate, was a schoolmaster before joining the Continental army at the age of 21. At Washington's request, he ventured behind enemy lines on Long Island; he was captured by the British and executed in Manhattan as a spy on the site of the present Yale University Club. Captain Hale's last words, "I only regret that I have but one life to lose for my country," have been a lasting inspiration to American patriots. He taught at this school, known as Union School, from 1774 to 1775.

✐ **Eugene O'Neill Statue**, New London. An appealing statue of the young Eugene in his schoolboy cap and first long pants, sitting on a rock overlooking New London Harbor and scribbling in his notebook. Connecticut sculptor Norman Legassie modeled the statue after an 1895 photo of a 7-year-old O'Neill sketching on the banks of the Thames River.

♿ ✐ **Fort Trumbull State Park** (860-444-7591), 90 Walbach St., New London. Grounds open year-round, daily 8 AM–sunset; free admission. Fort and visitor center open Memorial Day weekend–Columbus Day, Wed.–Sun. 9–4. Adults $5; children 6–12 $2; 5 and under free. From the days of the Revolutionary War, when New London was attacked by the British, a fort has stood here guarding the entrance to New London Harbor at the mouth of the Thames River. Named for Connecticut's Revolutionary War governor, Jonathan Trumbull, the fort was an early home of the U.S. Coast Guard Academy and an integral part of the nation's coastal defense system. It was built in 1839 of huge granite blocks with an Egyptian Revival entrance. In the visitor center, interactive exhibits tell the story of military history from the American Revolution to the Cold War. Visitors can also access a boardwalk and fishing pier along the river.

Old Burying Ground, East Town St., Norwich. A colonial burying ground whose ancient headstones, complete with hand-carved inscriptions and images of cherubs and winged skulls, are considered a form of early American sculpture. Norwich's earliest residents were laid to rest here, including Connecticut governor Samuel Huntington, signer of the Declaration of Independence, and Hannah Arnold, mother of Benedict Arnold.

Beebe Phillips Farmhouse (860-442-2707), CT 156 and Avery Lane, Waterford. Open June 15–Sept. 15, Mon.–Fri. 1–4. Free admission. A complex of 18th- and 19th-century buildings, including the **Jordan Schoolhouse**, **Stacy Barn Museum**, and **Miner Education Center**. Youngsters will enjoy the early horse-drawn farm vehicles and equipment. For Mom and Dad, an authentic colonial herb garden.

LIGHTHOUSES **New London Harbor Lighthouse**. This tall, octagonal white lighthouse at the entrance to the harbor, opposite the Lighthouse Inn, is not open to the public, and the 19th-century keeper's house is privately owned, but it's lovely from afar. It opened as a lighthouse station in 1760; the light was automated in 1912 and is still functional.

FLOWER POTS ADD AN EXTRA GLOW TO STREET LIGHTS IN NEW LONDON'S INVITING HISTORIC DISTRICT.

Kim Grant

New London Ledge Lighthouse (860-442-2222), at the mouth of the Thames River. Open June–Sept. Unlike conventional lighthouses around the world—tall spires arching into the sky—the Ledge Lighthouse is a brick French Second Empire Mansard-roofed "house" that sits on an 18-foot foundation at the entrance to New London Harbor. Since 1909 its light has guided vessels, from tall ships to nuclear submarines, around the harbor's dangerous ledges. Automated in 1987, it was the last staffed light on Long Island Sound. Maintained by the New London Ledge Lighthouse Foundation, it may be visited by boat (see *Boat Excursions* in the Mystic chapter). Over the years, its friendly foghorn has lulled millions of Connecticut shore visitors and residents to sleep.

✳ To Do

BALLOONING **Eastern Connecticut Balloon Services** (860-376-5807;

www.easternctballoon.com), P.O. Box 628, Jewett City 06351. Scenic hot-air balloon flights over eastern Connecticut, Apr.–Dec.

BOAT EXCURSIONS **Captain John's *Sunbeam* Fleet** (860-443-7259; www.sunbeamfleet.com), 15 1st St., Waterford. Call or check the Web site for rates and schedules. The 149-passenger *Sunbeam Express* has heated cabins, comfortable seats, even bunks and a full galley. It's a special treat when Captain John is on board; he's the kindly ancient mariner with the scalloped beard of a Maine fisherman. Excursions include lighthouse and fireworks cruises, nature cruises, and fishing trips; others head out in search of harbor seals.

***Mystic Whaler* Cruises** (860-535-1556; 800-697-8420; www.mysticwhaler.com), P.O. Box 189, Mystic 06355. Sails out of City Pier, New London. Modeled after the trading schooners that served ports along the New England coast, the *Whaler* offers adventures under sail with cruise-ship amenities. Schedules have been designed to suit every taste, from one-day on up to five-day sails that put in at such interesting ports of call as Block Island, Shelter Island, Sag Harbor, Cuttyhunk, Newport, and Martha's Vineyard. There are lighthouse cruises (see *Special Events*), full-moon cruises, lobster dinner trips, and twilight sails. Help veteran captain John Eginton, at the helm since 1993, and his friendly crew work the rigging, or just relax as the *Whaler* heels nicely in the cooperative winds of the waters off southern New England.

SeaPony (860-440-2734; www.seapony.com), City Pier, State St., New London. Cruise around New London Harbor and then up the Thames River aboard *SeaPony*, a 64-foot dinner tour boat. Trips include lobster bakes, lighthouse cruises, harbor tours, and sunset or moonlight excursions.

BOATING If you're towing or sailing your own craft, several marinas are located on the New London waterfront, including **Crocker's Boat Yard** (860-443-6304) on Howard St.; **A. W. Marina** (860-443-6076), **Burr's Marina** (860-443-8457), and **Thamesport Marina** (860-437-7022) are all on Pequot St. There's also a marina at **Fort Trumbull** (860-443-6020) in New London, and **Marina at American Wharf** (860-886-6363; 888-489-4273) is at the head of the Thames River in Norwich. **Mago Point Marina** (860-442-2710), 20 1st St., Waterford, is on the Niantic River.

FISHING Anglers head to the Thames River in late spring for striped bass. A variety of charter and party boats sail out of harbors along the coast of southeastern Connecticut from New London, Niantic, and Waterford, as well as Stonington, Mystic, and the Noank section of Groton. Charter boats are small, usually carrying four or five anglers, and reservations are a good idea; larger party boats operate on a first-come, first-served basis and accommodate a larger crowd. They include:

Charter fishing in New London

Captain Bob II (860-434-5681), Thames Inn Marina; ***Carolyn Ann*** (860-444-8760), ***After You, Too*** (860-537-5004), and ***Good Company II*** (860-443-0581), all tying up at Captain Scott's Lobster Dock; ***Lady Margaret*** (860-739-3687), Thamesport Landing; ***Marlintini*** (860-917-5893), ***M and M*** (860-447-8490), and ***Brothers Too*** (860-437-3491), all out of Crocker's Boatyard; ***A'Vanga*** (860-848-0170), Burr's Yacht Haven.

Charter fishing in Niantic and Waterford

Captain John's *Sunbeam* Fleet (860-443-7259), and ***Osprey*** (860-739-4129), both out of Captain John's Sport Fishing Dock, Waterford. ***Fishpot*** (860-563-4006), Niantic Bay Marina, Waterford. ***Dot-E-Dee*** (860-739-7419) Niantic Fish Dock, Niantic. ***Atlantic Flyway*** (860-442-6343), Port Niantic Marina, Niantic.

Party fishing in Niantic/Waterford

Captain John's ***Sunbeam Express*** (see above); ***Mijoy 747*** (860-443-0663), Mijoy Dock, Waterford; ***Black Hawk II*** (860-443-3662), Niantic Beach Marina, Niantic.

GAMING **Mohegan Sun** (888-777-7922; www.mohegansun.com), 1 Mohegan Sun Blvd., Uncasville. The new Casino of the Wind opened in late 2008.

Ten miles southwest of Foxwoods Resort Casino and only a mile from the interstate (I-395). The Mohegan tribe received federal recognition in the 1990s; since then, it's evolved into a flourishing gambling empire, and one of the largest gaming facilities in the world. Thousands of visitors come 24/7 to try their luck at 550 gaming tables and 5,780 slots grouped into three artfully decorated casinos with Native American themes. Serious players crowd the green-felted poker, craps, roulette, and blackjack tables, while older folks like to wager on simulcast races and play keno. Headlining entertainment, restaurants, a convention center, and a 1,200-room hotel and luxe spa keep everyone occupied, gambler or not.

GOLF **Cedar Ridge Golf Course** (860-691-4568; www.cedarridgegolf.com), 34 Drabik Rd., East Lyme. This 18-hole course is shorter than most, making it ideal for beginners or those looking for a quick round.

Norwich Golf Course (860-889-6973; www.norwichgolf.com), 685 New London Turnpike, Norwich. Par 71, 18 holes, 6,200 yards. Municipal golf course.

HAYRIDES AND SLEIGH RIDES **Blue Slope Country Museum** (860-642-6413; www.blueslope.com), 138 Blue Hill Rd., Franklin. Horse-drawn wagon and sleigh rides through cornfields and along wooded carriage trails and quiet country roads.

MINIATURE GOLF **Yankee Clipper Mini Golf** (860-739-9634), 157 West Main St., Niantic.

Miniature Golf at Ocean Beach Park (800-510-7263), 1225 Ocean Ave., New London. Kids love the course's famous whale.

SPECTATOR SPORTS **Connecticut Defenders** (860-887-7962; www.ctdefenders.com), Dodd Stadium, 14 Stott Ave., Norwich. Games are played Apr.–Labor Day weekend. This San Francisco Giants AA team is the first professional baseball in eastern Connecticut.

Connecticut Sun (877-786-8499; www.connecticutsun.com), Mohegan Sun Casino, Uncasville. The Women's National Basketball Association's Connecticut Sun plays its home games to huge crowds at Mohegan Sun Arena. The roster includes several former UConn Huskies.

Waterford Speedbowl (860-442-1585; www.speedbowl.com), 1080 Hartford Ave. (CT 85), Waterford. Open Apr.–Oct. NASCAR stock-car racing on Sat. nights.

SWIMMING Swimming opportunities are limited along the Connecticut shore. In the southeastern quadrant, most town beaches are open to nonresidents for a fee. **Ocean Beach**, owned and operated by the town of New London, is open to the general public. Nearby **Crescent Beach**, at Niantic, is open to anyone owning or renting a cottage in the community or staying in local lodging. A mile-long boardwalk was built with walkway perches on the edge of Niantic Bay, with views of Long Island Sound. The boardwalk is near the village's Main St., which is lined with restaurants, shops, a movie theater, and the Children's Museum of Southeastern Connecticut. **McCook Point Park**, also in Niantic, has a pair of beaches linked by a bluff, a popular spot for picnics.

Ocean Beach Park (860-447-3031; 800-510-7263; www.ocean-beach-park.com), 98 Neptune Ave., New London. Just beyond the Monte Cristo Cottage, this is arguably one of the finest beaches on the Connecticut coast. At the eastern end of Long Island Sound, it's washed by the rolling waters of the Atlantic but still protected enough so the surf isn't dangerous. For nearly a century, Ocean Beach was a cottage colony. Wiped out in the 1930s by a devastating hurricane, it was rebuilt along the lines of Long Island's Jones Beach. In addition to the boardwalk and 0.5-mile-long crescent-shaped beach, there is miniature golf, an Olympic-sized pool, a waterslide, a carousel, a nature walk, a health club, and an arcade.

Rocky Neck State Park (860-739-5471), 244 West Main St. (CT 156), Niantic. Open year-round, daily 8 AM–sunset. Seasonal parking fee on weekends and holidays: residents $10, nonresidents $15; on weekdays: residents $7, nonresidents $10. Rocky Neck is one of four major state park beaches on Long Island Sound, and the only one east of the Connecticut River. It's bounded by salt marsh on one side and a tidal river on the other. Children and train buffs enjoy watching the occasional Amtrak train rumble by on the main rail line linking Boston and New York that splits the park. In addition to the mile-long sandy beach, there are nature trails for hiking, fishing, a large campground, and a 1930s pavilion for picnicking.

Green Space

Connecticut College Arboretum (860-439-5020; www.arboretum.conncoll.edu), 270 Mohegan Ave., across from the U.S. Coast Guard Academy, New London. Open May–Oct.; guided tours on Sun. Free admission. A 750-acre tract of labeled native trees and shrubs. Birders and hikers can meander by themselves or follow a self-guided tour brochure available at the main entrance. See one of the last stands of virgin pine in the state; some trees tower as high as California redwoods. Across from the college's main entrance, the 5-acre **Caroline Black Garden**, established in 1920, has a diversity of woody plants in a garden setting. Special programs include lectures, tours, and guided walks.

New London Waterfront Park (860-437-6346), 111 Union St., New London. Open daily dawn–dusk. In addition to becoming a major transportation hub for trains, buses, and ferry boats, New London's once grungy port has been landscaped into an inviting waterfront park with a 0.5-mile promenade along the water. Docks have been refurbished and now welcome occasional cruise ships.

Mohegan Park and Memorial Rose Garden (860-886-2381), 50 Clinton Ave., Norwich. Open daily 9 AM–sundown. Free admission. This 500-acre park in the heart of Norwich is a gem. In the 2-acre, beautifully designed formal rose gar-

Kim Grant

HARKNESS MEMORIAL STATE PARK IN WATERFORD

den, you'll find more than 200 varieties (2,500 bushes) of the world's favorite flower. Summer concerts are given by the Norwich City Band. The walking paths, pool, and children's playground are popular with locals.

Norwichtown green, north of the present core city, is an ideal place to recapture the ambience of the first days of Norwich. Beautifully restored and maintained 18th- and 19th-century houses surround the green, or commons, as it was called. Revolutionary War veterans are buried in the adjacent cemetery.

Indian Leap at Yantic Falls off Yantic St. in Norwich. In 1643, according to legend, fleeing Narragansett warriors leaped to their deaths here to avoid surrender during their final battle with the Mohegans.

🐾 ✐ ♿ **Harkness Memorial State Park** (860-443-5725), 275 Great Neck Rd. (CT 213), Waterford. Seasonal parking fee: weekdays $5 residents, $7 nonresidents; weekends $7 residents, $10 nonresidents. The 230 seaside acres at this former estate are magnificent; so is Eolia, the restored mansion open for summertime tours. The perennial borders, designed by famed landscape architect Beatrix Farrand, invite strolling and quiet contemplation. You can also picnic or fly a kite on the great lawn that slopes down to Long Island Sound.

✷ Lodging

RESORTS ❀ **The Spa at Norwich Inn** (860-886-2401; outside Connecticut 800-275-4772; www.thespaatnorwichinn.com), 607 West Thames St. (CT 32), Norwich 06360. Built in 1929—just before the stock market crash—by the city of Norwich, the Georgian-style inn is one of the most elegant resorts in Connecticut. Today it's owned by the Mashantucket Pequot Tribal Nation, of Foxwoods Resort Casino fame. A full-service spa, with 36 treatment rooms (facials, hydrotherapy, massage) and a health club with indoor and outdoor pools. Those who like their workouts outdoors can enjoy tennis, cross-country skiing, and golf. The adjacent inn has 49 rooms and four suites, all with four-poster beds, plush robes, and spa amenities; villas have kitchenette, working fireplace, and private balcony. Kensington's (see *Dining*

Out) offers innovative gourmet fare for breakfast, lunch, and dinner, as well as seasonal outdoor dining. $175–900.

♿ **Mohegan Sun Hotel** (888-226-7711; www.mohegansun.com), Mohegan Sun Casino, 1 Mohegan Sun Blvd., Uncasville 06382. A 1,200-room luxury hotel with a range of accommodations, from standard rooms to opulent suites, all tastefully furnished. The 20,000-square-foot Elemis Spa has 13 private treatment rooms; there's also a fitness room and indoor pool. A 300-room House of Blues–themed hotel, part of a larger 1,000-room hotel, is in the works.

Lighthouse Inn Resort (860-443-8411; 888-443-8411; www.lighthouse inn-ct.com), 6 Guthrie Place (off Pequot Ave.), New London 06320. A restored 1902 mansion at the mouth of the Thames that takes its name from nearby New London Light. This is Connecticut's only inn designated by the National Trust for Historic Preservation as a Historic Hotel. Fifty-one guest rooms and a highly regarded restaurant, Timothy's (see *Dining Out*). There's a private beach here, and Ocean Beach Park is just a few blocks away. Continental breakfast. $95–395.

BED & BREAKFASTS In addition to the listings below, a number of B&B reservations services offer access to rooms available in establishments throughout the state. For a list, see *Bed & Breakfasts* in "What's Where in Connecticut."

The Inn at Harbor Hill Marina (860-739-0331; www.innharborhill .com), 60 Grand St., Niantic 06357. A pleasant port of call for the Top-Sider set. Walk to Niantic shops, restaurants, and theaters. Nine rooms with bath, air-conditioning, and cable TV, all overlooking the inn's marina and the Niantic River, named for New England lighthouses. Transient slips are available, or arrive by car. Kayaks and beach passes for guests, beautiful gardens and gazebo, picnic area. Enjoy continental breakfast indoors or on the wraparound porch. $135–255.

Fourteen Lincoln Street (860-739-6327; www.14lincolnstreet.com), 14 Lincoln St., Niantic 06357. A converted 19th-century church is a fitting sanctuary for guests to rest and realign their priorities. The four suites are elegantly furnished with an eye to comfort. If a Jacuzzi tub and crystal chandelier are among your criteria, opt for the Three Angels Suite, which occupies the church's original choir loft. Outdoors, the garden-filled grounds invite wandering. The boardwalk, downtown shops, and local beaches are within easy walking distance. Full breakfast, and afternoon coffee, tea, and made-right-here desserts. $195–250.

Uncasville B&B (860-848-3649), 1851 CT 32, Uncasville 06382. Four nicely decorated guest rooms, each with private entrance and private bath. A few minutes' drive from Mohegan Sun Casino. Continental breakfast. $75–140.

Fitch Claremont Vineyard B&B (860-889-3748; 877-889-0266; www .fitchclaremonthouse.com), 83 Fitchville Rd., Bozrah 06334. A comfy bed & breakfast at a family vineyard. Four guest rooms, each with private bath, fireplace, air-conditioning, free WiFi, and a complimentary bottle of wine from the vineyard. Full breakfast. $149–169.

HOTELS AND MOTELS 🐾 **Oakdell Motel** (860-442-9446; 800-676-7378; www.oakdellmotel.com), CT 85, Waterford 06385. Twenty-two tidy and comfortable rooms, all with microwave, refrigerator, air-conditioning, and cable TV, in a semicircle centered on the outdoor pool. Continental breakfast. $60–145.

Niantic Inn (860-739-5451; www.theniantcinn.com), 345 Main St., Niantic 06357. Offers 24 spacious studios, each with dining and living room areas and refrigerators. Across the street from a sandy beach. Continental breakfast. $100–195.

Rocky Neck Inn & Suites (860-739-6268), 237 West Main St., Niantic. Offers 31 rooms, most of them efficiencies. McCook Point Beach is right across the street; passes are available. $49–129.

♿ **Courtyard by Marriott** (860-886-2600), 181 West Town St., Norwich 06360. The 120 rooms, including 24 efficiencies, offer standard amenities, plus free high-speed Internet access. Restaurant and outdoor pool. $99–219.

♿ **SpringHill Suites by Marriott** (860-439-0151), 401 North Frontage Rd., Waterford 06385. The 80 studio suites have free high-speed Internet access, ergonomic work desks, a wet bar with microwave and mini fridge, and a pullout sofa bed. Fitness room, laundry facilities, indoor pool and whirlpool. Continental breakfast. $119–199.

CAMPGROUNDS **Rocky Neck State Park** (860-739-1339), 244 West Main St. (CT 156), Niantic 06357. Open May–Sept. 160 open and wooded sites for RVs and tents. Wide beach with lifeguards; food concessions; hike to a salt marsh and fishing. $15.

Aces High RV Park (860-739-8858; 877-785-8478; www.aceshighrvpark.com), 301 Chesterfield Rd., East Lyme 06333. Tent and RV camping on 93 wooded acres. There are three ponds for fishing and swimming (you can rent paddleboats, too); a game room and playground for the kids. Free WiFi. $49–54.

Camp Niantic by the Atlantic (860-739-9308; www.campniantic.net), 271 West Main St. (CT 156), Niantic 06357. Open mid-Apr.–mid-Oct. If the campground at Rocky Neck State Park is full, this 135-site wooded campground is within walking distance. $30–38.

Salem Farms Campground (860-859-2320; 800-479-9238; www.salemfarmscampground.com), 39 Alexander Rd., Salem 06420. Families take note: With two pools, two playgrounds, hayrides, a petting zoo, nature trails, mini golf, and volleyball, there's plenty for young campers to do at this family-owned campground. $30–42.

Odetah Campground (860-889-4144; 800-448-1193; www.odetah.com), 38 Bozrah St. Extension, Bozrah 06334. Open May–mid-Oct. A sandy beach and 269 campsites on a picturesque 30-acre lake. There's boating, fishing, and swimming on the lake; you'll also find a swimming pool, tennis courts, recreation hall, basketball court, and hiking trails. Planned activities run the gamut from arts and crafts and potluck suppers to hayrides. Adirondack-style cabins and yurts are available. Sites $38–48; cabins $75–90; yurts $90–130.

Witch Meadow Lake Campground (860-859-1542; www.witchmeadowcampground.com), 139 Witch Meadow Rd., Salem 06420. Open May–mid-Oct. Complete family resort with a 14-acre lake for swimming, boating, and fishing. A full range of recreation facilities includes a new children's playscape and miniature golf course. Nature trails through 122 acres of wooded parkland. The restaurant is famous for—dare we say it—"batwings and witchburgers"! $40–50.

✷ Where to Eat

DINING OUT

In New London

On the Waterfront (860-444-2800; www.onthewaterfrontnl.com), 250 Pequot Ave. Open Tue.–Sun. for lunch and dinner; closed Mon. Dinner reservations are strongly recommended. A multitude of windows frames a lovely view of a boat-filled marina. Inside, there's nautical decor and a menu of seafood, steaks, and chops. This is a popular dinner stop before a show at the Garde Arts Center. $15–22.

Lucca Wine Bar & Grill (860-444-0333), 165 Bank St. Open Mon.–Sat. for lunch and dinner; closed Sun. Part busy Manhattan-style bistro, part friendly neighborhood grill. The bustling open kitchen churns out a daily-changing repertoire that might feature lobster bisque, lobster and avocado salad, or smoked salmon over spinach ravioli with arugula pesto. $14–26.

Tony D's (860-443-9900), 95 Huntington St., across from the courthouse. Open daily for dinner. Generous portions of Italian fare accompanied by piped-in Sinatra tunes. You can start with a hearty antipasto, bruschetta, or fried calamari. For dinner, signature dishes like braised short ribs or "Italian macaroni and cheese," studded with bacon and Gorgonzola cheese, accompany daily specials. $15–30.

Bangkok City Thai Restaurant (860-442-6970), 123 State St. Open for lunch and dinner Mon.–Sat.; closed Sun. Thai pepper reputedly is the hottest in the world, and if your tastes incline that way, here's a chance to scorch your stomach (milder renditions are prepared on request). A house specialty: spicy salad with seafood or meat. The pumpkin custard dessert is yummy. $10–21.

Café 57 Restaurant and Bar (860-442-5282; www.cafe57.net), 381 & 385 Bank St. Open Wed.–Mon. for dinner; closed Tue. Steaks are hand cut and trimmed here; there's also a nice selection of seafood and pasta dishes, and lighter fare in the bar. $11–35.

Dev's on Bank (860-442-3387; www.devsonbank.com), 345 Bank St. Open for dinner Mon.–Sat.; closed Sun. Regulars love this new spot in the center of town because, they say, staff have a knack for making diners feel like family. You can opt for Mediterranean tapas-style small plates with Spanish and Asian touches, or main courses such as Spanish paella, lime-crusted salmon, and wasabi sea scallops. $16–24.

Timothy's (860-443-8411), 6 Guthrie Place (off Pequot Ave.), at the Lighthouse Inn. Open for lunch Mon.–Sat.; dinner daily; Sun. brunch. Dine on chef Timothy Grills's seasonal American specialties and—as befits the location—fresh seafood in a beautifully restored Victorian mansion overlooking Long Island Sound. $19–33.

In Norwich

Daniel's On the Waterfront (860-887-8555; www.lisaanddaniels.com), 1 American Wharf. Open daily for lunch and dinner. A casual café with a nice view of the bustling harbor and the head of the Thames River. The menu includes French and Italian dishes, traditional New Orleans dishes, and many pastas, salads, and sandwiches. $13–21.

Kensington's (860-886-2401), the Spa at Norwich Inn (see *Lodging*), 607 West Thames St. (CT 32). Open daily for breakfast, lunch, and dinner. Chef Daniel Chong-Jimenez's creative menu features naturally raised poultry, beef, and pork—even game, in-season—as well as light-and-healthy dishes (low-cal, low-fat, low-cholesterol) popular among spa guests. $19–42.

In Uncasville

Todd English's Tuscany (860-862-3236), Mohegan Sun Casino, 1 Mohegan Sun Blvd. Open for lunch Mon.–Fri.; dinner daily; Sun. brunch. In tune with its name, celebrity chef Todd English presents rustic Tuscan cuisine. You might start with crispy oyster salad, beef carpaccio, or chilled tomato soup. For entrées, try the signature handmade spinach ravioli or potato gnocchi and you'll swear you've never had better. The fallen chocolate cake, a house specialty, is to die for. $23–40.

The Longhouse (866-226-7711), Mohegan Sun Casino, 1 Mohegan Sun Blvd. Open for dinner Thu.–Mon.; closed Tue. and Wed. A steak house that caters to a highbrow crowd without being snooty or stodgy. Chef Aiman Saad offers hearty American cuisine: dry-aged steaks, seafood, chicken, and chops. Decadent chocolate mountain cake or, on the lighter side, house-made gelato tops off the meal. $16–45.

Pompeii & Caesar (866-226-7711), Mohegan Sun Casino, 1 Mohegan Sun Blvd. Open for dinner Wed.–Sun.; Sun. brunch; closed Mon. and Tue. For high rollers, hot dates, and gourmands, this is the ultimate for regional Italian cuisine. Start with hearty antipasto or Tuscan sweet sausage and kale soup, then choose from a menu of elegant dishes such as osso buco or seared Chilean sea bass, which are beautifully presented and indulgently delicious. $22–40.

Elsewhere

✐ **La Belle Aurore** (860-739-6767; www.labelleaurorebistro.com), 75 Pennsylvania Ave., Niantic. Open for breakfast Thu.–Sun.; lunch Wed.–Fri.; dinner Mon., and Wed.–Sat.; closed Tue. Reservations are strongly recommended. A charming café with a seasonal bistro-inspired menu that utilizes top-notch ingredients, such as locally grown organic veggies and herbs. The build-your-own salad is a fun lunch alternative. For dinner, start with chopped veggie salad with watermelon, feta, and mint; then try roasted rainbow trout with fresh herbs and lemon, Niman Ranch filet mignon with roasted fingerling potatoes, or mussels with andouille sausage in a curry tomato broth. $16–28.

Frank's Gourmet Grille (860-739-0600; www.franksgourmetgrille.com), 135 Boston Post Rd. (US 1), East Lyme. Open for lunch Mon.–Sat.; dinner Tue.–Sun. The mood is set by white linen and candlelight; the creative bistro menu is accompanied by a nice selection of affordable wines. Offerings might include pan-seared coconut shrimp atop butternut squash risotto, or grilled flatbreads with prosciutto, poached pears, roasted garlic, and other gourmet toppings. Housemade tiramisu and lemon mascarpone cake for dessert. $18–32.

EATING OUT

In New London

The Broken Yolk Café (860-437-0898; www.brokenyolkcafe.net), 825 Montauk Ave. Open Tue.–Sun. for breakfast and lunch; closed Mon. The Broken Yolk is, as its name suggests, a breakfast joint. It's tiny, painted an appropriate yellow, and most definitely open for lunch, too. Regulars belly up to the counter or fill wooden booths for specialties such as shirred eggs, huevos rancheros, and croissants stuffed with eggs, tomatoes, scallions, and cream cheese. Wraps, salads, and sandwiches are whipped up later on. $5–9.

Hanafin's Irish Pub (860-437-9724; www.hanafinspub.com), 310 State St. Open daily for lunch and dinner;

brunch on Sat. and Sun. Hanafin's follows squarely in the tradition of Irish public houses, being as it is a friendly local gathering spot. There's ale and traditional Irish fare (bangers and mash, shepherd's pie, Guinness cake), live music, and sporting events on TV. Traditional Irish breakfast on Sun. $8–10.

Zavala (860-437-1891), 2 State St. Open Mon., Wed.–Fri. for lunch; Wed.–Mon. for dinner; closed Tue. A little jewel of a restaurant across from Union Station, where authentic Mexican dishes (cactus salad to tuna seviche) are prepared with fresh ingredients. For less adventurous palates, Tex-Mex dishes fall squarely in the comfort food category. $10–20.

Singapore Grill (860-442-3388), 938 Bank St. Open daily for lunch and dinner. Be prepared to wait on weekends, or make reservations. From the outside, it looks like a fast-food joint, but inside is small and intimate, and a local favorite. Chef-owner Sonny Chok's eclectic menu of Pacific Rim fusion cuisine includes well-prepared sushi and sashimi. He's often in the dining rooms chatting with guests. $10–20.

Captain Scott's Lobster Dock (860-439-1741), 80 Hamilton St. Open May–Oct., daily for lunch and dinner. *Shore dinner* is the operative term in this landmark alfresco waterfront eatery, where anything that swims could end up on your plate. Start off with a lobster roll, lobster bisque, or steamers dipped in melted butter. Then turn your attention to sea scallops, whole-belly clams, or the Captain's Combo—a medley of all of the above plus clam fritters and shrimp. Tucked between the railroad tracks and Crocker's Boatyard, it's off the beaten path but worth finding. $8–15.

Mangetout Organic Café (860-444-2066; www.mangetoutorganic.com), 140 State St. Open Mon.–Sat. 8–4; Sun. 11–4; reduced off-season hours. *Mangetout* is French for "snow pea," a nod to the café's simply prepared fresh organic food. The daily-changing menu might have frittatas and apricot-orange muffins at breakfast; ginger chicken and tomato soup, blue cheese and red onion quesadillas at lunch; and vegan chocolate mint tofu pudding for dessert. $5–8.

Monica's State Street Diner (860-701-0573), 138 State St. Open daily for breakfast; lunch Mon.–Fri. Extensive menu of classic diner fare, from omelets that span the globe to deli sandwiches piled high with corned beef, pastrami, turkey, ham, or beef. $3–8.

The Recovery Room Restaurant (860-443-2619), 445 Ocean Ave. Open Mon.–Sat. for lunch; dinner daily. The specialty at this popular pizzeria is the thin-crust pies with gourmet toppings (think artichoke hearts, feta cheese, and steak). $10–20.

Elsewhere

Flanders Fish Market & Restaurant (860-739-8866; 800-242-6055; www.flandersfish.com), 22 Chesterfield Rd. (CT 161), East Lyme. Open daily for lunch and dinner; seafood buffet on Sun. Take out or eat in. Either way, the lobster and shrimp dishes have won raves from seafood lovers all over the state. The seafood bisques are exceptional and filling; the fish-and-chips was featured on the Food Network's *Best of Fingerlickin' Favorites*. $16–33.

Jasper White's Summer Shack (860-862-9500; www.summershackrestaurant.com), Mohegan Sun Casino, Uncasville. Open for lunch Mon.–Fri.; dinner daily. Jasper White, aka Boston's "King of Seafood," lends his famous name to the casino's boisterous seafood joint. In addition to the extensive raw bar, signature dishes such as wood-grilled fish and pan-roasted lobster share billing with venison, wild rice salad, and other Native American–inspired dishes. $15–30.

Sunset Rib Co. (860-443-7427; www.sunsetribs.com), 378 Rope Ferry Rd., Waterford. Open Apr.–Oct. Pasta dishes, chicken, seafood, and, of course, ribs dominate the menu at this fun, lively bar. Live music. $13–26.

J. R.'s Shack (860-442-6660), 131 Boston Post Rd. (US 1), Waterford. Open Mon.–Sat. for breakfast, lunch, and dinner; breakfast on Sun. This no-frills, family-friendly place, known simply as "The Shack," is also known for its hearty breakfast. As at all the best breakfast places, be prepared to wait. There's a second location in East Lyme at Flanders Four Corners (860-739-8898). $10–14.

Unk's On The Bay (860-443-2717), 361 Rope Ferry Rd. (CT 156), Waterford. Open for lunch and dinner Wed.–Mon.; closed Tue. There are enough starters, soups, and salads on Unk's extensive roster to fill the entire menus of other restaurants. Clam fritters, deep-fried mozzarella, and saffron steamed mussels are some of the specialties. For entrées consider the Portuguese seafood stew, Unk's lobster pie, or coconut fried shrimp. If these don't suit your palate, there is a wide selection of beef, chicken, and seafood dishes. $16–21.

Filomena's (860-437-1010; www.filomenascafe.com), in the Utopia Centre, 262 Boston Post Rd. (US 1), Waterford. Open Mon.–Sat. for lunch and dinner; closed Sun. This upscale market and candlelit café gives Italian cuisine a fresh spin. Among the starters, the polenta fries with Gorgonzola dipping sauce is a must. Lunch is grilled bread salad, chicken Parmesan ciabatta, or handmade potato gnocchi. For dinner, penne comes with grilled chicken and artichokes; the porterhouse steak is topped with roasted garlic butter; and the pistachio-crusted tuna is among the creative seafood dishes. $8–22.

Caffe NV (860-444-8111), 57 Boston Post Rd. (US 1), Waterford. Open for lunch and dinner. Just a hop, skip, and jump west of New London, you can enjoy such Greek specialties as gyros, pork or chicken souvlaki, and an authentic Greek salad topped with creamy feta cheese. Run by four Greek sisters who started this restaurant in 2001 in a former beauty salon. Blackboard specials change daily. $9–16.

SNACKS

In New London

Michael's Dairy (860-443-2464; www.michaelsdairy.com), 629 Montauk Ave. Open daily 11–10. A landmark red barn on the campus of Mitchell College offers 41 flavors of homemade ice cream, frozen pudding, and frozen yogurt. The older crowd indulges in familiar flavors like chocolate, while the young'uns go for Monster Mash and Moose Tracks. An adjacent café is stocked with baked goods and coffee. There's a satellite location downtown at 60 Bank St. (203-443-2464).

Bean & Leaf (860-701-0000; www.bean-leaf.com), 13 Washington St. Open daily. As you'd expect, you can get really good coffee and tea here, but that's not nearly all. They offer pastries and other sweets, and a full menu of paninis, sandwiches, soups, and salads. Sunday-night movies, poetry and comedy open-mike nights, and live music fill the entertainment calendar.

Muddy Waters Café (860-444-2232), 42 Bank St. A heart-of-downtown coffee bar—a short walk from the train station and ferry dock—that's fun, friendly, and popular with locals as well as visitors from out of town. A full menu of lattes, espressos, cappuccinos, and other hot and cold coffee and tea drinks, not to mention yummy treats to go with them.

Brie & Bleu (860-437-2474; www.brieandbleu.com), 84 Bank St. A gourmet cheese shop that prepares lunches and light suppers to eat here or take home. You can grab a bottle of wine from the shop next door and dine on the open-air deck overlooking the harbor.

Chester's Barbecue (860-447-1406; www.chestersbbq.com), 549 Bank St. New location in Groton (860-449-6868) at 943 Poquonnock Rd. Wood smoke emanates from the smoker in front of this tiny building. Pulled pork, smoked meats, beef brisket, and baby back ribs come with potato salad, baked beans, coleslaw, and other homemade sides.

Fred's Shanty (860-447-1301; www.fredsshanty.com), 272 Pequot Ave. Open for lunch and dinner daily, Mar.–late Oct. There's no denying the summery pleasure of doing your eating outdoors, and locals love this waterfront drive-in for its seafood, burgers, lobster rolls, and soft-serve ice cream.

Elsewhere

East Coast Taco (860-739-8770), 51 West Main St. (CT 156), Niantic. A California-style taquería offering Tex-Mex fare by way of hearty stuffed burritos, tacos, and enchiladas. Do as the locals do: Sit outside (BYOB) or take your meal to go and stroll the boardwalk.

Dad's (860-739-2113), 147 Main St., Niantic. Open Apr.–Sept. for lunch and dinner. A family favorite on the Niantic boardwalk for more than 40 years. Dad's is known for its generous seafood platters, as well as burgers, lobster rolls, and ice cream.

David's (860-442-7120), 1647 CT 85, Chesterfield. Open for lunch and dinner in summer. Drive-in standbys, from fried seafood (the whole-belly clams are a must-try) to hot dogs and fresh-cut fries. Spinach pie and gyros are among the Greek specialties. Across from Nature's Art.

Entertainment

MUSIC AND THEATER **onStage at Connecticut College** (860-439-2787; www.conncoll.edu), Palmer Auditorium, 270 Mohegan Ave., New London. Dance, music, and theatrical performances Sept.–May.

Garde Arts Center (860-444-7373; www.gardearts.org), 325 State St., New London. Downtown performing arts center housed in a magnificently restored 1920s-era vaudeville theater. There's an annual concert series by the **Eastern Connecticut Symphony Orchestra**, as well as Broadway musicals, ballet, and children's theater.

U.S. Coast Guard Band (860-444-8468; www.uscg.mil/band), Leamy Hall Auditorium, on the campus of the U.S. Coast Guard Academy, 15 Mohegan Ave. (CT 32), New London. Full schedule of free concerts, but the band also performs at special events and celebrations throughout the country; check to see if it's in residence when you're in town.

Mohegan Sun Casino (888-777-7922; www.mohegansun.com), Mohegan Sun Blvd., off CT 2A, Uncasville. The casino has a variety of entertainment venues: the 10,000-seat **Mohegan Sun Arena** is the setting for concerts, world-championship boxing, and the home court for the Connecticut Sun basketball team. The **Cabaret at Mohegan Sun** is an intimate 300-seat theater with comfy banquettes; and the **Wolf Den** offers free shows in the Casino of the Earth. A new 1,500-seat

House of Blues music hall is slated to open in 2010.

Monte Cristo Cottage (860-443-0051), 325 Pequot Ave., New London. Lectures of particular interest to writers and students of literature are held regularly at Eugene O'Neill's boyhood summer home. (See also *To See.*)

Eugene O'Neill Theater Center (860-443-5378; www.theoneill.org), 305 Great Neck Rd., Waterford. This waterfront, Tony Award–winning theater is committed to nurturing new works. Professional readings of newly written plays and musicals, selected the previous fall, are read here at the playwriting and musical theater summer conferences and the annual Eugene O'Neill Celebration in October (see *Special Events*). Many have gone on to fame and fortune on Broadway.

Spirit of Broadway Theater (860-886-2378; www.spiritofbroadway.org), 24 Chestnut St., Norwich. A converted historic brick firehouse is now a 74-seat black-box theater in downtown's historic Chelsea Arts District, devoted to cutting-edge new works and Off-Broadway theater productions. It's not named for Broadway hits, as many assume, but for Norwich's old Broadway Theater.

✴ Selective Shopping

Crystal Mall (860-442-8500), 850 Hartford Turnpike (CT 85), Waterford. Open daily 9:30–9:30; Sun. 11–5. Major department store chains such as Sears, Macy's, and JCPenney, along with more than 130 specialty shops. There are market pushcarts in the corridors, plus a variety of vendors in the Food Court—Chinese, Japanese, and American—to stave off the appetite of even the most ravenous teenager. See the world's largest Waterford crystal chandelier.

The Book Barn (860-739-5715; www.bookbarnniantic.com), 41 West Main St., Niantic. Open daily 9–9; closed Christmas and Thanksgiving. Weary of big-box bookstores? This complex of buildings is a bibliophile's dream: some 350,000 gently used books start at $1. A great place to spend a rainy day; outside, gardens invite strolling.

The Shops at Mohegan Sun (888-226-7711; www.mohegansun.com), Mohegan Sun Casino, 1 Mohegan Sun Blvd., Uncasville. More than 40 retail shops provide ample opportunity to spend your casino winnings.

Nature's Art (860-443-4367; www.enaturesart.com), 1650 CT 85, Montville. Gift shop open daily 10–6; activities on Sat. and Sun. Kids learn about fossils, gems, rocks, and bones through interactive exhibits. Next door, **Dinosaur Crossing** (860-443-4367; http://thedinosaurplace.com) has more than 25 life-sized dinosaur replicas along a mile of wooded nature trails; **SplashPad** focuses on watery interactive play stations. Open mid-Apr.–Oct., daily 10–6.

Bayberries Fine Gifts (860-739-2977; www.bayberriesfinegifts.com), 32 Pennsylvania Ave., Niantic. An interesting selection of items in all price ranges, from home decor and gifts to pottery, greeting cards, and linens.

Grace (860-739-4333; www.gracestores.com), 51 Pennsylvania Ave., Niantic. A showcase for an array of furniture, home decor, fun gifts, women's apparel, and jewelry.

Defender (860-628-8225; www.defender.com), 42 Great Neck Rd., Waterford. For more than 70 years, Defender has been outfitting the boating set. Here, a warehouse outlet store is stocked with more than 20,000 marine products, including closeouts and discontinued items.

ART AND ANTIQUES

In New London

New London Antiques Center (860-444-7598), 123–131 Bank St. More than 30 dealers have set up booths offering antique treasures, including furniture, paintings, frames, glassware, jewelry, and lamps.

Captain's Treasures (860-442-2944), 165 State St. Antiques, furniture, collectibles, and decorative accessories.

Ya-Ta-Hey (860-443-3204; www.yahtaheygallery.com), 279 State St. Choice Native American pottery, jewelry, sculpture, rugs, and paintings.

Hygienic Artist Cooperative Galleries (860-443-8001; www.hygienic.org), 79–83 Bank St. For folks more interested in art than attitude, good news: This nonprofit gallery is a casual venue for local artists to display their work. Changing exhibits focus mostly on the work of young artists bursting with new ideas. An abandoned parking lot next door is now Hygienic Art Park, a European-inspired garden.

Golden Street Gallery (860-444-0659; www.goldenstreetgallery.com), 94 Golden St. Open Fri.–Sun. and by appointment. Paintings, sculpture, and prints by regional artists.

Elsewhere

Price Fine Arts (860-691-0223; 888-628-9278; www.danielprice.com), 205 Upper Pattagansett Rd., East Lyme. Exhibitions of maritime and military art: aviation, lighthouses, sailboat racing, and local scenes.

FARMS **The Salem Herb Farm** (860-859-3344; www.salemherbfarm.com), 320 Hartford Rd. (CT 85), Salem. This is the go-to spot for culinary, ornamental, and medicinal herbs, as well as a nice selection of annuals and perennials. An inviting gift shop in a restored 19th-century barn is stocked with plants, gifts, and gourmet food items. Demonstration gardens are outside, as well as emus, sheep, and other farm animals.

✸ Special Events

January: **Sun WineFest** (860-728-5700; www.sunwinefest.com), Mohegan Sun, Uncasville. Celebrity chefs and more than 1,000 fine wines from around the world.

Late April: **Connecticut Storytelling Festival** (860-439-2764; www.connstorycenter.org), Connecticut College, New London. A weekend of storytelling, workshops, and concerts at the college's Connecticut Storytelling Center.

June: **Yale–Harvard Regatta**, Thames River, New London. Traditional rivals in crew racing meet in the oldest intercollegiate competition in the United States. View from shore or from chartered observation boats. **Norwich River Fest** (860-887-1647), Norwich Harbor. Chinese dragon-boat racing, live entertainment, and food from local restaurants.

July: ✐ **Sailfest** (860-444-1879; www.sailfest.org), New London waterfront. Three days of live entertainment, tall ships, food, games, amusement rides, harbor tours, and fireworks over the Thames River. ✐ **Norwich Independence Day Celebration** (860-886-6363), Norwich Marina at American Wharf, Norwich. Entertainment and food during the day; fireworks at night. **LobsterFest** (860-908-2247), East Lyme. Lobster barbecue, and arts and crafts, on the town hall grounds.

July through August: ✐ **Ocean Beach Park Summer Festival**, New London. A variety of special celebrations, from games, shows, and movies for families to dancing and DJs for teens. **Eugene O'Neill Playwrights**

Conference (860-443-5378), Eugene O'Neill Theater Center, Waterford. Readings of new plays, many of which go on to fame and fortune on Broadway.

August: **Montville Fair** (www.montvillefair.org), CT 163, Oakdale.

September through June: **Food for Thought**, Lyman Allyn Art Museum, New London (see *To See*). Bring lunch and enjoy lectures on a wide variety of subjects.

September: **Annual Arts and Crafts Show**, Ocean Beach Park, New London. **Historic Norwichtown Days**, on the Norwichtown green, Norwichtown. Reenactments of life during the Revolutionary and Civil War periods. Demonstrations of bygone handicrafts, woodworking, outdoor cooking, weaving, and blacksmithing. ✎ **Ledyard Fair** (www.ledyardfair.org), CT 117, Ledyard Center. A traditional three-day country fair. **Books, Brushes, Jazz, & Blues** (860-444-2489), New London. A celebration of the city's maritime heritage with music, literary events, art, and food in the waterfront district.

October: ✎ **Fall Festival** (860-642-6413), Blue Slope Country Museum, Franklin. A two-day celebration with horse-drawn wagon rides, draft horse demonstrations, pie-eating contests, and historic reenactments. The **Mystic Country Marathon** (www.mysticcountrymarathon.com) is a scenic waterfront run that starts at Rocky Neck State Park in East Lyme and winds through downtown Niantic before returning to Rocky Neck. There's also a children's fun run and a festival in downtown Niantic. **Eugene O'Neill Celebration** (see *Entertainment*). **Lantern Light Graveyard Walk** (860-886-4683), Norwich. Led by a ghost hunter, a guided tour of Old Norwichtown Burial Ground and the Norwichtown green.

December: **Wassail Party**, Smith-Harris House, Niantic. The house is decorated in the style of the mid-1800s. **Winterfest**, Norwich; parade through downtown. ***The Holly and the Ivy: A Living History Play*** (860-444-2489; www.newlondonmainstreet.org), New London. Scenes from the play are acted out at historic sites downtown. **Celebration of Lights & Songs by the Sea** (www.newlondonmainstreet.org), New London. Ice-carving exhibition, gallery tour, music, community carol sing, and tree lighting in the historic waterfront district. **Niantic Light Parade** (www.eastlymelightparade.com), Niantic. A parade of some 60 floats down Main St.

The Lower Connecticut River Valley and Shoreline

THE LOWER CONNECTICUT RIVER VALLEY

THE CENTRAL SHORELINE, OLD LYME TO BRANFORD

Kim Grant

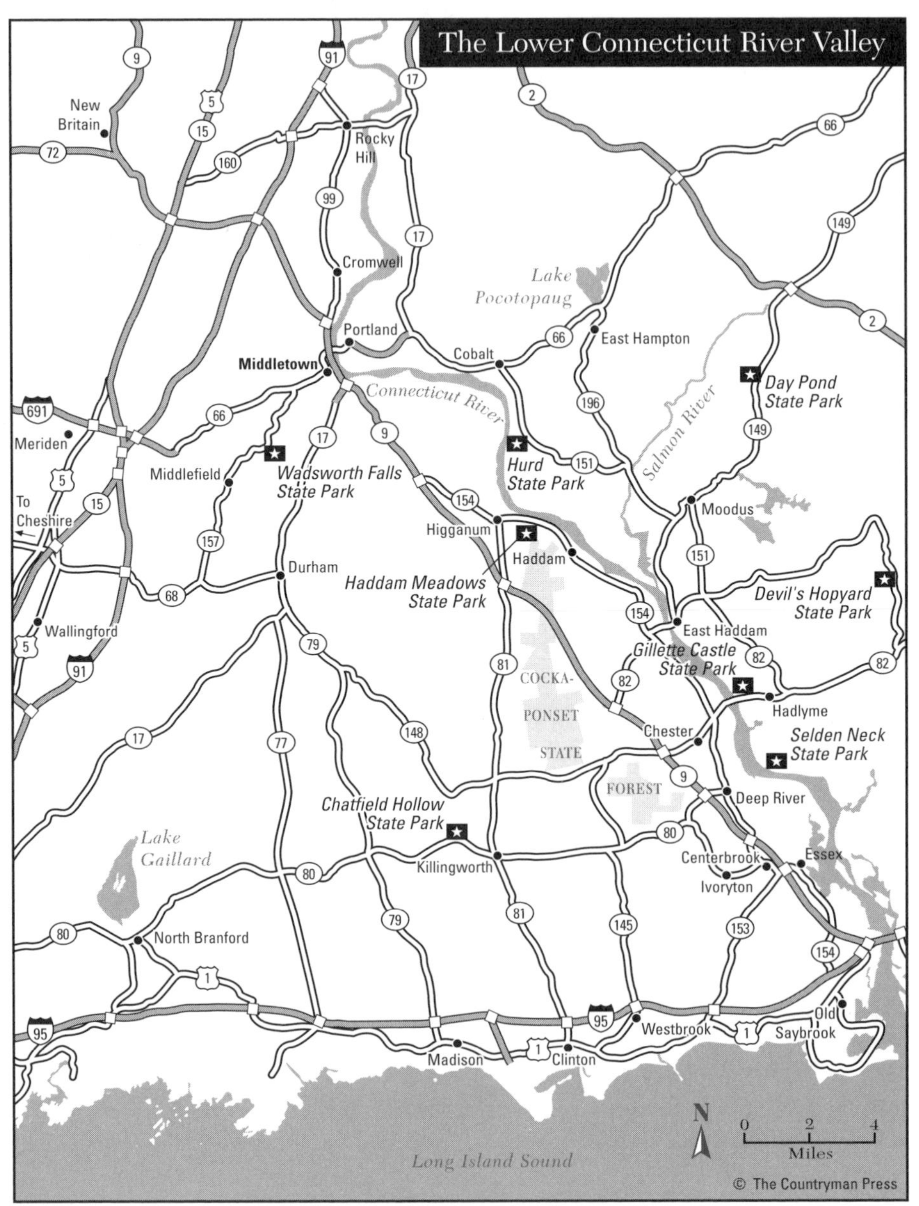

The Lower Connecticut River Valley
New Britain
Rocky Hill
Cromwell
Portland
Middletown
Lake Pocotopaug
East Hampton
Cobalt
Connecticut River
Salmon River
Day Pond State Park
Hurd State Park
Meriden
Middlefield
Wadsworth Falls State Park
To Cheshire
Higganum
Haddam
Haddam Meadows State Park
Moodus
Devil's Hopyard State Park
East Haddam
Gillette Castle State Park
Hadlyme
Durham
Wallingford
COCKAPONSET STATE FOREST
Chester
Selden Neck State Park
Deep River
Chatfield Hollow State Park
Lake Gaillard
Killingworth
Centerbrook
Essex
Ivoryton
North Branford
Westbrook
Old Saybrook
Madison
Clinton
Long Island Sound
N
0 2 4
Miles
© The Countryman Press

THE LOWER CONNECTICUT RIVER VALLEY

New England's longest river trickles out of a spring-fed pond near New Hampshire's Canadian border, and cuts a 410-mile-long liquid highway through the heart of New England before emptying into Long Island Sound. The two waterways—the river and the Sound—attracted the state's first settlers and later provided an avenue of trade for adventurous Yankee merchants and sailors.

Because the mouth of the river is relatively shallow in most spots, and sandbars are hidden menaces, freighters and other deep-water ships couldn't navigate very far. Thus industrial cities couldn't take root at the mouth of the river or in the lower valley. Instead of urban sprawl, there unexpectedly is a 40-mile stretch of shoreline green with trees, the peace and quiet of the river punctuated occasionally by the mournful sound of a historic steam engine. This section of Connecticut, nestled between the river and the Sound, is iconic and timeless, dotted by a scattering of charming maritime villages, complete with demure white clapboards, stately mansions, sharp-steepled churches, and neat picket fences.

Visitors to Connecticut familiar with the hills of Litchfield, the glamour of the Gold Coast, and the high-energy casinos in the southeast are uniformly surprised and delighted when they literally discover the lower Connecticut River Valley. Here is an area unbelievably rich in beauty and history, but also in its passive and active recreational possibilities: kayaking, biking, bird-watching, walking, riding a train or a riverboat, not to mention unique theater, art and artists, an extraordinary museum, and superb dining and charming inns.

The Indians knew whereof they spoke when they named this river the Connecticut "the Long Tidal River." In the 1970s, however, industrial dumping and general misuse polluted the river, with disastrous results for its wildlife and water quality. Thanks to a determined cleanup effort, the river underwent a renaissance; as a result, The Nature Conservancy has designated the tidelands of the Connecticut River one of the hemisphere's 40 Last Great Places. Ospreys and bald eagles are now a common sight on tidal creeks and salt marshes, as are swimmers and anglers. A wintertime festival in Essex celebrates America'a symbol of freedom, back in healthy numbers and off the federal endangered species list.

Along the riverbank lies the history of a region. Middletown, once the largest, busiest port on the river, has kept its splendid 19th-century mansions of successful traders and merchants, now incorporated into the leafy 290-acre Wesleyan University campus. The university has left its thumbprint on the city in the way of several art galleries, a children's museum, and a youth theater, as well as a grassroots art and music scene supported by downtown bookstores and coffeehouses. Across the Arrigoni Bridge, east of the river, the quarries of the town of Portland have given their name to the brownstone of New York City's familiar row houses. Farther downstream, on a bluff in East Haddam, broods the outlandish castle that the actor William Gillette designed as a monument to his eccentricities; its stone terraces boast one of the most spectacular vistas of the river valley. Steam-driven locomotives of the old Connecticut Valley line still rumble along the 19th-century roadbed, now hauling tourists to Deep River, where they can board the *Becky Thatcher*, a Mississippi-style riverboat that plies the Connecticut River. Theatergoers flock to East Haddam to savor the excellence—architectural as well as theatrical—of the Goodspeed Opera House, a Victorian gem known as the birthplace of the American musical. Theater troupes once arrived here from New York City on Captain Goodspeed's steamboat to perform. Visitors can cross the Connecticut River on an antique swing bridge, or board the Chester–Hadlyme Ferry, a transportation option here for more than 200 years. Also in town is the tiny schoolhouse where Revolutionary War hero Nathan Hale once taught; today it's open to visitors.

Chester is one of the state's most charming villages; its quaint and historic Main Street is home to a thriving community of artists, artisans, designers, craftspeople, chefs, and others blessed with exquisite talents. On the wall of the Pattaconk 1850 Bar & Grille, a Main Street restaurant, is a lighthearted "Non-Historical Marker" announcing that on this spot on February 29, 1778, absolutely nothing happened. Essex, with a maritime legacy older than the country, was captured by British marines during the War of 1812 and all its shipping burned; but the inn the redcoats commandeered for quarters still offers lodging and hearty meals. Deep River and Ivoryton once thrived by importing and manufacturing ivory piano keys; today they are among the valley's quieter villages with antiques shops, cafés, and a luxuri-

ESSEX'S HISTORIC MAIN STREET IS A PRISTINE EXAMPLE OF A CONNECTICUT RIVER TOWN.

Kim Grant

ous inn with award-winning cuisine. Deep River was a major shipbuilding center and the country's largest manufacturer of ivory piano keys; today it's a quiet blue-collar town whose must-see event on the third weekend in July is the Deep River Ancient Muster, where traditional fife and drum corps parade down Main Street. And then there's shad, Connecticut's official state fish, which returns to the lower Connecticut River every spring. The arrival is celebrated with shad suppers, derbies, a festival, even a tiny seasonal shad museum in Haddam.

Even towns one tier removed from the river have clung to their 18th-century roots. Wooded hills are dotted with farms, historic villages, acclaimed restaurants, and charming inns tucked away off winding country roads. Much of the river valley is protected state land, providing visitors with miles of forest trails for hiking and mountain biking. Lyman Orchard in Middlefield, a family enterprise dating back some 200 years, contradicts the usual New England image of rocky, barren hillsides with its bounty of apples, peaches, and berries. Cheshire, awash in greenhouses, is the self-styled Bedding Plant Capital of Connecticut. In springtime, town roads are alive with flats of colorful annuals to brighten winter-weary yards.

Entries in this section are arranged in alphabetical order.

AREA CODES 860 and 203.

GUIDANCE **Central Regional Tourism District** (860-244-8181; 800-793-4480; www.enjoycentralct.com), 31 Pratt St., Hartford 06103. The district publishes comprehensive brochures and guides listing lodgings, attractions, restaurants, theaters, galleries, charter boats, golf courses, and other travel information. They also supply literature from individual establishments, giving excellent one-stop service that includes referrals to specific local sources.

State highway centers. The main center for this region is at Westbrook on I-95 eastbound. Many towns staff small information booths in the warm season.

GETTING THERE *By air:* The state's major airport is **Bradley International Airport** (860-292-2000; 888-624-1533; www.bradleyairport.com), north of Hartford off I-91 in Windsor Locks. **Groton–New London Airport** (860-445-8549) is used only by charter and corporate planes. **Tweed–New Haven Regional Airport** (203-466-8833; www.flytweed.com) is served by US Airways Express. Private planes may land at **Chester Airport** (860-526-4321; 800-752-6371) and at **Goodspeed Airport** (860-564-2359) in East Haddam.

By bus: **Peter Pan Bus Lines** (800-343-9999; www.peterpanbus.com) stops in Meriden and Middletown. **Greyhound Lines** (800-231-2222; www.greyhound.com) stops in Middletown.

By car: Drive into the area from either New York City or Boston via I-95 or, if you prefer more leisurely driving, by US 1, the legendary old Boston Post Rd. CT 9 is the major north–south route, a limited-access divided highway connecting I-84 in Farmington and I-95 at Old Saybrook.

By train: **Amtrak** (800-872-7245; www.amtrak.com) runs between New York City and Boston with stops in Mystic, New London, Old Saybrook, and New Haven. **Shore Line East** (203-777-7433; 800-255-7433; www.shorelineeast.com) offers weekday commuter rail service between New London and New Haven, with several local stops along its shoreline route.

GETTING AROUND *By taxi:* **Executive 200 Transportation** (860-347-4222) serves Middletown, Durham, Middlefield, Cromwell, Haddam, and the central river valley area. If you plan a stay at one of the major inns or resorts, inquire about pickup service at the nearest railroad station, or when you are making your lodging reservation.

MEDICAL EMERGENCY The statewide emergency number is **911**.

Middlesex Memorial Hospital (860-344-6000), 28 Crescent St., Middletown. The emergency number is 860-344-6686.

Middlesex Hospital Shoreline Medical Center (860-767-3700), 260 Westbrook Rd. (CT 153), Essex.

MidState Medical Center (203-694-8200), 435 Lewis Ave., Meriden. The emergency number is 203-694-8911.

✱ To See

MUSEUMS 🖍 **Allegra Farm Horse-Drawn Carriage and Sleigh Museum** (860-537-8861; www.allegrafarm.com), 69 Town Rd. (CT 82), East Haddam. Open by appointment. Tour a restored 19th-century livery stable, complete with a coach house full of antique carriages, a restoration and wheelwright shop, and a gift shop. Afterward, check out the post-and-beam carriage barn, which houses antique horse-drawn vehicles, including hearses and a U.S. mail wagon. Western chuck-wagon events and country carriage rides and hayrides. Many of the wagons have been used in movies and TV shows.

🖍 **Barker Character, Comic and Cartoon Museum** (203-699-3822; www.barkermuseum.com), 1188 Highland Ave. (CT 10), Cheshire. Open Wed.–Sat. 11–5; closed Sun.–Tue. Free admission. If you like to play, this is your place. Herb and Gloria Barker have amassed a staggering collection of toys, as well as comic strip, cartoon, television, and advertising memorabilia—some 80,000 items in all. About 350 lunch boxes hang from the rafters; display cases are crammed with rarities like a 1940 Fisher-Price train, a Dick Tracy wrist radio set from the 1950s, Howdy Doody talking dolls, and tin toys from the early 1900s. When was the last time you saw a 19th-century Yellow Kid gumball machine or found a Lone Ranger flashlight ring in your cereal box? A surreal fantasy world for the young and young at heart. See also Barker Animation Gallery under *Selective Shopping*.

Connecticut River Museum (860-767-8269; www.ctrivermuseum.org), 67 Main St., Essex. Open year-round, Tue.–Sun. 10–5; closed Mon. and major holidays. Adults $7; seniors $6; children 6–12 $4; under 6 free. The museum building is a well-kept 1878 Yankee dock house, situated on the water's edge at the old Essex Steamboat Dock. It's now the repository for nautical paintings, photographs, ship models, and antique objects that illuminate the maritime history of the lower river valley before and after Adriaen Block's historic voyage of discovery in 1607. Among the exhibits is a replica of David Bushnell's 1775 underwater vessel, the *Turtle*—recognized as the world's first submarine. Big enough for a crew of one (preferably smallish) human, it carries no lights and no oxygen supply and is powered by foot pedals. It attacked a British warship in the battle of New York during the first days of the American Revolution, but the explosive failed to dent the protective copper plates around the hull. The *Turtle* was an ingenious precursor of the nuclear subs built nearby in Groton today. Nature tours (see *To Do*) aboard *RiverQuest* leave from Steamboat Dock.

Haddam Shad Museum (860-267-0388), 212 Saybrook Rd. (CT 154), Higganum. Open mid-Apr.–June, Sun. 10–4 and by appointment. Free admission. When American shad begin their annual spring migration, swing by this tiny one-room museum housed in a former shad shack. Memorabilia tells the story of shad fishing on the Connecticut River.

🖍 ♿ **Kidcity Children's Museum** (860-347-0495; www.kidcitymuseum.com), 119 Washington St., Middletown. Open Sun.–Tue. 11–5; Wed.–Sat. 9–5. Admission $7; children under 1 free. An imaginative, hands-on museum for children from 1 to 8 years old. Three floors of unique exhibits and programs—a video theater and science-themed area among them—encourage creative thinking and interactive play.

Museum of Fife and Drum (860-767-2237), 63 North Main St., Ivoryton. Open late June–Labor Day weekend, Sat.–Sun. 1–5. Adults $3; seniors and students $2; children 12 and under free. The Company of Fifers and Drummers is credited with preserving the tradition of mustering fife-and-drum corps for parades and concerts; this is the only museum in the world dedicated to the music of the ancient fife and drum. Exhibits trace the importance of fifing and drumming to military strategy from colonial days through the Revolutionary War. Today's civilian corps keep alive this musical symbol of American patriotism with annual musters held around the state, drawing corps from all down the eastern seaboard and beyond. Performances are scheduled in July and Aug. (see *Special Events*).

HISTORIC HOMES **Amasa Day House** (860-247-8996), on the Moodus town green, Plains Rd. (CT 151), Moodus. Hours change seasonally; phone ahead. Adults $7; seniors and students $6; children 6–18 $4; 5 and under free. This 1816 Federal-style white-clapboard classic, property of the Antiquarian and Landmarks

KIDCITY MUSEUM IN MIDDLETOWN

Cory Mazon

Society, features original stenciling on the floors and stair risers. Many of the furnishings and toys belonged to the Day family, who lived here for three generations. In the restored barn, the East Haddam Historical Society exhibits trace local twine and textile mills of the 19th century.

General Mansfield House (860-346-0746), 151 Main St., Middletown. Museum tours Wed. 1–5; Tue., Thu., and Fri. 11–5; closed Sat.–Mon. Adults $5; children 11 and under $1. A Federal-style redbrick home built in 1810 and furnished with both 18th- and 19th-century pieces, this house has another appeal: As headquarters of the Middlesex County Historical Society, it contains a genealogical library that attracts visitors from all over. Exhibits focus on Middletown history, particularly the Civil War era.

 **Gillette Castle** (860-526-2336), 67 River Rd., East Haddam. The grounds are open year-round, 8 AM–sunset; the castle is open Memorial Day weekend–Columbus Day, daily 10–4:30; Columbus Day–late Dec., weekends 10–4. Adults and children 14–18 $5; children 6–12 $2; 5 and under free. There is no charge to visit the grounds. This not-to-be-missed site should be on every New Englander's to-do list. After its completion in 1919, this fieldstone oddity, perched high above the Connecticut River, was home to Hartford native and playwright William Gillette, whose fame and fortune rested on his portrayal of Sherlock Holmes from 1899 to 1932. His granite-and-timber mansion is a collection of eccentricities, replete with such curiosities as a dining table on tracks; guests were seated on a bench against the wall, and the table was moved into place, effectively trapping them through dessert. Hidden mirrors allowed the host to spy on guests in the bar or living room, then seize the correct moment for a dramatic entrance. And what would a castle be without hidden rooms, secret passageways, and a miniature railroad that chugged around the estate? Upstairs is a replica of Sherlock Holmes's study at 221B Baker St., with the Persian slipper of tobacco, the violin ready to play, the chemistry lab set up, and newspapers scattered about, as if the game were once more afoot and Holmes and Watson outside hailing a hansom cab. Extend your visit by picnicking or exploring the hiking trails in the 125-acre state park surrounding the castle.

WILLIAM GILLETTE USED THE FORTUNE HE AMASSED PORTRAYING SHERLOCK HOLMES ON THE STAGE TO BUILD THIS CURIOUS EAST HADDAM CASTLE.

Kim Grant

Hitchcock Phillips House (203-272-8771), 43 Church Dr., off CT 10, Cheshire. Open Sept.–May, Sun. 2–4, or by appointment. A 1785 Georgian mansion on the town green built by a wealthy merchant, it was later part of the Cheshire Academy but is now home to the Cheshire Historical Society. The house features wood paneling, period furnishings, and a fireplace with beehive oven in the keeping room. Historical exhibits highlight locally manufactured wares such as campaign buttons, watches, and oyster kegs.

Pratt House Museum (860-767-1191), 18 West Ave., Essex. Open for tours June–Labor Day, Sat. and Sun. 1–4 or by appointment. Admission by donation. A handsome 1732 home—one of the oldest homes in this historic town—built in sections throughout the 18th century; operated by the Essex Historical Society.

Thankful Arnold House (860-345-2400), Hayden Hill and Walkley Hill Rds. (CT 154), in the Higganum section of Haddam). Hours vary; phone ahead. Adults $4; seniors $3; children $2. A somewhat unusual, three-story, gambrel-roofed house dated 1794 to 1810 and built right on the street with entrances on two levels. The deep sand color of the clapboards may surprise you if you expect all early homes to be restoration white or colonial red. The furnishings reflect two centuries of changing tastes on the part of the owners. Like the house itself, the period herb, vegetable, and flower gardens have been carefully researched. Summer visitors can tour the Colonial Revival–style gardens.

ꝏ **The Wadsworth Mansion at Long Hill Estate** (860-347-1064), 421 Wadsworth St., Middletown. Grounds open year-round, sunrise to sunset; tours of the mansion Wed. 2–4 and by appointment; phone ahead. Free admission. A grand hilltop estate designed in 1897 in the opulent style of the Gilded Age and built by Colonel Clarence Wadsworth to rival Newport's palatial summer "cottages." Landscaping by the Olmsted brothers. Visitors can tour the mansion or explore the grounds on walking trails that wind through 103 acres of mixed forest and past stone walls, a tennis pavilion, and landscaped gardens.

HISTORIC SITES **Comstock Covered Bridge** (860-267-2519) spans the Salmon River near the Colchester town line in East Hampton. Just off CT 16, this 1873 bridge is open to pedestrians only; it's one of three covered bridges left in the

THE MOODUS NOISES

No Connecticut mystery has caused more fear, and speculation, than the mysterious and relatively minor but continuing earth tremors known as the Moodus Noises. Centered in East Haddam where the Salmon and Moodus rivers meet, the Noises have startled all who have heard them. For the Pequot, Mohegan, and Narragansett tribes, the thundering and quaking were caused by the displeasure of their god Hobomoko, who reigned below on a sapphire throne. The Indians called the area *Matchemadoset* or *Matchitmoodus*—now *Machimoodus*—meaning, literally, "Place of Bad Noises." When the first white settlers came to the region in the 1670s, they were shaken by the Noises. Those devout Puritans were certain that Hobomoko and their own Satan were the same. Many other horror stories revolve around the Moodus Noises. You may still hear them when you visit the region. Calm your fears. We have not yet lost a tourist in the "Place of Bad Noises."

state. An excellent spot for souvenir pictures and for examining the lattice-truss design, devised by Connecticut architect Ithiel Town to enable early bridge builders to span rivers without suspension cables or complicated machinery. The adjacent **Salmon River State Forest** has picnic sites; the stocked river is a favorite spot for local anglers, so you may want to bring your fly rod.

Lock 12 Historical Park (203-272-2743), 487 North Brooksvale Rd. (CT 42), Cheshire. Park open daily, sunrise to sunset; museum tours by appointment. An authentically restored section of the once bustling Farmington Canal. The success of New York's Erie Canal inspired area entrepreneurs to build their own avenue of waterborne commerce. From 1827 to 1848, barges carried passengers and cargo through 60 locks up and down the 83-mile-long, hand-dug canal between New Haven and Northampton, Massachusetts. The waterway eventually succumbed to the faster, more efficient locomotive. Today the canal's stillness makes it hard to believe that it was once a major transportation system. The park features a small museum, lock keeper's house, and picnic areas.

Nathan Hale Schoolhouse (860-873-3399), 29 Main St. (CT 149), East Haddam; behind St. Stephen's Episcopal Church (see below). Open Memorial Day–Columbus Day, weekends and holidays noon–4. Free admission; donations accepted. Local history records that the 18-year-old Yale graduate taught in this one-room school for five months, from 1773 to 1774. Later he became a Revolutionary War hero—and later still, Connecticut's state hero—and the school assumed his name. On display are the schoolmaster's possessions and relics of local history.

St. Stephen's Episcopal Church (860-873-9547), 31 East Main St., East Haddam. The belfry of this stone church houses an ancient bell dated AD 815, thought to be the oldest such bell in the New World. It was cast for a Spanish monastery destroyed in the Napoleonic Wars and later shipped to the colonies by a Yankee sea captain in need of ballast. The best vantage point for viewing the bell is from the hillside path to the Nathan Hale Schoolhouse (see above), behind the church.

WINERY **Priam Vineyards** (860-267-8520; www.priamvineyards.com), 11 Shailor Hill Rd., Colchester. Tasting room and vineyard open Fri.–Sun.; extended summer and holiday hours. In the winery, surrounded by 24 acres of grapes, you can sample Priam's 13 handcrafted wines—five reds and eight whites—and enjoy the work of regional artists. Visitors are welcome to picnic on the grounds; there's a farmer's market here July–Oct.

* To Do

AIRPLANE RIDES **Chester Airport** (860-526-4321; 800-752-6371), 61 Winthrop Rd., Chester. A 20-minute plane ride—a good idea at any time of year, but spectacular in fall. Passengers can choose an open-cockpit plane in spring, summer, and fall, or an enclosed aircraft year-round. With prior arrangement, you can also hire pilot and rent plane, and create your own flight plan for a one-hour trip.

BALLOONING **Above Earth's Plane Balloons** (860-857-8757), 12 Blue Grass Rd., Middletown. Scenic champagne flights over central Connecticut year-round.

Balloon Rides by Castle View (203-272-6116; www.castleviewballoons.com), 1476 Highland Ave. (CT 10), Cheshire. Daily sunrise or late-afternoon flights Apr.–Dec.; call ahead for reservations. Trips over central Connecticut offer views of the Berkshire foothills and Long Island Sound.

BOAT EXCURSIONS **Chester–Hadlyme Ferry** (860-443-3856), CT 148, either shore. Operates Apr.–Nov., daily except Thanksgiving Day, Mon.–Fri. 7–6:45; weekends 10:30–5. Car and driver $3; additional passengers and walk-ons $1. Follow the signs to the dock and read the instructions posted there. The short river crossing on the *Selden III*—the second-oldest continuously operating ferry in the nation—is truly one of life's simple pleasures. During the three- to five-minute trip to the opposite shore, take in views of the Connecticut River and the towering hills called Seven Sisters, one of them crowned by Gillette Castle.

Connecticut River Expeditions (860-662-0577; www.ctriverexpeditions.org), 67 Main St., Essex. Year-round; check the Web site for a schedule. *RiverQuest* leaves from Steamboat Dock at the Connecticut River Museum (see *To See*). River tours and sunset cruises on the still waters of the lower Connecticut River. From February to mid-March, the boat heads out in search of bald eagles (reservations are recommended); bring your camera and binoculars and dress warmly.

Lady Katharine Cruises (866-867-4837; www.ladykatecruises.com), Harbor Park Landing, off CT 9, Middletown. Public cruises May–Oct. A variety of excursions—brunch, moonlight, foliage, and the like—on the Connecticut River aboard *Mystique*.

Valley Railroad Riverboat Ride (860-767-0103; www.essexsteamtrain.com) is an optional addition to the steam train excursion that departs from Essex (see *Train Ride*). From Deep River, the 70-foot-long Mississippi-style riverboat MV *Becky Thatcher* heads up the Connecticut River to East Haddam. The two together produce an appealing half-day journey mixing transportation nostalgia and scenic discovery.

BOATING **Brewer Deep River Marina** (860-526-5560), 50 River Lane, on the Connecticut River in Deep River, and **Brewer Dauntless Shipyard** (860-767-0001), 37 Pratt St., on North Cove in Essex, are full-service marinas with transient slips, swimming pools, picnic areas, shower facilities, and other amenities.

In **Deep River**, you can launch a boat at Deep River Landing; in **Essex**, there's a boat launch at the foot of Main St. There are many more places to launch car-top boats; check the **Connecticut Coastal Access Guide** (www.lisrc.uconn.edu/coastalaccess) for a comprehensive online listing by town.

CANOEING AND KAYAKING Canoeists and kayakers can explore the **Quinnipiac River Canoe Trail**, a self-guided 3-mile stretch of flat water between the towns of Cheshire and Southington. Guidebooks at the launch sites provide details about 14 natural areas marked along the route, as well as wildlife, erosion, and river ecology. Begin the trail in Southington at the CT 322 commuter parking lot, or at the junction of CT 70 and Cheshire St. in Cheshire. In this part of the river valley, the **Connecticut River** is wide and rural, perfect for day-tripping canoeists out for a leisurely paddle or accompanied by children or pets. Canoe-camping enthusiasts can paddle to **Selden Neck** (860-424-3200), an island in the Connecticut River off Lyme. The primitive campsites in this 528-acre state park are accessible by water only; open May–Sept.

FISHING There's a boat-launching site on the Moodus Reservoir in **East Haddam**, and fishing is permitted in state parks and forests, including: Day Pond and the Salmon River, **Colchester**; Haddam Meadows State Park, on the Connecticut River, **Haddam**; Wadsworth Falls, **Middlefield**. The waterways are stocked by the Department of Environmental Protection. Fishing for striped bass on Connecticut River in late spring. See also *Swimming* and *Green Space.*

GOLF **Banner Country Club** (860-873-9075), 10 Banner Rd., Moodus section of East Haddam. Par 72, 18 holes, 6,300 yards.

Fox Hopyard Golf Club (860-434-6644; 800-943-1903; www.golfthefox.com), 1 Hopyard Rd., at the junction of CT 82 and CT 156, East Haddam. A new course with an elegant clubhouse whose dining room is open to the public; next to Devil's Hopyard State Park. Par 71, 18 holes, 6,912 yards.

George Hunter Memorial Golf Club (203-634-3366), 688 Westfield Rd., Meriden. Par 71, 18 holes, 6,593 yards.

Indian Springs Golf Club (860-349-8109), Mack Rd., Middlefield. Par 72, nine holes, 5,922 yards.

Lyman Orchards Golf Club (860-349-8055; 888-995-9626; www.lymangolf.com), at the junction of CT 157 and CT 147, Middlefield. Two separate courses, each 18 holes.

Portland Golf Club (860-342-6107; www.portlandgolfcourse.com), 169 Bartlett St., Portland. Par 71, 18 holes, 6,213 yards.

HAYRIDES AND SLEIGH RIDES ✐ **Allegra Farm** (860-680-5149; 860-537-8861; www.allegrafarm.com), CT 82 between the Goodspeed Opera House and Gillette Castle, East Haddam. Call for reservations. This 42-acre livery stable offers hayrides, sleigh rides, and carriage rides. Choose from some 30 vehicles on the premises, and John Allegra and a team of horses will take you on an excursion around the 19th-century farm.

HIKING For **waterfall aficionados**, **Devil's Hopyard State Park** in East Haddam (see *Green Space*) has a particularly scenic one; **Wadsworth Falls State Park** in Middlefield (see *Swimming*) has two waterfalls. In Cheshire, you can hike to **Roaring Brook Falls**, a picturesque set of cascades off Roaring Brook Rd. At 80 feet, the main waterfall is the second largest in the state.

Mount Higby, off CT 66 in Middlefield. Park behind Guida's Dairy Bar at the junction of CT 66 and CT 147 and walk along CT 66, going west, for less than 0.25 mile to the blue-blazed **Mattabesett Trail**. It's a mile-long climb to the Pinnacle, which the *Connecticut Walk Book* calls the "best viewpoint on Mount Higby"—a nearly 360-degree sweep. From here you walk along the cliff (beware if you have trouble with heights) among laurel bushes, with unfolding views as you go. After 1.5 miles or so, the trail takes you down the slope and up again to another cliff with more views and a natural bridge (nicely labeled N.B.). You can keep walking if you wish—the Mattabesett Trail continues to Chauncey Peak and Lamentation Mountain—or you can retrace your steps at any point.

See also *Green Space* and *Swimming* for additional hiking in state parks.

ICE SKATING **Champions Skating Center** (860-632-0323; www.championsskatingcenter.com), 6 Progress Dr., Cromwell. Public skating sessions are held daily on two rinks; pro shop, snack bar, skate rentals.

MOUNTAIN BIKING With more than 200,000 acres of state forests and parks, Connecticut offers many opportunities for off-road cyclists. Although hiking trails are closed to mountain bikes, many miles of old logging roads, cross-country ski trails, and other paths are yours to explore. Look for maps at the entrances to these areas, or visit a local bike shop for advice on places to ride. The knowledgeable staff at **Pedal Power** (860-347-3776), 359 Main St., Middletown, can help plan rides in the river valley.

Across the river from Middletown, **Meshomasic State Forest** (860-424-3200) in Portland offers a network of trails through 8,000 acres of hardwoods. At **Cockaponset State Forest** (860-424-3200), CT 148, Haddam, trails wind through 15,652 quiet, wooded acres in the state's second-largest forest. In Cheshire, the **Farmington Canal Linear Park** (860-225-3901) features an 8.5-mile paved bike path along the historic Farmington Canal waterway. Parking lots are on Cornwall Ave. (off CT 10) and at the Lock 12 Park, 487 North Brooksvale Rd. (CT 42).

CROSS-COUNTRY SKIING See **Haddam Meadows State Park** under *Green Space.*

DOWNHILL SKIING **Powder Ridge Ski Area** (860-349-3454; 877-754-74343), 99 Powder Hill Rd. (CT 147), Middlefield. Powder Ridge, one of the oldest and most active ski areas in the state, closed in 2006 and, as of press time, its future remains uncertain. Local skiers, especially those with children, keep their fingers crossed—the hills are of a size that makes for perfect family skiing—fun but not threatening.

SWIMMING **Day Pond State Park** (860-295-9523), Day Pond Rd., off CT 149, Colchester. Open year-round, daily 8 AM–sunset. Admission is charged on weekends and holidays: residents $7; nonresidents $10. Day Pond, which is stocked with trout, is popular with anglers, but it's also a favorite local spot to cool off on a summer day. The pond once turned an overshot waterwheel that powered a sawmill; the stone foundations remain.

Wadsworth Falls State Park (860-663-2030), 721 Wadsworth St. (CT 157), Middlefield. Open year-round, 8 AM–sunset. Parking fees on weekdays: residents $5, nonresidents $7. On weekends and holidays: residents $7, nonresidents $10. The falls are the main attraction in this 285-acre park but by no means the only reason to visit. A man-made swimming pond is popular with families.

Wharton Brook State Park (203-789-7498), US 5, Wallingford. Open year-round, 8 AM–sunset. Parking fee on weekends and holidays: residents $7; nonresidents $10. This small, 96-acre park started out as a rest stop for travelers in the pre-superhighway era—1918. A lovely, low-key area for swimming.

Kim Grant

ALL ABOARD THE ESSEX STEAM TRAIN FOR A TRIP BACK IN TIME.

TRAIN RIDE **Essex Steam Train and Riverboat** (860-767-0103; 800-377-3987; www.essexsteam train.com), 1 Railroad Ave., Essex. Open May–Sept.; foliage excursions and holiday trips Oct.–Dec.; call for information, or check the Web site for details. The conductor wears the regulation black suit and stiff cap, the engine belches black smoke, and authentic coal-fired steam powers the mighty engine and sounds the whistle's lonesome call. If you remember real trains, or if you'd like to, here is your outing. Odds are that, after settling into a seat in the restored 1920s coach, you'll discover within earshot a former switchman or engineer, perhaps a news butcher from the old days, who'll spellbind you with tales of fun and danger from the heyday of the New York Central or the Wabash. When the train reaches Deep River Landing, you can disembark and board the MV *Becky Thatcher* for a Mississippi-style riverboat cruise on the Connecticut River, to view the exotic Goodspeed Opera House perched on the riverbank. Then return to Essex by train. The station, Valley Railroad, has a gift shop where you can purchase railroad memorabilia and other collectibles. Before or after your ride, you can refresh yourself, and your siblings, with a hot dog or a variety of sandwiches or salads in the station's café. The train also runs specials, such as North Pole Express, Day Out With Thomas, Caboose Weekend, and the Dinner Express, a five-course meal aboard a handsomely restored 1920s Pullman car. (See also Valley Railroad Riverboat Ride under *Boat Excursions.*)

✷ Green Space

Devil's Hopyard State Park (860-873-8566), 366 Hopyard Rd., off CT 82, East Haddam. Open daily year-round, 8 AM–sunset. Free admission. After negotiating a 60-foot drop at Chapman Falls, the Eight Mile River continues through this heavily wooded, 860-acre park, one of the river valley's most popular hiking areas. Pack a picnic lunch, find a rock at the base of the falls, and enjoy an idyllic summer day. The park's curious name is also notable as a focus for area mythology. Potholes at the base of the falls are explained by some local historians as the footprints of the devil, hopping from one ledge to another so as not to get wet, although a plethora of legends abound. Stream fishing is permitted; there are 21 campsites.

🐾 **Haddam Meadows State Park** (860-663-2030), CT 154, Haddam. Open daily year-round, 8 AM–sunset. Free admission. One of the few truly flat areas in the state, this park consists of 175 acres of former farmland on the banks of the Connecticut River, offering picnicking, fishing, field sports, boating (there's a boat-launching ramp), and cross-country skiing, depending on the season. This is a great spot for a riverside picnic.

🐾 **Hubbard Park** (203-630-4259), West Main St., Meriden. This is Meriden's green space: 1,800 acres divided by I-691. There's a network of hiking trails in the wooded northern tract; a pavilion, playgrounds, tennis courts, and Mirror Lake (popular among swimmers, anglers, and ice skaters) in the southern portion. The park's highest elevation, East Peak at 976 feet, is crowned by Castle Craig, a replica of an ancient stone castle that affords a sweeping view of the surrounding land—and of Long Island Sound on clear days. The park is the focus of the city's Daffodil Festival in spring, the site of summer outdoor concerts, and at holiday time festooned with lights and decorations (see *Special Events*).

See also *Fishing*, *Hiking*, and *Swimming* under *To Do*.

✳ Lodging

RESORTS The Moodus section of East Haddam was the state's major resort area during the era when many families spent their vacations in a full-service summer haven. Several of these resorts remain, offering rooms or cabins, meals, swimming, a playground, and other amenities such as fishing, boating, organized activities, tennis and other games, and entertainment. Keep in mind that these are not resorts in the luxe sense; rather more casual, family-oriented places. For specifics, contact **Sunrise Resort** (860-873-8681; www.sunriseresort.com), P.O. Box 415, CT 151, Moodus 06469; and **Cave Hill Resort** (860-873-8347; www.cavehillresort.com), 138 Leesville Rd. (CT 151), Moodus 06469.

INNS ♿ **Copper Beech Inn** (860-767-0330; 888-809-2056; www.copperbeechinn.com), 46 Main St., Ivoryton 06442. A stately 1890s country house and adjacent carriage house—the former estate of a prominent ivory comb and keyboard manufacturer—have been fitted out comfortably with suitable antiques and traditional furnishings. There are 13 guest rooms and suites, all with private bath, telephone, and air-conditioning; 9 with Jacuzzi. Guests can stroll the serene grounds and gardens (the inn's grand 200-year-old namesake spreads its copper limbs over practically the entire front yard) or relax in the plant-filled Victorian conservatory. There's a new bistro, and the dining room's French country cuisine continues to win awards (see *Dining Out*). Honeymooners and other romantics find the inn a perfect getaway spot; the Connecticut River and Long Island Sound are a short drive away. Full breakfast. $195–375.

♿ **The Griswold Inn** (860-767-1776; www.griswoldinn.com), 36 Main St., Essex 06426. Claiming a history back to 1776, "the Gris" (pronounced *Griz*) is an adored landmark in the lower river valley. Standing near the riverfront at the foot of Main Street, it's essentially a three-story clapboard colonial manse behind a latter-day wraparound porch. The building survived an attack on Essex by British marines in 1814, who burned all the boats in the harbor but not a shingle in the town. Then the officers commandeered the inn, ate a nice meal, left a generous tip, and departed the next morning. Reminders of a long history are evident in the collections of Currier and Ives prints and ancient firearms, the steamboat mural (that moves), the old popcorn cart, and the potbellied stove. The restaurant is especially known for its Sunday Hunt Breakfast (see *Dining Out*) and for the rousing music in the Taproom—banjo, sea chanteys, and such. The new Wine Bar is attracting attention. There are 31 guest rooms and several suites, each with private bath, telephone, air-conditioning, and classical music. Some have fireplace. Continental breakfast. $100–370.

HOTELS ♿ **Courtyard by Marriott** (860-635-1001), 4 Sebethe Dr., Exit 21 off I-91, Cromwell 06416. Designed for business travelers, but tourists are most certainly welcome, too. There's a business center, a fitness center, and a swimming pool in the hotel; Courtyard Café serves American cuisine for breakfast and dinner daily; drinks, snacks, and food items are available around the clock at a small store. $119–199.

♿ **Crowne Plaza** (860-635-2000; 800-308-4589), 100 Berlin Rd. (CT 372), Cromwell 06416. The 215 guest rooms and common areas are fresh off a $5 million renovation; there's also a pool, whirlpool, fitness center, and sauna. $109–199.

Inn at Middletown (860-854-6300; 800-637-9851; www.innatmiddletown.com), 70 Main St. (just off CT 9), Middletown 06457. The city's historic National Guard Armory has been transformed into a five-story, 100-room luxury hotel. Offering a fitness center, indoor pool, and a Jacuzzi full-service restaurant and lounge will make your stay a pleasant one. Also nearby: Kidcity Children's Museum and Wesleyan University with its cultural resources. The inn's **Tavern at the Armory** offers pub fare and American cuisine. Rooms and suites $119–289.

🐾 ♿ **Residence Inn** (203-634-7770), 390 Bee St., Exit 16 or 17 off I-91, Meriden 06450. The 106 guest suites are clean and nicely furnished, and outfitted for business travelers with voice mail, work desks, and wireless Internet access. There's a fitness center, restaurant, and outdoor swimming pool. Continental breakfast. $119–209.

BED & BREAKFASTS In addition to the listings below, B&B reservations services offer access to rooms available in establishments throughout the state; see *Bed & Breakfasts* in "What's Where in Connecticut."

Bishopsgate Inn (860-873-1677; www.bishopsgate.com), Goodspeed Landing, P.O. Box 290, East Haddam 06423. The Kagel family and their handsome 1818 colonial inn have been cited for excellence by prestigious publications and by celebrities who are in town to perform at the Goodspeed Opera House. In winter, fires crackle in the fireplaces of the public rooms; four of the six very individual guest rooms also have working fireplace, and each has a private bath. The Director's Suite boasts an outside deck, sauna, and private entrance. Bishopsgate is about one city block from the opera house, making it perfect for a theater weekend. Full breakfast. $125–205.

Riverwind Inn B&B (860-526-2014; www.riverwindinn.com), 209 Main St., Deep River 06417. A country B&B weaving together New England country antiques and an informal homey atmosphere. Guests enjoy the warmth of a wood fire in winter, a breezy sunporch in summer. Four of the common rooms have fireplace. There's a piano and places to play checkers, read, or simply relax. Antiques are everywhere—collectibles, exquisite quilts, and folk art. Innkeepers Elaine and Leo Klevens extend their hand of welcome. Massive cooking fireplace in the 18th-century keeping room. Each of the eight guest rooms has a different decorating theme; three have fireplace, all have private bath, wireless Internet, and air-conditioning. Full breakfast. $128–240.

CAMPGROUNDS Several private campgrounds in this region are members of the **Connecticut Campground Owners Association** (CCOA) (860-521-4704; www.campconn.com) and meet that group's standards. These are:

🐾 **Little City Campground** (860-345-8469), 741 Little City Rd., Higganum 06441, with 50 sites. Open May–Sept.

🐾 **Markham Meadows Campground** (860-267-9738; www.markhammeadows.com), 7 Markham Rd., East Hampton 06424, with 100 sites. Open mid-Apr–mid-Oct.

🐾 **Nelson's Family Campground** (860-267-5300; www.nelsonscampground.com), 71 Mott Hill Rd., East Hampton 06424, with 315 sites. Open mid-Apr.–mid-Oct.

🐾 **Wolf's Den Family Campground** (860-873-9681; www.wolfsdencampground.com), 256 Town St. (CT 82), East Haddam 06423, with 205 sites. Open early May–Oct.

State park and forest campgrounds (reservation information: 877-668-2267) offer fewer amenities than do the private campgrounds, but they are also more rustic, less expensive, and allow for more solitude. Camping is permitted, with reservations advised, at the following state parks: **Devil's Hopyard State Park**, **Cockaponset State Forest**, and **Haddam Meadows State Park**. In addition, **Selden Neck** and **Hurd State Park** offer canoe camping.

✷ Where to Eat

DINING OUT

In Chester

✐ **Lupo** (860-526-4400; www.luporestaurant.com), 189 Middlesex Ave. Open for dinner Tue.–Sun.; closed Mon. Mediterranean fare that wins raves from local epicures and clued-in tourists alike. The creative menu is full of the kind of unique culinary twists that make dining out fun. Start with lobster ravioli with browned butter and garlic, or bruschetta topped with sautéed spinach, golden raisins, and pine nuts. Then, dine on grilled porterhouse pork chop with mango salsa and lemon couscous, or sautéed chicken, artichokes, and sun-dried tomatoes over linguine. A nice touch: Net proceeds from the children's menu are donated to charity. $16–28.

Restaurant du Village (860-526-5301; www.restaurantduvillage.com), 59 Main St. Open for dinner Wed.–Sun.; closed Mon. and Tue. Reservations are recommended. Painted a cheerful blue, this restaurant's many-paned windows are accented with well-tended flower boxes. Inside, the surroundings are quaint and charming, the service thoughtful and perfectly timed, the menu imaginative French country, the food and wine excellent. The menu may offer leg of lamb marinated in herbes de Provence, and salmon pot-au-feu with fresh tomato and basil coulis. Specialties reflect authentic French country cuisine—cassoulet and choucroute garnie. Marvelous crusty breads and pastries are made on the premises. To wit: chocolate génoise filled with orange-liqueur-scented chocolate mousse and raspberry jam, covered in a Belgian chocolate ganache. $26–34.

River Tavern (860-526-9417; www.rivertavernchester.net), 23 Main St., Chester. Open for dinner Tue.–Sun.; closed Mon. You wouldn't expect to find a chic New York City–style bistro in a historic quiet river town, but that's exactly what you get at River Tavern. The tasteful contemporary decor of polished wood and bright primary colors lends an air of sophistication, but it's casual and friendly nonetheless. The menu changes according to what's fresh and available. The handful of carefully selected main courses might include grilled swordfish with a curried zucchini puree and ginger-sautéed green beans, or house-made pork chorizo with grilled onions and crispy potatoes. End with house-made peach ice cream, or a baked-to-order bittersweet chocolate soufflé. $25–28.

THE SAGE AMERICAN BAR AND GRILL IN CHESTER

Kim Grant

♿ **Sage American Bar and Grill** (860-526-9898; www.sageamerican.com), 129 West Main St. Open daily for dinner. Diners looking for solid American fare that's consistently well prepared come to this longtime favorite, housed in a former 19th-century brush mill and decorated with local artifacts. Expect top-notch steaks, seafood, prime rib, and rack of lamb, plus 40 wines by the glass. Live music on Fri. nights. $15–39.

Middletown

Amici Italian Grill (860-346-0075; www.amiciitaliangrill.com), 280 Main St. Open daily for lunch and dinner. People wait in line here for generous portions of regional Italian cuisine. The menu runs the gamut from fried clam strips to pasta primavera, providing something to please everyone at the table. The bar has a creative martini menu. $15–22.

Forbidden City Bistro and Art Gallery (860-343-8288; www.forbiddencitybistro.com), 335 Main St. Open for lunch Mon.–Sat.; dinner daily. Snazzy black awnings grace the entrance to this Main Street bistro, where stellar Chinese cuisine is paired with an award-winning wine list. It's a favorite among dates, Wesleyan students, and gourmands from all over. The kitchen's artful presentation is evident in the fruit-glazed crispy shrimp, wok-seared flank steak with jalapeño peppers and onions, and spice-rubbed grilled salmon with shallot fried rice. The walls are hung with the work of upcoming Chinese artists. $15–25.

Luce (860-344-0222; www.lucect.com), 98 Washington St. Open daily for lunch and dinner; brunch on Sun. Upscale Tuscan cuisine in a cozy space done in exposed brick, hand-hewn beams, and a massive stone fireplace. Aged steaks, fresh seafood, and pasta dishes are prepared with imported Italian olive oils, cheeses, and other top-notch ingredients. You might have a grilled chicken panini for lunch; porcini mushroom ravioli or the signature porterhouse steak for dinner; or, at the bar, raw oysters, burgers, and calamari. $15–32.

♿ **Tuscany Grill** (860-346-7096; www.tuscany-grill.com), 120 College St. Open for lunch Mon.–Sat.; dinner daily. Housed in what was once an opera house, the Tuscany has an intriguing interior, with a huge central bar and several dining areas, including a high gallery that must have been the auditorium balcony. From the dining room, watch the chefs in the open kitchen turn out creative Italian dishes with a California accent: hoisin-glazed tuna steak over toasted orzo, for example, or smoked mozzarella ravioli with roasted red pepper sauce. $13–25.

Elsewhere

♿ **Bistro du Glace and Patisserie** (860-526-2200), 156 Main St., Deep River. Dinner Tue.–Sun.; closed Mon. Patisserie open Tue.–Sun. 6–6. This new French bistro occupying a Main Street storefront is one of the most romantic cafés, some say, this side of the Seine. Start with the bacon leek tart before trying coq au vin, ragout, or cassoulet. Chef Bill Von Ahnen is a veteran of the Copper Beech Inn; so is his wife, Jackie, who's at the helm of the next-door patisserie. $17–29.

♿ **Copper Beech Inn** (860-767-0330; 888-809-2056), 46 Main St., Ivoryton. Dinner Tue.–Sun.; closed Mon. Reservations recommended. Over the years the restaurant of the Copper Beech Inn (see *Lodging*) has earned a reputation as an elegant establishment with an ambitious French menu, and as a prime pick for a romantic getaway. Linen, crystal, and silver table service; wall sconces for muted lighting; and a Victorian-style conservatory where you can enjoy an aperitif. Staff are extremely knowledgeable and attentive—you will be pampered. You might find on the menu French-country-style appetizers such as pumpkin gnocchi with walnut sage butter, or sautéed foie gras; dinner specialties include Dover sole with truffle mousse, or brine-cured pork loin over creamy polenta. Desserts range from a simple artisanal cheese plate to exquisite French classics like *glace au gingembre*—a crisp pastry filled with ginger-caramel ice cream and served with a warm apple-raisin-pecan compote. $26–38. A new bistro serves more casual fare (see *Eating Out*).

Gabrielle's (860-767-2440, www.gabrielles.net), 78 Main St., Centerbrook. Lunch Tue.–Sun.; dinner daily; closed Mon. When friends and relatives visit, this Victorian-era house restaurant will win their praises for its Mediterranean-influenced contemporary American cuisine. Lunch opens with cornmeal-crusted fried oysters or the chef's signature mussels and thin fried potatoes (or *frites*, as any French chef will tell you). Other small plates join the appetizers at dinner; start with asparagus and shiitake mushroom spring rolls, then try the grilled lamb chops or pan-seared sea scallops with lemon-basil crème fraîche. Round out the meal with profiteroles or crème brûlée. $18–25.

♿ **The Gelston House** (860-873-1411), 8 Main St., next to the Goodspeed Opera House, East Haddam.

Open for lunch Tue.–Fri.; dinner Tue.–Sun.; brunch Sat. and Sun.; closed Mon. This landmark 1853 Victorian on the Connecticut River recently reopened after being shuttered for more than a year. Starters like beef tartare and Gelston House mussels lead to such entrées as New England cod and Australian free-range lamb. They're used to catering to theater crowds, so they'll get you to the show on time. $18–29.

♿ **The Griswold Inn** (860-767-1776), 36 Main St., Essex. Open for lunch and dinner daily; breakfast on Sun.; wine bar open evenings Wed.–Sun. Reservations suggested. Known far and wide as "the Gris" (see also *Lodging*) and renowned for its opulent Sunday Hunt Breakfast, here is the essence of Connecticut Yankee innkeeping: welcome, warmth, and bounty. Specializes in such solid fare as venison, meat pies, prime rib, and baked stuffed shrimp. The decor itself is worth the visit, with maritime art, American memorabilia, an old-fashioned corn popper, and cozy fires in the several dining rooms. The mural that covers an entire wall in the Steamboat Room undulates just enough to give you the illusion of dining on deck. A new wine bar features more than 50 wines by the glass and an extensive bottle list, as well as tapas-style small plates. In keeping with its nautical theme, live entertainment sometimes features authentic sea chanteys. $18–30.

La Vita Gustosa (860-873-8999; www.lavitagustosa.com), 9 Main St., East Haddam. Open Tue.–Sun. for lunch and dinner; closed Mon. A cheery butter-yellow house in view of the Connecticut River sets the scene for home-cooked Italian dishes. Panini, pizza, and other light meals for lunch; dinner features chicken, steak, and seafood. $13–25.

♿ **Nu Nu's** (860-537-6299; www.nunusbistro.com), 45 Hayward Ave., Colchester. Open for lunch Tue.–Sat.; dinner Tue.–Sun.; Sun. brunch; closed Mon. Reservations are recommended for dinner on weekends. Regular customers love this out-of-the-way bistro tucked beside the town green for the generous portions of well-prepared southern Italian cuisine, from steaks and seafood to lamb, chicken, and veal. BYOB. $13–28.

EATING OUT

In Middletown

Coyote Blue Tex-Mex Café (860-345-2403; www.coyoteblue.com), 1960 Saybrook Rd. Open for lunch and dinner Tue.–Sun.; closed Mon. A local favorite known for its friendly staff and generous portions of fajitas, burritos, enchiladas, and other dependable Tex-Mex favorites. Start with nachos, guacamole and chips, or chili con carne, then try the healthy spinach and feta quesadilla or one of the hearty combo platters. $8–17.

Eli Cannon's Tap Room (860-347-3547; www.elicannons.com), 695 Main St., Middletown. Open daily. Nothing fancy, just well-prepared pub fare: burgers, wraps, and ribs, plus three dozen brews on tap and a fun, energetic atmosphere. $7–15.

Harbor Park Restaurant (860-347-9999), 80 Harbor Dr. Lunch and dinner are served daily; Sun. brunch. Built in 1915 as a home for the Middletown Yacht Club, the three-level building facing the river is now part of Middletown's Harbor Park. You can stroll along the harbor, take a cruise, or just watch the river traffic ripple the water. On the second level is the main dining room, and outdoors is a patio where drinks and light fare are served in good weather. The maritime motif extends to the menu, which features seafood and shellfish. American cuisine with an emphasis on steak and seafood. You can get prime rib, pasta, and chicken dishes as well. Sandwiches galore and salads at lunchtime. $16–25.

It's Only Natural (860-346-9210; ww.ionrestaurant.com), Liberty Square, at the corner of Liberty and Main streets. Open for lunch and dinner Mon.–Sat.; brunch on Sun. This is arguably the best-loved spot in the city for creative and delicious good-for-you food, not to mention one of Connecticut's top vegetarian restaurants. In 2008, it moved from its longtime spot on Main Street, but regulars love the juice and coffee bars at the new digs. At the deli counter, you'll find rich-tasting but very wholesome desserts, baked goods, and innovative sandwiches such as blackened tempeh. Then there's the restaurant itself, serving unique culinary treats like *gado gado*, mixed vegetables in a spicy Indonesian peanut sauce; tasty spinach pierogi stuffed with sautéed garlic greens; and chocolate cream couscous cake as a sweet-and-healthy end to everything. $10–15.

Mikado Japanese Restaurant (860-346-6655; www.mikadoct.com), 3 Melilli Plaza. Open for lunch Mon.–Sat.; dinner daily. The area's only Japanese restaurant, Mikado serves an impressive variety of tempura, teriyaki, and grilled dishes, as well as traditional sushi with flavored rice. Quilts on the walls denote common cultural ground, and the extensive menu caters to many tastes. With a bow to the current emphasis on healthy foods, chef Teddy Endo features grilled rather than fried dishes. While the cuisine is exquisite, prices are reasonable. $11–19.

O'Rourke's Diner (860-346-6101; www.orourkesdiner.com), 728 Main St. Open daily for breakfast; lunch Mon.–Sat.; dinner Thu.–Sat. This landmark diner reopened in 2008 after a devastating fire closed it to the dismay of legions of fans. The O'Rourke family has catered to a loyal following of Wesleyan University students and professors, tourists, fishermen, and locals for more than 50 years. Breakfast is anytime you want it, and standard diner fare such as burgers and chili fills the menu; but Brian O'Rourke's inventive specials eclipse the traditional standbys. Try the Parmesan polenta topped with roasted portobello mushrooms and poached eggs, served with grilled eggplant; or an omelet of farmer cheese and watercress, with grilled turnips and brown bread. Other favorites have a Cajun twist—poached eggs with crawfish and spiced grits. The diner—a fixture at the end of Main Street since the 1920s—is one of only a handful in the nation listed on the National Register of Historic Places. Muffins, breads, and jams are made on the premises. Service is fast, informal, and friendly, and the portions are generous and cheap. Meals are up to $12; sandwiches and breakfast items up to $7.

Thai Gardens (860-346-3322), 300 Plaza Middlesex. Serving lunch and dinner Mon.–Sat.; dinner on Sun. Reservations suggested. Thai food, with its delicate and sometimes breathtaking flavorings, makes for a memorable feast. The menu lists jasmine rice, Asian noodles, crisp steamed vegetables, and a variety of meats. For dessert, try the butternut squash custard, made with a typical Thai ingredient: coconut milk. $9–20.

Elsewhere

Brasserie Pip (860-767-0330; www.brasseriepip.com), at the Copper Beech Inn, 46 Main St., Ivoryton. Open for dinner Tue.–Sun.; closed Mon. Gourmands cheered the opening of this Old World–style bistro, a casual alternative to the venerable country inn's formal dining room (see *Dining Out*). Homey fare ranges from oysters on the half shell and steamed mussels to *pommes frites* and foie gras. At the copper-topped bar, the martini inspired by Charles Dicken's *Great Expectations* is a must, but the real star is the wine list, with more than 500 labels. $9–25.

The Cabin (203-237-7471), 103 Colony St., Meriden. Open daily for lunch and dinner. A large but cozy restaurant facing the railroad station, where trains rumble past from time to time. A definite Italian flavor marks the offerings—fried calamari, rigatoni porcini, pasta Genovese. Also on the menu are lamb, Long Island duckling, Maine lobster, Cajun-style swordfish steak, chicken, and veal. A bevy of appetizers, a surfeit of desserts. $12–20.

Oliver's Restaurant & Taverne (860-767-2633; www.oliverstavern.com), 124 Westbrook Rd., Essex. Open daily for lunch and dinner. Feeding locals and vacationers in the Essex area for two decades, pleasing their guests with a long list of dependable American classics. They've got burgers and sandwiches for a quick, light meal; entrées like barbecued pork ribs and New England scrod if you're in the mood for something more. $10–20.

Funky Monkey Café and Gallery (203-439-9161), 130 Elm St., in the Watch Factory Shoppes, Cheshire. Open for lunch and dinner Tue.–Sun.; closed Mon. The decor is funky indeed (zebra rugs, lime-green chairs), but the homegrown menu is yummy and healthful, from salads and homemade soups to New England beers and fair-trade coffee. House-made pastries and local ice cream for dessert. $8–15.

The Whistle Stop Café (860-526-4122), 108 North Main St., Deep River. Open Thu.–Mon. for breakfast and lunch; closed Tue. and Wed. Step into this tiny house and enter a tropical oasis—the bright pastel decor is reminiscent of the islands, where owner Hedy Watrous ran a Key West restaurant before returning to Deep River to continue a family tradition (her grandparents opened Ed's Diner on the site in 1936). Enjoy scrumptious breakfasts and filling soups, salads, and deli sandwiches at a handful of tables and stools in this friendly, casual spot. $6–10.

SNACKS **Blackie's Hot Dog Stand** (203-699-1819), 2200 Waterbury Rd., Cheshire. A no-frills drive-in (since 1928) where there are no fries and the ingredients in the homemade pepper relish are a secret. Hummel franks are boiled in oil, grilled, and tucked into a side-split roll. Want to sound like a regular? Belly up to the counter, announce how many dogs you want, and hold up the corresponding number of fingers. Your order will be shouted into the kitchen. $4–9.

The Blue Oar (860-345-2994), 16 Snyder Rd., at Midway Marina, Haddam. Open May–Columbus Day, daily for lunch and dinner. A laid-back and always-packed BYOB alfresco spot on the Connecticut River with hot dogs, burgers, ribs, fish, steamers, and lobster rolls on the menu. $7–15.

Crow's Nest Gourmet Deli & Bakery (860-767-3288), in Brewer's Dauntless Shipyard, Pratt St., Essex. Open daily for breakfast and lunch; dinner on weekends. A clean, pleasant deli that boasts the only waterfront dining in town. Families are welcome; notice the old standbys—peanut butter and jelly and grilled cheese—on the menu. For the more adventurous, tasty homemade soups and a variety of sandwiches, as well as fresh-baked goods. $3–8.

Feast Gourmet Market (860-526-4056; www.feastgourmetmarket.com), 159 Main St., Deep River. Open Mon.–Sat.; closed Sun. A specialty food shop with an always-changing menu of local and seasonal dishes to eat here or take home. Watch them use a vintage machine to crank out fresh pasta in creative flavors ranging from whole wheat to savory chocolate. $7–12.

Perk on Main (860-349-5335), 6 Main St., Durham. Open daily for three meals; breakfast is served all day. A bustling order-at-the-counter eatery where delicate crêpes are the specialty. Watch them being made and stuffed with spinach and Brie—or the classic banana-and-Nutella dessert version. This is a breakfast spot mostly, but there's a light menu of salads and sandwiches and the like for lunch and dinner. $4–8.

Praline's (860-347-2663; www.pralinesct.com), 170 Main St., Middletown. Open daily. There's no better cool-down than ice cream, and creative flavors like honey coffee have made this little ice cream shop a favorite among locals kids and Weslyan students alike. Cakes, pies, and frozen yogurt round out the tempting menu. A second location in Wallingford (203-269-1869).

Spencer's Shad Shack, CT 154, Haddam. In spring, while driving along CT 154—the street nearest the river—watch for this roadside stand offering smoked shad, a seasonal and increasingly rare southern New England delicacy. American shad, which make their annual run up the Connecticut River in May (the season for legal shad fishing is Apr. 15–July 1), have been sold at this local landmark since 1930. It's Connecticut's only remaining shad shack.

Ted's Restaurant (203-237-6660; www.steamedcheeseburger.com), 1046 Broad St., Meriden. Open daily. Many a foodie has Ted's on their short list. It's been a local institution since 1959, and the specialty is the steamed cheeseburger.

Harry's Place (860-537-2410), 104 Broadway St., Colchester. An old-fashioned roadside gem serving burgers and dogs, ice cream and milk shakes.

COFFEE AND TEA **Essex Coffee & Tea** (860-767-7804), 51 Main St., Essex. Open daily. A casual neighborhood spot with hot and cold coffee drinks, an espresso and tea bar, and a light menu of sandwiches, salads, and desserts.

Javapalooza (860-346-5282), 330 Main St., Middletown. Open Mon.–Fri. until 9 PM, 11:30 PM on weekends. Local art adorns the walls; live entertainment, from comedy to open-mike nights, packs the place on weekends; and Wesleyan students spend hours here with their laptop computers.

Klekolo World Coffee (860-343-9444), 181 Court St., Middletown. Open daily. All day (and night) long, students pack this friendly, bustling coffeehouse near the university for their organic and fair-trade java and the extensive menu of coffee and pastries.

✷ Entertainment

MUSIC AND THEATER **The Buttonwood Tree** (860-347-4957; www.buttonwood.org), 605 Main St., Middletown. A former storefront church is now an eclectic performance space, art gallery, and bookstore, a popular venue for local talent as well as artists and musicians from around the country.

Wesleyan University Center for the Arts (860-685-3355; www.wesleyan.edu/cfa), 283 Washington Terrace, on the campus of Wesleyan University, Middletown. Taking its cue from the wide-ranging interests of this prestigious university, the arts center mounts dance programs, concerts, and theatrical productions representing the familiar and the exotic and mixing many genres and cultures. **Davison Art Center** features several exhibits per year, and the **Zilkha Gallery** shows contemporary works in various media.

♿ **Chevrolet Theatre** (203-265-1501), 95 South Turnpike Rd., Wallingford. The Chevrolet presents the stars of popular music, covering the styles and signature personalities of the 1940s to the present. A veteran of the performing arts scene in Connecticut, it started out in 1954 as the Oakdale, a classic summer theater, striped circus-style tent and all; it has since graduated into a year-round performance venue.

The Goodspeed (860-873-8668; www.goodspeed.org), Goodspeed Landing (CT 82), East Haddam. Guided tours available Sat., mid-June–Oct. An architectural feast for the eye, the opera house was built in 1876 by Captain Goodspeed to entertain theater lovers who came from New York City on his steamship. The dignified but whimsical white Victorian structure set on the banks of the Connecticut River has been compared to a wedding cake, and a sweet sight it is. Like their predecessors, today's audiences can walk out on the balcony at intermission and enjoy the play of light, the soothing ripple of the moving river, the spectacle of waterborne traffic coming and going. The Goodspeed, since its 1963 reincarnation—saved from demolition by local preservationists—is devoted to American musical theater. And fittingly, the Goodspeed delivers the true excitement of live performance: Audiences experience the songs, music, and speech directly, unmiked. Revivals are carefully staged, and new musicals are selected and launched, many to resounding and continuing acclaim. *Man of La Mancha*, *Shenandoah*, *Annie*, and *The Most Happy Fella* are among the Goodspeed's premieres that went on to Broadway and theaters nationwide.

♿ **Ivoryton Playhouse** (860-767-7318; www.ivorytonplayhouse.org), 103 Main St., Ivoryton. A Connecticut classic, the playhouse—the nation's oldest professional, self-supporting theater—has helped launch many a showbiz career, from Marlon Brando and Groucho Marx to Christopher Reeve and Hartford native Katharine Hepburn.

Norma Terris Theatre (860-873-8668; www.goodspeed.org), North Main St., Chester. This offspring of the Goodspeed Opera House (see above) is housed across the Connecticut River in a converted knitting factory. It's an intimate 200-seat theater that experiments with new musicals; some go on to larger venues and audiences.

🖍 **Oddfellows Playhouse Youth Theater** (860-347-6143; www.oddfellows.org), 128 Washington St., Middletown. The state's most active year-round youth theater, started in the 1970s by a group of Wesleyan University students committed to involving children in the performing arts. Several productions are staged each year, including Shakespeare, original musicals, plays, even a children's circus.

✷ Selective Shopping

ANTIQUES Here, as elsewhere in the state, many roads yield their share of antiques dealers, particularly on CT 154 between Old Saybrook and

Chester. In the list below we've included some; you'll find many more.

Black Whale Antiques (860-526-5073; www.rattleberryfarm.com), 5 Town St. at Hadlyme Four Corners, Hadlyme. English, American, and European antiques; hand-painted furniture.

Brush Factory Antiques (860-767-0845), 33 Deep River Rd. (CT 154), Centerbrook. Open daily 11–5. Thirty dealers offering antiques, home decor, and collectibles in a 19th-century mill on the banks of the Falls River.

Don Slater & Son's Irish Country Antiques (860-526-9757; www.irishcountryantiques.com), 246 South Main St. (CT 154), Deep River. Open Wed.–Sun. 10-5; closed Mon. and Tue. Antiques, pottery, and furniture (think farm tables, armoires, cupboards) from the Emerald Isle.

River Wind Antiques (860-863-9660), 68 Main St. (CT 154), Deep River. Three floors of furnishings, books, china, silver, jewelry, collectibles, quilts, linens.

T. F. Vanderbeck Antiques (860-526-3770), 32 Town St. (CT 82), Hadlyme. Furnishings, decorative objects, lamps, chandeliers; Asian ceramics, Venetian glass, and vintage lighting are specialties.

Valley Farm Antiques (860-767-3007), 134 Saybrook Rd. (CT 154), Essex. A multidealer shop with a something-for-everyone mix that includes furniture, clocks, rugs, toys, books, coins, and art.

ART GALLERIES **Barker Animation Gallery** (203-272-2357; 800-995–2357), 1188 Highland Ave. (CT 10), Cheshire. Original drawings and production cels of cartoon characters—Mickey Mouse, Bugs Bunny, and so on—for sale. Also character toys and cartoon memorabilia. The outside stage area offers live plays and readings. (See also *Museums.*)

Connecticut River Artisans (860-526-5575; www.ctriverartisans.com), 5 West Main St. (CT 148), Chester. Open June, Aug., Nov., and Dec., daily 11–6; Jan.–May, and Sept.–Oct., Wed.–Sun. 11–6. This nonprofit cooperative shows and sells works by local artisans: jewelry, paintings, pottery, handwoven goods, and more. The shop features guest artists from the area and special theme displays. Next door, the **Mill House** exhibits fine art.

eo art lab (860-526-4833; www.eoartlab.com), 69 Main St., Chester. Open Tue.–Sun.; Mon. by chance. Emerging and established artists working mostly in abstract art.

Essex Art Association Gallery (860-767-8996; www.essexartassociation.org), 10 North Main St., Essex. Open mid-Apr.–Oct., daily 1–5. Exhibits featuring the work of local artists and artisans, as well as special exhibitions mounted throughout the year featuring painting, photography, ceramics, and sculpture.

Gallery 53 (203-235-5347; www.gallery53.org), 53 Colony St., Meriden. Changing exhibits of work by area painters, photographers, and artisans. Ask about poetry slams and other special events.

Gallery at 85 Main Street (860-304-6206; www.galleryat85main.info), Centerbrook. Open Apr.–Dec., Thu.–Sun. 11–5. A 200-year-old barn on the Falls River has been cleverly converted into a gallery. The handsome space showcases local and regional artists working in the style of traditional Connecticut River Valley impressionism. Plein air painting on the lovely grounds is encouraged.

Hammered Edge Studio & Gallery (860-526-1654; www.hammerededge

.com), 14 Main St., Chester. Handmade jewelry by artist-owner Kathryne Wright, as well as new and antique beads, and hand-carved objects from around the world.

Nilsson Spring Street Studio and Gallery (860-526-2077; www.nilsson studio.com), 1 Spring St., Chester. In his studio-gallery, artist Leif Nilsson specializes in Connecticut impressionist landscapes in oil and watercolor, and shows works in progress and others for sale.

Wesleyan Potters (860-344-0039; www.wesleyanpotters.com), 350 South Main St., Middletown. Open Wed.–Fri. 10–6; Sat. and Sun. noon–4. Changing exhibits and a variety of crafts for sale. Wesleyan Potters took its name not so much from the local university as from the fact that many of the original crafters were wives of Wesleyan faculty members. Over the past 60 years, the reputation of Wesleyan Potters has grown, and the operation has increased in size without losing its original intensity. Tours of the pottery and weaving studios are available on request. Call for information on workshops and courses.

BOOKSTORES ✐ **The Alphabet Garden** (203-439-7766; www.the alphabetgarden.com), 132 Elm St., in the Watch Factory Shoppes, Cheshire. Open Mon., Tue., and Sat. 9:30–5:30; Thu. and Fri. 9:30–8; Sun. 10–4; closed Wed. Primarily a children's bookstore, but there are books for grown-ups, too.

Centerbridge Books (860-767-8943), 33D Deep River Rd. (CT 154), Centerbrook. Open Wed.–Sun. 11–5. A comprehensive selection of old, collectible, and rare books. Specializes in art, children's literature, and New England titles. Many first editions.

Broad Street Books (860-685-7333), 45 Broad St., Middletown. Open weekdays 8–8; Sat. and Sun. 9–5. Because it's owned by Wesleyan University (college bookstore on the lower level), it stocks an unusually wide range of works, making it exceptionally attractive to readers both academic and otherwise. College gear and gift items are also available. After book browsing, relax in the small but lively café with coffee, a sandwich, a bowl of soup, or a fresh pastry.

SPECIAL SHOPS **Essex Mariner** (860-767-7805; www.essexmariner .com), 51 Main St., Essex. An inviting shop with an interesting collection of ship models, as well as barometers, clocks, and other nautical items.

Scensibles (860-767-7877; www .scensibles.com), 2 Main St., Essex. Here you'll find Free People jeans and camis, Archipelago candles and body products, and jewelry by local artisans. Weekend trunk shows in summer.

Ceramica (800-270-0900; www .ceramicadirect.com), 36 Main St., Chester. A small shop specializing in handcrafted Italian tableware and accessories. Exquisitely hand-painted maiolica pottery is imported from the Amalfi and Umbrian regions of Italy.

Thompson Candy (203-235-2541; 800-648-4058), 80 South Vine St., Meriden. Open Mon.–Sat. 9–5; closed Sun. A universal favorite among residents, Thompson is a longtime local maker of chocolate novelty candies. Holidays like Easter, Christmas, and Mother's Day bring out the creativity in the candy designers. The company has been headquartered here since 1879.

FARMS AND GARDENS ✐ **Lyman Orchards** (860-349-1793), junction of CT 147 and CT 157, Middlefield. Open daily 9–7 in summer; call for winter hours. A Lyman family operation for more than 250 years, Lyman Orchards is an area institution. More than 1,000 acres with 25,000 fruit trees, mostly apple trees, that you can tour in spring to smell the blossoms or in late summer to pick the fruit. The **Lyman Farm Store** has, besides fresh produce, pies (apple pie sales top 15,000 annually), cookies, tea, cheese, cider, gift items, and an offer to ship your gift direct. Enjoy your goodies on a sprawling deck overlooking the fruit orchards. Two golf courses are part of the complex.

Hickory Hill Orchards (203-272-3824; www.hickoryhillorchards.com), 351 South Meriden Rd. (CT 70), Cheshire. Open daily 10–5:30. On weekends, tractor-pulled hayrides head out to apple and pear orchards.

Sundial Herb Garden (860-345-4290; www.sundialgardens.com), 59 Brault Hill Rd. (off CT 81), in the Higganum section of Haddam. Open Sat. and Sun. 10–5. Admission to the gardens. A little off the beaten track, but well worth the trip; the gardens are formal but inviting. In the main garden, geometric walkways radiate from a sundial; you can stroll through a 17th-century Persian-style knot garden, or another garden featuring topiary. The plantings evoke tastes in landscapes over three centuries. Herbs grown on the premises are available in the shop, along with 20 varieties of tea. Seminars on herb gardening, tea, baking English scones, chocolate, and other topics are held during the year; call for information.

Cato Corner Farm (860-537-3884; www.catocornerfarm.com), 178 Cato Corner Rd., Colchester. Open Sat. and Sun. 10–3. Mother-and-son cheesemakers craft a dozen varieties of aged farmhouse cheeses with raw milk from their herd of 40 Jersey cows.

✷ Special Events

February: **Connecticut River Eagle Festival** (860-434-6095), downtown Essex. A celebration of the resident and migratory bald eagles that inhabit the lower Connecticut River each winter. **Winter Carnivale** (860-526-2077), downtown Chester. A longtime village outdoor event with a tractor parade, gallery openings, dancing, food, and an ice-carving competition.

April: **Daffodil Festival** (203-630-4259), West Main St., Meriden. Plantings at Hubbard Park (some 600,000 daffodils, we're told) inspire an annual welcome to spring. Features arts, crafts, music, a parade, fireworks, and the crowning of Miss Daffodil.

May and June: Celebrating the return of American shad to the Connecticut River each spring are two local favorites. In May, the **Shad Festival** (860-767-8269) at the Connecticut River Museum in Essex offers activities and demonstrations featuring Connecticut's official state fish. The Essex Rotary Club holds an annual **Shad Bake** (www.essexrotary.com) in Centerbrook in June.

June: **Travelers Championship** (860-502-6800; www.travelerschampionship.com), Tournament Players Club at River Highlands, Cromwell. Connecticut's stop on the PGA tour. **Hot Steamed Jazz Festival** (800-348-0003; www.hotsteamedjazz.com), Valley Railroad, Essex.

Summer: **Summer Sounds Concert Series** (203-630-4259), Hubbard Park, Meriden. Bring a lawn chair or blanket for free concerts in the park.

July: **Deep River Ancient Muster**, Deep River. An annual event since 1953; traditional fife-and-drum corps march in a rousing parade down Main Street. The oldest such gathering in the world.

Late July: **Great Connecticut Traditional Jazz Festival** (800-468-3836; www.ctjazz.org), CT 151, Sunrise Resort, Moodus. Features jazz bands and performers from around the world.

August: **Chester Fair** (860-526-5947), at the fairgrounds, CT 154, Chester. A traditional country fair, here since 1877. **Westbrook Muster**, Westbrook. Fri. and Sat. events centered on a grand parade of the region's best fifers and drummers. **Peach Festival** (860-349-1793), Lyman Orchards, Middlefield. All things peachy: pie, shortcake, sundaes, and pick-your-own fruit.

September: **Haddam Neck Fair** (860-267-5922; www.haddamneckfair.com), 26 Quarry Hill Rd., Haddam. A traditional Labor Day weekend event. **Durham Fair** (860-349-9495), at the junction of CT 68 and CT 79, Durham. Connecticut's largest agricultural fair, since 1916, takes place on the last weekend of the month.

October: **The Head of Connecticut Regatta** (860-346-1042), Harbor Park, off CT 9, Middletown. An annual Columbus Day weekend and internationally recognized rowing competition: singles, doubles, fours, and eights from around Connecticut and the world—some 600 boats in all—race 3.5 miles up the Connecticut River.

November through December: **Wesleyan Potters Exhibit and Sale**, 350 South Main St., Middletown (through mid-Dec.); see *Selective Shopping*. **Festival of Lights** (203-630-4259), in Hubbard Park, West Main St., Meriden. More than 350,000 lights on display, with 250 winter figures around the park.

THE CENTRAL SHORELINE, OLD LYME TO BRANFORD

With Long Island as a buffer against the Atlantic's nastier moods, the Connecticut shoreline is visited by water somewhat warmer and often calmer than the open sea. The absence of deep harbors brings water traffic in the form of pleasure boats and an occasional oil barge headed for Middletown, and the nearly uninterrupted line of cottages hugging the coast from the mouth of the Connecticut River west to Branford is filled year after year by summertime vacationers. As a result, the Boston Post Road is rife with purveyors of fried clams, soft-serve ice cream, miniature golf, and other family attractions that cater to the annual tourist tide. But tucked slightly inland is a rural tableau of salt marshes, meadows, stone walls, forests and gentle hills, the landscape that the American artist Henry Ward Ranger declared was "waiting to be painted" when he first arrived in 1899. Not coincidentally, it's common to see artists setting up easels and oils or pastels to paint en plein air. Centuries-old village greens and picture-postcard scenes have been preserved in pristine splendor. In and around them, romantic inns and sophisticated eateries abound. These colonial-era shoreline towns may be lined up cheek by jowl, but each maintains its own particular flavor, making them ideal for exploring.

Old Lyme sits on the east side of the river as it enters Long Island Sound. This maritime village has a certain cachet in the art world, thanks to Miss Florence Griswold, who turned her father's splendid late-Georgian mansion on the Lieutenant River into a boardinghouse for summering artists (the likes of Childe Hassam, William Metcalf, and the aforementioned Henry Ward Ranger) and effectively turned her town into a major hub of American impressionism. Today the Griswold home, with a splendid museum in its backyard, is one of the foremost small art museums in the country. Its neighbors on historic and lovely Lyme Street include a renowned art association, a gallery selling paintings from the 19th and 20th centuries, and a fine arts college. On the west bank of the river's estuary, pleasure boats and fishing vessels ply to and from the marinas that dot Old Saybrook's shoreline. The Outer Lighthouse, at the end of the Old Saybrook Breakwater, is an iconic beacon featured on the state's popular SAVE THE SOUND license plates. Meanwhile, the lovingly restored homes and immaculate churches on Main Street are a testament to the town's colonial past. The secluded and gentrified borough of Fenwick is where Katharine Hepburn spent much of her life in a rambling house overlooking the Sound.

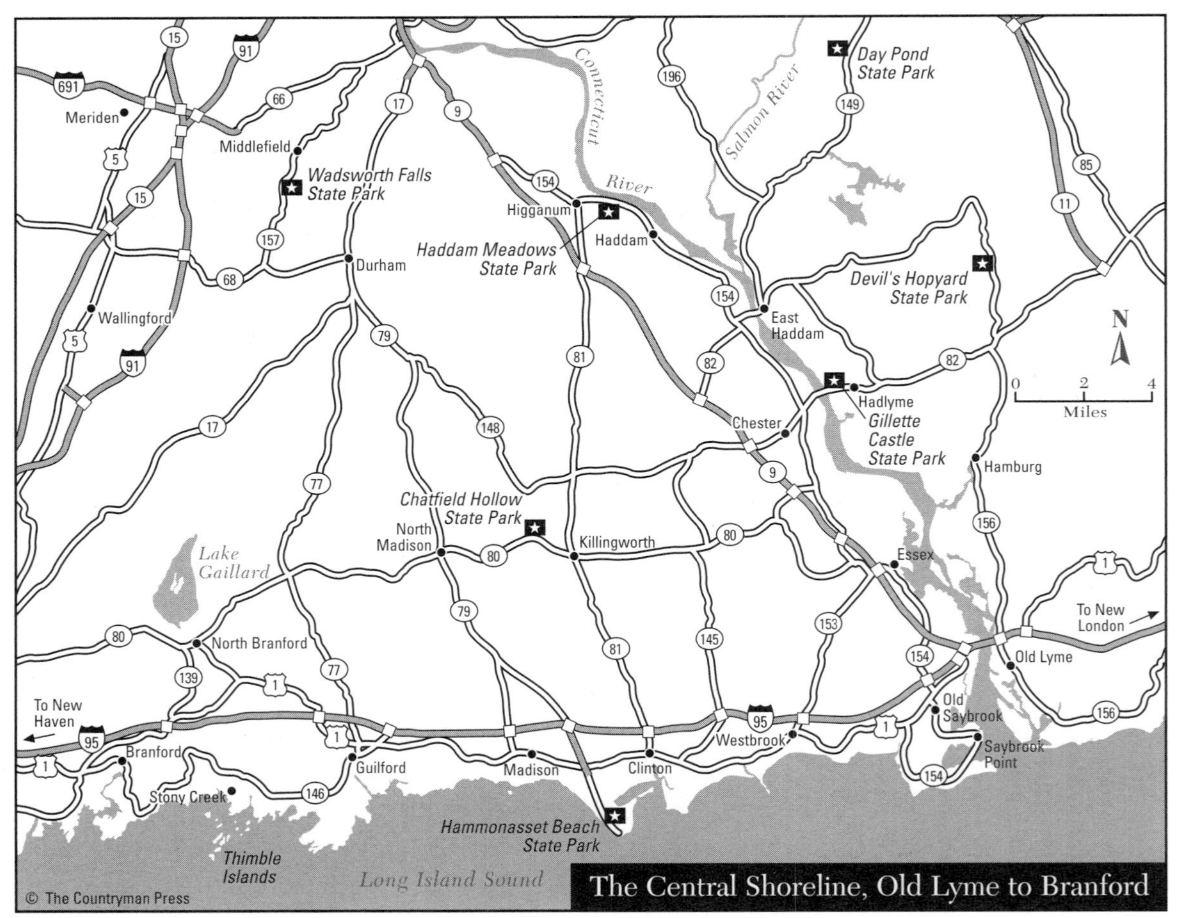

The Central Shoreline, Old Lyme to Branford

Continuing west along the coastline, US 1, or the Boston Post Road (named for the route that early settlers used to travel to and from New York to Boston), will lead you to the beach towns of Westbrook and Clinton, which boast a sprawling seaside resort, a noted vineyard, antiques shops, and, most recently, two bustling factory outlet centers. The latter is a popular destination for tourists, particularly on those rainy beach days that drive vacationers off the beaches and into the stores in droves. Farther along is Madison, named for the nation's fourth president and centered on a dignified green set about with the grand homes of former sea captains and shipbuilders. Its waterfront boasts a magnificent 2-mile stretch of sandy beaches, salt marshes, and dunes; in fact, 936-acre Hammonasset Beach is the state's longest beach and—with more than a million annual visitors—busiest state park. Whatever you do, be sure to make time après-beach for Madison's galleries, eateries, shops, and the Sculpture Mile, an eclectic variety of art in and around the town center.

Equally walkable is neighboring Guilford, a community founded by a band of Puritans in 1639. Here you'll find New England's oldest stone house, Civil War homes, and in true past-meets-present fashion, boutiques and galleries offering modern art and cutting-edge fashions. It also boasts one of New England's prettiest town greens, a stately tree-shaded expanse modeled after a 17th-century English common, flanked on all sides by steepled churches, classic New England clapboard dwellings, and a kitsch-free lineup of shops, bistros, galleries, and a renowned crafts center. In Branford, the timeless fishing cove of Stony Creek harbors a string of offshore jewels—the Thimble Islands, home to celebrities and other solitude seekers, as well as the legendary stamping grounds (according to local lore) of Captain Kidd and his treasure-toting cutthroats. Hop aboard one of the narrated boat excursions for good looks at this timeless archipelago.

Entries in this section are arranged in alphabetical order.

AREA CODES 860 and 203.

GUIDANCE **Central Regional Tourism District** (860-244-8181; 800-793-4480; www.enjoycentralct.com), 31 Pratt St., Hartford 06103, and the **Greater New Haven Convention & Visitors Bureau** (203-777-8550; 800-332-7829; www.visitnewhaven.com), 169 Orange St., New Haven 06510, provide tourism information in the central shoreline region.

A **state highway welcome center** (860-399-8122) on I-95 northbound at Westbrook offers Connecticut vacation guides and maps, as well as respite from the interstate blues. The center is run during summer months by tourism staffers who provide assistance and answer questions.

Several towns maintain their own **information centers**, which operate during the summer months. One is on the town green in Old Saybrook, where you can pick up a brochure that outlines self-guided walking tours of Main Street's historic buildings. Another is on the Clinton green, where information is available at the re-created 1630 House.

GETTING THERE *By car:* I-95 is the north–south corridor along the Atlantic coast, although it runs east–west in Connecticut—something that happens in a state where the Atlantic Ocean is, in a sense, to the south. CT 9 is a north–south route along the Connecticut River, joining I-95 in Old Saybrook; and I-91 comes from northern New England to New Haven at the western end of this region.

By air: **Bradley International Airport** (860-292-2000; 888-624-1533; www.bradleyairport.com) in Windsor Locks is the state's principal airport, with more than a dozen airlines scheduling flights in and out. US Airways Express serves **Tweed–New Haven Regional Airport** (203-466-8833; www.flytweed.com). At present, **Groton–New London Airport** (860-445-8549; www.grotonnewlondonairport.com) accepts only charter and corporate planes. Rental cars are available at all three airports.

By rail: **Amtrak** (800-872-7245; www.amtrak.com) runs from New York City along the Connecticut coast with stops at New Haven and Old Saybrook. On weekdays, **Shore Line East** commuter trains (203-777-7433; 800-255-7433; www.shorelineeast.com) stop in Branford, Guilford, Madison, Clinton, Westbrook, and Old Saybrook on their route between New Haven and New London.

MEDICAL EMERGENCY The statewide emergency number is **911**.

Hospital of St. Raphael (203-789-3000), 1450 Chapel St., New Haven. The emergency number is 203-789-3464.

Middlesex Memorial Hospital (860-344-6000), 28 Crescent St., Middletown. The emergency number is 860-344-6686.

Yale–New Haven Hospital (203-688-4242), 20 York St., New Haven. The emergency number is 203-688-2222.

Yale–New Haven Shoreline Medical Center (203-688-4242), 111 Goose Lane, Guilford. The emergency number is 203-688-2222.

✷ To See

MUSEUMS ♿ **Florence Griswold Museum** (860-434-5542; www.florencegriswoldmuseum.org), 96 Lyme St., Old Lyme. Open Tue.–Sat. 10–5; Sun. 1–5; Jan.–Mar.: Wed.–Sun. 1–5; closed Mon. and major holidays. Adults $8; students and seniors $7; children 6–12 $4; 5 and under free. Art lovers take note: This is a gem in the state's collection of art museums. Around the turn of the 20th century,

THE FLORENCE GRISWOLD MUSEUM IN OLD LYME CONTAINS MANY EXAMPLES OF PAINTINGS BY THE AMERICAN IMPRESSIONIST PAINTERS WHO FLOCKED TO MISS FLORENCE'S SUMMER SALONS.

Kim Grant

THE HENRY WHITFIELD STATE MUSEUM IN GUILFORD IS REPUTEDLY THE OLDEST STONE BUILDING IN NEW ENGLAND.

Miss Florence opened her home as a salon for artists summering in the community. They were so inspired by the accommodations and the setting that they formed what came to be America's best-known impressionist art colony and founded a local school for artists that still flourishes. Some paid the rent in original works on doors, mantels, and paneling. Meanwhile, the house—a late-Georgian mansion of considerable elegance—has become a National Historic Landmark combining history and art, with original paintings by American impressionists Henry Ward Ranger, Childe Hassam, and Wilson Irvine, among others. On the grounds, the **Chadwick Studio** has been renovated and opened to both visiting artists and museum visitors from mid-May through October. Changing exhibits year-round. Behind the museum, the stunning **Nancy and Robert Krieble Gallery** houses a trove of American art, 188 paintings collected by a former president of the Hartford Steam Boiler Insurance Company and presented to the Griswold in 2002.

Henry Whitfield State Museum (203-453-2457; www.whitfieldmuseum.org), 248 Old Whitfield St., Guilford. Open Apr.–mid-Dec., Wed.–Sun. 10–4:30; closed mid-Dec.–Mar., and major holidays. Adults $4; seniors and college students $3; children 6–17 $2.50; 5 and under free. Here's a rare gem: Connecticut's oldest house—1639—and reputedly the oldest stone building in New England, now a National Historic Landmark. Though much of the structure is restored and recreated, this house is indeed a relic of early New England. Designed to serve as a pastor's home and fortress, it has two enormous fireplaces in the main chamber, thick walls, and small windows. Furnishings reflect three centuries of its residents. If you're interested in restorations, this house has seen more than one: Frederick Kelly, the controversial authority on early Connecticut architecture, directed a 1930s restoration here. The visitor center has changing exhibits, as well as a gift shop with crafts, books, maps, and souvenirs. A research library is open by appointment.

WINERIES **Bishop's Orchards Winery** (203-453-2338; www.bishopsorchards.com), 1355 Boston Post Rd. (US 1), Guilford. Winery open daily; free tastings on Sat. noon–4. The popular sweet cider, aged to apple wine blended with various fruits from the orchard, including peach, raspberry, and pear.

Chamard Vineyard (860-664-0299; www.chamard.com), 115 Cow Hill Rd., Clinton. Open year-round, Tue.–Sun. 11–5; closed Mon. One of the state's shoreline wineries that take advantage of the rich, stony soil of the coastal slope and temperatures moderated by the waters of Long Island Sound. Visitors tour the inviting winery, which incorporates stonework and antique beams in typical New England style. Chamard's winemaking process combines modern technology with traditional methods, and tasting rooms afford a chance to judge for yourself the prizewinning Connecticut Chardonnay, Chamard's best-known and most popular wine. They grow seven grape varieties, including Cabernet Franc, Pinot Noir, and their acclaimed Estate Reserve Chardonnay, and produce upward of 6,000 cases of wine every year.

HISTORIC HOMES AND SITES **Allis-Bushnell House and Museum** (203-245-4567), 853 Boston Post Rd. (US 1), Madison. Open May–Sept., Wed., Fri., and Sat. 1–4, and by appointment. Free admission. A handsome 1785 home with unusual corner fireplaces and original paneling. Displays of ship models, toys, china, clothing, kitchenware. This is said to have been the home of Cornelius Scranton Bushnell, Civil War–era shipbuilder, president of the Union Pacific Railroad, and chief sponsor of the USS *Monitor*.

Deacon John Grave House (203-245-4798), 581 Boston Post Rd. (US 1), Madison. Open on Sat.; call for hours. For more than 300 years, descendants of local magistrate John Grave occupied this center-chimney survivor, which served variously as school, inn, tavern, courtroom, and wartime infirmary and weapons depot. The house, built in 1675, retains the framed overhang, clapboard siding, and small-paned windows typical of the era.

Fort Saybrook Monument Park (860-395-3152), Saybrook Point, CT 156, Old Saybrook. Open year-round; free admission. Eighteen acres, with boardwalks, trails, great views of the mouth of the Connecticut River, and a permanent display on the origins and controversial early history of Saybrook Colony—founded in 1635 by John Winthrop Jr., scion of the Massachusetts Winthrops.

General William Hart House (860-388-2622), 350 Main St., Old Saybrook. Open mid-June–mid-Sept., Fri.–Sun. 12:30–4. Admission $2; children 11 and under free. In 1767, Hart built this high-ceilinged, center-hall Georgian "mansion," now on the National Register of Historic Places, to impress upon his associates the extent of his success in life. Transfer-print tiles, eight corner fireplaces, splendid period paneling indoors, and a restored garden outside memorialize the general, who was actually a major in the Revolutionary War. In true entrepreneurial fashion, he also dabbled in real estate, shipping, trade, even politics. A model of perseverance, he ran for governor five times and lost five times.

Harrison House Museum & Barn (203-488-4828), 124 Main St., Branford. Open June–Sept., Sat. 2–5 and by appointment. Free admission. Built in 1724, this well-kept traditional saltbox has the characteristic steep roof slope, as well as the center chimney and clapboard siding typical of colonial homes. A bonus is the herb garden, and in the barn is a display of antique farm implements.

Hyland House (www.hylandhouse.com), 84 Boston St., Guilford. Open June–Labor Day, Tue.–Sun. 10–4:30; Labor Day–Columbus Day, Sat. and Sun. 10–4:30. Free admission. A circa-1700 red-clapboard gem near the green with early colonial artifacts on display in the parlor, bedrooms, and lean-to kitchen. Outside, a garden features the herbs and flowers colonists commonly grew for culinary and medicinal uses.

Stanton House (860-669-2132), 63 East Main St., Clinton. Limited hours; phone ahead. Free admission. Eighteenth- and 19th-century furnishings enhance the interior of this big, solid 1790 manse. One of the exhibits is a collection of Staffordshire, and there's a re-created general store with period merchandise. Guides will show you the room where Yale University's first classes met. The peripatetic college, founded in Saybrook, had a way stop in Clinton before it finally settled in New Haven.

Thomas Griswold House (203-453-3176), 171 Boston St., Guilford. Open June–Sept., Tue.–Sun. 11–4; Oct., Sat. and Sun. 11–4. Adults $3; students and seniors $2. A carefully restored 1774 saltbox featuring costumes, furniture, and a historic herb garden from the period of 1810, when George and Nancy Griswold lived here. (The Griswold family occupied the house until 1958.) Special features include a blacksmith shop with anvil at the ready, and the large barn full of farming implements.

SCENIC DRIVES A 12-mile stretch of **CT 146**, as it wanders south of the interstate through Branford to the junction with US 1 in Guilford, has been designated one of the state's scenic roads. And rightly so; this route travels through the true New England coastal plain—windswept trees, low vegetation, shorebirds, salt marsh, and an occasional glimpse of cottages and grand summer homes. This is also the road to **Stony Creek**, a cozy harbor village where you catch the sightseeing cruises around the tiny **Thimble Islands**. It's well worth a detour to drink in the sights, sounds, and smells of coastal Connecticut.

Guilford is the starting point for another official state scenic road, **CT 77**, which intersects with CT 146 at the Guilford town green. From there it runs north to the Durham town line, a distance of just under 12 miles. Rural landscapes and rising hills in this sparsely settled section provide a peaceful interlude and tempt you to long for the times we like to think were simpler.

✷ To Do

BIRDING **Hammonasset Beach State Park** (203-245-2785), 1288 Boston Post Rd. (US 1), Exit 62 off I-95, Madison. Shorebirds in the tidal marsh; in fall, migrating ducks, loons, and gannets off Meigs Point, flocks of snow buntings, larks, and sparrows in the grassy fields.

In Guilford, the **East River Salt Marsh** on Meadowlands Rd. is a prime birding spot that's frequented mostly by local birders. Hike the mile-long Anne Conover Nature Education Trail for good looks at resident and migrant songbirds and waterfowl. In Old Lyme, fittingly—home to the late naturalist Roger Tory Peterson, author of *A Field Guide to the Birds*—there are two prime birding spots, accessible only by boat: the Roger Tory Peterson Wildlife Area on Great Island, as well as Griswold Point, a mile-long barrier beach favored by nesting endangered piping plovers.

BOAT EXCURSIONS One of the state's most popular offshore excursions is cruising the **Thimble Islands**, the windswept archipelago off the coast of Branford in the picturesque village of Stony Creek. It's home to an exclusive summer colony where an invite is required to step ashore, but if none is forthcoming, no matter: Hop aboard one of the boat tours that motor past dozens of granite islands with names such as Potato, Mother-in-Law, and Money. Some are barely large enough to hold a single house; others are sizable enough for a dozen cottages. Boat captains spin fact and lore about hidden pirate treasures and notables who have found the Thimbles inviting, from Tom Thumb to Captain Kidd.

Leaving from the town dock are Captain Bob Milne's ***Volsunga IV*** (203-488-9978; 203-481-3345; www.thimbleislands.com) and Captain Mike Infantino's ***Sea Mist* Island Cruise** (203-488-8905; www.thimbleislandcruise.com). Both offer 45-minute narrated cruises as well as private charters from May to September, and in October if the weather permits. Contact each boat for specific information on schedules and prices.

BOATING **Old Lyme** has three boat-launching areas—the Great Island boat launch on Smith Neck Rd., Pilgrim Landing on CT 156, and the Four Mile River boat launch on Oak Ridge Dr. In **Clinton**, the Town Marina boat launch is on Riverside Dr.; **Guilford** has two launching spots: the Town Marina on Whitfield Street, and on the East River at Neck Rd. In **Branford** you can put in on the Branford River at Goodsell Point Rd.; **Old Saybrook** has two boat-launching areas: the Baldwin Bridge launch on Ferry Rd., and the town launch on North Cove Rd. In **Westbrook**, Kirtland Landing on Old Clinton Rd. has a boat launch.

There are many more places to launch car-top boats; check the **Connecticut Coastal Access Guide** (www.lisrc.uconn.edu/coastalaccess) for a comprehensive online listing by town.

CANOEING In Guilford, canoeists can paddle a 1-mile route through farmland down the East River into Long Island Sound. Another 4-mile paddle heads to Tunxis Island, off the coast of neighboring Madison. **North Cove Outfitters** (860-388-6585; www.northcove.com), 75 Main St., Old Saybrook, hosts canoeing demonstrations and can point you to local hot spots. The **Thimble Islands** archipelago, just off the coast of the Stony Creek section of Branford, is a haven for paddlers.

FISHING Fishing is permitted in Chatfield Hollow State Park, **Killingworth**, and in Hammonasset Beach State Park, **Madison**. Streams are stocked by the Department of Environmental Protection.

Bluefish and stripers on Long Island Sound

Charter boats are for hire for half- or full-day trips on Long Island Sound and beyond. Captains are licensed by the U.S. Coast Guard and registered by the state of Connecticut. In this area are the following: In Westbrook, ***Catch 'Em*** (860-223-1876; 860-399-5853) at Pilot's Point Marina, and ***Rumrunner*** (860-307-2603) out of Pier 76 Marina. In Old Saybrook, the ***Sea Sprite*** (860-669-9613) is docked at Saybrook Point Marina; **North Coast Charters** (203-378-1160) runs from Saybrook Point Inn & Marina; **Eden Charters** (860-388-5897) is at Ferry Point Marina; and **Islander Sport Fishing Charters** (860-663-3844) departs from 2 Clark St.

In Clinton, **Bluefin Sportfishing Charters** (203-421-7981; 877-259-9920) runs from Grove St.

HIKING In the shoreline region, **Chatfield Hollow State Park** in Killingworth and **Hammonasset Beach State Park** in Madison (see their descriptions under *Green Space*), in addition to the local land preserves listed below, offer hiking trails and, in some cases, other outdoor activities.

Branford Land Trust (203-483-5263; www.branfordlandtrust.org), P.O. Box 254, Branford 06405. The land trust protects 800 acres of land in some 90 parcels; their Web site has a comprehensive list of trails for walking and cross-country skiing.

Madison Land Trust (www.madisonlandtrust.org), P.O. Box 561, Madison 06443, has blazed trails for hiking and cross-country skiing. Guided hikes are scheduled throughout the year, including moonlight walks and family-friendly hikes.

Westwoods Trails (www.westwoodtrails.org), P.O. Box 200, Guilford 06437, maintains 39 miles of hiking trails spread across 1,200 acres. Trail maps are available online and at various locations around town.

MOUNTAIN BIKING **Hammonasset Beach State Park**, Madison, has an easy 2-mile trail through dunes, with water views at every turn. Park at any of the lots near the trail. Miles of wooded fire roads are waiting for offroad cyclists at **Chatfield Hollow State Park**, Killingworth (see *Green Space*). **Zane's Cycles** (800-551-2453), 105 North Main St., Branford, has friendly, resourceful staff who can help you plan a ride, or at least tell you where to find the trailheads.

✷ Green Space

Chatfield Hollow State Park (860-663-2030), 381 CT 80, Killingworth. Parking fee on weekdays: $5 residents, $7 nonresidents; on weekends and holidays: $7 residents, $10 nonresidents. Open year-round, daily 8 AM–sunset. More than 350 acres of wooded land, rife with natural caves and rocky ledges, along with Native American stories. Families come for the swimming pond; outdoor enthusiasts love the network of hiking trails that extend into adjacent Cockaponset State Forest.

Hammonasset Beach State Park (203-245-2785), 1288 Boston Post Rd. (US 1), Exit 62 off I-95, Madison. Parking fee weekends and holidays, $10 residents, $15 nonresidents; weekday fees: $7 residents, $10 nonresidents. A sanctuary on Connecticut's otherwise heavily developed coastline. The 2-mile stretch of beach is the focal point, but this 923-acre oasis—Connecticut's largest shoreline park—adds a number of other inducements. **Meigs Point Nature Center** (203-245-8743), open during summer, offers exhibits and interpretive programs, including guided walks. Programs illuminate the abundance of birds, fishes, crustaceans, and other life-forms that thrive in the salt marshes and along the beach. Camping, picnicking, saltwater fishing, scuba diving, hiking, boating, swimming, and food concessions are available. The park is open year-round, so if you're an off-season beach walker, solitude can be found here.

Watch Rock Nature Preserve (www.old-lymeconservtrust.org), Joel Dr., Exit 70 off I-95, Old Lyme. Open daily year-round, 6 AM–sunset. Free admission. This 25-acre property of the Old Lyme Conservation Trust sits at a pretty off-the-beaten-path spot

Kim Grant

HAMMONASSET BEACH STATE PARK IN MADISON OFFERS A 3-MILE STRETCH OF BEACH AND ENCOMPASSES THE MEIGS POINT NATURE CENTER.

on Duck River, where the Connecticut River joins Long Island Sound. A short loop trail through woods and tidal marsh heads to the water, where a cluster of rocks is a perfect spot to contemplate the coastal landscape and enjoy a picnic.

✷ Lodging

RESORTS 🐾 **Saybrook Point Inn & Spa** (860-395-2000; 800-243-0212; www.saybrook.com), 2 Bridge St., Old Saybrook 06475. This European-style inn with marina and spa has been named a AAA Four Diamond historic hotel—a deluxe accommodation—by the AAA. It's sited at the "point" where the Connecticut River enters Long Island Sound; views, from either the grounds or inside the inn, are remarkable. The inn has set out to offer guests every comfort, including working fireplaces, sitting areas, Italian tile in the bathrooms, whirlpool tubs, swimming pools outside and indoors, and upscale dining (see Terra Mar Grille under *Dining Out*). The luxe spa provides all forms of pampering. A nationally recognized 120-slip marina is available for those who arrive by water. There are 80 rooms and suites, many with water views and fireplace; one is a unique lighthouse suite at the end of the marina dock. $219 and up.

⚭ ♿ **Water's Edge Resort and Spa** (860-399-5901; 800-222-5901; www.watersedgeresortandspa.com), 1525 Boston Post Rd. (US 1), P.O. Box 688, Westbrook 06498. Once an estate, now an inn-resort complex with a health spa and fitness center in a beautiful shoreline setting. The sprawling central building, set on a bluff, overlooks Long Island Sound. Whether you stay in one of the inn's 170 guest rooms and suites, or opt for one of the spacious oceanfront villas, you can enjoy the private beach, tennis courts, outdoor and indoor pools, whirlpool, sauna, steam room, and award-winning restaurant (see *Dining Out*). Continental breakfast. $209 and up.

INNS **Bee and Thistle Inn** (860-434-1667; 800-622-4946; www.beeandthistleinn.com), 100 Lyme St., Old Lyme 06371. A 1756 yellow-clapboard house on the banks of the Lieutenant River in Lyme's picturesque historic district. Well-tended gardens and handsome old trees grace the 5-acre property. Porches and windows have been added, not to mention private baths; the 11 luxurious guest rooms are comfortably fitted out with antiques, and some have four-poster or canopy beds. It's one of the shoreline's top romantic retreats, as is the acclaimed restaurant, a longtime favorite for elegant dining (see *Dining Out*). $150–275.

Inn at Lafayette (203-245-7773; www.innatlafayette.com), 725 Boston Post Rd. (US 1), Madison 06443. At the heart of pretty historic upscale shoreline town, behind two-story fluted columns supporting a lofty portico, this carefully restored church meetinghouse is as gracious outside as it is inside. The furnishings reflect the inn's quiet elegance—intricate handwoven rugs and painted armoires, first-edition books and an antique writing table, have all been chosen with care and taste. The five guest rooms are appointed with marble bath (one with a Jacuzzi), telephone, and color TV. Lunch and dinner in the elegant Café Allegre Tue.–Sun. (see *Dining Out*). $125–150.

🐾 ♿ **Old Lyme Inn** (860-434-2600; 800-434-5352; www.oldlymeinn.com), 85 Lyme St., Old Lyme 06371. Across the street from the Florence Griswold Museum, where a group of American impressionists, also known as Old Lyme artists, spent their summers. Some of their works adorn the walls of this gracious, rambling 1850 home-turned-elegant inn. The 13 antiques-filled rooms and suites are spread across the main house and a more modern wing. Each room has a private bath, air-conditioning, telephone, and TV. The furnishings evoke Empire and Victorian styles. Adirondack chairs and park benches on the lawn invite relaxation. The restaurant serves continental breakfast to guests, and is open to the public for lunch, dinner, and Sun. brunch (see *Dining Out*). $135–185.

Scranton Seahorse Inn (203-245-0550; www.scrantonseahorseinn.com), 818 Boston Post Rd. (US 1), Madison 06443. The 1833 Greek Revival home of a prominent local family now provides charming in-town lodging. All seven guest rooms have private bath, Internet access, and cable TV; some have a Jacuzzi tub or fireplace. Continental breakfast. $100–200.

THE BEE AND THISTLE INN IN OLD LYME

Kim Grant

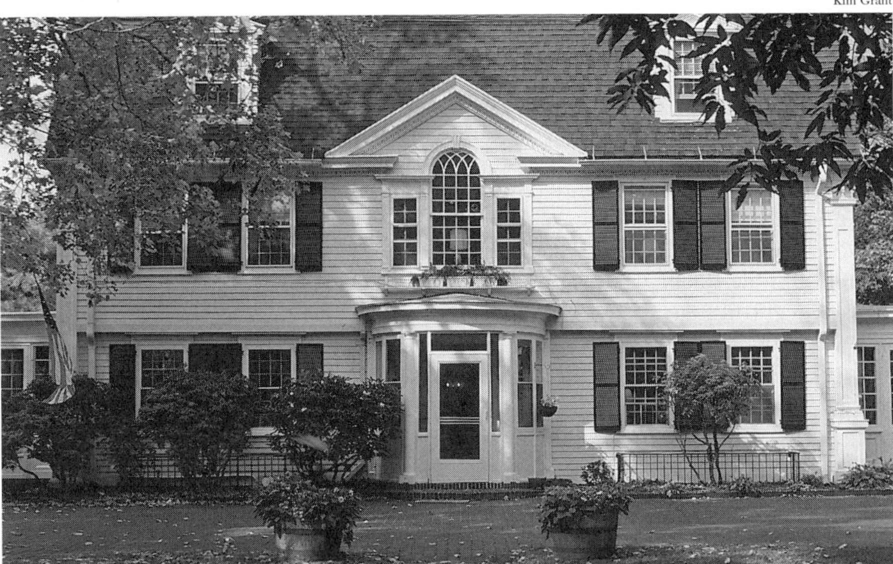

BED & BREAKFASTS **Angel's Watch Inn Bed & Breakfast** (860-399-8846; www.angelswatchinn.com), 902 Boston Post Rd. (US 1), Westbrook 06498. A historic 1880 Federal home built by Horace Kelsey. Guests are welcome to relax in the elegant yet welcoming common rooms, where they will find a variety of delicious treats, perhaps strawberries dipped in chocolate, or fresh fruit, champagne, and soft drinks. They can also stroll in the quiet backyard, relax at a picnic table or park bench, or make use of the outdoor grill. The inn makes bicycles available as an alternative mode of transportation to nearby beaches; beach towels, blankets, and passes are provided. Five guest rooms with fireplace and refrigerator stocked with complimentary refreshments. Full breakfast. $125–195.

The B&B at Bartlett Farm (203-457-1657; www.thebartlettfarm.com), 564 Great Hill Rd., Guilford 06437. A lovingly restored 1784 farmhouse on a working farm offers three guest rooms with private bath, air-conditioning, and television. Innkeepers Sam and Diana Bartlett, who are descendants of the farm's original settlers, raise sheep, pigs, fallow deer, even a buffalo. A full breakfast includes farm-fresh eggs. $115–140.

Bushnell House Inn (860-; 800-342-3162; www.bushnellhouse.com), 106 South Main St., Westbrook 06498. *Elegant* and *comfy* characterize these three comfortable guest rooms and suites, most with chandeliers, decorative granite fireplaces, and pine floors; all have fine linens and tasteful decor (the heated tile floors in the bathrooms are a thoughtful touch). Beach passes, towels, and totes are provided. Full breakfast. $230–280.

Captain Stannard House (860-399-4634; www.stannardhouse.com), 138 South Main St., Westbrook 06498. The 19th-century ship's captains who did well built homes that announced their success. Captain Stannard's four-square colonial home is enhanced with ornate brackets under the deep eaves, double doors under a fanlight window, a cupola—from which supposedly the womenfolk might watch for his sails on the horizon—and several additions, one a distinctly Victorian tower. The attractive whole, a commodious lodging, has been completely renovated. Each of its nine guest rooms has a private bath and is nicely furnished with New England antiques. Full breakfast. $145–205.

Deacon Timothy Pratt Bed & Breakfast (860-395-1229; 800-640-1195); www.pratthouse.net), 325 Main St., Old Saybrook 06475. This 1746 home, which is on the National Register of Historic Places, features seven exceptional period-style guest rooms with private bath, working fireplace, four-poster or canopy bed, and whirlpool tub. From the wide-board floors and original hand-forged door latches to the beehive oven and cooking fireplace in the kitchen, no detail has been overlooked in restoring this grand center-chimney colonial. Folk art and antiques fill the inviting common rooms, where guests can read, mingle, or relax by a roaring fire. Breakfast is a grand occasion here—the table is set with silver and china for dishes such as heart-shaped pancakes, Belgian waffles, eggs Benedict, fresh fruit, and muffins on weekends. Continental breakfast during the week. $140–240.

Griswold Cottage (203-453-1488; www.griswoldcottage.com), 296 Boston St., Guilford 06437. A chef-owned B&B in a charming 19th-century clapboard farmhouse. A light-filled upstairs suite is spacious and private, with areas for sitting and dining and a full private bath. Stroll to the town green for boutique shopping, cafés, and galleries, or take a cooking class here. Full breakfast. $125.

Sound Reach (203-457-0415; www.bbhost.com/soundreach), 50 Christmas Hill Rd., Guilford 06437. Three guest rooms in a Swiss-style log home perched on a secluded hilltop 10 minutes from the village green. Guests can stroll the perennial and herb gardens and enjoy views of Long Island Sound in the distance. Hiking and cross-country ski trails are close by. Continental breakfast features raspberry corn bread and cranberry scones, among other delicacies. $95–115.

♿ **Talcott House** (860-399-5020; www.talcotthouse.com), 161 Seaside Ave., Westbrook 06498. The inn is open Apr.–Oct. On the beach, facing the water, this 100-year-old former summer home is designed to bring the outdoors inside. Each of the three guest rooms has a view of the Sound and a private bath. Guests in the first-floor room have a private, brick-floored porch with immediate access to sun and ocean breezes. A fireplace in the living room provides cozy warmth in winter. A continental breakfast is served in the large common room or on the screened porch. A sandy beach is right across the street. $195–225.

3 Liberty Green (860-669-0111; www.3liberty.com), 3 Liberty St., Clinton 06413. Make this comfy bed & breakfast your headquarters and you'll be well poised for the upscale everything (galleries, boutique shopping, gourmet dining) of the area. The handsome 1734 colonial on Liberty Green in the historic district has four guest rooms, no two of which are alike; each has double Jacuzzi tub, canopy bed, private bath, and sitting area. Wireless Internet access and other high-tech touches keep the inn firmly rooted in the present. $120–220.

Tidewater Inn (203-245-8457; www.thetidewater.com), 949 Boston Post Rd. (US 1), Madison 06443. This handsome B&B was a stagecoach stop in the 1890s; today it offers eight antiques-filled guest rooms and one suite, all with private bath, TV, air-conditioning, and telephone; the Curtis Cottage suite has a Jacuzzi. Some rooms have working fireplace, as does the beamed sitting room, where guests enjoy a hearty breakfast. A couple of minutes' walk from the center of Madison and close to several beaches. Passes are available to guests. Full breakfast. $110–245.

Welcome Inn Bed & Breakfast (860-399-2500; www.welcomeinnbandb.com), 433 Essex Rd. (CT 153), Westbrook 06498. This cozy 1895 farmhouse has received loving care and skillful restoration. A fireplace in the sitting room guarantees instant relaxation, and the four guest rooms are furnished with family heirlooms and fine reproductions; three have private bath. Continental breakfast. $99–165.

Westbrook Inn (860-342-3162; 800-342-3162; www.westbrookinn.com), 976 Boston Post Rd. (US 1), Westbrook 06498. A lovely Victorian with perennial gardens, a wicker-filled porch, working gas fireplaces, and period Victorian decor. Nine guest rooms and a two-bedroom cottage might have a working fireplace, balcony, or kitchenette; all have private bath. Walk to the beach (beach passes, towels, and chairs are provided) or take one of the inn's bikes. Full breakfast; wine and cheese on Saturday night. Rooms $100–229; cottage $226–299.

HOTELS **Best Western Stony Creek Inn & Suites** (203-488-4991;

www.bwstonycreekinn.com), 3 Business Park Dr., Exit 56 off I-95, Branford 06405. The 85 guest rooms and suites, in an office park just off the interstate, are close to the Thimble Islands boat cruises and just outside New Haven. There's a small indoor pool and fitness center, and free WiFi. Continental breakfast. $79–129.

Madison Beach Hotel (203-245-1404; www.madisonbeachhotel.com), 94 West Wharf Rd., Madison 06443. Facing Long Island Sound, directly on the beach, this three-story, porch-wrapped hotel has a history stretching back to the whaling era, when it opened in 1800 as a boardinghouse for shipbuilders. Open Mar.–Nov., it has 35 rooms and suites, all with private bath, TV, and water views. An ideal base for strolls on the beach, swimming, basking, fishing. Nothing fancy, but great on-the-beach location. Continental breakfast is served to guests; **The Wharf** restaurant serves lunch and dinner. $149–299.

Sandpiper Inn (860-399-7973; www.sandpiperinnct.com), 1750 Boston Post Rd. (US 1), Old Saybrook 06475. This longtime shoreline hotel was newly renovated in 2008. Rooms and suites have standard amenities; some have Jacuzzi tub. Heated outdoor pool. Continental breakfast. Children stay free. $99–199.

MOTOR INN **Heritage Motor Inn** (860-388-3743; www.heritagemotorinn.com), 1500 Boston Post Rd. (US 1), Old Saybrook 06475. A family-owned and -operated motel for more than 40 years. The clean and comfy rooms all have private bath, air-conditioning, refrigerator, cable TV, and colonial-style decor. A pool and patio are on site, and beaches and shopping are close by. Continental breakfast. $99–155.

CAMPGROUNDS **Hammonasset Beach State Park** (203-245-1817; reservations 877-668-2267), 1288 Boston Post Rd. (US 1), Exit 22 off I-95, Madison 06443. Open mid-May–Oct. The only state park campground in this area, Hammonasset Beach is on Long Island Sound and has 558 grassy sites. Amenities include a dump station, flush toilets, showers, a concession, swimming, boating, fishing. No individual connections to electricity, and no firewood. Direct access to the 2-mile-long beach and boardwalk. $15.

Riverdale Farm Campsite (860-669-5388; www.riverdalefarmcampsite.com), 111 River Rd., Clinton 06413. Open year-round. Riverdale Farm has 110 sites, plus facilities for trout fishing, ball games, tennis, and swimming; planned activities round out the amenities. Sites $40–45; cabins $100–120.

COTTAGES **Beech Tree Cottages** (203-245-2676; www.beechtreecottages.com), 1187 Boston Post Rd. (US 1), Madison 06443. Open May–Oct. Clean and simply furnished guest rooms and four efficiency cottages are available to rent by the night or week on quiet parklike grounds right off US 1. Walk or bike to Hammonasset Beach State Park. $100–125.

Where to Eat

DINING OUT **Aspen** (860-395-5888; www.aspenct.com), 2 Main St., Old Saybrook. Open for lunch Tue.–Sun.; dinner daily. One of shoreline's newest restaurants sits next to the Shops at Saybrook Country Barn. It's a sophisticated space, with floor-to-ceiling windows, a double-sided fireplace, and a granite bar. The menu of contemporary American cuisine with global accents keeps pace with the surroundings. Consider a grilled flatbread with shrimp, fig puree, and Gorgonzola for lunch, or grilled chili-rubbed steak with truffled *pommes frites* for dinner. Either way, you'll get a taste of what the kitchen can do. Be sure to save room for desserts such as mascarpone cheesecake, dark chocolate mousse tart, and bittersweet chocolate soufflé. Creative cocktails in the Amber Lounge. $19–29.

The Back Porch (860-510-0282; www.backporcholdsaybrook.com), 142 Ferry Rd., Old Saybrook. Open daily for lunch and dinner. The "porch" is actually an expansive outdoor deck overlooking a bustling marina on the Connecticut River. The seafood-leaning menu has simple, well-executed raw bar selections, as well as fried seafood and dressed-up dishes such as wasabi-crusted tuna. Many just stop by for the upscale bar bites and drinks. $12–31.

Bee and Thistle Inn (860-434-1667), 100 Lyme St., Old Lyme. Open daily for breakfast, lunch, and dinner. Reservations are recommended. Set in a colonial inn (see *Lodging*) and offering a sophisticated menu of eclectic choices, it's no wonder the Bee and Thistle is often cited as one of the top romantic spots for dining in Connecticut. Cocktails are served in the parlor or, weather permitting, in the exquisite perennial garden. Starters sometimes include chilled melon gazpacho, or Thai fish cakes. Dinner might feature seared Stonington sea scallops with an heirloom tomato salad, or filet mignon with red bliss potatoes and peach chutney. A selection of homemade desserts changes seasonally, but the specialty is the pecan diamond: a shortbread base studded with nuts and basking in caramel sauce. Entrées $25–40; prix fixe (Fri. and Sat. only, reservations required) $65–90.

♿ **Café Allegre** (203-245-7773; www.allegrecafe.com), 725 Boston Post Rd. (US 1), Madison. Open daily for lunch and dinner; on Sunday, for Harvest Brunch and dinner. Call for reservations. The inn that houses the café (see Inn at Lafayette under *Lodging*) declares its elegance with a noble Greek Revival facade. The interior is even more striking: The walls of the four dining rooms are done in pale salmon; underfoot are handwoven rugs; tables are set with Limoges. The many windows invite the sun. The cuisine, with both regional and Italian overtones, does not disappoint. Your dinner might start with shrimp stuffed with goat cheese and wrapped in pancetta, or wild mushrooms atop polenta. Entrées are expertly prepared; try the seared salmon in a cognac cream with mushrooms and shallots, or the braised lamb shank with garlic and fresh herbs. $16–27.

♿ **Café Routier** (860-399-8700; www.caferoutier.com), 1353 Boston Post Rd. (US 1), Westbrook. Open daily for dinner. This elegant bistro was once known, unbelievably, as the Truck Stop Café. Today the always-changing menu takes a three-tiered approach: You can choose from a selection of seasonal offerings (heirloom tomato risotto), sample classic French bistro dishes (grilled steak with *pommes frites*), or try the featured global cuisine (Peruvian-style bouillabaisse). Lemon crème brûlée and chocolate banana bread pudding are among the desserts made on the premises. $19–32.

♿ **Foe** (203-483-5896; www.foeamericanbistro.com), 576 Main St., Branford. Open for lunch Tue.–Sat.; dinner Tue.–Sun.; closed Mon. Reservations are recommended for dinner. "Foe" is the nickname of chef-owner Alfonso Iaderosa. His cozy bistro not far from the green serves innovate takes on bistro favorites; you can't go wrong with the hanger steak, fresh pasta, or thick juicy burgers. The warm and friendly atmosphere is perhaps why this place is often packed with regulars. $18–27.

Jack's Saybrook Steak (860-395-1230; www.jackssaybrooksteak.com), 286 Main St., Old Saybrook. Open for lunch Mon.–Fri.; dinner Mon.–Sat.; closed Sun. Reservations recommended on weekends. Traditional chophouse fare that's exceptional, albeit pricey, and well worth the wait for a table. Summer crowds fill it up; try a meal during the week. $19–40.

Le Petit Café (203-483-9791; www.lepetitcafe.net), 225 Montowese St., Branford. Open Wed.–Sun. for dinner. Reservations are essential. A small café in the best style of a French bistro that entices devoted gourmands to drive miles for a unique culinary experience. The talented chef-owner Roy Ip trained at the French Culinary Institute under Jacques Pepin. The superb four-course, prix fixe menu changes seasonally. Some recent examples: sautéed French escargots with blue cheese and creamy polenta, roasted Canadian halibut with baby root vegetables, warm apple tart with caramel sauce. $49.

Liv's Oyster Bar (860-395-5577; www.livsoysterbar.com), 166 Main St., Old Saybrook. Open for dinner Wed.–Mon.; closed Tue. Food-savvy locals and vacationers flock to this newer culinary rave for its market-fresh seafood menu and icy shellfish at the raw bar. Stonington scallops, lobster risotto, panko-crusted lemon sole, and roasted halibut appear on the fish-centric menu. $19–26.

♿ **Old Lyme Inn** (860-434-2600; www.oldlymeinn.com), 85 Lyme St., Old Lyme. Serving lunch Mon.–Sat.; dinner daily; brunch on Sun. Reservations are recommended on weekends. One of the state's most charming country inns (see *Lodging*) features chef Joe Hill's Continental cuisine, and white-linen service, in the formal Winslow Room. Appetizers celebrate seafood: Try the New England clam chowder, or perhaps Hudson Valley foie gras. For entrées, enjoy a wealth of choices: paillard of veal, Parmesan-crusted halibut, Stonington sea scallops. You can finish off with traditional favorites such as apple crisp, chocolate mousse, or bread pudding. There's also a Grill Room for more casual fare, and a flagstone café for outdoor dining. $17–34.

♿ **Penang Grill** (203-488-6171), 1205 Main St., Branford. Open Wed.–Sun. for dinner; live jazz on Sun. An eclectic seasonal menu that is expertly prepared and stylishly presented. Venison roulade with roasted sweet potatoes and mushrooms in a sauce of lingonberries and pears; Gulf shrimp in orange juice, sake, and ginger; or brown-and-green-striped ravioli stuffed with shiitake mushrooms and asparagus might be among the dinner offerings. Extraordinary desserts. $13–16.

♿ **Quattro's** (203-453-6575; www.quattrositalian.com), 14 Water St., Guilford. Open for lunch and dinner daily. A delightful trattoria in a 19th-century storefront near the town green. Chef Luis Rojas's well-prepared, traditional Italian fare can be found on the regular menu, but his creative daily specials shine here. They might include grilled prosciutto-wrapped Gulf shrimp stuffed with fresh mozzarella, or Chilean sea bass topped with crabmeat and scallops and sauced with vodka cream. $17–22.

♿ **Restaurant at Water's Edge** (860-399-5901; 800-222-5901), 1525 Boston

Post Rd. (US 1), Westbrook. Breakfast, lunch, and dinner served daily, with a popular brunch on Sun. Reservations suggested. A splendid glass wall gives patrons a view of the Sound. In summer, you can dine outside the wall, on the deck, where a grill provides suitable fare. In the dining room, the atmosphere is more formal: white linen and an elaborate menu featuring seafood, pasta dishes, prime rib, duck, and lamb. $16–40. (See also *Lodging.*)

♿ **Stone House Restaurant** (203-458-3700; www.stonehouserestaurant.com), 506 Whitfield St., Guilford. Open year-round for lunch and dinner. A waterfront dining landmark since the 1940s, the Stone House is deservedly well known for its innovative dishes such as roast sea bass with fennel and Chardonnay butter, or diver scallops with asparagus risotto, as well as impeccable service. Next door, the **Little Stone House** serves lighter fare. $20–28.

Whitfield's on Guilford Green (203-458-1300; www.whitfieldsonguilfordgreen.com), 25 Whitfield St., Guilford. Open for lunch Mon.–Sat.; dinner daily; breakfast and brunch on Sun. Contemporary American cuisine in a handsomely restored Victorian with big windows overlooking the green. Start with steamed sweet potato dumplings with Gorgonzola sage sauce, then lobster ravioli with asparagus and black mission figs, or pepper-crusted steak with garlic mashed potatoes. Artwork is on display inside on the walls, and outside in a sculpture garden. $18–30.

Terra Mar Grille (860-395-2000; 800-243-0212; www.saybrook.com), 2 Bridge St., Old Saybrook. Open daily for breakfast, lunch, and dinner; Sun. brunch. This highly rated American cuisine restaurant in the Saybrook Point Inn and Spa (see *Lodging*) is sophisticated and seasonal, albeit pricey. The dinner menu may feature Maine lobster bisque, or grilled Block Island swordfish. Save room for the must-have chocolate caramel mousse torte. Unmatched views of the mouth of the Connecticut River from the windows. From the other side of the dining room, you can see the last home of Katharine Hepburn on Fenwick Point on the shores of Long Island Sound. $26–40.

EATING OUT

In Old Saybrook

🏵 ♿ **Alforno Brick Oven Pizzeria** (860-399-4166), 1654 Boston Post Rd. (US 1). Open for lunch and dinner daily. Don't let Alforno's strip-mall location fool you; you'll pass the critics' rave reviews posted by the front door and enter a chic eatery. The homemade Tuscan bread and pizzas are works of art. Inventive toppings include asparagus with caramelized Vidalia onion, or wild mushrooms and fresh herbs. Other menu items are equally noteworthy: The homemade pistachio sausage and handmade gnocchi in an artichoke-basil cream sauce are among the more popular dishes. This spot appeals to families, tourists, and foodies alike. Pizzas $11–23; entrées $14–23.

🍼 ♿ **Cuckoo's Nest** (860-399-9060; www.cuckoosnest.biz), 1712 Boston Post Rd. (US 1). Open daily for lunch and dinner; Sun. brunch. A popular shoreline cantina among locals and summer visitors for 30 years. Traditional and exotic Mexican specialties, with Creole and Cajun creations as well. Colorful surroundings in a comfortably weathered barn, with south-of-the-border textiles and crafts. Specialties include Cajun prime rib, fresh seafood, and, of course, fajitas, empanadas, and enchiladas. For gringos, the menu includes a glossary defining terms from *burrito* to *sopaipilla* to *tostada.* Mexican combination plates. $15–25.

Dock and Dine (860-388-4665; www.dockdinect.com), Saybrook Point, at the end of Main Street. Open daily for lunch and dinner; closed Mon. and Tue. in winter. Reservations suggested. A friendly bar and lounge, entertainment on weekends, and water views from every table in the dining room. Seafood is a specialty on the extensive menu. After your meal, stroll the docks along the Connecticut River and watch the procession of waterborne traffic ply its way past Saybrook Point to and from the Sound. $17–30.

Pat's Kountry Kitchen (860-388-4784), 70 East Mill Rock Rd. (CT 154). Open daily for breakfast, lunch, and dinner. Diner and pancake house, lots of kitsch and cuteness. Pat's has a statewide reputation as a fun place for good food. Homemade soups and pies; seafood specials like shrimp with clam stuffing, and flounder stuffed with fresh veggies. Famous for her clam hash and potato skins. $7–15.

Penny Lane Pub (860-388-9646; www.pennylanepub.net), 150 Main St. Open daily for lunch and dinner. A family-friendly English-style pub and restaurant with an authentic menu of fish-and-chips, burgers, nachos, and shepherd's pie. Live music from Celtic to jazz keeps everyone entertained on weekends. $10–25.

In Branford

Auberge d'Asie (203-643-8067), 284 East Main St. Open for lunch and dinner Mon.–Sat.; closed Sun. Reservations are suggested for weekends. Chef Sophie Nguyen's casual-yet-sophisticated eatery serves authentic Vietnamese cuisine, a favorite among locals and foodies. $16–22.

Darbar India (203-481-8994; www.darbarindia.com), 1070 Main St. Open for lunch and dinner daily. Critics agree that this is one of the best Indian restaurants in the state. Authentic dishes, from tandoori and biryani to curries, plus lots of vegetarian options. $10–20.

Lenny's Indian Head Inn (203-488-1500; www.lennysnow.com), 205 South Montowese St. Open daily for lunch and dinner. Another large family-friendly fish restaurant where the deep fryer is kept bubbling with clams, shrimp, and fish-and-chips. Enjoy your dinner in the waterfront dining room or, in-season, on the spacious deck overlooking a salt marsh. The made-from-scratch clam chowder (clear broth) is a family recipe. Live music and lively bar crowd. $15–27.

Mango's Bar & Grille (203-483-7700; www.mangosbarandgrille.com), 988 Main St. Open daily for lunch and dinner. Dining on conch fritters and key lime scallops under ceiling fans in this sunny yellow café is like taking a trip to the Caribbean via Connecticut. The laid-back island vibe extends to the lively bar and the Key West/Cuban menu. $15–23.

Parthenon Diner-Restaurant (203-481-0333; www.parthenondiner.com), 324 East Main St. Open daily, 6 AM–midnight. If you are tired of fish and seafood shoreline dinners and are yearning for moussaka, spanakopita, a gyro, or some other Greek specialty, this is the place. The menu is a gigantic pastiche of sandwiches, burgers, soups, and salads that rivals the menu of any other traditional diner in America. $8–18. Another location in Old Saybrook (860-395-5111) at 809 Boston Post Rd. (US 1).

Su Casa (203-481-5001), 400 East Main St. (US 1). Open for lunch and dinner daily. Muted adobe-colored walls sport tapestries, pottery, masks, and murals in this locally acclaimed restaurant serving up traditional Mexican fare. Two fireplaces and live guitar music add to the festive ambience. $8–16.

Elsewhere

Bill's Seafood Restaurant (860-399-7224; www.billsseafood.com) 548 Boston Post Rd. (US 1), Westbrook. Open daily for lunch and dinner. This family-friendly, flip-flop-casual place next to Westbrook's "singing bridge" has been a shoreline favorite for decades. Lobster rolls, fried seafood platters, and clam chowder are served with a heaping side of atmosphere; snag a picnic table on the outdoor deck overlooking the Patchogue River. There's an outdoor bar with live music in summer, and an ice cream and gift shop. $6–25.

Café Grounded (203-453-6400; www.cafegrounded.com), 20 Church St., Guilford. Open Mon.–Sat. for breakfast and lunch; dinner Thu.–Sat.; Sun. brunch. A unique airplane-hangar-inspired restaurant, where patrons with pets can sit on the patio and kids can nosh on hot dogs while their parents dine on osso buco. Omelets, French toast, and pancakes in the morning; paninis and light fare at lunch; steak, pasta, and seafood at dinner. For dessert, orange Creamsicle smoothies for the kids, chocolate mousse lasagne for adults. $16–28.

Lenny & Joe's Fish Tale (860-669-0767; www.ljfishtale.com), 86 Boston Post Rd. (US 1), Westbrook; also on US 1 in Madison (860-245-7289). Open daily for lunch and dinner. Hot lobster roll, shore standbys. Everyone comes here for the fried seafood and seasonal specials like bluefish and Connecticut River shad. One of the favorites in the state. $12–22. T-shirts and hats are sold.

Cheryl's Corner Cafe (860-399-7130), 4 Westbrook Place, Westbrook. Open daily for breakfast and lunch. Egg dishes and sandwiches are on the menu at breakfast and lunch, but most know this homey spot for its homemade muffins. Signature flavors like morning glory and blueberry are not to be missed. On request, they'll butter yours and throw it on the breakfast grill to give it a satisfying crunch. $3–9.

M. Sarba Fine Art Café (860-669-5062; www.sarba.com), 95 East Main St., Clinton. A charming café in a lovingly restored 1807 homestead that's filled with a collection of museum-quality contemporary art. Owner-artist Marek Sarba's nautical-themed oil paintings are on display in the upstairs gallery; downstairs, a creative menu of salads, sandwiches, and coffee drinks is served in the dining room and on the outdoor patio. $6–15.

SNACKS Along US 1 (the Boston Post Rd.) you'll find, in summer, a succession of hot dog, clam roll, fried shrimp, and ice cream stands. Nobody drives hungry through Connecticut's shoreline towns.

Bread Star Bakery (203-488-2536), 1008 Main St., Branford. Open Tue.–Sun.; closed Mon. The raison d'être here is, simple yet exquisitely, bread—hearty herb, pumpkin nut, blueberry sourdough, and four-seed, to name a delicious few. Also soups and wraps along with baked goods.

Bruehwiler's Bakery & Café (860-388-0101), 247 Main St., Old Saybrook. Open Tue.–Sat.; closed Sun. and Mon. European-style bakery-café known for its cakes, cookies, breads, and scones. Coffee, espresso, and a small menu of sandwiches and soups for lunch.

Clam Castle (860-245-4911), 1324 Boston Post Rd. (US 1), Madison. This breezy seafood shack has been a Madison institution since the 1960s, dishing out hefty lobster rolls and mounds of fresh-fried golden-crusted bivalves to locals, tourists, kids in bathing suits, and Sunday drivers.

Cohen's Bagel Company (203-318-5090; www.cohensbagelcompany.com), 1347 Boston Post Rd. (US 1), in the Marketplace of Madison, Madison. Open daily. A new location in Branford (203-488-6200) at 1008 Main St. A must-stop for breakfast on the go. Bagels—sun-dried tomato, cinnamon crunch, Asiago, cranberry orange, and the usual varieties—plus a nice variety of breads and pastries. Bagel sandwiches for breakfast; paninis, sandwiches, soups, and salads for lunch. The cashew chicken salad on focaccia is a must.

Edd's Place (860-399-9498), 478 Boston Post Rd. (US 1), Westbrook. Open daily. Tables by the water and homemade pies; if you bring your own caught fish, they'll cook it up and serve it with salad and sides for a reasonable price. This is a casual take-out shack where most come to get food to go, but there's a patio. The perfect after-beach stop with the kids. Signature lobster roll, chowders, burgers and dogs, nightly dinner specials. $3–16.

Hallmark Drive In (860-434-1998), 113 Shore Rd., Old Lyme. Being in business since 1909 tells you that this drive-in is doing something right. Sure they make sandwiches, and good ones too, as well as fried seafood, burgers, and dogs, but generations of families have come here for ice cream, happily braving the line for a supremely satisfying single scoop.

James Gallery and Soda Fountain (860-395-1229), 2 Pennywise Lane, Old Saybrook. Open year-round, except Mon. Seasonal hours. A gift shop with an authentic old-fashioned Vermont marble soda fountain dispensing genuine old-fashioned ice cream treats. Gourmet coffee, pastries, and sandwiches are also available. Located in the Deacon Timothy Pratt B&B (see *Lodging*).

La Rosticceria (203-458-8885; www.guilfordtakeout.com), 500 Village Walk, off US 1, Guilford. Open Tue.–Sat.; closed Sun. and Mon. The gourmet lunch and dinner take-out items may tempt you to never cook again, but not to be missed is the house favorite: cupcakes in flavors like carrot cake and chocolate that locals line up for. They also run the cozy café in the back of R. J. Julia Booksellers in Madison.

Lobster Landing (860-669-2005), 152 Commerce St., Clinton. Open daily Apr.–Dec. This tiny spot a stone's throw from Long Island Sound is a "shack," as the locals call it. Join the laid-back sun-and-sand crowd at the plastic tables outside. Those in the know order Connecticut-style lobster rolls (think hot, buttery chunks of lobster meat stuffed into a grilled split-top bun). And in case you aren't tipped off by the name, you can pick up live lobsters, too.

Old Lyme Ice Cream Shoppe & Café (860-434-6942), 34 Lyme St., Old Lyme. Open daily in summer; reduced off-season hours. You know it's been a good day when your toughest decision is deciding what flavor of ice cream to order. Here traditional standbys share the roster with seasonal flavors like apple pie, black raspberry crunch, pumpkin, spiced chai, and Guinness, a house specialty. A good stop after exploring the Florence Griswold Museum.

Pasta Vita (860-395-1452; www.pastavita.com), 225 Elm St., Old Saybrook. Open Mon.–Sat.; closed Sun. When pasta pangs hit after a day at the beach, stop in for handmade pastas, as well as entrées, salads, soups, and desserts. The eggplant rollatini and spinach and cheese manicotti are delicious, but the kitchen really shows its pizzazz with ravioli filled with wild mushroom and spinach, smoked salmon with dill, roasted eggplant with garlic, artichoke and Fontina, or broccoli rabe.

Red Rooster Baking Co. (203-533-4330; www.redroosterbaking.com), 2614 Boston Post Rd. (US 1), Guilford. It's near impossible to decide which of the 16 varieties of freshly baked oversized gourmet cookies to take home. Glazed in Bailey's Irish Cream? Loaded with Kahlúa espresso beans? The signature cookie is studded with white and milk chocolate, butterscotch morsels, and cranberries. Yum.

Stony Creek Market (203-488-0145), 178 Thimble Islands Rd., Stony Creek, Branford. Open daily only in summer. The handwritten menu posted on the wall in this pleasant, unpretentious eatery-store changes daily, featuring terrific breakfast items, soups, sandwiches, and pizzas. Eat on the deck looking out at the Thimble Islands.

♿ **Tastebuds of Guilford** (203-453-1937; www.tastebudsgourmetcafe.com), 51 Whitfield St., Guilford. Tempt your taste buds with the unusual soups and sandwiches this little café is known for. On one visit, pumpkin butternut bisque was on the specials board, as was a strawberry and Brie melt on French bread with honey mustard. Grab a white-chocolate brownie or a slice of cheesecake, and you have the makings for a picnic on the nearby village green.

The Place (203-453-9276), 901 Boston Post Rd. (US 1), Guilford. A delightfully unassuming summer-only, roadside drive-in sort of place, where you snag a seat on a tree stump, or eat in the car and be on your way. First-timers can't go wrong with a plate of littleneck clams roasted on the open-air wood grill. Lobster, steak, chicken, and corn on the cob are all here, too.

COFFEE **Ashlawn Farm Coffee** (860-434-3636; www.farmcoffee.com), 78 Bill Hill Rd., Lyme. Open Wed.–Sat. For coffee, cappuccino and espresso, they roast beans—mostly organic and fair trade—in small batches to ensure freshness. The farm is a gorgeous backdrop for the Lyme Farmers Market. If you come, do what the regulars do: Grab a cup to go and sip while you check out the bounty of local produce.

Common Grounds (203-488-2326), 1096 Main St., Branford. Open daily. A good place to start the day, if only for its homey baked goods and excellent coffee. A variety of delicious international and flavored coffees, and all manner of specialty coffee drinks.

Madison Gourmet Beanery (203-245-1323), 712 Boston Post Rd. (US 1), Madison. Open daily. This cozy, aromatic café features seven flavored coffees daily, a light breakfast menu, muffins, scones, and other tasty goodies. The quiet, casual surroundings are adorned with paintings and photographs by local artists. Breakfast sandwiches around $4.

Willoughby's Coffee & Tea (203-481-1700; www.willoughbyscoffee.com), 550 East Main St., Branford. Open Mon.–Sat.; closed Sun. This is also the plant where they roast the coffee. Other locations in Madison (203-245-1600) at 752 Boston Post Rd. (US 1) and New Haven (203-777-7400).

✷ Entertainment

MUSIC **Branford Folk Music Society** (203-488-7715), First Congregational Church, 1009 Main St., Branford. Vocal and instrumental tradition-based performers from the United States and abroad are presented in monthly concerts, Sept.–May.

Chestnut Hill Concerts (203-245-5736; www.chestnuthillconcerts.org), at the First Congregational Church on the green, Madison. A long-standing shoreline summer chamber music festival featuring world-acclaimed classical musicians. Concerts the first four Fridays of August, 8 PM. Preconcert picnics on the church grounds are encouraged; box suppers are available by reservation.

THEATER **Opera Theater of Connecticut** (860-669-8999; www.operatheater-ct.org), Andrews Memorial Theater, 54 East Main St. (in the town hall), Clinton. Fully staged operas with orchestra in an intimate 500-seat theater.

Puppet House Theatre (203-488-5752), 128 Thimble Island Rd., Stony Creek, Branford. Operating year-round, this nationally acclaimed company presents both plays and concerts as well as workshops and classes by professional puppeteers. A collection of life-sized Sicilian puppets is on display inside the theater.

* Selective Shopping

ANTIQUES SHOPS On CT 154 between Old Saybrook and Chester, you'll find antiques dealers, alone and in group shops, at just about every turn in the road. Many specialize in New England antiques. We singled out these to get you started:

Clinton Antique Center (860-669-3839), 78 East Main St. (US 1), Clinton. Home to more than 85 dealers offering a large variety of antiques and collectibles.

The Clocktower Antiques Group (203-488-1919), 824 East Main St. (US 1), Branford. A multidealer shop with an emphasis on furniture, early iron, glass, china, and architectural items, as well as carriages and sleighs.

John Street Antiques (860-669-2439), 23-A West Main St. (US 1), Clinton. Both small and large items: jewelry, toys, furniture, architectural items, and advertising memorabilia.

Madison Trust Antiques—Consignments (203-245-3976), 891 Boston Post Rd. (US 1), Madison. Quality paintings, prints, silver, rugs, furniture, crystal, china, and lamps.

Old Saybrook Antiques Center (860-388-1600), 756 Middlesex Turnpike (CT 154), Old Saybrook. Open daily 11–5. A trim, brown, barn-shaped building houses more than 125 dealers in fine glass, porcelain, jewelry, American and European silver, 18th- and 19th-century furniture, and an unusually large selection of original artworks.

Trolley Square Antiques and Collectibles (860-399-9249), 1921 Boston Post Rd. (US 1), Westbrook. A general line of furniture, accessories, and unique items.

ART AND ARTISANS **Central Gallery** (860-510-0432; www.centralgallery.net), 270 Main St., Old Saybrook. Contemporary paintings, sculpture, ceramics, and unique gifts on display in a vintage-style space.

The Cooley Gallery (860-434-8807; www.cooleygallery.com), 25 Lyme St., Old Lyme. Open Tue.–Sat. 10–5; closed Sun. and Mon. Fine art from the 19th and 20th centuries, including Connecticut impressionism and Hudson River School painters.

Gallery 12 (203-458-1196), 29 Whitfield St. (on the Guilford green), Guilford. Selected works of contemporary craftspeople.

Guilford Art Center (203-453-5947; www.guilfordartcenter.org), 411 Church St. (CT 77), Guilford. Open year-round, Mon.–Sat. 10–5; Sun. noon–4; closed major holidays. Free admission. A favorite among fine arts and crafts aficionados. At this prestigious crafts center, visitors may observe classes and artisans at work. The gift shop, open year-round, features work of American artists: pottery, quilts, textile and fiber creations, woodenware, glass, toys, and jewelry. The **Mill Gallery** hosts changing exhibitions throughout the year, featuring fine arts and crafts by members, and the work of regional and national artists. A prestigious outdoor show draws thousands of visitors to the Guilford town green (see *Special Events*).

James Gallery (860-395-1406), 2 Pennywise Lane, Old Saybrook. Open daily in summer, weekends in winter; call for hours. In the gallery, you'll find marine art and river scenes and an old-fashioned soda fountain. According to lore, General Lafayette visited in 1824 when he was touring the new United States. The French hero of the American Revolution apparently spent a night in town and came to what was then a general store to buy supplies (historians can't agree on Lafayette's purchase—wool stockings and saddle soap are two ideas bandied about). In this century, that general store became a pharmacy and soda fountain. It was eventually owned by Anna James—Connecticut's first female African American pharmacist—who ran the James Pharmacy for some 50 years.

Lyme Academy College of Fine Arts (860-434-5232; www.lymeacademy.edu), 84 Lyme St., Old Lyme. Gallery is open Mon.–Sat. 10–4; closed Sun. Changing exhibits year-round; admission by donation. An art school perpetuating the town's tradition of nurturing the arts. Steps away from the Florence Griswold Museum.

Lyme Art Association (860-434-7802; www.lymeartassociation.org), 90 Lyme St., Old Lyme, across from Old Lyme Inn. Open Tue.–Sat., 10–5; Sun. 1–5; closed Mon. Artists—including some of the impressionists who summered at the Griswold mansion—have been exhibiting their work here for nearly 100 years. Today several exhibitions are mounted every year.

Ruggiero Studio and Gallery (203-710-5502; www.ruggierogallery.com), 33 Wall St., Madison. Contemporary works by artists with ties to the Lyme Academy College of Fine Arts (see above).

BOOKSTORES **Breakwater Books** (203-453-4141), 81 Whitfield St. (on the Guilford green), Guilford. A full-service independent bookstore, in town since 1972.

Harbor Books (860-388-6850; www.harborbooks.com), 146 Main St., Old Saybrook. Open Tue.–Fri. 10–5:30; Sat. 10–4:30; closed Sun. and Mon.; extended summer hours. A friendly neighborhood bookshop with a special emphasis on nautical and local interest titles.

R. J. Julia Booksellers (203-245-3959; 800-747-3237; www.rjjulia.com), 768 Boston Post Rd. (US 1), Madison. Open daily. Local bibliophiles agree that this is one of the state's finest bookstores. Thoughtful staff picks and a full roster of author events. Coffee, soups, sandwiches, and pastries are available in a tiny café at the rear of the store; look for the hanging teacup. A beloved institution among those who eschew big-box bookstores.

The Turning Page (860-434-0380; www.theturningpage.com), 62 Halls Rd., in the Old Lyme Marketplace,

Old Lyme. Open Mon.–Sat. 10–6; Sun. in Dec. 10–4. Lots of new and used titles; fiction and children's literature, in particular.

FACTORY OUTLETS **Clinton Crossing Premium Outlets** (860-664-0700), 20-A Killingworth Turnpike (CT 81), Exit 63 off I-95, Clinton. The shoreline's mecca of upscale bargain shopping. A great source for affordable designer finds. Seventy stores—Kate Spade, Donna Karan, Juicy Couture, Saks Fifth Avenue, Crate and Barrel, to name a few. Food court to nourish hungry shoppers.

Tanger Outlet Center (860-399-8656), 314 Flat Rock Place, Exit 65 off I-95, Westbrook. Sixty-five outlets—clothing, housewares, specialties—also a food court and 12-screen movie theater. Reebok, Rockport, Corning-Revere, Oneida, Pfaltzgraff, Leather Loft, Boston Traders, Dockers, Carter's Children, Oshkosh, L'eggs-Hanes-Bali, J.Crew, and more.

FARMS AND GARDENS ✐ ♿ **Bishop's Orchards Farm Market** (203-458-7425; www.bishopsorchards.com), 1355 Boston Post Rd. (US 1), Guilford. Open daily. Five generations of the Bishop family have been providing shoreline customers with farm products since 1871. Today they operate a farm market, bakery, and winery. Pick-your-own fruits in-season, and farm-fresh produce year-round. For a tasty snack, try a perfect apple or peach, fresh-baked bread, apple cider, a wedge of cheese—and maybe a packet of fudge. (They also make pies, including the sugar-free variety.)

Dudley Farm (203-457-0770; www.dudleyfarm.com), 2351 Durham Rd., Guilford. Open May–Oct, Mon.–Sat. 10–1; grounds open year-round. Adults $3; children 15 and under free. A 19th-century working farm on 10 acres. You can come to simply tour the barns and the 1844 farmhouse or take part in a variety of interesting programs, from winter farmer's markets in the barn to live music and workshops on history and agriculture.

SPECIAL SHOPS **The Audubon Shop** (203-245-9056; 888-505-9056; www.theaudubonshop.com), 907 Boston Post Rd. (US 1), Madison. Birders take note: This small shop is worth seeking out for its mix of scopes and tripods to feeders and field guides.

Azul Fine Clothing (860-399-0099; www.azulclothing.com), 1587 Boston Post Rd. (US 1), in the Shops at

PICK YOUR OWN APPLES AT BISHOP'S ORCHARD.

Cory Mazon

Waters Edge, Westbrook. Fashions at this women's clothing boutique range from classic to cutting edge.

The Cedar Chest (860-669-9425; www.thecedarchestresale.com), 85 West Main St., Clinton. Open daily. A consignment shop featuring upscale women's clothing, accessories, jewelry, and furniture.

The Shops at Saybrook Country Barn (860-388-0891; www.saybrookcountrybarn.com), 2 Main St., Old Saybrook. Open Tue.–Sun.; closed Mon. Known mostly for its furniture, but also home decor, linens, outdoor lighting, prints, and women's clothing.

The Herbery (860-388-4753; www.theherberyonline.com), 1001 Middlesex Turnpike, Old Saybrook. Open Tue.–Sun.; closed Mon. and Jan.–Mar. A whimsical cottagelike shop that's made for browsing. Potted herbs, gardening books, Harney and Sons teas, and tea accompaniments are on display in a reproduction Victorian barn. Out the door, gardens overflow with 50 varieties of herbs.

Glee (203-453-2554), 71 Whitfield St., Guilford. The go-to spot for unique, funky, elegant clothing and accessories for women. You're bound to find something that will add pizzazz to your look.

Southern Exposure (860-399-4445; www.shopsouthernexposure.com), 1587 Boston Post Rd. (US 1), in the Shops at Waters Edge, Westbrook. Open daily. Native American jewelry, wildlife prints, pottery, furniture, and collectibles from the Southwest.

The Bowerbird (860-434-3562; www.thebowerbird.com), 46 Halls Rd., in Old Lyme Marketplace, Old Lyme. Open daily. Unique gifts—what they call "impulsive necessities"—include toys, baby gifts, home and garden accessories, and gourmet food items.

The Pink Sleigh (860-399-6926), 512 Essex Rd. (CT 153), Westbrook. Open early July–Dec. An 1830s barn-turned-gift-shop that's been revered by locals and vacationers for more than 40 years. It's all about Christmas: themed trees, gifts, holiday decorations, and collectibles.

North Cove Outfitters (860-388-6585; www.northcove.com), 75 Main St., Old Saybrook. Open daily. Clothing and gear for hiking, cycling, paddling, fishing, and other outdoor pursuits.

✱ Special Events

April: **Guilford Antiques Show**, Adams Middle School, 233 Church St. (CT 77), Guilford. More than 40 antiques dealers from around the Northeast come to this antiques show that features lectures on the care of old houses and collections and benefits the Hyland House Museum.

May: **Meet the Artists & Artisans** (203-874-5672), on the Milford green, Milford. A juried arts and crafts show with more than 200 exhibitors.
Planked Shad Supper (860-873-9525), Fireman's Field, Old Saybrook. Local shad cooked on seasoned aged oak planks.

June: **Lobsterfest** (203-453-4733; www.guildfordrotary.com), Guilford Rotary Club, Guilford Fairgrounds. ✐ **Branford Festival** (203-488-5500; www.branfordfestival.com), town green, Branford. Music, food, and family activities.

July: **Guilford Art Center Craft Expo** (203-453-5947; www.guilfordartcenter.org) on the Guilford green, Guilford. Handmade contemporary crafts by more than 180 artisans from around the country; an annual juried show on the town's historic green for more than half a century. ✐ **Clinton**

Bluefish Festival, on the town dock, Clinton. A celebration of the catch of the season, with live music, a seafood chowder cook-off, and a fishing tournament on the Sound. ✐ **Midsummer Festival**, along historic Lyme St., Old Lyme. Victorian children's games, concerts, art shows, storytelling, and other activities.

August: ✐ **Westbrook Fife & Drum Muster** (860-399-6436), Ted Lane Field (behind the town hall), Westbrook. More than 50 fife-and-drum corps from around the world participate in this annual parade and muster. **Antiques Fair** (203-245-4567), Madison town green, Boston Post Rd. (US 1), Madison. A 35-year tradition, sponsored by the Madison Historical Society; more than 100 antiques dealers; country store and bake shop. ✐ **Hamburg Fair** (860-434-9497; www.hamburgfair.org), Lyme Grange Fairgrounds, Hamburg Rd. (CT 156), Lyme. Agricultural exhibits, farm animals, children's games, animal pulls, and a Revolutionary War encampment.

September: ✐ **Guilford Fair**, Lover's Lane, Guilford. This three-day event is not only one of the state's major country fairs, but also its second oldest (established in 1859).

November through December: **Artistry** (203-453-5947; www.guilfordartcenter.org), 411 Church St. (CT 77), Guilford. Juried exhibit and sale; through Christmas Eve.

December: ✐ **Old Saybrook Torchlight Parade of Fife and Drum Corps**, Main St. More than 40 fife-and-drum corps, their uniforms enhanced by seasonal decorations, strut down Main Street, sometimes amid falling snow. Spectators bring candles or flashlights to provide illumination. Caroling at the end of the parade on the Old Saybrook town green. A local holiday tradition.

INDEX

C

F

H

I

J

K

M

O

P

S

T

U

V

W